THE TEACHER'S GUIDE TO SUCCESS

ELLEN L. KRONOWITZ

Professor Emerita

California State University, San Bernardino

second edition

Boston Columbus Indianapolis New York San Francisco Upper Saddle River
Amsterdam Cape Town Dubai London Madrid Milan Munich Paris Montreal Toronto
Delhi Mexico City São Paulo Sydney Hong Kong Seoul Singapore Taipei Tokyo

This book is dedicated to the hard-working teachers who make a difference every day.

Vice President and Editor in Chief: Jeffery W. Johnston
Senior Acquisitions Editor: Meredith D. Fossel
Development Editor: Bryce Bell
Editorial Assistant: Nancy Holstein
Vice President, Director of Marketing: Margaret Waples
Senior Marketing Manager: Darcy Betts Prybella
Marketing Manager: Danae April
Senior Managing Editor: Pamela Bennett
Senior Project Manager: Mary M. Irvin
Senior Operations Supervisor: Matt Ottenweller
Senior Art Director: Diane Lorenzo
Cover Designer: Candace Rowley
Cover Art: istock
Photo Researchers: Lori Whitley, Carol Sykes
Composition: S4Carlisle Publishing Services
Printer/Binder: R.R. Donnelley & Sons Company
Cover Printer: Lehigh-Phoenix Color Corp
Text: Times

Every effort has been made to provide accurate and current Internet information in this book. However, the Internet and information posted on it are constantly changing, so it is inevitable that some of the Internet addresses listed in this textbook will change.

Photo Credits: The list of photo credits can be found on p. 486.

Library of Congress Cataloging-in-Publication Data
Kronowitz, Ellen L.
The teacher's guide to success/Ellen L. Kronowitz.—2nd ed.
p. cm.
Includes bibliographical references and index.
ISBN-13: 978-0-13-705074-1
ISBN-10: 0-13-705074-7
1. Teaching—United States—Handbooks, manuals, etc. 2. Teachers—United States—Handbooks, manuals, etc. I. Title.
LB1025.3.K76 2012
371.102—dc22
2010027024

10 9 8 7 6 5 4 3 2 1

PEARSON

www.pearsonhighered.com

ISBN 10: 0-13-705074-7
ISBN 13: 978-0-13-705074-1

ABOUT THE AUTHOR

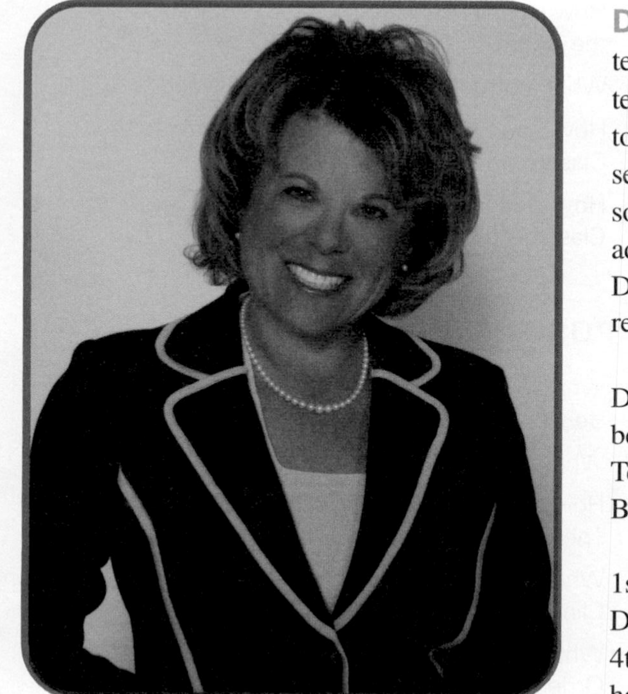

DR. ELLEN KRONOWITZ epitomizes what it means to be a teacher of young people. As a long-time educator as both a teacher and a teacher educator, Dr. Kronowitz brings a passion and dedication rarely seen today. At California State University, San Bernardino, Dr. Kronowitz has served as a member of the multiple subjects credential program, instructor of social studies methods, and supervisor of student teachers and interns. In addition, she has served as the CSUSB liaison to the Hillside-University Demonstration School, an award winning partnership that has been recognized nationally and internationally.

A graduate of the Columbia University Teachers College, Dr. Kronowitz began her career as an elementary school teacher and later became program development specialist for a New York University Teacher Corps Project. She has also served as a full-time lecturer at Brooklyn College, City University of New York.

In addition to the publication of *A Teacher's Guide to Success*, 1st and 2nd editions, and *The Substitute Teacher's Guide to Success*, Dr. Kronowitz has written *Your First Year of Teaching and Beyond*, 4th edition, *Beyond Student Teaching*, and other titles, some of which have been translated into Chinese and Korean. She has co-authored three resource books for teachers, *Pathways to Poetry* and, with her graduate students, published a teacher resource book about Native American cultures, *Circle of Tribes*. She also has written books for early readers in the Dominie Factivity Series, published by Pearson.

Dr. Kronowitz continues to reach out to educators by conducting workshops for new teachers and mentors and presenting on various topics, including teacher induction, social studies methods, and research-based teaching strategies.

CONTENTS

UNIT 1 YOUR INDUCTION INTO TEACHING 1

Chapter 1 Are You Ready for the Journey? 1

Chapter 2 What Does Research Show About the Induction Year? 9

Chapter 3 What Are Some Challenges for the Reflective Teacher? 15

Chapter 4 How Can I Plan Ahead for My First Day? 24

UNIT 2 FIRST DAY 35

Chapter 5 What Can Help Me Through My First Day? 35

Chapter 6 How Do I Arrange and Assign Seats? 54

Chapter 7 What Should I Wear and What Should I Say? 63

Chapter 8 How Do I Learn My Students' Names and How Do They Learn Each Other's Names? 71

Chapter 9 How Do I Establish Rules and Discipline on the First Day? 78

UNIT 3 CLASSROOM ORGANIZATION AND MANAGEMENT 92

Chapter 10 How Do I Accessorize the Classroom with Bulletin Boards and Extras? 92

Chapter 11 How Do I Establish and Maintain Routines for Entrances/Exits, Beginning and Ending the Day? 105

Chapter 12 How Do I Move Materials and Students Around the Room? 114

Chapter 13 What Instructional Routines Will I Need? 124

Chapter 14 How Can I Engage Students in Operating the Classroom? 134

Chapter 15 How Do I Manage Technology in My Classroom? 141

UNIT 4 POSITIVE DISCIPLINE 159

Chapter 16 What Are the Main Views of Changing Behavior? 159

Chapter 17 What Are Some Causes of Misbehavior? 171

Chapter 18 How Can I Prevent Discipline Problems Before They Start? 181

Chapter 19 What Teacher Behaviors Lead to a Positive Classroom Climate? 191

Chapter 20 What Are Some Nonverbal Strategies to Maintain Order and Some Responses to Avoid? 204

UNIT 5 PLANNING AND ORGANIZING SUBJECT MATTER 218

Chapter 21 How Do I Align Standards and Fit Everything In? 218

Chapter 22 How Do I Write Unit, Weekly, and Daily Lesson Plans? 232

Chapter 23 How Do I Gather Materials and Resources to Support My Instruction? 263

Chapter 24 How Do I Plan for Classroom Aides and Substitutes? 279

UNIT 6 ENGAGING ALL LEARNERS 293

Chapter 25 How Do I Communicate Positive Expectations to My Students? 293

Chapter 26 What Research-Based Strategies Should I Consider? 305

Chapter 27 How Do I Combine Research-Based Strategies with Cooperative Learning Groups? 320

Chapter 28 How Do I Differentiate Instruction to Meet the Needs of All Learners? 331

Chapter 29 What Are Effective Strategies for English Language Learners? 351

UNIT 7 ASSESSING AND COMMUNICATING STUDENT PROGRESS 368

Chapter 30 How Can I Assess Student Performance? 368

Chapter 31 How Can I Assess Student Interests and Attitudes? 382

Chapter 32 How Do I Manage Paperwork and Homework? 391

Chapter 33 How Can I Prepare My Students for Taking Standardized Tests? 405

Chapter 34 How Can I Enlist Support from and Communicate with Parents and Guardians? 412

UNIT 8 A PROFESSIONAL LIFE IN BALANCE 427

Chapter 35 What Is Reflective Practice and How Do I Engage in It? 427

Chapter 36 How Do I Establish Relationships with Administrators and Colleagues? 434

Chapter 37 How Can I Manage My Time and Balance My Life? 443

Chapter 38 What Professional Opportunities Are Open to Me? 453

EPILOGUE FINAL TIPS 465

Chapter 39 The Last Days of School 465

Chapter 40 Now It's Time to Teach! 471

REFERENCES 477

INDEX 481

PHOTO CREDITS 486

PREFACE

This handbook was written expressly for the new teacher, kindergarten through high school, in all regions and settings. It is a quick and easy reference to support novices before and during their first years in the classroom.

Supervisors, administrators, curriculum coordinators, mentor teachers, in-service support providers, university methods course professors, and student teaching seminar leaders will find that this handbook facilitates their work with pre- and/or in-service teachers.

Research on the challenges teachers face in their first years of teaching often concludes that a balance of research and practical advice makes for a successful induction into the teaching profession. The content of this handbook presents that balanced approach, using essential knowledge derived from those engaged in research and those engaged with students in the classroom. Therefore, the advice and guidelines provided in this handbook reflect not only a review of the available literature on the new teacher experience, but the collective wisdom of resourceful and experienced teachers as well.

This handbook is as comprehensive as the format allows, and readers seeking more information may read the books or visit the websites recommended at the end of each unit or refer to the reference listing at the end of the handbook.

Content and Organization

The 40 chapters divided into 8 units and an Epilogue address the most practical and research-based aspects of the first year of teaching. These chapters will simplify the complex challenges ahead, including having a successful first day, organizing and managing your classroom, respectfully disciplining students, mapping out a differentiated curriculum, teaching with proven, research-based strategies, assessing student learning, preparing students for standardized tests, and addressing your own personal and professional development needs.

The content has been keyed to the NBPTS standards that guide the professional education of teachers. You will find the chart showing the correspondence of the Handbook chapters to these standards in Chapter 3. The tabs and index guide you to material on your immediate concerns, although some readers may prefer the cover-to-cover approach.

New to This Edition

With every new edition, the author has a chance to incorporate suggestions from readers and reviewers and to expand on topics and examine new issues, policies, legislation, research and innovative ideas and programs. This new edition also features additional input from a variety of voices such as parents, principals, teachers, educational consultants, experts such as Carol Tomlinson, and students.

New features in the second edition:

- **Summaries** at the end of each chapter highlight the main ideas
- The new **Reflect!** feature invites the reader to synthesize the information and apply it to their teaching situation
- New video clips have been added on a **Companion Website** to elucidate the new material in the second edition
- The **Principals' Perspectives** feature has been added to reflect administrators' points of view
- Many more **classroom artifacts** such as lesson plans and unit plans are incorporated
- **Journal articles** on differentiated instruction and homework in a responsive classroom are built in

The content has been expanded to include more extensive discussion of the following topics:

- English language learners and models that facilitate proficiency such as SIOP

- Expanded information, examples, and suggestions for middle and high school teachers
- Updated research, websites, resources, references, and current statistics provide additional perspectives
- Differentiated instruction is explained through text and an interview with Carol Tomlinson
- Homework policies are new to this edition and include an interview with Cathy Vatterott
- There is a greater focus on diversity throughout the second edition
- RTI, or Response to Intervention, is included as a separate topic
- Professional learning communities are discussed from the practitioners' perspectives
- The technology section has been updated to include newer technologies and issues arising from student use of cell phones and social networks
- Adaptations for "floaters" are included for the first time
- More serious behavioral challenges such as bullying and drug use are included

Unique Features

The Teachers Guide to Success contains a variety of unique features that will help you make the most of your reading.

- **Effectiveness Essentials** at the beginning of each chapter outline the key concepts within the chapter.
- **Apply It!** activities provide ideas for the reader to work through with or without instructors or supervisors.
- **Avoid It!** features provide tips about mistakes teachers should try to avoid.
- **Classroom Artifacts** features include lesson plans, syllabi, and handbooks that have been used in the classroom shared by practicing teachers and principals.
- **Watch It!** icons call out video clips that can be accessed in the Classroom Videos section of the Companion Website that accompanies this book.
- A series of features offer quotes and shared stories from veterans in the field and students. These include **Myth Busters!** with advice from veterans that dispel common misconceptions and myths; **Teacher Talks** . . . filled with anecdotes from experienced teachers; and **Student Says** . . . reflections from students of all ages on school and schooling.
- Each unit ends with a **Unit Checklist** to help in-service or pre-service teachers prepare and an **annotated list of recommended readings and websites** for use in professional development or in the classroom.
- A **Technology Advantage** is realized with the inclusion of the robust Companion Website (www.pearsonhighered.com/kronowitz2e) which accompanies *The Teacher's Guide to Success.* Divided into three main sections, this valuable resource is designed to help you prepare for day-to-day instruction and plan for the days ahead, as well as inspire you. After a general introduction by Dr. Kronowitz, you have access to:
  - **Hear from the Experts:** Video clips of various researchers in the field of education speaking on critical issues in education today
  - **Watch It! Videos:** Over 60 video clips of concepts-in-action in live classroom settings
  - **Your First Year Teaching:** additional tips from other educators to set up your classroom, manage student behavior, and learn to more easily organize for instruction and assessment

Adapt the guidance in *The Teacher's Guide to Success* to your teaching circumstances and subject area. Use the resources provided to help you identify, clarify, solidify, and/or modify your currently held beliefs about instruction, discipline, management, assessment, working with parents, and working with colleagues. Use this Handbook as your roadmap to successful first years of teaching beyond which are the rewards that first motivated your choice of this exciting, challenging profession.

ACKNOWLEDGMENTS

It takes a committed team of professionals to tend this project from start to finish and I was fortunate to have the best. I would like to thank Meredith Fossel, Senior Acquisitions Editor at Pearson. I am endebted to Mary Irvin, Senior Project Manager; I relied throughout on her expertise and sound advice. Bryce Bell, Development Editor, provided feedback and suggested changes for the better. I am grateful to Pam Bennett, Senior Managing Editor, who coordinated the artistic team that brought the manuscript to life. The marketing team, Danae April and Darcy Betts Prybella, devised a cutting-edge and inventive approach to bring the book to its audience. To all of you at Pearson who helped along the way I offer my deep appreciation and heartfelt thanks.

I want to thank the following reviewers whose attention to the big picture as well as the details made this a much better book. I am grateful to all of you: Peggy DeLapp, University of Minnesota; Libby Hall, George Mason University; and Laura McClain, Indiana University.

My final thank you is to all of the administrators, teachers, students, and others who added the spice and flavor to this Handbook with your anecdotes. The following principals, teachers, and students from many parts of the country have given freely of their advice.

Students . . . Adam, Lexington, NC; Alicia, Tucson, AZ; Allie, Edmonton, OK; Andrew, Redlands, CA; Coco, Edmonton, OK; David, Satellite Beach, FL; Debbie, Silverbell, AZ; Drew, Edmonton, OK; Erik, Brookline, MA; Erin, Glenview, IL; Holland, Redlands, CA; Jack, Redlands, CA; Jeremy, Klamath Falls, OR; Kathleen, Glenview, IL; Kendall, Aurora, CO; Kira, Arcata, CA; Kurt, Plano, TX; Mackenzie, Aurora, CO; Mark, Orlando, FL; Megan, Glenview, IL; Natalie, Yucaipa, CA; Niki, Redlands, CA; Riley, South Charleston, OH; Walker, Redlands, CA

Teachers . . . Abby Ungefug, Student teacher, Montana State University, Lewistown, MT; Abby Volmer, MO; Andy Slavin, Bend, OR; Angel Van Horn, Riverside, CA; Ann Kocher, San Bernardino, CA; Art Eustace, Fontana, CA; Art Gallardo, San Bernardino, CA; Barbara Arient, San Bernardino, CA; Barbara Benjamin Trevino, Arlington, TX; Becky Monroe, San Bernardino, CA; Beth Ann Willstrop, San Antonio, TX; Beth Williams, Mobile, AL; Betty Rosentrater, Santa Barbara, CA; Brandi Stephens, Mebane, NC; Brenda Downs, Minden, NV; C. Francine Apacible, San Bernardino, CA; C. L. Lopez, San Bernardino *Sun*; Camille Napier, Natick, MA; Carla McClain, West. TX; Charles Skinner, South Carolina State Department of Education, Cottageville, SC; Cheryl Ayala, San Bernardino, CA; Cindy Brewer, Mebane, NC; Colleen Flavin, Hemet, CA; Corinne Gregory, Bellevue, WA; Dave Emrick, Redlands, CA; Debora Ondracek, Madison, GA; Deborah Lichfield, St Johns, AZ; Delaine Zody, Fresno, CA; Diane Amendt, Colton, CA; Dion Clark, San Bernardino, CA; Dottie Bailey, Colton, CA; Eileen Mino, Colton, CA; Elizabeth Hodgson, Durham, NC; Francesca Sweet, Redlands, CA; Frank Geiger, Mountainside, NJ; Gabe Aguilar, San Bernardino, CA; Dr. Gary Negin, Redlands, CA; Gaynor Morgan, Oostende, Belgium; Gordon MacDonald Montvale, New Jersey; Heidi Thompson, Yucaipa, CA; Hester Turpin, Colton CA; Ingrid Munsterman, Bloomington, CA; Ivania Martin, Benicia, CA; Jan Christian, San Bernardino, CA; Jason Paytas, Arcata, CA; Jennifer A. Ponsart, Davenport, FL; Jennifer Lytle Begonia, Barnegat Light, NJ; Joan Marie Smith, Colton, CA; Joan Prehoda, Palm Springs, CA; Joe Nutt, Surrey, England; Julie Prater, Hemet, CA; Johnna DeBella, Denver, CO; Karla McLain, Cromwell, CT; Kathleen Beard, Morongo Unified, CA; Kathleen Cave, Sparks, MD; Kelly Rubio, Manhattan Beach, CA; Kevin Jarrett, Northfield, NJ; Kevin White, Charlottesville, VA; Kim Bridgers, Hermitage, TN; Kim Ciabettini, Highland, CA; Kris Ungerer, San Bernardino, CA; Laura Civitano, Yonkers, NY; Laura Graham, Ontario, CA; Laurel Garner, Duluth, GA; Laurie Wasserman, Medford, MA: LeTiqua Bellard,

Charlotte, NC; Linda Meyer, San Bernardino, CA; Loretta Gomez, San Bernardino, CA; Lynn Sleeth, Fontana, CA; Maria Cleppe, San Bernardino, CA; Marian Casey, Evanston, IL; Marsha Moyer, San Bernardino, CA; Martinrex Kedziora, Hemet, CA; Mary Hall, Eastbourne, NZ; Mary K., Wellman, IA; Matt Villasana, Columbia, MO; McKayla Beach, Palm Springs, CA; Michelyn Brown, Grass Valley, CA; Molly Bendorf, Aurora, CO; Nancy DeMaggio, Redlands, CA; Nancy Derksen, San Bernardino, CA; Natalie Ruddell, Hemet, CA; Nikki Shull, Denver, CO; Nina Conine, Principal, Olivehurst, CA; Perry Lopez, Bronx, NY; Rachel Vogelpohl Meyen, Durham, NC; Robin Smith, Hollidaysburg, PA; Sandra Stiles, Sarasota FL; Sarah Barten, Desert Sands, CA; Sarah Dominick, Preschool aide, Stockholm, ME; Shannon Vanderford, West Memphis, AR; Shelley D. Howell, Morongo Unified School District, CA; Shirley Byassee, Colorado Springs, CO; Shirley Casper, Sydney, Australia; Shirley Clark, Sun City, CA; Stephen Pulliam, Stony Brook, NY; Steven Podd, St James, New York: Storme Freeman, Hemet, CA; Susan Johnson, Richwood, WV; Sylvia Maisano, Roseville, MI; Tamara Remhof, Mesquite, TX; Thomas Kaszer, Lodi, CA; Tiffany Gammaro, Sarasota, FL; Dr. Virginia S. Newlin, Rock Hall, MA.

FROM THE AUTHOR

Hello, my name is Ellen Kronowitz, the author of *The Teacher's Guide to Success.* As a longtime teacher, I can honestly say that working with students and helping to shape their futures was some of the most satisfying and fulfilling work I could have asked for. I have never regretted that initial decision to teach. It started me on a sustained and exhilarating journey around the world of education.

Whether experienced or new to teaching, as that first day of the school year approaches, you may feel some apprehension, regardless of your preparation to this point. Having been through this experience myself, I know that anxiety and apprehension. Teaching, after all, is the only profession I know of that has a first day every year! That's why I wrote *The Teacher's Guide to Success* and created the accompanying Companion Website. If I'm able to help you feel just a little bit more ready for that first day of school, well, then we both will have succeeded.

The good news is that there is only one very first day in the first year of teaching. The better news is that although each subsequent year evokes the same anticipation and feelings of excitement, each year also produces fewer jitters. Many first-year, novice, and even experienced teachers spend restless nights before that first day of school. But I assure you that with each year, it gets easier and easier. Trust your training, and remember that you know more and are better prepared than you feel. Also remember that there is always a lot of help around you. Mentors and colleagues ensure that no teacher is alone.

There are challenges, and there will be obstacles that will get in the way of your efforts to teach effectively. But along with those challenges come many individual joys and opportunities to develop your skills as a teacher. Each year brings new students, new opportunities for personal growth, and new colleagues. Daily you will delight in the small successes of your students, knowing you have made a difference. Your students bring something new to the classroom, and they are why no school year is ever the same. The key is spending time getting to know and appreciate the various personalities and racial, ethnic, and cultural influences students have on your classes. You have the most sacred trust imparted with your credential—influencing the lives of young people—and the benefits of your efforts may not be known for years. For every feeling of apprehension, it is equally important to remind yourself why you chose this profession.

Concerns about the first years of teaching bring back memories of sleepless weeks prior to my first teaching assignment. I was anxious and sick to my stomach that first morning until I walked through the door and saw my class. My mother always told me to put my right foot forward before any new endeavor, and that's what I did as I stepped into the classroom.

As years go by, you may not remember each and every student you encounter, but rest assured that they will remember you. Some of your students will keep in touch. Some won't. But students never ever forget a teacher who has touched their lives. To paraphrase Christa McAuliffe, You touch the future. You teach.

As you look around the faculty meeting or the staff room, know that at one time all teachers experienced the same apprehension. Beyond all the anxiety of the first days and months of school lie all the rewards that motivated your choice of this exciting, challenging profession.

While I cannot be there in the classroom with you, I believe you will find *The Teacher's Guide to Success* the next best thing.

Now, as my mother used to say, put your right foot forward and do it!

Ellen Kronowitz

UNIT 1

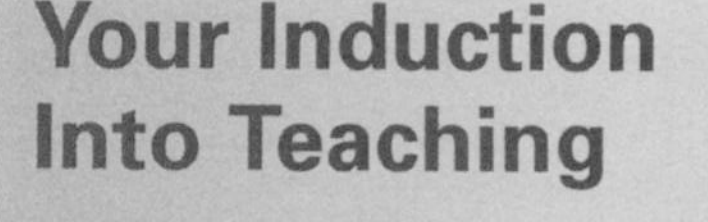

Your Induction Into Teaching

CHAPTER 1

ARE YOU READY FOR THE JOURNEY?

Effectiveness Essentials

- Teacher preparation and credentialing are only the beginning steps of a long journey.
- There are multiple pathways into teaching.
- Part of the challenge of the first year is fear of the unknown.
- Teachers are a diverse group, although not as diverse as their students are.
- Teachers have to assume multiple roles.

I touch the future. I teach.

Christa McAuliffe

UNIT 1

STUDENT SAYS . . .

I have modeled myself after you as a teacher of my own children. You were a patient teacher that gave each person a chance to reach their potential even if it was not evident initially. . . . Any public school teacher that does this gives each student a fighting chance. You gave me confidence that continues to this day. You weren't afraid to love the students in your charge. To a little child with as many challenges in life as I had, this can mean everything.

Much love,
DEBBIE BRADSHAW
Silverbell, Arizona

Why Don't I Feel Prepared to Start Teaching?

This question, often posed by students in the last phase of the teacher preparation program, gives me pause each time I hear it. Having been through this experience myself, I know exactly what they mean. They're anxious and scared. The valuable information they have learned and are still learning doesn't make them feel competent and confident in light of their upcoming first solo day in a classroom.

Listening to my students' concerns about the first years of teaching brings back memories of sleepless weeks prior to my own first teaching assignment. I had many methods courses under my belt but had not the vaguest idea of how to combine instructional ingredients to meet my students' needs. I was anxious and sick to my stomach that first morning until I walked through the door and saw my class. My mother always told me to put my right foot forward before any new endeavor, and that's what I did as I stepped into the room. I never regretted my decision to teach, and I remember each one of the students in my first class. I guarantee that you will too!

As years go by, you may not remember each and every student you encounter, but rest assured that they will remember you. I recently contacted a former student, an environmentalist and a mother of three, and asked her to collect her own children's comments about their favorite teachers.

Here's my unforgettable second class.

Debbie was a fifth grader in my third year of teaching. We have kept in touch over all these years. She was the student who needed the extra attention and the extra push to excel. I pushed, and she resisted. Finally, she gave in and accepted my challenges to excellence. And, despite a very difficult childhood, she authored some of the most creative stories and poems I have encountered as a teacher.

I have kept Debbie's letters over the years. Each one reminds me of the intangible rewards of teaching. Sometimes your students will keep in touch. Sometimes they won't. But students never, ever forget a teacher who has touched their lives.

This was Mark then.

Another former student, Mark Young, pictured below as a third grader and today (and in the class photo on page 2), surprised me by writing to me a few months ago. (See the Student Says feature in the outside column.)

Teacher Preparation Is Only the Beginning

The proliferation of induction and mentoring programs and the new standards for the teaching profession all suggest that success in the first year is dependent on having certain knowledge, skills, and dispositions, as well as a great deal of support. Luckily, today there is a greater emphasis on helping new teachers through the challenges of the first year.

Here's Mark now.

STUDENT SAYS . . .

I came across your name within a listing of teacher resources and stopped dead in my tracks. I attended public school in New York City in the 1960s, and had a third-grade teacher named Ellen Kronowitz. My Miss Kronowitz was a young and spirited teacher who stood out among the rest of the faculty, and made a very lasting impression on me.

I went to P.S. 15, Queens, and had the same teacher for both first and second grade. My report cards were filled with comments remarking on my inability to focus, my talking out of turn, my tendency to daydream, and other habits now often associated with ADD. I fear she almost had my mother convinced that I just wasn't very bright, until I finally entered the third grade.

Miss Kronowitz, on the other hand, told my mother that she thought that I was quite bright indeed and that difficulties in second grade were likely the

(continued on following page)

UNIT 1

STUDENT SAYS—*continued*

result of boredom and a need to be challenged academically. And challenge me she did. Looking back, I realize that Miss Kronowitz taught with a fresh enthusiasm and not only fostered in me a lifelong love of learning but also the freedom and courage to march to the beat of my own drummer.

MARK YOUNG
Orlando, Florida

STATISTICS

How prepared do you feel for the first year of teaching? According to the National Comprehensive Center for Teacher Quality and Public Agenda (2008), these are some reponses:

Very prepared	42%
Somewhat prepared	38%
Somewhat unprepared	16%
Very unprepared	3%
Don't know	1%

After all of the educational psychology and methods courses, and the internship or student teaching experience, you still may feel uneasy. But you actually know more and are better prepared than you feel. Ask any veteran teachers you know, and they will tell you that it takes at least five years to build your confidence. We have all experienced the pre-service jitters. The treatment for this affliction is experience in the classroom.

There Are Multiple Pathways Into Teaching

Student teaching and traditional teacher preparation programs are just one avenue for becoming a teacher. Today, multiple pathways into the profession exist for teachers. Alternative credential programs abound. Some are tied to districts through internships, while others are free-standing and privately administered. Some of these programs have special emphases, such as Teach for America, Troops to Teachers, and the New Teacher Project. The responsibility for the entire day and all it entails is yours from the outset.

If you are a student teacher in a traditional program, your supervising teacher can catch you when you fall and cheer you on during rough times. The curriculum has been set, and you are responsible only for portions of students' education. During your practicum, the ultimate accountability lies with the master or supervising teacher. In contrast, once you have your teaching credential in hand, the responsibility is all yours.

If you are an intern teacher in an alternative program, earning a credential while teaching and without benefit of a traditional supervised student teaching experience, you may find that guidance and supervision are less intense than you need during your first year. It is understandable why many first-year teachers spend restless nights before that first day of school. The good news is that, after the first year, it gets easier and easier, and there is a lot of help available to you.

APPLY IT!

Take a few minutes to reflect on the program that is currently preparing you. Or, if you are teaching, reflect on the strengths of the program that prepared you. Write down what you believe could have made you feel more confident in your first year(s) (see Figure 1.1).

Figure 1.1
Program Preparation

Strengths of Program	Additional Preparation I Need
Reading methods	*Technology update*

We Fear the Unknown

Part of the challenge of the first year is fear of the unknown. What will it be like when you have to assume total responsibility for a class? Here's what lies ahead (the scary stuff):

- You are accountable for the planning, organization, instruction, and assessment of students.
- You are responsible for your classroom environment and the routines that keep it operating efficiently.
- You are asked to assume non-teaching duties such as lunch, yard, and bus duty.
- You need to meet new colleagues and possibly explore an unfamiliar community.
- You need to establish and maintain communication with parents and perhaps supervise aides.
- You are responsible for record keeping and ongoing diagnoses.
- You are assigned a challenging variety of students.
- You may have to teach unfamiliar material.
- You may experience impediments such as lack of parental support; overcrowded classrooms; outdated equipment; lack of adequate texts and materials; poorly maintained campuses; and some students who are disrespectful, angry, disengaged, or even violent.

TEACHER TALKS . . .

I always remind myself of the "why" in my teaching. I love my "babies," who happen to be 16–17 years old; and I must remember that they are experiencing my themes, writing requests, and choices in literature for the first time rather than for the hundredth-plus time as I am doing. If my "why" is for money, then I am in the wrong position. If my "why" is job security, then I say thanks to my profession. If my "why" is because I love to watch my "babies" struggle with thinking and adjusting earlier thoughts with new information and synthesizing those thoughts into their own new forms that transfer to other disciplines and their own lives and that from them I also learn, then I'm in Nirvana.

BETH ANN WILLSTROP
Reading and Literature Teacher
Health Careers High School
Grades 9–12
San Antonio, Texas

UNIT 1

TEACHER TALKS . . .

I became a teacher because I was inspired by my own teachers in middle school and high school. I had a passion and talent for music that was fostered by them and knew I wanted to affect students in the way that they had affected me. It also helped that I liked to be in charge of things.

The challenges of the first year of teaching are so great! I think the biggest ones by far are classroom management and learning to deal with parents. No one can teach you how actually to manage a classroom—I think it just takes trial and error and finding your own style. I also remember so clearly being nervous if I had to call or speak with a parent about a child, especially because I was a young teacher. Now, more than ever, we deal with pressures such as testing and No Child Left Behind. I don't remember there being so much focus on them when I started, and now they are all you hear about, even in the arts.

KARLA MCCLAIN
Music Teacher, Middle School
West Hartford, Connecticut

Here's what also lies ahead (the fun stuff):

- The joy of watching your students "get it"
- The thank-you notes and letters from students and grateful parents
- The eagerness and excitement you see on students' faces
- The letters of acceptance to college your high school students share with you
- The painting or drawing a student offers as a gift
- The affectionate comments you receive as the students leave your classroom
- The growth and development you see every day
- A letter from students like Debbie or Mark many years later
- The small successes and the large leaps
- The knowledge that you will make a difference and "touch the future"
- The joy of sharing a joke with your students
- The chance to celebrate your students' achievements with them
- The ability to attend student performances, proms, festivals, homecoming, sports events, carnivals, and other significant schoolwide events
- The gratification of attending awards assemblies, promotions, and graduations honoring your students
- Lasting friendships and collegiality with the school's staff
- Pride in your own professional accomplishments

Who Are We?

We Are a Diverse Group

However, we are not as diverse as the students we teach. A key to being a great teacher is spending time getting to know and appreciate the various racial, ethnic, and cultural groups represented in our classes.

We Have to Assume Multiple Roles

All teachers have to be cheerleaders, interior decorators, artists, systems analysts, efficiency experts, performers, nurturers, assessors, judges, mediators, diagnosticians, psychologists, communicators,

bookkeepers, managers, and friends—to name just a few. Many of these roles come naturally to teachers. Good communication skills, for example, are associated with the teaching profession. Other roles, such as assessor or diagnostician, are practiced during teacher preparation. Some roles, such as mediator and efficiency expert, are often learned on the job.

Every teacher you know was once a novice. As you look around the faculty meeting or the staff room, you need to realize that at one time all teachers experienced the same apprehension that you do now. Beyond all the anxiety of the first days and months of school lie all the rewards that motivated your choice of this exciting, challenging profession in the first place.

STATISTICS

A 2007–2008 profile of a public elementary school in southern California:

Group	Percentage of School Population
African American	14.2
American Indian or Native Alaskan	.39
Asian	.13
Filipino	.13
Hispanic or Latino	59.34
Pacific Islander	.13
White	21.05
Multiple or no response	4.16
Special needs	13
Economically disadvantaged	70
English learners	36

TEACHER TALKS . . .

Every teacher must decide who to be—sculptor chiseling hard stone, potter molding yielding clay, cowboy herding wild bulls, pied piper leading the eager, mama nurturing the helpless, pioneer leading the way, clown entertaining the masses, doctor healing the damaged. Any of these or all of these? One at a time or simultaneously? No wonder new teachers are jittery.

(continued on following page)

UNIT 1

TEACHER TALKS—*continued*

To make the job even more exciting, the students don't come homogenized and labeled. They, too, are trying to figure out who they are, where they are going, and how to get there. Is teaching them scary? Yes! Is it worth it? Yes! Where else can one engage all of their being, talents, skills, and hopes; contribute in such an exciting variety of ways; and find such satisfying results!

BETTY ROSENTRATER
Elementary/High School Teacher, Retired
U.S. and International Schools
Moreno Valley, California

WATCH IT! video

Becoming a Teacher
Teaching Fifth Grade

Two teachers talk about why they became teachers, how they decided on a grade level, and the challenges and joys they discovered. Compare and contrast their motivations, and then write about your own motivation for becoming a teacher.

Summary

Teacher preparation courses and internships leading to your teaching credential are the beginning steps of a long and worthwhile journey. There are multiple pathways into teaching. Among these are traditional programs and alternative programs such as Troops to Teachers and Teach for America. Part of the challenge of the first year is fear of the unknown. Teachers are a diverse group, although not as diverse as their students are. Teaching requires the assumption of multiple roles.

Reflect!

Review the statistics regarding teachers' satisfaction with their preparation that appeared in the chapter on page 4.

1. How would you have responded to the question?
2. If you were to choose a metaphor for your teaching role, what would it be?
3. What are your greatest fears about your first year of teaching, and how will you go about facing them?

CHAPTER 2

WHAT DOES RESEARCH SHOW ABOUT THE INDUCTION YEAR?

Effectiveness Essentials

- The beginning teacher dropout rate is alarmingly high.
- Districts recruit quality teachers and want to hold on to them.
- The first year of teaching has its ups and downs.
- Be sure to identify your support system at the school and district levels.
- Adequate preparation can diminish your apprehension.

The beginning is the most important part of the work.

Plato

STATISTICS

According to the National Commission on Teaching and America's Future (2007),

- In the United States, 46% of all *new* teachers leave the profession within five years.
- The national cost of public school teacher turnover could be more than $7.3 billion a year.
- Teacher attrition has grown by 50% over the past fifteen years.
- The national teacher turnover rate has risen to 16.8%.
- In urban schools the turnover rate is more then 20%.
- In some schools and districts, the teacher dropout rate is actually higher than the student dropout rate.

The Teaching Profession As a Leaky Bucket

The beginning teacher attrition rate is alarmingly high. As more teachers are hired, too many spill out of the profession. School district administrators increasingly realize that the effort to recruit new teachers needs to be combined with an effort to retain and support these teachers during the first years, when the going gets a little rough.

Research Is Needed to Stem the Attrition and Retain Effective Teachers

In some areas, there is a severe teacher shortage resulting from growing pupil populations, teacher retirements, class-size reduction, and competition from other fields for the pool of candidates who traditionally have entered teaching. Because of the increasing need for new teachers, districts are working very hard to retain the teachers they recruit. That means finding new and improved ways of making the induction year a successful one. Current research focuses on why teachers leave, the cost of teacher attrition to the districts, and the elements that constitute effective induction, including timing and sequencing of inservice instruction and the role of administrators and mentors during the induction process.

myth BUSTER

Teaching is a lonely profession.

It certainly can be lonely if you isolate yourself from your colleagues and the community. Reach out to form alliances and bonds with people you believe to be like-minded. Become involved in a project with other teachers, other grade levels, other subject specialists, and community members. Projects that invite participation may include a global fair, a technology showcase, a writer's festival, or a play. Schoolwide events, though hard work, can help pull teachers together. Teaching is as lonely as you want it to be.

Andy Slavin
Sixth-Grade Teacher
Bend, Oregon

The Prevailing Emphasis Is on Recruiting *Quality Teachers*

In January 2002, George W. Bush signed into law the No Child Left Behind Act mandating that a "highly qualified" teacher staff every classroom by the 2005–2006 school year. According to the official No Child Left Behind website (U.S. Department of Education, 2002), the act provides grants to recruit and train quality teachers, especially in specific areas of need; creates tax deductions for out-of-pocket teaching-related expenses; and establishes loan forgiveness programs for teachers. The secretary of the U.S. Department of Education, Arne Duncan, and the Obama administration have raised the stakes with Race to the Top, formally known as the American Recovery and Reinvestment Act (2009), which will provide $4.35 billion in grants to districts that lead the way in school reform in four areas: documenting their past success and outlining plans to extend their reforms through standards and assessments, building a workforce of highly effective educators, creating educational data systems to support student achievement, and turning around their lowest-performing schools (U.S. Department of Education, 2009).

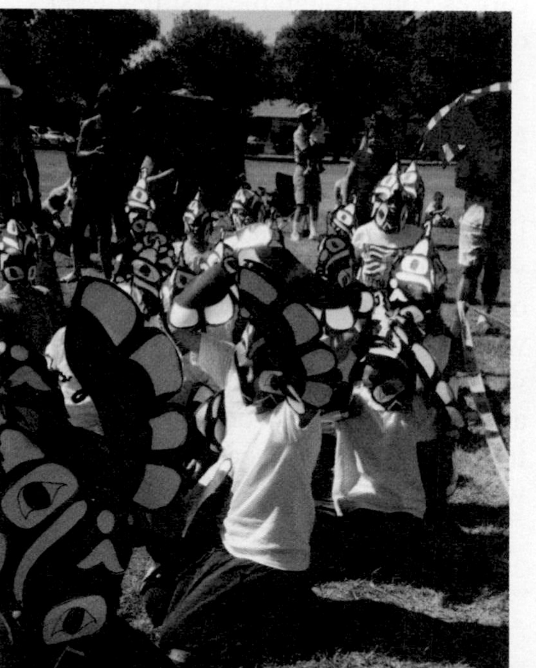

Schoolwide events bring teachers and students together.

The Race to the Top's most debated provision requires that districts develop plans to evaluate teachers and principals based on student performance. You can read about all the provisions of this extensive plan at http://www.ed.gov/programs/racetothetop/index.html. These initiatives address the quality issue while school districts work on recruitment and retention challenges.

Why do teachers who have studied so hard, endured student teaching, and even survived the first year leave the field?

In a California State University study of teacher attrition, Futernick (2007) reported that 22% of teachers in California leave after four years. This statistic contrasts with the central finding that 81% of teachers who participated in the survey said they entered the profession because they wanted to make a difference to children and society. The reasons for

STATISTICS

According to the National Center for Educational Statistics (2008), by the end of the 2003–2004 school year,

- 17% of the elementary and secondary teacher workforce left the public and private schools where they had been teaching.
- 8% of the teacher workforce transferred to a different school.
- 9% of the teacher workforce left teaching in order to take a job in another field; return to school for further education; take care of family; retire; or for reasons such as starting their own business, taking a sabbatical or leave of absence, or joining a religious community.
- In public schools, the turnover rate for high-poverty schools was greater than for low-poverty schools (21% versus 14%).

leaving were all subsumed under "the teaching and learning environment" and had nothing to do with pay. The main subreasons were an inadequate support system from the district, inadequate time for planning and professional development, lack of collegial support, not enough textbooks, excessive paperwork, and too many unnecessary meetings. Conversely, if turned into positives, they become the reasons why teachers stay and the reasons why 28% would return to the classroom before retirement if these issues could be resolved.

Other explanations cited in the literature on attrition include

- Lack of physical and mental conditioning
- Isolation
- Value conflicts
- Assignment to teach the most disruptive and least academically able students
- Lack of long-term commitment
- The differential between beginning teacher salaries and the first-year salaries of other college graduates
- Idealistic and unrealistic expectations
- Inadequate resources

The First-Year Roller Coaster

The first year of teaching has its ups and downs. Ellen Moir and her colleagues at the University of California at Santa Cruz (1990) identified a five-phase cycle of that first-year roller coaster.

The First Phase Is ANTICIPATION

When your job offer arrives, you are higher than a kite. No more part-time jobs at the supermarket, no more moonlighting as a security guard, no more living from hand to mouth to pay for courses. You have a job! This phase carries you through the first few weeks of school.

Next Comes the SURVIVAL Phase

During the first weeks of school, you scramble to keep one step ahead of the kids, staying up too late to write lesson plans, worrying about what your principal thinks of you, and so on. In other words, you are trying to keep your head above water!

The DISILLUSIONMENT Phase Arrives Next

This phase kicks in when your responsibilities outstrip your energy. This phase can set in six to eight weeks into the school year, and it varies in length and intensity. To your current anxieties, you have to add preparing your room for open house, principal evaluations, and parent conferences. You are exhausted! The job as a supermarket checker or night security guard begins to look appealing. You start to question your commitment, and your morale sinks.

The Next Part of the Cycle, REJUVENATION, Coincides With Your First Sustained Rest

It might occur during winter break or even Thanksgiving. You can reintroduce yourself to your family, read a book for enjoyment, and generally relax and enjoy a few minutes to yourself. You begin to see the big picture and, after a well-deserved rest, you are ready to seek out new solutions.

In the Spring Comes the REFLECTION Phase

Reinvigorated, you can reflect on some of your practices. By now, you may have gotten good advice, attended inservices, and gotten a handle on some of your paperwork. You begin to think about how you would do things differently next time, and you begin to look forward to next year!

Recognize and Identify Your Own Concerns

The most important thing you can do is to recognize and address your fears before you begin teaching. Help is

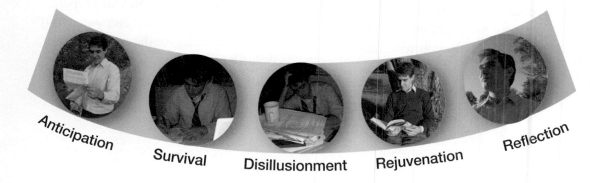

Anticipation Survival Disillusionment Rejuvenation Reflection

STATISTICS

How did teachers respond to a Met Life (2009) Survey? Compare their 1984 and 2009 answers.

	2009	1984
Teachers are very satisfied with their careers.	62%	40%
Teachers feel respected in society today.	66%	47%
Teachers agree that their jobs allow them the opportunity to earn a decent salary.	66%	37%
Teachers agree that the training that they now receive does a good job of preparing them for the classroom.	67%	46%
Teachers report that they would advise a young person to pursue a career in teaching.	75%	45%
Principals report that the quality of new teachers entering the profession is strong.	51%	44%

UNIT 1

TEACHER TALKS . . .

After my first year of teaching was over, I wanted to write an apology letter to all my students for making so many mistakes that first year. I didn't, but maybe I should have.

DOTTIE BAILEY
English and Speech Teacher, Middle School
Colton, California

STATISTICS

According to the National Education Association (2009), these states offered the top-10 beginning teacher salaries in 2007–2008:

1. District of Columbia $42,370
2. New Jersey $41,802
3. Hawaii $39,901
4. Maryland $38,985
5. California $37,795
6. Alaska $36,700
7. Delaware $36,629
8. Wyoming $36,305
9. Rhode Island $36,141
10. Pennsylvania $35,782

APPLY IT!

Prepare for the induction year by making a list of behaviors, thoughts, and feelings that might go along with each phase of the first-year teaching cycle shown on pages 12 and 13. For example, in the Survival phase:

"I am a nervous wreck, I have to get some help, I'm drowning in paper, I can't sleep, I'll never get these plans written, etc."

available at the school and district levels. You may have mentors, buddy teachers, and/or formal induction programs. Your grade-level colleagues in elementary school, your team in middle school, and your department at the high school are your "first responders" when you want to put out fires or lay your concerns to rest. Most important, you can, on a personal level, be prepared. Your concerns can be substantially reduced by appropriate preparation. This handbook is intended to help you with that preparation.

AVOID IT!

Do not suffer in silence. Ask for help when you feel overwhelmed.

Do not give in to disillusionment. This, too, shall pass.

Summary

The beginning teacher dropout rate is alarmingly high for a variety of reasons. The first year does have its ups and downs, but you can prepare yourself by identifying your concerns and seeking help from your support system at your school and district and among your peers.

Reflect!

How prepared do you feel for your first year, and how can you prepare yourself further? How can you avoid or at least mitigate the roller coaster described here?

CHAPTER 3
WHAT ARE SOME CHALLENGES FOR THE REFLECTIVE TEACHER?

Effectiveness Essentials

- Standards help you reflect on your teaching practice.
- It is never too early to begin to reflect on your teaching.
- All teachers face common challenges.
- Balance research with practical advice.

What teachers know and can do makes the most difference in what children learn.

Linda Darling-Hammond

The Reflective Teacher

John Dewey's (1933) definition of *reflective thinking* has been the basis of a teaching construct that we refer to as *reflective practice*: "active, persistent, and careful consideration of any belief or supposed form of knowledge in the light of the grounds that support it and the further conclusion to which it tends." Reflective teachers, therefore, think about and analyze their own teaching for the purpose of improving practice and becoming the best teachers they can be.

The Biggest Challenge Is Becoming the Best Reflective Teacher You Can Be

The National Board for Professional Teaching Standards (NBPTS, 1989) has identified five core propositions that can help you meet this challenge. Each proposition pinpoints an essential aspect of teaching that will enhance student learning. They are listed in Table 3.1, along with references to which chapters of this handbook are relevant to learning more about them.

Standards Help You Reflect on Your Teaching Practice

Standards help you set new goals to improve and assist you in monitoring your practice to meet your professional goals throughout your career. The NBPTS list of standards can be downloaded in its entirety from the Internet at http://www.nbpts.org/the_standards. The Interstate New Teacher Assessment and Support

APPLY IT!

Before you begin reading this chapter, take a piece of paper and jot down what you believe teachers should be able to do to make a difference in students' lives and learning. Then check your responses against the professional standards mentioned in this chapter. Comparing and contrasting your own perceptions with national standards will enable you to reflect on what you know vis-à-vis the expectations for a first-year teacher.

APPLY IT!

Write down your biggest fears about being a first-year teacher. Then compare your responses with the following sections, selected from recent reports, that highlight concerns. This activity will convince you that your anxieties are shared by many first-year teachers.

Table 3.1 NBPTS Standards and Corresponding Handbook Chapters

NBPTS Five Core Principles	Correlations in This Book
Teachers are committed to students and their leaning.	Chapters 15–34
Teachers know subjects they teach and how to teach those subjects to students.	Chapters 15, 21–34
Teachers are responsible for managing and monitoring student learning.	Chapters 5–20, 30–34
Teachers think systematically about their practice and learn from experience.	Chapters 1–4, 35–40
Teachers are members of learning communities.	Chapters 8, 14, 34, 36, 38

Consortium (INTASC) proposes standards that are very similar. Additionally, many states have their own set of professional teaching standards that you will need to know.

It Is Never Too Early to Begin to Reflect on Your Teaching

A simple six-step process for reflection is shown in Table 3.2.

WATCH IT! video

Developing a Philosophy of Education

Teachers reflect on their philosophies and tie them into the standards for the profession. How does your philosophy of education compare?

Main Concerns and Challenges

If you are not too worried about the challenges you are facing, you are a phenomenon, a rare individual who has it all together. You are definitely atypical. When I look back on my first year of teaching, the first word that comes to mind is *trepidation*. Also, *delight, success,* and *fun*.

Table 3.2 Reflecting on Your Teaching

The Steps	Sample Responses to Each Step
1. Clarify your beliefs.	All kids can learn. Parents must partner with teachers.
2. Own up to your strengths.	I know my subject matter. I am funny and explain things well. I am able to sense who needs a kind word.
3. Give up perfectionism.	I will never be able to carry a tune. My desk will never be as neat as I would like.
4. Question your beliefs and actions.	Maybe I shouldn't use time-out as a strategy. How can I find more time to work with individuals?
5. Devise a five-year professional development plan.	I will use more research-based teaching strategies. I will differentiate learning more effectively. I will get a master's degree in counseling. I will take more courses in special education. I will learn American Sign Language.
6. Toot your own horn.	I will invite administrators and parents to performances/debates/culminating events, etc. I will have business cards made up to hand out. I will send student work to the district office for display. I will call and invite the newspaper education reporter to special events or demonstrations.

All Teachers Face Common Challenges

More than a decade ago, Brock and Grady (1996) reported that principals and beginning teachers rank classroom management and discipline as the number-one problem, and most current research suggests that this holds true today. In addition to discipline, there are other perceived challenges during the first year and beyond:

- Dealing with individual differences
- Meeting No Child Left Behind and Race to the Top requirements
- Implementing standards
- Assessing students
- Preparing students to do well on standardized tests
- Motivating students
- Establishing good relationships with parents
- Organizing classwork
- Grading papers
- Making do with insufficient materials and supplies
- Dealing with individual student problems
- Juggling heavy teaching loads
- Having insufficient preparation time
- Establishing relationships with colleagues
- Planning lessons and preparing for the day
- Being aware of school policies and rules

How would your own list of challenges compare to the bulleted list? What challenges would you add? These are the types of concerns addressed throughout this handbook. Research-based ideas and practical solutions from veterans will be presented throughout the book to allay the anxiety you may be experiencing.

Initially, New Teachers Request Help With the Most Practical Teaching Tasks

These include locating and using teaching resources and materials, securing emotional and instructional support, getting advice about classroom organization and discipline/management, gathering information about the school system, and establishing a classroom environment.

In the Middle of the First Year, Instructional Needs Move to the Top of the List

These may include conferring with your team or department head about best practices, best strategies, and teaching resources. Effectively teaching essential curriculum standards and benchmarks and test preparation take center stage. Securing adequate resources and materials, emotional support, and classroom management assistance continue as midyear needs.

TEACHER TALKS . . .

How many people can honestly say that they love their job? I can. When I am enjoying what I do the kids get so much more out of it. They can tell when I am enthusiastic about something and in turn they get excited about it. When a child turns to me at the end of the school day and says, "Today was fun," it makes my day.

KELLY RUBIO
Fourth-Grade Teacher
Manhattan Beach, California

STATISTICS

Between 2004 and 2008, the Center for Teaching Quality (CTQ) studied teachers' working conditions across the nation, surveying more than 200,000 educators in an effort to identify factors that may impede maximum student learning. In a recent review of its studies in seven different states, the CTQ compiled a top-10 list of trends and issues:

1. Most teachers want to remain in teaching and are committed to their students.
2. Teachers who intend to leave their schools and teaching are more likely to have grave concerns about their lack of empowerment, poor school leadership, and the low levels of trust and respect inside their buildings.

(continued on following page)

STATISTICS—continued

3. Teachers and administrators view teaching and learning conditions differently—and often dramatically so.
4. New teachers who have quality support are more likely to report they will remain in teaching.
5. Teachers who report relatively low levels of satisfaction with their professional development often do not have access to the kinds of training they believe they need.
6. Except in a few instances, and not surprisingly, new teachers are less concerned about issues of empowerment.
7. Elementary school teachers are far more positive about their working conditions than are their middle and high school counterparts.
8. Teachers with different preparation and career intentions view their working conditions differently, which can have consequences for whether they stay in teaching.
9. Out-of-field assignments and teaching in high-stakes grades can have a powerful impact on teachers' perceptions of working conditions—and subsequently on their willingness to stay in a certain school.
10. Teachers' working conditions may vary more inside of schools than between them.

mythBUSTER

Teaching is easy. Anybody can do it.

First and foremost, teaching is not for everyone. Good teachers make teaching look easy, but it's not. Teachers are responsible for molding and shaping students through academics as well as character building. Sometimes the best lessons are not planned. However, a good teacher knows how to use these teachable moments and tie them into the state standards. Having good classroom management skills is an essential part of teaching. Without classroom management in place, the class will not run smoothly, nor will any learning take place. The students also have to know and feel that the teacher respects and cares for them. This is not as easy as it sounds. Teachers can develop this by being fair, firm, and consistent with all students. It takes a lot of work, but the time and effort you put into doing this will pay off in the end. Believe it or not, students know when teachers genuinely care about and respect them.

LeTiqua Bellard
Math and Science Teacher, Grades 7–9
Charlotte, North Carolina

This suggests that only after teachers have control of areas such as resources and materials are they ready for assistance with instruction.

Achieving a Balance Between Subject Matter and Student Needs Is Another Challenge

Some beginning teachers are subject-centered and some are student-centered. Lidstone and Hollingsworth (1992) were the first to identify this duality. The first group needs help in establishing routines and management, advice on attending to student learning, and encouragement to reflect on their practice and rely on themselves for answers. The latter group, already focused on the students, needs support in management and curriculum, encouragement to balance idealism and pragmatism, and support to avoid excessive self-criticism.

To find out which type you are, ask yourself whether you spend more time organizing the content or figuring out the learning styles of individuals. Do you talk to colleagues about individual kids or your subject area? Are you more concerned with the "what" of teaching than the "how to" of teaching? Not surprisingly, secondary teachers tend to be subject-centered and elementary teachers, especially primary teachers, tend to be student-centered. Which type are you?

As you plan your lessons, make sure that you are balancing both the content and your students' needs. Your lesson plan should include a section for "differentiating instruction"—the means by which you will adapt the content for specific student groups or individuals. You will read more about differentiating instruction in Chapter 28 of this handbook.

New Teachers Face Daunting Challenges, but Help Is Available

Schools and districts offer a variety of assistance. Mentor and buddy teacher programs help ease the way in more and more districts, and orientation sessions are scheduled for new teachers. Your principal and other administrative and instructional personnel are there to help.

Formal School District Induction Programs Are Very Common

These programs assume that the credential is just one stepping stone on the long journey to becoming an accomplished teacher. You may be required to attend presentations, demonstrations, and informal meetings with other new teachers. You may be assigned a mentor, who will do everything from providing a sympathetic

TEACHER TALKS . . .

You've known yourself for a long time. Think about your personal strengths and weaknesses and how to apply them in the classroom and when working with the staff. Look bravely into the mirror with a glowing smile and say, "I can do it." Remember, you are a person, so care for all of you, not just the teacher part. Know you will have a rewarding experience but that it's impossible to feel fulfilled at the end of the first week. Love and be patient with yourself even as you are loving and patient with your growing, striving, bungling, maturing students. Yes, chances are you'll have butterflies in your stomach each year; but as you think of the beautiful butterflies, you'll calm and relax.

BETTY ROSENTRATER
Elementary and High School Teacher, Retired
Moreno Valley, California

UNIT 1

AVOID IT!

Comparing yourself to more experienced teachers and becoming self-critical are self-defeating, so accept your novice status and do the best you can each day.

Complaining is considered to be unprofessional. Seek solutions from mentors instead.

shoulder to actually demonstrating effective strategies and classroom management techniques. In some states, your mentor may follow a sequence of state-mandated, beginning-teacher standards and track your progress toward meeting them. If your district has not yet formalized an induction program, seek out a buddy on your grade level, on your team, or in your department. An experienced teacher on the staff will be a great source of succor, support, and information.

Research Is Valuable, but Practical Advice Will Assuage Immediate Concerns

Research on the challenges teachers face in their first years of teaching often concludes that a balance of research and

mythBUSTER

If you ask for help, you will be perceived as incompetent.

I would say that if you don't ask for help in your first year of teaching, the principal will think you are incompetent, unaware of the challenges that you are facing, and possibly arrogant!

Teaching is always a challenge . . . because the challenges are not just the kids we teach but are the intellectual challenges of understanding how individuals learn, how we can provide the best environment and stimuli for them to learn, how we as individuals can enrich the lives of our students, how we can encourage our colleagues to do the best they can, how we can learn from our colleagues . . . and the list goes on.

Shirley Casper
Science Teacher, Grades 7–12
North Sydney Boys' High School
Sydney, Australia

practical advice makes for a successful induction into the teaching profession. You will find recent research with practical applications throughout the handbook from such prominent figures as Robert Marzano, Carol Ann Tomlinson, Fred Jones, William Glasser,

Table 3.3 Reflecting on Your Teaching

The Steps	Your Responses
1. Clarify your beliefs.	
2. Own up to your strengths.	
3. Give up perfectionism.	
4. Question your beliefs and actions.	
5. Devise a five-year professional development plan.	
6. Toot your own horn.	

Jacob Kounin, and others. Advice from veteran teachers combined with research results will provide a well-balanced set of guidelines for the new teacher to follow. Balancing research and practical advice is essential for your success.

Summary

Start early to reflect on your own teaching practice and to face the challenges that come with the profession. Help is available, and you are not alone.

Balancing research with what works and with practical advice will get you through the first year and beyond.

Reflect!

It is never too early to begin reflecting on your own teaching. Table 3.3 is a version of the table shown on p. 18, with room for you to fill in your own responses. Keep this in your journal and from time to time, note any changes as you progress in your induction.

CHAPTER 4

HOW CAN I PLAN AHEAD FOR MY FIRST DAY?

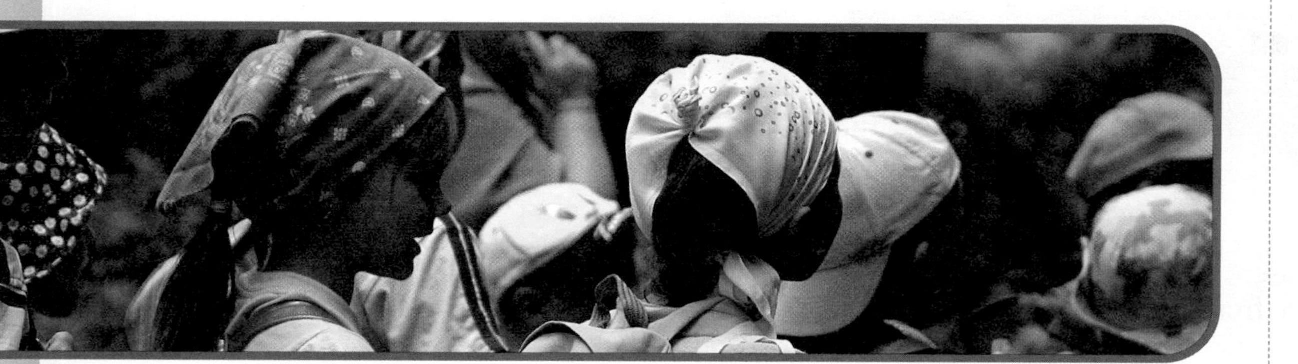

All the resources we need are in the mind.

Theodore Roosevelt

Effectiveness Essentials

- Mental planning and detailed plans in black and white are keys to success.
- Gather teachers' editions, planning documents, and supplies.
- Reach out to your students and parents.
- Familiarize yourself with your district, your school, and its community.

Plan Ahead for Success

The two keys to success in teaching are mental planning and detailed written plans. The minute you secure your teaching position is not too soon to begin preplanning for your first year and first day of teaching. Before school starts, you have an opportunity to plan the year ahead by visualizing yourself at work in your classroom and then writing down on paper those ideas and tasks that need to be accomplished before the first day. You will probably revise your drafts, so keep them in a loose-leaf binder.

Ways to Prepare for the First Day

Somehow, "firsts" seem magical: first date, first prom, first baby, first house. These moments are etched into memory. But the reality is that the first day of school is like any other, and if you are well prepared, the day will pass very quickly, and you will be on to the second!

Gather Resources

These are some resources to help with preparations:

- **Success-of-the-day journal.** Buy yourself a blank journal, and then write the date and three successes of each school day (see Figure 4.1). It might be that your class responded favorably to your poetry lesson. Perhaps your principal gave you a much valued compliment or a colleague told you how well behaved your students were. Or a parent may have commented on how much his child looks forward to coming to school each day.

  This will become your reflective journal, and initially you are allowed to write down only your successes. Later, you can add suggestions for improvement as you reflect on your day. As you reread the journal at the end of each week, you will see written proof that you know what you are doing.
- **A day planner/calendar or electronic organizer.** You probably used some sort of calendar, date book, or electronic

APPLY IT!

Ask at least three veteran teachers how they prepare for the first day of school. Every teacher, new and experienced, can always use some fresh ideas. Make a list of relevant, useful, and constructive advice and keep adding to the list as you pick up more tips along the way. The ongoing list will serve as a reminder of tasks still to be done.

NOTES

Date	Success
9/5	*First day over!*
	Plans were appropriate
	I remembered most students' names

Figure 4.1
Success-of-the-Day Journal Entry

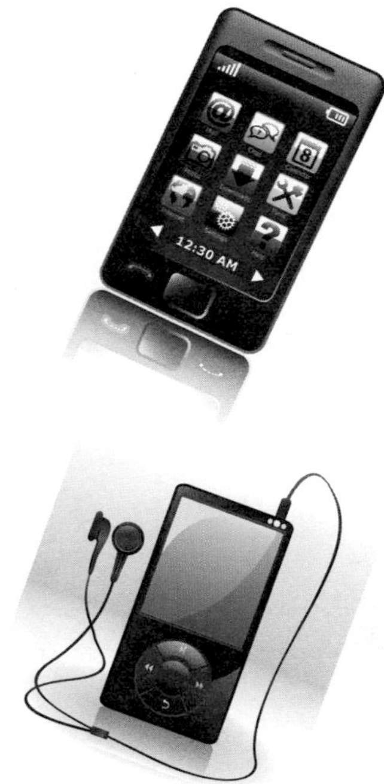

organizer to keep track of appointments, exams, and work during your college years. Now you need to think about a planner in which you can list open house dates, parent conferences, inservice seminars, faculty meetings, and other school events. Calendar apps on MP3 players, computers, iPads, and smart phones can help you keep track of important dates and events.

- **Just-in-case kit.** Keep a personal "just-in-case kit" in your desk with items such as a change of socks or hose, a toothbrush and toothpaste, sewing kit, Band-Aids, pain relievers, deodorant, cologne, breath mints, etc. If you teach a messy subject like art or chemistry or teach early grades, you may want a change of shirt or blouse in case of accidental spills. Or keep an oversized shirt around that you can wear in those messy situations. You may want to keep an extra sweater and an umbrella in your classroom and a few snack bars in case your lunch is interrupted. Pretend you are delayed at school for an evening meeting or during an emergency. What would you need to get through that day? Think of this as your school emergency/teacher survival kit.
- **Autobiographical bulletin board.** Gather materials for an autobiographical bulletin board. You might include a report card from your own school days; photos of family, pets, and travels; a list of favorite books; special quotes; certificates you have earned; a statement of your teaching philosophy; and anything else you want to share with your students. This board will serve as a visual when you introduce yourself to your class on the first day of school.

Reach Out to Your Students and Their Parents Before School Starts

Here are some ideas:

- **Parent and student letters.** Compose a parent letter that will go home on the

Introduce yourself.

first day of school. You can make templates for the rules, policies, newsletters, and open house schedule way before school starts. You can send a postcard, or a letter, to parents or to your students expressing your anticipation of the new school year (see Figure 4.2). If email addresses are available, use technology.

- **One-on-one visits.** One teacher I know makes home visits or telephones parents at the start of the school year. Although this is unusual in this day and age, you can imagine how impressed a parent would be at your level of commitment.

Take the Time to Get to Know Your School and the Surrounding Community if You Are Unfamiliar With Them

- **Attend a school board meeting.** You can even introduce yourself informally to the board members. They will be impressed that you took the time to attend.
- **Visit your school.** Take some time to visit or revisit your school site. This will enable you to find the school and see how long the commute takes. Try out your route to school during the times you will be traveling back and forth to

TEACHER TALKS . . .

Call parents the first week of school. Let them know something great you have observed about their child. This will start the year off on a positive note, and if you have to call about some problem later, you will have already established a good relationship.

LINDA MEYER
Resource Teacher
San Bernardino, California

TEACHER TALKS . . .

During your work days before school begins, seek out other teachers and take the initiative to introduce yourself. You will need the support that they have to offer, and they will appreciate your support as well.

BECKY MONROE
Language Arts and Reading Teacher
Grades 7–9
San Bernardino, California

WELCOME TO
ANCIENT HISTORY CLASS!
MR. VAN
Dear Student,
Choose a time period you would like to have lived in for an activity on the first day of class. Be prepared to tell us why you chose that time period.
I look forward to meeting you in person.
Sincerely,
Mr. Van
EUROPA
ITALIA 500

Figure 4.2
Back-to-School Postcard

see what traffic is like or how to time your arrival by rapid transit. In addition, visiting the site early will help you feel more comfortable in your new surroundings. Find out how to get your own school email and web addresses.

- **Get to know your community.** Many teachers will relocate to a new state, city, or region. Settle down as soon as possible so you can get a feel for the community and learn where best to make friends. Check out key locations in town like the public library, and meet key people, including the movers and shakers. Making friends in and out of school will give you a sense of belonging. Investigate community organizations and other activities that might interest you and enable you to connect with others.
- **Surf the school and district websites.** You will find a great deal of information here that you will need to know, such as test scores, school policies and procedures, etc. Ask about any procedures that are unclear. Learn the reasons for any policies that don't seem to make sense. Every school has its own history and challenges. You'll be better equipped to follow policies and procedures correctly if you understand the reasoning behind them.

APPLY IT!

Become an architect. Take a piece of graph paper and decide what furniture arrangement best reflects your instructional and management goals. Is your designated space a science or technology lab? In your history classes, do you want your students facing one another across a divided room? Will you be using PowerPoint as a primary instructional tool, and do you want all students facing the screen? Will you be using cooperative learning strategies? Do you need areas for small-group instruction and differentiated learning? Does your plan encourage or discourage interaction? Planning your room out on paper will save you time when you actually get into your classroom to move furniture. Create alternative plans just in case one doesn't work out.

- **Read the community phone directory, local newspaper, and website.** You will glean a great deal of information about an unfamiliar community by reading these sources of good information. Learn the history of the town and read the local newspaper to find out what the local issues are. What are the unique features of the community? What are the after-school opportunities you can refer parents to? What special services are offered to families?

Make Your Classroom a Space You Look Forward To Coming To

You will spend more hours at school in your classroom than you will at home from Monday to Friday. If you are sharing a room, you need to meet with your "roommates," negotiate some private desk and bulletin board space, and discuss sharing computers, file cabinets, storage cabinets, and technology such as the projection device. If you are a "floater" with no permanent room, buy a rolling cart to take with you as you move from room to room.

Gather Materials and Supplies for Your Students

Teacher supplies you may need include a plan book, a journal, pens and markers, a stapler and staples, paper clips, tape, rubber bands, a seating chart, subject-specific materials, a substitute teacher folder, and a substitute goodie bag. This last item should be packed with new and different materials that pertain to your subject or subjects and supplement the plans you have prepared in advance. It might include a History Channel video

TEACHER TALKS . . .

I went out and spent $1,700 on supplies and posters for my room. What I did not take into consideration was that the students did not want to see posters. They wanted to see their own work up. I did not need to spend all that money.... Another thing that I did not realize was that other teachers would be more than happy to share what they already had with me. The thing that I should have been working on was where to put all the things that I wanted up. Space is very limited in a classroom.... After the first quarter, I'm a little more choosy about what and where I put things up.

CHERYL AYALA
First-Year Teacher, Grade 5
San Bernardino, California

UNIT 1

TEACHER TALKS . . .

I teach English to second, fourth, and sixth graders at Escuela Concepción in Costa Rica. Only the sixth graders have four thin, photocopied textbooks. There are no textbooks for students in the other elementary grades. Teachers get one piece of chalk per day. This is back-to-basics teaching—the students, a blackboard, and me.

DR. GARY NEGIN
Volunteer English Teacher
Grades 2, 4, 6
San Carlos, Costa Rica

for your American history class, play scripts for an English class, an edible experiment for a middle school science class, or special arts or crafts projects and one-minute mysteries for elementary students. See Chapter 24 for information on preparing for subs.

Stock up on student supplies at discount or warehouse-type stores. A *Los Angeles Times* article (Hayasaki, 2004) reported that teachers commonly dip into their own pockets for supplies, and one profiled teacher spends as much as $2,000 of her $48,000 salary. A science teacher was quoted as spending $3,000 on special equipment and supplies. First, check out what the school provides and then, depending on the grade level of your students, you may need to supplement these supplies with some that you provide. YOU DO NOT NEED TO BUY WHEN FREE IS BETTER. There are suggestions for securing free and inexpensive materials in Chapter 23.

AVOID IT!

Don't be in denial about what lies ahead.

Don't wait until school starts to prepare yourself.

Don't wing it.

Visit your school supply room early.

Get a Copy of the Teachers' Editions of Your Textbooks Early

This is the best way you can adequately prepare your curriculum. Many teacher materials can be complex. So you will need time before school begins to get the big picture of all you are expected to teach that first year. This will also give you time to think of additional strategies or activities you can use in your lessons.

Summary

The better prepared you are with concrete plans for your first days and weeks, the more successful you will be. Gather all your materials, such as teachers' editions, planning documents, supplies, and so forth. Familiarize yourself with the context for teaching—that is, the community, the district, and the school site. Reach out your hand to parents and students even before school starts.

Reflect!

1. What preparations have you made for the first day?
2. What do you still need to do?
3. Imagine yourself setting foot in the classroom for the first time. What do you see, hear, feel? Write a reflection using all of your senses.

UNIT 1 CHECKLIST

Preplanning for First Day Checklist	For more information go to:
☐ Have I read all the state and district standards?	Chapters 3, 21
☐ Have I read school and district procedures and policies?	Chapters 4, 9
☐ Do I have an overview of the year's curriculum, including texts?	Chapters 21, 23
☐ Have I designed my classroom environment?	Chapter 10
☐ Do I have a discipline plan consistent with the district/school?	Chapter 9
☐ Have I familiarized myself with the school and community?	Chapter 4
☐ Do I have a plan for reaching out to students and families?	Chapters 4, 9
☐ Have I gathered teaching resources, including planning materials?	Chapters 4, 23

Further Reading: Books About the First-Year Teaching Experience

Baldacci, L. (2003). *Inside Mrs. B's classroom: Courage, hope and learning on Chicago's South Side.* New York: McGraw-Hill. A journalist gives up her job to teach middle school in an urban school that is overwhelmed by problems. This is a realistic view of teaching in the inner city by a teacher who faced all of the challenges head-on and eventually triumphed.

Brown, D. (2008). *The Great Expectations School: A rookie year in the new Blackboard Jungle.* New York: Arcade. Dan Brown writes about his experiences as a teaching fellow in a New York City public school. His fourth-grade class has an assortment of challenging students, and this idealistic teacher manages with humor to convey the first-year teacher's struggle to make a difference against tough odds.

Codell, E. R. (2009). *Educating Esmé: Diary of a teacher's first year* (expanded ed.). Chapel Hill, NC: Algonquin. Esmé Raji Codell compiled this diary during her first year of teaching in a Chicago public school. Madame Esmé, as she likes to be called, uses unconventional teaching methods to reach her students while bucking the status quo. This diary is a window into a very gifted first-year teacher.

Esquith, R. (2007). *Teach like your hair's on fire: The methods and madness inside Room 56.* New York: Penguin. In his fifth-grade class in Los Angeles, this passionate teacher uses innovative methods with poor immigrant children to give them confidence in their abilities to master Shakespeare, Vivaldi, and so forth.

Goodnough, A. (2006). *Mrs. Moffett's first year: Becoming a teacher in America.* New York: PublicAffairs. This is an account of a legal secretary turned teaching fellow in a pilot program in New York City. She signs on as first-grade teacher in an underperforming school in Brooklyn.

Kane, P., Ed. (1996). *My first year as a teacher.* New York: Signet. This is a collection of 25 first-year teacher accounts spanning all grade levels and all kinds of classrooms.

Kozol, J. (2008). *Letters to a young teacher* (reprint ed.). New York: Three Rivers. This book is composed of letters to a young first-year teacher in an inner-city school in Boston. In the letters, the author reflects on his days as a teacher as he offers counsel and encouragement to teachers who are passionate about making a difference.

Ladson-Billings, G. (2001). *Crossing over to Canaan: The journey of new teachers in diverse classrooms.* San Francisco: Jossey-Bass. This is an account of the challenges and rewards of teaching diverse learners in real-life situations.

Ladson-Billings, G. (2009). *The dreamkeepers: Successful teachers of African American children* (2nd ed.). San Francisco: Jossey-Bass. This book combines scholarship and the inspiring stories of eight teachers who are succeeding with their students in a predominantly African American school district.

McCourt, F. (2005). *Teacher man: A memoir.* New York: Scribner. This is the third in McCourt's series of memoirs and humorously recounts inspirational stories from his 30 years spent teaching in New York City high schools.

Michie, G., and Cisneros, S. (2009). *Holler if you hear me: The education of a teacher and his students* (2nd ed.). New York: Teachers College Press. A primarily Mexican American middle school classroom of challenging students in Chicago is the context for this inspiring account of the tribulations and rewards of teaching.

Reed, K. (1999). *Rookie year: Journey of a first-year teacher.* Boston: Peralta. A first-year teacher recounts the personal and professional challenges in his first year of teaching a fifth-grade class, known as "The Wild Bunch," in a Boston school.

First-Year Teacher Websites

Advice for First-Year Teachers

http://www.educationworld.com/a_curr/curr152.shtml

This website is geared to the needs of first-year teachers and includes survival guides, tips, resources, and links to other first-year teacher sites.

Middle Web: The First Days of Middle School

http://www.middleweb.com/1stDResources.html

This website is geared to the middle school teacher but has ideas relevant for high school as well. There is a multitude of short articles about discipline, icebreakers, connecting with parents, successful first-year and first-day advice, etc.

National Education Association

http://www.nea.org

This comprehensive website for educators features ideas, archives of research articles, education statistics, and links to classroom ideas.

New Teacher Resources

http://www.teachersfirst.com/new-tch.shtml

This website will be especially helpful to secondary teachers and includes topics such as the first day of middle school and do's and don'ts for success in middle school, along with many other useful resources, with links to the U.S. Department of Education publications for new teachers.

New Teacher Survival Guide

http://www2.ed.gov/teachers/become/about/survivalguide/index.html

This site shows how new teachers can work effectively with veteran teachers, parents, principals, and teacher educators.

Resources for New Teachers

http://www2.ed.gov/teachers/become/about/survivalguide/resources.html

This is a section of the just-mentioned survival guide that lists websites that new teachers will find useful.

What to Expect Your First Year of Teaching

http://www2.ed.gov/pubs/FirstYear/index.html

This website offers advice and strategies from first-year teachers and veterans and includes a checklist of tips.

UNIT 2

First Day

CHAPTER 5 WHAT CAN HELP ME THROUGH MY FIRST DAY?

You don't have to see the whole staircase, just take the first step.

Dr. Martin Luther King, Jr.

Effectiveness Essentials

- All new teachers are nervous as the first day approaches.
- Ten basic principles can guide you to a successful first-day experience.
- Teachers set the tone for the year on the very first day.
- You will have many opportunities to address first-day slip-ups.

UNIT 2

NOTES

All New Teachers Are Nervous as the First Day Approaches

You are not alone. The night before your first day will be a sleepless one as you worry about what to wear, what to say, whether the students will stay in their seats, and whether your plans will run out before recess or the period ends. Remind yourself that you are as prepared as you can be without actually meeting your students, and then engage in your favorite bedtime stress buster like taking a warm bubble bath or listening to music.

Most teachers do not have a first-day experience before their very own first day as an intern or as the fully credentialed teacher. Only after you have succeeded in your very own first-day experience will you finally relax. You have all the ingredients, but you still worry about whether the recipe will turn out. The first day is an untried recipe. And you can always change, adapt, and revise your plans on days 2 through 188. Your students are checking you out and trying to figure out what your expectations will be, and they may be as nervous as you are.

Ten Basic Principles Can Guide You to a Successful First-Day Experience

Incorporating and following these principles will give you a sense of control over that first day, and each principle conveys an important message to students that will help set the tone for the coming year. Although sample first-day schedules can be helpful, it is often more useful to provide you with a list of 10 fundamental ingredients for the first day. Then you can create your own gourmet dish (see Table 5.1).

Be Overprepared

Arrive very early. You will feel more confident if you can spend time checking out the classroom(s) and feeling comfortable. Make sure your name is on the board along with the daily schedule, a welcome sign is on the door, all your name tags are carefully prepared, the desks are arranged to your satisfaction, all your instructional materials are ready, your bulletin boards are fresh, and your plans are summarized for easy reference.

The one certainty for the first day is that you will forget to do something! On my first day of class, I always forget something. My students never know

Table 5.1 First-Day Principles

Guiding Principle	Message Sent to Students
1. Be overprepared.	Teacher has it all together.
2. Motivate.	School will be exciting.
3. Establish routines and a schedule.	School is organized.
4. Establish classroom rules.	I will be safe and responsible.
5. Orient students to school and classroom.	I belong and am comfortable.
6. Preview the curriculum.	I will gain mastery of new subjects.
7. Let students choose and decide.	I am part of a community of learners.
8. Include a literacy experience.	Reading and writing are keys to learning.
9. Acknowledge every student.	I am unique and special.
10. Review and assign easy work.	I can succeed. It's a snap!

because I adapt. Write a summary of your first day or first period plan on an index card and keep it close at hand. Write the outline of activities or schedule on the board as another cueing device for you and a reminder to your students that you are well organized and have given a great deal of thought to this first day. Because you have!

Message sent to students: *This teacher has put effort into this first day or period and really is businesslike. She knows what she is about and has thought this through. This teacher doesn't wing it. So I better not either.*

Motivate

Capitalize on students' anticipation and excitement on the very first day. Provide a variety of highly motivating experiences. Keep the pace moving and overplan so you never drag anything out to fill time. One kindergarten teacher brings in a chicken and eggs it has laid that week. The students talk about chickens using descriptive words, follow directions to cook the eggs, read *Green Eggs and Ham* by Dr. Seuss, make mosaics with the eggshells, and write about their experiences. That's a first day to remember! Although you need not bring in an elephant to teach the color gray, you may want to think about an exciting activity to start the day.

Students have fun while learning.

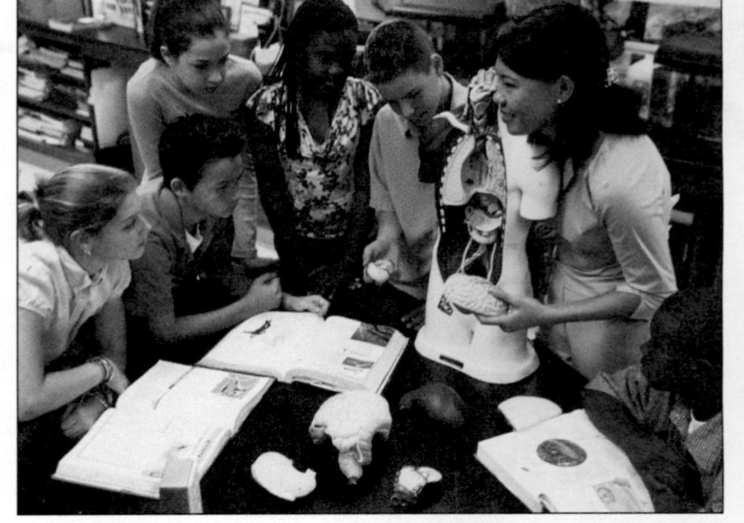

A middle school social studies teacher I know dresses up like a Roman senator, complete with toga and laurel wreath, and tells students all about the social studies curriculum. A high school earth science teacher brings in frozen models of the earth made out of melons that have been halved, hollowed out, and filled with different flavored ice creams to represent the layers. Of course, the students eat the earth after this motivating presentation. At all levels you need to motivate in some way. If you are not comfortable with a flashy activity, at least tie an ice breaker to the subject matter and make an impression. In middle and high school every one of the teachers is trying hard to get students' attention that first day.

> ***Message sent to students:*** *This class will be exciting, and the teacher has made an effort to convey that he will do his utmost to keep things moving along so we won't be bored.*

Establish Routines and a Schedule

Begin to establish a set of daily routines that first day. Unit 3 will discuss routines at length. Routines are your tools for saving time and ensuring smooth functioning, structure, and security. Introduce some routines on that first day as they are needed; others can be introduced as the week progresses.

> ***Message sent to students:*** *School is organized and predictable. This teacher will help me keep all my assignments straight and stay structured.*

Establish Classroom Rules

No matter what grade level or subject matter you teach, you will need to establish the rules of the classroom that first day. You will have an opportunity to learn about rule making in Chapter 9, and Unit 4 is devoted to discipline and classroom management. Begin to implement your strategies and create a positive discipline system based on mutual respect, responsibility, and dignity. Don't let infractions slide that first day. Thirty pairs of eyes (or more) will be watching!

> ***Message sent to students:*** *I will be safe, and I will be responsible for my actions.*

Orient Students to School and Classroom

The easiest way to orient elementary students—whether new, second language learners, or returning students—to their school is to take a walking tour that first morning, pointing out such places of interest as the rest rooms, water fountains, principal's office, and nurse's office. You also may need to show students school bus stops, places to line up after lunch, the cafeteria, assigned fire drill locations, and appropriate exits. Let the students know what the bells or other signaling devices mean. Take an "eyes only" tour of the classroom as well. Make sure that

APPLY IT!

On the first day, design a class motto, class flag, or class mascot to establish a sense of community. Cut up a huge rectangle of butcher paper into puzzle pieces and have every student write his or her name on the piece and decorate it. Call students up to add their piece to the puzzle of friendship. Have each student make a silhouette using a light source projecting the image on black construction paper (see Figures 5.1 and 5.2). Hang these around the room. Younger students can draw their images on paper plates. Or design your own motivating and inspiring beginning that is subject matter and/or age appropriate.

TEACHER TALKS . . .

I learned the importance of "The Rules of the Room" my first semester teaching high school, when I didn't establish any right at the start. I soon learned that it's much easier to ease off on rules than it is to establish them after the fact. Fortunately for me, I taught just semester-long courses, no full-year courses. So before the start of the second semester, I clearly wrote out the guidelines or rules for my classroom, and that was the first thing we went over after first introductions. It was perhaps the most important on-the-job lesson I learned throughout all my time teaching. There's just no anticipating what that first day is going to be like, and the most important thing you can do is make sure there's order in your room. It carries over for the rest of the semester . . . or year.

MARY
High School Science Teacher
Wellman, Iowa

Figure 5.1
Silhouettes

Figure 5.2
Class Puzzle

your English language learners understand what you are saying. Use gestures, visuals, and peer translators. As you look around your own classroom and study the one shown in Figure 5.3, consider which locations should be pointed out to students.

Middle and high school students also can be oriented to the school, but not in the same way. In large schools, you may discuss key landmarks near your classroom or pathways to the bathrooms, cafeteria, or main office. Make sure your students have a campus map and go over it. This is particularly helpful to students who are new to the school, such as recent elementary or middle school graduates. Orient your secondary students to the classroom and discuss how it is set up for learning.

> ***Message sent to students:*** *I belong, and I am comfortable. I know my way around the school and the classroom.*

Preview the Curriculum

Preview some of the topics students will cover and introduce them to at least one of their textbooks or readers

APPLY IT!

Young students can make a simple map of the classroom or the school grounds (see Figure 5.4 on p. 42). Or have them pinpoint their houses with stickers on a local map of the community. Older students can use Google Maps to locate their houses in relation to the school on a community map. School maps should be distributed to middle and high school students and key locations should be highlighted.

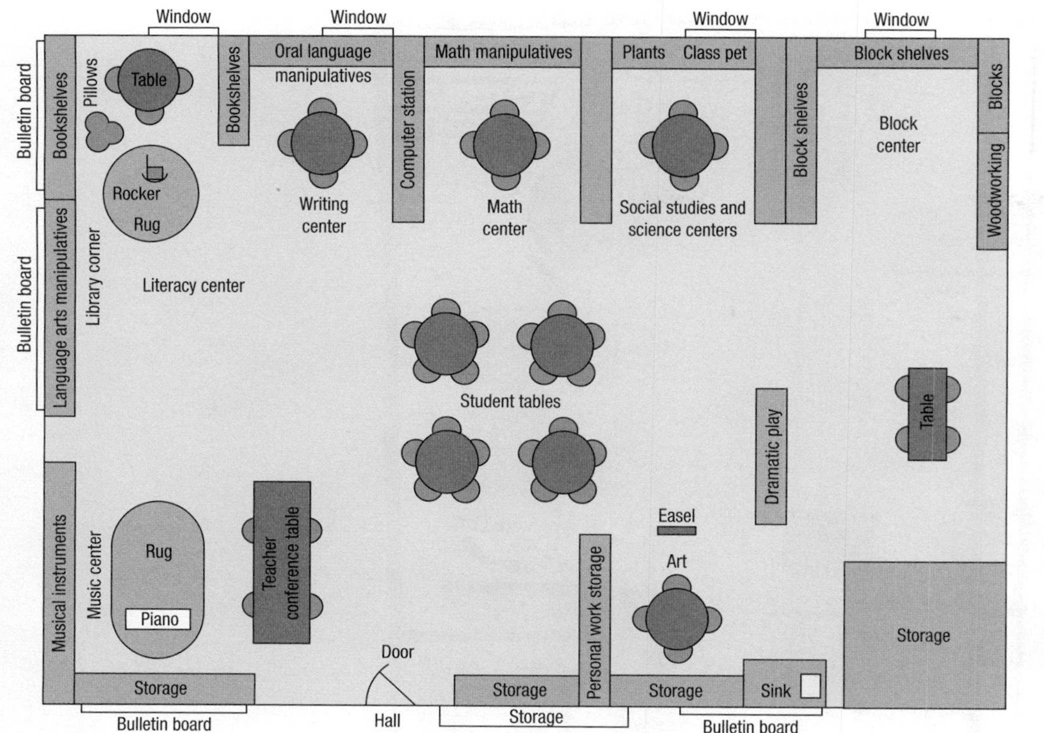

Figure 5.3

Floor Plan for a Kindergarten Classroom

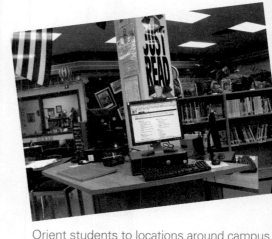

Orient students to locations around campus such as the library and the cafeteria.

that first day. Hand out the textbook(s) and take a brief survey of the table of contents. You also can construct a bulletin board that previews the curriculum and highlights the year's or semester's topics, field trips, and upcoming special events. This is the time to present the big picture and connect the content with the students' experience. Think of the first day as a splashy advertisement of the content and what it can do for students later in life.

Message sent to students: *I will gain mastery of this new material, and it looks like the subject(s) will be interesting.*

Figure 5.4
Classroom Map

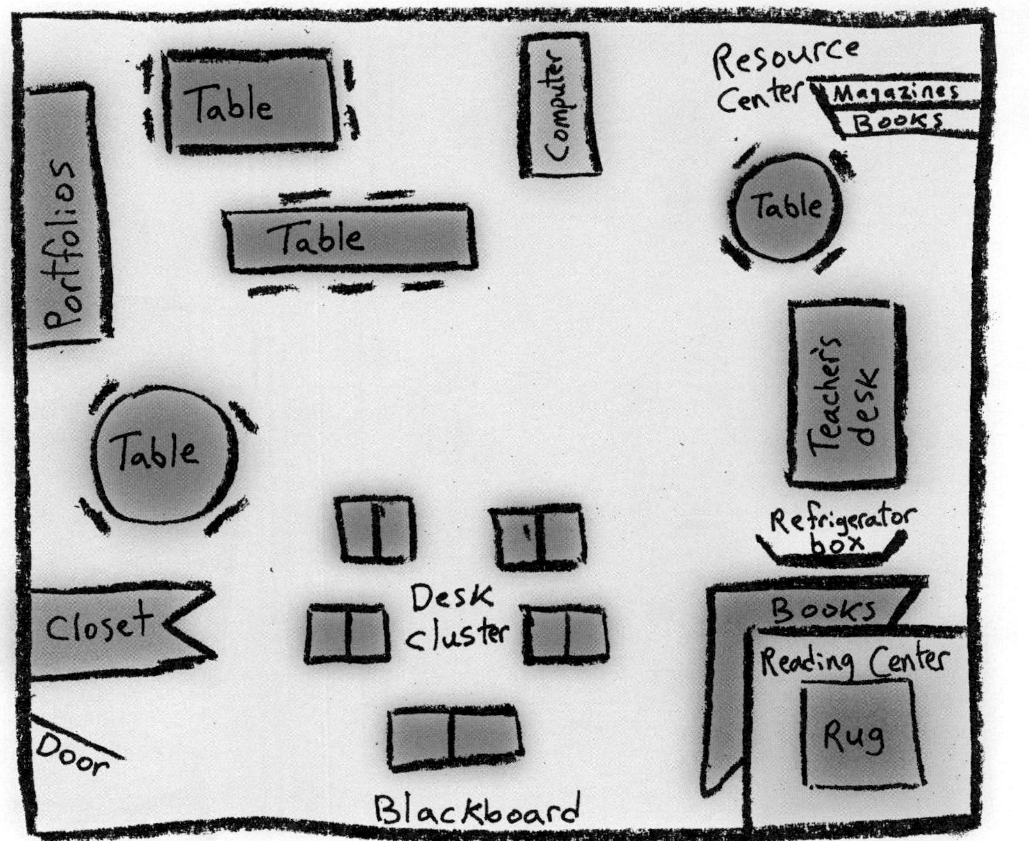

Let Students Choose and Decide

Share responsibility for decision making from the outset. Let students know they will be encouraged to make choices and participate in classroom processes. Participatory experiences that first day might include choosing seats, writing classroom rules, and so forth. In secondary school, ask the students what most interests them about the first topic or unit. Seek their input on the subject matter within the parameters of the standards. Let them know that they will have a choice on projects in terms of both content and presentation modes.

Message sent to students: *I am part of a community of learners, and I will have input and will be invited to participate in my own education.*

Include a Literacy Experience

Demonstrate the value you place on literacy by incorporating some reading-related or writing activity into your plans, no matter what grade level or subject you teach. You can turn the tide toward literacy by showing great wonder and enthusiasm for the world of books yourself. For example, read "First Day of School" in Aileen Fisher's book of poetry, *Always Wondering* (1991), to primary students after asking them to describe or write about what they are wondering on this first day of school. Table 5.2 lists some books that are appropriate to read on the first day of school, with approximate grade levels.

Message sent to students: *Reading and writing are keys to learning and to success.*

Acknowledge Every Student

Let each student know with a verbal or nonverbal response from you that she or he is welcome, valued, and special. It

APPLY IT!

Have your older students write a thank-you letter or card to a previous year's teacher. This will provide you with a purposeful writing sample.

can start with an individual greeting to each student on the way into the room. A greeting in the primary language of second language learners will make them feel welcome.

A high school government teacher I know gives his students note cards and has them write "I (name) am, beyond a shadow of a doubt, cool." Then he signs the cards and laminates them. He tells students to keep the cards with them at all times, and randomly throughout the year, he gives them extra credit if they have the cards with them. Some of his students keep those cards for years.

Message sent to students: *I am unique and special, and this teacher cares about getting to know me as a person, not just as a student.*

Review and Assign Easy Work

Prepare work for the first day that is slightly below the anticipated level of the

TEACHER TALKS . . .

Every fall I look forward to a teacher's "New Year": a fresh beginning; an opportunity to greet my new middle school kids as their sixth-grade teacher and get to know their wonderful, unique personalities as we go through their first year together. I love watching them grow and change. There's a feeling of excitement and anticipation as I go in to school a few weeks before the year starts: setting up my room, thinking of ways to get the kids energized about learning, and watching their transformation from being elementary kids from our district's four different schools into a group of middle schoolers who care about one another, help one another, and become friends for many years.

LAURIE WASSERMAN
Learning Disabilities Specialist
National Board-Certified Teacher (NBCT)
Medford, Massachusetts

Table 5.2 Books About School

		Primary (K, 1, 2)	
Minerva Louise at School *Janet Stocke*	Ella Sarah Gets Dressed *Margaret Chodos-Irvine*	The Principal's New Clothes *Stephanie Calmenson*	The Teacher From the Black Lagoon *Mike Thaler*
Starting School *Janet Ahlberg*	This Is the Way We Go to School *Edith Baer*	Officer Buckle and Gloria *Peggy Rathmann*	
Will I Have a Friend? *Miriam Cohen*	Lily's Purple Plastic Purse *Kevin Henkes*	Never Spit on Your Shoes *Denys Cazet*	
		Grades 3, 4, 5	
I'm New Here *Bud Howlett*	Math Curse *Jon Scieszka*	Amber Brown Series *Paula Danziger*	Class Clown *Johanna Hurwitz*
My Teacher Glows in the Dark *Bruce Coville*	Sixth Grade Can Really Kill You *Barthe DeClements*	Junie B. Jones Series *Barbara Park*	
		Middle School	
Merlyn's Pen: Fiction, Essays, and Poems by America's Teens *R. James Stahl*		Soft Hay Will Catch You: Poems by Young People *Sanford Lyne and Julie Monk*	
Olive's Ocean (chapter book) *Kevin Henkes*		Ten-Second Rainshowers: Poems by Young People *Sanford Lyne*	
Chicken Soup for the Teenage Soul *Jack Canfield*		Poems From Homeroom: A Writer's Place to Start *Kathi Appelt*	
How I Survived Middle School Series *Nancy Krulik*		Swimming Upstream: Middle School Poems *Kristine O'Connell George*	
		High School	
Depending on your subject matter, select a short biography of a scientist, historical figure, mathematician, athlete, writer, health worker, political leader, etc., and have your students read and respond orally or in writing with a prompt from you. You can search for biographies at http://www.biography.com.			

class. Why? Everyone should go home that very first day feeling successful, believing that he or she has accomplished something. Step in when you see that a given task is too difficult or frustrating. You have the whole year to challenge students and expand their capacities and talents.

Message sent to students: *I can succeed. It's a snap!*

Teachers Set the Tone for the Year on the Very First Day

The first day should be framed within the regular class schedule you have worked out. The students should experience a routine sequence of activities from the outset. Your new colleagues can help here. Many schools and/or districts will have orientations and teacher-only workday before students arrive. At that time, you can speak with teachers at your grade level or in your department and survey them about what they actually do step by step on the first day. Take very careful notes. Typical first-day schedules for elementary and secondary teachers follow.

Here's a Generic Elementary First-Day Schedule

This schedule is a template of common first-day activities. Your grade-level colleagues will be able to help you adapt this generic agenda since they know about the bell, recess, and lunch schedules and other special first-day events you should anticipate.

Welcome. Post a welcome sign on the door. Welcome your students at the door and direct them to take a seat. Have your name on the board and pronounce it for your students. Let them choose seats or have the seats already assigned. See Chapter 6 for ideas on assigning or choosing seats.

Routines/morning exercises/flag. Have a list of what must be accomplished during the morning routines and establish a sequence that will become habitual after the first few days.

Orientation to classroom/school. Take a walk around the school site and orient the students to the classroom, stressing what is yours, what is theirs, and what materials are available to use with and without teacher permission.

Rule making. Either present the rules or engage in rule making with your students. You will read more about this in Chapter 9.

Recess/snacks. Find out ahead of time what (if any) snacks are allowed and how the snacks are provided. Will

TEACHER TALKS . . .

On my first day of teaching first grade, a little boy went missing after lunch. I didn't notice until the end of afternoon recess around 2:00 P.M. He was simply doing what he had done in kindergarten the year before at lunchtime. He went home! In a panic I called the principal. She went to his house and found him sleeping on the porch because his parents hadn't expected him home until 3:30.

P.S. I wasn't fired and am still teaching 20 years later.

LINDA MEYER
Resource Teacher
San Bernardino, California

UNIT 2

STUDENT SAYS . . .

On the first day of school the teacher welcomed us. I was calm. She was easy on us. I felt happy. She explained the rules to us. She told us who our three teachers were. I was really bored. She told us what they taught. I felt interested. She reviewed a lot of things. I felt as if I knew everything. Love, Riley.

RILEY
Third Grade, Age 8
South Charleston, Ohio

parents take turns bringing in snacks? Will you have rules about what kind of snacks are acceptable? Avoid snacks such as peanut butter that may trigger potential allergic reactions. Will milk money be collected? Where is recess equipment stored? Will you have ball monitors?

Language arts/reading. Distribute literature books, read aloud, or have the students write for diagnostic purposes.

Centers for kindergarten or math. Decide which centers you will have and shorten the time for students' first experience. Most of your center time will be taken up with an explanation of the rotation. A math diagnostic test may be administered on the first day, but also excite students' imaginations with some special math activity.

Lunch. Students go to lunch or go home after morning kindergarten.

Science/social studies/art. On the first day, introduce your first science or social studies unit and combine it with artistic expression.

Wrap up/clean up. Summarize the day so students will remember what they did when parents ask the question, "So what did you do in school today?"

Preview the next day. Tell your students what exciting lessons they will be learning tomorrow so they will return to school eager to see what you have planned.

Here's a Generic Secondary First-Day Schedule

Consult with your team or department colleagues after you have a tentative agenda. They will help you adjust the agenda since they know about the bell and lunch schedules as well as other special first-day happenings you should anticipate.

Welcome. Welcome your students at the door and direct them to take a seat. Have your name on the board and perhaps a welcome sign on the door. Have students fold index cards and make nameplates or provide nametags. You might take digital photos of the students to help you remember who's who. Small versions can be pasted on the seating chart you develop. Have a mini-agenda of the class session on the board.

Administrative tasks. Take attendance. Check the pronunciation of the names and ask if there is a nickname or shortened form the student prefers. Make a tentative seating chart.

Introductions. Use any of the introductory devices described in Chapter 8. Tell the students something about yourself and about how you got interested in teaching this particular subject area. Include your schooling background and your approach to teaching.

Expectations. Discuss your expectations and class rules. These should conform to the school and district rules and be posted on the bulletin board. Make sure to let the students know that mistakes are permitted in class but there is only one pass for each rule that is broken. Discuss the consequences for failure to follow the rules. Discuss your policy for late work, make-up work, absences, etc.

Routines. Let the students know what they will need to bring to class each day, how you or the teaching assistant will take attendance, how to set up their notebooks, homework policies, general expectations, procedures for sharpening pencils, bathroom pass policy, throwing items in the wastebasket, raising hands, and generally what will happen routinely each class period.

Preview curriculum. Tell students your goals and objectives and give an overview of the content they will master during the semester. Let them know what big projects are coming up and how your grading system works. Display sample projects from last year to set the standard high. Most teachers distribute a mini-syllabus similar to the ones you have been given in university classes. Syllabi make assignments clear; discuss assessment and grading policies; set due dates; detail penalties for late work, tardies, and absences; spell out rules; list needed supplies; and explain procedures for make-ups, etc., all in one place. See the following Classroom Artifacts for a step-by-step description of a first day and an actual high school syllabus.

Short activity. Try to fit in one very short activity related to your subject. Enforce all the rules you have just set down regarding hand raising, calling out, listening, etc. Possibilities include

- A jazzy science experiment
- A math puzzler or shortcut students don't know about
- A two-minute mystery to solve

See Apply It! for an example of a simple inquiry activity.

APPLY IT!

This is a short, generic inquiry activity that can be applied to any subject area on the first day. Hide an item related to your subject matter in a mystery box. Before the item can be revealed, make the following rules clear:

1. Everyone must get a turn.
2. Only yes/no questions are allowed. (Is it alive? Is it made out of metal? Is it found in a house?)
3. The teacher will not answer the same question twice.
4. Each student gets to write down his or her answer on a sticky note.
5. Prizes can be awarded.

CLASSROOM ARTIFACTS

I am a high school Spanish teacher who used to teach ESL. Here are a few things that I do on the first day of school in my Spanish classes:

1. I let students sit where they want initially. This helps me know who is friends with whom and who should *not* sit near each other.
2. I introduce myself and have students do a quick-write (something quick and about themselves but a little zany)—like "Pick an object you have on you or with you and describe how it went about its first day of school." This gets them thinking and keeps them quiet and focused while I take attendance. I always have extra paper and pencils in my community area for those who come unprepared.
3. Then I do a team-building activity. We might line up shortest to tallest or by birthday months or something. Then I have them create a double line and share their quick-writes—but in the form of musical chairs. I play some music, they move, and then they stop when the music stops and introduce themselves and share their piece with the person across from them. Sometimes we share the funniest responses with everyone.
4. From there, I go over my rules and expectations. This can be a bit boring, so I tend to infuse my monologue with funny, practical statements at the end of a detailed list—like "Be cool, don't mess up." Some teachers try to have a buy-in, something that makes the kids feel like they are in the presence of greatness and that this class is going to be awesome. I think there is a place for that, but it's not my personality. I try to make the kids feel like our classroom is a community; and while I am in charge, they have the power to make or break their final outcome in our class as individuals because of the way they contribute (or don't contribute) to the whole as members of a family or community. There are a few other ways that people do this. One teacher I know gives out a list of 64 rules. These span "Wash your hands after you use the bathroom" to "Don't use glitter on projects or in life." Ha! Another teacher says that he will out teach anyone at any point and challenges the kids to find someone who wants to take him on. He then tells them that they can earn extra credit by telling him that he looks nice and by saying it as if they mean it. In both cases, these teachers are adding something quirky to their first day hoopla, and this makes them memorable and implies a sense of confidence that can deeply influence student behavior.

(continues)

5. Next, I usually make the class do an evacuation drill practice, even if it's not required, because it makes them move (after my boring monologue on expectations). It also makes me feel better because then I know they understand what to do in an emergency and I don't have to think about it again.
6. I always assign homework on the first day. I usually have students read over and sign off on a syllabus expectation sheet, and then I have them write me a short letter. I ask them to tell me the most extraordinary thing about themselves and anything that will help me meet their needs.
7. I pass out participation points throughout the period. Participation is a big deal in my class. As we go through our first class, I start giving out points to demonstrate how students can earn them. I don't give out candy (I don't think we need to eat junk or suggest that it is a reward), but I do give out points for appropriate interaction.

ESL is a very different situation from Spanish class. I usually spend my first day going over basic introductions and basic school vocabulary (like *bathroom, office,* etc.), and I do that by giving a tour of the building. I spend a lot of time on that first day helping students figure out the building and things like lockers and school norms (dress code, materials, school ID, etc.).

Nikki Shull
High School Spanish Teacher
Denver, Colorado

CLASSROOM ARTIFACTS

A Real Syllabus
U.S. History: Class Rules and Policies

Place this sheet in the front of your notebook.

Notebook: Taking notes is an essential skill and can be acquired only by experience. Every student must take notes and keep a notebook. A notebook is helpful in developing habits of good organization; good organization means time saved and no searching for papers. Students should take notes from class lectures and discussions. At least 60% of the objective test questions will come from matters discussed in class—topics that may not be covered by the assigned readings. A carefully kept notebook will make studying for

(continues)

TEACHER TALKS . . .

I realized that high school students didn't like a lot of rules, so I had three rules that I gave them on the first day, and they worked out really well. The rules were

Respect yourself
Respect others
Respect property

Everything could be broken down into these three rules, and they did help the students become responsible for their own behavior. They could always figure out which rule they had broken and took responsibility for things.

JOHNNA DEBELLA
Teacher Educator
Denver, Colorado

CLASSROOM ARTIFACTS—*continued*

tests much easier. Notes may be used on the test for the last 20 minutes. If you are absent, it is YOUR responsibility to copy the notes you have missed from another class member.

Tests: The tests will generally be objective, with at least 40% of the multiple-choice questions coming from the assigned reading. Some of the questions will not be discussed in class, but if you have done the assigned reading, you should do well on them. The remaining 60% of the questions will come from the notes. Some unit tests may have both objective and essay portions. I will usually tell you ahead of time what the essay question will be so that you may prepare for it. I expect that all rules of English will be followed on all essays, along with good organization (i.e., introduction, body, conclusion).

Make-up tests: Anyone who misses a regularly scheduled test for any reason must make up the test. The make-up test may or may not be the original test. No notes may be used on the make-up test. Make-up tests may be taken during the class period in another room or after school (my choice).

Quizzes: Quizzes may come at any time and may cover lectures, discussions, readings, videos, and assignments.

Homework: All homework assignments will be done in ink (blue, black, or purple). Assignments done in pencil or other colors will NOT be accepted. All assignments must be turned in on time—no late papers will be accepted! There is no penalty for excused absences—papers will be due upon your return to school. If you are absent either on the day an assignment is given or on the day that assignment is due, the assignment will be accepted only if your absence is excused. Note: If you attend school for any portion of the day but miss my class, you must turn in that assignment or receive a zero.

Copying: While you may desire to work with a friend on an assignment, I expect you to do your own work. Any form of copying will result in zeros for all parties involved. This, of course, does not include any group assignments that might be made.

Attendance: In a class such as history, being in class is very important. Absences do tend to reduce a student's learning and subsequently lower his/her grade. This is especially true because much of the test material is covered in class.

Suspensions and cuts: No credit will be given for work missed if you are suspended or cut class.

Field trips, sports, and activities: All absences must be prearranged before you may be excused from class. Failure to prearrange any absence will result in a cut being issued. Any assigned work due on the day of your prearranged absence must be turned in before you leave on your trip or you will receive no credit.

(continues)

Tardies: It is essential that students arrive on time, are prepared, and are ready to work. If you arrive late, you cause the instructor (that's me, hint, hint) extra work (which I detest) and waste valuable class time. If you are not in your seat when the bell rings, you are tardy! If you are detained by another teacher or school staff member, be sure you have a pass. Find your seat with the least possible disruption. If you arrive tardy (unexcused) for the THIRD time during a grading period, you will be given a choice to either stand up in the back of the room for the entire period and lose your Off Campus Card or spend one hour of detention after school with me. Standing for the period or one hour of detention will erase the tardy for that day only. You may stand one more time or spend one hour in detention to erase the next (fourth) tardy; after that you will lose your Off Campus Card and the opportunity to do extra credit. The next tardy (really your fifth tardy of the quarter), you will spend one hour after school on either a Tuesday or Thursday in detention with me! Failure to spend the assigned detention will result in a one-day suspension for defiance. Each quarter begins with no tardies.

Class rules

1. Come prepared with notebook, pencil or pen, and paper.
2. Bring your textbook to class every day. If you do not bring your textbook, you will be sent back to your locker to get it and receive a tardy.
3. Be in your seat when the bell rings.
4. Be courteous and raise your hand if you wish to speak.
5. Follow school rules.
6. You will be treated as an adult and will be expected to act accordingly. The rules of common sense and courtesy will be followed by all.

Grade sheet and scale: Each student must keep his/her own point totals and grade average. You should therefore be aware at all times of how well you are doing. A cinch notice (my vernacular for "progress report," which is sent out halfway through each quarter) or poor grade should not come as a surprise. This course is not graded on a curve: each student earns a grade based on his/her individual performance.

90–100 = A   80–89 = B   70–79 = C   60–69 = D   59% and below = F

Pluses and minuses are added as follows:

0, 1, 2 =	(–)	80% 81% 82% =	B-
3, 4, 5, 6, =	straight grade	83% 84% 85% 86% =	B
7, 8, 9 =	(+)	87% 88% 89% =	B+
.5+	round up to next number		

(continues)

UNIT 2

TEACHER TALKS . . .

Tell the students they all have an "A+" on this first day. It can go down only if they don't do all assignments on time, pay attention, do extra credit work, and pass all tests with a "B" or better. By doing this they are protecting their grade. All responsibility is on them. They have no excuse to get a poor grade or fail, even if their test scores aren't perfect.

NANCY DEMAGGIO
High School Physical Education Teacher
Redlands, California

CLASSROOM ARTIFACTS—*continued*

Research paper: It is the policy of the Social Science Department that a research paper be done during one of the semesters. We will do the research paper during the SECOND semester. Topics and format will be discussed during that time.

Extra credit: Extra credit is available only to those students who do the assigned classwork and homework. Only students who have successfully completed 80% of their assignments AND have perfectly cleared attendance will be eligible to do extra credit. Incomplete assignments will diminish your opportunity to do extra credit. Extra credit may be used only to raise your grade from "F" to "D," "D" to "C," or "C" to "B." You may not raise your grade from "B" to "A" with extra credit. Extra credit is limited to a maximum of 10% of the points per quarter and must pertain to what has been studied during that quarter. All projects, research reports, drawings, etc., must be approved by the instructor and are due one week before the end of any grading period.

Teacher assistance: Students who find the work difficult should see the instructor early in the quarter. Help will be made available before or after school. It is essential for any student experiencing difficulty to do all the assigned work. It is possible for a student who has difficulty on tests to pass the class by doing all the assignments and extra credit.

My class teaching schedule is

Periods 1, 2, 3	U.S. History CP	Room SS-6
Period 3–6	Work Experience	Work Exp. Office
Period 7	Work Experience	Classroom SS-2 (Tues. & Thurs. 2:20–3:15)

Work experience office phone # ___________. Call anytime after 10:45 A.M.

Parent and student signatures: The purpose of these rules is to inform all concerned as to what I expect and how I intend to run the class. I believe it is important for everyone to know ahead of time what the class policies are so that confusion and future problems can be eliminated. If you have read and understand your responsibilities for being a member of this class, please sign. A parent or guardian must also read and sign this paper.

Thank you.
Mr. Thomas Kaszer
Tokay High School
Lodi, California

Student's name ______________________________
Date ______________________________
Parent/guardian signature ______________________________
Comments or suggestions: ______________________________

AVOID IT!

By all means, when parents ask your students what they did in school or in a certain subject, you *do not* want them to utter the dreaded words, "Nothing much." When you look over your plans for the day, put yourself into your students' shoes and ask yourself, "Would I go home and talk about an exciting day, or would I yawn and say the dreaded words?"

Wrap up. Set a timer to let you know the period is coming to an end. Have students gather materials, clean up, and wait for your signal to leave. Remind them of what to bring to class the next day and give a very short homework assignment. Review all rules and procedures every day that week to reinforce them and orient any new students.

Oops, I Forgot Something

Remember, Rome wasn't built in a day, and you don't have to accomplish everything in one day either. Unlike other firsts—first date, prom, graduations from high school and college, job interview, car purchase, birth of a child—you can redo the first day of school over and over again for the rest of the semester or school year. First days have a funny way of erasing themselves, and you can start anew each and every day.

Summary

All new teachers are nervous as the first day approaches. Teachers set the tone for the year on the very first day. If you slip up, you will have many opportunities in the coming weeks to correct the missteps. Some key principles will make your day go more smoothly:

1. Be overprepared.
2. Motivate.
3. Establish routines and a schedule.
4. Establish classroom rules.
5. Orient students to school and classroom.
6. Preview the curriculum.
7. Let students choose and decide.
8. Include a literacy experience.
9. Acknowledge every student.
10. Review and assign easy work.

Reflect!

How comfortable are you feeling about the first day of school? What concerns are uppermost in your mind? To allay those concerns, design a first-day or first-period schedule. Use the guidelines and examples in this chapter as models for your own first day or period.

TEACHER TALKS . . .

On the first day of middle school, I ask the students to brainstorm all of their concerns about middle school. Some of those most frequently mentioned are getting lost, mean teachers, gangs, getting on the wrong bus, too much homework, and being offered drugs. They record their lists, and on the second day the students take out their lists and we have a reality check to see which of these things actually occurred. Then the students are asked to turn the two lists into an essay. This process serves two purposes: it alleviates anxieties and puts them at ease and, secondarily, I have an initial writing sample from each student.

KATHLEEN BEARD
Middle School Social Studies/
English Teacher
29 Palms, California

CHAPTER 5

CHAPTER 6

HOW DO I ARRANGE AND ASSIGN SEATS?

At a round table, every seat is the head place.

German proverb

Effectiveness Essentials

- Your seating arrangement should be consistent with your instructional philosophy.
- Choosing seats can be a first exercise in responsible decision making.
- Teachers should move students who make bad choices.
- Seat students with special needs and second language learners to optimize learning.
- When sharing a room, establish ground rules openly and honestly.

When I attended public school, there was one seating design—bolted-down desks—and two schemes for assigning seats: alphabetical or size order. A saving grace was poor eyesight, hearing impairment, or behavioral problems. Those students were placed up front, close and personal, next to the teacher's desk. My bottle-thick glasses gave me a front-row seat. Some might say it was because I talked too much, but I will never admit to that.

It is time to put on your designer's hat and think about your room arrangement and how you can fit the 20–40 students into the space that will be your home away from home for the year. In this chapter you will encounter some considerations that should guide your blueprints.

WATCH IT! video

Classroom Arrangement and Arranging Furniture and Materials

Teachers discuss how classroom arrangement is dependent on the age of students and type of instruction taking place. After watching the videos, make at least two tentative and different floor plans for your room.

Your Seating Arrangement Should Be Consistent With Your Instructional Philosophy

Another way of saying this is that your seating arrangement should be determined by how you want to conduct business in your classroom. Your classroom reflects your personality and instructional style and takes into account the needs (intellectual, emotional, and social) of your students. If you plan on lecturing using PowerPoint, you may want your students in rows, all facing forward for optimal viewing. If you are a cooperative learning advocate, you can minimize disruption by having students already seated in clusters. Clusters also facilitate the learning center approach favored by many elementary teachers and accommodate differentiated learning at any grade level.

Seating Arrangements Vary From Classroom to Classroom

A first step is to look at various arrangements in classrooms around the school to see the alternatives available. Ask your colleagues which arrangements

TEACHER TALKS . . .

My students are always clustered in groups. I always have at least one high and one low per group. That way the students have someone to scaffold with when they begin independent work.

KRIS UNGERER
Kindergarten Teacher
Riverside, California

seem to work best for them and why they arranged the desks or tables as they did. Collect as many ideas as you can. Find out how many students are on your class list and see which configurations accommodate that number best. There are some basic configurations to consider.

Rows or Modified Rows Will Reduce Distraction and Social Interaction

You will find desks arranged in rows or tables oriented toward the front of the room in many classrooms (Figure 6.1a). This arrangement tells the students that you are in charge and literally at the head of the class. This is a way to curb discipline problems at the outset, and many novices rely on this seating arrangement to diminish talking and distractions.

Row upon row of seats may convey the message that cooperative work is not the priority and that students work independently. However, effective teachers model moving desks quietly and quickly to form clusters or groupings when collaborative activities are planned.

Figure 6.1a
Rows

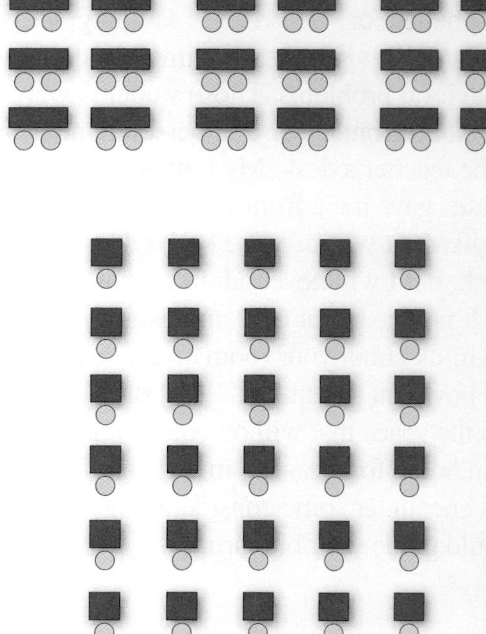

Clustering Facilitates Differentiated Learning for Students With Special Needs and Second Language Learners

Clustered tables or desks (Figure 6.1b) provide a social environment conducive to projects, cooperative learning, and differentiated learning. This configuration allows for sharing of materials

WATCH IT! video

Take Some Classroom Tours

Watch the video clips that pertain to the grade or grades you will be teaching. As you watch the clips, write down the classroom features/ideas that you would like to emulate and add some ideas of your own. What did you see in the clips that you had not seen before? Would you like to be teaching in this classroom setup? Why or why not?

- Summit Elementary School, kindergarten
- Summit Elementary School, grade 2
- Rees Elementary School, multi-grade 3, 4, 5
- Cairo Middle School, seventh-grade math
- High school world history (Specially Designed Academic Instruction in English [SDAIE])

and more interaction. The downside is that clustering may create management and even discipline problems. Make sure students at clustered tables can see the board and all technology and

Figure 6.1b
Clusters

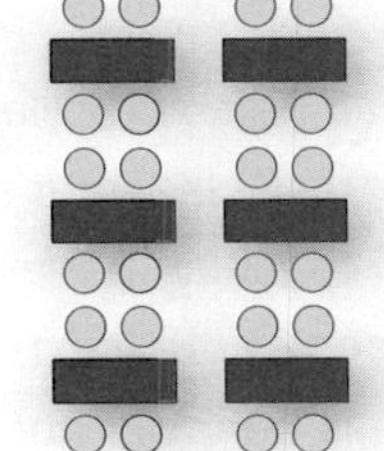

instructional locations without twisting into pretzels. No student should have his or her back to the instructional sites.

The Horseshoe Configuration Allows for More Space and Reduces Interaction

More students are oriented toward the front of the room, and the teacher has greater access to all students (Figure 6.1c). The horseshoe configuration can be used on a larger scale, or students can

TEACHER TALKS . . .

As an upper elementary teacher, I understand that the days of nametags and all the books stacked neatly on each desk are no doubt passé, and certainly not my style. I am concerned about arranging my room so every seat is relatively good and so that my independent work areas are accessible. As far as seating goes, I let students find their own with the warning to find something that fits because it might be a long time before I make changes. Then I adjust seating to compensate for social irresponsibility, language help, or physical difficulties (hearing, "lost" eyeglasses, etc.). I also radically change around the seating at least once a month to promote more diverse social interaction. Also, at my present school the difference between initial class lists and who actually shows makes a lot of preplanning in

(continued on following page)

UNIT 2

TEACHER TALKS—*continued*

this area a waste of time. I do listen to the moms who tell me on the first day not to let their child sit by. . . . That is almost always good advice.

ART EUSTACE
Fifth-Grade Teacher
Fontana, California

sit in a circle to encourage debate and discussions—especially in middle and high school classes (Figure 6.1d). On the negative side, one high school teacher cautions colleagues to stay alert as students in this configuration now

APPLY IT!

Your seating chart can be a valuable assessment tool as well. Use your seating chart to assess *your* teaching behaviors, patterns, and practices as well as monitor your students' in-class behavior and response patterns.

Make several copies of your finalized seating chart. Use the copies to put some symbol next to the students you call on. This will help you identify who is responding the most and who needs to be encouraged to respond more. You want to ensure equity in your questioning. You can also use copies of the seating chart to identify your pattern of movement around the room. Attach a copy of the seating chart to a clipboard every so often and draw lines to see how well you are circulating around the room. Use seating chart copies for other notations as well, such as inattention, rule breaking, unique responses, etc.

Figure 6.1c
Horseshoes

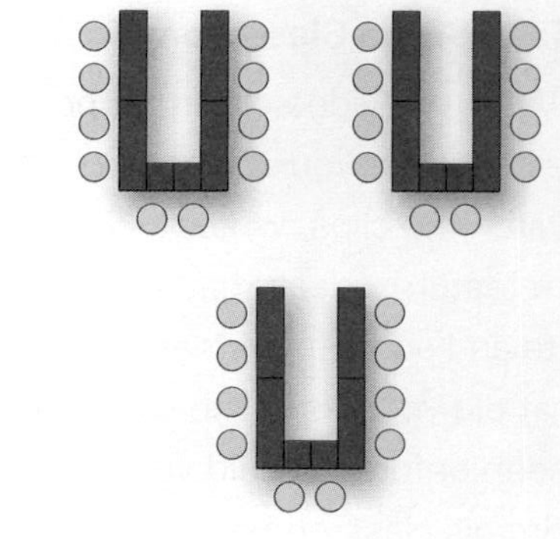

Figure 6.1d
Circles

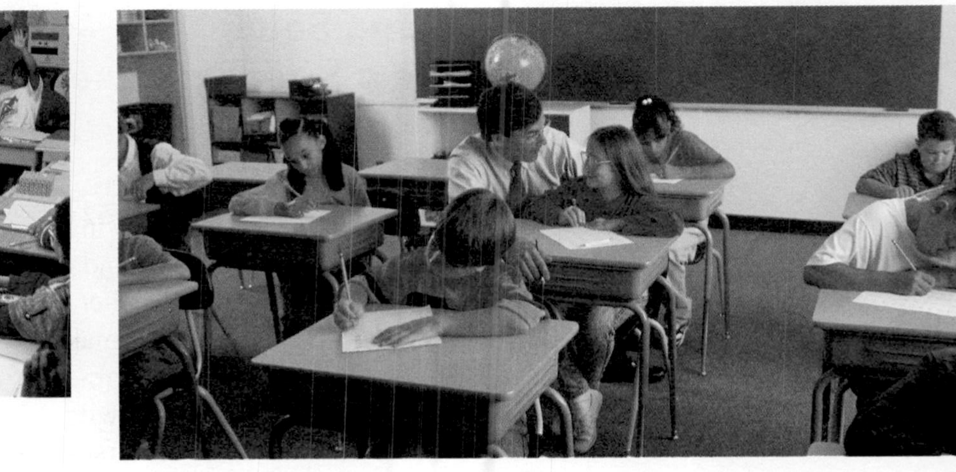

have an easy opportunity to communicate nonverbally with each other.

These basic building blocks—the individual desk, the cluster, the mini-horseshoe, and the circle—can be arranged in any number of ways. Or the elements can be combined in the same classroom.

If you are working in a team in block schedules, you will want to confer with your teammates about their methods of arranging and assigning seats. Check to see how seats are arranged in the classroom(s) you are assigned to. Since you are sharing space, your choices may be limited. Secondary school teachers generally use a seating chart and/or use nameplates for the desks or tables that facilitate attendance taking. Students take their index cards or nameplates from a table or pocket chart, so you will know who is absent at a glance. Use different colors for each period, and your nametags or nameplates can be easily sorted if they get mixed up.

Different teachers prefer different room arrangements.

UNIT 2

TEACHER TALKS . . .

At the beginning of the year, I assign seats to my students. Midway through the semester, I rearrange the assignments, but I turn it into a logistical challenge. My room has three large tables (islands really); two of them have six seats and the third has four seats. I allow the students to sit anywhere they want with the following. restrictions: They cannot sit at the same table. They cannot sit across from or beside anyone whom they were previously across from or beside. It is not that hard for them to figure out, and they have fun figuring it out.

STEPHEN PULLIAM
High School Science Teacher
Stony Brook, New York

Choosing Seats Can Be a First Exercise in Responsible Decision Making

Choosing your own seat is increasingly common in elementary, middle, and even high school classrooms. The teacher should emphasize good decision making and remind students that bad or irresponsible choices are subject to swift teacher modification before the first week of school has ended. From the following options, choose the one that is age appropriate. The first two are suggestions for elementary school teachers:

1. Draw numbers from a hat and the number 1 gets to choose first, number 2 second, and so forth.
2. Determine criteria for choosing first, such as white tennis shoes, red clothing, sayings on shirts, etc.
3. Let the students come in and choose a seat, temporarily or permanently.
4. Have nametags on the predetermined seats.
5. Allow free choice, but during the first week reseat any students with special needs or those with obvious incompatibilities with seatmates before finalizing your seating arrangement.

Move students who make bad choices. In other words, free seating choices are not final until the teacher says they are final. And even then, students are reminded that seating charts are written in pencil and may be changed at any time. New seat selections can be made every few months or at midsemester in the interest of fairness. Students can make new friends and have a new classroom vantage point.

APPLY IT!

If you have students sit in clusters or grouped at tables, you might ask them to come up with names for their table groups or clusters related to the curricular content. They can be names of constellations, continents, mythological figures, desert animals, etc. Then they can make nametags reflecting their table, row, or cluster identity or hang a cluster identity sign from the ceiling.

Students With Special Needs and Second Language Learners Should Be Your Main Concern

Seat non-native speakers next to native speaker buddies and make sure your students with special needs have their individual circumstances accommodated. The cumulative record card, parents, teachers, administrators, and your own observations may help you identify those who need special accommodation. If you are using self-selection as your seating method, you need to use utmost sensitivity when reseating students with special needs so as not to draw undue attention to them. Since you have already stated that seat selections are not final until you say they are, making changes of this sort can appear routine.

When Sharing a Room, Have an Open and Honest Discussion to Establish Ground Rules

You may want to address topics such as leaving the room clean and ready for the next occupant, returning moved furniture to an agreed-upon arrangement, turning off all computers, removing personal materials to a storage container, use of common supplies, allocation of board and bulletin board space, etc. Another topic to address is how the teacher(s) with whom you share a room feel about your remaining in the room to prep. Some teachers don't want to be watched, and you need to be up front with colleagues about your feelings and theirs.

AVOID IT!

Do not isolate any student based on hearsay, rumor, or gossip. Give every student a chance to start anew.

Do not hesitate to modify a dysfunctional seating arrangement.

Do not be afraid to modify student seating if you see obvious cliques developing based on race, culture, school social status, etc.

FLOATER FUNDAMENTALS

A floater is a migrating teacher, one without a permanent classroom who occupies rooms vacated by teachers at lunch or during prep periods. It's hard enough being a new teacher without having to float.

But there is good news:

- You get to see other teachers' classroom arrangements and bulletin boards.
- You don't have to decorate the space.
- You get a lot of exercise running across campus to your next room.

Here are a few survival tips for floaters:

- Buy a sturdy rolling cart for transporting materials.
- Stay very organized.
- Color-code all materials by period—e.g., all period 1 folders, assignments, seating chart, and lesson plans are on blue paper; all period 2 instructional items are on green paper.
- Use transparencies instead of writing on the board.
- Use a flash drive for your lessons.
- Befriend your classroom mates. You may be able to negotiate a small space on the bulletin board and a place to store your stuff.
- Maintain a positive attitude so you can graduate to a room of your own.

Summary

Your seating arrangement should be consistent with your instructional philosophy. You can teach and reinforce with your students how to rearrange the furniture quickly and quietly to facilitate group work or other instructional purposes. Seat students with special needs and second language learners to optimize learning; and when sharing a room, establish ground rules openly and honestly.

Reflect!

You were invited to draw two floor plans after viewing the video clips "Classroom Arrangement" and "Arranging Furniture and Materials." If you haven't drawn tentative floor plans, you can do so now. If you have, evaluate your plans on their approach to visibility and mobility and on their ability to allow easy reconfiguration of the room for another type of instructional activity.

CHAPTER 7
WHAT SHOULD I WEAR AND WHAT SHOULD I SAY?

Effectiveness Essentials

- Let students, parents, and administrators know you are a professional through dress, words, and deeds.
- Balance professional dress with comfort.
- Develop rapport with your class.

> Clothes make the man.
>
> *Anonymous Latin proverb*

> Clothes make the man. Naked people have little or no influence on society.
>
> *Mark Twain*

Your dress should be professional or business casual.

Your First Impression Will Be a Lasting One

Veterans recommend dressing as professionally as possible. Professional dress will help with classroom discipline. When you dress casually, the students perceive you as casual and may not take you as seriously as they should. Model the dress of your principal or administrators to be on the safe side. You need not run out to a color consultant or buy a dress-for-success manual. A few low-cost upgrades to your wardrobe will give you confidence. Try for the "business casual" look.

Even if "all the other teachers are wearing them," save your sweats and shorts for the gym and your flip-flops and backless shoes for the weekend. Think about how midriff-baring tops and very short skirts will look in your classroom, especially when you lean over. Although jeans are worn at some schools, your students will be wearing them and you want to distinguish yourself from them. Students will make judgments about you on that first day, and you can gain an advantage in the respect department by dressing like you deserve it.

myth**BUSTER**

Students like a teacher who is with it and can relate to them as a peer.

I remember the principal of the school where I did my practice teaching 30 years ago reminding me that the students have friends; they do not need me to be their friend—they need me to be their teacher. That means compassion, wisdom, and experience on my part, but I do not need to be their buddy.

Beth Ann Willstrop
English and Reading Teacher.
Grades 9–12
San Antonio, Texas

Let Students, Parents, and Administrators Know You Are Professional Through Dress, Words, and Deeds

Plan what you will wear on the first day to look your professional best. You will feel more confident, and those you encounter will make judgments about your professionalism based solely on your looks, rightly or wrongly, since they have no other data. Consider what message you want to send to others and let that be a guiding principle of how you dress.

Balance Professional Dress With Comfort

Whereas some veterans suggest a dressy dress or suit and tie on the first day, most stress comfort. You will have to take into consideration climate, school norms, and grade level as well as your own personal taste. Sitting on the floor or handling art materials may dictate more casual clothing or, better yet, a smock that suits you. Think about your poor feet, too! Wear comfortable shoes!

It's Okay to Be a Little Playful

Wearing subject-related clothing shows you have a sense of playfulness while still being professional. This might include a tie with global themes or a dress with a book pattern. Science teachers may wear a lab coat. You can accessorize with scarves or pins to advertise your subject area. One elementary teacher I know wears various styles of socks with her outfits. Her students always look to see which unique pair she is wearing that day. Another has a sweater for major holidays. In high school, especially, don't overdo the playfulness lest you be considered just plain weird or dorky.

mythBUSTER

How a teacher dresses is not important.

The kids notice everything about you. My high school students commented on every aspect of my clothes, nails, shoes, hair. Teachers are idols until they prove themselves otherwise. Don't try to look like your students. It rings false for them. They don't want another peer because they are struggling with peer relationships as it is and you can be the bellwether of fine fashion for them. Keep the sweats in your gym bag. Dress comfortably but do dress up. I always feel better about myself when I look my best.

Dottie Bailey
Speech Therapist/Teacher
Colton, California

Establishing Rapport With Your Students

The first days and weeks of school are the time to establish an authentic connection with your students. Even as you are presenting yourself as a businesslike professional, you can convey to your students that you are an approachable human being who is

TEACHER TALKS . . .

My first principal walked into my classroom one afternoon and took a good look at me and told me sternly that she wanted to see me after school. I spent the rest of that afternoon anticipating what job I could get after she fired me. At 3:30 I went to the office and waited to see her. She came out moments later and said, "Oh, I thought you were wearing culottes. I see it is only a pleated dress." That's the way it was back then. No pants, ever!

ELLEN KRONOWITZ
Former Third-Grade Teacher
Springfield Gardens, New York

A CROSS-CULTURAL CONSULTANT COUNSELS . . .

With the press of activity on the first day of school, you will want to be prepared to help the English language learners in the classroom succeed. Be aware that the norms influencing communication vary from culture to culture and person to person. Your students will act in ways consistent with the cultural norms they've absorbed growing up, as will you. Focus on relationship building first, rather than just content.

The key to establishing rapport with students and families from other cultures is to demonstrate respect. Make it a point to address each one personally. If you don't know how to pronounce their names, just ask. Even if you don't succeed in pronouncing the names precisely, you will get an "A+" just for trying. The initial goal is to make the student feel welcome in the class. Just as you would take pains to prepare

(continued on facing page)

Some teachers might choose to wear a lab coat or a school-themed sweater.

genuinely interested in them. The open communication channel begins with your very first words.

The First Words Are the Hardest

You can no doubt remember your first public speaking experience. It may have been the first time you made a speech, read a poem aloud, stood before your class to read a passage, or participated in a play or debate. You probably felt like you would freeze up or run off to hide. The reality is that you are well prepared to address your first class. Your students will likely not remember what you said first, but because it is of primary concern to new teachers, here are some common introductions:

- **The welcomers** attempt to make the student feel right at home and set a positive tone at the outset.
  "Good Morning. I know we are going to have a good year and lots of fun."
  "Hi, I'm so glad to see all of you. We are going to have a super year."
  "Welcome to chemistry. It's not as hard as people think."
  "Welcome to geometry class. See these models? You will make them this year."

- **The introducers** get right to the point and launch into a formal introduction of the classroom personnel.
  "I'm Mrs. ____________, your ____________ teacher, and this is Ms. ____________, our aide, who will help you also."
  "I'm Mr. ____________ and here are Boris and Natasha, our classroom pet rats."
- **The managers** put classroom management, rules, and discipline right out there and convey the expectation that the class will be well organized and well behaved.
  "The line is very straight, and I appreciate how quietly everyone entered the room."
  "Pick up your nametag and take a seat."
- **Other unique first words** are offered by teachers who share their values, ideals, and/or enthusiasm with their students.
  "I'm happy and excited to be your teacher."
  "Mistakes are permitted in this class."

Secondary students may not remember what you said first, but they will be evaluating you on the cool and professional scales. Younger students may express their concerns differently, but all students will be more concerned with the issues that directly affect them than they are with your first words. Homework load, the difficulty of subject matter, your grading practices, and discipline policy are all concerns that matter on that first day. Deep inside, however, students of any age are curious about your personal life, and you should share something with them.

It Is Most Appropriate to Be Called by Your Last Name Preceded by Mr., Mrs., or Ms.

These are the customary titles and they convey professional respect. Many

APPLY IT!

Introduce yourself with an autobiography poem and then have the students follow suit. This would make a great initial bulletin board, along with photos of each student.

First name	Ellen
3 traits	Funny, loving, friendly
Relative of	Wife of Gary
Who loves . . .	Family, friends, and horses
Who feels . . .	Fortunate
Who fears . . .	Losing loved ones
Who needs . . .	A kind word
Who gives . . .	A helping hand
Who would like to see (3) . . .	Peace, clean air, no hunger
Resident of . . .	Redlands
Last name	Kronowitz

for a guest coming to your home for any holiday, approach the task of integrating the student into your class the same way. Choose verbal methods of communication first. Use props, graphics, visual aids, and similar methods around which to converse. Don't worry about not understanding the precise content of the communication. It's important just to break the ice. Assign a buddy to each ELL student; you can even rotate buddies once a week or once a month. Pair the ELL student with a local student whose first language is English, not another ELL student, not even one with the same first language.

BARBARA BENJAMIN-TREVINO
Founder, Bentiva Education Solutions
Arlington, Texas

UNIT 2

TEACHER TALKS . . .

I teach general music to 600 students in two different schools. Parents often comment that music with me is their child's favorite subject. I have found the way to success is

1. *Know their names.*
2. *Bring a lot of energy to the classroom.*
3. *Focus on making it fun.*
4. *Be silly.*

An enthusiastic approach is the only way! And get plenty of rest the night before!

KEVIN WHITE
Music Teacher
Charlottesville, Virginia

STUDENT SAYS . . .

Teachers shouldn't use very loud voices because they can sound rude and are disrespectful to the class. And it is important for teachers to say "please" and "thank you" to the kids.

ERIK
Grade 5
Brookline, Massachusetts

middle and high school teachers call on their students using Mr. or Miss/Ms. and the students' last names to convey mutual respect. Some primary teachers use only a last initial or first name preceded by a title if their name is especially hard to pronounce. In all cases, write your name on the board and pronounce it with your students. During attendance, students can easily learn your name by responding to your salutation, "Good morning, Juan," with "Good morning, Mrs. Matsumoto."

A Little Disclosure Goes a Long Way

Tell your students something about your personal life and professional background. The majority of teachers commonly tell their students about their family, pets, hobbies, why they love teaching, why they became a teacher in the first place, and any apparent physical disabilities. Some teachers decorate a biographical poster with photos of family, pets, favorite hobbies, sports, foods, and so on. You might bring in five

APPLY IT!

Convey your educational beliefs to your students with a clear sandwich baggie or small manila envelope that contains items such as these:

Rubber band	To remind them to be flexible
Paperclip	To remind them to stay connected to the class community
Eraser	To remind them that everyone makes mistakes
Sticky note	To remind them to stick to the goal when things get tough
Penny	To remind them they are valued
Hershey's Hug	To remind them that we all need hugs
Lifesaver candy	To remind them you are there to help
One homework pass	To remind them that mistakes are permitted
Noodle	To remind them to use their noodles

objects that will serve as props as you tell about yourself. My objects would be an album of family photos, a horseshoe or horse figurine, a swim cap and goggles, a map with places I've traveled to circled, and a book I am currently reading.

Even minimal self-disclosure (the type and name of your pet, your favorite hobby) will ease the tension, satisfy curiosity, and bring you down to earth and make you more approachable. Consider the activity in the Apply It! on page 68 as a way to communicate your philosophy and put your students at ease. You can substitute items to reflect your grade level.

Create Your Own Unique Way of Breaking the Ice

Generally, you're safe if you take one element from every category in this acronym: WISHES—welcome, introduction, share hopes, and establish standards. This is your formula for a good start on the first day.

APPLY IT!

After reading the Teacher Talks on this page, design an engaging initial activity for the first day of school, one that will showcase your subject matter in secondary school or create excitement in the elementary classroom.

AVOID IT!

Your students are not your friends, and you can convey your role as teacher by your dress, demeanor, behavior, and words on the first days and weeks of school. The clothing and words you choose will often determine how much respect and status your students accord you. Facial piercing and tattoos may be acceptable in some circles, but remove piercings and cover tattoos as best as you can during the workweek.

TEACHER TALKS . . .

I always give a brief synopsis of the subject and my approach to teaching it. Make your presentation one that is short on boring details and long on experiences to look forward to. Use visuals such as PowerPoint or videos to highlight some projects or exciting moments that will captivate your students. You can use props to introduce the course. Since I taught social studies, I would bring in a cultural object that I knew would intrigue students. And my first activity would be an inquiry about the object. You can bring in a Mobius strip in a math class, generate an eye-catching chemical reaction in a chemistry class, share a model of a heart in biology, and so forth.

How much you tell about yourself is up to you, but if you can share some anecdotes that relate to your subject matter, all the better. For example, if you are teaching civics, you might recount a family trip to Washington, D.C., and even

(continued on following page)

TEACHER TALKS—*continued*

include some humorous anecdotes, like the day you got lost and separated from your family in the Smithsonian. I recounted how, during a homestay in Japan, without a common language, we resorted to pantomime and a Japanese-English dictionary. And it worked!

ELLEN KRONOWITZ
Author
Redlands, California

Summary

Strive for a professional first impression with students, colleagues, administrators, and parents through your dress, words, and deeds. Look for a balance between professional dress and comfort. Introduce yourself and your subject(s) to the students in a manner that will motivate them and start the process of building rapport.

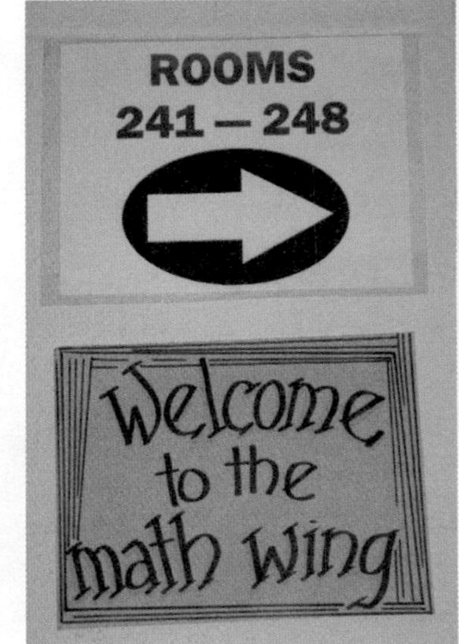

Reflect!

How will you welcome your students on the first day? How will you introduce yourself? What hopes will you share with the class? What standards will you emphasize? Jot down a few ideas.

Welcome ____________________

Introduction ____________________

Share hopes ____________________

Establish standards ____________________

CHAPTER 8

HOW DO I LEARN MY STUDENTS' NAMES AND HOW DO THEY LEARN EACH OTHER'S NAMES?

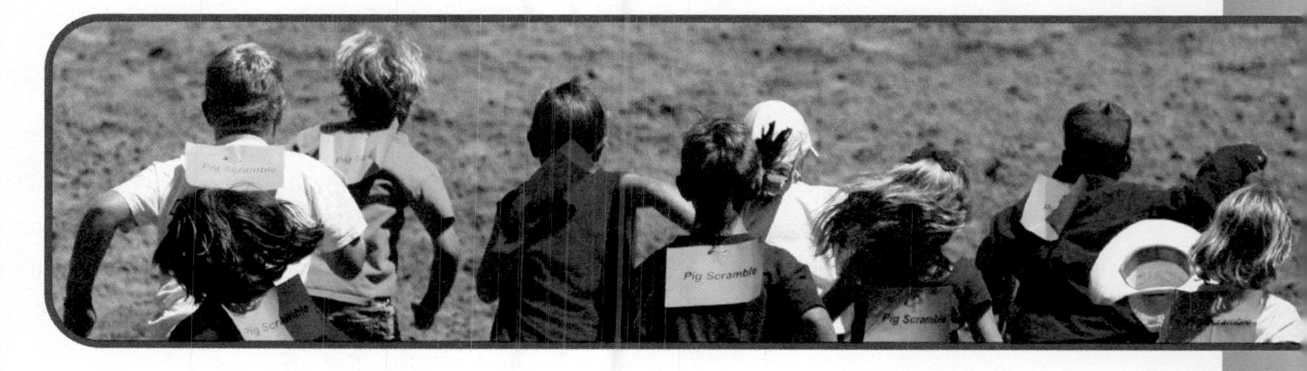

We could learn a lot from crayons; some are sharp, some are pretty, some are dull, while others bright, some have weird names, but they all have learned to live together in the same box.

Anonymous

Effectiveness Essentials

- Knowing students' names is a powerful way of validating them.
- There are a variety of grade-appropriate devices to help everyone to learn names quickly.

Make a Concerted Effort to Learn Your Students' Names as Soon as You Can

This is a powerful way to connect with your students and acknowledge them personally. It requires concentration and extra effort, but it can be done. Always check the pronunciation. All students should have the option of going by a nickname or shortened version.

Knowing Students' Names Is a Powerful Way of Validating Them

There is no greater compliment to a student than calling him or her by name at the end of the first day or week in middle and high school. You can associate the names with faces from school photos. In many districts, individual photos are taken at the time of the class picture, and they are attached to the permanent record cards. Take time to make the name-face association before school starts. Students will be shocked and pleased to be recognized. Or buy an inexpensive digital camera and take the photos yourself.

Using Nametags and Nameplates. Nametags and nameplates are very popular aids for learning names. Teachers place them on desks or on the front of desks, pin them on the children's clothing, or string them around primary youngsters' necks. Students can make their own nametags or nameplates. Overcome the reluctance of secondary students to wear nametags by explaining that they are common in the workplace. Your school may require teachers to wear nametags, and that will support your request.

APPLY IT!

You can use a digital camera and take instant pictures of the students, table by table or individually. Writing the names below the faces will help you remember who's who, and you can memorize the photos. Once the photos have served their purpose as memory aids, you can use them to create a Welcome Back bulletin board bearing a subject-grade-level–relevant caption. Or you can attach the photos to your seating chart to help you associate names and faces when you have multiple sets of students.

Using the Seating Chart. One of the most useful devices for learning students' names is the seating chart. You can get a jump on the process by having the blank chart or map ready to go (see Figure 8.1). The names just have to be filled in when you take attendance or look at the nametags. You can attach small digital images or write in some distinguishing characteristic such as "spiked hair" or "wears bright red glasses." Do not hesitate to ask students to identify themselves before responding. They will appreciate your attempts to learn their names.

Figure 8.1
Student Seating Chart

Help Everyone to Learn Each Other's Names

There are a variety of grade-appropriate devices to help everyone learn names quickly. It's important for you to know your students, but it is just as important for them to get to know one another as individuals. This decreases the likelihood of fights and arguments. Here are some additional suggestions from veterans.

Try This in the Primary Grades, K–1

The teacher holds up name cards, and the children recognize their names,

STUDENT SAYS . . .

On the first day of middle school I was really nervous—not about the teachers but about the students. You see, almost everyone in my old school was going to the new middle school, which left me here with only four other girls from my old school. "Will I make new friends? Who will help me know where my class is? Are the students there nice?" These questions ran through my head on the way to school. When I got to school, the first thing I did was look for one of my friends from my old school. When I found her, I felt better, but almost all the people around me had big groups of friends. Then, when the bell rang, I ran straight to my class. All the classes had nice teachers, and at lunch I found my friends quickly. At the end of school I felt proud of myself for surviving the first day of school.

NIKI
Age 12, Grade 6
Redlands, California

UNIT 2

Student photos decorate a bulletin board.

> The most important single ingredient in the formula of success is knowing how to get along with people.
>
> *Teddy Roosevelt*

retrieve the cards, and place them in the designated spot. The teacher can call the names as well at the beginning but should encourage recognition solely by visual cues early in the year.

Here's an Idea for the Intermediate Grades, 2–3

Students introduce themselves to the class. They can be given some guidelines and time constraints:

1. Tell us your name.
2. Tell us something about your family and pets.
3. What do you do after school?
4. What are your favorite sports?

Or review alphabetical order by having children come up in small groups and alphabetize themselves, using their tags or cards.

A child who is "It" leaves the room and is assigned a partner in the room. When the child who is "It" returns, he or she must ask questions to find out who the partner is:

Is my partner a girl or a boy?
Is my partner in the first row?
Does my partner have long hair?
Is my partner wearing blue?

Students can interview a partner, following a set of guidelines, and then introduce the partner to the rest of the class. Guidelines can be distributed or invented by the class.

1. Partner's favorite and/or least favorite subject in school
2. Partner's career goals
3. Partner's pets
4. Partner's favorite sports or hobbies
5. Partner's favorite foods

A Scavenger Hunt Is Fun in the Upper Grades, 4–6

Students have to find someone in the class who corresponds to one of the descriptions provided, and then they put that student's initials next to the description on a prewritten grid. Figure 8.2 shows what this might look like.

These Activities Work for All Grades, Including Secondary

The Name Game. Each person introduces all the others preceding, going around the room or up and down the rows in the following manner:

Maria: I'm Maria.
Jason: This is Maria; I'm Jason.
Eric: This is Maria, Jason; and I'm Eric.
Isabella: This is Maria, Jason, Eric; and I'm Isabella.

Time Lines. Divide an 11 inch × 14 inch sheet of construction paper in half the long way and have each student divide his or her strip into six equal parts (fraction review). In each segment students illustrate a significant event in their

Figure 8.2
Classmate Scavenger Hunt

who hates pizza	*who plays the drums*	*whose favorite color is purple* NP	*who has ridden a horse* RP	*who owns more than three pets*
who can do a magic trick	*who has lived in another state*	*who has a library card*	*who has lived in another country*	*who has a five-letter name*
who speaks two languages	*who wants to be a teacher*	*who has a birthday in September* RW	*who has a skateboard*	*who snowboards* BM
who is wearing blue shoes JTC	*who has a reptile as a pet*	*who has snorkeled*	*who plays soccer*	*who plays tennis*
who likes spinach	*who has two sisters*	*who is wearing a ring*	*who is wearing a necklace*	*who has a green backpack*

STUDENT SAYS . . .

From the moment my mom dropped me off until the end of the day . . . it was nerve-wracking! The whole day, the other puny sixth graders were looking up at me hoping at any moment that I wouldn't turn around and accidently stomp on them. (I'm almost 6 feet tall.) My teachers had to play it safe and be mean until they knew what kind of kids we were. After that it was fine. At lunchtime I walked around in circles looking for my friends, trying not to look like I didn't have any. I was glad that day was over. Then I had a whole year of adventures ahead of me!

JACK
Age 12, Grade 6
Redlands, California

TEACHER TALKS . . .

For the first week or two of classes, I require that the first words out of each student's mouth is her name when she asks or answers a question. The game becomes quite fun and forces me into the habit of calling on students equally from day 1.

STEPHEN PULLIAM
High School Science Teacher
Stony Brook, New York

TEACHER TALKS . . .

In one of my grad classes I kept calling Debra "Marjorie," although the students looked nothing alike. I was so focused on not doing it that I did it repeatedly. Each time, I apologized profusely, remembering how I felt when my mother frequently called me by my sister's name.

ELLEN KRONOWITZ
Author
Redlands, California

life—e.g., born, started school, moved to a new house, etc. They share these in class, a few each day during the first week of school. Figure 8.3 shows a sample.

Adjectives. Have your students describe themselves to the class using only three adjectives. You should model the exercise first.

Cooperative Groups. Have your students get into small groups and discuss their favorite music group, sport, movie star, TV program, etc. They will need to answer the questions about commonalities and differences (see Figure 8.4). This will help them learn about one another, key to foming a classroom community.

What do group members have in common?
Where are the main differences?
What three things can you say about your group?

Interviews. Students can generate interview questions and then interview and introduce a partner to the rest of the class. Or you can provide interview forms with items like these:

My hero or heroine is ______________ because ______________________.
My career goal is __________________.
My favorite subjects are ____________.
My least favorite subjects are ________.
My pet peeve is ___________________.
I am known for ____________________.
I laugh when ______________________.
I would like to know more about ______ ____________________________.
I excel at _________________________.
Three words to describe me are _______.
Something I want to get better at is ____ ____________________________.

Figure 8.3
Sample Time Line

Figure 8.4

Worksheet for Cooperative Group Activity

Student Names	Music	Movie	Food	Sports

You don't want to spend a great deal of time on introductions that first period of the first day, but some of these simple icebreakers will create a cooperative climate in which students feel they have gotten to know at least one other student in the class.

Summary

Validate your students by learning their names and addressing them by name as soon as possible. There are a variety of techniques for learning names, and you can ask your colleagues how they manage to learn the names of so many students, especially in middle and high school.

AVOID IT!

Don't get to the end of the semester or the year without knowing who is who.

Avoid mispronouncing names.

Work hard not to confuse one student with another.

Reflect!

Which techniques for learning names seem most efficient, given your grade level/subject matter or your potential grade level/subject matter? Search on the Web for at least two more icebreakers that seem appropriate.

CHAPTER 9

HOW DO I ESTABLISH RULES AND DISCIPLINE ON THE FIRST DAY?

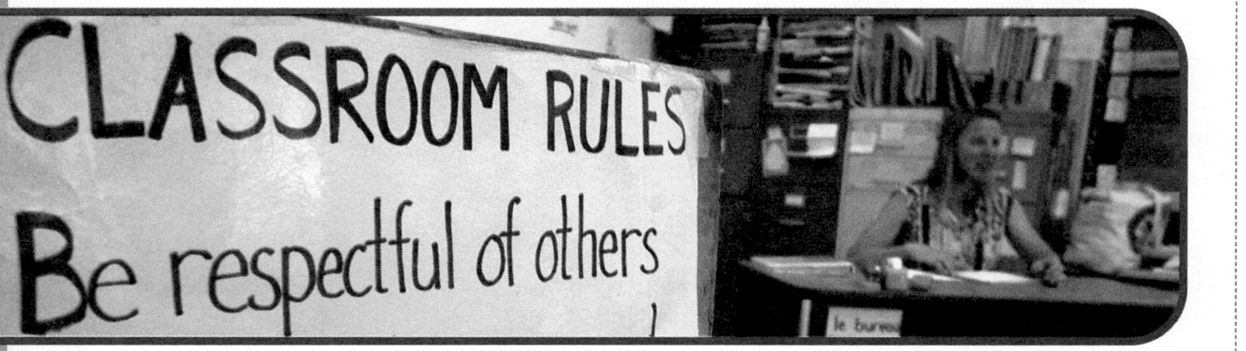

No one is ever old enough to know better.

Holbrook Jackson

Effectiveness Essentials

- On the first day your students will be judging your management style.
- Ascertain what the school norms are regarding discipline and rules.
- Good rules are fair, understandable, respectful, accommodate students with special needs, and don't create more work for the teacher.
- Strictly enforce the rules on the first day and in the weeks ahead.
- Communicate the rules to parents as soon as possible.

Students Will Be Judging Your Classroom Management Style on the First Day

There will be anywhere from 20 to 40 pairs of eyes staring at you, and although they will never appear more angelic, beware! They will be watching and waiting to assess your toughness or easiness. While they are at their best and paying close attention to your words and deeds, it is your time to make a firm stand about your standards and expectations. All but the kindergarteners have great experience in sizing up their teachers on the first day, and with each year their skills in this area improve. By their senior year, they are experts. You are one in a line of teachers they have scrutinized and judged at first glance. You need to pass the rule-making/discipline test with flying colors.

Ascertain What the School Norms Are Regarding Discipline and Rules

Your discipline plan must conform to those norms. Don't reinvent the wheel. How can you learn what the norms are? First, speak with your principal or resource teachers about the generic school and district rules with regard to discipline. Check out the website where the discipline policy is often posted and read the district/school policy manual. Ask colleagues what their rules are and how they abide by the generic and district rules. After learning about school and district policy regarding discipline, experienced teachers report setting rules on the first day of school. Common practices include:

- Eliciting classroom rules from the students
- Ranking the rules with your students and selecting a maximum of five
- Telling the students that, as school progresses, the teacher and students can add or delete rules
- Stating rules positively—e.g., *raise hands* rather than *no calling out*

The challenge secondary school teachers face results from the multiple sets of rules other teachers may set forth, often dictated by the subject matter. This can be confusing to your students. That is why, in secondary school, it is essential that you determine what the district and school givens are before you go it alone with

STUDENT SAYS . . .

When students break the rules, the teacher sends them to the thinking chair where they sit and think about it, and then in a short time they can come back.

DREW
Kindergarten, Age 6
Glenview, Illinois

UNIT 2

STUDENT SAYS . . .

On the first day of school, the teacher goes over the rules and regulations.

HOLLAND
Grade 10, Age 15
Redlands, California

APPLY IT!

Think back to a teacher you respected. What personal attributes made you want to come to class? What were his or her management strategies? What happened when kids misbehaved? Now think about the opposite teacher, whom no one respected or listened to. What personal attributes did he or she exhibit? What were this teacher's management strategies? What conclusions can you draw from this comparison?

your own rules. Here are some typical secondary school rules gleaned from high school teachers:

1. Obey all school rules.
2. Be in your seat when the bell rings.
3. Bring all required materials, books, and homework to class.
4. Raise your hand to speak, and be an attentive listener.
5. Be responsible and respectful.
6. Plagiarism and cheating result in failure.

Students in high school want to know the rules and the consequences up front for not adhering to them. In other words, they may not care what the rules are; they just want to know what the penalties are for not following them. Stating the rules and consequences on that first day will put the decision making in their hands.

Seven Principles Should Guide Your Rule Making on the First Day

These principles are ones found in most discipline guides, and they will serve you well as you consider your own rules, whether you allow your students to help create them or you write them yourself. It is key to remember that an elementary classroom is like a family, and since the students are with you all day, the rules you devise together or set down can be reinforced all day long. In middle and high school, the rules may be different from class to class, depending on the subject matter. That is why it is essential that there be a generic set of rules that can be added to if need be. So again, check out what essential rules the district and school prescribe.

Good Rules Tend to Be Needed, Fair, Applied Equally, Consistently Enforceable, Age-Appropriate, Reasonable, and Respectful

Any rules you impose on your students or ones they create themselves with your assistance should meet these criteria. The most common rules in classrooms are listed below:

1. Respect rights and property of others.
2. Follow directions.
3. Work quietly in the classroom.
4. Be a good listener.
5. Raise hands to speak or leave seat.

One year I decided to do something different. On the first day of class I told the sixth graders there would be no rules until we found a need for them. After three days of chaos and my nagging, and worse, I had them come to the class meeting space and we talked about how things were going. Everyone, including me, worked on a list of problems that we had noticed with no rules in place. They recognized the need for rules and came up with two: "Clean up the mess you make" and "Be responsible." Although I would not recommend this exercise in anarchy to novice teachers, you might consider leading your students in a guided fantasy about a class with no rules.

APPLY IT!

Before you begin your rule-making discussion, ask your students to close their eyes and imagine what it would be like to have a classroom with no rules. List the pros and cons on the board. Ask them which list is more likely to help them learn. Once they recognize the need for rules, you can ask them to identify five rules that would make for a good classroom community. In middle and high school, ask your students what additions they would make to the generic district/school rules to enable them to remain safe—for example, in a science lab—or to best use their time in an art class or gym class or any other specific discipline. They can do this in groups, and additional subject-specific rules can be gleaned from the group efforts.

TEACHER TALKS . . .

Well, for my class, I like to let us come up with rules together. During the first day of school, we come up with a list of things that are not correct behaviors to do and we draw a picture of them—for example, running in the hall. After we have a list of bad behaviors we create our own classroom rules together. The students write them in a contract, sign them, have their parents sign them, then return them for their file. It has worked so far. This is my sixth year of teaching third grade.

BETH WILLIAMS
Third-Grade Teacher
Mobile, Alabama

Post classroom rules in plain sight.

WATCH IT! video

Succeeding in Your First Year of Teaching

As you watch this clip, write down at least three recommendations this new teacher offers for making your first year a successful one. What were the high and low points of this teacher's first year? Especially note comments about classroom management and discipline.

Good Rules Are Understandable to Non-Native Speakers and Are Sensitive to Cultural Norms

Make sure that you translate as necessary all rules for the students and their parents. The translation website http://babelfish.yahoo.com/ will serve you well. Rules should be posted in a prominent place in the room. In their book *Managing Diverse Classrooms,* Rothstein-Fisch and Trumbull (2008) provide a multicultural frame of reference for classroom management. Some cultures value saving face and indirect communication, so you may not want to engage in public and direct confrontation. Some cultures are taught not to make direct eye contact as a sign of respect to elders, so the teacher who says, "Look at me," may interpret failure to do so as disrespect. This is just one valuable resource you will need to read to prepare yourself to deal appropriately with diverse student populations.

Good Rules Respect and Accommodate Students With Special Needs

You will have students in your class who may not be physically or emotionally able to comply with your rules. For example, a student with Tourette syndrome will be unable to keep from making uncontrollable utterances and even cursing. Students with physical disabilities may not be able to raise hands before speaking. Help your students realize that each one of us is special in some way and we need to be considerate of those who are allowed some leeway on some rules.

Good Rules Don't Create More Work for the Teacher

Your plan should be easy to administer. That is, you need to make sure that you are not overwhelmed by counting

APPLY IT!

Another way to drive home the need for rules is to make up a list of age-appropriate "silly" rules and discuss what is wrong with each one. Once your students identify what is wrong with each rule, they can turn it around and use the opposites as criteria by which to judge their own rules. Some examples follow:

Rule	Weakness	A good rule is . . .
Only boys get bathroom passes.	Not equal	Equal for everyone
No sneezing in class.	Not possible	Possible
Late students have detention all year.	Too harsh	Fair
Be nice.	Vague	Specific

TEACHER TALKS . . .

As a sixth-grade teacher, I posted the following as the sole guiding principle:

> *When I am responsible, I will have a good day. When I am irresponsible, I will pay the consequences.*

And below this rule were the following words:

> *Whatever you believe about yourself, you will become.*

ART GALLARDO
Former Sixth-Grade Teacher
Principal
San Bernardino, California

CHAPTER 9

UNIT 2

TEACHER TALKS . . .

I write a list of "Classroom Manners and Expectations." I include things like "I will say thank you when I am given a gift or a piece of candy for a test." I explain it will be taken back if they "forget their manners." They will raise their hand and wait to be called on if they want to share something. If they don't observe these expectations, a point will be taken off of their behavior and classroom preparation grade. I explain how important it is for them to help each other if someone is confused, or struggling, or doesn't understand. I print out two copies for each student, which I sign. I hold a classroom meeting, explaining this will be a written, signed agreement among all of us, and I require that they sign it too. I keep a copy, and they keep the second copy in their binders. I emphasize that if any of them "forget their manners or classroom expectations," I will

(continued on facing page)

points, doling out candy, or punishing rule breakers during your recess or lunch period. Students who break a rule should be asked to tell you which rule they ignored or forgot. In this way they learn to monitor their own behavior. If you prominently display the rules and go over them as needed, perhaps even every day at the beginning of the year or semester, you will make your students more responsible. You will learn more about this in Unit 4, Positive Discipline.

Strictly Enforce the Rules on the First Day and in the Weeks Ahead

Rules need to be indelibly written in the minds of your students. Catch all infractions immediately, restate the rule, check for understanding, and liberally praise students for following the rules. Adopt this motto, "It's easier to ease off than it is to crack down." Have the students memorize the rules. For example, in elementary grades, call out the number of the rule and have students respond with the rule or an example of obeying or disobeying it. In middle and high school, the rules should be written in student notebooks or binders, highlighted on the syllabus, enlarged on a poster, or tacked to the bulletin board.

myth BUSTER

Rules stifle creativity and self-direction.

Nonsense! Kids thrive in an environment where they feel safe. Kids often test structure and limits as a way to check to see if the boundaries are still in place. In a structured environment, kids can express themselves while all moving in the same direction.

Jason Paytas
Middle School Teacher
Arcata, California

Communicate the Rules to Parents as Soon as Possible

On the first day, most teachers send a note home to parents (in translation, if needed) explaining the classroom rules, or they have the students rewrite the rules for their parents to sign. Parents need to know the ground rules so they can help you out. Middle and high school teachers include this information in the syllabus or student handbook, but it would be useful to send out a separate letter regarding rules that will not get lost in all the other information that handbooks and syllabi contain. Should infractions occur, parents will have been forewarned about rules and will more likely accept the news that their youngster or teen has broken one.

APPLY IT!

Students are apt to be more cooperative if they have a hand in making the rules. You can combine creativity and rule making by asking students in groups to come up with five rules they think will lead to a productive learning environment. Each group writes its five rules on a chart you will hang up in the room. Then the charts are compared and commonalities are circled in red marker. The most effective rules, agreed upon by students and teacher, become the rules of the classroom as long as they are consistent with school rules and district policy. Facilitate group work by posing some key questions like these:

Describe a classroom, free from distractions and disruptions, where all students can learn.

What rules would you need to maintain this productive classroom learning environment?

Are your rules fair to everyone, enforceable, reasonable, and respectful?

Are your rules stated in positive terms?

Condense your rules to five essential ones that cover the bases.

stop the class, and we will review them again.

In a very short time, my students start to change. They start to demonstrate a desire to become well-mannered young ladies and gentlemen. They change from a class into a respectful, caring community.

The most wonderful and touching moment came this past week, when one of my students baked and decorated a birthday cake for one of her classmates. The recipient asked to make a speech. She said, "Thank you for baking me a birthday cake. No other student has ever done something this thoughtful for me before. Last year when I was in fifth grade I didn't have any friends. Now I do. Thank you."

My wonderful, loving, caring students burst into applause, and one young man (one of my "tough boys") said, "That made me cry, Ms. Wasserman." It doesn't get any better than that.

LAURIE WASSERMAN
Learning Disabilities Teacher
National Board-Certified Teacher
Medford, Massachusetts

TEACHER TALKS . . .

High school students are just taller elementary school students. Don't be fooled by their size. I have to repeat the rules so often that first week of school, I feel like I am back teaching elementary school again. On the other hand, high school students devise more devious methods of circumventing the rules and invent more creative excuses for not following them than my elementary students did.

ANONYMOUS

CLASSROOM ARTIFACTS

Dear Parent or Guardian,

Thank you for sharing ____________ with me this school year. I will do my best to help ____________ reach his or her full potential. In order to have a safe, secure, productive learning environment, we have written these classroom rules:

1. Respect rights and property of others.
2. Follow directions.
3. Work quietly in the classroom.
4. Be a good listener.
5. Raise hands to speak or leave seat.

I know the students will work hard to follow the rules they developed. At school, I will encourage them in their efforts at self-control. If I need your help at home, I will be in touch with you by phone or note. If you have any questions or wish to speak with me, I can be reached at the school phone number ____________ between 8:00 and 8:30 A.M. and during recess (10:00–10:15 or 2:15–2:30). If these times are inconvenient for you, please leave a message and I'll return your call as soon as possible. You can reach me by email at ____________ @yahoo.com. I look forward to working with you during the coming school year.

Sincerely,

Name
Grade Room School

Please keep the letter and return the signature portion by the end of the week in the envelope provided.

. . . .

I have read this letter and we will support the rules regarding behavior.
Parent or guardian's signature ____________ Phone____________ Email ____________
Student's signature ________________________
Comment, questions, or conference request: ________________________________

Summary

Ascertain what the school norms are regarding discipline and rules, and make sure your rules fall within those norms and school/district policies. The students will be judging your adherence to rules from the outset, so communicate the rules clearly and concisely and then post them in the room, on the syllabus, and on the letter that goes home. Rigorously enforce your rules so students know you are serious about compliance. Communicate rules to parents or guardians as soon as possible so there are no surprises should you have to contact them.

Reflect!

What are the bottom-line rules for your school or district? Write these down and then add to the list any additional rules or policies that are peculiar to your subject or grade.

UNIT 2 CHECKLIST

Preplanning for First Day Checklist	For more information go to:
Planning	
☐ Did I overplan and include doable homework?	Chapters 4, 5
☐ Are my activities motivating?	Chapter 5
Materials	
☐ Do I have all materials I will need *with* me?	Chapter 5
☐ Do I have enough textbooks and furniture?	Chapters 5, 6
Classroom Environment	
☐ Are my name and schedule on the chalkboard?	Chapter 5
☐ Are bulletin boards ready to go?	Chapters 5, 10
☐ Do I have the routines set in my mind?	Unit 3
☐ Is my furniture arrangement consistent with my instructional goals?	Chapter 6
☐ Have I decided on a seat-selection method?	Chapter 6
☐ Have I identified and accommodated my students with special needs and ELL students?	Chapter 6

UNIT 2 CHECKLIST

Preplanning for First Day Checklist	For more information go to:
Rapport With Students	
☐ Is there a welcoming atmosphere in the room?	Chapter 10
☐ Have I decided how to break the ice?	Chapter 7
☐ Have I determined a method for learning names?	Chapter 8
Rules and Regulations	
☐ Do I have a way to establish rules that conforms to district and school policies?	Chapter 9
☐ Are my rules easily communicated to students and parents?	Chapter 9
☐ Is my plan age-appropriate and flexible enough to accommodate all students' needs?	Chapter 9
And Most Important	
☐ Will students give a positive first-day report back home?	Unit 2
☐ Will they look forward to returning to school on the second day?	Unit 2

Further Reading: Books About the First Days of School

Charles, C. M., & Senter, G. W. (2007). *Elementary classroom management,* 5th ed. Boston: Allyn & Bacon. The authors provide essential advice for organizing and managing an elementary classroom. They include information within the context of the standards-based movement and No Child Left Behind.

Emmer, E. T., & Evertson, C. M. (2008). *Classroom management for middle and high school teachers,* 8th ed. Boston: Allyn & Bacon. The authors communicate 25 years of experience-based research including planning instruction, setting up the secondary classroom, establishing rules and procedures, and much more. The authors encourage teachers to embrace the challenge of teaching diverse students and those with special needs.

Evertson. C. M., & Emmer, E. T. (2008). *Classroom management for elementary teachers,* 8th ed. Boston: Allyn & Bacon. The authors provide practical and experience-based suggestions for organizing the elementary school classroom, including communicating with students, planning, managing behavior, establishing rules and procedures, and much more.

Kellough, R. (2009). *What every teacher should know about your first year of teaching: Guidelines for success*, 5th ed. Upper Saddle River, NJ: Prentice Hall. This is a concise and very practical text that covers managing your first day, coping with testing, differentiating instruction, classroom management, and other first-year challenges, including working well with parents and colleagues.

Kronowitz, E. (2004). *Your first year of teaching and beyond,* 4th ed. Boston: Allyn & Bacon. This text addresses the concerns of first-year and novice teachers, including classroom organization, the first day, discipline, communicating with parents, working with colleagues and your principal, getting to know the school and community, and balancing a professional and personal life.

Schell, L. (2000). *Countdown to the first day: NEA checklist series.* Washington, DC: National Education Association. This is a checklist of tasks teachers should accomplish leading up to and including the first day of school. Although it is not newly published, it remains relevant.

First Day of School Websites

Babel Fish Translation

http://babelfish.yahoo.com/

This website enables you to translate up to 150 words of the most common languages into any of those same languages, including Chinese, Spanish, French, Korean, Italian, Greek, German.

Varied Teacher-Oriented Ideas for the First Days and Beyond

http://atozteacherstuff.com/

At this general website, you will find ideas for starting off the school year, thematic units on every conceivable topic, lesson plans, worksheets, teacher-tested ideas, online chat rooms for teachers, and much more.

A Teacher Network

http://teachers.net

At this generic website, you will find free printable worksheets, chat rooms, web tools, lesson plans, job listings, articles, and links to other sites for teachers.

Middle School Teacher Resources

http://www.middleweb.com/

This website is geared to the middle school teacher and includes ideas for the first day of school, chat rooms, articles on middle school reform, book reviews, and links to other useful sites.

Grades 7–12 Website

http://712educators.about.com/

This is a website geared to the middle and high school educator. You can access articles, lesson plans, teaching tips, curriculum ideas, and teaching strategies.

Education World at Your Fingertips

http://www.education-world.com/

This is a website for all teachers at all levels and administrators. You will find lesson plans, articles, technology updates, discussion forums, and much more. It is a website that you can enjoy browsing as well as searching for specific topics.

UNIT 3

Classroom Organization and Management

CHAPTER 10

HOW DO I ACCESSORIZE THE CLASSROOM WITH BULLETIN BOARDS AND EXTRAS?

Knowledge is always accompanied with accessories of emotion and purpose.

Alfred North Whitehead

Effectiveness Essentials

- Classrooms reflect the personality and instructional style of the teacher and the needs of students.
- Setting up and arranging the furniture are your first and most important tasks.
- Arrange for some private spaces and a quiet reading area.
- Bulletin boards deliver very powerful nonverbal messages to your students.

Classrooms reflect the personality and instructional style of the teacher as well as the needs of the students. As you walk around your school, you will see that no two classrooms look exactly alike. Even when teachers collaborate in planning, the individual rooms still reflect the personality of each teacher and the needs of the particular group of students. Your room environment speaks volumes, not only to your students but to their parents, the principal, other staff members, and other students around the school. We get quick impressions when we visit our friends' homes, our doctors' offices, and new restaurants. Décor counts! Make yours appealing and inviting.

Create a Physical Space Conducive to Learning

It's time to call upon your "inner classroom interior decorator" because that richly decorated space you may have been shown during prior visits now has bare walls and the furniture arranged helter-skelter. Confront the work involved with the underlying motivation to create an organized, efficient, attractive home away from home for both you and your students. You are creating a space that gives them the best opportunities to learn.

Setting Up and Arranging the Furniture Are Your First and Most Important Tasks

You should already have a well-developed plan for arranging the furniture after reading the first two units of this handbook. Pretend it's moving day, arrange the furniture according to your plan, and keep rearranging it until you feel it's workable. Put on your oldest clothes and try out the various arrangements at school, sampling every seat to assure visibility. You may need to allow space for some of these areas: computers, library, teacher/small-group instruction, aide work station, art center, listening center, writing center, storage, and technology equipment.

Arrange for Some Private Spaces and a Quiet Reading Area

If your principal permits, build yourself a loft or raised platform for reading. If you can't do this or don't know how, you

TEACHER TALKS . . .

Don't do this! Every afternoon before leaving the classroom in a laboratory school at a major university the students—4th, 5th, and 6th graders—moved all the furniture out into the hallway. Then each morning we planned the day and only brought in the furniture we needed. If we were painting large murals, we left all the furniture in the hallway. If we were taking tests, we brought in all the tables and chairs. This plan did not sit well with the fire department or the university administrators. The principle was a good one—use furniture functionally—but the implementation was a disaster. So we just learned to move furniture within the room to meet our instructional needs.

ELLEN KRONOWITZ
Laboratory School Teacher
New York City

CHAPTER 10

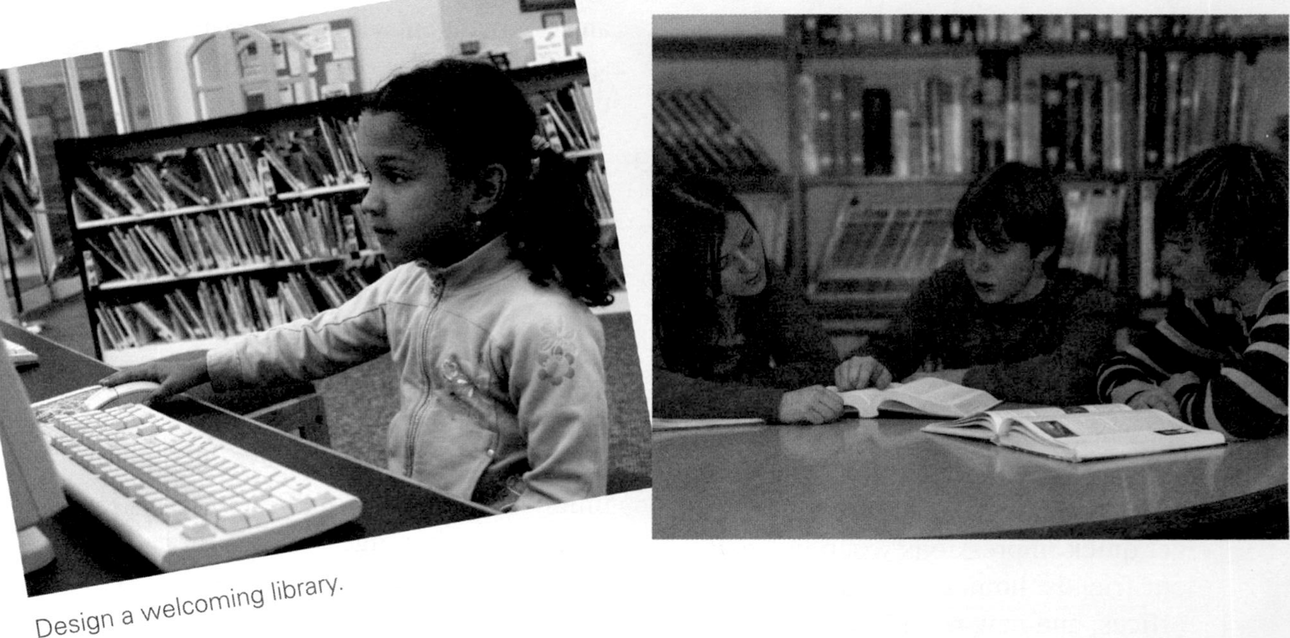

Design a welcoming library.

might bring in an old mattress and cover it with a pretty floral sheet and use it for a reading area. One resourceful teacher I know uses an old-fashioned bathtub filled with pillows for a special reading space. Bring in a small inflatable pool or rubber dinghy for the same purpose. Display magazines on a magazine rack or a narrow shelf. Recycle the older magazines into art or language arts projects. Every secondary school classroom should also have a library area. Middle and high school students welcome private study carrels.

Keep Your Room Arrangement Dynamic

At the outset, you can arrange your desks in rows for maximum control,

APPLY IT!

Take some graph paper and add to your furniture arrangement the other centers and spaces that you define as needed. This will be your blueprint. See Figure 10.1 for an example.

Figure 10.1
A middle school classroom blueprint

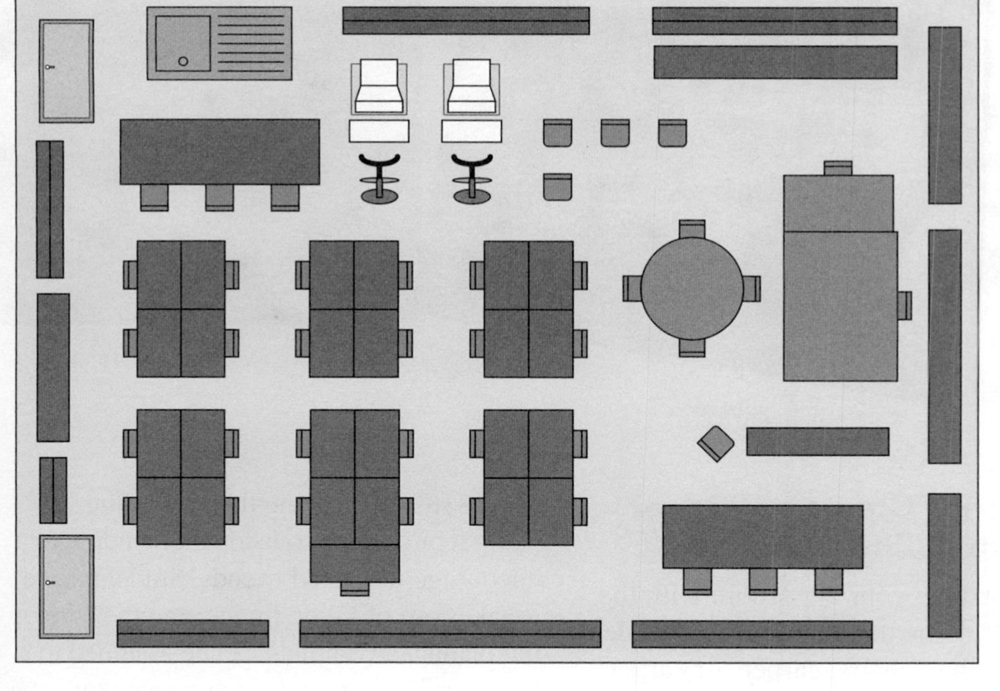

and then you can relax and create a more open environment as the school year progresses. You can relocate the library area to another part of the room. You can change where the pet is located to keep interest high and boredom low. Every few months, surprise the class with an all-new room arrangement. Of course, this depends a great deal on what the space of your room will allow.

Decorating the Space Is Your Next Challenge

Think of the walls, windows, ceilings, and bookshelves as canvases for your artistry.

STUDENT SAYS . . .

When I was in kindergarten somebody brought in silk worms. We also had trout, baby chicks, and hermit crabs.

NIKI
Third Grade, Age 8
Satellite Beach, Florida

A classroom should be designed for learning.

Sit right down and read.

Students enjoy a pet hamster.

Accessories Create a Unique, Stimulating Environment

You can jazz up your classroom with the addition of some thrift store or yard sale items. Beanbag chairs, carpets or carpet remnants, a small sofa, and perhaps a discarded lamp or two will create a warm and homey atmosphere. Reading lamps rest the eyes from the fluorescent lights and can calm students. These items are particularly useful in a library corner separated from the rest of the room. After all, how many of you read while seated in a straight-back chair with your feet flat on the floor?

A fish tank or even one beta fish or a goldfish will provide endless entertainment for the students during their free time. Hang a bird feeder outside the window to encourage feathered friends. Students love to take care of living things, and the care of the plants and animals can be assigned to a monitor. During my teaching years my students cared for rats, hamsters, a tortoise named Yurtle, tadpoles that developed into frogs, and assorted fish.

Student preferences need to be considered in light of your overriding responsibility for creating an environment that reflects and supports your educational goals and teaching style. Leave some leeway for student input on room accessories, ornamentation, and even pets.

The Décor Can Deliver Very Powerful Nonverbal Messages to Your Students

You and your students spend approximately 30 hours each week in classrooms, and an aesthetically pleasing environment can do much to stimulate the senses and teach at the same time. The physical environment is the first thing students and observers notice about a classroom, and you want yours to deliver the message that exciting and sound instruction is going on there. Before you utter the first word on that first day of school, you will have delivered your message nonverbally to students through your attention to the door, ceilings, and walls of your classroom.

In elementary grades bulletin boards that focus interest on students—a "Star of the Week" board and a "Good Work" board—tell them they are important. A "Helper's Chart" tells them they will share in the responsibilities for their classroom with you. In primary grades, the calendar and weather chart will let students know you provide the security of routines they are used to. A subject-matter bulletin board clues them in to the mysteries that will be unraveled as the year progresses. A word wall makes them more independent as they master the basics of literacy. Labels on all the objects in the room and the cardinal directions posted on corresponding walls will let primary students and English language learners feel confident that they will learn to read these markers soon.

At the high school level, bulletin boards can be used as a way to showcase the talents of the students who enter your room, whether they feature classroom work or announcements of upcoming extracurricular events, such as games of school teams, concerts, plays, or contests. Such displays send the message to your students that you know what they're involved in and you know what is going on in school.

From the very first moment—at the doorstep—you can greet them with a door sign that says:

Welcome to My Stars, with digital photos and/or names on star shapes
Fall Into ________ *Grade,* with names on leaves
Future Nobel Prize Winners Inside
Look Who's Mixing It Up in Chemistry, with names or digital photos on cutout flasks
Welcome to the Ancient World

Strike a balance between excitement and quiet, restful places. Looking at the four walls is the only respite students

TEACHER TALKS . . .

I don't like putting up a lot of professionally made materials; they reflect what you can buy. I prefer to cut 3.5-inch strips of colored paper and have the students write their names, alphabet, math problems, definitions . . . on them and use them as bulletin board borders. These reflect student learning and their environment. By having their work displayed, there is pride in all of us in the final product.

KRIS UNGERER
Kindergarten Teacher
Riverside, California

TEACHER TALKS . . .

Keep up current work and display all levels so students know what kind of work you expect from them. Do not just display "A" and "B" work examples. You can cut out names from work that is not as exceptional so as to not embarrass students. Do not overstimulate students with too much to look at in the room. Keep it interesting and neat.

BARBARA ARIENT
Special Education Teacher
Grades 9–12
San Bernardino, California

have from their daily work. Create warm, bright spaces that instruct and motivate, but don't overdo it. Veteran teachers caution you not to overstimulate the senses of your students.

Design and Construct Some of Your Bulletin Boards Before School Starts

Some teachers purchase or order from catalogs a great deal of prepackaged material, including bulletin board borders; others use available materials so they can draw or construct their own. You can copy and make transparencies of images and then project them onto the wall using a projection device if you feel you can't draw. It's a less expensive solution than buying a multitude of materials that will stay up for only a few short weeks.

Careful lettering will tell your students you are precise and want them to take pride in their work. Bright colors will tell them you have a vibrant and exciting program planned. Mounting pictures on black paper creates contrast on bright bulletin boards and gives depth to your creations. Die-cut presses, available in many districts, turn out borders and bulletin board letters with no fuss or bother.

Maintain a fresh look for your bulletin boards. Try out some different ideas for bulletin board backgrounds instead of the likely-to-fade butcher paper.

- Fabric of all sorts
- Wallpaper
- Wrapping paper
- Newspaper/comics section
- Burlap
- Indoor/outdoor carpeting

Welcome to our class.

Here's our best work.

Instead of buying packaged borders, consider these ideas other teachers have suggested:

- Wide wire ribbon
- Photos of the students
- Old greeting cards/calendar pages
- Old CDs from the computer center
- Laminated gift wrap strips
- Newspaper cartoon strips
- Paint sample cards from home improvement stores
- Number lines/rulers
- Monopoly money

Consider These Suggestions for Secondary Schools

The Kottlers (2003) suggests that in secondary schools, bulletin boards serve nine purposes: information giving, rule reminders, demonstrations, motivation, stimulation, student work display, teacher interests, reinforcement, and entertainment. The same could be said for elementary schools.

Teachers at the middle and high school levels suggest the following bulletin boards:

- Lists of assignments
- Standards
- Calendar
- Inspirational sayings
- Student work
- Motivational posters
- Rules
- Current curriculum topics
- School news/booster activities

Here Are 10 More Bulletin Board Ideas

1. **Birthday board.** This is a listing of all students' birthdays by month. In secondary schools, the teacher passes around a calendar and has each student note his or her birthday. This can be celebrated with a card from the teacher or a small gift.
2. **Tooth fairy report.** In the primary grades, a bulletin board marks the loss

APPLY IT!

For each of the nine purposes shown in Table 10.1, jot down some age- and subject-appropriate ideas for classroom bulletin boards. Some examples have been provided.

A high school bulletin board encourages literacy.

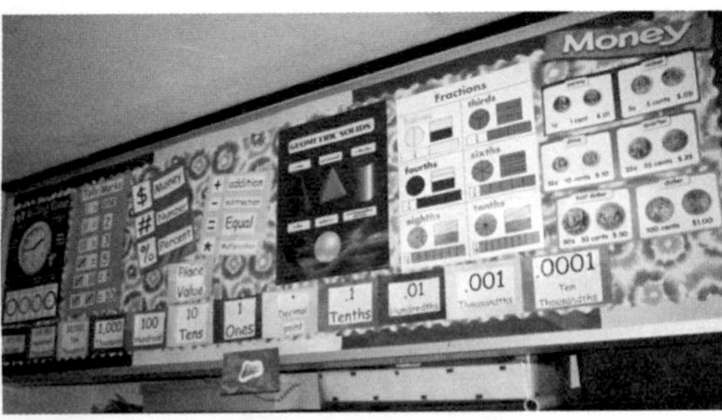

A middle school bulletin board highlights numeracy.

Table 10.1 Purposeful Bulletin Board Ideas

Purposes for Bulletin Boards	Bulletin Boards Ideas
1. Information giving	*How to solve a math word problem*
2. Rule reminders	*Classroom rules*
3. Demonstrations	*Steps in drawing a portrait*
4. Motivation	
5. Stimulation	
6. Student work display	
7. Teacher interests	
8. Reinforcement	
9. Entertainment	

of each tooth. A large cutout tooth for each month lists the name and date of each event. Students enjoy marking these important milestones in their lives.

3. **Star(s) of the week.** Highlighted students decorate the board with photos, hobbies, work, or whatever they choose.
4. **Baby picture—guess who?** Students at all grade levels can bring in a baby picture, which is then posted on a bulletin board with number identification only. A contest can be held after two weeks to see who has correctly identified the most classmates and the teacher.
5. **Student self-portraits or silhouettes.** These are described in Chapter 5 as suggested activities for the first day of school.
6. **Teacher autobiography.** A bulletin board introducing the teacher is also suggested in Chapter 7. You might include photos, samples of your hobbies, a favorite poem, or other information about you.
7. **Encouragement to read.** Book jackets make an effective display. Some teachers use the bookworm idea and encourage students to read a book and add a segment to the worm.

I sat in a fourth-grade classroom recently and checked out the walls. This is what I saw:

- Focus wall for academic standards
- A calendar
- Pledge of Allegiance and pressed American flag
- Current events bulletin board
- Globe and maps
- Cursive alphabet
- "How to Treat Others" poster
- "Rules for Homework" poster
  1. Leave time.
  2. Take home what you need.
  3. Find a quiet place.
  4. Follow directions.
  5. Ask for help.
  6. Keep your homework in the same place.
  7. Return it to school on time.
- Class procedures
- Class rules
- Daily schedule
- Friendly letter format
- Homophone, antonym, and synonym charts
- Helper's chart
- Helping verbs chart
- Outline of math chapter on a graphic web
- Star of the week
- Subject matter bulletin boards
- Poems on posters
- Free time chart
- Getting help chart
- Class photos
- Inspirational sayings
- Huge ruler in centimeters
- Parts of speech poster
- Screen
- Teacher information board with lunch menus, bus schedules, bell schedules, school map, various notices
- Parts of a folktale poster
- Teacher-made curtains geared to the social studies theme
- Book jackets
- A huge bulletin board with an individual space for each student's work

An elementary bulletin board is a learning tool.

8. **Current events.** Another suggested theme is current events at the school, local, national, and international levels. "Nose for News," "News Roundup," or "News Hound" banners can evoke charming, simple drawings or cutouts you've done using an opaque projector.
9. **Instructional boards.** These boards either introduce some concept or provide an overview or preview of some content area. Primary teachers use color, shape, or alphabet bulletin boards, while middle or high school teachers might highlight the first unit or theme. An overview of the semester or year can be attractively depicted under a headline, "Preview of Chemistry," with a glitzy movie poster format.

Meet the class.

10. **Individual bulletin board spaces.** Many teachers solve bulletin board worries by dividing the largest wall in the classroom into equal sections, one for each student. This can be done with colorful yarn. Inside the rectangles, each student displays his or her best work, a photo, a favorite item from home, an art project or a creative writing assignment. The display can be changed according to a schedule or when the student decides to display some other aspect of his or her life at home or at school.

Whatever your initial bulletin boards turn out to be, make sure they are neatly lettered; thoughtfully arranged; have attractive, brightly colored backgrounds; and can be read from all parts of the room. Finally, consider using the space overhead for displaying student work. Wires strung across the room enable you to hang student artwork from the wires with paper clips.

APPLY IT!

Search "classroom bulletin boards" on the Internet and start collecting ideas. Or use the websites listed at the end of this unit for bulletin board ideas.

AVOID IT!

You do not have to take all the responsibility for bulletin board construction. The students can work with you or on their own to construct bulletin boards in cooperative groups. Your role is to suggest the theme and then okay the plan and design they come up with. This activity requires that they research the topic, choose the graphics, and make sure that the board is visually appealing and easy to read. You can develop with them a set of questions such as the following, and they can then assess their work and make adjustments before the actual board is constructed.

Bulletin Board Proposal

1. What is the purpose of your proposed bulletin board—e.g., curriculum and standards, motivation, showcase student work or other?
2. Will your proposed bulletin board feature student work as well as related illustrations?
3. Does your plan include borders and lettering?
4. What will students learn from the bulletin board that they didn't know before?
5. Do you have a plan for gathering needed materials and visuals?
6. Write down the names of team members and their assigned tasks.
7. Date of completion is ______________.
8. Attach a sketch of your bulletin board.

AVOID IT!

Avoid spending money on prepackaged bulletin boards.

Do not allow your boards to become dog-eared, faded, and tattered.

UNIT 3

Summary

Your classroom is your home away from home, and the way you arrange the furniture should complement and facilitate your instructional plan. Individualize your classroom with unique accessories, such as rugs, beanbag chairs, lamps, pets, and so forth. Use bulletin boards to instruct, motivate, and showcase student work.

Reflect!

What would a visitor see on the walls of your classroom? Make a list similar to the one on page 101. Also review Table 10.1, which outlines the nine purposes of bulletin boards, so you can cover all the bases.

CHAPTER 11

HOW DO I ESTABLISH AND MAINTAIN ROUTINES FOR ENTRANCES/EXITS, BEGINNING AND ENDING THE DAY?

A student wants some kind of undisrupted routine or rhythm. He seems to want a predictable, orderly world.

Abraham Maslow

Effectiveness Essentials

- Routines in the classroom enable the teacher and the class to function smoothly and provide the safety and security students need.
- The way in which students enter the room sets the tone for how the day will go.
- Ingrain an exit procedure, so when a real emergency occurs, everyone will get out safely and quickly.
- Normally, the day should begin in the same way every day and should include many rituals.
- The end of the day needs to be planned for as carefully as every other part of the day.

UNIT 3

TEACHER TALKS . . .

The best piece of advice I can give to teachers is something I learned my first year of teaching fifth grade. Routine is a MUST. Students need to know what's going on to feel involved and important. The more the kids know the routine, the more able they are to help when the teacher is out or conflicts arise. My kids practice everything (lining up, changing classes, packing up to go home) during the first week of school. We literally hold drills to practice these things.

I write the next day's schedule on the board at the end of every day. I show the kids how to look in my plan book and write up our activities. They have been able to write up the daily schedule when I am absent. They enjoy this routine and thrive on it. They try to be the first to ask me to "write the schedule." It makes them feel important and involved. After all, if kids aren't actively involved, they will actively try to create trouble!

LAUREL GARNER
Fifth-Grade Teacher
Duluth, Georgia

Routines Serve a Vital Function

Because they are habitual and can be performed automatically, routines set our minds free for more creative and critical thinking activities. While one part of our brain mechanically performs our routines in the morning, the remainder is free to plan the day's activities, consider problems, and anticipate whatever challenges await us.

Humans Are Creatures of Habit and Adhere to Certain Routines and Procedures Throughout the Day

When my alarm goes off, it sets in motion a unique and regimented set of procedures for meeting my day. Almost with eyes closed I perform the daily rituals, day in and day out, in the same order without fail. If I lose a half hour, some of my daily rituals have to go. Either the cats don't get any petting, or I can't have fresh-brewed coffee. I can't read the morning headlines, or I can't do my workout DVD. In short, my day gets off to a bad start.

Routines in the Classroom Will Enable You to Provide the Stability, Safety, and Security Your Students Need

The more stability there is in the classroom, the less likely it is that disruptions will occur. If certain activities or procedures are learned and practiced in rote fashion, the time saved and effort spared can be used for more stimulating instructional activities and events. Routines create order, and when the basic operation of your classroom is under control, you and the students will feel less stressed. In this chapter and the ones that follow, you will learn about routines for

- Entering and exiting the classroom
- Beginning and ending the day
- Materials storage and distribution
- Bathroom and water fountain permission
- Movement within the room
- Getting help
- Hand raising
- Noise control
- Free time
- Collection, distribution, and labeling of papers
- Instructional management

When students act confused or unsure of what to do or how to do it, this is a good sign that you have to think through or create another routine or procedure.

Entrances and Exits

The beginnings or endings of any endeavor are important bookends for what comes in between. Although technically your interest is in what happens in between, paying attention to the entrances and exits will serve you well.

The Way in Which Students Enter the Room Sets the Tone for How the Day Will Go

Meeting your students at the door helps you establish your presence and allows you to greet each one individually. This is the perfect time to say something positive to each student. It may simply be "Good morning" (in the student's native language as appropriate) or "I like your new haircut" or "That's a neat sweater." At the high school level, this can be a fine time to acknowledge accomplishments from the night before, such as "Nice game last night" or "I heard the math club trounced its opponents."

Have Your Students Form Lines Outside the Classroom Prior to Entering

Although school rules may be more relaxed, lines diminish pushing and shoving and discourage barreling into the room. Lines also help to make a smooth transition from socializing outside to work inside the classroom. These same procedures can be followed during any entrance into the room, whether from recess, physical education, or another part of the building. Students can be shown how to line up (not by gender because of Title IX regulations), and this expectation is most easily

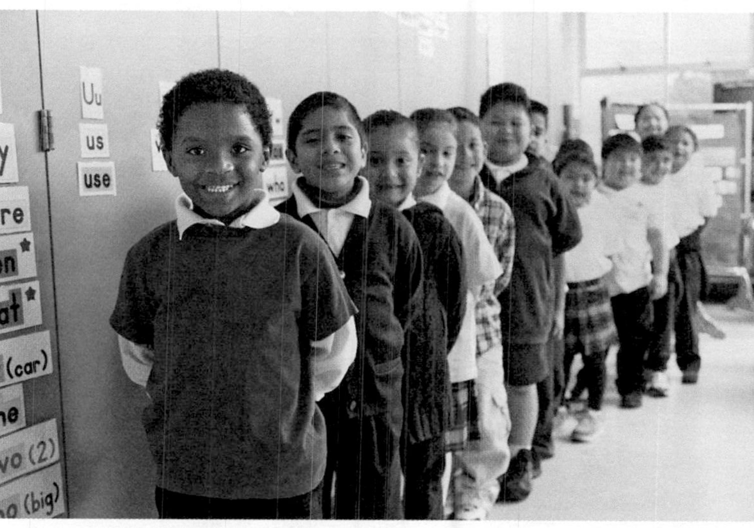

These students are off to a good start.

UNIT 3

TEACHER TALKS . . .

During my first month of teaching in my first year, the school at which I taught had a lap-running fundraiser. As our P.E. activity that day we went out to practice running. I decided to take the classroom wall clock out with us so the students could easily see how long the event took. When we returned to the classroom, I noticed a stony silence coming from the other classrooms. Apparently, the clock had stopped and it wasn't until another teacher noticed my students that I realized that my entire class had missed their buses to go home.

HEIDI THOMPSON
First-Grade Teacher
Yucaipa, California

imprinted when it applies to all situations involving entrances into the room. Although this is most readily enforced in elementary and middle school, at the high school level the same purpose is served by meeting your students at the door, where you can more easily monitor and assure an orderly entrance.

Establish a Procedure for What You Expect Your Students to Do When They Enter the Room

Turn off all lights when you leave the room and establish the turning on of the lights as a signal that the next activity is about to begin. Or, better yet, have an activity on the desks or on the board for your students to do as soon as they enter the room. Some teachers have students write in their journals first thing in the morning and read their books first thing after lunch. These alternatives give you a few minutes to collect your thoughts, especially in the morning and after lunch, when clerical tasks may command your attention.

For middle and high school students, use entrance and exit routines that are customary in your school, but be sure your students enter your room ready to learn. Every moment counts in a short period. You don't want to waste half the period quieting rowdy students—and one way of avoiding this is insisting on an orderly entrance.

Design the quickest method to take attendance in high school so as not to waste time. If kindergarten students can turn name cards over in a pocket chart themselves (see Figure 11.1) and take their own attendance, then middle and

Figure 11.1
Pocket Chart

APPLY IT!

What can you have your students do in the first few minutes of school or for the first few minutes of the period? This should be an ongoing assignment that has both a management and an instructional purpose.

high school students can do the same. For each period have a sign-in sheet or have a seating chart that is on a clipboard that students must sign in on. Write your seating charts in erasable pen. Seats will change. You can count on it! You may choose to call roll each and every day to help you learn the names, but after a while, you can simply scan the room and see who is missing. Keep a tardy list at the door that late students must sign. TAs in high school use the computer to take attendance, and elementary teachers often submit attendance using their computers.

Teachers Suggest Dismissing by Table or Row, With the Quietest One Leading the Pack

Combining the group dismissal with the line is another alternative. By table, students line up for P.E., recess, lunch, library, assembly, or final dismissal. Transitions are unstable times in a classroom. No matter what the grade level, the more structure you give to the situation, the more likely it is that safety and low noise level will prevail. This is true especially when the exit from the room is required for simulated (or real) emergencies such as fire drills. In large gatherings, such as assemblies or rallies in high school, there is usually an established order of dismissal. Find out what it is and take note.

You can dismiss by some clothing attribute: students wearing stripes or red tops, white tennis shoes or a sweater, for example. This is not only a good way to have students line up for dismissal, but it also provides a nonthreatening way to teach basic concepts to English language learners. In secondary classrooms, you don't have the luxury of a slow dismissal because it is essential that students get to their next class on time. You need to establish a quick method such as dismissing by those rows or tables that are packed up and ready to go.

Ingrain an Exit Procedure, So When a Real Emergency Occurs, Everyone Will Get Out Safely and Quickly

Make sure your students know the signals and frequently practice the procedures used in your school for emergency situations. Even if your school does not require it, keep a copy of the class roster accessible so you can grab it in case of emergency and count heads immediately. Carefully review and reinforce these

STUDENT SAYS . . .

Question: How does your teacher dismiss the class? *She tells us to put our heads on our desk. Whichever table is the quietest goes first.*

WALKER
Second Grade, Age 7½
Redlands, California

procedures in the first days and weeks of school and then intermittently after that.

When moving around the school with your class, walk in the middle, not at the front. When you lead the line, the students at the back of the line will create their own party. When you bring up the rear, the students in the front will get away from you. Give clear directions about stopping points along the way. For example, "Stop at the water fountain or stop in front of the office and wait for me." Line leaders should be responsible for following your directions.

Beginning and Ending the Day

Students of all ages enjoy the safety and predictability of morning and end-of-the-day routines. How important are these routines? Try an experiment and "forget" something on purpose. You will experience for yourself the uproar that ensues! Students will let you know if you have forgotten something. They expect certain things to happen in a certain order.

In middle and high school, homeroom teachers are responsible for beginning the day and implementing the routines, such as attendance taking, collection of monies, announcements, etc., that elementary teachers are solely responsible for. However, the beginning of each period in secondary school requires planning and order on your part. And the last moments of the period or the class are key to orderly dismissal and everyone getting to their next destination.

The Day Normally Begins in the Same Way Every Day and Includes Many Rituals

Typical rituals elementary teachers use to begin the day in the same order every day can include many tasks such as these:

- Collection of money, permission slips
- Attendance, pupil counts
- Flag salute and song
- Announcements
- Homework collection
- Explanation of the day's schedule or period agenda and the standards that will be addressed
- Birthdays, tooth fairy update, calendar, weather, etc., in primary classrooms
- Sharing, current events, or a classroom meeting
- Journal writing

Middle and high school teachers should have a routine for what students do upon entering that is appropriate to your subject area.

Closure Is Important at the End of the Day

Use the last 5–10 minutes for a quick review of the day's activities with your students, discussing what they learned or enjoyed most that day. Present an exciting preview of the next day. Use the time for clearing off tables, cleaning out desks, tidying up the room, and making sure that all papers and notices that need to go home are distributed. Set a timer or use an alarm clock to remind you and the students that it is time to clean up. Buses run on schedules, and they can't wait for students to clean up after an art lesson. Add a special, individualized, and positive comment to as many students as time allows as you dismiss them.

Many of the same routines for ending the day also pertain to ending the period in middle and high schools. You can set a timer and, when it rings, have the students clean up, gather their

WATCH IT! video

Modeling and Building Respect and Establishing Routines and Transitions

In this video, you will see a fourth-grade teacher using effective instructional routines and procedures. If you were his supervisor, what strengths would you observe and commend him on? What would you offer as additional suggestions or alternatives? How will you apply the very consistent routines he demonstrates to your grade level or subject area?

APPLY IT!

A pleasant way to end each day is the compliment activity. Randomly distribute the nametags, cards, or sticks you use to call on students (Chapter 13). Everyone in turn compliments the student whose name he or she receives. Thus, everyone gives and gets a compliment. For example, John gets Steve's stick or card and says, "I would like to compliment Steve for. . . ." Steve says, "Thank you," and then gives the next compliment to the person whose name he has been given. And so on. In this way, the students leave school with a positive outlook for the next day.

STUDENT SAYS . . .

Question: How does your teacher end the day? *At the end of the day when our desk is clean, she tells us to pack up.*

DAVID
Sixth Grade, Age 11
Satellite Beach, Florida

UNIT 3

STUDENT SAYS . . .

Mrs. H. greets the class and asks everyone to sit on the rug. She takes attendance, and then we listen to the announcements of the day and participate in the Pledge of Allegiance, which is led by a fifth grader over the intercom. After this, we continue to sit on the rug and review what day it is and the date . . . and what day of school it is. For instance, today was our 100th day of school, and we had a little party.

Toward the end of the day we visit a center: for example, computers, Polly Pockets, Legos, reading corner, imagination corner. When this free time is up, the teacher starts to sing, "It's clean up time, clean up time; sorry, but it's clean up time, time to clean up." She'll ask everyone to clean up their space and get a wipey to wipe down their desk. She then asks us to put on our backpacks and line up at the door.

KENDALL
Kindergarten, Age 6
Denver, Colorado

Five Ideas for Beginning the Period

1. Copy the period outline from the board into your notes.
2. Write a question that comes to mind when you read the period standards or objectives.
3. Summarize yesterday's notes into a paragraph.
4. Fill out a feedback form for yesterday's session (see Figure 11.2).
5. Make yourself a set of flashcards based on what you learned the previous day.

papers, and make sure they have copied the homework; then summarize the lesson, review the homework, and tell the students what to bring the next day. If you have time, you can ask them to describe what was most interesting, tell you what idea was completely new to them, ask any remaining questions, predict what they will learn the next period, etc. Remember that *you* signal the end of the period—*not* the bell. In high school, the last-period teacher, especially at the end of the week, has the biggest challenge of corralling the students who are antsy to get to after-school jobs, practices, pep rallies, games, or just to leave. You will need to plan accordingly for those last 10 minutes of the final period of the day and the week.

Figure 11.2
Period Evaluation

Subject ______________ Date __________

Period _____ Teacher ________________

What were the three most important things you learned yesterday (today)?

What questions do you still have?

What will you do to resolve these questions?

Do you have any suggestions for improving the lesson?

AVOID IT!

Among the errors to be avoided at the beginning of the year are:

- Letting infractions slide because you are too busy
- Not taking enough time to check for understanding of the routines
- Introducing too many routines at once
- Thinking that your students don't need to practice

Summary

Students need the security and safety that routines provide. The way in which students enter the room sets the tone for the day, so you need to establish a routine for how they will enter the room. Similarly, you want them to leave the room in an orderly fashion so they can get to where they are going efficiently and safely. The exit procedure is especially important in the event of a real disaster. Begin the day with a consistent set of procedures that students will come to expect and rely on. The end of the day or the period should be planned to alleviate a chaotic rush to the door.

Reflect!

Make a list of standardized procedures for beginning and ending the day or period that are appropriate for the age, grade, and subject matter you teach. What questions do you still have about entrances, and starting and ending the day or period? Write these down and make sure that you consult other teachers for additional ideas.

TEACHER TALKS . . .

Regardless of how your day has gone, before students leave, give positive affirmations either to the whole class or to individuals. Students leave the classroom with positive feelings and will be happy to start a new day tomorrow.

MARSHA MOYER
Fifth-Grade Teacher
San Bernardino, California

CHAPTER 12

HOW DO I MOVE MATERIALS AND STUDENTS AROUND THE ROOM?

For every minute spent in organizing,
an hour is earned.

Anonymous

Effectiveness Essentials

- Establish which materials and equipment may be accessed by students, and set up distribution and collection procedures.
- Establish routines for purposeful out-of-seat activities such as bathroom, water fountain, pencil sharpening, and so forth.
- Establish routines for moving to small groups/centers.

By now, you are well on your way to becoming a logistics expert. You will need to establish just a few more routines for materials distribution, bathroom and water fountain privileges, and movement around the room. In the next chapter, you will learn about instructional routines.

Materials and Equipment

Schools are not yet paperless environments. There is much teacher stuff in classrooms that needs to be accessed, monitored, distributed, and collected efficiently. Student stuff in desks, in cubbies, on hooks, or in lockers presents yet another organizational challenge.

Establish What Materials May Be Accessed by Students

The teacher's desk and file cabinet or special supply shelf should be off-limits to the students unless they have your permission. Similarly, their cubbies, desks, and coat hooks are their private spaces. Shared paper supplies should be pointed out during your room environment orientation, and you need to be clear about how these supplies are to be distributed. Will your students be allowed, for example, to get whatever papers they need when they need them, will monitors hand out papers, or will you pass the papers out yourself to individuals or to monitors?

In most high schools and middle schools, lockers are assigned to all students. In some schools where the privilege has been abused, students must carry all of their books with them all day. Ouch! You should emphasize that personal lockers are off-limits to other students out of respect for privacy and that students should not share lockers or their lock combinations. Since lockers and contents are joint student and school district property, the courts have consistently ruled that administrators may search lockers based on "reasonable suspicion." Check out what constitutes reasonable suspicion for locker and other searches in your district. Tell your students that inappropriate pictures or photos on the outside or inside of lockers are not acceptable.

Establish Procedures for Materials Distribution and Collection

Will monitors collect papers, or will you collect them? Will you have a central collection tray that individuals can use when they finish their work? How will students get pencils, crayons, scissors, and paste? Will these items be on the

TEACHER TALKS . . .

We are "Garner's Gators" and we have a "Gator turn-in box." It's a large wooden bookcase (sponge-painted with gators) and each section is labeled. The kids know to turn in their work to the "Gator turn-in box." They like to say the name aloud and it helps them associate our name with their work.

My fifth graders know the importance of organization. They are immersed in organization from day 1 of school. We spend the first two days organizing and color coding our materials—books, folders, materials, coats, backpacks, etc. Blue social studies book goes with blue folder and notebook, red science book goes with red folder and notebook, etc. I even have them help me color-code the art supply cabinet. They have learned to do this on their own and will sometimes come up with an organization system that we can all use!

LAUREL GARNER
Fifth-Grade Teacher
Duluth, Georgia

TEACHER TALKS . . .

Use a computer program to collect and keep track of grades and turned in materials.

BARBARA ARIENT
Special Education Teacher
Grades 9–12
San Bernardino, California

UNIT 3

APPLY IT!

Create a worksheet such as the one shown in Table 12.1, adding other materials as needed, to get a handle on how to organize and distribute your supplies. This activity will help you make some decisions about materials location and distribution.

desks or at a central location? Will students be allowed to come up at will to get what they need, or will supplies be distributed by you or by a monitor?

Bathroom and Water Fountain

You have been planning out routines and procedures at your desk for two hours, drinking lots of water, tea, or coffee, and all of a sudden your bladder reminds you that you have to establish some biology-related rules for bathroom and water fountain use. Accidents are common in primary grades, and your rules should take this into account. At secondary levels, at certain times of the month, the girls may need to use the bathroom *now!* Every student now and then has an

Table 12.1 Location and Distribution Chart

	Location		Distribution	
Supplies	Each Desk	Central Location	Monitor	Teacher
1. Paper				
2. Pencils				
3. Rulers				
4.				
5.				
6.				
7.				
8.				

emergency. Water is key to health, and you need to achieve a balance between intake and output!

Establish a Fair and Equitable Policy for Bathroom Breaks

Recesses, lunch, and between periods are the specified times for bathroom breaks. However, realistically, you may have to deviate from these norms and establish some bathroom rules because students have special needs and nature does not always adhere to schedules. Before creating your own rules about bathroom use during class time, ask colleagues or department heads what the school norms are. You do not want to deviate from them.

Most teachers use a pass system. Only two students at a time (different genders) are allowed out of the room so that they do not fool around in the restroom with a friend. Some teachers fashion large passes out of wooden blocks. Others suggest that, since the pass often ends up on the floor of the restroom, you should consider passes on lanyards or bracelets (see Figure 12.1). Make sure your name and/or room number is on the pass, that there are only two of them, and that students understand these procedures:

- They should not leave during instructional time or when directions are being given.
- They must wait until a pass is available.
- They must keep all restrooms neat and tidy for others.
- They must leave and return without disturbing others.

Figure 12.1
Bathroom Passes

STUDENT SIBLINGS SAY . . .

We have a bathroom sign-out sheet at the back of the classroom. We can get up whenever we want, and if nobody else is out we can sign out and go.

DREW
Fourth Grade, Age 10
Edmond, Oklahoma

If Mrs. K is teaching us something, we're not allowed to go to the bathroom because she doesn't want us to miss something. If she's not teaching us something and we're having free time, we put the bathroom pass on our desk and go.

ALLIE
Second Grade, Age 8
Edmond, Oklahoma

We can only have four people in the bathroom at a time. We have to stay quiet. We go to the bathroom as a group after a lesson. We have to make sure we wash our hands good. We have two bathroom breaks every day.

COCO
First Grade, Age 6
Edmond, Oklahoma

CHAPTER 12

UNIT 3

TEACHER TALKS . . .

No restroom passes the first and last 10 minutes of the passing period for middle and high schools, since students just had the opportunity to use the restroom. Some teachers only allow two per quarter and keep track in a grade book. Have a special pass that you can have the students use so you do not have to be interrupted to write a pass every time, and have a sign-in-and-out log book that you can show to parents if it becomes an issue of too much time out of the room or asking every day! Only allow five minutes to use bathroom.

BARBARA ARIENT
Special Education Teacher
Grades 9–12
San Bernardino, California

Students who abuse your bathroom policy should be dealt with individually so as not to cause embarrassment. After an incident, and periodically thereafter, review bathroom rules without mentioning specific offenders. In my experience, the less fuss you make about the bathroom policy, the less likely it is that students will use passes when they really don't need to.

Here are some other teacher suggestions. You can combine any number of them to meet your grade-level needs:

1. Assess a penalty for leaving the room during instruction. Students may have to stay in for five minutes or give up earned tickets or reward "bucks" to leave the room.
2. Give each student three bathroom passes for the semester. When they use them up, that's it!
3. Teach your students to use American Sign Language to signal that they need to use the restroom. The sign is the one for the letter "T." Make a fist with the thumb between the index and middle fingers and move it side to side. This will be a silent signal that will not disturb others (Figure 12.2).
4. Require students to leave a placeholder on their desks when they need to use the restroom. This lets you know who is out of the room and why, especially in large classes where a visual reminder may be needed (Figure 12.3).
5. Limit the number of times a student may sign out to the restroom in a week, and require students to record their comings and goings in a log or on a timesheet.

Although some of these suggestions may sound harsh, you do not want your students to miss valuable instruction, especially in light of two recesses and a lunch break in elementary school and time between periods in secondary schools. In special cases, you can bend the rule.

Remind kindergarten parents to make sure boys and girls know how to undo their belts or, better yet, encourage parents to consider elastic-waist pants. In kindergarten, look for signs of imminent bathroom need. By the time these busy folks in kindergarten raise their hands, it is sometimes too late.

Figure 12.2
ASL Signs for "Toilet" and "Water"

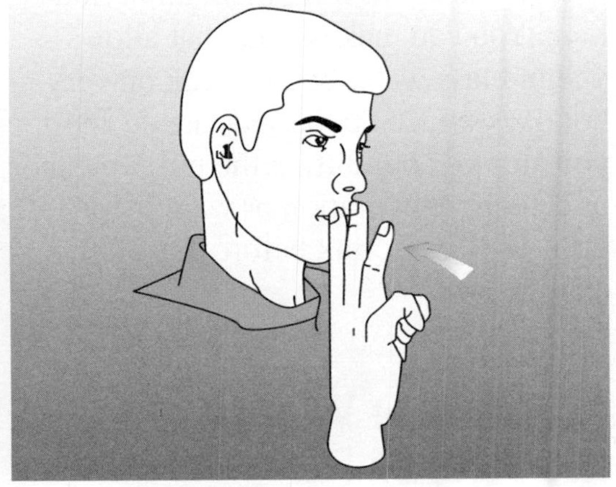

Water Access Is Not as Necessary as Bathroom Breaks

Water is always available at recess and at passing times. When fountains are in the room, you may choose to allow students to drink as they require liquid nourishment, but beware! Since there is a direct connection between drinking and bathroom requests, you may be adding to your own management problems if you provide access to water all day, even within the room. A compromise would involve water lineup after transitions into the room for those who need it. On very hot days, in very hot classrooms, you can always suspend the rules or allow students to have individual water bottles at their desks. When you buy the water in pint bottles in bulk you can affix name labels and have students refill them, assuring equal access.

Figure 12.3
Placards to Put on Tables When Students Leave the Room

TEACHER TALKS . . .

Because I teach kindergarten, and there is no bathroom in my room, I send pairs of students to the bathroom at one time. That way, if one gets stuck in the bathroom because the door is heavy, there are two people to try to open the door. Also, an added benefit—they tell on each other immediately upon reentry if either was naughty.

KRIS UNGERER
Kindergarten Teacher
Riverside, California

In high school, depending on the rules, students carry big, bulky water bottles and drink from them all period long. You can make a rule that allows one in-class water bottle break on very hot days. Since the periods are so short, you are not committing the misdemeanor of student dehydration or water deprivation. They can drink before and after class.

Movement Within the Room

Your students, especially the energetic ones in elementary school, need teacher-sanctioned opportunities to stretch and amble. Secondary students move about between classes, but the elementary students need to move about periodically, too.

Incorporate Structured Movement

You can structure periodic in-class exercise routines. There are several excellent DVDs that feature classroom-appropriate controlled exercise routines. When you provide the opportunity for exercise, fewer students are likely to make their own individual opportunities, which can disrupt and cause delays.

In middle school or the upper grades, after establishing a signal such as a bell for returning to work, schedule periodic five-minute mini-breaks to enable this peer-dependent group to socialize.

Manage Pencil Sharpening

The constant grinding noise of a sharpener can grate on the ears and disrupt instruction. The extreme position some teachers hold is that all broken pencils and wastebasket material must be held until specified times, usually early morning and after lunch. Better yet, have a supply of pencils at each table in a coffee can. One table leader is responsible for sharpening them at the start of the day. During the day, students can exchange their broken pencils for a sharpened one.

Allow Access to the Wastebasket

You can't totally eliminate the need to get rid of dirty tissues or paper scraps. Equip each table cluster with a cheap plastic wastebasket from a bargain store and have the students dispose of their refuse without leaving their seats.

Control Movement to Groups

If your classroom is typical, you will need to establish routines for moving to groups. No matter what the grade level is, when your students work in groups, you must provide clear instruction about the groups they are to work in, even posting the groups so there is no confusion and the transition to groups is quick. To ease transitions from groups to seatwork to activity, you will need to make two charts, one listing the names of all members of each group and another that signals what activity each group is engaged in. A wheel arrangement or pocket chart works very well.

You can make a rotation chart by listing the centers down the left side and the students who will be at each center on the right side. Use Velcro or magnetic strips to attach the names or even laminated digital photos of your students (Figure 12.4).

Another popular device is the rotation wheel. Cut out two large circles. Divide the outer circle into your centers and the inner circle into groups. You will also need a chart of who belongs in each group. Just turn the wheel to show where each group should be (Figures 12.5 and 12.6).

When you have established your schedule, set up a procedure for changing to another group efficiently and quietly. Some teachers use a timer,

Figure 12.4
Center Rotation Chart

Teacher	Karen, Paul, Laticia, Jacob
Teacher/aide	Linda, Len, Don, Juan
Spelling	Maria, Liz, Jake, Eric
Writing	Bella, Sue, John, Steve
Reading games	Paul, Gary, Donna, Jan
Computer	Niki, Allen, Rachel
Listening	Ruby, Denny, Ryan, Jason
Library	Sam, David, Elena, Juanita

AVOID IT!

Make sure your policy for bathroom privileges isn't too strict and rigid. You do not want to humiliate your students, and sometimes there is a real emergency. Don't adopt a policy you can't enforce or one that is so inflexible that you will be hard pressed to explain away accidents to parents and administrators, not to mention the students.

Figure 12.5
Center Rotation Wheel

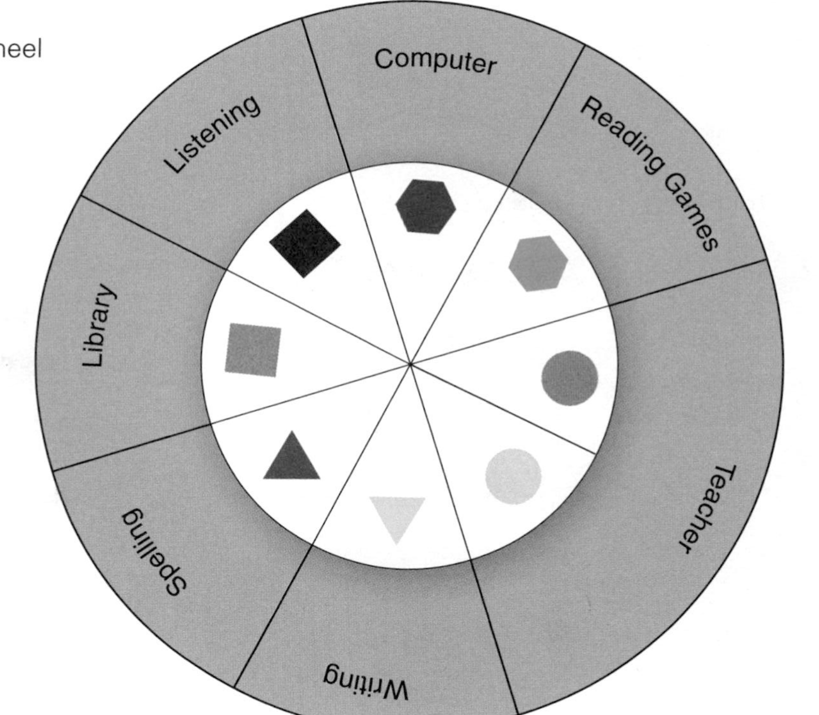

Figure 12.6
Groups and Symbols Chart

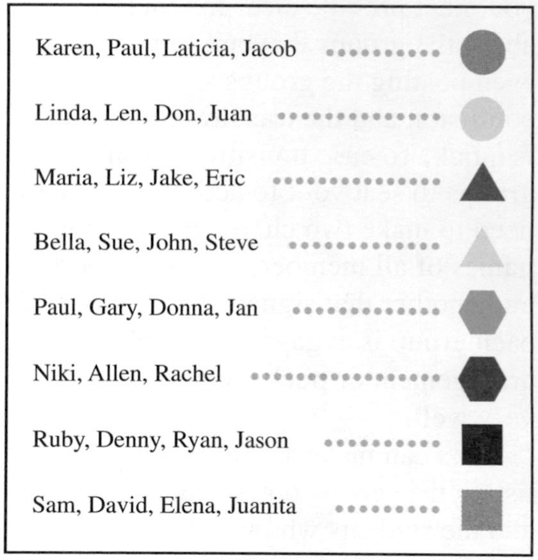

Karen, Paul, Laticia, Jacob
Linda, Len, Don, Juan
Maria, Liz, Jake, Eric
Bella, Sue, John, Steve
Paul, Gary, Donna, Jan
Niki, Allen, Rachel
Ruby, Denny, Ryan, Jason
Sam, David, Elena, Juanita

WATCH IT! video

Making Transitions

This teacher is giving very explicit directions prior to a cooperative learning activity on life cycles.

What techniques does he use to move the students to a new activity? Do you think he overexplains? Why or why not? How might you do this differently?

others a bell; and many simply announce that it's time for a change. You will want to post rules for working in groups. Consider these:

1. Help each other.
2. Share and take turns.
3. Compliment each other.
4. Talk quietly.
5. Evaluate how the group worked.

Summary

The less movement around the room, the better; but sometimes students need to access materials, or they need a sharpened pencil, or they have to throw something in the wastebasket. Carefully consider bathroom and water fountain rules and the potential consequences of your decisions. Students also rotate to centers at the teacher's direction. The more thought you put into movement around the room, the fewer distractions you will have and the more instructional time you will save.

Reflect!

Find out about bathroom policies at your school site or ask several teachers what their rules are regarding bathroom use since you don't want to impose conflicting rules. Determine which suggestions in this chapter meet your need for accessing materials, distributing materials, using the wastebasket, sharpening pencils, and so forth. How will you rotate students through centers if you plan to use centers in your classroom? Ask colleagues for alternatives to the system described in the chapter. This is the time to create your own American Sign Language dictionary using resources online or by buying an ASL reference book.

CHAPTER 13
WHAT INSTRUCTIONAL ROUTINES WILL I NEED?

Habits are cobwebs at first; cables at last.

Chinese proverb

Effectiveness Essentials

- Good discipline is dependent on effective instructional management.
- Teachers learn many routines by trial and error, common sense, or observation of other teachers.
- At the very start, establish and rehearse procedures for
  Getting help
  Quieting classroom chatter
  Asking or responding
  Free time
  Labeling papers
  Collecting and distributing papers
- Use visual aids to teach and reinforce procedures for English language learners.

Teachers learn many routines by trial and error, common sense, or observation of other teachers. One teacher reported "stumbling into what worked best." A *reliable* student assisted one new teacher by recounting how the class did things last year. You may be thinking that a tactical operations degree would be a useful supplement to a teaching credential after reading about routines. In fact, logistics are a major factor in any complex endeavor, but especially in teaching. There are still a few more routines to consider, and they apply to instruction.

WATCH IT! video

Modeling Mutual Respect, Routines, and Transitions

In this video, you will see a fourth-grade teacher using effective instructional routines and procedures. He is using some of the techniques suggested by Jacob Kounin. Which techniques can you identify? What are the strengths of his approach, and what would you do differently? How will you apply the very consistent routines he demonstrates to your grade level or subject area?

Effective Instructional Management

With a central tenet that "good discipline is dependent on effective instructional management," Jacob Kounin (1977) developed a set of principles for instructional management. His work will be discussed in greater detail in Unit 4, Chapter 18, but because these principles are so important, they are briefly noted here.

Take Advantage of the Ripple Effect

This occurs when a teacher corrects or praises one student and thus influences other students to shape up or correct misbehaviors to earn the same praise. For example, she might say, "See how quietly table 1 is waiting for instructions." Students at all other tables then come to attention with hands folded.

Cultivate Withitness

Withitness is defined as having eyes in the back of your head or being aware of the entire class at all times. Before you begin, make sure all eyes are on you and keep scanning the room for potential disruptions.

TEACHER TALKS . . .

The best advice I can give a new teacher is to forget teaching academics for the first week or two, especially in the younger grades. What needs to be focused on is modeling, modeling, modeling, and then some more modeling! After routines and expectations are in place, then the academics will happen. Time can now be spent on teaching and having fun instead of constant interruptions for behavior or the "what am I supposed to do now?" questions. Happy teaching!

SHIRLEY BYASSEE
Third-Grade Teacher
Colorado Springs, Colorado

Group Alerting Is Key

Keep everyone on task and make every class member accountable for responding. Using name cards or sticks (described on page 129) is a great way of applying this concept.

Watch for Satiation

Satiation occurs as boredom sets in or when the students have had enough. Leave them wanting more.

Overlappingness Can Save Time

This concept is defined as the ability to attend to two activities at once—for example, walking over to a student who is playing with a puzzle or a phone application and confiscating the item without missing an instructional beat.

Be Aware of Pacing and Transitions

Teachers should be aware when lessons have gone on for too long. Transitions between activities should be smooth and include closure as well as an introduction to what is coming next.

Instructional Routines

The more you can routinize the procedures that support your instruction, the more smoothly the instructional period or day will go. You won't have to ask yourself every day, for example, "Now how will I collect papers today?" It will be automatic, as will the other instructional support routines in this section.

Routines are only as effective as their constant reinforcement. So as you consider each and every routine that follows, apply these principles:

1. Begin on the first day to establish the procedures that will be in use for the whole year or semester.
2. Be very specific about how you want things done.
3. Have the students practice each procedure until they get it right.
4. Liberally compliment students when they follow procedures.
5. Reteach the routines and quickly deal with deviations from established procedures. For example, "I hear a good answer, but I won't call on anyone who doesn't raise his or her hand."
6. Give rational reasons for each routine as it is introduced.

Establish How Students Can Get Help

You need to establish how your students can get help when you are busy. I found it frustrating to have students tugging at my sleeve when I was involved in a lively discussion during a small-group session. Secondary students will just sit there with raised hands or find more amusing things to do when they are stuck and you are busy. Clearly explain the objective, encourage procedural questions, ask one student to repeat the directions, write all assignments on the board, identify alternative sources of help, and provide something meaningful for students to do when their work is completed. Then you can really enjoy and profitably use the time spent in small-group instruction. Create a "When I Need Help Chart" and select your own age-appropriate alternatives from this list:

When students need your help and you are unavailable, two systems seem to work better than raising hands. The first involves the "take-a-number" method. To facilitate service, many businesses use preprinted numbers to serve customers. Prepare a duplicate set of numbers on cards, laundry tags, or sticky notes. When students need help, they take a number from the pad or a laundry tag from a hook and go on to something else while they wait. You simply call out the numbers in order or put the duplicate numbers up on a hook one at a time. Students then come up to your desk when they see or hear their number. This works very well and provides a first-come, first-served, fair method of getting help (Figure 13.1).

Since a raised hand can get very tired, an alternative method is to give each student a red and green Lego block or Unifix cube. When help is needed, the red cube or block is placed on top of the

- Ask the monitor of the day.
- Ask a cross-age tutor.
- Ask one of the volunteer parents.
- Do what you can and skip the hard parts.
- Use the word wall, instructional charts, spelling journal, dictionary, or thesaurus.
- Whisper to a neighbor for help.
- Consult appendices in your text for formulas or conversions.
- Consult maps in your text.

TEACHER TALKS . . .

I had a student teacher who followed all of the aforementioned advice and told me nothing worked. I went to see for myself. After a terrific lesson, she gave clear directions about what to do next, had the students repeat them, asked for questions, and then sat down at her desk. Students immediately came up to her desk with questions. "See," she said, "it doesn't work." I asked if I could try. She said yes. When the next one approached her desk, I simply pointed back to his seat and mimed writing. Like magic he returned to his seat. This was no magic at all! I simply affirmed her directions nonverbally and wouldn't be sidetracked since I knew my student teacher had given clear directions and checked for understanding. Sometimes I tell teachers to sit at their desk and write while students are writing or read something while

(continued on following page)

TEACHER TALKS—*continued*

students are reading. This will also cut down on attention-getting behaviors that masquerade as interminable questions.

ELLEN KRONOWITZ
Student Teacher Supervisor
Redlands, California

Figure 13.1
Materials for the "Take-a-Number" Method

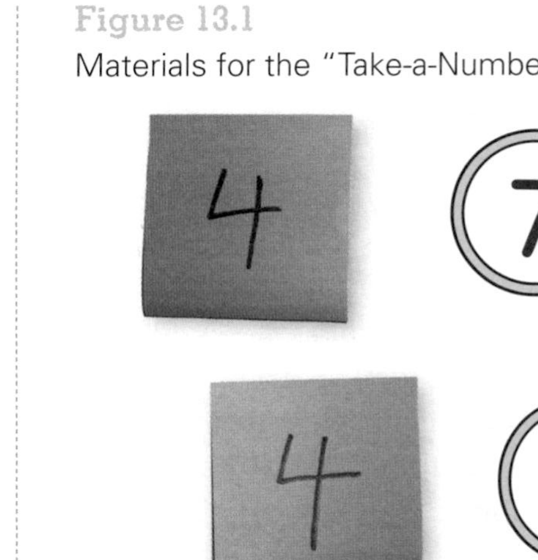

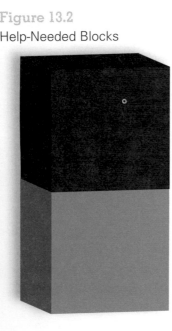

Figure 13.2
Help-Needed Blocks

green one. At all other times, the green is on top. You can see this easily and the student can keep on working until you get there. This has worked so well for so many of my student teachers that I encourage you to try it. I have made these red/green signaling devices out of toilet paper rolls with red masking tape on one end and green on the other. The devices can be used in the computer lab as they fit nicely on top of a computer (Figure 13.2).

One teacher wears a sign that says, "Please see me later," when she is involved in small-group instruction and wants to discourage interruptions. She points to the "When I Need Help Chart" when students come up to her. This may sound extreme, but you are actually establishing independence and making it more likely that students will solve the problem themselves, learn to rely on peers for instruction, or discover the virtue of patience. If too many of your students are baffled, you need to reteach the material to the entire class or work with a small ad hoc group.

Control Noise

The best way to abate noise and chatter is to differentiate among whispering, talking, and silence. This is a useful distinction to make because total silence is hard to maintain during an entire day. Try it yourself sometime! Using a home-made cardboard traffic light can help control the noise level—green signifying talking, yellow for whispering, and red for silence (Figures 13.3 and 13.4). Have your students practice differentiating between whispering and talking. You can make a game of this. Have them say their names with their voice and then whisper their names, using only their breath. Teachers usually have a signal for total silence, like lights off, a bell, or a hand signal, and allow whispering at all other times.

Figure 13.3
Traffic Signal

Specify the acceptable noise level for each activity beforehand. Be realistic about how much silence can be expected in the classroom. If you teach your students to whisper, you will have a quiet classroom—not a silent classroom, but a quiet one. One teacher puts a doll in a basket and announces that the baby is sleeping. Another cautions students not to awaken the rabbit (stuffed animal or real classroom pet). Still another cautions that the canary is getting nervous. These techniques work well, even with older students.

Figure 13.4
Noise-Level Circles

Plan for Hand Raising

Be consistent about hand raising and avoid questions that elicit choral responses. Called-out responses or questions frustrate beginning teachers. Preface your questions with "Raise your hand and tell us. . . ." Always compliment and encourage students who remember to raise hands, especially at the beginning of the year. During a dynamic discussion, debate, or brainstorming activity, you can always suspend the rules.

No matter what level, consider using a system for calling on students that assures equity. With young students, teachers might write the names of students on sticks and place these in a coffee can. These craft sticks or tongue depressors are chosen on a random basis and may or may not be removed from the can. Another teacher uses a deck of cards and writes a student's name on each card (Figures 13.5 and 13.6).

STUDENT SIBLINGS SAY . . .

Question: *What happens when you need help with your work?*

I ask my teacher.

DREW
Fourth Grade, Age 10
Edmond, Oklahoma

Sometimes we ask a friend, and if the friend doesn't know it, we ask Mrs. K. (head teacher) or Ms. M. (student teacher).

ALLIE
Second Grade, Age 8
Edmond, Oklahoma

I'll ask a friend, and if she doesn't know, I ask a different friend. I ask my teacher only if two friends don't know.

COCO
First Grade, Age 6
Edmond, Oklahoma

Figure 13.5
Playing Cards

Figure 13.6
Can With Name Sticks

The cards are used in the same way as the sticks but are more compact and more age-appropriate for intermediate grades and secondary students.

Use American Sign Language

In Chapter 12, you learned the signs for water and bathroom. Other signs that will help you manage the classrooms are those for "sit" and "quiet." These and other signs can be accessed online and will enable you to send nonverbal cues to your students without interrupting the flow in instruction. See Figures 13.7 and 13.8.

Have a Free Time Policy

To cut down on disruption when students finish quickly, you need to have a free time policy. Note that if your students are finishing too quickly, this may be evidence that the work is too easy or insufficient in volume. Establish a routine for what your students do when they finish work, and post this on a bulletin board in plain view. Some suggestions include:

Figure 13.7
The sign for "sit" is the verb form of the sign for "chair." You just do the first half of the "chair" sign in one quick motion.

TEACHER TALKS . . .

Students put their work at the end of the table, all headings going one way, and one student brings up the stack. The reasoning is it's neat and only a few people are moving around the room at time, which works well in classroom management.

KRIS UNGERER
Kindergarten Teacher
Riverside, California

- Read a book.
- Play a game quietly.
- Work on some other unfinished project.
- Make up a crossword puzzle or acrostic.
- Work at the computer station.
- Play with class pets, clean cages, and feed the animals.
- Help others with their work or with learning English.
- Listen to a story using headphones.
- Tidy up your desk.
- Review your portfolio.

Figure 13.8

To tell someone to be quiet, just use the "shhhh" sign.

APPLY IT!

What are some age-appropriate ideas for your free time poster? Take into consideration your subject area and age group. Design some extension or reinforcement activities. Consider that most students love game formats, extra computer time, and creative curriculum applications. Jot down your grade- and subject-specific ideas for later transfer to a poster.

Label Papers

Schools, grade levels, departments, and teams often decide to have uniform labeling of papers. Check with your colleagues to see what the norm is.

In general, you will most likely need student name, date, subject, and, for secondary students, the period and your name on each paper for easy identification when the papers get mixed up.

UNIT 3

TEACHER TALKS . . .

Color-code everything. For example, period 1's handouts are all on blue paper. Their hanging file folders are blue. The drawer they turn their work in to has a blue dot on it. This has saved me hours of sorting and stress. I can instantly spot a pink paper (fourth period) in the blue pile and place it where it belongs without even reading a name. Middle schoolers are not that far removed from kindergarteners when it comes to organizational issues.

SHELLEY D. HOWELL
Science and Pre-Algebra Teacher
Grade 7
Yucca Valley, California

APPLY IT!

Brainstorm all the other possible routines and procedures that you may need and that have not been covered, given your subject or grade level. Think back to your observation, student teaching, or own experience in school. List as many situations as you can that may necessitate other routines or procedures.

AVOID IT!

Don't introduce all routines at once, especially on the first day. For example, movement to and from centers need not be discussed right off. However, bathroom routines are a priority on the first day. Don't stick with routines if they are not working for you or are no longer needed. Don't be afraid to encourage students to suggest better ways of doing things.

Don't encourage learned helplessness by jumping up every time you see a student who needs help. Provide clear directions, check for understanding, elicit questions, and then let the students do some self-help before you intervene.

Color coding the papers by period is very useful. Use a different color of copy paper for each period. (See Teacher Talks on this page.) Middle and high school teachers will need to add some additional routines for setting up a notebook, labeling assignments, turning in projects, making up assignments, going to lockers, storing backpacks, etc.

Consider Collection and Distribution of Papers

You need to consider how you will collect and redistribute homework and assignments. In order to maintain privacy, you might assign everyone a random number and set up your grade book with these numbers. In that way, you can have a student monitor put the papers in numerical order for you and you will know immediately whose assignment is missing. When the papers are returned, students can look for their numbers and not invade anyone else's privacy when they look through the folder. You may want to have in and out boxes in a convenient location. Some teachers have student mailboxes for return of papers.

Summary

Jacob Kounin's work offers you some very concrete and proven techniques to guide your effective instructional management. The more you can routinize your classroom procedures, the more time you will have for your instruction. At the very beginning of the school year or semester, establish your routines, reteach them until they are set, and consistently reinforce them every day. Time you spend at the outset will save you instructional time throughout the year or semester. Make sure that your English language learners comprehend your routines, and use visuals and modeling when needed.

Reflect!

After reading about all the routines that will make your classroom run smoothly, create your own mini-manual for procedures and routines that will work for you, given your grade level or subject areas. Here is a table of contents for your mini-manual. For each of these classroom situations, create a routine that works for you.

Getting help
Noise control
Asking or responding
Free time
Labeling of assignments
Collection and distribution of papers
Other

CHAPTER 14

HOW CAN I ENGAGE STUDENTS IN OPERATING THE CLASSROOM?

Great discoveries and improvements invariably involve the cooperation of many minds.

Alexander Graham Bell

Effectiveness Essentials

- Many of your routines can be handled through delegation of authority.
- Make sure that your second language learners and students with special needs participate fully in monitorial duties.
- There are many ways to create classroom cohesion.
- Read and talk with experienced teachers about alternative routines and procedures that facilitate class cohesion.

Good managers know how to delegate authority. Teachers who want to delegate can use monitors to manage a great many of the routines of classroom life. Besides reducing your own role as manager, you are enabling students, through the monitor or helper system you set up, to assume responsibility, gain independence, enhance self-concept, and practice leadership skills.

Types of Monitors

Think up as many jobs as you can so every student feels a responsibility for maintenance of the classroom community. Following is a list of possible jobs. Most teachers rotate these jobs on a weekly or semimonthly basis:

Messenger service
Paper passer
Pencil sharpener
Homework handler
Sports equipment supervisor
Board eraser
Pet caretaker
Gardener
Doorperson
Lunch counter
Snack server
Flag bearer
Calendar changer
Librarian
Clean team
- Chairs
- Sink
- Floor
- Wastebasket
- Shelves

Table or row leaders
Unofficial teaching assistant

Some high schools give students credit for being a teaching assistant, or TA. What do TAs do? You need to check with your department head, but often they take attendance, run errands, make copies, and give you administrative support that doesn't compromise the privacy of your students.

Although you may not need all the monitors just listed, the opportunity is there for more than half the students to be involved in running the classroom at any one time. Use this list when deciding on monitors. You can make badges for your monitors or create paper visors with job titles on them for your elementary students (see Figure 14.1). Certificates of appreciation for a job well done will be welcomed by your students and their parents.

TEACHER TALKS . . .

From the first day of school I tell my students that our classroom is their daytime home. Involving the students in the classroom setup and bulletin board decorating is only a part of keeping the classroom orderly and making all students feel as if they belong. They are always ready to show off their new writing or works in a clean, nicely decorated classroom.

LORETTA GOMEZ
Fourth-Grade Teacher
San Bernardino, California

Figure 14.1
Monitor Visor and Monitor Badge

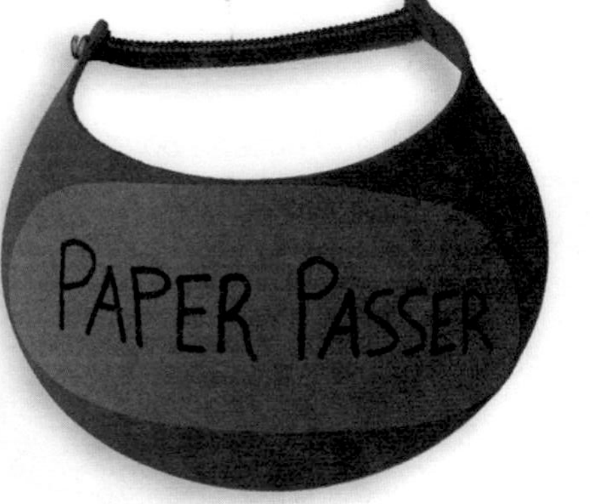

Attendance Monitor

Include English Language Learners Fully in Monitorial Duties

This will help them feel part of the social fabric of the classroom and assist them in gaining a sense of belonging and acceptance vital to their self-esteem. Embrace this motto as well: less work for teacher and more independence and responsibility for students.

Include Students With Special Needs in All Leadership and Monitorial Roles

Give students with special needs the opportunity to work as partners with a monitor, who can help them with tasks that are challenging for their given disability. But never assume that they cannot perform the task.

APPLY IT!

Make a subject- and age-appropriate list of monitors that would be useful in your classroom.

Assigning Monitors

Most teachers rotate jobs on a weekly or semimonthly basis, with the changing of the guard usually occurring on Monday. Your students should sample each job throughout the course of the year; alternative methods of assignment, with pros and cons, follow.

Students Volunteer for Positions

Many students enjoy volunteering for positions, but this method may discourage shy students from participating.

Hold a Lottery

Each student's name is on a craft stick in a can or on a card in a fishbowl. As names are chosen, the student gets to choose the job he or she would like to do. Once the names have been drawn, they are removed from the lottery until all students have had a turn. This provides randomization with equal access. However, favorite jobs may be taken first.

Create a Class List

The names are taken in order from a class list displayed on the bulletin board. Clothespins with the job titles are attached to the chart in order next to the name of the person (see Figure 14.2). The clothespins are moved down a notch each week so everyone gets to sample each job. This is the fairest method I know of. Table leaders are rotated weekly as well and fall into a separate category.

Avoid the Reward System

Some teachers attach monitorial positions to good behavior. This system discriminates against the poorly behaved student who just may need the chance to exercise some responsibility in order to change his or her behavior. This student never gets the opportunity in the reward system.

A Predetermined Schedule Reduces Student Choice

Each week, the teacher selects students for each job and makes sure everyone has an opportunity. Although this may assure the "right person for the job," it takes the choice of position out of the students' hands.

Elections Can Be a Popularity Contest

Some teachers hold elections for class officers or leaders—some using very sophisticated ways, simulating the election process in our democracy, including nominations, campaigns, and secret ballot elections. This can become a popularity contest, and we all know how it feels to be on the losing end.

Use an Application Process

Some teachers simulate the entire job-hunting process. This is a good time to teach youngsters how to fill out a simplified application, write a cover

Figure 14.2
Class List With Job Titles on Clothespins

Names	Jobs
Steve	MESSENGER
Maria	GARDENER
Juan	BOARD CLEANER
Laticia	SNACKS
Kathy	LIBRARIAN
Sam	PENCILS
Karen	PET

We all help.

STUDENT SAYS . . .

We had pet hamsters. It made me feel very responsible to help take care of them and other stuff.

ERIK
Grade 5
Brookline, Massachusetts

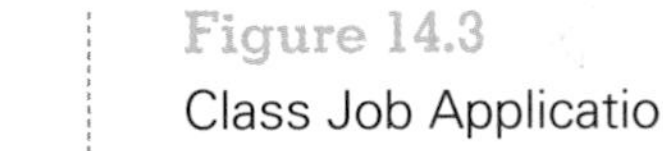

Figure 14.3
Class Job Application

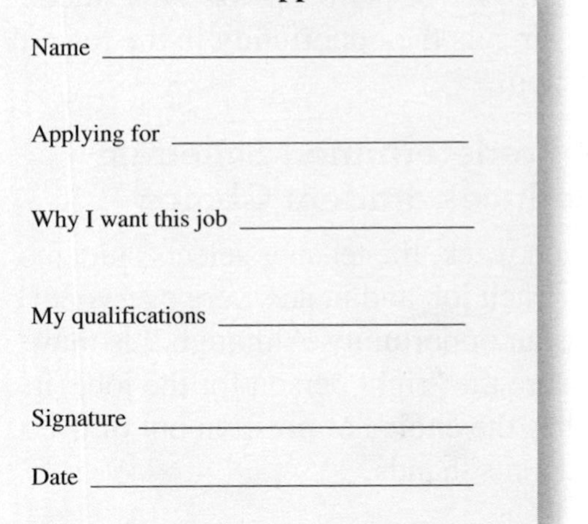

Class Job Application

Name ______________________

Applying for ______________________

Why I want this job ______________________

My qualifications ______________________

Signature ______________________

Date ______________________

letter, and even make up a résumé. A student committee can interview each prospective job applicant and select the most experienced and qualified student for each job (see Figure 14.3).

Other Opportunities for Creating a Cohesive Classroom Community

You are with your students almost as many hours Monday through Friday as you are with close family members, unless you don't sleep at all. The same is true for your students in elementary and middle school. Your class can become a sort of family that cares about and supports one another. A cohesive classroom community will provide a sense of belonging that your students desperately need. In high school, the allegiance is to the peer group and to the school as a whole. But you can still encourage a sense of community with any number of activities.

The Most Essential Way of Engaging Your Class as a Community Is the Rule-Setting Activity

Let your students have a say in rule making. From the first day, if they are involved in setting the rules, it is more likely they will buy into and follow them.

Have Your Students Vote on Everything That Involves Them

For example, I was helping prepare students for a global festival. We were going to make falafel and learn a traditional dance. I had the students vote on which they wanted to do first, even though I suspected the outcome. They counted the votes and proceeded to cook and eat. No surprise, but the students had a say in an outcome that neither the teacher nor I held strong opinions about. Of course, there are some things that are solely determined by you, but when it comes to which of two plays to perform or which story should be in the listening center, let them have a say.

Have Your Students Plan Events With You

If there is to be a winter festival, sit in a circle and discuss what the options are before putting them to a vote. If you are planning a toy drive for the holidays, give students a voice in planning and decision making. If they are making baskets for the needy, have them decide what items should be included. If you are sending disaster relief, let students decide on the nature of the fundraiser.

Display a Suggestion Box in Your Classroom and Let Students Make Suggestions to Improve Any Aspect of Classroom Life

A suggestion box empowers your students to participate in the life of the classroom and express opinions that they may hesitate to communicate openly. It also is a way to encourage good citizenship in our participatory democracy.

A suggestion box empowers students.

Create a Class Identity Through a Logo, Class Mascot, Class Motto, Class Emblem, and Class Meetings

The best way I know of to create classroom cohesion is the class meeting. That's how I started every day in the classroom. Students came to the circle to discuss morning routines and then current events or whatever was on their minds. The classroom meeting has many purposes—e.g., planning together, talking about current issues, and discussing curriculum topics. Most important, classroom meetings are a key channel for optimizing student involvement in and responsibility for classroom management. You will read more about

UNIT 3

Figure 14.4
Sample Class Mascot

classroom meetings and other ways of creating a positive and cohesive classroom in Chapter 19.

Students can enjoy a sense of cohesion through team-building activities. They can engage in friendly competitions to design a class logo or motto (see Figure 14.4). They can design bulletin boards in teams. They can compete in instructional games and contests. They can vie to have the most innovative suggestion for improving the class.

Read all you can and talk with experienced teachers about how they establish routines and procedures to create a cohesive classroom community. Although the tasks described in this unit may seem a bit overwhelming at first, the time and effort you expend at the beginning will allow you the freedom to enjoy and exercise your primary function—instruction.

AVOID IT!

Avoid choosing only your "teacher's pets" or the most well-behaved students for the classroom jobs. The student who never gets chosen for special recognition is probably the one you should choose. This could mark a turning point in the student's behavior and/or attitude toward school. Make sure everyone has an equally vital role in classroom functioning.

Summary

When students have a stake in the classroom and how it runs, they are more likely to cooperate. Classroom cohesion is cemented in many ways. Monitors or teaching assistants assume responsibility for the smooth functioning of the room, and this responsibility is very affirming and empowering. Make sure that students with special needs and those who are learning English are included as equal participants in the community. There are many ways to establish a unique classroom identity that leads to unity and solidarity, including class meetings.

Reflect!

After reading about how students can participate in the classroom community, think of all the ways that you can facilitate cohesion, given your grade level and subject area. Ask all the teachers you know how they achieve harmony, and then start to plan how you will go about making your class more than a collection of individuals but instead a community of learners.

CHAPTER 15

HOW DO I MANAGE TECHNOLOGY IN MY CLASSROOM?

Never trust a computer you can't throw out a window.

Steve Wozniak

The Internet is a giant international network of intelligent, informed computer enthusiasts, by which I mean, "people without lives." We don't care. We have each other.

Dave Barry

Effectiveness Essentials

- Most of the students in your class are technology savvy.
- Technology can support your curricular objectives and help with noninstructional tasks.
- Students are motivated to learn and benefit from the use of technology.
- Projection devices enable you to conduct whole-group lessons with word-processing programs, simulations, web-based lessons, and so forth.
- Students deserve equal access to the limited number of computers in the classroom.
- There is divided opinion on the use of cell phones as instructional tools.
- Preview and evaluate every technology application and device you use.

UNIT 3

STATISTICS

According to the Kaiser Family Foundation study *Generation M2* (2010), the percentage of students ages 8–18 who own technological devices rose dramatically between 2004 and 2009.

Device	2004	2009
iPod or mp3 player	18%	76%
Cell phone	39%	66%
Laptop	12%	29%
Time spent consuming media each day	6 hr 2 min.	7 hr 38 min.

Researchers for the Kaiser Family Foundation explain that the 2009 figure of 7 1/2 use hours per day is more like 10 hours, 45 minutes' worth of media use since the students are multitasking with more than one medium at a time. In other words, they are packing 10 hours, 45 minutes' worth of media use into 7 1/2 hours.

APPLY IT!

Conduct or adapt a student survey like this one:

Do you have a computer at home?
yes ☐ no ☐
If yes, what kind of computer?
laptop ☐ desktop ☐ PC ☐ Mac ☐
Do you have an iPad or e-reader?_______
What peripherals do you have on or for your computer? CD burner ☐ DVD drive ☐ speakers ☐ digital camera ☐ digital video camera ☐ other ☐ ______
What computer programs do you use?
____
What websites are your favorites?
____
Do you use email? yes ☐ no ☐
How many hours per day do you work on your computer? ________
Do you have a cell phone?
yes ☐ no ☐
If yes, what do you use your cell phone for?
texting ☐ web browsing ☐ email ☐
What apps are on your cell phone? ________
What is your email address for our class email list? _________ *(optional)*
Do you have an iPod or an mp3 player?
yes ☐ no ☐
What apps are on your music player?
____
What game boxes do you have?
Wii ☐ XBox? ☐ other _______
What games do you play on your computer?
____

Most of the students in your class have a better handle on technology than you do. Not only can they set the time on the VCR to something other than a blinking 12:00, but DVRs, Wii games, Xboxes, iPods/mp3 players, cell phones, and thousands of applications are now their staples. Use the survey in the Apply It! box to find out exactly how much technology expertise and how many devices your students have.

Using Technology to Enhance Teaching

Technology is one loyal classroom assistant that doesn't earn a salary. It will save you time, that rare and

Students use handhelds, iPods, and laptops.

valuable commodity in the busy classroom. Technology supports your curricular and personal objectives and augments instruction to meet the needs of *all* students, including English language learners and students with special needs.

Computers Are Teacher Time Savers

Your computer can actually ease the burdens of some of your most time-consuming teacher tasks. These include record keeping; parent communications; planning and locating resources to support your curricular objectives; and locating activities and resources to meet individual differences, particularly those of students with special needs. Think of your computer as a robot at your beck and call—a tool that serves and doesn't dictate your needs.

Your Computer Can Support Your Curricular and Personal Objectives

On page 144 are 25 things your plastic and metallic servant can do to meet your instructional and personal productivity goals. On page 145 are 30 student uses of computers.

STATISTICS

According to a PBS (2009) survey,

- 76% of K–12 teachers use digital media in their classrooms.
- In 2008, the figure was 69%.
- 80% are frequent or regular users.
- Elementary teachers report the most frequent use.
- More than 44% of teachers report using digital media in their classrooms two or more times per week.
- Teachers are using technology to access
  - Lesson plans
  - Videos
  - Images
  - Interactive simulations
  - Student-focused multimedia
  - Social networking sites

UNIT 3

STATISTICS

According to a PBS (2009) survey, the following percentages of teachers value particular types of digital media:

Media	Percentage
Games or activities for student use in school	65
Interactive lesson plans	59
Research information for student use	58
Current events information	57
Image collections	57
Games or activities for student use out of school	55
Information for own professional development	53
Online video library/exclusive content	53
Primary source materials	50
Interactive simulations	49
Online video library/ previously aired content	48
Student-produced multimedia	43
Data sets	39
Student-created websites	38
Opportunities to interact with experts	35
Student submission websites	29
Noninteractive lesson plans	20
Audio on handheld devices	16
Blogs	15
Facebook, Wiki, social media communities	14
Video on handheld devices	12

25 Teacher Time Savers Provided by Your Computer

1. Managing electronic portfolios
2. Researching content or finding lesson plans and thematic units hot off the web
3. Generating tests
4. Making PowerPoint presentations and slide shows for your students
5. Locating and/or constructing curriculum-related games, crossword puzzles, word searches, worksheets
6. Creating a digital address book or spreadsheet for each class period in middle and high school so that you can e-mail and send notices to parents and/or students who have internet access at home.
7. Creating a course overview using Moodle, a course management system (http://moodle.org)
8. Finding unique graphic organizers of all sorts
9. Accessing and evaluating websites for student research
10. Creating certificates, homework passes, thank-you notes, lesson plan templates
11. Creating scavenger hunts and WebQuests
12. Downloading photos, clip art, and other graphics for stationery and bulletin boards
13. Finding thoughtful and inspiring quotations for your class
14. Networking with teachers who are engaged in similar projects
15. Previewing a field trip site
16. Downloading game formats such as *Jeopardy*
17. Taking an online course or webinar to improve your skills or meet further certification requirements
18. Designing your own business cards
19. Locating conferences and/or proposing a workshop or session
20. Reading online newspapers and magazines
21. Designing a class website
22. Keeping track of student assignments and grading using spreadsheets or software programs such as E-Z Grader, Gradekeeper, or Gradebusters
23. Creating and updating a substitute teacher file
24. Downloading e-books
25. Shopping online ☺

30 Student Instructional Uses for the Computer

1. Supporting and extending curriculum through motivational software
2. Facilitating cooperative learning, socialization, and English language acquisition when one computer is used as a shared tool
3. Connecting your class with others across the country or the world to share information—as "key" pals
4. Researching using tools such as multimedia encyclopedias, CD-ROMs, and the web
5. Providing problem-solving opportunities through simulations
6. Encouraging the use of information databases
7. Facilitating communication skills by enabling student participation in forums for students such as Kidlink
8. Promoting writing and desktop publishing
9. Printing a map of your town or of places you are studying
10. Viewing live webcams of volcanoes, animals, the space station, etc.
11. Visiting a museum
12. Using drill and practice games
13. Touring the White House, Senate, House of Representatives, National Archives
14. Creating spreadsheets for math and science
15. Utilizing digital photography applications
16. Reading e-books online
17. Creating time lines
18. Playing subject-matter games such as *Jeopardy* with a PowerPoint template you can create by going to http://www.graves.k12.ky.us/tech/jeopardy_instructions.htm or playing "Homeworkopoly," a game format you can download at www.teachnet.com/homeworkopoly/
19. Downloading clip art and graphics to illustrate stories
20. Creating PowerPoint projects/slide shows in cooperative groups
21. Creating thematic webs with Kidspiration or Inspiration
22. Taking a virtual field trip
23. Going on a scavenger hunt or WebQuest
24. Researching an author or historical figure
25. Preparing current events reports with online newspapers
26. Using an online thesaurus, a dictionary, or Wikipedia
27. Getting help with homework
28. Printing maps/directions for real or simulated journeys
29. Sending one another e-cards or postcards
30. Downloading free educational games

TEACHER TALKS . . .

Student daily reporters contribute to our website blog that highlights the events of the day. These reporters take pictures to go along with their writing to create an authentic article. The blog offers the students and me a record of their writing improvement. Parents and other visitors enjoy reading the blog to learn about what we do at school and also to see how much the student writing improves over the course of the year. The website offers an authentic audience for my developing writers.

MATT VILLASANA
Fourth Grade Teacher
Columbia, Missouri

Visit us at Studio Four:
www.columbia.k12.mo.us/she/mvillasa

UNIT 3

Principal's Perspective . . .

There is very real tension between techno-zealots—who see phones as "cool" tools—and skilled teachers who fully understand their potential social and educational risks. The cell phone, for example, is the best bullying tool ever invented, as many teenage girls will sadly testify. A school policy has to be simple, clear, and practical. Insisting that phones are turned off during all lesson time is sensible. Teachers can make an exception when there is a need—for example, a quick internet search, under strict guidelines for the period—but most phone screens are still too small to make any kind of real textual reading meaningful. The argument that cell phones are needed in case of emergency is a nonstarter, given the close proximity of responsible adults.

JOE NUTT
Former Principal
Senior Education Consultant
Kingston upon Thames, United Kingdom

Keep up with the kids when it comes to technology! Know how they are using their phones to constantly text, and be familiar with the acronyms like *btw*. Try to use their technology ability in your lesson planning. For example, let them do an information search on their iPhone, post a question/survey on their Facebook page, use their phone (or other video device, like the new FLIP cameras) to record speeches or instructions to an assignment. Additionally,

1. If it's out there in "pay-for-it format" online, it's out there for free. For example, try *Moodle,* a free course management alternative to Blackboard.
2. A good website for finding graphic organizers: http://www.sanchezclass.com/reading-graphic-organizers.htm
3. Locate and adapt PowerPoints for the classroom rather than starting from scratch! Use Google, go to advanced search, change the number of hits per page to 50 or 100, and switch the file format to *.ppt* so that you receive back only PowerPoint files. This is an amazing way to get ready-made *ppts* on any topic, and once saved can easily be adapted to your needs.
4. http://books.google.com can get you a gazillion books online—even old and out-of-print editions and magazines, too! Students can download audio books to their iPhone/iPod or mp3 player at http://openculture.com and http://freeclassicaudiobooks.com
5. I would never have the students do a Google search . . . too many inappropriate sites. Always use onekey.com or some other kid-safe search engine.

Angel Van Horn
Coordinator, Teacher Support Center
Riverside County Office of Education
Riverside, CA

The Great Cell Phone Controversy

They do it in restaurants. They do it while crossing the street. They do it at the dinner table. They do it in the movie theater during the movie. They do it in the bathroom stall. They do it under their desks or even through their jeans in the classroom. Yes, the middle and high school students and even some elementary students are texting on their phones. I heard someone say that it is the new email. I guess email is outdated already.

The great cell phone controversy comes down to whether to outlaw them from school or harness the energy of cell phone users and put the phones to work in the service of learning. Throughout the chapter, you will read a sampling of responses I received on an educator's networking site recently in response to the query "What is your school's cell phone policy?"

APPLY IT!

Highlight 15–20 activities from the list on page 145 that you would like your students to engage in. Then turn those items into a survey for your students. Ask students to rate each one on a scale from 1 to 3. Start with those activities that receive the highest rating. Secondary students can do the data analysis for you.

STATISTICS

According to a PBS (2009) survey,

- 93% of K–12 teachers report that their schools have computers with Internet access.
- 81% say they have computer Internet access in their classrooms.
- 91% of teachers report that their schools have DVD players.
- 76% report that their schools have computers with DVD drives.
- 61% have DVD players or computer DVD drives in their classrooms.
- 78% access digital content from DVDs.
- 72% of teachers stream or download content from the Internet.

In contrast, only 36% of pre-K teachers have computers with Internet access in their classrooms.

As in All Things, Your Students With Special Needs Must Have Equal Access to Technology

No one expects you to go it alone. Collaboration with the special educators at your site is key. They will know about the adaptive technologies that fit your students' needs. Adaptations may be as simple as using the largest fonts in word processing or as complex as voice recognition software. As soon as you identify your

WATCH IT! video

An Adaptive Keyboard

In this video clip, a student with a physical disability uses a word prediction/synthesizer program to type on the adaptive keyboard.

Word Processing

In this video clip, a student with use of one hand is empowered by using a word-processing program to express her thoughts about and feelings of isolation.

After watching these two clips, discuss how the students with special needs are accommodated and talk about the benefits of inclusion in technology.

STUDENT SAYS . . .

I like using the computer for schoolwork because typing is faster than writing down a lot of stuff. Computers are good for research because you can find an infinite amount of information, but in a book you can only find what's in there.

ERIK
Grade 5
Brookline, Massachusetts

students with special needs, arrange a meeting to go over their IEPs and determine what, if any, technology adaptations are needed.

English Language Learners Can Use Audio Devices to Help Facilitate Language Acquisition

Books can be downloaded from http://books.google.com to mp3 players or iPods. As the students hear as well as read the book, they can follow the flow of language, hear how difficult words are pronounced, and go back as many times as they need to.

Gearing Up for Integrating Technology

You do not need some rare, innate technology gene. You can learn more about technology through effort, trial and error, inservices, networking with colleagues, technology journals, and visiting technology websites. You may feel overwhelmed just by reading this chapter. The way I control my anxiety is

STATISTICS

According to a PBS (2009) survey, many K–12 teachers have strong positive attitudes about particular uses of digital media. Following are the percentages of teachers who agree with each survey statement:

Statement	Percentage of Teachers Who Agree
Digital media:	
Are more effective when integrated	78
Are preferred by students over other types	66
Increase student motivation	65
Help teachers to be more effective	60
Help teachers to be more creative	57
Stimulate student discussions	55
Stimulate student creativity	54
Directly increase student achievement	44
Are more effective than other types	40

A Reporter Writes . . .

iPod-Enhanced Reading a Hit

C.L. Lopez
Staff Writer

San Bernardino Sun 10/13/2005
Excerpted with permission

REDLANDS. Silence enveloped the classroom.

Students listened raptly as pet mongoose Rikki-tikki-tavi fought a battle to the death with Nag, the cobra.

Rikki-tikki-tavi won, as the 19th-century story was brought to life on a 21st-century device for the 15 children in Linda Bomar's seventh-grade English class at Clement Middle School.

. . . The widely publicized iPod is the latest alternative to books on tapes or compact discs. Since its arrival at Clement, pupils are finding it easier to tune in to the audio versions of books and stories.

The children listen to the stories through earphones as they read it from the book. It gives each student the power to move at his or her own pace, moving ahead or going back to listen again to an earlier segment or skip around in the story, something that is awkward to do on a tape or CD.

. . . The iPod also allows the pupil to learn the pronunciation of difficult words as they are read by actors, professional storytellers and sometimes by the author.

10 Steps to Computer Confidence and Competence

1. Survey your classroom, school computer lab, or district resource center to see what hardware is available to you.
   - Computers in classroom? How many?
   - Computers in lab? How many?
   - CD drive/burner?
   - VCR/DVR?
   - AlphaSmarts?
   - PC Tablets?
   - iPods or mp3 players?
   - Whiteboards—e.g., SMART boards?
   - TV and connector to computer?
   - Digital cameras?
   - Scanner?
   - LCD projection device?
   - Digital video cameras—e.g., Flip video?
   - Internet access?
   - Mobile computer labs?
   - Wireless technology?
   - Other?
2. Survey the resources for the preceding hardware, such as software programs of all sorts, including interactive books, skills programs, word processing, graphics and art programs, databases, spreadsheets, simulations, etc.
3. Next, commit some time to teacher utility programs so you can see immediate benefits. *Teachers Tool Kit* (Hi Tech of Santa Cruz), for example, enables you to design word searches, word scrambles, and multiple-choice tests. *Grade Busters* (Jay Klein Products) is an example of an easy-to-use database for recordkeeping and grading. A program such as *The Print Shop Deluxe* (EdMark) or *Kid Pix* (Broderbund) can help you design fliers, invitations, bulletin board banners, and awards. Suggested software for beginning computer users who have money to spend can be found in a variety of educational catalogs.
4. Inform yourself step by step as the need arises. When I needed to communicate with colleagues from home, I learned how to set up my email and read messages from home. Saving time and energy can be a terrific source of motivation for learning new things.
5. Ask for help from teachers and tech-savvy students at your school.
6. Plan to enroll in a technology course, workshop, or inservice seminar.
7. Attend a technology conference or sessions at teacher conferences that focus on technology applications to your subject matter.
8. Join a computer users group and swap public-domain software. Computer-Using Educators (CUE), http://www.cue.org, can point you to a local group.
9. Teacher magazines such as *Instructor* or *Teaching K–8* often include ideas for using your computer effectively, and specialized computer magazines, such as *Tech & Learning* (http://www.techlearning.com), supply lesson plans and teaching strategies, even on managing the one-computer classroom.
10. Finally, take every opportunity to play around on the computer yourself. There are many resource directories of websites specifically geared to teachers who want to integrate technology. Many of the websites have prepackaged time-saving lesson plans that you can adapt.

Principal's Perspective . . .

Cell phone use is troubling and not allowed during school hours. I do not yet view the technology safe enough to be used as a classroom tool. We ask that cell phones are off and out of sight.

If a student is seen using a phone, it is taken until the end of the day. The third time it is taken, a parent must come to pick up the phone. I view the use of cell phones during an exam as potential for plagiarism, and the student's grade could be lowered based on that policy.

The office phone is accessible to students, but parents do sometimes come to school to bring something from home because the kid called from a cell phone. And yes, parents do sometimes call their kids directly, rather than the office. That I don't get at all.

Middle School Principal
New Jersey

by taking one step at a time when I have time and typing in keywords or phrases in a search engine such as Google (http://www.google.com). Type the term in the search region, and away you go. At Google, you can also click on images and get pictures of anything you put into the search region.

Evaluate Software Programs

You need to preview and evaluate every software program you use. There are some terrific software programs on the market. Some are not so good. Ask yourself these questions when you are assessing software:

- Does the program support and expand the educational goals you have set?
- Is the program attention grabbing as well as instructionally sound?
- Are activities developmentally appropriate?
- Does the program have open-ended opportunities so that students can reuse it?
- Are there several levels of increasing difficulty?
- Is the program student-friendly and easy to use?
- Does the program give immediate feedback in a positive way?
- Can the program be run without sound so the noise does not disturb the class?

TEACHER TALKS . . .

Educators fear new technology instead of embracing its potential. And our students have a better grip on the current technologies than we do. Instead of using the new tools, we ban them, threatened by their very presence. Until we open our minds, the use of technology will continue to fall further behind in the educational world.

SYLVIA MAISANO
Secondary Technology Instructor
Roseville MI

APPLY IT!

Go to the search engine http://www.google.com and choose a topic to research. Insert the topic keywords into the search region and see what comes up. Then search for images you can download related to the topic. Next time, type in your topic followed by these terms, one at a time: lesson plans, units, WebQuests, scavenger hunt, virtual field trips, games, simulations, books. You will be shocked at how efficiently your computer can help you create a unit of instruction. If you are really adept at using search engines, try your hand at creating a PowerPoint presentation in a content area.

Free iPhone Apps

There are an overwhelming number of applications for cell phones, and more are being created every day. Here is a small sample of free educational apps for the iPhone that are available online.

- Language tutors: French, Spanish, German, Arabic, Japanese, Italian
- Mathematical formulas
- History, such as maps of the world
- SAT vocabulary challenge
- States and capitals
- Periodic table
- iSign (sign language)
- StarLite (star charts)
- USA factbook
- Today in History
- Free flashcards
- NASA
- History classics (books)
- Art history, including the Louvre
- My Homework

Managing the Computer-Assisted Classroom

The main question teachers have about computers in the classroom, once they have some basic knowledge of their operation and applications, is "How do I manage computer-assisted instruction with 30 or more students and only one computer, or maybe two or three, if I am very lucky?"

Use the Computer as One of Many Learning Centers to Which Students Rotate

The program is demonstrated to everyone in the class using an LCD or DLP projection device. Then the students rotate to the center in groups of two to work on the activities. Aides, parent volunteers, and cross-age tutors can help you manage computer-assisted instruction in the lower grades.

Projection Devices Enable You to Conduct Whole-Group Lessons With Word-Processing Programs, Simulations, or Educational Games

Students take turns suggesting the next sentence, editing documents, or volunteering answers while the whole class watches the screen.

TEACHER TALKS . . .

Great tools are available for Web 2.0 use in the classroom—for example, cell phones as polling devices that create a graph able to be projected (http://www.polleverywhere.com/). Also Google Mobile is a resource. Many blogs also offer updating through texts. Example: Students on a field trip to a Holocaust museum—text to my blog number (pre-assigned of course!) a description or picture of something interesting or moving from your field trip. Instant accountability! Why NOT?

TIFFANY GAMARRO
Technology Teacher
Temple Beth Sholom
Sarasota, FL

UNIT 3

A PARENT'S POINT OF VIEW . . .

Texting is the big problem with cell phones. My children took summer school at the local high school they will attend this fall. In class, students were texting back and forth to each other under their desks. The teacher caught some students, but others were able to hide their phones. My son was distracted by this texting, not only because of the clicking keys but because of the guffaw let out by a classmate receiving the text.

But as an e-Learning Specialist . . .

I'm a strong supporter of incorporating technology into the classroom. Two important issues are providing educators with the resources they need to use technology and teaching students about the proper use of technology. First, rules can be created for the appropriate use of technology tools (iPhones, iPads, iPods, iTouch, computers, etc.) in the classroom, just as they have

(continued on facing page)

Students Can Work in Groups at the Computer During Center Time or on a Rotating Schedule That Provides Equal Time and Access

Two or three students can work together on a simulation or educational game. Start slowly with peer tutoring or by matching a computer-using student with a novice. These sessions may be structured as cooperative learning sessions with rules, specified tasks, and group interdependence assured through the assignment of specific roles: the facilitator who seeks everyone's input, the keyboarder who inputs the data, and the recorder who summarizes the steps and results on paper. These roles will shift each time. Here are some tips:

1. Focus on one curriculum area at a time.
2. Choose a program that enhances instruction in that area.
3. Learn the program thoroughly yourself and diagnose any potential difficulties.
4. Teach this program to a few students, who can then teach it to others.

AVOID IT!

- Viruses are a serious issue. To avoid contamination, make sure that students do not insert flash drives or external drives from home into the class computer.
- Make sure that the computers are covered and that someone who has been trained to do so uses computer wipes to clean the screens and the keyboard. This can be one of your classroom monitorial duties. You might also establish a routine of washing hands before computer use to avoid a sticky keyboard.
- At the end of the week, make sure you check computers for any inappropriate content entries and for temporary files and caches that are no longer needed.

Develop a Rotation Schedule for the Computer(s) in Your Classroom and Appoint a Monitor

This classroom "tekkie" sees to it that the rotation schedule is followed and that each student on the list gets his or her allotted computer time.

Devise a Routine to Allow Equity in Access to Computers

Identify students who have personal computers at home. You may want to provide more classroom computer access to those who do not. Here are some ways to ensure equity in computer usage:

1. **A pocket chart with names on cutout apples.** When a student completes his or her work, the apple is turned and the next one on the list has a turn (see Figure 15.1).
2. **A clothespin chart divided down the middle into "waiting" and "completed" sections.** When the students go to the computer in order, they move their name clothespin from "waiting" to "completed" (see Figure 15.2).
3. **Post a class list and have students check off their turns.** You will also need to decide if and how you will time students. A kitchen timer works well, as does dividing the day into segments and

Figure 15.1
Computer Access Chart

been created for other new technologies over the years. Second, many teachers will resist the use of technology for various reasons, which may include their own comfort with technology or a belief that their current teaching methods are effective. Teachers will not only need resources and training on the use of technology in the classroom, but they will also need a change process that provides them with the support they will require to adapt to this paradigm change.

MARIAN CASEY
eLearning Speciaist
Evanston, Illinois

CHAPTER 15

UNIT 3

ELEARNING SPECIALIST AND SPOUSE SPEAKS . . .

My husband is a high school art teacher, and cell phone use is the bane of his existence. His large regional public school's policy is no cell phones during school, but this rule is not consistently enforced. Unless they are being used for instructional purposes—assuming equitable access—I think cell phones should be banned from the classroom. There are other procedures in place for emergencies.

JEN LYTLE BEGONIA
eLearning Specialist
Barnegin Light, NJ

Figure 15.2
"Waiting" and "Completed" Chart With Names on Clothespins

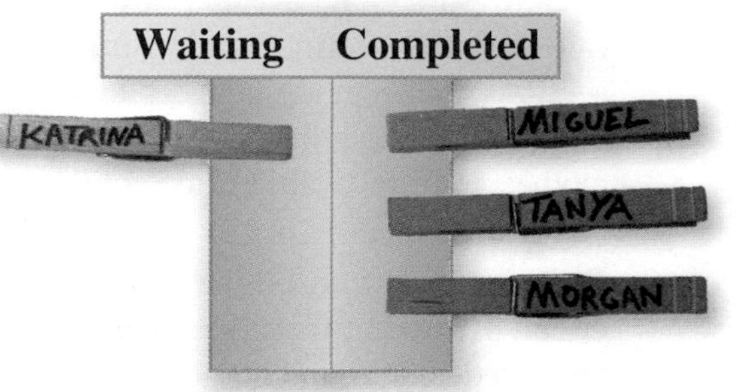

assigning students to segments based on their access chart.

4. **Use Popsicle sticks or a deck of playing cards.** Draw names for computer time and exhaust the sticks or cards before starting over.
5. **Assign students numbers as in a bakery or at the post office.** Let the students know whose turn it is by their assigned number.
6. **Rotate students in pairs on to the computer.** This is useful during learning center time.

Summary

The students in your class are technology savvy and often spend more time multitasking with their media than they do in school. You can support your instruction with available and emerging technologies and create a learning environment that motivates your students, connects them to applications that facilitate learning, and, above all, harnesses their interest in all things technological. Technology affords you time-saving opportunities to integrate your standards-based instruction with web-based instructional tools and applications. Equal access to technology for students who don't have the latest gadget is an issue that can be overcome in cooperative learning groups. Students with special needs should have adaptive devices, and English language learners can benefit from language immersion through technology. This chapter may already be out of date, so you need to keep up with the latest innovations.

Reflect!

Create a two-year technology plan for your own professional development. Use the following list to decide what devices or applications you need to learn more about. Join the International Society for Technology in Education

(ISTE), Computer-Using Educators (CUE), or another technology interest group. See the website addresses in the references.

- Whiteboards/SMART Boards
- Tablet PCs
- Skype
- Webinars
- RSS feeds
- Blogging
- Wikis
- AlphaSmarts
- Podcasts
- mobile learning
- WebQuests
- Twitter
- Facebook/My Space/LinkedIn
- Electronic gradebook
- Parent portals
- iPad or e-reader

ELEARNING SPECIALIST AND SPOUSE SPEAKS . . .

There is a lot of good literature and research out there about harnessing the power of the cell phone to improve kids' connection with schooling through mobile learning and innovative lesson design. As long as we persist in thinking of mobiles as a useless distraction rather than a core technology, we will continue to alienate our students and prove that we and our school system is irrelevant to their lives. Effective teachers make learning relevant to their students, and harnessing the power of the mobile is part of that process!

MARY HALL
Education Innovator, Analyst, and Writer
Eastbourne, New Zealand

UNIT 3 CHECKLIST

Classroom Organization and Management Checklist	For more information go to:
☐ Is my arrangement conducive to my instructional plan?	Chapter 10
☐ Have I decided on bulletin boards and accessories?	Chapter 10
☐ Can I see everyone and can they see me?	Chapter 10
☐ Have I established routines for entrances, exits, beginning and ending the day or period?	Chapter 11
☐ Do I have routines for materials, movement around the room, bathroom, and water fountain?	Chapter 12
☐ Have I decided on instructional routines?	Chapter 13
☐ Have I decided on monitors and how to select them?	Chapter 14
☐ Have I designed activities to promote cohesion?	Chapter 14
☐ Have I conducted a survey of the hardware available?	Chapter 15
☐ Have I checked the availability of standards-based/curriculum-appropriate software?	Chapter 15

Further Reading: Books About Classroom Organization and Management

Diffily, D., & Sassman, C. (2004). *Teaching effective classroom routines.* New York: Scholastic. This book describes how to create spaces conducive to good management and discipline and covers the routines that will help the day flow smoothly.

Emmer, E. T., & Evertson, C. M. (2008). *Classroom management for middle and high school teachers* (8th ed.). Boston: Allyn & Bacon. The book addresses all the tasks involved in setting up an environment for learning in middle and high schools, including but not limited to arranging the physical space, creating a positive climate, establishing expectations, rules and procedures, encouraging appropriate behavior, addressing problem behavior, and using good communication skills.

Kolb, L. (2008). *Toys to tools: Connecting student cell phones to education.* Eugene, OR: International Society for Technology in Education. This book addresses head-on the common response of banning cell phones in the classroom and suggests ways of overcoming the resistance. The author provides mini-lessons using cell phones that are useful within and outside the classroom and are adaptable for any grade level. The title conveys the essence of the book.

Morrison, G. R. & Lowther, D. L. (2010). *Integrating computer technology into the classroom: Skills for the 21st century* (4th ed.). Boston: Allyn & Bacon. This book explains and expands on the NTeQ (iNtegrating Technology for inQuiry) model for integrating computers into the K–12 classroom. The model involves the following components: specifying objectives, specifying the problem, manipulating the data, presenting the results, and assessment. It is a road map for teachers who want to learn more about effectively integrating technology into their curriculum.

Richardson, W. (2010). *Blogs, Wikis, podcasts, and other powerful tools for the classroom* (3rd ed.). Thousand Oaks, CA: Corwin. This is an easy-to-understand introduction to the educational uses of current technologies, especially the ones mentioned in the title. It has examples and covers all grade levels but would be most useful for middle and high school teachers.

Williams, J. (2004). *How to manage your middle school classroom.* Westminster, CA: Teacher Created Materials. This is a very practical and easy-to-use guide for the middle school teacher, and covers most aspects of classroom organization and management. It includes ready-to-use forms and a great many easy-to-follow guidelines.

UNIT 3

Classroom Organization and Technology Websites

Bulletin Board Ideas

http://www.kimskorner4teacherstalk.com/classmanagement/bulletinboards.html

http://school.discovery.com/schrockguide/ bulletin/index/html

http://www.teachnet.com/how-to/decor/bboards

These websites have classroom management and bulletin board ideas.

Virtual Field Trips

http://www.theteachersguide.com/virtualtours.html

This is one of many virtual field trip websites you can visit. It will give you an idea of what is available.

Museum Resources

These and many other museum websites are available to you and your students. These are some of my favorites.

American Art Museum at the Smithsonian

http://americanart.si.edu/index2.cfm

Metropolitan Museum of Art

http://www.metmuseum.org

Exploratorium, San Francisco

http://www.exploratorium.edu/

Natural History Museum at the Smithsonian

http://www.mnh.si.edu/

Keypal/e-Pal Sites

http://www.epals.com/

http://www.un.org/cyberschoolbus

These and other sites will enable your students to interact across the world with others their age.

Technology Center at Education World

http://www.educationworld.com/a_tech/

At this location, you will find articles, tips on blogging, techtorials, WebQuests, technology lesson plans, technology tools, tips of the week, and more.

International Society for Technology in Education

http://www.iste.org/

The International Society for Technology in Education (ISTE) provides leadership to improve technology teaching K–12. There are a great many resources and links on this website.

Computer-Using Educators

http://www.cue.org

This organization provides leadership and support to the tech community to advance student achievement.

UNIT 4

Positive Discipline

CHAPTER 16

WHAT ARE THE MAIN VIEWS OF CHANGING BEHAVIOR?

It is our continuing love for our children that makes us want them to become all they can be, and their continuing love for us that helps them accept healthy discipline—from us and eventually from themselves.

Fred Rogers (Mr. Rogers)

Effectiveness Essentials

- Most teachers combine elements of many approaches to discipline.
- Most approaches fall into two camps: the behavior modification camp and the logical consequences camp.
- In behavior modification systems, incentives or rewards and penalties are imposed by the teacher to modify behavior extrinsically.
- In logical consequence approaches, encouragement is the alternative to praise and logical consequences are the alternative to punishment.
- Logical consequences are always related to the offense, reasonable, and respectful.

Even experienced teachers are concerned about discipline. In fact, teachers are more fearful of the "D" word than are students. There has been a proliferation of discipline models in recent years, and the subject can get very confusing. But it's important to put discipline into the context of the entire educational experience. In addition to studying subject matter and acquiring academic skills, students are at school to learn the lifelong skills of self-discipline and accepting responsibility for their actions.

- **Safety.** Students need to feel physically safe, emotionally secure, and free from threat and intimidation both inside the classroom and outside. School may be the safest place in their lives.
- **Limits.** Students need to abide by limits and learn what is appropriate and inappropriate behavior. This is the other side of the safety issue. To ensure an environment that is safe for everyone, each student must conform to appropriate behavior standards.
- **Acceptance.** Students need and desire the approval of others. When they behave in a socially acceptable manner, they will earn acceptance from others and feel a sense of belonging in the classroom.
- **Self-esteem.** Self-esteem needs closely follow those of acceptance (Maslow, 1987). Students who can control their behavior will gain a sense of mastery and will feel competent and respected in their classroom community. Feeling competent in one area of life can help shore up poor self-esteem in other areas.
- **Learning.** Your students have both the need to reach their potential and the right to an orderly classroom environment free from distractions, interruptions, and behavioral disruptions that interfere with their learning.
- **Responsibility.** Students need to learn that for every action there is a logical and sometimes equal reaction. Taking responsibility for one's actions is a cornerstone of democratic society.
- **Democratic training.** In a workable discipline system, students learn about democratic principles and concepts such as

  1. One person, one vote
  2. Rule of law
  3. Self-responsibility
  4. The rule of the majority, with respect for minority views

APPLY IT!

Take a few minutes to think about reasons to support the need for discipline and order in the classroom. Then compare your answers to those in the bulleted items on this page.

UNIT 4

STATISTICS

The U.S. Department of Education's Institute of Educational Sciences (2009) reported on indicators of school crime and safety:

- Overall, 34% of teachers agreed or strongly agreed that student misbehavior interfered with their teaching.
- 32% reported that student tardiness and class cutting interfered with their teaching.
- 72% of teachers agreed or strongly agreed that other teachers at their school enforced the school rules.
- 89% reported that the principal enforced the school rules.

When the survey results were sorted by elementary and secondary school teachers, the percentages of perceived rule enforcement by other teachers and principals dropped to 56% and 86% respectively.

5. Consequences for actions against the greater good
6. Individual freedoms balanced against the common good
7. Respect for all, regardless of viewpoint

Most teachers combine elements of many approaches to discipline. You have probably read a great deal about approaches to discipline. If not, I would urge you to spend time reading some of the books or visiting the websites that are listed at the end of this unit. Before you adopt any one system, spend some time clarifying your own beliefs about discipline by doing the Apply It! activity on this page.

It was probably hard for you to rank these statements, as most teachers are eclectic in their beliefs and practice, walking the thin line between a laissez-faire approach and total authoritarianism. In between you will find statements reflecting common approaches to discipline. Most approaches fall into two camps: the behavior modification camp and the logical consequences camp. These two divergent viewpoints for changing behavior can be compared and contrasted. Other systems derive from the two approaches, and they will be mentioned where they apply.

APPLY IT!

Take some time to work through this discipline clarification activity. Rank-order these positions vis-à-vis discipline from 1 to 7, with 1 being the position most like your own.

______ I'll figure out discipline as I go along.

______ I believe in counseling individuals about their behavior.

______ Students should participate in making rules and solving classroom problems.

______ Discipline entails helping students make good choices.

______ Students should experience the logical consequences of their behavior.

______ Students respond best to rewards and punishment.

______ A classroom is a dictatorship, and I make the rules.

Behavior Modification: Incentives and Penalties

In a speech, a prominent psychiatrist and expert on discipline remarked that, if Pavlov had experimented with cats instead of dogs, his behavior reinforcement theories would have been long forgotten. I have two cats, so I know that

NOTES

Figure 16.1
Positive Rewards

Elementary

Individual
Certificates
Special activities
Stickers, small gifts
Food
Homework exemption
Verbal praise
Honor roll

Whole Class
Popcorn parties
Field trip
Extra P.E. time
Ice cream party
Special cooking activity
Verbal praise
Preferred Activity Time (Jones et al., 2007)

Middle and High School

Individual
Computer time
Recognition certificates
Fast-food coupons
Homework passes
Gel pens, key chains
Posters

Whole Class
Activities the students enjoy
Free time

the psychiatrist was probably right. But Pavlov didn't use cats, and behavior modification techniques are very much in vogue in schools today.

In behavior modification systems, incentives or rewards and penalties are imposed by teachers to modify behavior extrinsically. After the rules are handed down (or, in some instances, established with your students) and then practiced, an intricate system of rewards and penalties is initiated. Canter's (2009) work in assertive discipline and Jones, Jones, Jones, and Jones's (2007) work are examples of systems based on rewards and penalties. One reward Jones et al. suggest is Preferred Activity Time (P.A.T.), in which teachers use a stopwatch to either subtract or add free-time minutes. If students take away teaching minutes through misbehavior or inattention, then they are docked free-time minutes. Some of the other positive rewards that teachers use for appropriate behavior are listed in Figure 16.1.

We all respond to positive rewards. For adults, it may be a certificate of appreciation, a bonus, or a sincere "You did a great job." For students, a homework pass, a trinket, or a certificate also work wonders to shape positive behavior. And not just in elementary school.

I recently visited a classroom that had a token economy in place. Students earn tickets (raffle type available at office supply stores in rolls) for positive on-task behaviors. They write their names on the tickets; and at the end of the week, a drawing is held, and those whose names are drawn get to choose something from the treasure chest that contains a variety of items. The small and inexpensive items are greatly valued by the students, and the system works very effectively, especially because tickets are given to students who are "caught doing the right thing."

AVOID IT!

Incentive programs take time, and you must be consistent and fair in using them. Students will clamor for points and keep you on your toes if you forget. Beware of addicting your students to rewards. Otherwise, it will be hard to tell if they have really internalized controls or are simply behaving in anticipation of material rewards. If the purpose of discipline is ultimately self-control, you may be acting counterproductively by relying too much on extrinsic motivation. The management of these systems may cause more disruption in your class than the behaviors they were designed to correct in the first place.

Students earn tickets for positive, on-task behaviors.

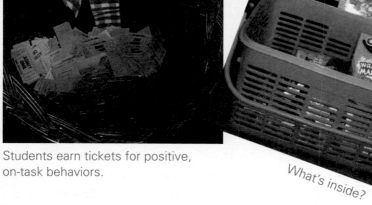

What's inside?

Choose a prize!

Rewards Can Be Earned Individually, in Groups, or as a Whole Class

Designing a record-keeping system is fairly easy; maintaining it is difficult. Teachers make a chart of students' names and attach stars, move pushpins, or color in the spaces when students earn points. If the record keeping is done by groups at a table, the entire table is listed, and points accrue when all the students at the table are doing the right thing. Some teachers run the system by total class behavior and add marbles or popcorn kernels to a jar when everyone is behaving appropriately. A full jar means a popcorn party or special treat. Some teachers announce the number of points or marbles to be earned before each activity begins.

STUDENT SAYS . . .

When the class misbehaves, we have to put our heads down for a couple of minutes. Some teachers make us sit out some minutes of recess.

KURT
Third Grader, Age 8
Plano, Texas

UNIT 4

TEACHER TALKS . . .

I had a student in class who was constantly in trouble during the day and after school in extended day (an after school day care program). I devised a system of rewards with the approval of his parents whereby I awarded him from 1 to 5 points after consulting with my student teacher, aide, and recess personnel and his extended day worker also awarded him from 1 to 5 points each day. This made for a possible total of 50 points for the five days of school. I printed out the tickets on purple paper and dated them in advance. His parents knew to ask for the purple ticket (see Figure 16.2). At the end of the week, if he had accumulated more than

(continued on facing page)

On the Flip Side of the Rewards System Are the Various Penalties That Teachers Assess for Infractions of the Rules

When students break the rules, depending on the system, students gather negative checks on the board or on a teacher's clipboard that translate into ever-more negative consequences. These may include staying in for recess, staying after school, going to the principal's office, carrying a note home, or missing favorite activities.

Penalties in middle and high school may include detention, isolation, fines, and suspension, combined with parental notification. You will be expected to follow the referral procedures and be in line with the other staff members in identifying those behaviors that mandate suspension as punishment. In California, a student can be suspended for infractions that seem unimaginable and unlikely, but they happen.

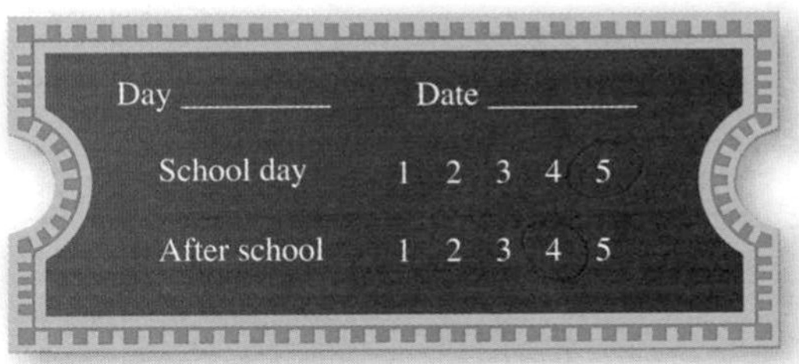

Figure 16.2
Behavior Modification Daily Accounting

mythBUSTER

Rewards aren't needed in high school. That age group is above it.

Some people might say that motivation should be intrinsic, particularly when it comes to learning. However, most people, no matter their age, enjoy receiving tokens of appreciation for their efforts. In a school setting, giving rewards can actually increase self-efficacy if done well. By using external factors to engage students, teachers help them achieve goals they might not always aim for and potentially help them see themselves and their abilities in a different way.

High school students need rewards just like younger students do . . . and just like most adults do. As long as the reward connects to the learning, the desired behavior, or the specific interests of a student, it can truly motivate students in a healthy manner. Rewards can be small or large—from pieces of candy or a few extra-credit points, to iPods or a change in privileges. They are useful tools for teachers and students because they help learners push beyond their perceived limits. Like people of all ages, high school students need their efforts to be noted and validated from time to time.

In order for rewards to work, they can't be given out too frequently. They should either be

(continued on facing page)

mythBUSTER

expected (students know in advance they can receive a little extra for their efforts), or they should be unexpectedly bestowed—given to those students who are just doing the right thing or doing exceptionally well without thinking they are going to receive anything unique for their efforts.

Rewards add to the sense of community in a classroom, support the teacher's need to manage the environment effectively, and engage students by pushing them to do their best while valuing their efforts along the way.

Nikki Shull
High School Spanish teacher
Denver, Colorado

Denying Preferred Activities or Meting Out Punishment Has a Downside

Although punishment may stop the behavior immediately, Nelsen (2006) cautions that, in the long haul, punishment results in the four "Rs": revenge, resentment, rebellion, and retreat. One teacher has reversed the pocket chart suggested by Lee Canter and associates from ever-increasing color-coded negative cards to ever-increasing positive ones. She flips the card when the student or group is doing the "right thing." The first color stands for good, the second for great, the third for excellent. Special rewards are given to those who reach excellent. This turnaround on ever-increasing negatives to ever-increasing positives has had a profound effect on the climate of the classroom (see Figure 16.3 on p. 167).

Encouragement and Logical Consequences

Encouragement is offered by Dreikurs, Grunwald, and Pepper (1998) as an alternative to praise. Encouragement means that you don't have to be 100% perfect. It means you have made progress along the way and that progress is noted and supported. Encouragement gives you the will to continue on the right path. Praise suggests completion, approval for a job well done, or an achievement.

Dreikurs et al. believe that all students want to be recognized and to feel that they belong. Their model is

45 points, his reward was to go out to dinner at his favorite restaurant. If he had received less than 35, his favorite activity (Wii) was denied to him for the weekend. From 35 to 45 was a neutral zone, and there was neither a reward nor a penalty. Now he usually accumulates more than 45 points but never less than 35. A success story!

JASON PAYTAS
Sixth-Grade Teacher (Formerly First Grade)
Arcata, California

STUDENT SAYS . . .

My teacher finds fun ways for us to work together. . . . Each of us has an envelope with colored cards inside. Each color has the following special meaning: yellow = doing well, orange = a warning, green = extra homework, blue = miss recess, pink = phone call home. We get points for the days when the whole class has yellow cards. When we have enough points, we get to have a party.

ERIN
Third Grader, Age 8
Glenview, Illinois

STATISTICS

The U.S. Department of Education's Institute of Educational Sciences (2009) reported on indicators of school crime and safety during the 2007–2008 school year:

- 10% of male students in grades 9–12 reported being threatened or injured with a weapon on school property in the past year, compared to 5% of female students.
- 10% of black students, 9% of Hispanic students, 7% of white students, and 6% of American Indian/Alaska Native students reported being threatened or injured with a weapon on school property.
- 8% of secondary school teachers reported being threatened with injury by a student, compared with 7% of elementary school teachers.
- 6% of elementary school teachers reported being physically attacked by students, compared with 2% of secondary school teachers.

What conclusions come to mind when you read these statistics?

CLASSROOM ARTIFACTS

California Education Code With Reasons for Suspensions From A-Q 48900

A pupil may not be suspended from school or recommended for expulsion, unless the superintendent or the principal of the school in which the pupil is enrolled determines that the pupil has committed an act as defined pursuant to any of subdivisions (a) to (q), inclusive:

(a) (1) Caused, attempted to cause, or threatened to cause physical injury to another person.
    (2) Willfully used force or violence upon the person of another, except in self-defense.

(b) Possessed, sold, or otherwise furnished any firearm, knife, explosive, or other dangerous object. . . .

(c) Unlawfully possessed, used, sold, or otherwise furnished, or been under the influence of, any controlled substance. . . .

(d) Unlawfully offered, arranged, or negotiated to sell any controlled substance. . . .

(e) Committed or attempted to commit robbery or extortion.

(f) Caused or attempted to cause damage to school property or private property.

(g) Stolen or attempted to steal school property or private property.

(h) Possessed or used tobacco, or any products containing tobacco or nicotine products. . . .

(i) Committed an obscene act or engaged in habitual profanity or vulgarity.

(j) Unlawfully possessed or unlawfully offered, arranged, or negotiated to sell any drug paraphernalia. . . .

(k) Disrupted school activities or otherwise willfully defied the valid authority of supervisors, teachers, administrators, school officials, or other school personnel engaged in the performance of their duties.

(l) Knowingly received stolen school property or private property.

(m) Possessed an imitation firearm.

(n) Committed or attempted to commit a sexual assault. . . .

(o) Harassed, threatened, or intimidated a pupil who is a complaining witness or a witness in a school disciplinary proceeding. . . .

(p) Unlawfully offered, arranged to sell, negotiated to sell, or sold the prescription drug Soma.

(q) Engaged in, or attempted to engage in, hazing. . . .

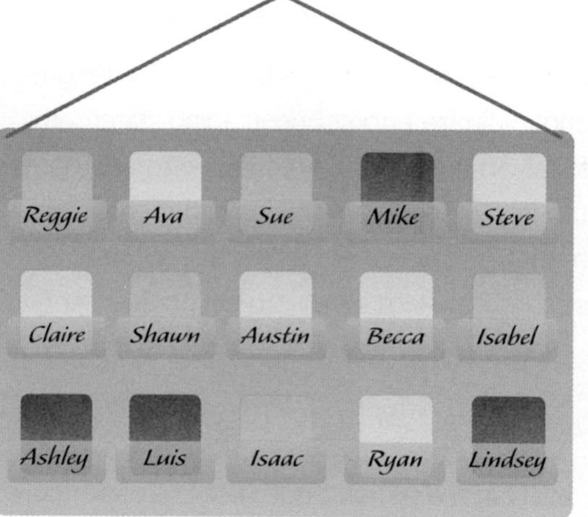

Figure 16.3
Pocket Chart With Color-Coded Cards

based on mutual respect, encouragement, and taking responsibility. It is a model that encourages good citizenship when no one is looking. Students do the right thing because it is the right thing to do as opposed to students who do the right thing because they are intimidated by the fear of getting caught. Some people drive at 80 miles per hour until they see the flashing lights. Others drive at a safe speed all the time because it is the reasonable and responsible thing to do.

Teachers Need to Provide Students, and Especially the Discouraged Ones, With Opportunities to Experience Success

Dreikurs et al. (1998) believe that students can be made responsible for their behavior as they experience the logical consequences of that behavior. Praise is easily showered upon those who succeed, but those who have not yet succeeded also need encouragement. Encouraging the small steps on the way to success is as important as acknowledging the completion of a whole task. If a misbehaving student is a discouraged student, as Dreikurs and colleagues assert, then the teacher's goal is not to give false praise that the student knows is not deserved but rather to help him or her achieve small victories through encouragement. Some ways of encouraging students include the following:

- Recognizing effort as opposed to success
- Pointing out helpful contributions
- Highlighting the improvements you observe
- Assigning special jobs that your student can succeed in
- Having your student share a special interest or talent with the class

TEACHER TALKS . . .

I tell my students that when they wake up each morning and come to school, they spend six to seven hours with me, which is usually more time than they spend with their parents. They may be in the same house with them, but that does not mean that they spend time with them. After all, they are busy with homework, outdoor time, TV time, phone time, etc. I told them that they should therefore think of me as their mom away from home. My job was to teach them, comfort them, encourage them, and, yes, discipline them as needed. However, my most important job was to love them so that they could put away all other thoughts and prepare to learn. I have no losers in my class. Over the years many of my students slip up and call me mom in the classroom. I tell them that is all right because I love them all as if they are my own and consider it an honor.

SANDRA STILES
Reading Remediation Teacher, Grades 6–8
Sarasota, Florida

As seen on http://www.LessonPlansPage.com

- Asking students to assist others who need help
- Displaying the student's work
- Demonstrating in word and deed that you believe in him or her

Your encouraging words might include

Don't give up. I know you can figure it out.
You have improved in. . . .
Let's try it together.
You do a good job of. . . .
You can help me by. . . .
I'm sure you can straighten this out.

Just as Encouragement Is an Alternative to Praise, Logical Consequences Are an Alternative to Punishment

Whereas punishment is applied by an outsider and may be generic (miss recess, call to parent, visit to principal or dean), in the logical consequences approach (Dreikurs et al., 1998), the student experiences the natural or logical consequences of his or her own behavior, and the consequence is not generic. The consequence is always related to the offense. For example, a student who trashes her textbook needs to share with someone else until restitution is made. A student who is abusive to a classmate may have to write a letter of apology.

APPLY IT!

Encouraging statements build upon strengths and minimize errors. Encouraging statements focus on the activity, not the end result. Identify the following statements as either encouragement (E) or praise (P). If they are praise statements, turn them into encouragement.

1. You have taken a good deal of care with your handwriting. Now work harder on your spelling. P/E
2. That's a difficult question, but I am sure you will figure out the answer. I'll give you a hint. P/E
3. You are the smartest science student I ever had. P/E
4. You are a terrific athlete. P/E
5. Your help giving out the papers was much appreciated. P/E
6. Today you raised your hand to answer questions most of the time. P/E
7. You are the greatest helper in the class. P/E
8. You worked quietly during language arts time today. P/E
9. Take another look at your computation to find a small error. P/E
10. Super-duper job on that! P/E

(Answers: encouragement 1, 2, 5, 6, 8, 9; praise 3, 4, 7, 10)

A student who is disrespectful in the library is denied access to library books that week.

Logical Consequences Are Always Related to the Offense, Reasonable, and Respectful

A student who writes graffiti on the bathroom wall cleans it up during recess. A student who fights on the playground sits on the bench for a day or two. A student who spills the paint mops it up. Students are usually given the choice between stopping the misbehavior or accepting the logical consequence. Logical consequences are never humiliating, and they teach students about responsibility and the relationship between actions and consequences. Remember to use the phrase "make a better choice" before you try anything else.

To implement the strategy, follow these steps:

1. Make behavioral expectations clear.
2. Make clear the logical consequences of not meeting the behavioral expectations.
3. Base your relationship on trust and respect.
4. Identify misdirected behaviors and problem-solve with the student.
5. Encourage students instead of always praising them.

APPLY IT!

For each of these mini-case studies, speculate how teachers would use, first, behavior modification and, second, logical consequences to address the problem behavior:

Case 1 Susan doesn't complete any assignment and/or homework and doesn't seem to care very much. She dawdles and daydreams and feels no compunction to finish her work.

Case 2 John is relatively quiet, never raises his hand, and is mostly invisible and not motivated at all. He seems withdrawn and depressed at times, but he doesn't really cause any disturbance.

Case 3 Liz is the class clown. She mugs and makes funny noises during instructional time.

Case 4 Sandy is the class bully, pushing and shoving in line and threatening to beat up students on the way home.

AVOID IT!

I recently compiled a list of penalties teachers use. Here are some of the most severe punishments:

I keep a cell phone on my desk and have the misbehaving kid call home on the spot.

I add or take away the letters that spell QUIET. If they are all erased, the class gets no free time.

I make the "bad kids" sit in the middle of the circle.

I saw my mentor teacher construct a faux dungeon complete with paper shackles.

Summary

The subject of discipline is always a daunting one for all teachers, but especially for new teachers. The most important reasons we need to be concerned about discipline are the safety of the students and the creation of a learning environment free from the distractions that inhibit learning. This chapter sets out an overview of the main views of discipline that you will encounter as you read and reflect on your own personal belief system. The main views under which most discipline plans can be categorized are behavior modification and logical consequences. Your ultimate goal is teaching students to be responsible citizens in a democratic society.

Reflect!

Think back to the teachers you have encountered in your own schooling or some you have recently observed. How would you categorize their approaches to discipline? Were they behavior modification advocates, or did they focus on logical consequences and encouragement? Which way are you leaning now?

CHAPTER 17

WHAT ARE SOME CAUSES OF MISBEHAVIOR?

Effectiveness Essentials

- You can prevent discipline problems by looking for underlying causes and dealing with them.
- Disruptive behavior results from four misdirected goals.
- Look for root causes when students exhibit extreme behaviors or affect, and get them help.

People's behavior makes sense if you think about it in terms of their goals, needs, and motives.

Thomas Mann

All human actions have one or more of these seven causes: chance, nature, compulsion, habit, reason, passion, and desire.

Aristotle

BE A DETECTIVE!

Look at the faces of these students. Be a detective and make a list of possible causes of the emotions shown. You can't know what is going on, but making some hypotheses before having a private talk with the student will help you initiate the conversation with comments such as "You seem unhappy." "You appeared to be very tired in class today." "You seem very angry today."

After you are sure that your classroom management plan is effective, and if you are still having difficulty with some of your students, it's time to look at the students and become a detective in addition to being a good manager.

Be Aware of Underlying Causes of Misbehavior

To prevent discipline problems, look for underlying causes of misbehavior and deal with them before they break out into more serious, attention-seeking behavior. Dreikurs and colleagues (1998) tell us that all behavior is related to goals we are seeking. The primary goals we all seek are to belong and to feel significant. A misbehaving student is a discouraged student who, when thwarted from seeking these primary goals, substitutes four mistaken goals: attention, power, revenge, and assumed inadequacy.

You need to be a good detective and find the mistaken goal so that students' behavior can be redirected (primarily through encouragement, mutual respect, and understanding) to return to the original goals. You have three clues to go on:

1. **The recognition reflex.** This is a student's smile, the one you receive when you seek and get permission from the student to guess why he or she is behaving this way.
2. **Your visceral reaction to the misbehavior.** This is how the teacher feels when the behavior occurs.
3. **What the student does when told to cease and desist.** This is the student's reaction to correction.

Some Students Seek Attention

Johnny is tapping his pencil and the teacher says, "Please stop tapping your pencil." Johnny stops for a minute or two and starts humming. Janice tips back in her chair and rocks back and forth. The teacher, afraid Janice will tumble and hit her head, tells her to sit up straight and stop. She does but soon resumes her rocking.

Attention-getting behaviors say, "Look at me." An attention-seeking student irritates or annoys you; and when told to stop, he or she ceases and then resumes or substitutes another attention-getting behavior. These behaviors are directed at the teacher or other classmates. Although they are not that serious, if they are not dealt with, they progress into more serious problem behaviors.

Instead of asking the student to stop, try saying, "Could it be that you want to have my attention now?" or "Could it be that you are finished and want to move on to something else?" The student's smile will tell you that you hit the nail on the head.

Remedies include spending special time with the student; redirecting the behavior; ignoring the behavior; imposing a consequence that is related, respectful, and reasonable; and presenting choices to the student (Nelsen, 2006). A now-retired kindergarten teacher was often heard to tell her block-throwing students, "Either you share and play nicely, or you will have to leave the block center. Make a better choice," and they did. The language of making choices is key to teaching your students about being responsible for the decisions they make, both now and in the future.

Other terminology is "make a different choice," or "make a wise choice." Or "either you (fill in the expected behavior), or you (fill in the consequence)."

APPLY IT!

Try framing some choices for these behaviors. "Make a choice, either _______ or _______."

1. Talking to neighbors
2. Calling out
3. Forgetting homework
4. Getting out of seat and walking around
5. Combing hair or sprucing up in class
6. Coming to class late
7. Engaging in name calling

Some Students Seek Power

Lynn is defiant. "No one tells me what I can and cannot do. I don't have to play by the rules, not at home, not at school." This is the tug-of-war student who challenges your every directive. A power-seeking student intimidates you and, when told to stop, may passively resist or defy you even more. This is the "you can't make me" kind of misdirected goal. Arrange a time to meet with the student. Remedies include withdrawing from the situation, cooling off first, problem solving with the student, redirecting the student's power needs, focusing on what you will do instead of what you will make the student do, and scheduling special time with the student (Nelsen, 2006).

Think of a student you encountered with a serious power issue. Write down a dialogue for a conversation

TEACHER TALKS . . .

I had a sixth-grade student who loved to show me his artistic creations. I would have heaped praise on him for his creativity, except that the pictures he drew were all X-rated. So I glanced at them and registered no reaction. Later I suggested that he draw a cover for our poetry anthology, and he set about doing this with the same effort he had expended on his inappropriate artwork. The imaginative poetry anthology cover was a hit with all the other students, and he never shared another explicit drawing with me or his classmates after that.

ELLEN KRONOWITZ
Middle School Teacher
New York City

Ask these students to make a better choice.

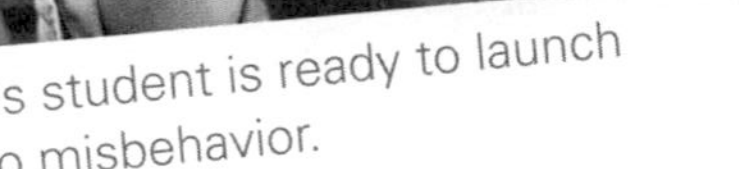

This student is ready to launch into misbehavior.

Redirect or ignore this conversation.

you might have had with him or her using the 10-step process in the Apply It! on page 175.

Some Students Seek Revenge

Pat will get revenge on you for forcing him to back down in a confrontation. He has lost the battle but tries to win the war. He is saying to himself, "I will have the last laugh." You may find your tires slashed in the parking lot or a nasty anonymous note on your desk. You may be accused of hitting, pinching, or even worse by the parents who unwittingly buy into the revenge scenario.

A revenge-seeking student hurts your feelings and, when asked to stop, is destructive or spiteful. Remedies include allowing a cooling-off period, engaging in problem solving with the student, giving encouragement, and scheduling special time with the student (Nelsen, 2006). The same 10 steps can be followed for this student, although serious revenge takers might need to be seen by the principal or school counselor if they have caused

APPLY IT!

In a nonconfrontational conversation, follow these 10 steps:

1. Begin by telling the student all the positives you see (talents, skills).
2. Describe the negative behavior in question.
3. Seek verification from the student and accept no excuses. Just ask, "Is this happening?"
4. Encourage the student to name the costs of continuing the behavior. List them on paper.
5. Encourage the student to talk about the benefits of desisting. List them on paper.
6. Compare the two lists and discuss which list is more productive.
7. Brainstorm together what better choices the student could make.
8. Offer assistance to the student.
9. Sign a contract indicating what each of you will do to make the better choice a reality.
10. Revisit the issue after a week's time by asking, "How's it going? Have you fulfilled your part of the contract? Have I?" Revise the contract if need be.

serious damage, either verbally or to your property.

Some Students Exhibit Assumed Inadequacy

I had a student whom I will call Alex. His response to every threat, every bribe, every entreaty, every punishment was, "I don't care." And he didn't. One day, three classes were watching a current film that was the culminating activity for a literature unit. I said, "Either you respect the other kids and watch the film silently, or you will have to sit in the office." His response: "I don't care." "You don't care?" I asked. "No, I don't want to watch this film anyway." So I marched him to the office where he sat for the rest of the film.

I have often regretted how I handled it because I knew how much attention Alex craved; but like many decisions we make as teachers, it seemed like the best thing to do at the time. I couldn't let him disrupt the enjoyment of the other students. However, I knew that inside there was a boy craving attention that he had all but given up on receiving. I should have asked him to be a film critic who could report back to the class on how well the film followed the book.

A student whose goal is assumed inadequacy makes *you* feel inadequate

TEACHER TALKS . . .

One student continued to misbehave during a lesson, so I sent him to the back of the classroom to stand for a time-out. Unfortunately, the fire extinguisher was housed at the back of the classroom too. The student proceeded to pick up the fire extinguisher and spray it all around the classroom! The room was filled with white dust and sand. I immediately removed the class from the room so we could breathe. Needless to say, that was the last time I ever used time-out. I restructured my entire discipline plan.

DION CLARK
Former Sixth-Grade Teacher
High School Vice-Principal
San Bernardino, California

NOTES

because you don't know how to reach him or her. You can't break through the wall of seeming indifference or passivity. The student remains unreceptive when confronted. Remedies include making success incremental, training the student in what to do, using encouragement, not giving up, and arranging for special time with the student (Nelsen, 2006).

Nelsen and colleagues (2000) present a very clear and concise discussion of the work of Dreikurs et al. (1998) and Glasser (1975, 1998). You may want to read more about them either in Nelsen's interpreted version or in the original works listed at the end of the unit.

This is just one framework for understanding your students' underlying motivation to misbehave. You need not accept it fully, but try in general to see things from the student's point of view. Ask yourself, "Why is the student doing this?" Make some good guesses. Instead of just meting out punishment, which works only in the short haul and may build up long-term resentment in students, stop and think about probable causes or motives. Your hypotheses may be incorrect some of the time, but there is a possibility that some of your theories may be tested out and even proven. You gain much more by canceling out a negative with a positive solution than by doubling the negativity by assessing an immediate penalty.

You need not be a fully certified counselor, but you could initiate a conversation with an observation and an open question like "You seem to be bothered (angry, sad, upset, concerned, distressed, etc.). Would you like to talk about it?" *Just listen*. You can reflect back the content and feelings articulated by the student and ask some probing questions. Be sure to let the student know that people are there to help; and if you feel you are in over your head, a referral to a school counselor is appropriate. Always speak respectfully.

Addressing the Challenges of Bullying

Bullying is one serious behavior you may encounter. The statistics on the next page suggest that bullying is quite prevalent. Preventing and dealing with instances of bullying require a coordinated and committed effort from parents, the community, the school district, the school, the individual teacher, and, of course, the students.

Cyber Bullying Is a Serious Problem

With the pervasive use of cell phones and other Internet connection devices and of social networking sites such as Facebook and MySpace, cyber bullying has become all too common. According to the National Crime Prevention Council (2010), cyber bullying occurs "when the Internet, cell phones or other devices are used to send or post text or images intended to hurt or embarrass another person." Cyber bullying can be as simple as continuing to send emails to someone who doesn't want them, but it may also include spreading rumors, sharing unwanted photos, sharing a victim's personal information, or assuming another identity for illicit purposes. While cyber bullying may take place out of school, the school has a responsibility to address this very serious issue by, according to the National Crime Prevention Council, raising awareness of the problem and its consequences to both the victim and the bully and by encouraging victims to come forward to a trusted adult.

You Will Need to Deal With Bullying at School

According to the National School Safety Council (2006), a group established by presidential directive in 1984, boys tend to bully in physical ways and girls tend to bully in emotional ways. Students can be both a target and a bully at the same time. Likewise, bystanders can be either active or passive observers. If the school is doing nothing about bullying, bystanders may think that it is acceptable and may join in. Or they may just watch passively, thinking that they may be the next victims if they intervene or that it's no big deal.

What can you do as a classroom teacher? Here are some suggestions from the National School Safety Council (2006) and other sources:

- Model desired attitudes and behaviors
- Foster students' shared responsibility
- Establish and communicate rules and consequences
- Apply classroom rules fairly and consistently
- Intervene when you see undesirable behaviors or attitudes
- Teach students how to ask for help and report acts of bullying
- Respond immediately to requests for help
- Promote social skills development
- Refer critical bullying cases to the administration and/or adult mentors trained as safe contacts
- Read all you can about bullying, and discuss this serious issue at staff meetings
- Conduct class meetings on the topic with your students

STATISTICS

The U.S. Department of Education's Institute of Educational Sciences (2009) reported on indicators of school crime and safety during the 2007–2008 school year. According to that study, 32% of students ages 12–18 reported having been bullied at school during the school year.

Type of Bullying	Percentage of Reporting Students
Made fun of	21
Subject of rumors	18
Pushed, shoved, tripped, or spit on	11
Threatened with harm	6
Excluded from activities on purpose	5
Forced to do things they didn't want to or property was destroyed on purpose	4

TEACHER TALKS . . .

I can tell you that the most effective anti-bullying program is one where positive social skills are taught and expected all the time. Too many times, our anti-bullying policies and programs treat the subject as an isolated topic—and that doesn't work. If you treat positive social skills, kindness, respect, compassion, and all those other virtues as a routine matter of what you do anyhow, you'll find a lot of bullying naturally goes away. You can deal with exceptions when they occur.

CORINNE GREGORY
Founder and President of SocialSmarts
Bellevue, Washington

TEACHER TALKS . . .

My classroom policy is simple: no put-downs. We lift each other up in our learning ventures and adventures. We cheer each other's successes and encourage each other in the face of disappointment. We chant, scream, and holler when milestones are passed. We peer-tutor and console each other when

(continued on facing page)

WATCH IT! video

Eliminating Bullying at School

In this video, the teacher engages middle school students in a discussion of bullying. They brainstorm a definition and come up with solutions. Would you engage your students in such a discussion? How might you do it differently? When the teacher speaks to the two boys who have been bullied, which effective communication skills did you see her using?

For other suggestions, read the Teacher Talks and Principal's Perspective features in the margins and watch the video "Eliminating Bullying at School." Several informative books and websites are listed at the end of this unit.

Symptoms of Other Serious Behaviors

The physical and emotional changes of teenagers present a particular challenge for those of you teaching at that level. Allow angry students to write about their feelings instead of taking them out on someone else. You may ask them to role-play and express the other person's point of view and vice versa. Use these techniques with all ages.

Some of the behaviors you might see have a basis in these hormone surges, but some of them are more serious. For more persistent or serious misbehaviors, you should immediately notify your counselor or administrator. You are not alone in dealing with serious behaviors. Your school counselor will be able to tell you if there is a behavior management plan in place, or he or she may provide information previously gathered on the student.

Check the discipline policy manual to see if the behavior is grounds for expulsion or suspension. This is important information to have at your fingertips, so all students can be held to the same account for these serious behaviors. Although the following list is far from complete, especially symptomatic behaviors to look for are:

- Anger
- Withdrawal
- Procrastination
- Lateness
- Bullying
- Defiance
- Clowning around
- Moodiness

- Abusive language
- Threats to do violence
- Threatening clothing and gang insignia
- Absences and excessive tardiness
- Signs of physical or mental abuse
- Depression
- Suicidal writings or comments, or drawings that depict suicide
- Violent drawings
- Any extreme changes in behavior
- Threats to other students
- Manic behavior

When you take the time to talk with your students, you may discover the root causes that underlie these symptoms and obvious manifestations. When these symptoms become apparent, confer with the appropriate resource person: principal, nurse, school counselor, social worker, school psychologist, or community worker. It is not unusual to find students in your class with serious attention-deficit/hyperactivity syndromes, students with parents who are in jail, homeless students, students living in group homes, students on probation, or students with a history of family violence and abuse. When you notice symptoms of these and other root causes, the best way to approach a student is to say, "I notice that you seem preoccupied (sad, angry, depressed, moody, etc.). Do you want to talk about it with me or with the counselor? We have support and resources here at school. We can help."

AVOID IT!

Some discipline plans require that you assess penalties swiftly and immediately and "take no nonsense." I would caution you to look a bit more deeply before you act. Kids are like icebergs. You can't see what's underneath the surface without teacher sonar. You may be the one person who takes an interest and who can get to the bottom of the problem. A kind word, an understanding look, a nonjudgmental attitude may unlock a closed door and make a difference in a student's life.

Avoid confrontations in front of the entire class. Conduct your discussions in private. You want to avoid having a student either lose face or strongly resist to show how tough he or she is in front of peers. Public humiliation is never an appropriate professional response.

Avoid going it alone. There are many resources at your site and at the district level to help you figure out appropriate interventions.

disappointments loom. If one cannot be trusted to speak kindly to others and follow classroom rules, one cannot be trusted out of my presence. I emphasize that trust and respect must be earned; and once lost, they take significant time to earn back. That means no recess, silent lunch, no permission to be in the hall without adult supervision, no fun stuff. And I make sure fun stuff is happening all the time!

DEBORA ONDRACEK
Fifth-Grade Teacher
Madison, Georgia

Principal's Perspective . . .

When I was housemaster at an English boarding school, I worked really hard to create a community to which other kids in the school wanted to belong. I gave them responsibility; I upgraded their facilities in every way I could think of; I provided them with a positive culture that they could feel proud of. Overarching this was one simple rule I repeated at the start of every term: "The one unforgivable crime was to deliberately make any student in the school unhappy."

(continued on following page)

Principal's Perspective—*continued*

Real bullying is a very unpleasant thing to witness and investigate; and in my experience, girls make boys look like amateurs at it. (The mobile phone could almost have been designed to help girls bully.) It is nearly always rooted in one thing: envy, sometimes triggered by the tiniest of things. It is very unusual to find any bully who actually knows she is bullying. The only way to put an end to it is to follow these steps:

1. *You need to investigate the events sufficiently to confirm to yourself that they are bullying.*
2. *You need to make all those involved aware that you are now treating the incident as bullying.*
3. *You need to spell out the harshest possible consequences to the bully if he continues. And when he does (as 99% of the time he will), you have to deal out those consequences to the letter.*

JOE NUTT
Surrey, England

Summary

One way of looking for causes of misbehavior is to use Dreikurs et al.'s (1998) hierarchy of causes of misbehavior: attention seeking, power, revenge, and assumed inadequacy. Beyond are those behaviors that threaten others, bullying being the most common in schools. While there are many programs that can diminish the frequency of bullying, the best offense is prevention and a classroom environment that promotes positive social interaction.

Reflect!

Complete this chart and keep it for your reference. For help, you can review the chapter at any time.

Mistaken Belief	Adult's Feelings	Student's Response When Corrected	What to Do
I belong when I have constant attention.			
I belong when I am powerful, and I have to win.			
You hurt me, and I will hurt you back.			
I don't really care anymore.			

CHAPTER 18

HOW CAN I PREVENT DISCIPLINE PROBLEMS BEFORE THEY START?

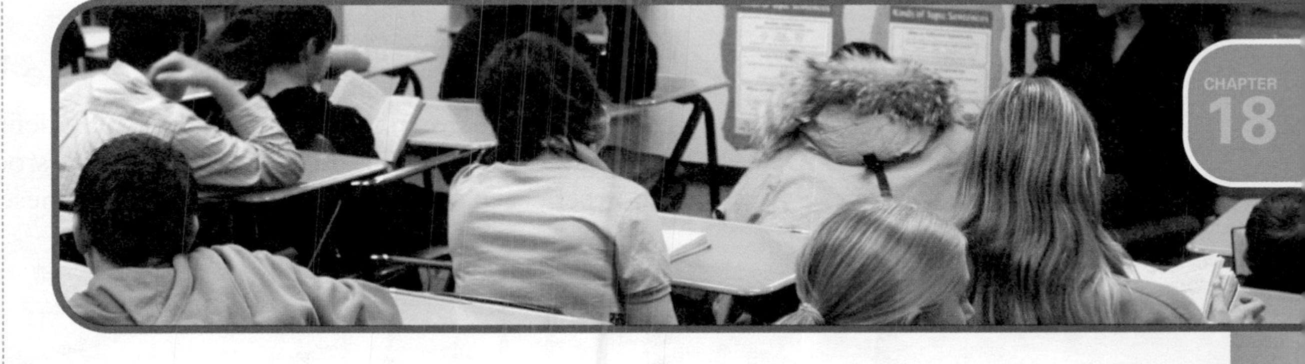

CHAPTER 18

Effectiveness Essentials

- Good teaching and organized, efficient classroom management will help to solve or prevent many discipline problems.
- Students learn best in a comfortable classroom environment.
- Some causes of behavior disruptions are related to instruction.
- Adhering to Kounin's principles during instructional time can cut down on potential disruptions.

Prevention is better than cure.

Proverb

No method nor discipline can supersede the necessity of being forever on the alert.

Henry David Thoreau

The best way to deal with discipline problems is to prevent them from happening in the first place. Marzano, Marzano, and Pickering (2003) analyzed more than 100 studies to identify principles that underpin effective classroom management. Among these are rule setting, appropriate and timely disciplinary interventions, positive student-teacher relationships, a teacher's positive or "can do" mental set, student cooperation in maintaining the positive learning environment, and emotional objectivity. Classroom management is under your control. It is how you do business in your classroom, and the principles that Marzano et al. (2003), Kounin (1977), and experienced teachers offer will make you an effective manager and prevent many of your discipline problems. Why? Because we all respond and react to the situation at hand, and the more you control the variables of instruction, including the physical arrangement of the classroom, the less likely it is that you will have to control or discipline the students. So it's best to start with a look at the context in which problems arise. That is effective classroom management!

The Physical Environment

Students learn best in a comfortable classroom environment. Paying attention to these parameters may increase the

Attractive classrooms assist with classroom management.

likelihood that students will attend to their learning tasks with minimum distraction and disruption:

- A well-ventilated room
- Glare-free lighting
- Colorful and informative bulletin boards
- A clean and orderly room
- Private spaces for students to get away from it all
- Visibility from all areas of the room for you and the pupils
- Compatible seatmates
- A teaching style conducive to your furniture arrangement

Meeting Individual Differences

Some causes of behavior disruptions are related to instruction, and you can do something about this by recognizing that, for some students, the assignments are not consistent with their abilities. These include students' inability to do the work, sheer boredom, lack of challenging assignments, and expectations that are too high. Counter these possibilities by recognizing each student's uniqueness. Unmet instructional needs may cause your students to engage in attention-getting behavior that undermines your classroom control. Here are some ideas for meeting instructional needs.

Make Differentiated Assignments

Make sure each student can succeed at the tasks you assign. This may necessitate rewriting some assignments, tape-recording assignments, or providing more challenging work for the advanced learner. Chapter 28 provides an in-depth look at differentiating instruction.

Group Students According to Specific Needs

Individual needs can also be met by grouping according to specific needs, abilities, and interests, when appropriate. Students with special needs should be seated with students who are considerate and willing to help out. This will be discussed further in Unit 6.

Give Students Opportunities for Choices and Decisions

Students' individual differences may also be met by providing choices whenever possible—in creative writing topics, in art assignments, in P.E. games, and in seating.

NOTES

Maintain Realistic Expectations

One of the ways to determine if your expectations are too high or too low is to put yourself in your students' place. Make revisions whenever you have the sense that you wouldn't be able to complete the assignment if you were in the students' shoes.

APPLY IT!

At the beginning of the year, have your students tell you what's in and what's out in their popular culture. Prepare an inventory with fill-in items such as these:

Favorite pop music stars
Favorite country music stars
Favorite hip hop music stars
Favorite movie stars
Favorite movies
Favorite books
Favorite television programs
What we are shopping for
What we like as gifts
What we like to eat
Favorite computer games
Favorite electronic devices
Favorite spectator sports
Favorite stores in town

Capitalize on Interests

Finding out what motivates each student and gearing instruction around common interests will accomplish two goals. First, you will capture students' attention more easily, and, second, you will convey the message that you care about your students. Developing rapport with your students is easy if you are honest, sincere, and genuine with them. Conduct an interest inventory (see the Apply It! feature). Using current fads as themes in your instruction may just be the spark you need to keep students involved and out of trouble.

Planning

Thorough and well-formulated planning will help you cut down on potential disruptions. If your planning allows every student to succeed, you are maximizing your chances for effective discipline. It is far better to underestimate your students' abilities during the first few days than it is to go over their heads. The worst thing that can happen is that they will feel successful!

Plan Meaningful Activities

Plan worthwhile and meaningful activities to cut down on behavioral problems. Design motivating lessons that hook the

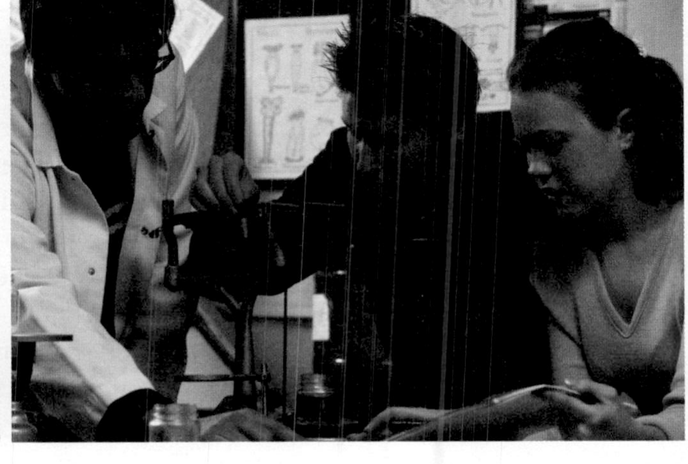

Engagement equals no time to misbehave.

students at the outset. Let your students know the purpose or objective of the lesson and point out which curriculum standards are being addressed. Use a variety of media and technology in your instruction, and vary your teaching strategies. Plan a balance among individual work, cooperative learning in groups, and teacher-directed instruction in order to create variety and to maintain involvement and interest.

Keep All Procedures Orderly

Orderly procedures facilitate the smoother operation of all activities within the classroom. Make sure you have gone through the lesson in your mind as well as written it on paper so you can anticipate any skipped steps or procedures that potentially will sandbag your lesson. Make sure materials are at the ready. If you have to go back to a cabinet to get supplies, you will interrupt the flow and undermine your lesson.

Engage Your Students

Engage your students and increase on-task behavior. Create a list of "things to do" for students who complete their work quickly. These activities must be rewarding in some way. Making more work the reward for early completion soon will lose its appeal. Students who are wise to your scheme will slow down and even avoid finishing in the allotted time.

TEACHER TALKS . . .

I have always found that engagement is the key. Getting the kids involved/interested in the activity is the way to deal with behavioral problems. We do make some rules each year, but these are generally safety rules because I always teach in a laboratory. As a more experienced, older teacher with a good reputation (the kids consider me cool!), I do insist that students do not speak while I am speaking, unless they are asking a relevant question, and then they wait

(continued on following page)

TEACHER TALKS—*continued*

until I have finished. I am quite strict about not speaking while others ask questions.

We do a lot of experiments. If students are doing anything that could be vaguely unsafe, they are told to sit at their desk immediately, and they miss out on the experiment and have to write it up after the event and often come back to clean some lab equipment.

Letting the kids know what you expect to cover in the lesson is another good idea. The students are able to pace themselves; and if they don't, you are able to say, "You didn't finish what we were supposed to do in class. It has to be done now . . . before you go to lunch/go home, etc., or for homework." To encourage them to complete the lesson, you might offer, "Complete this, and there's no homework today."

SHIRLEY CASPER
High School Science Teacher
Sydney, Australia

UNIT 4

Use Sponge Activities

Use sponge activities to reduce downtime. It's hard to think on your feet if you have an extra few minutes after you complete a lesson. Sponge activities are so named because they absorb the extra few minutes. If you don't have something to keep students actively involved, they may create their own diversions, ones you may not approve of. Sponges should relate to your curriculum, call for oral responses, and require no preparation on your part. Whether you teach at the elementary or secondary level, ready-made sponge activities can serve as good concept reviews or even nongraded quizzes. Make a quiz show out of the sponge activities. Some ideas for sponges are listed below:

- Name things that come in pairs.
- List one country for each letter of the alphabet.
- Name things that fly.
- Name solid geometry figures.
- Name characters in *Romeo and Juliet*.
- Name the constellations.
- Name rights guaranteed in the Bill of Rights.
- Name the Impressionists.
- Name the Greek/Roman gods and goddesses.
- Name the states in alphabetical order.
- Name presidents in chronological order.

APPLY IT!

Given your grade level or subject matter, list at least 10 sponge ideas you could use to soak up extra time.

Post a list of things to do when students are finished with their work.

Instruction

During instructional time, you can cut down on potential disruptions by adhering to principles of good teaching. Although good instruction cannot guarantee good discipline at all times, you

WATCH IT! video

Classroom Management

The high school teacher featured in Teacher Talks on page 185 asserted that engagement is the key to classroom management. In this video clip, you will see several scenarios that depict students willingly engaged in tasks. Explain the relationship between active learning and classroom management. What engaging activities do you see in the video? Do you subscribe to the notion that when students are creating their own meaning they are less likely to engage in negative behaviors? Why or why not?

can reduce potential problems by considering the possibility that a strong link exists between the two. It is even more important to minimize disruptions through effective classroom management or preventive discipline in middle and high school when the periods are so short. Time is of the essence in all grades, but in secondary school you don't want to spend the whole period settling the class down or trying to get their attention. In *Discipline and Group Management in Classrooms,* Jacob Kounin (1977) identified the following principles of good instruction.

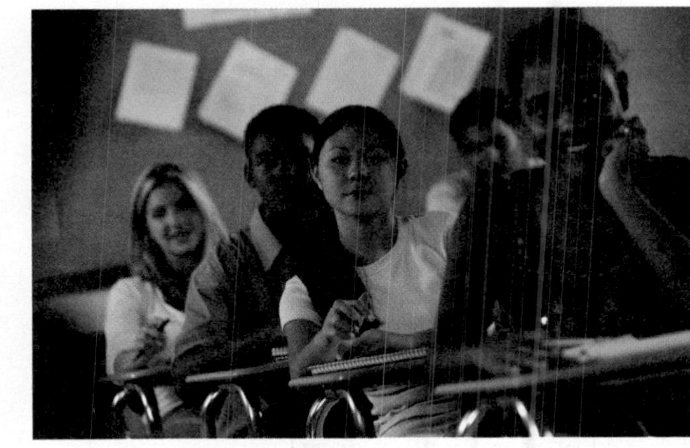

Students focus before a lesson starts.

Focus the Group's Attention

Before beginning any lesson, make sure the students are looking at you and that you have everyone's undivided attention. If you begin while students are talking or inattentive, the situation can only get worse. Keeping the group alert involves encouraging individual and unison responses and not calling on someone before you ask the questions; otherwise, the other 32 will tune out. Calling on students randomly with name sticks or a deck of individualized cards is one way of keeping them on their toes.

Be Careful of Overdwelling and Fragmentation

Make sure that lessons proceed at a steady clip. If you allow yourself to be

TEACHER TALKS . . .

My students in high school English classes would always notice when I changed the color of my nail polish and similar details of my dress and accessories. However, in order to focus their attention on the subject matter I often had to resort to dropping the metal wastebasket from the height of my desk.

DOTTIE BAILEY
Speech and English Teacher
Colton, California

Students often feel teachers have eyes in the back of their heads. Sometimes they need to!

distracted or slowed down, the delays will enable minor disruptions to erupt like mini-wildfires. A teacher engaging in overdwelling is spending too much time on directions, irrelevant details, or the physical props of the lesson. A teacher engaged in fragmentation divides the lesson into too many unnecessary steps or procedures or has each student do something individually when a group or the entire class could do it more efficiently all at once.

Practice Withitness

Observe and be alert during all presentations. Kounin (1977) invented the term *withitness* to describe teachers who have eyes in the back of their heads. Maintain eye contact with each student and move around the room. Pretend you are a bat hovering over the room with everyone under your wing. Students of all ages are less likely to act out when they feel they are in direct contact with you.

Consider Variety and Group Alerting

Vary the lesson formats, the group size, the media, and the materials. To keep everyone involved, ask stimulating and sometimes unpredictable questions. Use "every pupil response" techniques whenever possible, as these allow everyone to be involved in responding at the same time. They enable you to diagnose on the spot who understands the lesson and who doesn't, saving you hours of grading written work. Engage students by asking them to

- Say it aloud
- Use a finger signal (e.g., thumbs up or down)
- Display responses on individual sets of flashcards, chalkboards, or white boards
- Respond when their names are pulled from a bundle of ice cream sticks or a deck of cards

Practice Overlappingness

Practice multitasking or overlappingness. Kounin's (1977) term *overlappingness,* a key to effective classroom management, refers to a teacher's ability to handle two or more things at the same time. An example would be signaling a student who is tapping his or her pencil while still conducting the lesson, or checking a paper while working with a small math group and not missing a beat.

Make Smooth Transitions

Avoid dangles, flip-flops, thrusts, and truncations. *Dangles* and *flip-flops* occur when the teacher leaves one activity dangling or hanging, goes on to another, and returns once again to the initial activity. *Thrusts* occur when a teacher barrels into an activity without attention to pupil readiness. *Truncations* occur when a teacher aborts an activity and never returns to it. These erratic instructional shifts baffle students; and when students are confused, they may turn off and amuse themselves in inappropriate ways.

Know When to Stop

Terminate lessons that have gone on too long. Know when your students tend to reach their saturation point, and attempt to bring closure to the lesson before that time. Always leave students asking for more.

Check for Understanding

Before dismissing a group after a teacher-directed activity, make sure your students know what to do next. This can be accomplished by asking someone to summarize both the lesson's content and the directions for seatwork or follow-up. Always ask if anyone has any questions about what to do next. Do not give in to students who persist in asking interminable questions after you have answered them time and time again. Just tell them to pretend they know the answer. They will probably quit stalling and get to work. It's also helpful to model concentrating on a task by writing a letter to a friend during their writing assignment or reading silently a book of your choice while they are reading.

Emotional Objectivity

Emotional objectivity, along with withitness, according to Marzano et al. (2003), is a key construct of an effective classroom management plan. Emotional objectivity requires that no matter how upset you may be with a student, you continue to interact in a businesslike manner. If you are perceived as overreacting or biased, the offender will blame you for being "prejudiced" or "making a big deal out of nothing" instead of taking responsibility. When assessing a penalty or consequence, you need to be firm and clear without apologizing to or feeling sorry for the student. Focus on the behavior and the causes instead of personalizing the behavior as an attack on you,

AVOID IT!

During the first weeks of school, do not worry about how much you are teaching; rather, focus on preventive discipline and classroom management. The instruction will come soon enough in a well-managed classroom.

TEACHER TALKS . . .

Classroom management starts with discipline. To discipline, you have to show that you care about the child. You must discipline with love. Be tough. Stick to your classroom rules. Model these rules. If a rule is broken, there must be consequences. Apply the appropriate consequences. Always discipline with a hug afterward. Look the child in the eyes, and tell him that you care about him. Make sure he knows that you still care about him; you were just disappointed in his behavior. You are tough on him because you care. You will always care about him. That is discipline with love. A classroom cannot function without it.

LAUREL GARNER
Fifth-Grade Teacher
Duluth, Georgia

As seen on
http://www.LessonPlansPage.com

identifying with the student, or seeing the fault as your own. Anticipate which students might act out and then purposely talk yourself into positive expectations for the day or period.

Summary

Prevention is better than a cure. In this chapter, several precepts of effective classroom management were articulated that may help you avert serious discipline issues. The principles of effective and preventive classroom management are under your control; and before you look to the students and their misbehavior, consider checking whether you are consistent in implementing these guidelines.

Reflect!

Which precepts of effective and preventive classroom management are you using? Write them down and give an example of how you implement the principle. Then go through the chapter again and highlight those that you are not using or need more information about. For each of these, write down what you can do from here on out to make sure to incorporate that principle in your day.

Principles I Use Every Day	Principles I Need to Incorporate Into My Day

CHAPTER 19

WHAT TEACHER BEHAVIORS LEAD TO A POSITIVE CLASSROOM CLIMATE?

If I want to be great I have to win the victory over myself . . . self-discipline.

President Harry S. Truman

Effectiveness Essentials

- There are many ways to create a positive classroom climate.
- Model respect in order to establish a democratic classroom community.
- Show that you respect all students and value diversity through everything you do in the classroom.
- Empower students to resolve conflicts.

TEACHER TALKS . . .

Have clear, simple, and concise rules. Limit the number to no more than five. I chose (1) be respectful, (2) follow school rules, (3) do your best work, (4) no food or drinks. They are somewhat positive and broad enough to encompass my needs in the classroom. I also verbally go over the definitions with the students and constantly review them. I send home a syllabus to be signed by the parents, which includes a little more detail about the rules that are posted in my room and my contact information if they have any questions.

BARBARA ARIENT
Special Education Teacher
Grades 9–12
San Bernardino, California

The tone you set for your class is often referred to as "climate." No matter where you live, try to establish a climate more like Florida in February and less like Montana. The most attractive, well-designed room will lose its attraction if an icy, frozen, and rigid climate prevails. Establishing a warm, calming, neat classroom climate comes naturally to most teachers. Conveying a positive and enthusiastic attitude toward your students may alleviate many behavior problems before they begin (Marzano, et al., 2003). Marzano and colleagues cite teacher-student relationships as key to effective classroom management. This means that teachers should have equal parts of dominance (leading and in control of the class) and cooperation (willingness to take a personal interest in students and in the class as a whole).

A Baker's Dozen: Thirteen Ways to Create a Positive Classroom Climate

Think about how you greet dinner guests at your home. You meet and greet everyone, show them around, and make sure they are comfortable. You circulate among your guests and make introductions so that no one feels left out. On a less personal level, you want to make your students feel welcome in the shared space of the classroom. There are many ways to establish a warm, welcoming classroom climate.

1. Smile When Appropriate

When I started teaching, there were no discipline gurus to rely on and barely

Which teacher is more open to students?

any guidebooks on discipline. The conventional wisdom was "Don't smile until Christmas." The notion of the stern-faced schoolmarm of the nineteenth century prevailed. Students were to be intimidated by a stern approach. Think back on your own experiences in school. Were there teachers you were afraid of because of their dour demeanors?

More important, did you ever take advantage of teachers just because they had pleasant looks on their faces? The answer is probably no. Smiling when you greet your students tells them you are glad to see them. Adopt a businesslike yet friendly demeanor, the middle ground between the back-slapping, chummy teacher and the stern, prune-faced one.

2. Move Around the Classroom in Physical Proximity to All Students

University students typically take seats in the back of the room, far from me. Pity the poor latecomers who have to be up close and personal to the teacher. However, your students are usually not in the back by choice, and you need to make proximity a conscious effort. Most teachers talk to and walk to the middle of the class and across the front. Be aware that the students in the back need closeness to you as well. Keep moving around the room as much as possible.

I was observing a student teacher read a story to her kindergarten class and could see the big picture. It was quite entertaining from my vantage point in the back, watching the kindergarteners in the back row who couldn't see and couldn't be seen by the student teacher. Some were conducting beauty parlor, braiding one another's hair. Others were making faces or lying down. They couldn't see the action, so they made some of their own. They were quite surprised and embarrassed when they turned around and saw me watching them. They shaped up immediately. The student teacher could have walked around with

WATCH IT! video

Low-Profile Classroom Management

After viewing the video clip, divide a paper into three columns. In the first, write down all the distracting behaviors you witnessed. In the second, note the teacher's response to that behavior. In the third, write down what, if anything, you would have done differently.

Move to all sections of the classroom.

TEACHER TALKS . . .

I once read that the way to make friends and keep them is to say something genuinely kind each day. It takes time to develop the habit. It sounds corny to say, "I love your shoes, I wish I could wear them!" But you'd never expect the grin you get from a comment like that. I try to focus on their work. And when a student takes pride in her work, it fosters intrinsic goals to continue working well.

KRIS UNGERER
Kindergarten Teacher
Riverside, California

UNIT 4

the book or alternatively had the first row of students sit directly on the rug, the next row kneel above them, and the third row stand so everyone could see.

3. Maintain an Open Body Posture

Would you rather approach a principal who has her arms folded in front of her chest or one who extends a hand and greets you? Would you feel better about debriefing your lesson with a supervisor who sits across from you or next to you? These are two examples of opposite positions regarding body language. Whole books have been written about body language and non-verbal messages the body conveys. Be more aware of yours so that students and parents perceive you as open rather than self-protective. Come out from behind your desk. Walk among your students with your hands at your side instead of folded in front of you. Sit next to your students when you are counseling them, not across from them.

4. Listen Attentively to What Students Say

With 30-plus students, it is hard to find time to listen to their personal stories, especially when they are tugging on

What messages do these two postures send?

This teacher has open body posture.

Note the closed body posture.

your sleeve, saying, "Teacher, teacher." But you want to let them know that you are interested in them. Some ways you can include personal sharing during the school day might include having students sign up to tell you personal stories, maybe five minutes total per day. Or you might allow students in middle and high school to share news at the beginning of the period. Display a suggestion box, and encourage students to recommend alternative procedures or assignment options. Beware! Young students like to tattle on classmates and you don't have the time to referee all the squabbles. Instead, have them write out their grievances and deposit them in a "tattle tales" mailbox made from a shoebox (see Figure 19.1).

5. Share Appropriate Personal Stories About Yourself or Your Experiences

I always participate in introductions on the first day of class. Students often come up to me to share pictures of their horses when they find out I have two of my own. I award a small prize to the first student who guesses where I was born, not too difficult as I maintain my Brooklyn accent. I share my teaching mishaps and successes throughout the years. I have also asked students to make some reasonable guesses about me (my family, house, pets, interests, hobbies, genre of books I read, music tastes, etc.), and at the end of the day I tell them which ones were accurate. This would be

Figure 19.1
Cardboard mailboxes labeled "Suggestions" and "Tattle Tales"

TEACHER TALKS . . .

Besides knowing the subject matter really well, a good teacher must give his students the confidence to succeed. Praising your students goes a long way toward giving them confidence and the feeling of wanting to learn. If a student did not do well on a particular day, I could always find something to praise. It could be something like "That's a nice sweater," or "Your haircut looks very nice," etc. Naturally, a good teacher should have good discipline in his or her class. The discipline should be firm but fair.

GORDON MACDONALD
High School Band Teacher
Montvale, New Jersey

a fun activity for middle and high school students as well. In the younger grades, I avoid the guessing game and directly tell something about myself and my family, pets, hobbies, etc.

6. Say Something Complimentary to Each Student Each Day

Compliments are key to a positive classroom climate. You can give compliments during every exit from and entrance into the classroom. You can give compliments as you walk around the room. You can make a "compliment tree," a multi-branched dead tree limb secured in a planter from which students hang paper apples with written compliments for or from their peers.

APPLY IT!

Think about what you will tell your students about yourself. Will you use any props such as photos or other objects? Will you make it into a guessing game?

Make a "Star of the Week" bulletin board.

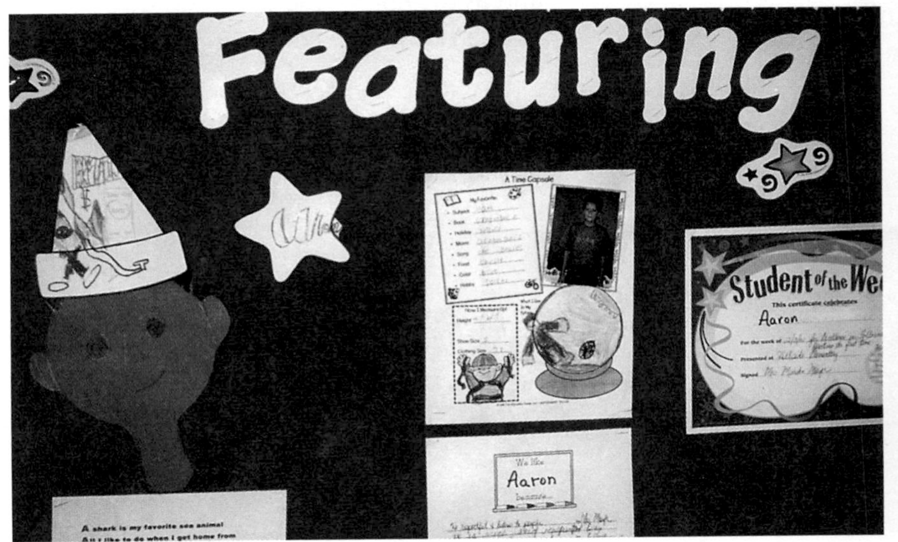

APPLY IT!

Recall that in Chapter 13 I suggested using sticks or a deck of playing cards to help you call on all students. Use these sticks or cards to call on students for end-of-the-day or -period compliments. Mark each student's name on a card or a stick. Each day, distribute the cards or sticks randomly. Start with the first student who says, "I want to compliment _____ for _____." The compliments should be a strong point or a positive attribute. Each student gives and gets one compliment. This is an effective way of alerting students to others' strengths.

Some teachers have a "Student of the Week" bulletin board. I would recommend a bulletin board divided into fourths so students don't have to wait so long for their turn. Their digital photo is posted along with special objects, awards, certificates, etc. The class gets to compliment the student of the week while the teacher writes down the comments. The comments are posted as well.

A teacher of students with special needs was concerned that his students found it difficult to be positive toward one another, so he devised a clever plan. He decorated soup cans with colorful sleeves, one for each of his ten students. At the end of the day, each student was given nine tokens to distribute in the cans of those students who had been nice or with whom they had gotten along during the day. The tokens were tallied at the end of the week, and the top five MVPs (most valued people) got to use the limited number of study carrels for the following week. Within weeks, his students were able to see the glimmerings of "what goes around comes around," and their behavior improved.

7. Empower Students to Resolve Conflicts

I have seen students as young as kindergarteners resolve conflicts with their peers. If they can do it, so can students in all grades, if given the proper guidelines. In the two video clips mentioned on page 198, you will see how teachers guide the students toward resolution of their differences. The teachers' role is that of facilitator and coach. The classroom meeting is a another vehicle for

Hold a classroom meeting.

resolving conflict in the classroom, and you will read about it later in the chapter. Teaching students to resolve conflicts on their own has implications far beyond the classroom. In the long term, disputes will inevitably occur in other grades and in contexts outside of school.

8. Use Teaching Strategies and Seating Arrangements to Create a Sense of Belonging

Cooperative learning strategies will break down isolation in a classroom and encourage a group identity. If students are also seated in table groups, they will

WATCH IT! video

Empowering Students to Resolve Conflicts

In this video, a fourth-grade teacher helps two students resolve their conflict. Afterward, he describes the steps in the process. What are those steps, and what are the pros and cons of using this approach? Would you be willing to try this? Why or why not?

Conflict Resolution

What are the long-term benefits of learning to resolve conflicts at an early age? How is this second-grade teacher's method different from the fourth-grade teacher's? Or is it the same? Do you think this teacher should have a rule about taking turns?

have a home base. Naming the groups will also encourage a group feeling. The names can reflect the curriculum—e.g., planets, Native American tribes, rain forest animals, famous artists, etc.

9. Allow Students Choices

You can encourage a warm classroom community feeling by letting students make simple choices that are important to them but inconsequential to you, such as which of two songs to sing, which game to play during physical education, or which poem to read aloud. It is important that students feel their opinions are valued and validated.

10. Call Each Student by Name

Your name defines you, and it is important that you call on your students using their names. This should be easy if you are using the sticks and card method described in Chapter 13. Your seating chart will cue you in to student names in middle and high schools. Monitor how often you call on students by making ticks on your seating chart, ensuring that your questions are evenly distributed.

11. Include Self-Concept Activities as Part of Your Everyday Program

Take some time to include self-concept activities in your day. Many are subject matter–oriented, such as personal time lines for math, self-portraits for art, or writing an ad for yourself for language arts. Or use a story starter or sentence stem each period or day for journal writing, such as

My proudest moment . . .
The greatest gift I ever received . . .
Wishes for my life . . .
The happiest time of my life . . .
My biggest strength . . .

12. Commit to Culturally Responsive Classroom Management

Weinstein, Tomlinson-Clarke, and Curran (2004) articulate five essential components of culturally responsive classroom management:

1. Recognition of one's own ethnocentrism
2. Knowledge of students' cultural backgrounds
3. Understanding of the broader social, economic, and political context
4. Ability and willingness to use culturally appropriate management strategies
5. Commitment to building caring classrooms

They posit that "we need to question traditional assumptions of 'what works' in classroom management and be alert to possible mismatches between conventional management strategies and students' cultural backgrounds" (p, 32). They offer examples such as the Hispanic student who has a cultural focus on collective rather than individual achievement and may find individual praise

STUDENT SAYS . . .

My perspective of a good teacher is one with lots of enthusiasm and lots of energy for learning, keeping us kids excited, and being there for us when we need help. I think it's important for teachers to accept the way we are as individuals and treat us all equally.

KIRA
Sixth Grader, Age 11
Arcata, California

Artifacts spark student interest.

embarrassing or the Chinese student who is reluctant to offer an opinion because culturally she has been instructed to listen and learn from elders. You will need to read much more about culturally responsive classroom management in the books listed in the Further Reading section.

13. Display Interesting Artifacts and Student Work Around the Room

In addition to displaying student work and projects, think of ways to make your room more visually appealing and homelike. Some teachers hang curtains. Some have plants or a fish tank. Others purchase exotic items from discount stores, museum shops, or flea markets. You may have items around your house, from your travels, or from import stores that are visually appropriate for classroom life. Change these around from time to time.

Respect and Responsibility

Modeling respect in your classroom is the most important thing you can do to establish a classroom community based on democratic values. How does the teacher model respect? The students will be watching your every word and deed. So . . .

1. Aspire to rate high on the fairness quotient.
2. Treat everyone as equally as you can.
3. Deal with confrontations privately.
4. Respect students' private spaces.
5. Show respect for all students and value diversity through the pictures on your

WATCH IT! video

Implementing Class Meetings

As you watch this video clip, how does the teacher set a positive tone at the outset? What are those positive statements? What problem is introduced? What suggestions do the students make to alleviate the problem? Can you allow your students to come up with their own suggestions? How did the teacher maintain a positive and respectful demeanor throughout? How do classroom meetings prepare students for their role as citizens in a democracy?

walls, the books you choose to read, and the lessons you plan.

6. Give students an opportunity to make things right before you resort to punishment.

Classroom Meetings

In democratic classrooms, students are encouraged to monitor and enforce the rules. Marzano et al. (2003) cite students' responsibility for classroom management as one of his five research-based constructs of effective classroom management. The classroom meeting has many purposes—e.g., planning together, talking about current issues, and discussing curriculum topics. But it is also a key channel for optimizing student involvement in and responsibility for classroom management. William Glasser (1975, 1998), the originator of the classroom meeting, believes that students can control themselves if their needs for survival, approval, love, power, fun, and freedom are met. Survival needs are up to the family and society, but the other needs can be met in the classroom setting when you lighten up, have some fun, provide love and approval, and enable students to have a say in how things are run.

The teacher's role is to help students make positive choices, and one vehicle for this is the classroom meeting. Jane Nelsen (2006) has simplified Glasser's

APPLY IT!

Post a sign like this: "The 3 'Rs'—Respect, Responsibility, Reliability." Discuss what each would look like when practiced. Then divide your class into six groups. Two groups write a list of 10 behaviors that show respect, two groups do the same for responsibility, and two groups tackle the concept of reliability. Share with the whole class after the groups complete their work.

Simplified Steps for a Classroom Meeting

1. Use a compliment circle or some positive activity to heighten class cohesion.
2. Expose the problem.
3. Seek verification that the problem exists.
   a. No excuses
   b. No blame
   c. No individuals singled out
4. Discuss the costs of continuing the behavior.
5. Discuss the benefits of desisting.
6. Make a value judgment about whether the costs outweigh the benefits.
7. Ask students to offer solutions and evaluate them.
8. Set the course of action and ask students to commit (often in writing) to follow it.
9. Have a follow-up meeting to assess the effectiveness of the solution.
10. Recycle the steps if necessary.

Classroom meetings can cover planning and discussing current issues and curriculum topics.

work on the classroom meeting by suggesting that entire class or individual conflicts be handled in class meetings, and the initiator can be the teacher or the students. Everyone sits in a tight circle; and although it is the teacher's role to facilitate the discussion, it is the students' role to make the value judgments and analyze the costs and benefits of continuing or desisting. Students brainstorm and evaluate the effectiveness of the proposed solutions to right the wrong; and after a solution is agreed upon, everyone commits to it. It is the act of problem solving itself that is important, not the efficacy of any one solution.

In secondary school, the classroom meeting is even more effective because teenagers are capable of abstract thinking and can better analyze and evaluate solutions. Then again, during classroom meetings, middle and high school students are more likely to be intolerant and forceful

AVOID IT!

Having a bad day is not an option for teachers. Leave your problems at home. Your students will expect some consistency in your mood and the way you respond to them. Students require stability in the teacher-student relationship; and if you are grouchy one day and happy the next, your reliability is at risk, and you may lose their trust.

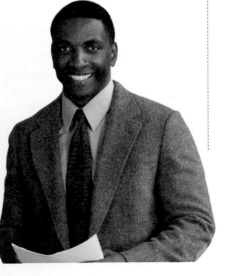

in their opinions. Because the classroom meeting is an age-appropriate forum for them to practice analytical and critical thinking skills, you will have to make a concerted effort to have them listen to one another. Use an egg timer to allow each one to have his or her say and then relinquish the soapbox. You will have to choose the issues carefully, given the time constraints. Most one-issue meetings can be compressed into 20 to 30 minutes.

You can be a hero to your students, whether they tell you so or not. The highest compliment you will receive may be "I want to be a teacher when I grow up." It won't be because you taught the causes of the Civil War or because you taught them two-digit division. It will be because you sent them forward as confident, positive, secure, respectful, and competent citizens in our diverse nation.

Summary

A positive classroom climate is one of the most important tools at your disposal for preventing discipline problems and resolving those that occur in a constructive manner. The chapter describes 13 strategies for creating an affirming classroom climate. You are challenged to implement culturally sensitive classroom management and to model respect in your diverse classroom. The classroom meeting and other conflict resolution strategies will help you empower students in the classroom to resolve conflicts on their own.

Reflect!

As you reflect on the 13 suggestions for creating a positive classroom climate, how will you implement them at your grade level or in your subject-specific classroom? What personal experiences have taught you about the norms and customs of a culture other than your own? What are the norms in your culture when conflicts occur? Research culturally sensitive classroom management and describe how you will go about implementing the concept in your classroom.

CHAPTER 20

WHAT ARE SOME NONVERBAL STRATEGIES TO MAINTAIN ORDER AND SOME RESPONSES TO AVOID?

When a teacher calls a boy by his entire name it means trouble.

Mark Twain

Effectiveness Essentials

- You can deal with minor infractions and distractions nonverbally without disrupting the entire class or instructional sequence.
- Effective nonverbal body language consists of teacher gestures, body posture, facial expressions, eye contact, and proximity control.
- Dealing with every minor infraction takes away from valuable instructional time.
- Serious acts need to be treated differently from rule-breaking behaviors but without overreacting.
- Avoid becoming obsessed with classroom discipline to the exclusion of instruction.

Nonverbal and Low-Key Interventions

You can deal with minor infractions and distractions nonverbally without disrupting the entire class or instructional sequence. Effective nonverbal body language consists of teacher gestures, body posture, facial expressions, eye contact, and proximity. The 10 suggestions that follow have no money-back guarantee that all misbehaviors can be handled without sacrificing instructional time. But try them first before resorting to harsher penalties or consequences.

Try Sign Language

Students can learn some simple signs in American Sign Language (ASL) to alert you to a need, and you can use signs to convey nonverbal messages without disturbing the class. Moreover, when students use this valuable communication tool, they may develop an interest in acquiring more signs. See Apply It! for ways to access ASL online or scan the library's catalog. Chapter 12 discusses using ASL for routines.

Use the "Look"

Establishing eye contact with the offender and staring until the behavior diminishes work for some teachers. Jones, Jones, Jones, and Jones (2007) advocate this practice, along with other nonverbal interventions. Remember that cultural norms may disallow the student from looking directly back at you.

Physical Proximity Can Help

Walking toward the offender will usually stop the behavior. You may need to move closer to the student and stand nearby. The increasing invasion of the student's space will usually cause him or her to desist. A hand on the desk as you pass is also effective, if moving to the edge of the desk hasn't achieved the desired outcome. You may want to learn more about nonverbal limit setting by reading

APPLY IT!

Go to a website such as http://www.masterstech-home.com/ASLDict.html or any dictionary of basic ASL terms, and find signs for "bathroom," "water," "quiet," and "sit down." You can also use Google Images to access visual representations of common signs. After you locate these terms, search for five others you may need in your classroom.

TEACHER TALKS . . .

Years ago I had to learn some American Sign Language including the alphabet, because I was temporarily assigned a partially deaf student. Since then I've incorporated the use of some sign language to quietly communicate back and forth with my students, thus not disturbing the whole class. We communicate things like "water," "bathroom," "recess time," "lunchtime," "concentrate/focus," "read," "write," "sit down," etc. The students seem to enjoy learning the alphabet and other signs.

GABE AGUILAR
Sixth-Grade Teacher
San Bernardino, California

Figure 20.1
Shh

Figure 20.2
Okay

Figure 20.3
Stop

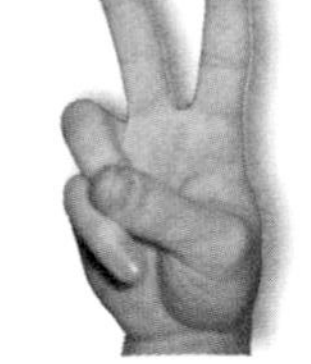
Figure 20.4
Quiet/Peace Sign

the work of Jones et al. (2007). They suggest nonverbal body language, incentives, and individual help to motivate on-task behavior and stop off-task behaviors such as talking and general goofing around. The end result is more time on task and thus more teaching and learning time. Here are some examples:

Jack and Steve are talking during a lesson. The teacher can

1. Make eye contact and let them know they are being watched.
2. Give a shake of the head while maintaining eye contact.
3. Hold up a hand, palm outward, signaling stop.
4. Move toward the offenders.
5. Stand next to the offenders.
6. Put hand on an offender's desk.
7. Look right at them and glare.

Jones and colleagues also believe in incentive or reward systems that include group and individual rewards and free time that is earned for favorite activities. A stopwatch is employed to gauge on-task versus nonproductive work. Students earn minutes for on-task behavior or lose minutes for preferred activity time (P.A.T.). It takes teacher commitment to use the stopwatch technique consistently. Jones et al. advocate quick and efficient individual help when students are stuck.

Establish Signals

Signals can be established ahead of time with individuals. A finger to your cheek tells John you see what he is doing and want him to stop. This helps John save face because the pre-established signal is private. Signals that work in general are a shake of the head, the raising of the eyebrows, a quick arc of the finger (see Figures 20.1–20.4).

Enlist Cooperation

You can nip the misbehavior in the bud by enlisting the student's aid for some small task relevant to the lesson. You might ask the culprit to erase the board or pass out materials. Whatever the job, both you and the offender will know why he or she has been chosen, and you still won't miss a beat in your instruction.

Ask a Question

Posing a question to the student who has just started to act out can redirect his or her attention to the task. Make sure it is a question that can be answered easily, as your goal is not to embarrass the student but to channel his or her attention in a productive way. If you feel the student cannot answer the question, have him or her select someone whose hand is raised to supply the answer.

Stay Alert for an Encouraging Moment

When you observe a potential offender doing something right or trying to do the right thing, offer praise. You are better off waiting for the moment when you get your chance to turn a student in the direction of success. Strike when the iron is hot, and encourage your student.

Create "See Me" Cards

You can duplicate cards that you can unobtrusively place on a student's desk that say something equivalent to "see me." You may also have a place for students to write in why they think they received the card and what a better choice would have been (see Figure 20.5).

Delay Your Reaction

Rather than interrupt the flow of instruction, simply and firmly tell the student in question that you wish to speak to him or her at the end of the lesson. This invitation to a private conference, only one sentence in length, may cause the student to shape up, negating the need for a long conference. The delayed reaction also gives you a chance to cool off and consider an appropriate response. Nelsen et al. (2000) suggest that this cooling off is most important when you are angry or frustrated and are likely to exacerbate the situation by responding in kind to the student's discouraging behavior.

Try Role Playing or Letter Writing

When there is a dispute, it's often useful for students to write out their angry feelings or express their point of view on paper. In the case of the upset student, writing it out is a more positive way of diminishing strong feelings. In a dispute, the two students can exchange their papers and read each other's description of the events leading up to the altercation. Sometimes I have put the two students on opposite sides of me and asked each to tell what happened from the other's point of view. This helps them to understand, if not empathize, with the other student and thus ameliorate the conflict.

Class and Culture Determine Reactions to Discipline

Before you decide on a strategy for changing, praising, or punishing the behavior of an individual student, recognize that the student comes to school with socially and culturally determined

See Me

Why?

____

____

____

A better choice would have been

____

____

____

Name ____________________
Date ____________________

Figure 20.5
"See Me" Card

UNIT 4

TEACHER TALKS . . .

One day it was particularly cold out, and I was not prepared with the warmest jacket. I told the class we would go out for P.E. if everyone completed the work and kept the noise level down. One student created a disturbance, and I said, "That's it, we aren't going to go outside for P.E. today." Was I looking for an excuse not to go outside? I'll never tell, but it wasn't my proudest teaching moment.

ELLEN KRONOWITZ
Former Third-Grade Teacher
New York City

reactions to discipline. For example, the Hispanic or African American student may not look you in the eye out of respect; and if you interpret this as further defiance, you will only escalate the situation.

Before you intervene in a serious situation, investigate the often hidden cultural and social norms and rules that may be determining the behavior. The school is just one influence on a student. The more you can learn about the culture and socioeconomic context your students come from, the easier the task of helping them learn that they may have to adapt their behavior or learn new rules of deportment in order to survive and succeed in school and work environments where unfamiliar rules may apply.

Beyond Rule Breaking: Crossing the Line

Serious acts need to be treated differently from rule-breaking behaviors or the manifestations of mistaken or misdirected goals. The most serious, unlawful offenses need to be dealt with swiftly according to your district's policy, which derives from your state education code or laws governing education.

It is possible that one or more of your students will be suspended or expelled from school because they have crossed the line. As you read about the offenses that are grounds for suspension in the Classrooms Artifacts feature in Chapter 16, you may have been surprised that such a listing exists and is necessary at all. It is best to know what may be considered grounds for suspension.

Many schools use a referral process. In middle and high school, where you only see the culprit for one or two periods, it is hard to follow up. Before you encounter your first severe behavior problem, find out what the policy is for serious infractions in your middle or high school and the steps you must take.

Students in middle and high school may take their offenses to a higher level than will students in elementary school. Behaviors that should concern you include fighting, name calling, stealing, cheating, plagiarism, destruction of property, constant defiance, bullying, refusal to work, profane language, and threats of violence, among others. There are no tried-and-true recipes for dealing with these behaviors either, but certain general principles obtain:

1. Except when students are in danger, it is best to deal with serious infractions when you are calm and better able to act in a rational manner.
2. Keep detailed records (anecdotal) of the student's behavior with dates, descriptions of behavior, and your response. Detailed anecdotal records will be helpful when discussing the problem and seeking solutions with school personnel or with parents.
3. When you suspect that a student will persist in the inappropriate behavior, ask for help early on. By using resource persons available to you at the school or district level, you are demonstrating that you are resourceful, not incapable. Most schools have a Student Study Team (SST), which is a group of professionals who work to solve behavioral and other problems. These teams generally are composed of the school psychologist, special education resource teachers, classroom teachers, and the principal. It's best to devise some long-range plans or strategies by enlisting the aid of the SST, your principal, school or district psychologist, counselor, special education resource teacher, and the student's parents.
4. Other, more experienced teachers can help as well, especially those who have encountered the student in earlier grades.

Schedule a parent/guardian conference.

Parent/Guardian Conferences

After speaking with the principal and the school or district counselor, enlist the aid of your student's parents or guardians. It is important for you to regard the conference or any contact with parents as a two-way communication channel. You have certain information, and the family has certain information. Adding your experience at school to the parents'/guardians' experience at home makes shared problem solving possible. That should be your message to parents.

Make your first contacts by phone; and if you need to, initiate a conference. Use an interpreter as needed, and make sure one is available during the conference. The parents/guardians should

TEACHER TALKS . . .

Being in a foul mood one day, I sent four kids to the principal for minor infractions. After school I was called in and given valuable guidance. When you send a student out of the room, you are seen as having less power. Not sending students to the office also keeps principals happy because you are not lining their office with students. On average I send only one student to the office per year. Sometimes I don't send any at all. Try to bring the student that's bothering you the most closest to you. Your proximity oftentimes brings the student into line.

KRIS UNGERER
Former Fifth-Grade Teacher
San Bernardino, California

A students sits in the "thinking chair."

already have a great deal of information from your prior contacts. During the conference, follow these six steps:

1. Make the parents or guardians comfortable. Say something positive about their son/daughter.
2. Describe the inappropriate behavior, using anecdotal data. Watch for overreactions by the parents or guardians and head them off.
3. Stress to the parents or guardians that their son/daughter is capable of behaving and has many positive attributes despite his or her negative behavior.
4. Elicit data from parents' or guardians' insights about their son's/daughter's attitude toward school, the student's behavior at home, how inappropriate behavior is dealt with at home, and what the parents or guardians see as possible causes of misbehavior at school.
5. Devise a plan together that is grounded in encouragement and logical consequences and does not run counter to cultural norms.
6. Follow up and inform parents or guardians about their son's/daughter's progress.

Responses to Avoid

The hardest part of dealing with discipline problems of the more serious kind is repressing some of the very human responses that serious offenses provoke. If there is ever a time to put on your angel's wings and sit under a halo, it's when a serious offense occurs in your classroom. A calm, cool manner on the part of the teacher will not only disarm the offender but also soothe the other students, who may be as upset as you are. What follows are various responses to avoid. Experienced teachers know that it is impossible to avoid all of them. But they try.

Don't Hold a Grudge

When the behavior has been dealt with, try to wipe the slate clean and forgive and forget. Begin each day anew. As one teacher phrased it, "Never let the sun go down on your anger."

Don't Take Misbehavior Personally

Separate yourself from the situation, and realize that the behavior is symptomatic of some disturbance within your student and doesn't necessarily reflect his or her attitude toward you. This may require that you schedule frequent pep talks with yourself.

Don't Make Everyone in the Class Suffer

It simply isn't fair to apply consequences to the entire class because a few of your charges are misbehaving. Discriminate between the offenders and the nonoffenders, and go on with business as usual.

Avoid Ejection From the Room or Time-Out

It is illegal in many districts to place your students outside the room unsupervised. Even if it is not, it is still not a good solution. Students will simply fool around in the halls or on the playground. You can be sure they won't stay where you put them. Avoid sending them to another classroom or to the principal, except in rare instances. Not only does this burden the other teachers and the principal; but if you exercise this option too frequently, your actions may send a message to your class and to your administrator that you cannot deal with misbehavior. Try to tough it out and deal with problems in your own classroom. Use a "thinking chair" for the young set and an isolated study carrel for older students.

Never Use Physical Contact

Corporal punishment is defined as punishment upon the body, and it is banned in many states. Although you may be driven to distraction, never grab, pinch, or hit your students. They will magnify some of the slightest restraining techniques, and you need to protect yourself from irate parents and even a lawsuit. Also, you don't want to model a physical response to the rest of the class because you are hoping to extinguish this kind of behavior in them.

Equally, in this day and age, a harmless touch, hand on the shoulder, pat on the back, hug, or any other positive physical contact may result in claims of sexual harassment. You have to be aware of the consequences of touching a student, no matter how harmless the intent.

Avoid Humiliation Tactics

Such tactics include sarcasm, nagging, requiring the wearing of a dunce hat, having the student stand in a corner, or imposing other public embarrassment. Your students need to save face; and if you can talk with the offender privately, you are denying him or her an audience for further defiance or face-saving entrenchment of the negative behavior.

Don't Assign More Work

Writing sentences 25 times or more or doing extra work may not change

A private conversation about behavior.

the behavior. Rather, it may negatively associate work, which should be intrinsically pleasurable, with punishment.

Don't Make Threats You Can't or Won't Carry Out

You will lose your credibility if you back down, so avoid this by thinking

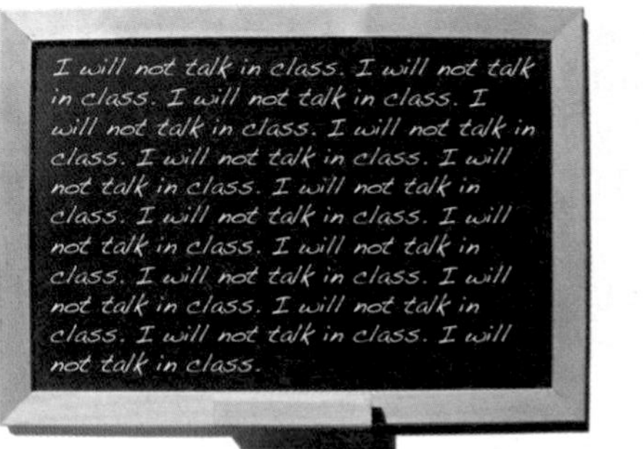

APPLY IT!

Consider the following 15 classroom behaviors, which vary in degree from minor to serious. Use all of the resources in this unit to brainstorm possible causes and possible solutions, whether through behavior modification, logical consequences, parent conferences, nonverbal interventions, or a combination approach. It's better to preplan possible interventions before they actually occur! Devise a plan for dealing with these situations at your potential or current grade level:

1. A student constantly rocks back and forth in her seat.
2. A student uses a racial epithet to you or another student.
3. A student says to the teacher, "You have bad breath."
4. A student destroys property of another student.
5. A student never brings her homework to class.
6. A student taps his pencil on the desk constantly.
7. A student says, "I don't care."
8. A student says, "You can't make me."
9. A student shoves another student in line.
10. A student won't share materials during a project.
11. A student brings a weapon to class.
12. A student throws objects at another student.
13. A student gets out of his seat and walks around the room.
14. A student makes fun of another student.
15. Add a behavioral problem you have experienced.

carefully about consequences before you announce them. Try withdrawing from the situation and establish a cooling-off period. Find a way out so that both of you can win if you are in a standoff situation. Simply saying, "I am choosing to let that go this time, John, although I expect that you will not be fighting on the playground again," allows both of you an easy out, yet you are still in control of the situation by making the choice. Or have your student choose between desisting and the logical consequence that pertains.

APPLY IT!

Now it is your turn to synthesize all you have read in this unit and in Chapter 9 and articulate your own comprehensive plan for discipline. Write a letter to parents articulating your plan and the philosophy underlying that plan.

AVOID IT!

Try not to become obsessed with classroom discipline matters. If you stop and try to deal with every misdemeanor in the classroom, you will never get any teaching done. There are times when it is best to just let it go. If you can't deal with it in using the strategies described in this chapter, and if the infraction is minor enough, then choose the unwritten discipline strategy and just let it go.

Although discipline is essential, it is only one component of effective instruction. If you are too focused on discipline and too concerned about control, you may not attempt some of the more active learning, inquiry, and cooperative learning strategies. Don't play it too safe and opt for a quiet classroom as your highest value.

If you make an error in judgment, you have the opportunity to recoup your losses the next day. Your students will be very forgiving and flexible. If you've been too lax, then tighten the discipline the next day. If you've been too harsh, then lighten up. Trust yourself and your intuition. Your experience, the experiences of colleagues, and the students themselves will help you figure out what works and doesn't work for you.

STATISTICS

According to the U.S. Department of Education's Office of Civil Rights (2008), among the 20 states that allow corporal punishment, the following 10 used it most often. The statistics show that many of the students who are punished also have disabilities.

State	**Number of Students Receiving Corporal Punishment, 2006**	
	Students with Disabilities	All Students
Texas	10,222	49,157
Mississippi	5,831	38,131
Alabama	5,111	33,716
Arkansas	4,082	22,314
Georgia	3,903	18,249
Tennessee	3,618	14,868
Louisiana	2,463	11,080
Oklahoma	2,249	14,828
Florida	1,331	7,185
Missouri	1,191	5,129

If we are ever to turn toward a kindlier society and a safer world, a revulsion against the physical punishment of children would be a good place to start.

Dr. Benjamin Spock

Summary

Because engaging students in instruction is your primary task, you want to identify the least obtrusive and therefore the most inconspicuous means of correcting behaviors that occur daily in most classrooms. Several suggestions for low-key and/or nonverbal strategies are described in the chapter along with responses that should be avoided whenever possible because they will have some unintended consequence that will do little to advance your commitment to positive, reasonable, and respectful discipline.

Reflect!

What are the low-key interventions that would be most useful to you, given your grade level or subject-matter area? Cite one instance in which you used a response that the chapter suggests should be avoided. Now what would you do instead? Research and identify other low-key interventions and start a list. Ask experienced teachers to review your list and add to it.

UNIT 4 CHECKLIST

Positive Discipline Checklist	For more information go to:
☐ Do I have a method for establishing rules that conforms to district/school policy?	Chapter 9
☐ Are my rules easily communicated to parents?	Chapter 9
☐ Does my discipline plan accommodate all students?	Chapter 9
☐ Have I checked for understanding of the rules and been consistent in enforcing them?	Chapter 9
☐ Am I looking for causes of the misbehavior?	Chapter 17
☐ Does my classroom environment promote good classroom management?	Chapter 18
☐ Do I follow Kounin's classroom management principles?	Chapter 18
☐ Am I promoting a positive classroom climate?	Chapter 19
☐ Is my overall plan culturally sensitive?	Chapter 19
☐ Have I examined and understood the school and district policies for serious offenses?	Chapters 16, 17, 20
☐ Have I ascertained the makeup of the Student Study Team at my site?	Chapter 20

Further Reading: Positive Discipline

Charles, C. M. (2010). *Building classroom discipline* (10th ed.). Boston: Allyn and Bacon. This text presents 18 models of discipline that have a solid theoretical base. The readers are challenged to synthesize models that meet their needs or situations from the variety presented in order to develop a comprehensive discipline system that works.

Emmer, E. T., & Evertson, C. M. (2009). *Classroom management for middle and high school teachers* (8th ed.). Boston: Pearson Education. Written for the new secondary teacher, this text covers the classroom management decisions that teachers make, especially in diverse and inclusive classrooms.

Evertson, C. M., & Emmer, E. T. (2009). *Classroom management for elementary teachers.* Boston: Pearson Education. Written for the new elementary teacher, this text covers the classroom management decisions that teachers make, especially in diverse and inclusive classrooms.

Jones, F. H., Jones, P., Jones, J. L., & Jones, F. (2007). *Tools for teaching.* Santa Cruz, CA: Fred Jones & Associates. This is a down-to-earth, practical guide that trains teachers in specific skills enabling them to deal with a wide variety of management issues.

Kaiser, B., & Sklar-Rasminsky, J. (2009). *Challenging behavior in elementary and middle school.* Upper Saddle River, NJ: Pearson Education. New and continuing teachers are helped to understand, prevent, and address challenging behaviors. The advice is practical, realistic, and evidence-based. The authors address working through challenges in a culturally responsive way and effectively dealing with the behavior of students with special needs.

Marzano, R. J., Gaddy, B., Foseid, M. C., Foseid, M. P., & Marzano, J. (2005). *A handbook for classroom management that works*. Upper Saddle River, NJ: Prentice Hall. In this companion volume to the 2003 edition, Marzano and colleagues describe the seven essentials that lead to a productive classroom environment. The descriptions are accompanied by case studies, worksheets, and other teacher-accessible materials to make this a practical and readable guide.

Marzano, R. J., Marzano, J. S., & Pickering, D. J. (2003). *Classroom management that works*. Alexandria, VA: ASCD. The authors have analyzed research from more than 100 studies on classroom management to distill which seven essential classroom management strategies are most effective.

Nelsen, J., Lott, L., & Glenn, H. S. (2000). *Positive discipline in the classroom* (rev. ed.). New York: Ballantine Books. This is a thorough explanation of positive discipline concepts with specific recommendations for implementing classroom meetings. The logical consequences approach is compared to behavior modification, and the four misdirected goals and how to identify them are covered.

Rothstein-Fisch, C., & Trumbull, E. (2008). *Managing diverse classrooms: How to build on students' cultural strengths*. Alexandria VA: ASCD. This book offers a framework for understanding cultural differences between those that value individual achievements and those that have a collectivistic orientation. The book presents strategies that build on cultural values.

Sprick, R. S. (2008). *Discipline in the secondary classroom: A positive approach to behavior management* (2nd ed.). San Francisco: Jossey-Bass. The author offers practical strategies for beginning the school year, classroom organization, and establishing rules and behavior expectations for students, accompanied by suggestions from successful classroom teachers and educational research.

Weinstein, C. S., & Romano, M. (2010). *Middle and secondary classroom management: Lessons from research and practice.* New York: McGraw-Hill. This book is a research-based guide on effective classroom management in secondary schools. It helps new and continuing teachers build a classroom management plan that focuses on building relationships with students and establishing a safe and caring classroom.

Informative Websites

Jane Nelsen/Positive Discipline

http://www.positivediscipline.com

This is the official positive discipline website with tips for teachers and parents, resources, articles, materials, and books to implement the approach.

Fred Jones

http://www.fredjones.com/

This is the official Fred Jones website where you can find articles, tips, and products.

Education World

http://www.educationworld.com/

This site contains excellent articles on classroom management and discipline issues. Be sure to register for and then access their free message boards, which contain valuable tips from teachers. The message board for classroom management is very informative.

National School Safety Center

http://www.schoolsafety.us/

This website provides information on bullying, creating safe schools, Safe Schools Week, and other important topics related to school safety issues. Article and book sources are cited as well as statistics on school violence.

The Teacher's Guide

http://www.theteachersguide.com/ClassManagement.htm

This website includes ready-to-use resources for elementary classroom management, including strategies, lessons, a teacher chat board, printouts, and book and discussion groups.

National Education Association

http://www.nea.org/tools/ClassroomManagement.html

The NEA offers articles about classroom management and character building. More specific articles such as addressing rude behavior and breaking up fights are also posted.

Middle Web

http://www.middleweb.com/

This website provides, among many other resources, a comprehensive section for middle school teachers on discipline and classroom management as well as suggestions for the first days of school.

UNIT 5

Planning and Organizing Subject Matter

CHAPTER 21

HOW DO I ALIGN STANDARDS AND FIT EVERYTHING IN?

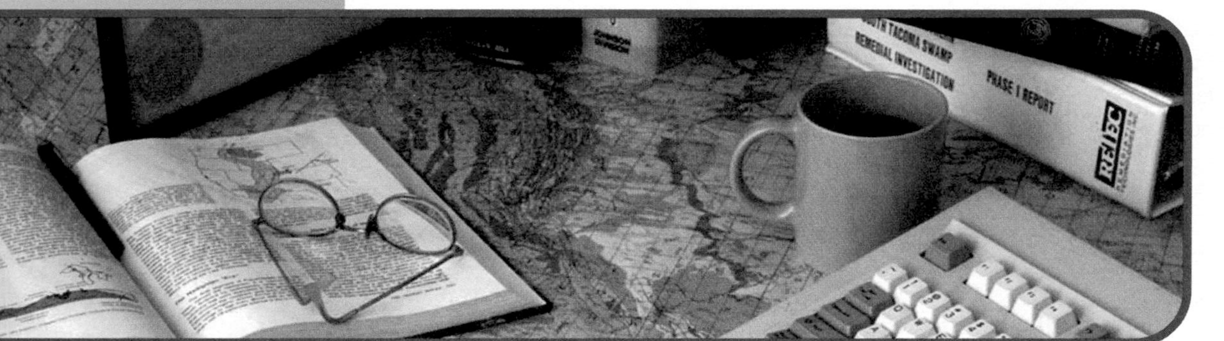

All states and schools will have challenging and clear standards of achievement and accountability for all children, and effective strategies for reaching those standards.

U.S. Department of Education

A man who does not plan long ahead will find trouble right at his door.

Confucius

Effectiveness Essentials

- Federal and state mandates have changed forever the way you and your fellow educators look at curriculum, instruction, and assessment.
- A standards-based curriculum sets uniformly high standards and expectations for all students.
- The first step in long-range curriculum planning is to become familiar with the relevant standards and expectations and the tests that assess them.
- Think of planning as a continuum from the general to the specific or from standards to your daily plans.
- Mapping out your year, month by month, can help you fit everything in.

When I began teaching, I was given a stack of curriculum materials, along with a class list, a record book, and a key to the teachers' rest room. Included in the curriculum materials were various guides (one each for social studies, science, and language arts). Inside each guide were the goals, content, and topics to be taught; suggested learning activities for each topic; and a bibliography of print resources that I could turn to if I ever had time. Math and reading curricula consisted of what the teacher's edition of the texts told me to teach, and art consisted of activities taken from *Instructor* magazine or borrowed from other teachers. Music and P.E. were hit-or-miss affairs. Each weekend I brought home curriculum guidebooks and manuals, and I labored to fit topics into little boxes in a weekly planning book. I hoped I was teaching what my third graders needed to know. But I always had my doubts! You see, I started teaching before there were the guidelines that exist today. There were no state standards, no benchmarks along the way, and no standardized assessments to measure just how much my students had learned. I had to rely on my teacher-made tests and judgment.

Of all the responsibilities that a new teacher has, none is less practiced during student teaching than curriculum planning. The period between the completion of

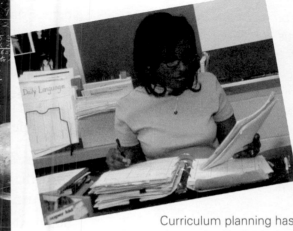

Curriculum planning has changed over the years.

your credential program and your first teaching assignment or internship is the time to reflect on what your curriculum will be during your first year(s) of teaching. All planning must be based on more than just your own desires for what you would *like* to teach. It must incorporate the requirements of national, state, and local interests, as well as the needs of your individual students.

Standards-Based Planning

Federal mandates have changed forever the way you and your fellow educators must look at curriculum, instruction, and assessment. They present challenges and opportunities that dictate how you do

CONGRESS SAYS . . .

In 1994, Congress enacted the Goals 2000 Educate America Act "to improve learning and teaching by providing a national framework for education reform . . . to promote the development and adoption of a voluntary national system of skills standards and certifications."

business in your classroom. These mandates establish a system of standards, along with accountability to ensure that all students meet them, regardless of any mitigating factors. Incrementally, federal legislation has completely changed how teachers today plan for the upcoming academic year (see Figure 21.1).

Goals 2000 Jump-Started the Standards-Based School Accountability Movement

Standards-based education requires that educators explicitly identify what students must know and be able to do. Goals 2000 supported comprehensive state- and district-wide coordination and implementation of programs focused on improving student achievement of state standards.

Under Goals 2000, standardized tests were given once per year. But they weren't always tied to the standards. As a result, there was inconsistency from district to district and state to state. Then Congress spoke again with one voice to ensure that every child should be educated to his or her full potential and dictated standards-based testing to ensure accountability with the No Child Left Behind Act of 2001.

No Child Left Behind Increases Educators' Accountability for Student Performance

The No Child Left Behind (NCLB) Act of 2001 ties federal monies to student performance. Under NCLB, states, districts, and schools that demonstrate improved achievement will be rewarded. On the other hand, schools that continually fail to meet set performance levels are sanctioned. Parents and communities will know how well their children are performing on annual state reading and math assessments in grades 3–8, and schools are held accountable for their effectiveness. Read about specific provisions of NCLB at http://www.ed .gov/nclb/landing.jhtml

A standards-based curriculum combined with the No Child Left Behind

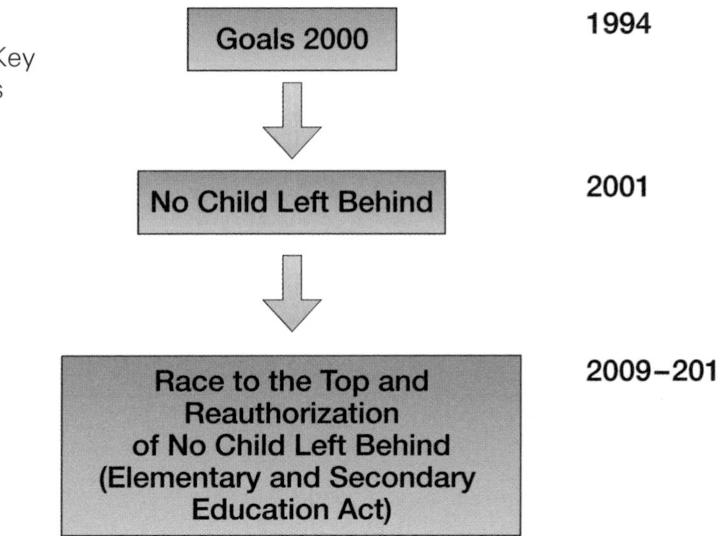

Figure 21.1 The Evolution of Key Federal Mandates

Basic Tenets of Goals 2000

1. All children in America will start school ready to learn.
2. The high school graduation rate will increase to at least 90%.
3. All students will leave grades 4, 8, and 12 having demonstrated competency over challenging subject matter, including English, mathematics, science, foreign languages, civics and government, economics, the arts, history, and geography; and every school in America will ensure that all students learn to use their minds well, so they may be prepared for responsible citizenship, further learning, and productive employment in our nation's modern economy.
4. U.S. students will be first in the world in mathematics and science achievement.
5. Every adult American will be literate and will possess the knowledge and skills necessary to compete in a global economy and exercise the rights and responsibilities of citizenship.
6. Every school in the United States will be free of drugs, violence, and the unauthorized presence of firearms and alcohol and will offer a disciplined environment conducive to learning.
7. The nation's teaching force will have access to programs for the continued improvement of their professional skills and the opportunity to acquire the knowledge and skills needed to instruct and prepare all American students for the next century.
8. Every school will promote partnerships that will increase parental involvement and participation in promoting the social, emotional, and academic growth of children.

(U.S. House of Representatives, 1994)

mandate can set uniformly high expectations for all students; provide educational equity; and make clear statements to parents, teachers, and students about what will be learned. In addition, this curriculum enables teachers and administrators to develop assessments directly related to the standards instead of relying solely on standardized achievement tests. You will

Four Pillars of NCLB

1. Stronger accountability for results
2. Flexibility for states and communities in how they use federal education funds
3. Determining and implementing research-driven educational methods and programs
4. More choices for parents

CONGRESS SAYS . . .

On January 8, 2002, President George W. Bush signed into law the No Child Left Behind Act, "an act to close the achievement gap with accountability, flexibility, and choice, so that no child is left behind. Be it enacted by the Senate and House of Representatives of the United States of America in Congress assembled."

THE PRESIDENT SPEAKS . . .

"[The Race to the Top] competition will not be based on politics, ideology, or the preferences of a particular interest group. Instead, it will be based on a simple principle—whether a state is ready to do what works. We will use the best data available to determine whether a state can meet a few key benchmarks for reform—and states that outperform the rest will be rewarded with a grant."

PRESIDENT BARACK OBAMA
July, 24, 2009

THE SECRETARY OF EDUCATION SPEAKS . . .

"All of these policy changes will support our effort to meet the President's goal that by 2020 America once again will lead the world in college completion. In particular, the ESEA [Elementary and Secondary Education Act] will set a goal that by 2020 all students will graduate ready to succeed in college and the workplace."

ARNE DUNCAN
U.S. Secretary of Education
March 17, 2010

read more about assessment and accountability under NCLB in Unit 7.

Schools and districts that don't meet their yearly improvement targets face intense scrutiny and potential repercussions. Often, school scores and district scores are published in the newspaper, and low scores or a lack of improvement can even lead to a principal's ouster or a takeover of the district by the state department of education. Schools also face the possibility of cutbacks in federal and state monies.

Race to the Top Offers States Competitive Grants

In a press release on November 12, 2009, President Barack Obama and U.S. Secretary of Education Arne Duncan announced that states will be eligible to compete for $4.35 billion in Race to the Top competitive grants, provided they are leading the way on school reform. The 2009 budget and the American Recovery and Reinvestment Act (ARRA) are the sources for the more than $10 billion in competitive grant money that will be available to states and districts. Within the Race to the Top, $350 million has also been set aside to help fund common assessments for states that adopt common international standards (U.S. Department of Education, 2009b).

Indicators of School Reform

Race to the Top requires that states and districts certify that they are implementing reform strategies in the following areas in order to be eligible for awards:

- Adopting internationally benchmarked standards and assessments that prepare students for success in college and the workplace
- Recruiting, developing, rewarding, and retaining effective teachers and principals
- Building data systems that measure student success and inform teachers and principals how they can improve their practices
- Turning around the lowest-performing 5% of schools, including high schools with low graduation rates, through one of four options:
  1. Closing a school and enrolling its students elsewhere
  2. Adopting a turnaround model that requires firing the principal and rehiring no more than half of the staff
  3. Reopening the school as a charter school or under new management
  4. Overhauling curricula, adding alternative pay systems, and introducing extended learning time (U.S. Department of Education, 2009b)

The Reauthorization of No Child Left Behind (Known as the Elementary and Secondary Education Act)

The reauthorization proposal seeks to overhaul the accountability system of No Child Left Behind: the primary recipients of federal resources will be schools that are struggling the most to improve student achievement. The proposal allows states and districts more leeway in determining how to intervene in schools that are performing well but may have trouble reaching students in particular subgroups, such as English language learners and students with special needs. The proposal would emphasize academic growth rather than compare groups of students with one another. However, it would retain NCLB's testing system and its requirement that states separate student-achievement data by racial and ethnic group and by other populations, such as students with special needs (U.S. Department of Education, 2010).

APPLY IT!

Find out where your district stands on Race to the Top. Has the district applied for an award? If so, how have the district and the state certified that they have met the four indicators of success? If the district has not applied or was not successful, find out why. What is the district's position on adopting national or common standards in language arts and math as required by a separate fund under the Race to the Top?

Long-Range Planning: The Year at a Glance

Before school begins, you will need to engage in long-term planning within these frameworks. During student teaching, your supervising teacher basically set the curriculum. Although you may have had some responsibility for designing units of study, an invisible structure was set up long before you arrived on the scene. Now it's your responsibility as a first-year teacher or intern.

Although it is impossible to plan down to the last detail until you have actually come face-to-face with your students, you can use the time before the beginning of the school year to sketch out a curriculum to ease some of the panic typically felt as opening day draws near.

Why do you need to plan ahead? In addition to alleviating butterflies, you need to plan because

STUDENT TEACHER TALKS . . .

While I want my future students to succeed on standardized tests, I want them to enjoy multifaceted, experience-based learning and not dread coming to school. As a beginning teacher, I want to be able to differentiate learning and reach them at their level while treating everyone equally.

ABBY UNGEFUG
Student at Montana State University
Credential Program
Lewistown, Montana

WATCH IT! video

Planning for Instruction

Two teachers plan a unit on civilization for secondary students. After viewing the video, write out the steps these teachers used in planning. Were any steps missing? How useful are graphic organizers in planning?

1. You will increasingly be required to meet the expectations of the major legislative mandates.
2. You don't want your students to miss out on necessary material on which they will be tested.
3. A well-thought-out curriculum, geared toward the needs, interests, and abilities of the students, will help you avoid many discipline problems.
4. Your district may have imposed a pacing schedule you are required to follow.
5. Planning will make you more confident and encourage you to learn new content and gather your resources and materials.

Become Familiar With Standards

There are multiple levels and sources of standards. Standards usually originate in professional organizations such as National Council for the Social Studies or National Council of Teachers of Mathematics. (Currently, there is a push from the U.S. Department of Education for states to adopt common standards in math and language arts.) Then the state education departments look at them and adapt or adopt them as their own. Finally, at the school district level, curriculum and instruction personnel further refine the standards so they can be allocated to grade levels and into courses.

The first step in long-range curriculum planning is to become familiar with the standards and expectations of your district for your grade level or subject matter. Collect all documents that are relevant, such as lists of state standards, benchmarks, pacing schedules, state frameworks, district standards, and teachers' manuals.

How do you get hold of these? The most practical way is to visit the school as soon as you receive your assignment and pick up all relevant materials. The website www.educationworld.com/standards/ enables you to access standards by state or by subject matter for all subjects and grade levels.

The more familiar you are with the upcoming curriculum, and especially the performance standards, the more comfortable and creative you can be in planning an overview of the year's instruction. After looking at this material, you may feel overwhelmed. How are you going to plan lessons in all curriculum areas, given 22½ hours or so of instructional time per week? This one question alone provides a substantial challenge to the first-year teacher (see Figure 21.2).

Planning Is a Continuum

Think of planning as a continuum from the general to the specific or from your state standards to the daily plans you follow every day in your classroom (see Figure 21.3).

1. Know the curriculum and standards.
2. Divide them among the months of the school year so everything gets covered.
3. Develop themes for each month from which weekly plans will be made.
4. Develop weekly plans.
5. Develop daily plans.

Standards From Professional Organizations and U.S. Department of Education

Examples: National Council for the Social Studies
International Reading Association
National Science Teachers Association
Association for the Advancement of Health Education
National Association for Sport and Physical Education

State adoption of national organization and federal standards

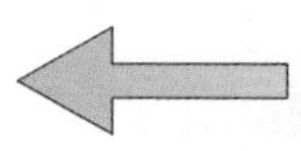

Textbook influence

District adoption of state standards

Figure 21.2
Working With Standards

STUDENT TEACHER TALKS . . .

My first-year worry is that I'll be given a classroom full of children and not know what to do. I know how to handle discipline problems, I know what to expect from parents, and whom to talk to in case of problems. What I don't know is what to teach! I have been observing, learning, and asking questions, but the one thing that I still don't know is what to teach. Where do teachers get their ideas for themes or units? Do they take them right out of the frameworks? Do they borrow from other teachers? How and when will I be given the golden key of knowledge? I am set for the first couple of weeks, but my biggest fear is that, after that, my lessons will be boring and not have a lot of substance because no one has ever taught me what to teach.

LAURA GRAHAM
Credential Candidate
Ontario, California

Figure 21.3
Nested Planning

State curriculum standards
Monthly
Weekly
Daily

Clothespins point to the day's standards.

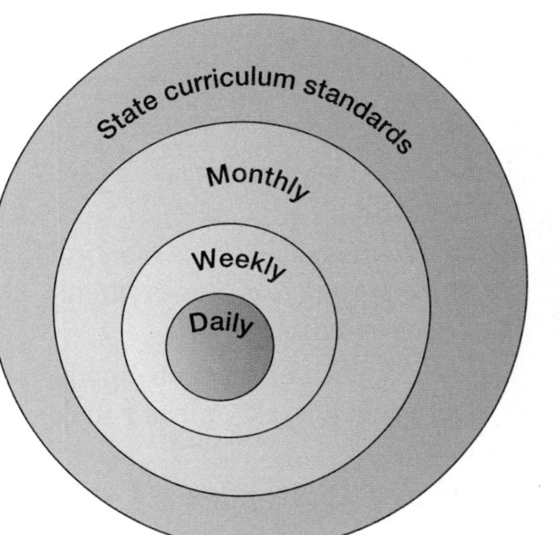

A math standards board helps everyone keep track.

Generally, you will find standards in all of the following curricular areas. The websites for all of these areas are listed in Chapter 38.

- English/language arts
- Mathematics
- Science
- Social science
- Physical development and health
- Fine arts
- Foreign languages

Managing Standards Can Be Complex

At the middle and high school level, standards can be managed more easily because teachers have only one or two subject areas; and within a discipline, such as math, the standards are similar even though the course name may be different. The real challenge is somehow dealing with the voluminous standards at the elementary level for each of the multiple subjects you teach. It has been suggested that it would take a 10-hour day to achieve all of the standards assigned to a grade level. In my local school district, the third-grade math standards break down as follows: 20 number sense standards; 9 algebra and functions standards; 12 measurement and geometry standards; 5 statistics, data analysis, and probability standards; and 14 mathematical reasoning standards. And math is just one of the multiple subjects an elementary teacher must address.

You may feel overwhelmed when you look at the curriculum materials and the standards documents in your new district. Some of them may not be clearly written in plain teacher talk. How will you manage all of them? If you are an elementary school teacher, many of the essential standards will be emphasized in your planning documents. These are the key standards that will be tested. You may be given a curriculum sequence to follow and/or a pacing guide to assist you. Also, turn to mentors, buddies, and support personnel to help you identify the critical standards.

In middle school, you will probably plan with others in your team because of block scheduling. The veterans on the team will be of great assistance to you as you plan a cohesive unit of study that addresses standards across the curriculum. At the high school level, your department colleagues may have already highlighted the essential standards.

APPLY IT!

If you are a middle or high school teacher, access the standards for one subject area and lay them out on the matrix as shown in Figure 21.4. If you are an elementary teacher, you will need to follow the suggestions for all your subjects but especially the ones that have benchmark assessments and, even more important, those that are tested at the state level.

STATISTICS

According to U.S. Secretary of Education Arne Duncan (2009c),

- 27% of America's young people drop out of high school. That means 1.2 million teenagers are leaving our schools for the streets.
- Recent international tests in math and science show that our students trail their peers in other countries. For 15-year-olds in math, the United States ranks 31st.
- 17-year-olds today are performing at exactly the same levels in math and reading as they were in the early 1970s on the NAEP test.
- Just 40% of young people earn a two- or four-year college degree.
- The United States now ranks 10th in the world in the rate of college completion for 25- to 34-year-olds.

Implementing a Standards-Based Curriculum

1. First, take a deep breath.
2. If you cover each standard in each curriculum area separately, you will go batty.
3. You will see that standards are generally arranged hierarchically.
4. There are some essential standards (generally the 1.0, 2.0), followed by many substandards under these items (e.g., 1.1, 1.2, 1.3).
5. Focus on the essential standards and you will see that the substandards add up to the larger one.
6. When your students are having trouble meeting the major standard heading, you need to look at the subheadings in your standards documents and pinpoint exactly where the problem lies.
7. Start with one curriculum area at a time (only a few for those lucky middle and high school teachers).
8. Lay out the standards in shortened form on a big piece of chart paper like the one in Figure 21.4. Use your own shorthand.
9. Then begin to look for any commonalties among the subject areas. For example, critical thinking standards such as "compares and contrasts" or "evaluates" may overlap in your curriculum.
10. Use a highlighter to accent those that you may be able to combine. Use a highlighter of another color to mark those that you find essential or that you have been told are essential because they appear on benchmark exams.

STATISTICS

Forty-eight states have formally agreed to join forces to create common academic standards in math and English/language arts. The two states not on board, as of this writing, are Alaska and Texas. Once the standards are agreed to, the states must then get them adopted. The common core must represent at least 85% of a state's standards, and the common core needs to be adopted within three years.

Figure 21.4

Example of Overlapping Standards in Two Curriculum Areas for Grade 6: Partial Listing

Language Arts Standards

2.0 Reading Comprehension (Focus on Informational Materials)

2.1 Identify the structural features of popular media (e.g., newspapers, magazines, online information) and use the features to obtain information.

2.2 Analyze text that uses the compare-and-contrast organizational pattern.

Comprehension and Analysis of Grade-Level-Appropriate Text

2.3 Connect and clarify main ideas by identifying their relationships to other sources and related topics.

2.4 Clarify an understanding of texts by creating outlines, logical notes, summaries, or reports.

3.0 **Literary Response and Analysis**

Students read and respond to historically or culturally significant works of literature that reflect and enhance their studies of history and social science. They clarify the ideas and connect them to other literary works. The selections in Recommended Literature, Kindergarten through Grade Twelve, illustrate the quality and complexity of the materials to be read by students.

Structural Features of Literature

3.1 Identify the forms of fiction and describe the major characteristics of each form.

Narrative Analysis of Grade-Level-Appropriate Text

3.2 Analyze the effect of the qualities of the character (e.g., courage or cowardice, ambition or laziness) on the plot and the resolution of the conflict.

3.3 Analyze the influence of setting on the problem and its resolution.

3.4 Define how tone or meaning is conveyed in poetry through word choice, figurative language, sentence structure, line length, punctuation, rhythm, repetition, and rhyme.

Social Studies Standards

6.4 Students analyze the geographic, political, economic, religious, and social structures of the early civilizations of ancient Greece.

1. Discuss the connections between geography and the development of city-states in the region of the Aegean Sea, including patterns of trade and commerce among Greek city-states and within the wider Mediterranean region.
2. Trace the transition from tyranny and oligarchy to early democratic forms of government and back to dictatorship in ancient Greece, including the significance of the invention of the idea of citizenship (e.g., from Pericles' *Funeral Oration*).
3. State the key differences between Athenian, or direct, democracy and representative democracy.
4. Explain the significance of Greek mythology to the everyday life of people in the region and how Greek literature continues to permeate our literature and language today, drawing from Greek mythology and epics, such as Homer's *Iliad* and *Odyssey,* and from Aesop's *Fables*.
5. Outline the founding, expansion, and political organization of the Persian Empire.
6. Compare and contrast life in Athens and Sparta, with emphasis on their roles in the Persian and Peloponnesian wars.

Look to Colleagues. The teachers in the grades below and above you have very similar standards, just at a lower or a higher level. Therefore, it would be very useful to look at the grade-level standards above and below your grade so you can see that key standards, topics, and skills are revisited throughout the grades. When you have done this, you will know how much you have to cover, and knowing the range is better than being caught up short at the end of the year or semester.

Look to Textbooks. The textbooks you are using identify the standards that are addressed. In some reading texts, standards are integrated, although there is no fully developed text that incorporates all of the standards in all of the curriculum areas for your grade level. That is up to you! Your resource teachers, principals, mentors, beginning teacher support team, curriculum coordinators, and new teacher in-service providers will help you navigate the sea of standards.

AVOID IT!

Do not be afraid to ask for assistance with the daunting task of long-range planning. Even the most experienced teachers are in uncharted waters because of standards-based instructional mandates. You can all work it out together. Help is available!

Map the Curriculum

The next step is to map out your year on a different piece of paper—this time, month by month (see Table 21.1). This will be a visual indication to you that you can fit it all in. You will need to pace your instruction according to your students' needs, interests, and abilities; but even a rough sketch of the entire year will be helpful, especially if you think about combining the essential standards into bigger units of instruction.

TEACHER TALKS . . .

If you try to teach every individual standard, you will go crazy. Instead, choose topics you are required to teach and review all your standards in light of that choice. You will begin to see opportunities to incorporate the essential standards from most curriculum areas into your unit of study. The little bits and pieces are really steps along the way to the big picture, so focus on the essential standards and the bits and pieces will fall into place.

JASON PAYTAS
Fourth-Grade Teacher
Arcata, California

Table 21.1 Partial Sixth-Grade Curriculum Map in Self-Contained Classroom, by Month

	Topics	Target Standards and Skills	Assessments	Activities/Resources/Technology
Sep.	Ancient civilizations—Egypt Reading for information Topography of Egypt Writing coherent essays	**Language Arts** Students write clear, coherent, and focused essays. The writing exhibits students' awareness of the audience and purpose. Essays contain formal introductions, supporting evidence, and conclusions. Students progress through the stages of the writing process as needed. **Social Studies** Students analyze the geographic, political, economic, religious, and social structures of Egypt. **Math—Pyramids** Students deepen their understanding of the measurement of plane and solid shapes and use this understanding to solve problems—creating a pyramid to scale. **Arts** Understanding the historical contributions and cultural dimensions of the visual arts. **Science** Topography is reshaped by the weathering of rock and soil and by the transportation and deposition of sediment. As a basis for understanding this concept: Nile River.	Writing rubric Group project on selected aspect of Egyptian culture Written tests on Egypt Map of Nile and explanation of importance to Egyptian life Building a pyramid to scale	Videos from *National Geographic* and PBS Word processing of reports on Egypt Print resources, including textbook Virtual tour of Egypt Hieroglyphic stamps Wall painting in Egyptian style Cooperative learning on Egyptian culture WebQuest
Oct.	Ancient civilizations—ancient Hebrews			
Nov.	Ancient civilizations—Greece			
Dec.				

Summary

Educational reform legislation and the resulting mandates have changed curriculum, instruction, and assessment in your state, district, school, and classroom. The major initiatives discussed in the chapter are the Goals 2000 Act, which promoted voluntary standards, skills, and certifications. Next came No Child Left Behind (2001), a reauthorization of the Elementary and Secondary Education Act (ESEA of 1965), which tied federal monies to stronger accountability and mandated that states adopt sets of standards and tests tied to them to show that they were effectively implemented. The latest reauthorization of NCLB-ESEA (2009) goes further by overhauling the accountability system and tying monies to school reform. As of this writing, 48 states have agreed to the development of a system of national standards, and national tests to measure student achievement will be designed. Failing schools will have a choice of transformation models, but the penalties range from total closure, to restaffing half of the school including the principal, to reopening as charter schools, to complete overhaul. Race to the Top is another initiative that has states and districts competing for grants based on their leadership in school reforms.

Reflect!

You are going to have to stay on top of the requirements because changes occur very quickly. Your principal and district curriculum coordinators will keep you informed. Colleagues will help you pace the curriculum, and your textbooks will usually have the standards indicated for each lesson. Now is the time to get ahead of the curve to ascertain what standards you are required to teach currently. The Education World website (http://www.educationworld.com/standards/state/toc/index.shtml) enables quick access to all the state standards by topic and grade level. You can access a state's main page from the pull-down menu or go directly to the standards for a particular subject. Go there now and check out the standards as they currently exist, and begin to get a handle on how you can integrate several standards at once.

CHAPTER 22

HOW DO I WRITE UNIT, WEEKLY, AND DAILY LESSON PLANS?

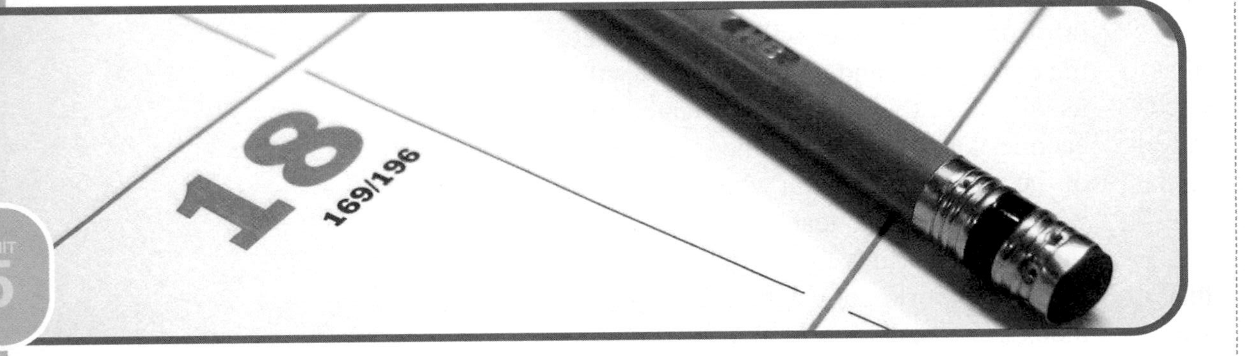

It pays to plan ahead.
It wasn't raining when Noah built the ark.

Anonymous

Effectiveness Essentials

- Plans are thinking maps that set an end point and steps along the way to reach the goal.
- There are at least two types of units: the teaching unit and the resource unit.
- The first-year teacher should approach curriculum integration slowly, with only one or two curriculum areas at first.
- District regulations and principal expectations vary when it comes to format and detail in lesson plans.
- Lesson plans should accommodate learning styles and the diverse needs of students in your classroom, including English language learners and students with special needs.

Your well-thought-out plans will be your security blanket during the first weeks of school and beyond. Careful planning does not mean that the resulting plans are indelible and rigid. They can and will change! But plan you must.

Plans will give you the confidence to step into your classroom as a well-prepared professional who is ready to make adjustments as you get to know your students. Your instruction will ultimately result from the dynamic interaction between your plans and the needs, interests, and readiness of your students. This chapter will enable you to translate your long-term plan into manageable unit, weekly, and daily lesson plans.

Unit Planning

Unit-based instruction is an option for those of you who wish to spend time thinking about curriculum delivery before the first day of school. Rather than following the manual for each separate subject area, unit-based instruction allows you to cluster some topics/standards into larger chunks of instruction (units) that enable you to cover multiple standards in several curriculum areas at the same time.

Although unit planning is time-consuming and challenging, it can save you countless hours of preparation later. You will have more fun, and your students will experience less curricular fragmentation. Even student teachers, as busy as they are, appreciate the rewards of unit-based instruction.

Once you have some idea of what you must teach, or the curriculum givens, sketch out a very brief beginning unit in social studies, science, literature, or whatever your area of instruction might be. Having one beginning unit roughly sketched out will enable you to start the year with confidence. For elementary school, consider a literature-based unit built around a favorite book you can secure in multiple copies from the book room or favorite student book club. If you teach a specific subject area in middle school or high school, map out your first introductory unit to the subject. Ultimately, this unit can ease the burden of that first week of school until your roster is set and you have all your teaching texts and materials.

There Are Two Types of Units

There are basically two types of units, the teaching unit and the resource unit. The teaching unit is much more specific than the resource unit is. As you read this section, think about

which type would best meet your needs and those of your students.

The teaching unit consists of a set of separate lesson plans that are all related to one topic and targeted to a specific group of students based on their needs, interests, and abilities. The teaching unit may include lesson plans in many or all curriculum areas. A unit on Mexico, for example, might include standards-based lesson plans for writing a letter to pen pals (language), designing bark paintings (art), learning a Mexican dance (physical education), counting in Spanish (math), and making tacos (math and cooking).

The resource unit is more general than the teaching unit is and can be adapted for any grade level. It is a compendium of ideas for teaching a particular topic through an integrated curriculum. The resource unit consists of a rationale, a content outline, a set of goals, brief descriptions of learning activities, an evaluation, and a bibliography. The activities span many curriculum areas, and you may need to expand lesson plans that are directed to a particular group of students in order to implement the unit.

Resource units challenge your creativity, and the out-of-the-box thinking required to implement them is so much fun. When you have a handle on the standards and skills that you must teach, the resource unit provides creative outlets for you and your students. Also, because they are not as specific as teaching units, resource units can be shared among colleagues who can adapt them easily to their own group of students.

There Are Steps to Designing a Resource or a Teaching Unit

The steps to designing a resource unit are easier to implement than you may think, especially as a novice teacher. If you follow this framework, you will experience the joy of seeing all of the disparate curriculum pieces elegantly melded into a whole unit.

Choose a topic based on the standards for your grade or subject area. Ask veteran teachers to share any subject or grade-appropriate units. Brainstorm with colleagues about topics and available resources. Excellent sources for units are the interests or cultural backgrounds of your students, provided they coincide with the standards. A mini-unit on cultures in your room might be an appropriate way for students to share and shine. A mini-unit on a literary work that has recently been made into a movie might hook students into English criticism.

Before you go any further with the topic you ultimately decide on, try it out on your audience to see what they already

CLASSROOM ARTIFACTS

First-Aid Resource Unit

Title: "Outline for an Integrated Academic Unit—Medical Innovations—First Aid"
Creator: Laura Civitano
Primary Subject: health/physical education
Secondary Subjects: social science, language arts, math
Grade Level: 9–12
Total Number of Sessions: third marking period—eight weeks
Time Estimate: 45 minutes per day

Goal/Purpose/Objectives of Sessions

Students will be able to:

- Recognize hazardous conditions in the home, school, workplace, and community.
- Develop and propose solutions to eliminate or reduce various hazards.
- Implement a plan to improve safety in the home, school, workplace, or community.
- Use universal precautions and apply first aid and other emergency procedures appropriately.
- Describe and demonstrate appropriate strategies to avoid or cope with potentially dangerous situations.
- Develop community approaches that enhance and protect the quality of the environment.
- Analyze how health laws, policies, and regulations protect personal and environmental safety.
- Demonstrate ways to care for and show respect for self and others.
- Evaluate personal and social skills that contribute to health and safety of self and others.
- Recognize how individual behavior affects the quality of the environment.
- Identify the collaborative role of team members among the systems that deliver quality health care.
- Use keyboarding skills to access, process, and retrieve information.
- Organize, write, and compile ideas into reports and summaries.
- Update their portfolios.
- Achieve first-aid certification—good for three years.

State Standards

Students will:

- Demonstrate personally and socially responsible behaviors. They will care for and respect themselves and others.

(continues)

CLASSROOM ARTIFACTS—*continued*

They will recognize threats to the environment and offer appropriate strategies to minimize them.

- Acquire the knowledge and ability necessary to create and maintain a safe and healthy environment.
- Understand and be able to manage their personal and community resources.

National Standards

Students will be able to:

- Demonstrate the ability to advocate for personal, family, and community health.
- Evaluate the effectiveness of communication methods for accurately expressing health information and ideas.
- Express information and opinions about health issues.
- Use strategies to overcome barriers when communicating information, ideas, feelings, and opinions about health issues.
- Demonstrate the ability to influence and support others in making positive health choices.
- Demonstrate the ability to work cooperatively when advocating for healthy communities.
- Demonstrate the ability to adapt health messages and communication techniques to the characteristics of a particular audience.

Products of Student Work

- Posters to be displayed within the school
- How-to skill sheets to be distributed within the school
- Portfolio development

Teacher Collaboration Suggestions

- Social studies teacher will introduce and offer a suggested list of historical medical innovations/innovators based on readings distributed by the medical teacher.
- English teacher will teach students how to write paragraphs and reports about medical innovations and/or innovators.
- Math teacher will use graphing and charts to compare accidents, injuries, diseases discussed in medical class.
- The library/media specialist will introduce research resources and skills.
- The inclusion teacher will assist English, social studies, math, and media teachers.

Prior Learning

- Previous first-aid skills (for students who have taken related courses)
- Oral communication skills
- Technology web searching
- Listening skills
- Note taking
- Writing processes
- Basic reading comprehension
- Summarizing

Lesson Activities

- Complete assigned readings ("The Beginnings of First Aid," etc.).
- Identify and describe modern first-aid kit materials.
- Create a first-aid kit from scratch.
- Learn and demonstrate various first-aid techniques.
- Compare old and new styles of bandaging and caring techniques.
- Create posters and packets for display and distribution within the school.
- Define important key terms and vocabulary.
- Discuss various career opportunities that use basic first-aid skills.
- Discuss health care trends.
- Complete other related activities:
  - Word search puzzle
  - Quizzes
  - Problem solving/scenario activities
  - Critical thinking activities

Classroom Materials

- Distributed worksheets
- Notebooks
- Pen/pencil

First-Aid Materials

- Adhesive strips
- Scissors
- Syrup of ipecac
- Flashlights
- One-way valve resuscitation mask (pocket mask)
- Antiseptic ointment
- Tweezers
- Activated charcoal
- Batteries
- Medical tape (waterproof/regular)
- Roller gauze
- Gauze pads
- Cold packs
- Disposable gloves
- Road flares
- Elastic bandages (Ace bandage)
- Mannequins
- Splints
- Heat packs
- Plastic bag
- Matches
- Triangular bandage (cravat)

Assessment

- Quizzes
- Class work
- Participation
- Demonstration

Homework

- Create a first-aid kit including the necessary materials discussed in class
- Write scenarios regarding emergency situations to be role-played by the students
- Actively promote the good habits of first-aid techniques in everyday life
- Promote the habit of noticing emergencies and assisting those in need
- Create "Check, Call, Care" posters to be displayed around school

(continues)

CLASSROOM ARTIFACTS—*continued*

- Create "how-to" posters—how to treat a small wound, perform the Heimlich maneuver, etc.

Classroom Management

- Continually acknowledge successful work, participation, and personal insight and reflection

Techniques for Differentiating Instruction

- Demonstration
- Readings
- Use of technology
- Video
- Worksheets

Resources

- Self-produced worksheets
- American Red Cross workbook/textbook: *First Aid: Responding to Emergencies* (2nd ed.)

(as seen on http://www.LessonPlansPage.com)

know, what they want to know, and what their level of interest in the topic is.

The next step is to find out about the topic if you are not already familiar enough with it to make your content outline. One of the major benefits of teaching is the opportunity to learn new things as you are conducting your unit research. Many gaps in my own education were filled in as I prepared for teaching. Search the Internet to amass information on your chosen topic.

Immerse yourself in the content by visiting libraries and checking out student-level books on the topic. In the interest of time, I found that if I went to texts and nonfiction accounts geared toward students, I would find

APPLY IT!

Sentence stems are effective tools for gathering information about prior knowledge. If the topic is the Civil War, you might write on the board, "When I think of The Civil War, . . ." or "What I want to know about Abraham Lincoln is. . . ." Similarly, you might put up two very large charts and have students brainstorm together. What do they already know, and what do they really want to learn about the topic? If you begin the unit by addressing students' initial questions, you will hook them in to study the rest (see Figure 22.1).

Figure 22.1
The Beginning of a KWL Chart (Ogle, 1986)

ABRAHAM LINCOLN AND THE CIVIL WAR

What I Know	What I Want to Know
• The Civil War was between the north and the south. • Slavery was an issue. • Lincoln was president. • Lincoln was shot. • He has a monument in Washington, D.C.	• Which were the northern and which were the southern states? • How many soldiers died? • What were the causes of the Civil War?

the material already predigested and written in a language that both they and I could readily understand.

Finally, sit down with a big piece of butcher paper and think of all the exciting ways you can carry through this unit. Make a web or map of your tentative ideas or simply write them all down and categorize them according to the curriculum areas that seem most dominant. If your topic derives from social studies or science, think back on all the ideas pertaining to language arts and art that might be germane. If your topic derives from literature, think of all the other curriculum areas, including language arts, that might pertain to the unit (see Figure 22.2).

Adapting the Unit Helps It Become More Focused

Only when the resource unit is adapted to a particular group of students through specific and complete lesson plans does it become more focused. If you are working with English language learners who are literate in their primary language, use some of the sheltered English techniques (see Chapter 29) when planning your unit activities. These strategies include good teaching techniques such as hands-on

Figure 22.2

Sample Concept Web for a Unit on America's Symbols

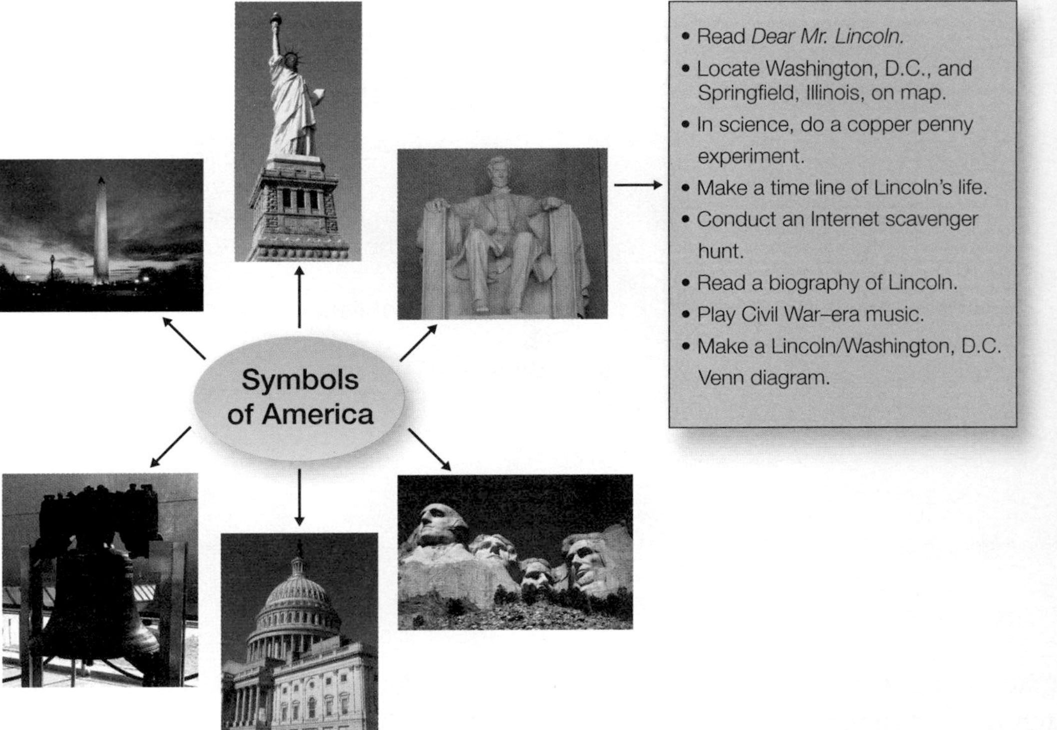

activities, use of visuals, cooperative learning, and similar projects. Students with special needs, including the gifted, should have differentiated assignments and activities built into the unit.

Symbols of America
• Read *Dear Mr. Lincoln.*
• Locate Washington, D.C., and Springfield, Illinois, on map.
• In science, do a copper penny experiment.
• Make a time line of Lincoln's life.
• Conduct an Internet scavenger hunt.
• Read a biography of Lincoln.
• Play Civil War–era music.
• Make a Lincoln/Washington, D.C. Venn diagram.

Integrate Curriculum Within Units

After you have brainstormed the activities to carry through the unit, go back to the list of standards you outlined for the year (see Chapter 21). You will notice that many of them fit right in. Let's say you are designing a self-concept unit. Your students need to write, so why not have them write autobiographies? In social studies, you are expected, according to the year-at-a-glance, to teach about time lines and to construct one, so why not begin the process with personal time lines? Although this is a case of the tail wagging the dog, you will not be the first or the last teacher to design your unit plans this way. Always keep in mind that students learn best when the material is meaningful to them.

The first-year elementary teacher should approach curriculum integration slowly, with only one or two curriculum areas at first. As a beginner who is unfamiliar with the curriculum for the grade level, you can try to integrate where possible and move at your own pace toward making other curriculum connections. For example, you can start by incorporating language arts, art, and music into a social studies unit on the American Revolution by having the students make era flags, sing popular revolutionary songs, and enact the Boston Tea Party. But there are some skills and concepts that defy integration, and you will feel more comfortable easing into integrated teaching slowly.

A single-subject teacher can integrate art, music, drama, math, and writing into the already-set curriculum in history, science, or math without having to worry about absolute coverage of the integrated subject standards.

A beginning teacher at any level would not be expected to teach the curriculum in an integrated fashion during the school year or semester. In fact, it is just as much of a burden to force integration of curriculum as it is to teach each curriculum area separately.

APPLY IT!

At this point, you may want to sketch out a unit that would be appropriate for a grade level or subject you may be teaching (see Figure 22.3).

Weekly Plans

It is easier to plan for the short haul when the entire structure, both content and organization, is laid out, even though this process is time-consuming. In the end, however, time spent planning for the big picture will save you countless hours on Sunday night when you sit down with a blank weekly plan book and have to fill in all those little boxes.

Plan Within School and District Parameters

When you sit down to write your weekly schedule, you want to have as much information about the parameters of your scheduling decisions as you can. School organization, the master school schedule, and curriculum time

STUDENT SAYS . . .

The most important advice I could give a new teacher would have to be to connect with the students. I know from experience that if a teacher doesn't connect with students, they will not pay attention and learn the lesson. If a teacher knows how to present material, it will stick with students for tests and for long-term use down the road. Stories will make information easier to remember for tests.

JEREMY O'NEILL
Twelfth Grader, Age 18
Klamath Falls, Oregon

Figure 22.3
Unit Planning Worksheet

Topic: Insects | **Grade:** 3 | **Subject:** Science

STANDARDS: Life Sciences, Grade 3
Adaptations in physical structure or behavior may improve an organism's chance for survival. As a basis for understanding this concept, students already know the following:

a. Plants and animals have structures that serve different functions in growth, survival, and reproduction.

b. There are diverse life forms in different environments, such as oceans, deserts, tundra, forests, grasslands, and wetlands.

c. Living things cause changes in the environment in which we live. Some of these changes are detrimental to the organism or other organisms, and some are beneficial.

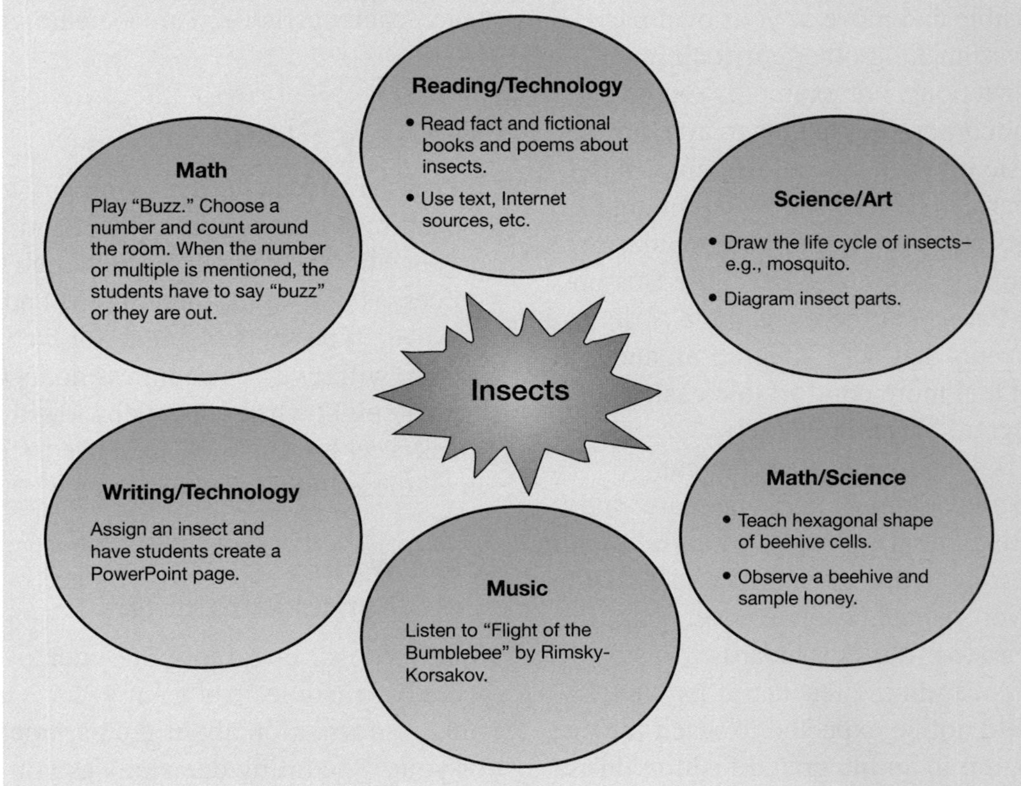
Insects
Reading/Technology
• Read fact and fictional books and poems about insects.
• Use text, Internet sources, etc.
Math
Play "Buzz." Choose a number and count around the room. When the number or multiple is mentioned, the students have to say "buzz" or they are out.
Science/Art
• Draw the life cycle of insects–e.g., mosquito.
• Diagram insect parts.
Writing/Technology
Assign an insect and have students create a PowerPoint page.
Math/Science
• Teach hexagonal shape of beehive cells.
• Observe a beehive and sample honey.
Music
Listen to "Flight of the Bumblebee" by Rimsky-Korsakov.

allotments and order will all influence the decisions you make about how your week will look. It's better to know at the beginning what the limitations will be to avoid constant changes in your schedule from unforeseen events.

But there will be unanticipated events nevertheless, and you need to be flexible and aware of what other teachers may be planning so you can coordinate. For example, you may come to school one day armed with a full day of plans, only to discover that a colleague has arranged for the fire department to bring its fire engine and adorable Dalmatian, Spot, to the playground to talk about fire safety. Or, in middle school, a special assembly may be called when the mayor makes an unscheduled appearance. In high school, the pep rally for that week's game may disrupt all of your plans if you have a last-period class. Or you may have shortened periods that day to equalize the lost time.

Obtain a copy of your district's calendar and schedule, and transfer it to your own master calendar or personal organizer. Include holidays, open houses, parent conferences, testing dates, inservice days, and special school- and district-wide events that will affect you and your class. Pencil in the big sports events, homecoming, etc., so you can anticipate a heightened level of excitement. Then, when you write up your weekly schedule, you can see if there are days or time slots in which you will have to adjust your instructional planning. Use sticky notes on your plans or in your plan book to indicate which lessons were shortened or abandoned altogether and need to be readdressed.

Holidays, or lack thereof for long periods of time, present another scheduling challenge. When a break is coming up, your students will need something extra-special to keep their attention on class work and away from holiday plans. Conversely, during the long periods between vacations, you will need to perk up weary students and energize yourself to keep them motivated.

A Master Schedule. On a master weekly schedule, write down the school schedule for a typical week. Include the times for lunch, preparation periods, assemblies, library, computer lab, and so forth. Then make a list of activities that will pull out some of your students, such as speech, band, lunch monitors, resource teacher, or the counselor. You don't want to schedule major new content lessons during these times if doing so can be avoided. Fill in these weekly givens on a schedule. Then you can duplicate these masters with key, immutable times already filled in. The

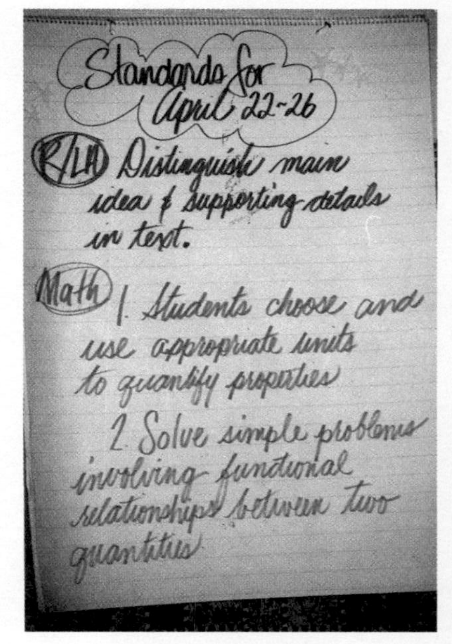

This weekly plan includes subject-matter standards.

VICE PRINCIPAL TALKS . . .

When I do my daily walk-throughs of classrooms, the first thing I look for is the lesson plan book. A lesson plan is like a blueprint for a great masterpiece. I want to see the groundwork. Teachers put a lot of time and effort into creating lesson plans; I absolutely want to see them!

DION CLARK
Vice Principal
San Bernardino, California

blank spaces are yours! You may feel as though the entire week is taken up with special functions, but so it is in a comprehensive elementary or secondary school where extracurricular activities, monitorial duties, and pullout programs round out the educational experience.

It is not unusual for states and/or districts to mandate the number of minutes for each school subject in elementary grades. You need to find out as soon as you can the time allotments for each subject area and if there is any prescribed order to the day.

Planning Oversight. District regulations and principal expectations vary when it comes to how much detail you are expected to include in your plans. Some principals collect the plans every week and look through each and every square. Others ask only that the plans be available in a prominent place on your desk. Principals and mentors will provide you with invaluable feedback about your planning. They may ask you to shorten or lengthen your plans and/or suggest alternative activities and resources you might consider.

It is important to ascertain the principal's planning expectations as soon as you find yourself with a teaching job. You want to get off on the right foot by providing your site administrator with the degree of specificity she or he expects to see in your plan book. If you have done your month-at-a-glance exercise, then it should not be too difficult to divide by four and make up your weekly plans. Use a plan book or word processing template with routine lessons already typed in. Keep your plans in a loose-leaf notebook so you can rearrange them as needed and add supporting materials easily.

Plan for Higher Levels of Thinking

Make sure you are considering various levels of thinking as you plan, ask questions during lessons, and design assignments. Bloom's taxonomy (Bloom, Mesia, & Krathwohl, 1964) is a very well established guide.

APPLY IT!

Select one of the lesson plans you have written in one of your classes and write at least two questions at each level of Bloom's taxonomy (see Table 22.1). Although you may not have the levels exactly right, that doesn't matter as long as your questions are varied, involve different thought processes, and require responses beyond yes, no, or simple recall.

Table 22.1 Bloom's Taxonomy

Level	Thinking Skill	Example	Outcome Verbs
Knowledge	Factual or recall level	Name the Great Lakes.	define, describe, identify, label, list, match, name, read, record, reproduce, select, state
Comprehension	Understanding	Explain the water cycle in your own words. Summarize the story we just read. Describe the political cartoon.	cite, classify, convert, describe, discuss, estimate, explain, generalize, give examples, make sense of, paraphrase, restate (in own words), summarize, trace, understand
Application	Transfer of information to a new situation	How would the story change if it happened here? Try out some new problems with this formula.	administer, articulate, assess, chart, collect, compute, construct, determine, develop, discover, extend, implement, include, predict, prepare, produce, project, provide, relate, report, show, solve, transfer, use
Analysis	Classification, compare/contrast	How is *Romeo and Juliet* like *West Side Story*? Put these rock specimens into groups that have common characteristics, and name the groups.	correlate, diagram, differentiate, discriminate, distinguish, focus, illustrate, infer, limit, outline, point out, prioritize, recognize, separate, subdivide
Synthesis	Creative or original response	Draw a portrait in the style of Picasso. Write a new ending for the story.	adapt, anticipate, categorize, collaborate, combine, communicate, compare, compile, contrast, formulate, integrate, model, modify, rearrange, reconstruct, reorganize, revise
Evaluation	Judgment based on criteria	Was Goldilocks justified in entering the bears' house and eating porridge, breaking their chair, and sleeping in the bed? Why or why not?	appraise, compare and contrast, conclude, critique, decide, defend, interpret, judge, justify, reframe, support

Source: Bloom et al. (1964).

Plan for Diversity

As your planning becomes more specific, make sure that you are meeting the diverse needs of students in your classroom. Davidman and Davidman (2001) demonstrate how most lessons, activities, and units can be transformed to reflect the diversity in your classroom. At the point at which you are translating your long-term and

CHAPTER 22

NOTES

midrange planning into actual classroom instruction, you need to think about how you will differentiate instruction. Consult Chapter 28 in Unit 6 if differentiated instruction is an unfamiliar term.

Accommodate Diverse Learning Styles

Keep in mind that students generally learn best from hands-on, concrete experiences and that Gardner's (1993) theory of multiple intelligences implies accommodations to the learning styles of your pupils. Gardner originally identified seven intelligences that can operate independently of one another. In 1999, Gardner added an eighth intelligence: naturalistic. The implications for teaching may be that,

AVOID IT!

A temptation you should resist when writing your weekly plan is to teach the entire year's curriculum in a week or a day. Instead, plan incrementally—that is, in bite-sized, easily digestible pieces.

Table 22.2 Gardner's Multiple Intelligences

Intelligence	Strength	Examples
Linguistic	Sensitive to word meanings and order, verbal	Writers, playwrights
Logical-mathematical	Thinks abstractly, logical	Mathematicians
Spatial	Thinks in pictures, images, and metaphors	Architects, artists
Musical	Learns through musical patterns	Composers, dancers
Kinesthetic	Uses body and movement in learning	Athletes, dancers
Interpersonal	Understands others	Politicians, therapists
Intrapersonal	Operates in sync with emotions	Poets, novelists
Naturalistic	Uses the natural environment to learn	Environmentalists

Source: Gardner (1993).

WATCH IT! video

Multiple Intelligence Learning Centers

In this video a team of teachers gets together to design multiple intelligence learning centers. For each of the centers, name the center and then the activity and its materials. For secondary students, choose a topic you plan to teach and create an activity and materials chart for each of the multiple intelligences. How does the implementation of the multiple intelligences theory improve comprehension for English learners? Do you think it is easier to work in a team to design the centers, or would it be best to design all of the centers on your own? Explain your reasoning.

because your students can be intelligent in many modes, instruction might be modified to develop and nurture individualistic, natural proclivities. You will have a more in-depth discussion of the intelligences in Chapter 28.

Daily Plans and Lesson Plans

A lesson plan is a kind of thinking map that sets an end point and designates steps along the way to reach the goal. It is for you more than for the students because you want to help them get from here to there in an efficient way while enjoying the activities along the route. If you were traveling across the country by car to a friend's wedding but didn't have a map, you might have quite an adventure wandering hither and yon. On the other hand, you might miss all the great sights along the way and the wedding as well!

A Lesson Plan Has Three Essential Elements

Once you get the hang of writing lesson plans, you will notice they consist of three essential elements: objectives that derive from standards, procedures, and evaluation.

1. Objectives that derive from standards: "Where do I want to go?"
2. Procedures (including materials): "How will I get there?"
3. Evaluation: "How will I know when I arrive?"

CLASSROOM ARTIFACTS

Multiple Intelligences Activities and Instructional Strategies

Abby Volmer, a literacy coach at Odessa Middle School in Missouri, shares activities in a unit plan that accommodates multiple intelligences.

Unit plan: Accommodating multiple intelligences
Title: "Capitalization of Direct Quotes"

Verbal/Linguistic

Instruction "Circle the Sage": Have six people who know the rules for capitalizing direct quotes stand at different points of the room. Teams split and gather around sages to hear info. They go back to teams and share and compare. (Interpersonal)

Activity Write a dialogue between two fictional characters. (Be sure to use before, after, and interrupting quotes.) Highlight the capitals in direct quotes. (Intrapersonal)

Logical/Mathematical

Instruction After "Circle the Sage," students look at sheets and decide on rules for capitalizing direct quotes. (Interpersonal)

Activity Read a dialogue page and highlight the capitals in the direct quotes. Graph how many times the direct quote was used and capitalized either before, after, or interrupting the quote.

Visual/Spatial

Instruction Cut and paste direct quotes in three categories (before, after, and interrupting).

Activity Create a cartoon strip that uses capitals in direct quotes. (Be sure to include before, after, and interrupting quotes.)

Musical/Rhythmic

Instruction Play background music during "Circle the Sage."

Activity Create rules sung to the tune of "Twinkle, Twinkle, Little Star."

Bodily/Kinesthetic

Instruction When a word is spoken, students stand each time they are to capitalize. (Whole group)

Activity Create either a dance or an exercise (movement) routine that would go with the direct quotes.

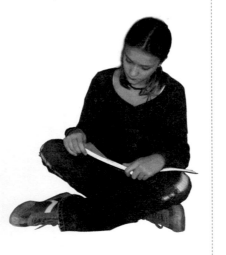

Naturalist

Activity Create a conversation that might occur between a predator animal and a prey animal. Somehow represent the animals with pictures, posters, puppets, etc. (Intrapersonal)

Interpersonal

Activity Same as verbal/linguistic, but have two people carry on a conversation on paper using capitals in direct quotes.

(as seen on http://www.LessonPlansPage.com)

APPLY IT!

Select a project that you are planning to assign to students. Let's say the topic is Westward Expansion. Think of alternative ways students can meet the requirement using Gardner's multiple intelligences. For example, if a subtopic is the life of a cowboy, students can write an essay, make a display of cowboy tools, play and analyze cowboy songs, write a play that exposes the feelings of cowboys, make maps of the major cattle routes, make a graph that depicts the rise and fall of cowboys in the west, write a diary of ranch life, write a poem, etc. This allows students to capitalize on their strengths and also to see the variety of responses that others come up with.

Topic ____________________

Assignment Choices

1. Linguistic
2. Logical-mathematical
3. Spatial
4. Musical
5. Kinesthetic
6. Interpersonal
7. Intrapersonal
8. Naturalistic

Districts and Schools Have Expectations

How detailed your daily lesson plans need to be depends on your department/school and/or district requirements. Certain lessons require more detailed planning than do others. Those that need extra planning include art, science experiments, social studies simulations, new physical education (P.E.) games and skills, and any other lessons that introduce a skill or concept unfamiliar to your students. Many a lesson has self-destructed because the procedures weren't clear in the teacher's mind, the teacher hadn't thought through the organizational pattern, or the teacher hadn't anticipated all the materials that would be needed. Write individual lesson plans on forms you are familiar with from your student teaching days or use the generic lesson plan form in Figure 22.4.

Lesson plans will allay your anxiety as well as provide a substantive instructional guide to a substitute or an administrator who takes over your class in an emergency. The lesson plans help the substitute get on the same page as you, and you don't lose as much time as a result of your own absence as you might if you didn't have the plans carefully written out. Use your weekly plan book to sketch in those lessons that are review or routine, such as spelling tests or math drill, or are clearly outlined in the various manuals. But make sure to indicate on your daily plans those lessons that clearly necessitate a more detailed instructional map for you to follow.

mythBUSTER

Principals never look at plan books.

I have asked my staff to put a plan book in front of me as soon as practicable when they see me come into the classroom in "observation mode," which in my case means "computer in hand." (Tenured teachers get two observations a year, and non-tenured teachers get four.) Then I can see what was planned for the lesson and (I hope) understand better what was intended and the depth of thought that went into it. I also ask for the first week's plan by the Friday before school starts and for a half-year lesson sequence (major topics) at the beginning of the year and again in January. The hope is that teachers will look toward the big picture—the essential questions—of their subject and how they can be answered during the course of the year.

Dr. Virginia S. Newlin
Principal, National Board-Certified Teacher
Rock Hall, Maryland

CLASSROOM ARTIFACTS

This week-long, standards-based lesson plan integrates social studies and technology into a familiar lesson plan format. Note the grading rubric and the adaptations for students with learning disabilities and the gifted. Also note the template that students will use to organize their information.

Title: "Tourist Advertisement for a Texas City"
Creator: Carla McLain
Primary Subject: social studies
Secondary Subjects: computers/Internet
Grade Level: 4
Estimated Time: One week
Concept/Topic: Students will create an advertisement for a city in Texas using Photo Story 3.
Texas Standards Addressed:

Social Studies

4.22 **Social Studies Skills.** The student applies critical-thinking skills to organize and use information acquired from a variety of sources including electronic technology. The student is expected to:

(A) differentiate between, locate, and use primary and secondary sources such as computer software; interviews; biographies; oral, print, and visual material; and artifacts to acquire information about the United States and Texas;

(B) analyze information by sequencing, categorizing, identifying cause-and-effect relationships, comparing, contrasting, finding the main idea, summarizing, making generalizations and predictions, and drawing inferences and conclusions;

(C) organize and interpret information in outlines, reports, databases, and visuals including graphs, charts, time lines, and maps;

(D) identify different points of view about an issue or topic.

4.23 **Social Studies Skills.** The student communicates in written, oral, and visual forms. The student is expected to:

(C) express ideas orally based on research and experiences;

(D) create written and visual material such as journal entries, reports, graphic organizers, outlines, and bibliographies.

(continues)

CLASSROOM ARTIFACTS—*continued*

Technology

5. **Information Acquisition.** The student acquires electronic information in a variety of formats, with appropriate supervision. The student is expected to:
   (A) acquire information including text, audio, video, and graphics.
6. **Information Acquisition.** The student evaluates the acquired electronic information. The student is expected to:
   (C) determine the usefulness and appropriateness of digital information.
7. **Solving Problems.** The student uses appropriate computer-based productivity tools to create and modify solutions to problems. The student is expected to:
   (B) use appropriate software to express ideas and solve problems including the use of word processing, graphics, databases, spreadsheets, simulations, and multimedia;
   (C) use a variety of data types including text, graphics, digital audio, and video.
11. **Communications.** The student delivers the product electronically in a variety of media, with appropriate supervision. The student is expected to:
   (A) publish information in a variety of media including, but not limited to, printed copy, monitor display, Internet documents, and video; and
   (B) use presentation software to communicate with specific audiences.

General Goal: Students will research a city in Texas and prepare an advertisement persuading tourists to spend their vacation in their city.

Specific Objectives

The students will gather information and photos about their city using the Internet, and cite resources.

The students will write an advertisement persuading tourists to visit their city.

The students will create the advertisement using Photo Story 3.

Required Materials

- Internet access
- Internet websites
  - Travel Texas website: http://www.traveltex.com/
  - Individual websites for city

- Photo Story 3 software downloaded on computer
- Photo Story 3 tutorial: http://millie.furman.edu/mll/tutorials/photostory3/index.htm
- Computer microphone
- Storyboard template
- Index cards
- Planning sheet
- Grading rubric

Anticipatory Set (Lead in)

1. Discuss how the tourist industry plays an important part in the success of a city.
2. Show an example of an advertisement in Photo Story 3.
3. Provide students with online tutorials for Photo Story 3.
4. Discuss copyright and citing resources for photos and music with students.

Step-by-Step Procedures

1. Allow students to choose the city in Texas they want to research for the advertisement.
2. Students will research their city and record information on a planning sheet.
3. Students will plan the advertisement by recording information for each frame on an index card.
4. Students will create the advertisement in Photo Story 3 using still photos and recording their information.
5. Students will share their advertisement with the class.

Independent Practice

1. Students will research information for their city.
2. Students will record information and gather photos for their city.
3. Students will create their advertisement in Photo Story 3.
4. Students will share their advertisement with the class.

Closure

1. The class will watch each other's advertisements.
2. Class members will ask each other questions about his or her city and vote if they want to visit the city.

Assessment Based on Objectives: Use the following grading rubric.

(continues)

CLASSROOM ARTIFACTS—*continued*

Total Points: ______ /15 Points

	5 Points	3 Points	1 Point	0 Points
Information	Information was effective in persuading tourists to visit, and sources were cited.	Information was somewhat effective in persuading tourists to visit, and sources were cited.	Information was not effective in persuading tourists to visit, and sources were cited.	Information sources were not cited.
Photos	Photos were effective in persuading tourists to visit, and sources were cited.	Photos were somewhat effective in persuading tourists to visit, and sources were cited.	Photos were not effective in persuading tourists to visit, and sources were cited.	Photo sources were not cited.
Advertisement	Ad as a whole was effective in persuading tourists to visit.	Ad as a whole was somewhat effective in persuading tourists to visit.	Ad as a whole was not effective in persuading tourists to visit.	Advertisement was incomplete.

Adaptations—Learning Disabilities:
Adaptations for students with learning disabilities will be based on Individual Education Plan (IEP).

Extensions—Gifted Students:

- Gifted students can scan pictures to use in their advertisement.
- Gifted students can add music to their advertisement.

Possible Connections to Other Subjects:
Language arts—students will demonstrate the use of grammar, spelling, sentence structure, and punctuation on index cards.

Planning sheet: each topic is one slide.

(as seen on http://LessonPlansPage.com)

Introductory Slide Introduce your city. (Why do tourists want to visit?)	
Map Tell where your city is located in Texas.	
History of City Brlefly tell the history of your city.	
Places of Interest 2–4 tourist sites (no more, no less) Talk about places to visit.	
Climate What is the weather like?	
Restaurants 2–4 restaurants (include addresses and phone numbers)	
Accommodations 2–4 motel/hotels (include addresses and phone numbers)	
Closing Slide Persuade tourists to visit. How about a catchy slogan for the city?	

Storyboard template: Cut out the template and paste on an index card. Complete the information on the index card to create your storyboard.

Frame Number ________ **Topic** ____________________

Narration/Script

Photo(s)

CHAPTER 22

Figure 22.4
Generic Lesson Plan Format

Teacher ____________ Subject ____________ Time requirements ______

Grade level ______ Period ______ Date ____________

Content standards	(List the standards that are being addressed in the lesson plan.)
Prerequisites	(This is the prior knowledge requisite for success.)
Instructional objectives	(These are derived from the standards and tempered by the students' prior knowledge.)
Adaptations	(These are accommodations for English language learners and students with special needs, including the gifted.)
Materials	(All specialized equipment and materials are listed here.)
Motivation	(This is a description of how you will engage the students.)
Procedures	(List the steps in the lesson.)
Assessment/evaluation	(This describes how you will determine the extent to which students have attained the instructional objectives.)
Follow-up activities	(These are indications of how to reinforce and extend this lesson, including homework, assignments, and projects.)
Reflection	(What went well, what adaptations should you make next time, and what needs to be retaught as a result of the assessment?)

There Are Several Available Formats for Lesson Plans

You may want to use the 5E lesson plan (Biological Sciences Curriculum Study, 1997) for discovery lessons. The steps include

Phase	Teacher Role
1. Engage	Motivates or captures the students' interest.
2. Explore	Enables the students to engage in a hands-on experience or experiment.
3. Explain	Introduces formal concepts and vocabulary.
4. Elaborate	Goes into greater detail using the concept in different contexts.
5. Evaluate	Assesses students' learning.

Or you might prefer the popular seven-step lesson plan developed by Madeline Hunter (R. Hunter, 2004), which prescribes the following stages:

Phase	Teacher Role
Anticipatory set	Motivates, focuses attention of students
Statement of objectives	Tells students what they will accomplish
Instructional input	Explains, lectures, demonstrates, gives instructions
Modeling	Demonstrates, shows
Check for understanding	Watches faces, asks questions, asks for summary
Guided practice	Guides and corrects students as they practice
Independent practice	Monitors students as they work on their own

Organize Your Lesson Plans

Duplicate whatever forms you plan to use, or mix and match forms as appropriate, with the key headings you need already in place. Then it is just a matter of filling in the blanks. Keep the plans in a loose-leaf folder.

Write your plans in pencil because they will change! Develop a code for identifying what was adequately covered, what needs to be retaught, and what never got taught because of interruptions or a special assembly. You also might want to identify those activities that didn't work,

CLASSROOM ARTIFACTS

Elizabeth Hodgson, a K–5 science teacher, and Rachel Vogelpohl Meyen, a fourth-grade teacher, both from Durham, North Carolina, share an example of a lesson plan that accommodates learners through multiple intelligences. This plan also demonstrates integration of social studies, language arts, and technology standards and team planning. The codes are mine and illustrate how you can mark your plans or code your plan book to remind you of where you stand vis-à-vis your plans. Notice that the standards are the same as the objectives.

Ran out of time ← *They liked this activity* ♥ *Need to return to this* ●

Topic: North Carolina
Curriculum areas: social studies, language arts, computers/Internet
Grade Level: 4
Standards/Objectives:

Social Studies

2.03 Describe the similarities and differences among people of North Carolina, past and present.

3.02 Identify people, symbols, events, and documents associated with North Carolina's history.

5.02 Describe traditional art, music, and craft forms in North Carolina.

English/Language Arts

4.02 Use oral and written language to present information and ideas in a clear, concise manner; discuss; interview; solve problems; and make decisions.

4.07 Compose fiction, nonfiction, poetry, and drama using self-selected and assigned topics and forms (e.g., personal and imaginative narratives, research reports, diaries, journals, logs, rules, instructions).

5.07 Use established criteria to edit for language conventions and format.

Technology

3.01 Create, format, save, and print a word-processed document.

Materials:

- Pencil
- Paper
- Computer with Microsoft Word software

- Tape recorder
- Blank tapes

Activities:

Diary entry writing continued

Students should finish creating their diary entries. They will continue to use their chosen medium from the day before. ♥

Publishing diary entries

Upon the completion of their writing, students should edit, save, print (rewrite or retell) their entries, depending on their chosen medium. The students should complete their entries by the time the presentations are scheduled to begin, though presentations should continue, with all students presenting their material, even if they have not fully completed their editing process.

Diary entry presentation ←

Group children (approximately eight to a group) so that one member of each WebQuest group is in each of the new, larger groups. Each student will read or play his/her diary entry for the group. At the end, each group will vote on one entry to be shared with the entire class.

Present the chosen entries to the class, and allow the students to ask and answer questions and comment.

KWL chart ○

Move the students' attention back to the original KWL chart. Add information to the "learned" column, and then begin a discussion and analysis of the misconception the students may have originally had about North Carolina's history of slavery and the Underground Railroad.

Multiple Intelligences:

- Verbal/linguistic (reading, discussing students' diary entries, presenting those entries to class)
- Intrapersonal (creation of own diary entry)
- Interpersonal (communicating/sharing entries in groups)

Note: Activity also appeals to auditory (listening to and discussing diary presentations) learners.

Assessment:

Assessment of students' diary entry, using the *diary-writing rubric*.

Affective assessment of *students' reflections* on the unit content, the teaching strategies employed, and their general interest levels will also be completed at this point.

(as seen on http://www.LessonPlansPage.com)

AVOID IT!

Teachers generally feel overwhelmed by writing so many plans, especially for an elementary class. Don't think of the time it takes. Think about the time it saves down the road for the current and upcoming years! You may choose to share your plans, use them again, or post them on one of the lesson plan websites cited at the end of this unit. If you are assigned the same grade level or the same subjects to teach in middle school or high school, you will have plans in your binder ready for some tweaking, but you won't have to start from scratch. Your subsequent years will be easier because you have committed your plans to paper and have kept them. Also, think about what would happen if you don't take the time! Winging it is for the birds!

The most common planning mistakes to avoid are

- Lesson objectives that do not specify a measurable or observable student outcome
- Assessments that are not linked or do not measure the specific behavior indicated in the objective
- Not collecting enough information about student readiness
- Activities that are not directly related to helping the students achieve the desired goal or objective
- Too much busywork and/or very time-consuming projects that lack substance

---

those that were great fun, and those that needed more time. Use symbols or differently colored checkmarks as you review the previous week's plan before you begin the following one. Sticky notes or flags are also very popular with teachers. Affix them to your plan book to help you remember what needs review, what needs total reteaching, what didn't get taught, and so forth. If you create a system that works for you, you will save yourself a great deal of time trying to remember whether you taught an activity and how well it went.

The software program *Inspiration* has some excellent planning forms that will enable you to just fill in the blanks and print them out. Many schools use this software, and it is popular with students of all ages, even the young

Figure 22.5
Lesson Plan Template

Benefits of using the Lesson Plan template

Keeping lesson plans in this way allows for consistency and easy transfer of assignments into the Makeup Work and Substitute Lesson templates. It is also a way for administrators to check and assimilate plans "at a glance."

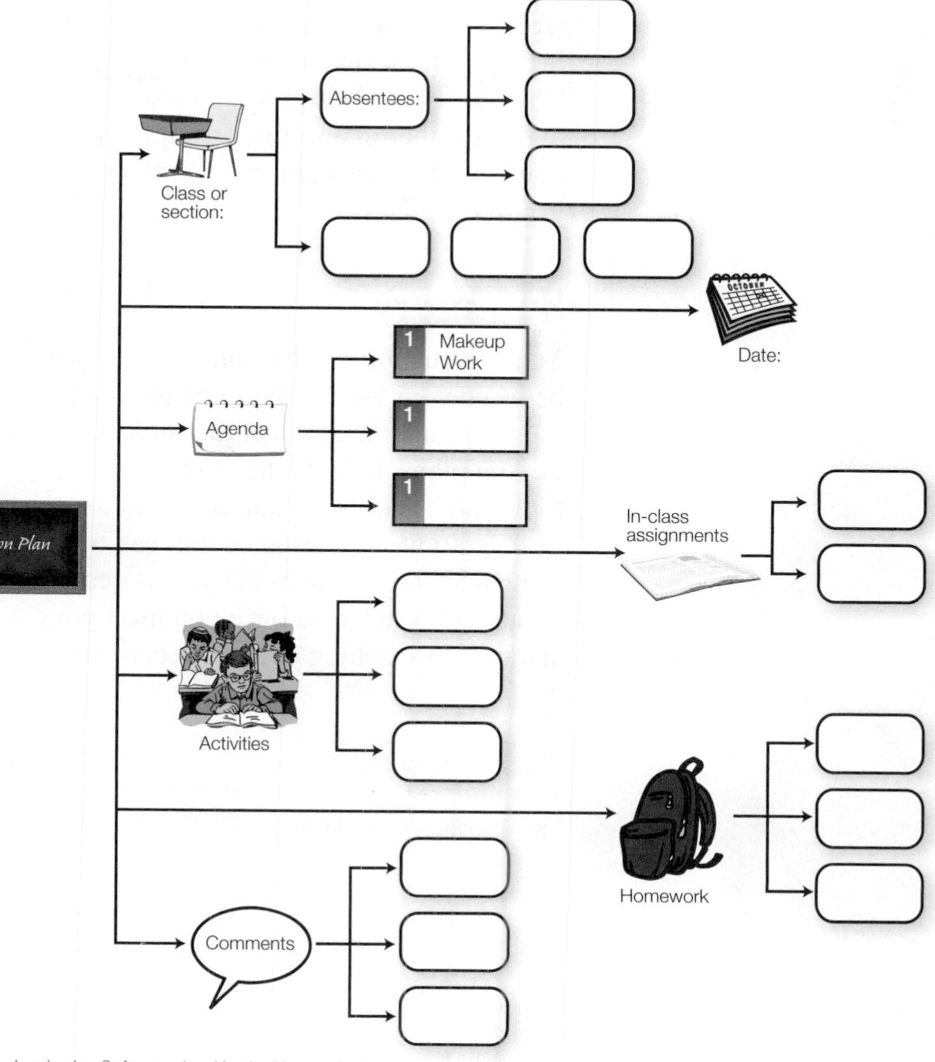

ones who have their own version called *Kidspiration. Kidspiration* enables young children to design thematic webs using pictures and symbols, even if they cannot read or write fluently. Consult the website http://www.inspiration.com and the example of one such lesson planning template in Figure 22.5.

Summary

Your instruction results from the interface between your lesson plans and the needs, interests, and readiness of the students. Lesson plans that all relate to a particular topic can be collected into a resource or teaching unit. The resource unit can be written ahead of time because it is general enough to be adapted once you meet your students. A teaching unit consists of set lesson plans targeted to a specific group of students. The related planning levels are the weekly plan followed by the daily plan.

Lesson plans come in a variety of formats and should take into account the diversity in your classroom and differentiate instruction for English language learners and students with special needs, including the gifted. Lesson plans should also accommodate learning styles and result in higher-order thinking.

Reflect!

Compare and contrast the lesson plans that have appeared in this chapter by developing a rubric for evaluating them. Assign points for each of the essential elements of a comprehensive and inclusive plan. For example:

3	2	1	0
Standards complete and integrated Clearly stated and numbered	Standards limited to one curriculum area Clearly stated and numbered	Standards very vague	No standards listed

UNIT 5

CHAPTER 23

HOW DO I GATHER MATERIALS AND RESOURCES TO SUPPORT MY INSTRUCTION?

The best things in life are free.

American proverb

Effectiveness Essentials

- Conduct an inventory of materials provided by the school, district, and resource centers.
- Carefully screen the materials you select for any gender, racial, ethnic, cultural, or age stereotypes and bias.
- Identify sources (including parents) of free materials, supplies, services, and field trips in your school community.
- Be resourceful and creative when it comes to securing teaching materials and supplies so you don't spend your own money needlessly.

You may arrive to find nothing but desks.

It's usually up to you to stock your room.

Visit your storage rooms ASAP.

UNIT 5

Unfortunately, as with most public and private organizations today, our nation's schools find themselves feeling the squeeze of budget cuts. This squeeze often filters down to each individual teacher. At the beginning of the school year, in a worst-case scenario, you may arrive to find an empty room with four bare walls and nothing but tables and chairs and a teacher's desk. Classrooms you have observed or student-taught in may have been chock-full of materials and supplies, and the resource centers and supply and storage rooms may have been veritable candy stores of resources, instructional materials, and supplies. But beware, on your first day of teaching, the cupboards in your classroom may be bare! And while you will likely have some materials to get started with, even in the best situations, the materials provided may not be as voluminous as you might prefer. Therefore, all teachers have to become resourceful and creative. This chapter will help you gather, order, buy, and use materials wisely.

Locating Resources and Supplies

An instructional resource is somebody or something that can be used as a source of information or help. Resources might include models for science, maps, globes, kits, DVDs, computer hardware and software, or human resources in the school or community. There are multiple resources available to you, and you just have to ask for them. Supplies are those tools that enable you and your students to conduct business. Included are crayons, pencils, paper, paste, rulers, bulletin board borders, art supplies, scissors, etc. Resources and supplies can be found or obtained in a number of places.

Check Your School Site First

Your school site is the first place to search for resources and supplies. You can ask for help from the principal, the resource specialist, the assistant principal, or one of the other teachers. They will be able to tell you where instructional materials, kits, media, and technology are located and how to secure what you need. They also can help you conduct an inventory of supplies provided by the school. You will need to conduct an extensive survey to establish what is provided so that you will know what you need to obtain elsewhere. Check with grade-level or same-subject colleagues for resources and supplies. Contrary to some myths, teachers do share.

The District Office Is Your Next Stop

Your next stop, after you have surveyed the resources at school, is your district's resource centers. Does your district have a media center from which you can borrow a digital camera, a digital video camera, or an LCD projector? Does the instructional materials resource center have that skeleton you have been seeking for biology class or the model of a volcano? Is there a curriculum library with instructional kits, idea books, and prepackaged units tied to the standards? These centers are repositories for instructional resources shared across schools, and it is important to determine the location of this gold mine, whatever name it goes by in your district. Make sure to ask about procedures for borrowing materials from the district, length of time they may be kept, and whether they can be renewed.

Survey all print and nonprint media, and carefully screen the materials you select for any gender, racial, ethnic, cultural, or age stereotypes and bias. Choose materials that reflect the diversity in schools and a modern worldview. Survey computer software, DVDs, photographs, CDs, posters, and other

TEACHER TALKS . . .

On that fateful day in February I got a phone call at 3:30 P.M. from my soon-to-be principal offering me my first job. They would be creating a new kindergarten class due to overflow, and I would be the teacher starting tomorrow! I rushed over to the school with eight hours of waking time before 24 kids would arrive. The room was bare—no tables, chairs, nor wall decoration. I quickly made friends with the other kindergarten teachers—begged and borrowed chairs, tables, minimal materials—and was ready to go at 8:30 the next morning.

JAN CHRISTIAN
First-Grade Teacher
San Bernardino, California

mythBUSTER

Teachers like to keep materials and ideas to themselves.

In my experience of 30 years as a classroom teacher I know that teachers like to share. Teachers are very creative people; and the more ideas we hear, the better we are able to adapt them to our own situations. I hear an idea, and it sends me off in thousand different directions. I may not be able to come up with the original idea, but I can spin off from other teachers. When another teacher asks for ideas or materials from me, I feel complimented. It makes me feel that I am pretty good, after all! Conferences are the way that teachers share all of their ideas. Every conference you go to, you write down all of the ideas and can't wait to get back to your own classroom to try them out.

Hester Turpin
Reading Specialist
District Resource Literacy Teacher
Colton, California

nonprint materials that relate to your grade-level or subject-matter standards. The resource center personnel will help you identify the most age-appropriate and relevant resources.

APPLY IT!

In your staff room, initiate a sharing system for instructional materials and/or supplies. A colleague who has what is requested simply signs the appropriate space, and the initiator now knows whom to contact (see Figure 23.1). Items are crossed out as the orders are filled. Use a chalkboard so items can be erased easily.

Look for Other Institutional Resources

Consider other, often overlooked sources of free instructional resources: public and university libraries and local museums. Universities are resources for special equipment in science or social studies. Public libraries have large selections of CDs, DVDs, and books for your standards-based units. Museums lend displays and kits to schools and often have a cadre of docents who bring everything from snakes to Native American artifacts to your classroom.

Parents Can Be Sources

The parents of students in your class are another source of supplies. Many schools send home a suggested supplies

Figure 23.1
Sharing System Among Colleagues

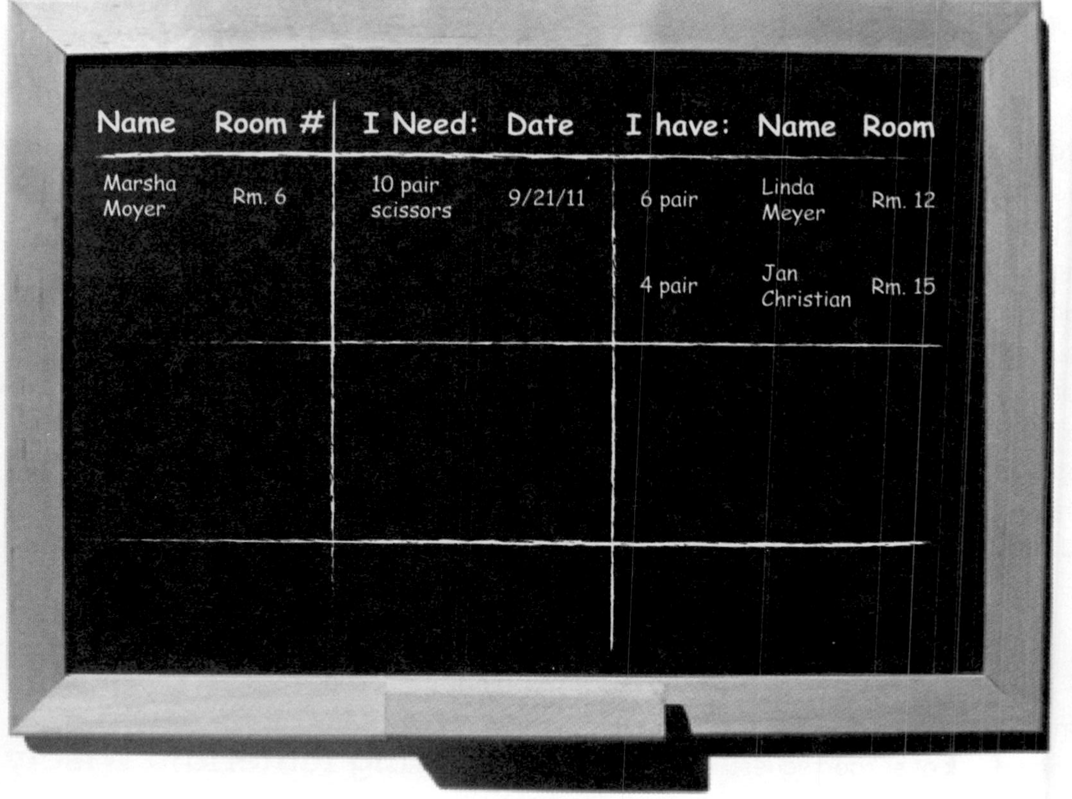

Name
Room #
I Need:
Date
I have:
Name
Room
Marsha Moyer
Rm. 6
10 pair scissors
9/21/11
6 pair
Linda Meyer
Rm. 12
4 pair
Jan Christian
Rm. 15

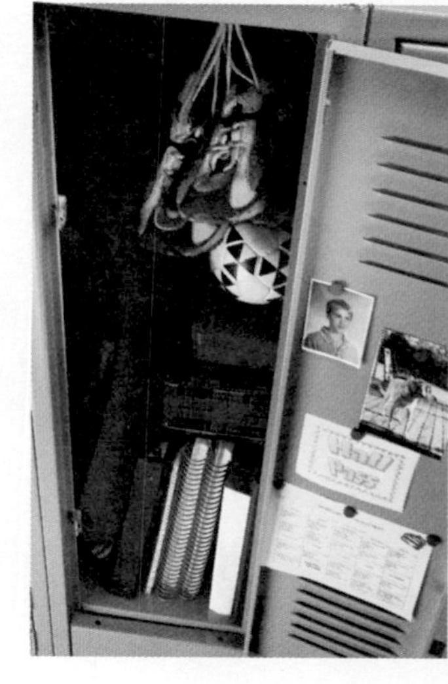

Supplies for high school (above) and elementary school (below) vary.

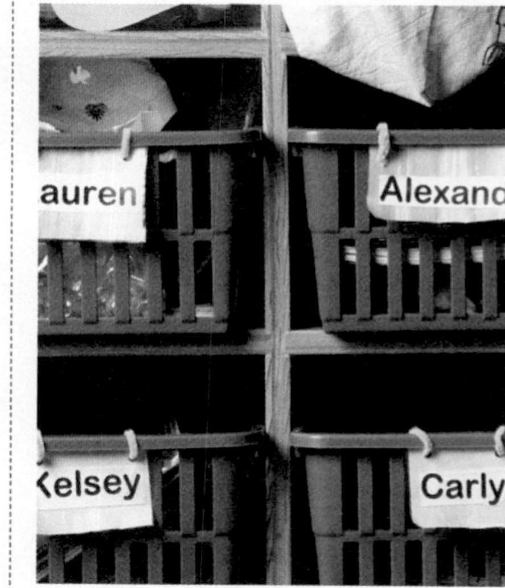

list by grade level (see Figure 23.2). Some school districts and schools post their lists on the school's website.

In addition, parents can collect cost-free supplies for class use. Large-sized ice cream vats, the type used at multiflavor-type stores, make wonderful storage cubbies when piled up on one another. Shoeboxes or milk cartons with the front ends cut out suit a similar

WATCH IT! video

Building Teacher Resources

This first-grade teacher describes how she collects and stores materials in her classroom. She emphasizes that you need not spend a great deal of money, and she gives examples of how to recycle materials to serve as containers. What advice does the teacher offer for assisting English language learners? At any grade level you will have materials to store inexpensively. What other resources and supplies in your home can you recycle as storage containers?

APPLY IT!

Compose a letter that can go home during the first week of school requesting materials and supplies unique to your subject matter and standards-based instructional needs.

purpose, as do wine cartons when the cross pieces are left intact. Large-size cereal or soap powder boxes, when cut on the bias, make sturdy file boxes, book holders, and paper caddies (see Figures 23.3 and 23.4). Duplicate (translate as appropriate) your own list of needed containers and send the list home to parents/guardians with a polite cover letter, samples of which are shown in the Classroom Artifacts on page 270. Here are a few suggestions:

Class Supplies	Containers We Need
Paste	Yogurt cups
Pencils and pens	Coffee cans
Math manipulatives	Berry baskets

And don't forget that parents can serve as good resources, too. Parents with jobs that tie into your instruction can be guest speakers. Or perhaps they can serve as good connections for obtaining needed resources.

Ordering Materials Wisely

Policies regarding the ordering of instructional materials and supplies differ greatly from district to district and from school to school. Usually, your principal will outline the ordering procedures at the first staff meeting. Information of this sort can also be obtained from the department head, staff members, the policy manual if one

Figure 23.2
School Supply Lists

Kindergarten/Grade 1
- White glue or stick
- Crayons
- Pencils
- Scissors
- Pocket folders
- Composition notebook (hardback black and white)
- Towel/rest mat
- Tissues
- Supply box
- Ruler (centimeter and inches)

Grade 3
- White glue or stick
- Crayons/colored pencils
- Pencils
- Scissors
- Pocket folders
- Composition notebook (hardback black and white) or spiral notebooks or binder
- Loose-leaf paper
- Tissues
- Supply box
- Pens
- Ruler (centimeter and inches)
- Highlighters
- Index cards

Grades 4–6
- White glue or stick
- Crayons/colored pencils
- Pencils
- Scissors
- Pocket folders
- Composition notebook (hardback black and white) or spiral notebooks or binder
- Loose-leaf paper
- Tissues
- Supply box
- Pens
- Ruler (centimeter and inches)
- Highlighters
- Index cards
- Protractor
- Backpack to carry items
- Day planner/organizer

Grade 8
- 2- or 3-inch 3-ring binder with dividers (science—stays in class)
- 1- or 1.5-inch 3-ring binder with dividers (math)
- Five-subject spiral notebook (world geography)
- 200–400 sheets of loose-leaf paper
- Several one-subject spiral notebooks
- One composition book (English)
- One dozen or more #2 pencils
- Bag of pens (blue or black)
- Box of colored pencils
- Box of markers
- Glue stick
- Calculator
- Protractor
- Two boxes of tissues for classrooms

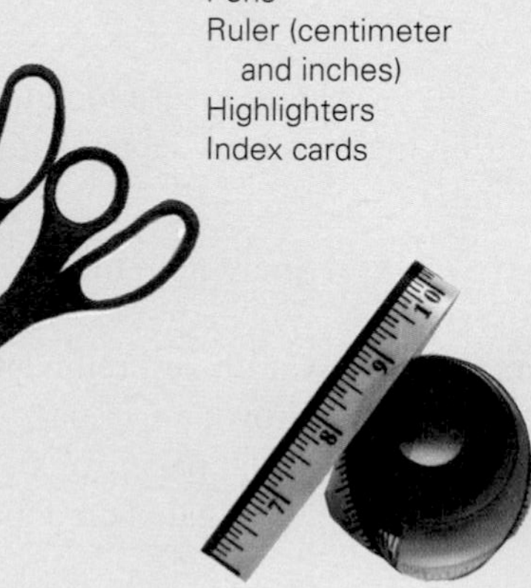

Figure 23.3
Cubbies From Ice Cream Vats

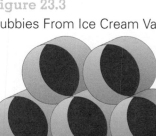

Figure 23.4
Folder Storage From Cereal Boxes

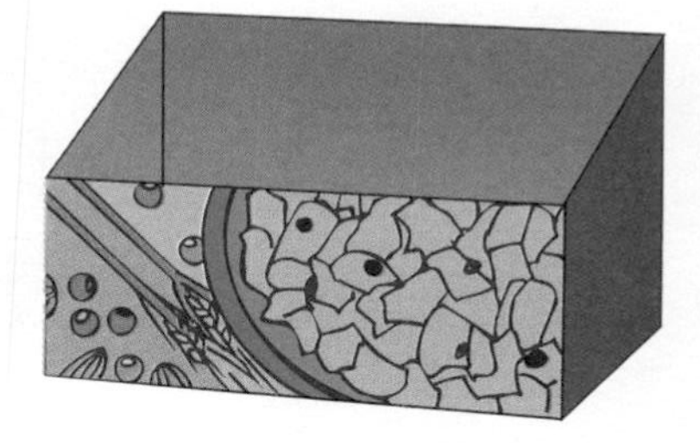

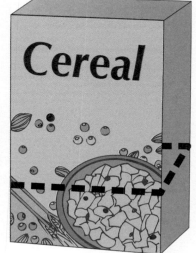

CLASSROOM ARTIFACTS

Dear Parent or Guardian,

We are setting up a classroom store to help us learn to add and subtract money. Will you please save, wash, and smooth the rough edges of cans of all varieties. Please leave the labels intact. We can also use empty food boxes and plastic containers. Please send the empties to school with your child during the first week in November, and please make sure to stop by toward the end of the week to see us operating our store. We thank you for your help.

Sincerely,
Mrs. Jan Garcia and Class 2-1
Parkville School

Dear Parents:

We are trying to gather a supply of art materials to use all year long. Please look through the list and send to school any that you have available during the month of September. We thank you in advance for helping us to make art more exciting.

- Scraps of fabric
- Old shirts for smocks
- Yarn
- Newspapers for papier-mâché
- Cotton batting
- Juice cans for paint containers
- Wallpaper remnants
- Bottle caps
- Margarine containers
- Wood scraps
- Coffee cans for brushes
- Greeting card fronts
- Wooden spools
- Shelving remnants
- Egg cartons
- Cardboard remnants
- Brown paper bags
- Toilet paper rolls
- Corrugated cardboard

Please pack like items together in a brown paper bag and label the bag as to its contents. This will make sorting materials easier. We thank you for your cooperation.

Sincerely,
Mr. Mark Horowitz
Art Teacher
Bridgeport Middle School

APPLY IT!

Your own ordering priorities will depend on how well endowed your school is, how much you can gather from other sources, and your own needs. Begin to list the items you would order if you could. These should be items not readily available from other sources. You can always add to your list or remove any items you happen to obtain elsewhere.

exists, the school secretary, the resource specialist, or the grapevine. It is important for you to know how monies are allocated.

1. Are all teachers allotted a sum solely for their own use?
2. Does the school principal rank your requests, along with all others, alone or with the help of a school committee?
3. Is the budget so limited that resources are doled out as long as they last?

If you gain support from co-workers and approach your administrator with a specified need, a list of instructional materials that will meet the need, the exact cost of such materials, and a list of colleagues eager to share the materials purchased, you have a better chance of having your request granted. Your principal may set forth criteria for ordering wisely, but here are three that might help you obtain what you need:

1. Ordered items should help differentiate instruction.
2. Ordered items should be nonconsumable.
3. Ordered items should be sturdy, long-lasting, and adaptable.

Sample items that meet these three tests of durability include

- Multicultural materials
- Computer software
- Globes, maps, atlases
- CDs, DVDs

- Manipulative materials
- Supplementary reading books
- Science equipment
- Teacher resource or idea books
- Storage and file cabinets
- Bookshelves
- Science and social studies kits
- Simulations and educational games
- Almanacs, thesauruses, dictionaries, other reference books

Going the Extra Mile for Materials

As an aspiring school supplies packrat, consider some outside sources of free and inexpensive instructional materials. If you are like most beginning teachers, your salary precludes excessive spending, and there is no reason to spend hard-earned dollars when there are many no- or low-cost options. Start with freebies and move into sources of inexpensive materials later.

Freebie Guides Contain a Wealth of Information

Although freebie guides are far from free themselves, they do contain a wealth of materials for teachers that more than makes up for the initial investment. You might suggest ordering one of each title for the school professional library or resource room. These are usually paperbacks with titles such as *Elementary Teachers' Guide to FREE Curriculum Materials, Middle School Teachers' Guide to FREE Curriculum Materials,* and *Secondary Teachers' Guide to FREE Curriculum Materials.* These titles are available from Educators Progress Service, Inc., at http://www.freeteachingaids.com

Book Clubs Sometimes Offer Free Books

Free books for your classroom can be slowly amassed by encouraging your students to subscribe to pupil book clubs, if district policy allows this. Some districts may not want to burden you with the extra responsibility for collecting monies, or they may feel that

APPLY IT!

Have your students practice business letter form, handwriting, grammar, and spelling by selecting a needed item and writing a letter requesting it as your representative. They can also write for innumerable items listed in their own freebie guide, *Free Stuff for Kids* (2001).

economically disadvantaged students will be left out. Usually, given a certain quantity ordered, the teacher can select a specified number of titles for free. This may seem like a small reward, but the books do pile up and they are free and current. Less current titles can be obtained from public libraries, which often cull their collections to make room for new titles. Inexpensive trade books can be found at swap meets, garage sales, and used-book stores.

The Local Community Is a Resource

No matter where you teach or at what level, you need to examine your local community for ideas to enhance your classroom instruction.

Source for Supplies. If you are searching for a real bounty of assorted free supplies and materials, look to all the various commercial establishments in and around your neighborhood. Many of the large office supply stores have set up special programs to help schools obtain supplies. Shoppers can earmark a specific school, and a portion of the receipts are donated to that school. Find out if businesses in your area have set up programs such as this. Also, feel free to ask about educators' discounts where you shop. My local chain bookstore offers teachers discounts, and so do other local businesses. You should always ask.

Your students can be excellent scavengers for freebies, and you can give them a list of needed materials that they can easily find and save at home or gather in the neighborhood. This will teach them a great deal about recycling opportunities in their very own homes.

Here are just a few examples of what a superb scrounger can obtain:

APPLY IT!

Check your local community directory and Yellow Pages to identify your own potential sources. The first time you ask, you will be embarrassed. The second time, you will be ill at ease. By the third inquiry, you will be a pro, reinforced by the positive responses you probably will receive. Start your own scrounging directory and keep adding to it. List the establishment, the address, the telephone number, and items received. Your students can write thank-you notes for each donation.

TEACHER TALKS . . .

Go to the thrift store. Buy clothing, big shirts for painting, costume jewelry, dramatic costumes for readings. Buy any electronic gadget kids can take apart. Buy puppets. I got some for as low as 17 cents each. Create a classroom veterinary office with secondhand and washed stuffed animals. Buy vases and cheap plastic flowers for a classroom florist shop.

KIM CIABETTINI
Fourth-Grade Teacher
Highland, California

Rug companies	Sample books for art projects Remnants to define areas Foam for stuffing projects
Wallpaper stores	Sample books for art projects Remnants to cover bulletin boards
Supermarkets	Cardboard cartons and boxes Styrofoam trays Plastic berry baskets Seasonal displays Old magazines
Lumberyard	Scrap wood Dowels for puppets Wood curls for class pets
Notions store	Buttons, sequins, glitter, yarn, tape, trimmings, needles, thread
Shoe repair shop	Scraps of leather, laces
Ice cream stores	3-gallon ice cream vats for storage
Cleaners	Wire hangers, plastic bags for clay projects
Copy/print shops	Paper of all colors, shapes
Tile companies	Scraps of mosaic tile for art projects
Garages/auto repair	Wheels, tires, assorted junk for construction
Telephone company	Colored wire, telephones on loan
Florists	Wire, foam blocks, tissue paper
Travel agencies	Travel posters, brochures

Local Field Trips. Your school community can also be a source of free field trips to support instructional goals. These off-the-beaten-path field trips often require no buses, no money, and no bother. They're good for business, excellent public relations, and, most of all, stimulating for both the tour guides and the student tourists. Here are a few examples of unusual, free field trips that can be arranged through local business establishments in my area:

Fast-food restaurant—tour
Florist—tour and corsage-making lesson
Tortilla factory—tour and samples
County courthouse—tour, including courtroom; visit to a trial in progress
Dairy—tour
Newspaper—tour
Radio station—tour
Post office—tour
Medical center—tour
Yardage store—tour, including discussion of different fabrics
Bakery—tour
Grocery chain—tour
Recycling plant—tour
Veterinary clinic—tour
Western Union office—tour and explanation of telegram delivery
City Hall—tour, including city council meeting when in session
Bank—tour
Stables—tour and presentation on care of horses
Pizzeria—tour and demonstration of pizza-making process
Police station—tour, often including fingerprinting
Fire department—tour
Sheriff's helicopter—tour and demonstration

WATCH IT! video

Field Trip

In this clip, the teacher prepares her secondary students for a field trip. The advice in the video pertains to all grade levels. What are the key pointers you have gleaned from this video in terms of pre-trip preparation, activities during the trip, and activities after the trip back at school?

APPLY IT!

Explore the free field trip options surrounding your school. I included only generic names in my list because the same services may not be available from a different branch of the same international or national chain in your area. Start your own directory of free local field trips. Begin with your friends or neighbors. Is one neighbor an optometrist? Ask if you can tour the office with your class. Does another work in a local hospital? Arrange a visit. Does another work in a bank? Get behind the scenes. Friends and relatives will be very understanding, as will local professionals and business people. A thank-you card or gift from the class will be much appreciated by those who offer their services and time as tour guides. What better way is there for incorporating career education into your curriculum? Share these sources with your colleagues. Get a schoolwide directory going.

TEACHER TALKS . . .

When I wanted the students to work in small groups in order to write or chart activities, I needed something they could use besides paper. I went to a home improvement store and bought two large shower boards. The clerks cut each large board into six smaller pieces (they are a nice size), so I now have 12 good-sized white boards for the students to use. When the students work in small groups, they each use a different dry erase marker on the board. They are great for small group activities such as Venn diagrams, character listings, math, and science. They are quite handy when the teacher is working with small groups and needs something to use besides paper and pencil. The students love using them, and they are really motivating.

IVANIA MARTIN
Former Fourth-Grade Teacher
Benicio, California

Visit Teacher Stores and Campus Stores

Many teachers spend money at local teachers' supply stores. If you have saved money by following the suggestions in this chapter, you can be a bit extravagant and feel comfortable doing so! You can probably find out from a colleague the name of the supply store frequented by most teachers in your area. These stores are to teachers what candy stores are to kids.

Middle and high school teachers should add any instructional resources and supplies that directly relate to their subject areas. In addition, you may want to consider ordering or buying more file folders, sticky notes, index cards, and dry erase markers. Look for teen-oriented posters and rewards. Use your funds sparingly here and make sure that items you are purchasing cannot be obtained free with a little ingenuity. Most often they can be!

Some middle and high schools have campus stores where students may purchase needed items. Encourage secondary students to purchase student planners so they can organize their assignments.

Discount and Warehouse Mega-Stores Offer Bargains

Other sources of inexpensive supplies are the various discount and warehouse stores in your neighborhood. These are

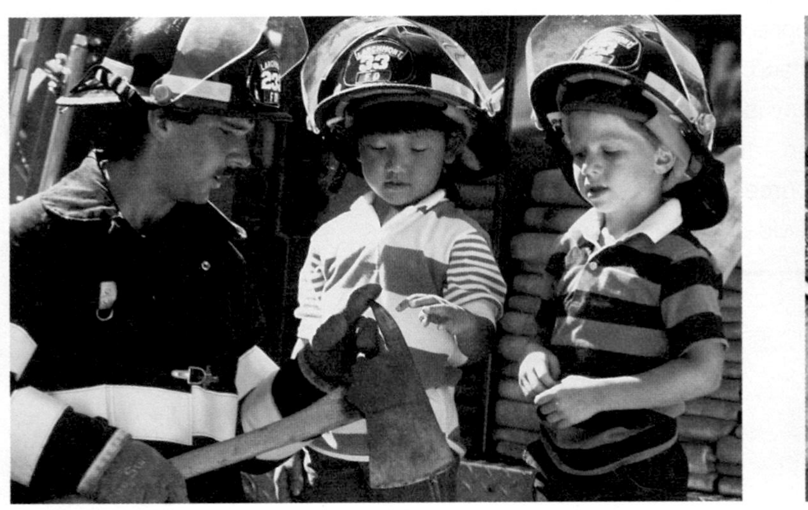

At the fire station.

Students enjoy a field trip.

the bottom-line stores, the bargain hunter's paradise, and the ultimate in cost cutting. Here, trade books for students may cost 99 cents as opposed to $8.50. Art supplies and food items may be bought in bulk at a fraction of the regular cost. Remember to shop for school supplies as you shop for large items for yourself. Look for the least expensive items that will hold up with constant use.

Recycled Merchandise Can Be a Low-Cost Treasure

Garage sales, thrift stores, swap meets, bazaars, and auctions are sources of inexpensive materials and low-cost treasures. Teachers find perfectly good chairs, tables, lamps, plants, and rugs at these venues. You can accessorize your classroom with recycled items that are as good as new. My house is furnished with cast-offs, but they are called antiques!

AVOID IT!

Don't be too concerned about not having everything you want during those first days and weeks of school. You will gather materials slowly, and pretty soon you will be competitive with the other packrats at your school. Remember that in ancient Greece, Socrates did pretty well without a fully stocked classroom—in fact, without a classroom at all!

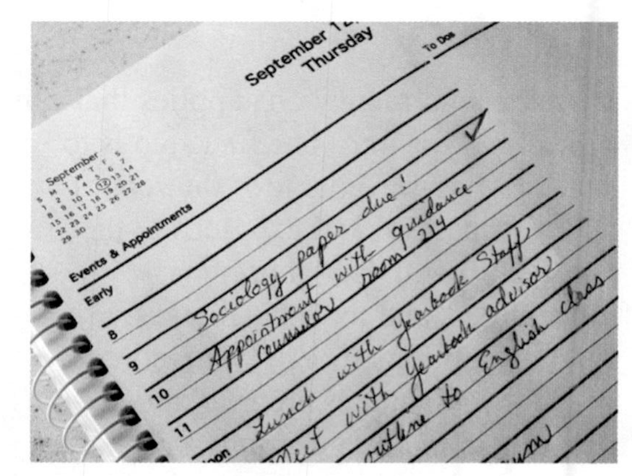

Students need planning tools too.

Buy what you need, buy what you anticipate needing, but remember that free is possible, preferable, and more gratifying. Organize your materials in large, colorful, and well-marked boxes so you can keep the clutter to a minimum at home and at school.

Summary

Do not spend money on supplies that can be secured for free. The first step is to survey what is available at the school and district level and then turn to the community—that is, museums, universities, and local businesses. Free field trip options should be explored because few monies are available to teachers in the best of times. All materials should be screened for bias and reflect the diversity of the student population.

Reflect!

Prepare a list of materials and supplies that are absolutely essential for your teaching. Next list those that you need but could do without if necessary. Then list those that are on your wish list. Finally, design a plan for obtaining these materials and supplies.

Essential	Need But Could Do Without	Wish List

UNIT 5

Effectiveness Essentials

- Instructional aides can offer both clerical and instructional support in your classroom.
- Establish a good working relationship with your aide, and clearly communicate your classroom systems, procedures, and instructional strategies.
- Provide the substitute with clear lesson plans and alternative motivating activities that you know your students enjoy.
- Talk to your class about the role of the substitute teacher and the need to respect him or her.

CHAPTER 24

HOW DO I PLAN FOR CLASSROOM AIDES AND SUBSTITUTES?

I am not authorized to fire substitute teachers.

Bart Simpson

A PRESCHOOL AIDE TALKS . . .

I've learned from my work with children with special needs to always have a backup plan and that changing focus mid-lesson is not only necessary sometimes but okay, too. Coming back to a lesson can be great, especially if there was a physical break in the meantime—e.g., drop the counting game to make a train with the children and march around the room before picking up the counting game again. It is surprising how often children's attention improves.

I've learned that an understandable and reliable routine helps students and teachers. Of course, flexibility is important, but flexibility within a predictable routine works best.

SARAH DOMINICK
Preschool Aide for Autistic Preschoolers
Stockholm, Maine

Working With an Instructional Aide

When a classroom or instructional aide is assigned to your classroom, you may feel anxious and delighted at the same time. You are delighted that you will have the additional help, but also you are likely to feel a little nervous about what to do with this extra person in light of your own concerns about beginning the school year.

What's the Role of the Instructional Aide?

Instructional aides, sometimes called *para-educators* or *paraprofessionals,* offer you clerical and instructional support in your classroom. Their assistance affords you additional time for planning and teaching. The best para-educators enjoy working with students from diverse backgrounds. They are expected to follow your directions for individual and small group instruction and to handle discipline with the same patience and sense of fairness that you do.

As more and more schools follow the inclusion model—that is, integrating students with special needs into general education classrooms—your para-educator is essential in helping you provide extra assistance and ensure the successful inclusion of students with special needs.

Let's plan together.

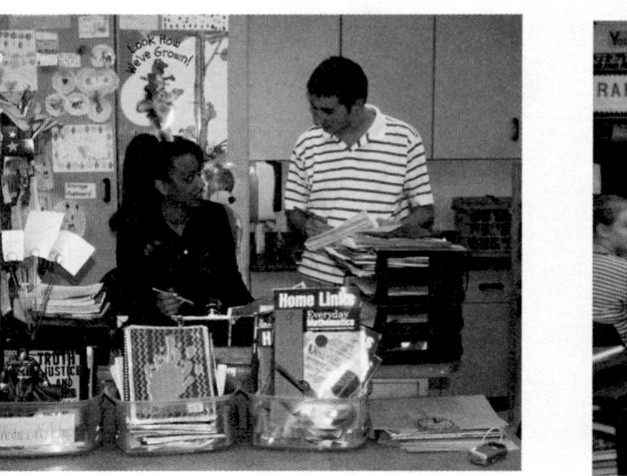

An aide offers two times the assistance.

Bilingual instructional aides also provide extra attention to your English language learners. They can communicate with parents, help your students transition to English, and assist you in establishing links with the community.

Instructional aides in secondary schools often specialize in a certain subject, such as math or science. They may assist with special projects, prepare materials and equipment, design and implement special exhibits, or set up a science experiment in a lab. A knowledgeable technology aide can lend support in the computer lab or in individual classrooms with hardware or software issues.

Prepare to Work With an Aide

Before working with an aide, ask some policy questions about traditional paraprofessional duties at your school site. Aides may talk among themselves, and you don't want to miss the mark with too little or too much initial responsibility. Find out the following:

1. How many hours per day/days per week will your aide be in your classroom?
2. What legal constraints exist vis-à-vis a paraprofessional's responsibilities in the classroom?
3. What duties do colleagues assign to their aides?

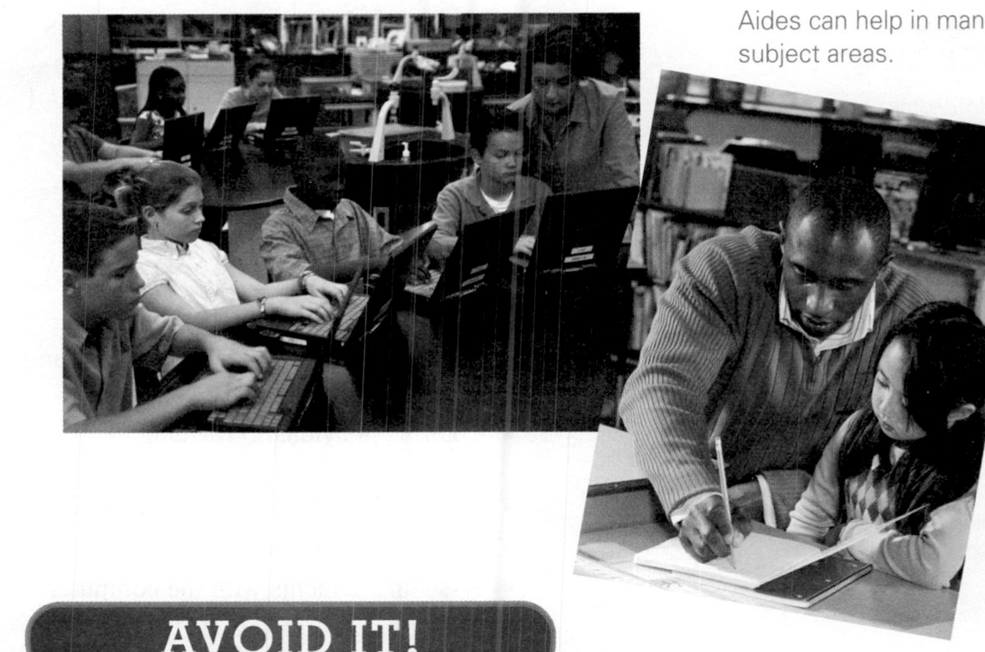

Aides can help in many subject areas.

AVOID IT!

Your aides, even the bilingual ones, should never work *exclusively* with English language learners or students with special needs. That sends a message to the students that they are somehow relegated to a lesser status with the assistant and do not have the attention of the "real" teacher. Aides serve an essential role as part of a team. However, they do not have your expertise; and while you may be giving them adequate or even excellent direction, your students' academic development may suffer.

UNIT 5

AN AIDE TALKS TO TEACHERS . . .

It is important to keep in mind that you, as the teacher, need to be flexible in working with your aides. People have their own personalities. Therefore, there is room for conflict. Just remember that you need to give and take throughout the time you work together. Dictatorships will not work.

C. FRANCINE APACIBLE
Classroom Bilingual Aide
San Bernardino, California

Have your aide spend as much of his or her time as possible working with students. Veterans were asked what roles and responsibilities aides or paraprofessionals generally assume in the classroom. Their responses follow:

- Reading with small groups
- Assisting individuals during seatwork
- Conducting drills in small groups
- Reinforcing and reviewing reading and math skills
- Tutoring individuals/providing enrichment
- Overseeing learning center activities
- Taking dictation for stories
- Assisting students with the computer
- Monitoring activities
- Correcting papers
- Entering grades
- Updating nonconfidential records
- Filing
- Repairing books
- Restocking from supply closet
- Changing bulletin boards
- Preparing materials for lessons
- Running off and collating copies
- Binding students' stories into books
- Laminating materials for class use
- Using your lesson plans to differentiate instruction
- Supervising students in the cafeteria and hallways
- Setting up equipment
- Preparing instructional materials

Orient Your Aide

Having another pair of eyes, ears, and hands will be a bonus in so many ways if you are approachable, flexible, clear, organized, and appreciative. The aide will be just as nervous as you are; but as a team, you can make the most of the instructional time in the classroom. Your students will be the beneficiaries.

1. The first step in establishing a good working relationship with your aide involves getting to know this individual as a person. If possible, before school starts, set aside a time to talk face to face about your mutual prior experience

working with students, your philosophies of education, your attitudes toward discipline, and the skills you both bring to the classroom.

2. Determine what the role and responsibilities of the paraprofessional will be, and write them down. Blank schedules, one per week, that clearly outline your aide's duties day by day, time slot by time slot, can be very helpful in delineating these tasks.
3. Establish an ongoing time during each week to sit down and plan for the following week. Charles and Senter (2005) suggest that you include a discussion of professionalism in your orientation, incorporating such items as appropriate dress, demeanor, promptness, dependability, and avoidance of gossip.
4. Discuss your record-keeping system, and orient the aide to your marking procedures and to the instructional materials he or she may be using. Supply a duplicate set of manuals if they are available. Provide a workstation for your aide and a place to store clothing and personal items. Post your aide's name on the door and chalkboard alongside your own. Make clear to your students that your aide is there as a second teacher and will enforce the same rules and discipline system.
5. Communicate appreciation to your aide frequently and in novel ways. Some teachers present aides with small gifts, award certificates, or recognition luncheons (see Figure 24.1).

Coach Your Aide

Offer suggestions regarding motivating activities and game formats, every-pupil response techniques, positive discipline strategies, and questioning techniques. If you are working in a special education full-inclusion classroom or simply with a mainstreamed population, your aide will prove to be that second pair of eyes, hands, and ears that you will desperately need. Provide coaching in the following areas and in others as needed:

- Technology and software applications
- Questioning and feedback strategies
- Motivational techniques and building on students' prior knowledge
- Game formats for drill and practice
- Every-pupil response techniques
- Your discipline plan and positive desist techniques
- The elements of lesson planning
- Facilitation of cooperative groups
- Shortcuts for checking student work
- The purpose and organization of student portfolios

STATISTICS

According to the U.S. Bureau of Labor (2010–2011),

- Almost 40% of teacher assistants work part time.
- Teacher assistants who work in Title I schools must have a minimum of two years of college or pass a rigorous state or local assessment.
- Teacher assistants held about 1.3 million jobs in 2008.
- Median aide wages in 2008 were $22,200.
- Full-time teacher assistants usually receive health benefits, but part-timers ordinarily do not.

UNIT 5

TEACHER TALKS . . .

I prepare my students for a sub. I am very stern about how they are to treat the sub and how they are to do their assigned work, or there will be hell to pay when I return. If the sub leaves a note about a student, I immediately call the parent; and if the violation was bad enough, I write a conduct referral. In 19 years of teaching I have had to do this three times, and I remember each time very well. My students know to behave, both with me and with subs. Because of that preparation, and the lesson plans I leave, I have subs wanting to come back to my classes. Some will only sub for me and my department, as we are all pretty much on the same page.

DELAINE ZODY
High School Teacher
Fresno, California

Figure 24.1
Appreciation for an Aide's Contributions

Certificate of Appreciation
Awarded to
Name
Date
For Outstanding Service in B3
Teacher and Students

Preparing for Substitute Teachers

The substitute teacher is a valued member of a classroom team, a pinch hitter in emergencies. The brave substitute may be unfamiliar with the school, the class, the grade level, the materials, and the content. In addition to all the ambiguity that goes along with the position, 30-plus students sometimes mistake the arrival of a substitute for party time. I have seen students who act like angels with their own teachers suddenly demoralize substitutes.

You need to help substitutes make their service to you and your class more effective. The substitute may be called in at the last minute, and you want to ensure that learning takes place in your absence. You don't want to have to pick up the pieces when you return to school, nor do you want to stay at home with the flu feeling guilty about what might be going on in your absence. There are a few guidelines that you can follow and certain preparations you can make. After that, sit at home, sniffle, and hope for the best.

AVOID IT!

Although your aide may have more school experience and be older than you are, remember that you have earned your credential. Stay calm and allay fears of being watched and judged. When you relax and maintain open communication channels with your aide, you'll find that two heads will accomplish far more than one. As your relationship with your aide deepens, you'll wonder how you ever managed or could manage alone.

Prepare a Substitute Folder

The more information your substitute has about your class, procedures, and schedule, the better this person will handle the other ambiguities. This information needs to be in concise form because the substitute may arrive five minutes before class and will not have much time to prepare. Have a brightly colored folder clearly marked for substitutes so they can find it without calling out the bloodhounds (see Figure 24.2). That folder should contain the following data:

- **Multiple copies of your class list.** On it the substitute can make notations of all sorts and check off the homework.
- **Seating chart.** A seating chart will help the substitute learn the names or at least call on your students with ease. The seating chart will also help the substitute quickly catch those who decide to pull a switcheroo and sit with a friend for the day.

Figure 24.2
Substitute Folder

- **School map.** Provide a map of the school site for the substitute so that she or he can easily find key school locations. You might circle key locations in red to be even more helpful.
- **Class schedule and comings and goings.** Provide a general class schedule and a schedule of out-of-room activities. Be sure to include days and times. There is often much confusion about comings and goings, and 35 voices expressing conflicting accounts of when they have library time can be most distressing to an already harried substitute.
- **Summary of your administrative duties by day.** Substitutes are expected to follow your schedule exactly, but they need to know what your extra school duties are so they can cover for you. You may have to change this schedule monthly, since your duties will change from month to month.
- **Discipline and organization.** You want to provide some information to your substitute about your discipline plan. Include in your substitute folder the letter regarding discipline that you sent home to parents.
- **Bus information in concise form.** You want to make sure that everyone gets on the right bus at the right time in your absence.
- **Buddy teachers, aides, and volunteer schedules.** Provide your substitute with the name and room number of a buddy teacher, the name of your aide and the aide's hours, the schedule of any expected

TEACHER TALKS . . .

I leave great substitute teacher plans, and I never labor over them for hours the night before. During the third or fourth week of school, after I have figured out the kids and we have established our procedures, I write my sub plans. They are in generic format that I will use for 90% of the days that I am absent. All of the subjects and routines are explicitly typed out. I include every detail of what we are accustomed to, things that only the students and I know out of habit because we are there. I leave space to highlight the particulars that change from day to day, like the title of the read-aloud book, the math work that we are on, or special events.

The night before the sub comes, I write in the order of the schedule and highlight the priorities. It leaves me confident that a new sub knows exactly what to expect, yet I have spent the same amount of time

(continued on following page)

planning that I normally do. The final special feature: I tell the sub to be very strict so that I get a warm welcome when I return.

SARAH BARTEN
Third-Grade Teacher
Desert Sands, California

STUDENT SAYS . . .

When we have an inexperienced substitute teacher, the class goes nuts. The students know they can get away with bad behavior because the subs act like big kids. When we have a sub who knows the ropes, students try to get away with it, but they don't succeed. The students can tell who is strict and who isn't in five minutes. Experienced subs act like professionals.

NATALIE GIBBS
Twelfth Grader, Age 17
Yucaipa, California

volunteers for the day, and the names of three students who can be counted on to give accurate and up-to-the-minute information about classroom life in general.

- **Notations about students with special needs.** Provide information about students with special needs. Some may need to see the nurse for medication or diabetic testing. Others may have adaptive P.E. Still others may have modified work programs and different behavior standards.

Some teachers will communicate all of this information to subs in a very concise fashion, covering all of the important information and giving it a name such as "Substitute Data Bank" (see Table 24.1).

Include Lesson Plans and Supplemental Materials

When you know in advance that you will need a substitute, you can leave up-to-the-minute lesson plans and review work for the class. You can write your plans with the substitute in mind and have all the materials at hand and ready to go. Some teachers, even in an emergency, will quickly write up-to-the-minute plans and send them to school with a friend or spouse that morning.

The lesson plans that you have already formulated should always be written in a form that would enable any reasonable person to decipher them and then teach

APPLY IT!

What would you put into your bag of supplemental materials for a substitute teacher? Make a list.

from them. In addition, include in your substitute folder many review sheets and activities for any possible emergency, and update the material every two weeks or so just in case.

Leave the substitute a box or bag of motivating activities that you know your students enjoy. Experienced substitutes have learned to bring their own supplemental materials; but if you provide your own, tailor-made to your class, you will be several steps ahead (see Figure 24.3).

Teach Respect for Substitutes

Talk to your class about the role of the substitute teacher and how that person is really an emergency teacher who saves the day for learning. Discuss specific ways the class can make it easier for this pinch hitter, and write them on a list. If your classroom discipline policy is based on a premise of self-responsibility, it is more likely that your students will not take too much advantage of the situation. Should you get a negative report upon

Table 24.1 Substitute Data Bank

What You'll Need	**Where You'll Find It**	
Lesson plans	Lesson plan book on teacher's desk	
Daily schedule	Lesson plan book on teacher's desk	
Weekly schedule	Lesson plan book on teacher's desk	
Additional duties	Notes section of lesson plan book	
Grade book	Top drawer of teacher's desk	
Attendance sheet	On the computer	
Seating chart	Front of plan book	
School map	Office	
Emergency procedures	Bulletin board beside teacher's desk	
Bus lists	Bulletin board beside teacher's desk	
Bell schedule	Bulletin board beside teacher's desk	
Emergency information cards	Office	
Materials and supplies	Teacher's desk and storage cabinets	
Procedures	**How We Do Them**	
For questions	Raise hand	
For answers	Use tongue depressors with student names	
Restroom	One person at a time, with pass	
Recess	Table by table, in order of quietness	
Entrances and exits	Same as above	
Lunch	Same as above	
Students With Special Needs	**Accommodation**	
Carlos	Asthma inhaler in nurse's office as needed	
Ella	Leaves for speech therapy at noon	
Discipline Policy	**Where You'll Find It**	
Letter outlining the policy	Inside each student's notebook, signed by the parent	
Rules and consequences	Poster at the front of the room	
Key People		
Reliable students	Secretary	Resource teachers
Buddy teachers	School nurse	School counselor
Principal		
Technology	**Where You'll Find It**	
Computer policy	Bulletin board above monitors	
Other equipment	Mr. Gold can help.	
Tech-savvy students	Calvin, Kayla	

TEACHER TALKS . . .

I had the worst case of the flu and spent the longest time preparing substitute plans and arranging my classroom so everything would be in perfect order when the substitute arrived. The next morning my school secretary phoned me 10 minutes before the bell. I thought that perhaps the plans weren't good enough. It turns out I had actually forgotten to call in for a sub!

MCKAYLA BEACH
Eighth-Grade Social Studies Teacher
Palm Springs, California

UNIT 5

Figure 24.3
Resources for Substitute Teacher

APPLY IT!

Start collecting materials for your substitute folder as soon as possible.

your return, despite all of your preventive measures, you can impose a logical consequence, such as requiring the culprits to write the substitute a letter of apology or bringing the whole issue up during a class meeting.

It is very important at the secondary level to instill respect for substitute teachers. These students are quite aware that the sub is vulnerable to their monkey business. Discuss in a meeting with students why you will be absent, rules of behavior, and positive and negative consequences depending on the report you receive from the substitute.

AVOID IT!

Don't let any mistreatment of substitute teachers go unnoticed. The work you do to instill respect for substitutes will long be remembered and appreciated by future substitutes in your classroom.

Summary

You may have an instructional aide assigned to you on a part-time or a full-time basis. This person will provide another set of eyes and hands, and you should prepare ahead of time to make this team member feel welcome with a comprehensive orientation and delineation of responsibilities.

It is almost certain that at some time in your first year you will have a substitute teacher take over your class due to illness, a scheduled inservice, a meeting with your mentor, a family emergency, or another unanticipated crisis. The sub saves the day for learning when you carefully set out a comprehensive substitute folder and a collection of additional materials and resources.

Reflect!

Reflect on your experiences with substitute teachers when you were in school. What can you do in your classroom to make the day you are absent productive? How will you prepare for subs, and how will you prepare your students?

UNIT 5 CHECKLIST

Planning and Organizing Subject Matter Checklist	For more information go to:
☐ Have I obtained all relevant planning documents?	Chapter 21
☐ Have I identified, with the help of others, the standards I need to address?	Chapter 21
☐ Have I consulted with other teachers about the preferred style of lesson plans and when they are reviewed?	Chapter 22
☐ Have I bought a plan book and/or organized a digital notebook to collect my lesson plans?	Chapter 22
☐ Do my plans differentiate instruction?	Chapters 22, 28, 29
☐ Have I conducted a school, district, and community survey of resources and supplies?	Chapter 23
☐ Have I planned for an instructional aide if one is assigned?	Chapter 24
☐ Have I organized a substitute folder and a collection of supplemental materials?	Chapter 24

Further Reading: Planning and Organizing Subject Matter

Armstrong, A. (2009). *Multiple intelligences in the classroom* (3rd ed.). Alexandria, VA: ASCD. This book updates multiple intelligences theory as expounded by Howard Gardner and provides many examples and applications of the theory to schools and classrooms.

Kronowitz, E. (2011). *The substitute teacher's guide to success*. Upper Saddle River, NJ: Pearson Education. This book is written for both substitute teachers and the teachers who rely on them to save the day for learning. The information on how to prepare for a sub is especially helpful for new teachers.

Marzano, R. J., & Haystead, M. W. (2008). *Making standards useful in the classroom*. Alexandria, VA: ASCD. This book helps teachers make sense of an overwhelming number of standards and recommends that teachers translate standards into useful guidelines and develop formative assessments and benchmarks to ensure student growth and achievement.

Nevin, A. I., Villa, R. A., & Thousand, J. S. (2008). *A guide to co-teaching with paraeducators: Practical tips for K–12 educators*. Thousand Oaks, CA: Corwin. This is a very easy-to-read guide for the teacher who will be working with a paraeducator. The information is up to date with many examples, resources, and case studies. The book exemplifies how the team approach is beneficial for all students, especially those with special needs.

Selected Websites for Lesson Plans and Lesson Planning Tips

Ed Helper

http://www.edHelper.com

This website was created by teachers and features lesson plans by subject matter, WebQuests, free worksheets, a grade book, puzzle maker, units, high school skills, and much more.

FREE (Federal Resources for Educational Excellence)

http://free.ed.gov

This website provides links to all educational resources from the federal government. All subject areas are covered, and secondary teachers will find it very useful.

Public Broadcasting Teacher Source

http://www.pbs.org/teachers

This website features PBS teacher resources by subject and curriculum ideas across grade levels. More than 3,000 lesson plans and activities are available to you.

Discovery Channel School

http://school.discoveryeducation.com/index.html

Lesson plans, teaching tools, and streaming video make this a very valuable resource for teachers of all grade levels.

The Lesson Plans Page
www.LessonPlansPage.com

Free lesson plans in all subject areas for all grade levels are included. They are well organized by subject matter and grade level. Science projects and inspirational stories are additional features.

Websites for Information on Standards

Developing Educational Standards
http://www.educationworld.com/standards/

This valuable website enables you to download national and state standards. State standards can be accessed by state or subject matter.

Department of Education
http://www.ed.gov

Here you will find the updated information on federal mandates, programs, grants, standards, statistics, and educational resources.

CHAPTER 25
HOW DO I COMMUNICATE POSITIVE EXPECTATIONS TO MY STUDENTS?

If you accept the expectations of others, especially negative ones, then you never will change the outcome.

Michael Jordan

A master can tell you what he expects of you.
A teacher, though, awakens your own expectations.

Patricia Neal

Effectiveness Essentials

- High classroom and schoolwide expectations can and do affect student achievement and attitudes.
- A *self-fulfilling prophecy* occurs when an initial perception of a situation or performance creates behaviors that make the original impression come true.
- By creating a positive classroom atmosphere, teachers play a critical role in helping students develop positive outlooks about themselves.

STATISTICS

Met Life's (2009) "Survey of the American Teacher" has found the following:

- Nearly nine in ten teachers (86%) and principals (89%) believe that setting high expectations for all students will have a major impact on improving student achievement.
- Most teachers (84%) are very confident that they have the knowledge and skills necessary to enable all of their students to succeed academically.
- Only 36% of teachers and 51% of principals believe that *all* of their students have the ability to succeed academically.
- Slightly more than half of students (53%) strongly agree that *all* of the teachers in their school want them to succeed.
- About two-thirds of teachers (64%) and principals (69%) strongly agree that it is important for all students to have one year or more of post-secondary education.
- On average, teachers expect that 50% of their students will attend a two- or four-year college, and principals expect 57% of their students to attend.
- Eight in ten students (79%) plan to attend a two- or four-year college after high school, but only about half of students (55%) are very confident that they will achieve their goals for the future.
- More girls than boys have aspirations to attend college (85% versus 73%) and believe they will achieve their goals (59% versus 50%).

(continued on facing page)

There was no question in my house about whether or not my sister and I would go to college. It was an expectation, reinforced from the time I was very young. I am sure that you have had similar experiences in your life. Either someone set the bar very high and you succeeded in jumping over it, or you were told, "No, that's not possible." When told that you could not do something, you may have either given up or tried to prove the naysayer wrong.

The Self-Fulfilling Prophecy

High classroom and schoolwide expectations can and do affect student achievement and attitudes. A key finding of effective schools research confirms that high expectations are a critical element for success. In effective schools, high expectations are communicated through policies and practices that focus on academic goals. For example, when schools raise their academic qualifications for student athletes, some students may feel unfairly targeted, but ultimately they can choose to adjust and work harder to meet the higher academic qualifications.

The general consensus is that a strong relationship exists between what we believe about students and what they can achieve. This is also known as a *self-fulfilling prophecy.* A self-fulfilling prophecy occurs when an initial perception of a situation or performance creates behaviors that make the original impression come true. Educators and the public in general have come to believe that the self-fulfilling prophecy is real and that both high and low expectations can affect student achievement. Consider the following hypothetical examples.

Let's say a student transfers into your math class from another high school and her records are late in arriving. You assume she is at grade level and make no accommodations in her program. You expect from her what you expect from all other students, and she performs up to speed. When her records arrive, you are surprised to find out that she is a student with special needs who is part of the special education math inclusion program. Was she misdiagnosed originally? Did she appreciate the challenge and rise to the occasion to meet your higher expectations?

On the other side, the brother of a student you had two years ago arrives in your sixth-grade class. You wrongly assume he is as disruptive as his older brother was. You seat him away from all the other students, praise him less than other students for the same positive responses and behaviors, and discipline him more harshly for ordinary offenses. Pretty soon you have a behavior problem on your hands, one of your own making!

There Is Early Evidence About the Power of Expectations

In their 1968 study, *Pygmalion in the Classroom,* Robert Rosenthal and Lenore Jacobson were the first to suggest that teachers' expectations have a tremendous effect on student achievement. The purpose of the study was to test the hypothesis that teacher behaviors and the resulting student outcomes could be influenced by the expectations of the teachers. Rosenthal and Jacobson predicted that when teachers were informed that certain students had more intellectual potential than others, the teachers might behave in ways that supported this expectation, which would then affect student scores on IQ tests.

In their study, two groups of students in grades 1 through 6 were evenly matched for intelligence. Teachers were given fabricated information about the learning potential of one group, the experimental group. Teachers were told that testing results showed these students to be on the verge of a rapid surge in intellectual development. Because teachers believed this assertion to be true, they challenged them more than they did students in the control group who were, in fact, no different intellectually. At the end of the experiment, the students in the experimental group, especially those in the early grades, displayed higher achievement on IQ tests than did the students in the control group. The results led the researchers to suggest that the high expectations teachers set for the experimental group and the teacher behaviors those expectations generated were responsible for the unusual growth.

How Do Expectations Affect Outcomes?

What parents and teachers believe and act upon makes an indelible impression on kids. The positive expectations as well as the negative ones or the expectations that are left unsaid all leave their mark.

Good (1987) describes the process by which teacher expectations affect student outcomes. (See Figure 25.1 for the circular process in graphic form.)

1. At the beginning of school, the teacher makes positive or negative judgments about expectations for student behavior and achievement from attributes such as gender, socioeconomic level, appearance, race, culture, language ability, etc. *(The math teacher believes boys are better at math than girls are.)*

- Nine in ten teachers (92%) and nearly all principals (96%) believe that having adequate public funding and support for education are very important for improving student achievement.
- Nine in ten teachers (88%) and principals (89%) believe that strengthening ties among schools and parents is very important for improving student achievement.

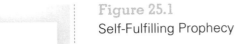

NOTES

Figure 25.1
Self-Fulfilling Prophecy

Teacher makes differing judgments about students.

Teacher behaves differently toward some students.

Students pick up on the positive or negative expectations.

They begin to act in accordance with the expectations.

Teacher expectations are confirmed.

Original expectations lead to low or high performance.

2. The teacher acts on those set attitudes toward some of the students based on preconceived notions about their race, socioeconomic level, gender, etc. *(The math teacher calls on boys more often or heaps more praise on the boys' responses.)*
3. The teacher's behavior communicates to the students his or her expectations for academic performance or behavior. *(Girls feel intimidated by being called on less often, and they stop trying. They begin to feel that they won't succeed in math, whereas boys are encouraged by all the attention and praise they receive.)*
4. When the teacher's behavior toward the students continues over time and is consistent, and if students do not actively resist or change it, their self-esteem, performance, and other behaviors begin to conform to the teacher's initial impression. *(The girls don't try as hard, stop listening in class, and lose interest. They stop raising their hands. Their grades begin to suffer.)*
5. The students' behavior then reinforces the teacher's perceptions, and the students conform even more to what has been expected. *(The girls' lower grades confirm the math teacher's initial perceptions.)*

Here is another example: A diminutive middle school student is told he will never make the varsity basketball team. The coach ignores him and doesn't let him play very often. The student gets the idea and stops practicing altogether. He comes to practice but doesn't even try. The coach thinks to himself, "I knew it." And the boy doesn't make the team. On the other hand, my son, relatively short in stature, practiced basketball from the time he was three years old with a toddler-sized hoop. He shot basket after basket; and when he went to high school, he threw his heart into it and let the coach know through attitude and performance that varsity ball was his goal and that his height wouldn't matter. He made the team. Was he more talented? Or did he just believe in himself more?

APPLY IT!

Think of a situation that you have been involved in where the original judgment led to either a positive or a negative self-fulfilling prophecy. You can choose any of the following factors, which often create self-fulfilling prophecies, or use any other factor that has led to positive or negative judgments.

Factors	Examples
Gender	Girls are more compliant and boys more resistant.
Race/ethnicity	Asians excel at science and math.
Socioeconomic status	Poor students don't have the means to go to college.
Grooming/ clothing	Boys who wear dark clothing are menacing.
School location	Violence is prevalent in urban classrooms.
Negative comments	Olivia's former teacher says that she is defiant.
Reading ability	Girls are better readers than boys are.

Researched-Based Practices for Conveying Positive Expectations

Being aware of any of your preconceived perceptions that are based on unfounded and unsupported evidence is a very important way to self-regulate and avoid negative self-fulfilling prophecies that will impede students' achievement. Conversely, when you focus on positive expectations, convey your belief that students will succeed, and structure learning to ensure success, your students will rise to the challenge. Research has

STUDENT SAYS . . .

My teacher is a good teacher because she makes you feel good about your work, so if you do something well she compliments and encourages you. When my teacher is happy, it makes the kids happy, and she is usually happy. She sets goals for the class, and the goals motivate our class to work like a team.

MEGAN
Seventh Grader, Age 12
Glenview, Illinois

NOTES

provided guidelines for conveying positive expectations in a proactive way.

Adhere to Standards

Adhere to standards without changing the expectations for your students based on prior achievement data or other teachers' opinions. Good (1987) suggests that goals be established without reference to prior achievement data that may set the bar too low. Take with a grain of salt other teachers' judgments about your students' learning potential. Find out for yourself where your students are vis-à-vis the standards. Don't lower the bar. Instead, communicate to your students in word and deed that they can and will achieve the standards and/or pass the exit exams.

Specify Objectives

Set objectives that are not too specific. Marzano, Pickering, and Pollack (2004) caution that when objectives are too specific or stated as behavioral objectives (measurable outcome, criteria, and conditions), the students may tune out the rest of the information while they narrowly focus on the stated objective. The goals, therefore, should be specific without being constraining and should allow students to adapt them to meet their own instructional needs. For example, an objective such as "students will name the planets" may cause the students to focus on memorizing them without regard to a more holistic understanding of the relationship of the planets to one another and to the sun.

APPLY IT!

Here are some incorrect responses you might receive in class and corresponding corrective feedback for two of them. How will you respond to the remainder?

Student Response	Teacher Corrective Feedback
There are 300 bones in the adult human body.	Actually there are 300 in kids and 206 in adults.
You spell assessment "A-S-S-E-S-M-E-N-T."	Try again with another *s* added.
There are six glasses in a quart.	
The president has the power to declare war.	
The square root of 144 is 14.	
The capital of New York is New York City.	

UNIT 6

Provide Effective Feedback

There are four types of feedback that teachers make use of: positive feedback (*Great!*), negative feedback (*No, that's not right*), neutral feedback (*restating the response or saying something noncommittal such as "Okay"*), and corrective feedback (*providing the correct answer*). Neutral feedback is effective when you want to promote multiple responses from your students. Corrective feedback puts students back on the right track and should be timely and specific to the response (Marzano et al., 2004). Tell students where they have gone right or wrong instead of just responding, "That's not right," or "Great!"

Teach Belief in Effort

Teach your students to believe in the value of effort. This means that you can provide encouragement for the little steps along the way to success, giving the "E for Effort!" Too little recognition is given for student efforts, according to Marzano et al. (2004), and students need to be made aware that efforts pay off. Very often, students do not see the big picture and give up when they make the slightest misstep. Your job is to stress again and again that mistakes are permitted. Make a poster to that effect to hang over the chalkboard. Respond to errors with either corrective feedback or comments such as "Let me help you fix that," or "Together we can figure this out." Have them recite this mantra every day: *What I believe about myself will affect how I perform and how successful I will be in school and in life.*

Provide Recognition

Provide recognition and dispel the notion that rewards decrease intrinsic motivation. Recognition should be given in nontangible form, whenever possible, and be tied to attainment of performance standards, according to Marzano et al. (2004). You can also dispense certificates, coupons, good-job stamps, stickers, and even treats or small prizes. These motivate students and reinforce the idea that there are rewards for a job well done or for sincere efforts along the way. Students will bask in the recognition, and the benefits in terms of self-worth and confidence are enormous.

Guard Your Instructional Time

Protect every minute of your instructional time. Time on task without disruptions will communicate positive expectations to your students. And positive expectations will convey to your students that they will succeed. When you make every minute

TEACHER TALKS . . .

I got a new homeroom class. I was kind of dreading it because a lot of teachers had been complaining about what a rough group these students are. I thought, "Oh God, can I handle this?" So I started preparing for the new class by asking our dean of students what the kids needed and which ones I had to keep my eye on. She spoke about one student who was failing on purpose because he wanted to live with his father who lives in a different state.

After meeting my homeroom students, I thought, "They aren't so bad! In fact, they're better than my first homeroom."

All special areas teachers have to spend 25 minutes out of 90 on preparation for the state's standardized tests. I was working with the kids, explaining how to read arithmetic questions. Then I called out some numbers to let them do some examples. The one who had been purposely failing last semester and another student kept raising their hands

(continued on following page)

TEACHER TALKS—*continued*

and answering questions correctly!

So during planning, I wrote them positive notes to take home to encourage their efforts. The one who had been failing was so excited when I talked to him and gave him his letter that he almost started to cry. He said, "I wish that I had you as my teacher last semester. You are the first one who has ever written my mother a positive note." At the end of study hall, he thanked me once again for the letter. I could tell that this is going to turn his year around. I know that this student will do great this semester even though he misses his father and wants to live with him. I could see it in his face. So often, teachers see the classification of their students rather than their potential. Too often, they see the negatives and not the positives. One positive thing can turn a student's lifetime of negatives around. The reward is awesome!

JENNIFER A. PONSART
Music Director
Davenport, Florida

(As seen on http://www.LessonPlansPage.com)

count, you are more likely to have students focused on the instruction without distractions. Strong school policies regarding lateness and absence will only increase the perception that school is important and that students need to be there in mind and body (Cotton, 1990).

Promote Literacy

Emphasize the importance of reading. Cotton (1990) reports that written policies regarding the amount of time spent on reading instruction daily, using a single reading series to maintain continuity, frequent free reading periods, and assigning homework that emphasizes reading will convey positive expectations. Reading is key to all learning; and the emphasis, time, and importance you allot to literacy, whatever subject you teach, will pay dividends in terms of student self-esteem.

Stress the Importance of Achievement Now and Later

Emphasize to your students the importance of academic achievement now and later in life. Some schools set minimal acceptable levels of achievement to qualify for participation in extracurricular activities and sports and notify parents when expectations aren't met (Cotton, 1990). There are too few students who believe that they can actually go to college. It is your challenge to make them believe they can do it and show them the baby steps along the way.

APPLY IT!

Go to www.biography.com and select some short biographies that show how people overcame initial difficulties to succeed later in life.

Take Responsibility

Take responsibility for the achievement of your students. Staff members who hold high expectations for themselves and for student performance are more likely to convey the message to students that they will succeed. Catch yourself when you want to play the blame game. Although there may be some valid reasons for students' earlier failures, big and small, it is your responsibility to take each student where he or she is and move that person forward. There is no greater compliment than a successful outcome that a student attributes to you.

Intervene Right Away

Intercede immediately when students need help. When students are having difficulty understanding a concept or demonstrating a skill, find out where the problem is and reteach in a different way, since the first way didn't work and merely repeating the same lesson will not help. Students have a variety of learning styles; and if you take into account the work of Howard Gardner (explained more fully in Chapters 22 and 28), you can offer the students alternative activities to meet the objectives you have set. Alternatively, cooperative learning groups (described in Chapter 27) are effective for students to help one another figure a problem out with minimal teacher intervention.

Connect Learning to Personal Experience

I remember someone telling me that you don't need to design dazzling enticements to motivate your students. Rather, just ask your students what they know, feel, or have experienced vis-à-vis a topic. The way to hook students into learning is to relate the topic to their experience or teach those subtopics that most interest them first.

Use the KWL strategy (Ogle, 1989), which requires a chart with three columns: What I Know, What I Want to Know, and later What I Learned. KWL is one specific strategy you can use to relate new material to prior experience and motivate your students to inquire more deeply. The students love to fill in the first column with all that they know from prior experience or instruction. As they activate their prior knowledge, they are motivated to learn about what they don't yet know or understand. Questions beget questions. Or use sentence stems like "When I think about democracy . . ." or "The questions that come to mind about the Civil War are . . ." (see Figure 25.2).

Use Heterogeneous Grouping and Cooperative Learning

Use heterogeneous grouping and cooperative learning activities. These strategies maximize students' strengths and minimize weaknesses. Everyone must pull together to succeed. *Either we all*

WATCH IT! video

Using KWL in Eighth-Grade Math

In this clip, the originator of the KWL strategy, Dr. Donna Ogle, discusses its usefulness in connecting students' experiences to learning. The strategy is demonstrated in an eighth-grade math class. What other curriculum areas lend themselves to using KWL?

STUDENT SAYS . . .

My social studies and science teachers are good at assigning special projects that we complete and then report on to the entire class. I think this is a good way to learn because you have to know the material well enough to be able to tell the entire class about the project. I like special projects best when they require sharing of information instead of a competitive situation. I think I usually learn a lot from listening to other students talk about their projects.

KATHLEEN
Ninth Grader, Age 14
Glenview, Illinois

STUDENT SAYS . . .

Mr. Peel is my P.E. teacher. We don't play traditional games. Mr. Peel makes up games by taking rules from two or three games and putting them together. He also gives the winning team's kids points, and at the end of the quarter he gives a soda to the kids with the most points. We made up a rhyme for him: "Deal with the Peel."

ALICIA
Fifth Grader, Age 10
Tucson, Arizona

Figure 25.2

Connecting to Personal Experience

K	W	L
What I Know About Penguins	What I Want to Know About Penguins	What I Learned About Penguins
They are birds.	*How big are they?*	*They walk long distances.*
They live in cold places.	*Do they fly?*	*Males sit on the eggs.*

sink or we all swim. The students help one another to accomplish the task, and the individual tasks are designed to play to each student's strength. Although the students are assigned individual tasks, there is group accountability for completion of the assignment and use of social conventions, and there is often one group grade. (See Chapter 27 for more about setting up and managing cooperative learning groups.)

Incorporate Diverse Learning Strategies and Problem Solving

Use diverse learning strategies and problem-solving tasks that have more than one answer. Stress to your students that they differ in their skills, abilities, talents, and approaches to learning. Make time for your students to examine one another's products, performances, solutions to problems, artworks, etc. This creates an atmosphere in which all students are equally valued, and no one is better or worse, just different. You will be pleasantly surprised when you break out of the "pour-and-store" mold and encourage creative responses or alternative solutions to problems. The students will be encouraged to recognize that diverse thinking and alternative responses are valued.

Establish a Positive Classroom Climate

Create a warm, friendly, and encouraging classroom climate. You will not compromise your authority when you show true concern for your students, act a little goofy, or do anything to help them learn, however silly it may look to others. You can return to Unit 4, Chapter 19 for suggestions.

mythBUSTER

Teaching is not a performance, and you are not an actor.

We were learning about the American Revolution in my fourth-grade classroom one year, and I could tell that my inner-city children were not getting it. They looked perplexed when we read about Paul Revere, Minutemen, and the Stamp Act, so I got creative! I told them about Paul Revere while pretending to ride my "horse" all over the classroom. Then they timed me as I "jumped out of bed" and "got dressed" as a Minuteman because the Red Coats were coming. They were delighted when I hopped up on one leg to get my boots on and nearly fell over in the process! It also took bringing in props and acting out all the various taxations, while rapping about "no taxation without representation" and the "bling-bling doesn't belong to the king-king" for my children to finally understand this piece of history. It may have looked crazy to anyone else, but it took acting out the revolution to make it real to my students.

Kim Bridgers
Fourth-Grade Teacher
Hermitage, Tennessee

APPLY IT!

Have your students create slogans, bumper stickers, badges, logos, tee shirts, etc. that communicate high expectations. These can be acronyms such as TOPS—Together Optimizing Pupil Success—or slogans such as Reach for the Stars!

Increase Your Wait Time

Allow students time to think before you expect an answer. Some students are quick on the draw, but others are more reflective. The fast responders can wait a little to allow the reflective responders to get a chance. You will encourage more student responses when you increase your wait time. The result will be greater participation and better responses (Rowe, 1972; Stahl, 1990). Wait at least three seconds before calling on a student, but the longer, the better. Count: 1 chimpanzee, 2 chimpanzees, 3 chimpanzees, 4 chimpanzees, 5 chimpanzees. That's about five seconds. Try it out!

You CAN Do It!

Dare to Dream
Reach for the Stars!

UNIT 6

STATISTICS

The U.S. Department of Education's National Center for Education Statistics (2009) offers these figures about the dropout rates of 16- through 24-year-olds:

Year	Total % of Students who Drop Out	White Students	Black Students	Hispanic Students
2000	10.9	6.9	13.1	27.8
2001	10.7	7.3	10.9	27.0
2002	10.5	6.5	11.3	25.7
2003	9.9	6.3	10.9	23.5
2004	10.3	6.8	11.8	23.8
2005	9.4	6.0	10.4	22.4
2006	9.3	5.8	10.7	22.1
2007	8.7	5.3	8.4	21.4

AVOID IT!

Avoid differentiating your high-expectation students from your low-expectation students in these ways:

- Calling on and waiting longer for responses from high-expectation students than from low-expectation students
- Praising high-expectation students more and criticizing low-expectation students more
- Seating low-expectation students in the back of the room farther away from you
- Giving less feedback and encouragement to low-expectation students
- Giving low-expectation students fewer opportunities than high-expectation students to learn new material
- Listening to lunchroom gossip about your students
- Giving less stimulating assignments to low-expectation students

Summary

Student achievement is influenced by the high expectations of both the classroom teacher and the school in general. The self-fulfilling prophecy occurs when an initial perception of a student or students creates teacher behaviors that make the initial impression come true. The self-fulfilling prophecy can be either a positive or a negative factor in the classroom, depending on the teacher's initial observations. Ways of conveying positive expectations include focusing on the standards, specifying objectives, providing effective feedback, providing recognition, teaching belief in effort, promoting literacy, guarding your instructional time, taking responsibility for your students' success, intervening when students experience difficulty, connecting learning to experience, using heterogeneous grouping, and offering strategies that engage students.

Reflect!

Reread and analyze the statistics throughout the chapter. Now draw some tentative conclusions, and consider the implications. For example, what conclusions can you draw from the Met Life survey of teachers', principals', and students' expectations? What interventions might be appropriate to raise the expectations for each of these groups? Likewise, what can you do to increase the retention rate for Hispanic students? How can you plan to create a positive classroom environment for your students?

CHAPTER 26

WHAT RESEARCH-BASED STRATEGIES SHOULD I CONSIDER?

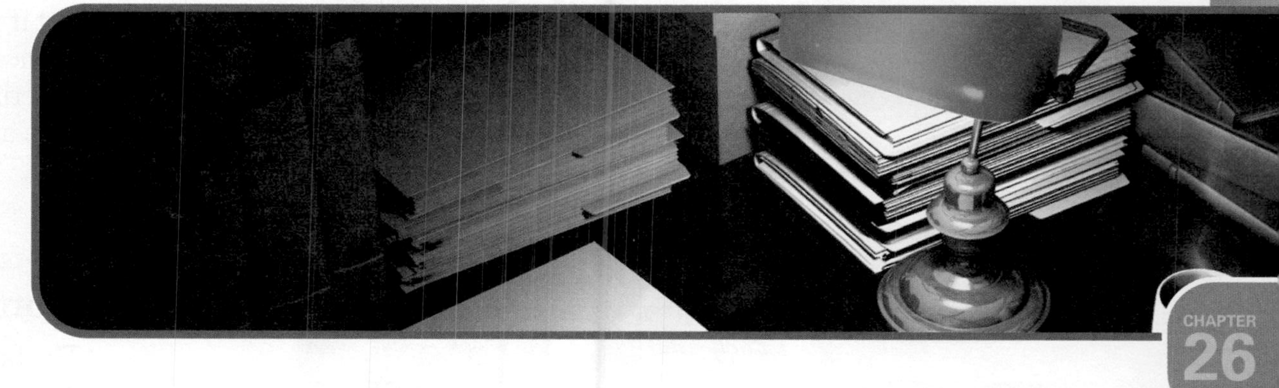

I never teach my pupils; I only attempt to provide the conditions in which they can learn.

Albert Einstein

Effectiveness Essentials

- Only recently have teaching strategies been put to the test of research.
- Some research-based strategies help students identify similarities and differences by comparing and contrasting material.
- Figures of speech have been proven to promote student creativity and to encourage student thinking.
- The use of graphic organizers has been proven to facilitate understanding.
- Advance organizers are general and higher-order concepts to which students can attach new information.

During your credentialing process, you likely have gathered an array of ideas, strategies, activities, and methods that purport to teach the concepts and skills you need to teach. In addition, you can go into any teacher supply store or read teacher magazines and come up with creative new ways to teach. However, today, teaching strategies have been put to the test of research. In fact, No Child Left Behind mandates that research-based strategies be implemented in classrooms. This is a cornerstone of the legislation. No longer can teachers just rely on strategies that have always worked for them. Now, by NCLB mandate, the strategies teachers use must be proven by research to be effective. In this chapter, you will learn some well-researched strategies, some of which are demonstrated in the video clips included on the website that accompanies this book.

In a nutshell, not only are these strategies based on research, but also they work because they actively engage students. These strategies require that students be connected to the material in ways that encourage their full participation. They are the opposite of passive lectures or demonstrations, although there is a place for those strategies in your repertoire as well. But if you want your students to be active learners and thoroughly engaged with the material, take a closer look at the video clips and the sample lessons that follow.

	Washington	Lincoln
Early Life		
Jobs		
Wars		
Successes		

Figures 26.1–26.4
Comparing and Contrasting

Comparing and Contrasting

The first group of strategies includes those that help students identify similarities and differences by comparing and contrasting. This skill is important at all levels and enables you to raise your students' thinking level beyond just knowledge and comprehension to analysis, the fourth level of Bloom's taxonomy (described in Chapter 22). They can do this on a Venn diagram or in chart form. Figures 26.1 through 26.4 identify some simple charts

APPLY IT!

Think about how you would design a classification activity. In teaching about ____ (fill in your topic) you might provide each group of students with envelopes containing words on pieces of paper and ask them to make categories. Or ask your students what they remember from a text segment, write all the words and phrases on the board, and then have them come up and use symbols to make categories. You can even play "Stump the Class" by having one student make a grouping and asking the rest of the class to guess the basis for the grouping. See Figure 26.5 on this page and Figure 26.6 on p. 310 for classification activities I have done with students, one on jobs in the community and one on jobs in ancient Egypt.

and graphic organizers you can use to help students distinguish the similarities and differences among several items. An example of a Venn diagram lesson is provided in the video clip.

Sorting Encourages Students to Look for Common Elements

Sorting is a strategy that encourages students to look for common elements

Figure 26.5
Job Classification Activity

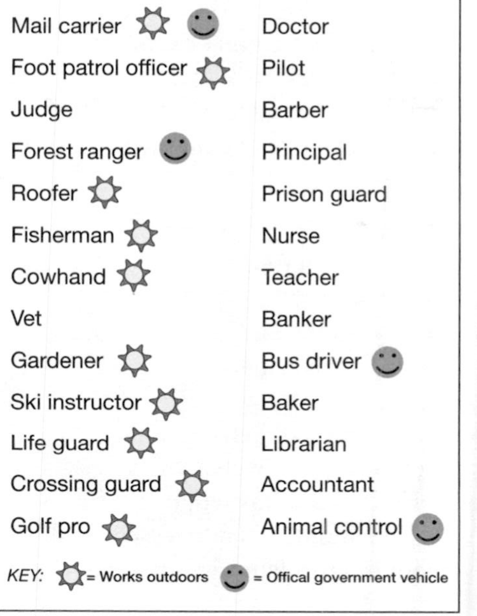

Mail carrier
Foot patrol officer
Judge
Forest ranger
Roofer
Fisherman
Cowhand
Vet
Gardener
Ski instructor
Life guard
Crossing guard
Golf pro
Doctor
Pilot
Barber
Principal
Prison guard
Nurse
Teacher
Banker
Bus driver
Baker
Librarian
Accountant
Animal control
KEY: = Works outdoors = Offical government vehicle

WATCH IT! video

Graphic Organizer: Venn Diagram
A teacher demonstrates use of a Venn diagram in literature class. After viewing the clip, create a lesson using any of the graphic organizers to enable your students to make comparisons among two or more items in any subject area. Fill in the diagram yourself to ensure that your students can make the comparisons.

CLASSROOM ARTIFACTS

This is a technology-based, integrated, five-step lesson plan that exemplifies comparing oneself to a character in a book. The plan includes adaptations for gifted students and students with learning challenges.

Title: "That's Me! No, It Isn't!"
Creator: Tamara Remhof
Primary subject: Language arts
Secondary subjects: Computers and Internet, social studies
Grade level: 9–10
Concept/topic to teach: how authors develop believable characters
Texas Essential Knowledge and Skills (TEKS) standards addressed: high school English language arts and reading, English I

(5) *Reading/Comprehension of Literary Text/Fiction*. Students understand, make inferences, and draw conclusions about the structure and elements of fiction and provide evidence from text to support their understanding. Students are expected to:

(B) Analyze how authors develop complex yet believable characters in works of fiction through a range of literary devices, including character foils.

General goal: Students will understand and explain what authors do to make their characters believable.
Specific objective: Students will develop a three- to five-minute presentation, using Photo Story 3, that describes five ways in which a character in a book is like them.

Required Materials:

- Photo Story 3
- Images and music from copyright-free sources
- Personal photos
- Book

Anticipatory Set (lead-in):

- What do you remember about the characters in your favorite book and why? Students can use this to start brainstorming ideas for their digital story.
- Show students a presentation made with Photo Story 3 that describes a character you are or are not like. (I'm very much like Neville Longbottom from Harry Potter!)

Step-by-Step Procedures:

1. **Brainstorm ideas.** Have students choose characters they think are or are not like them and discuss why. Students start listing the characters' attributes and their own.

(continues)

2. **Select character.** Students select a character from their list that is either very similar to them or opposite of them.
3. **Outline.** Students develop an outline for their digital story. They must include at least five images and two different transitions. The images can be personal photos, clip art, or copyright-free images from the Internet.
4. **Create storyboard.** Students will create a detailed storyboard that describes the images and a script for the narration that will be used on the project.
5. **Approve storyboards.** Review storyboards with students to be sure all elements are there and that students understand what is required.
6. **View projects.** After each class, view projects to ensure that students are following instructions and working through any technical difficulties.
7. **Add special effects.** Have students add the transitions, titles, credits, and special effects. Make sure they keep the projects to fewer than five minutes long.
8. **Copyright law.** Make sure students are following copyright law and crediting their sources.
9. **Save projects.** Have students save their projects after demonstrating how to do it.
10. **Deliver story.** Once the story is finished, make sure the students save the story as a ".wmv" file and turn it in to the completed projects folder.

Plan for independent practice: Students can use digital storytelling to describe their favorite books, music, etc.

Closure (reflect anticipatory set): Ask students if their friends would agree with them and why or why not. Do they see their friends like characters in a book?

Assessment Based on Objectives:

- Completed storyboard including script, narration, and timing instructions
- Content that demonstrates students' ability to compare real life with fictional characters
- Correctly documented copyrighted material
- Completed digital story no more than five minutes long, with five different images and two transitions and saved in ".wmv" format

Adaptations (for students with learning disabilities):

- Students work with a partner to develop storyboard and narration.
- Students have extra time to complete digital story.
- Students create a booklet that shows how they are like or not like a character.
- Students select a story and describe how a character is like or not like them.

(continues)

CLASSROOM ARTIFACTS—*continued*

Extensions (for gifted students): Students pick one element of the character they've chosen and describe how changing that element would change the story and why.

Possible connections to other subjects: Students can use digital storytelling for social studies, making connections in history and geography.

(as seen on http://www.LessonsPlanPage.com)

or attributes and sort them into the correct preestablished categories. Students may be asked, for example, to sort rocks into metamorphic, igneous, or sedimentary after learning the characteristics of each. Or they might be asked in math to sort pictures into color categories, shape categories, or number categories.

Classifying Enables Students to Form Their Own Concepts

Classifying is a similar strategy that enables students to form their own concepts, given just the data. This is a slightly higher order thinking strategy because the teacher does not provide the categories. The items to be classified may be actual items, pictorial representations, or words.

Figure 26.6
Classification Activity

Baskets	Sandals	Priests ♡	Papyrus	Pyramid
Scribe ♡	Pharaoh ♡	Desert	Nile	Delta
Mummy	Drought	Polytheism	Anubis	Scarab
Flood	Ra	Giza	Tut	Sphinx
Rosetta Stone	Farmer ♡	Tomb	Howard Carter	Artisan ♡
Valley of the Kings	Wall painting	Hieroglyphics	Rafts	Book of the Dead

KEY: ♡ = Jobs in ancient Egypt

WATCH IT! video

Animal Classification
Students sort pictures of animals in this elementary classification activity.

Figures of Speech

The use of certain figures of speech is another research-proven strategy that you may find useful in your practice. For example, Marzano and colleagues (2004) suggest that using metaphoric examples is yet another means of helping your students recognize similarities and differences. Joyce and Weil (2008) explain the use of figures of speech or metaphors in a teaching strategy called Synectics.

The use of figurative language can enliven learning by suggesting mental images that motivate and facilitate creative thinking. Three figures of speech commonly used in the classroom are similes, metaphors, and analogies.

A Simile Compares Two Unlike Things Using *Like* or *As*

A *simile* is a figure of speech that makes a comparison between two unlike things using the words *like* or *as*. "He acts like a couch potato," or "she is as silly as a goose." Here are some ways to formulate curriculum-based similes:

1. Simple comparison of two seemingly unlike specific things
   How is the heart like a pump?
   How is a volcano like a pimple?
   How is a cell like a factory?
   How is a teacher like a conductor?
2. Comparison of a category from which students choose an item to compare to a specific concept
   What fruit or vegetable is most like you? Why?
   What food is most like a diverse classroom? Why?
   What amusement park ride is most like life? Why?
3. Comparison of an abstract specific to a concrete specific
   Which is greener: jealousy or grass? Why?
   Which is thinner: an excuse or a piece of string? Why?
   Which is sweeter: a homecoming or a candy bar? Why?
   Which is denser: fog or an unwilling student? Why?

UNIT 6

APPLY IT!

1. Fill in these similes.

   As _______ as an ox
   As _______ as a bee
   As _______ as a feather
   As _______ as a cucumber

   As stubborn as a _______
   As wise as an _______
   As quiet as a _______
   As sly as a _______

2. Create similes to describe a diverse classroom.

   A diverse classroom is like _______.
   A diverse classroom is like _______ .
   A diverse classroom is like _______.

3. Underline and explain these metaphors.

   Sally and Jenny are two peas in a pod.
   The last test was a breeze.
   That hog ate the whole pizza.
   My boyfriend is a teddy bear.
   The mountain cabin was an icebox.

4. Now use the concept *middle school* to create metaphors.

   A middle school is a _______.
   A middle school is a _______.
   A middle school is a _______.

5. With your students, begin with questions like these and have them draw and write their responses.

   What fruit or vegetable is most like you? Why?
   What piece of furniture is most like you? Why?
   What musical instrument is most like you? Why?
   What appliance is most like you? Why?
   What crayon color is most like you? Why?
   What toy or game is most like you? Why?

Metaphors Require a Higher Level of Abstract Thinking

A *metaphor* is a comparison of two things using words that are not to be taken literally: "She is a fox," or "I'm drowning in work." Since they require a high level of abstract thinking, metaphors are perfect for your secondary students. You can give them metaphoric references in poetry and literature such as

The fog comes on little cat's feet.—Carl Sandburg
The heart is a lonely hunter.—Carson McCullers

Analogies Can Make Complicated Information Easier to Understand

An *analogy* is a comparison of two things that contain some similarities. Analogies are used to help explain something or make it easier to understand. Because analogies require such abstract thinking, only the simplest should be used with younger students.

Cat is to ______________ as *dog* is to *puppy*.
Paint is to *artist* as ______________ is to *potter*.
Hot is to *chili* as ______________ is to *ice cream*.
Barometer is to ______________ as *thermometer* is to *temperature*.
Humans are to *carbon dioxide* as *plants* are to ______________.

In all of these examples, "Why?" is the important question to ask.

For secondary students who are capable of abstract thinking, you might want to select examples from the Miller Analogies Test, which is used in graduate school admissions. The following list shows four examples for the comparison phrase "is to" or "are to." You can see the rest of the examples and test yourself at http://www.testprepreview.com/ Also, see the Apply It! on p. 314 for additional examples and a chance to design some of your own.

1. VASE : AMPHORA as FLOWERS : ______________.
   a. wine b. glass
   c. leaves d. grain
2. VINEGAR : ______________ as ACETIC : CITRIC.
   a. apple b. oil
   c. tea d. lemon
3. CONSTITUTION : MAGNA CARTA as UNITED STATES : ______________.
   a. Pilgrims b. Virginia
   c. England d. Rome
4. ___________ : ACROPHOBIA as SPIDERS : ARACHNOPHOBIA.
   a. water b. crowds
   c. noise d. heights

Answers: 1a; 2d; 3c; 4d

Graphic Organizers

The use of graphic organizers has been proven to facilitate understanding. Marzano et al. (2004) refer to them as nonlinguistic representations. Some already have been explained in this chapter. Several formats for you to consider are shown in Figures 26.7 through 26.10.

Figure 26.7
Sequence Chart

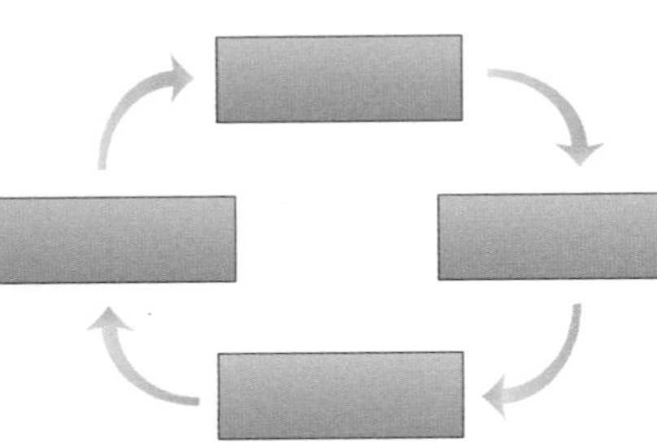

Figure 26.8
Circular Chart

APPLY IT!

Analogies can best be taught when students are asked to look at the relationship between the first and second half of elements, to state the relationship, and then to formulate a response. The elements can be related in many ways (adapted from Lewis and Green, 1982, and Marzano et al., 2004):

Synonyms (*Pleased* : *contented* as *sad* : *cheerless*.)
Antonyms (*Late* : *early* as *dog* : *cat*.)
Same class (*Hat* : *scarf* as *apple* : *pear*.)
Class name/specific (*Dog* : *Pekinese* as *cat* : *Siamese*.)
Part to a whole (*Slice* : *pizza* as *section* : *grapefruit*.)
Change (*Kitten* : *cat* as *puppy* : *dog*.)
Function (*Potter* : *clay* as *painter* : *oils*.)
Quantity/size (1/4 : 1/2 as 1/8 : 1/4.)

Now make up an analogy for each one of the possible constructions and leave out one element so you can challenge someone to complete it.

Sequence Charts Place Events in Order

Sequence charts help students place events in order. They can be used for:

- Time-lines
- Plot sequence
- Steps in an experiment
- Project procedures
- Storyboards
- Steps in problem solving
- Directions

Circular Charts Depict Cyclic Events

Circular charts can be used to help students visualize or depict cyclic events such as:

- The water cycle
- The food chain
- The seasons

Concept Maps Represent Ideas

Concept maps are another way to represent ideas in graphic form. *Kidspiration* and *Inspiration* (http://www.inspiration.com) are superb technological applications, but you can make webs on your board or on charts as well.

Advance Organizers

Advance organizers are general and higher-order concepts to which students can attach new information. They are

Figure 26.9
Concept Map

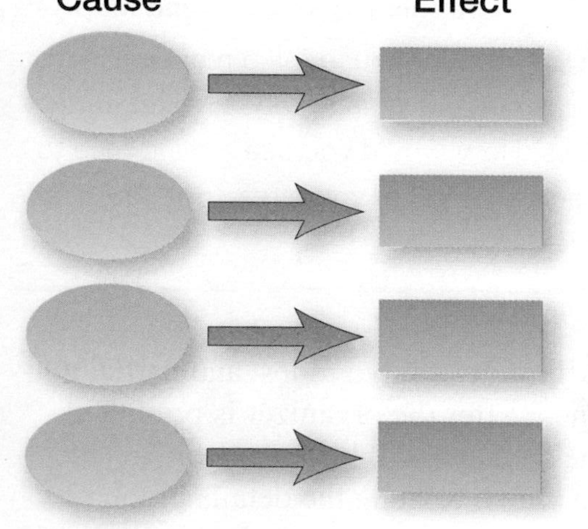

Figure 26.10
Large Wall Concept Map

typically the first step in direct instruction strategies and provide a framework or scaffold upon which subsequent information is hung. In other words, the advance organizer is the "big picture"—the large, important idea that is somewhat universal. Think of the advance organizer as the trunk of a tree. The subconcepts branch out from the trunk, and the supporting facts are the leaves on the branches.

Advance organizers were first introduced as a teaching strategy by David Ausubel (1968) and have been shown

WATCH IT! video

Fifth-Grade Strategies

The students are creating moon journals in the form of sequence charts. What would you do after they have created the sequence charts? This teacher has them choose a date and compare and contrast another date of their choosing.

by Marzano and his colleagues (2004) to be very effective in helping students to order or scaffold their learning. The use of advance organizers has also been shown to improve levels of understanding and recall, especially when the material is difficult to understand or disorganized.

Advance Organizers Require Hierarchical Structure

This strategy is the opposite of discovery learning. The advance organizer is presented first and explained up front. It can be in the form of a story, a personal narrative, or a graphic organizer and can involve previewing text material through skimming, study guides, and partial outlines. After the organizer is presented, the students will have a cognitive ladder on which to hang the details of the new material. The new material is presented in light of the advance organizer, so

WATCH IT! video

Graphic Organizer: Mind Map

Students use mind mapping in cooperative learning groups in literature class. How would you use a mind map to teach a lesson in your area or at your grade level?

APPLY IT!

Create a direct instruction lesson using an advance organizer. Where will you find these "big ideas"? They are usually highlighted in your textbooks or manuals. Use a story, photos, skimming, or narratives to introduce the big ideas. You will see that being up front with the main ideas will enable students to latch on more quickly than they might have otherwise.

APPLY IT!

Design a partial outline for your subject area. Try it out on your students and notice their enthusiasm for filling it in by skimming or reading the text. The outline becomes a tool for studying. Apply all of these strategies in one instructional unit, along with the two research-based strategies that lend themselves to cooperative learning, which are discussed in the next chapter.

there is no discovery or guessing game involved in this direct instruction strategy.

Let's take the example of *cultural diffusion*—that is, the influence of one culture on another through the spread of ideas, products, or processes. This is the advance organizer or "big idea." I once taught a lesson to sixth graders on how Greek culture influenced the Romans who followed them. I began by defining *cultural diffusion.* I showed students photos I had taken in China and Russia, which included several recognizable brands such as soft drinks, common brands of tennis shoes, and signs for our familiar fast-food restaurants. Then I asked them for examples of how other cultures have impacted our lifestyle. They gave me plenty of ideas—from food to music to clothing. At that point they were ready to learn how the concept of cultural diffusion was exemplified in the case of Greek and Roman culture.

There Are Several Types of Advance Organizers

Being up front with students about what you are trying to convey can also be accomplished through study guides, teacher-prepared notes, and partial outlines. Study guides ask focused questions so students know what is important to study. Teacher-prepared notes present the material in an outline or framework so students can easily ascertain what is essential and what is not. A partial outline is very useful because it gives away only part of the information and the students must do some detective work to fill it in. A partial outline for ancient Greek architecture might look like this example in Figure 26.11.

AVOID IT!

Avoid becoming set in your ways and using any one strategy, over and over again, no matter how effective it is. The research-based strategies in this chapter and the others presented in the next chapter should give you a better equipped toolbox to meet the differing learning styles of your students. Vary your instructional strategies to avoid boredom.

STUDENT SAYS . . .

Good teachers direct the class with note taking, and I end up with good notes that really help me when I study for a test. My best learning happens when my teacher is good at explaining a concept, just doesn't make me memorize a lot of facts I'll forget, and allows me to be creative.

KATHLEEN
Ninth Grader, Age 14
Glenview, Illinois

CHAPTER 26

Figure 26.11
Partial Outline

Parthenon

I. Rooms

A. Pronos - front porch
B. Naos - main room with statue of Athena
C. ________________ back room for offerings

II. __________ column
(Name of Greek column)

A. Number of columns in Parthenon
1. 8 at each end instead of the usual 6
2. __________ on each side
3. __________

B. Parts of a Doric column
1. capital define ___________________
2. abacus define ___________________
3. ______ define ___________________

Summary

When teaching strategies are put to the test of research, several emerge as the most effective for engaging students and connecting them to the material. Among the research-based strategies that Marzano et al. (2004) endorse and advocate are those that require students to compare and contrast, sort, classify, contemplate metaphors and other figures of speech, design or fill in graphic organizers, and apply advance organizers. Since these are all generic strategies, a teacher can use them in every grade level and curriculum area.

Reflect!

Depending on your grade level and/or curriculum area, you might favor some of these strategies over others. Which of the strategies explained in the chapter seem most adaptable to your teaching situation? Outline a mini-unit using at least three of them. Which strategies seem to be inappropriate for your instructional context? Try one of these out with students, and you may be surprised.

CHAPTER 27
HOW DO I COMBINE RESEARCH-BASED STRATEGIES WITH COOPERATIVE LEARNING GROUPS?

Great discoveries and improvements invariably involve the *cooperation* of many minds. I may be given credit for having blazed the trail, but when I look at the subsequent developments I feel the credit is due to others rather than to myself.

Alexander Graham Bell

Effectiveness Essentials

- Many classroom activities lend themselves to cooperative learning.
- Cooperative learning groups are heterogeneous groupings of students who work together to complete tasks while learning social skills that foster cooperation.
- Two research-based strategies that can be conducted in cooperative learning group format are reciprocal teaching and problem solving.

Cooperative learning is an effective research-based strategy that works with many classroom activities (Marzano et al., 2004). In particular, it can facilitate learning in a multicultural classroom and can help English language learners. In this chapter, you will learn to structure cooperative learning activities and implement two research-based strategies that use the format: reciprocal teaching and project-based learning. First, let's take a look at the basic principles of cooperative learning.

Principles of Cooperative Learning

Cooperative learning groups are heterogeneous groupings of students who work together to complete tasks while learning social skills that foster cooperation. Basic principles of cooperative learning include, but are not limited to, the following:

- Optimal group size is three to five students, according to most proponents.
- Each member of the group is an active participant.
- Membership in groups reflects heterogeneity with regard to ability, social class, gender, ethnicity, and language differences. In other words, cooperative learning groups reflect the real world.
- Cooperative groups foster interdependence among the members through the sharing of materials, group accountability, or individual contributions to one final product.
- Students practice social skills (for example, saying "please" and "thank you," using names, and making eye contact) in cooperative groups.
- Students are encouraged to solve their problems without teacher intervention.

Teachers who use cooperative learning begin with groups of three or four students. Some of the tasks students can work on in cooperative groups are preparing research reports, with each member becoming an expert on a part of the topic; editing stories; creating a crossword puzzle; deciphering a word search; making a collage; playing matching games; conducting experiments; brainstorming; making a chart or graph; and solving a puzzle.

TEACHER TALKS . . .

After input and a test on poetic devices and figurative language, I assign each student one poem. I group the poems by theme: love, death, war, nature, etc. Each group (four or five students in a group) discusses all the poems in the group to determine what theme they have in common. Group members also must decide how each poet treats the theme differently and come up with reasons why.

Then each group presents its poems and leads a class discussion. Members are required to read their poems aloud and use some kind of visual aid. (Students in one group wore berets and brought in coffee to create a coffeehouse setting.) After all groups are finished, each student writes a critical analysis of his or her poem.

When finished, each student has studied his or her own poem in great depth, the poems in his or her group in some depth, and

(continued on facing page)

WATCH IT! video

Cooperative Learning—Middle School

Students in a science lab work cooperatively and rotate to conduct experiments at several stations.

Cooperative Learning—Elementary

A fifth-grade teacher challenges students in cooperative groups to come up with story problems about fractions.

Cooperative Learning—Primary

In this clip you will see a primary-grades teacher using visuals to identify the roles in the cooperative groups. Can this technique be used with older students? How would you modify it?

Cooperative Learning—Middle School/Nonverbal Task

In this clip a middle school teacher uses puzzle pieces to teach the principles of cooperative learning to her students. She then discusses the positive attributes of cooperative learning.

After viewing the videos, what do you see as the advantages and disadvantages of the cooperative learning approach? Were the three pillars of cooperative learning—interdependence, accountability, and social or process skills—evident in the lessons?

Cooperative Learning Has Positive Outcomes

In cooperative groups, students can learn from one another while participating in ways that address their strengths. The value of the strategy for addressing diversity of all kinds cannot be overemphasized. Outcomes of cooperative learning may include:

- Increased understanding of differences and diversity
- Increased self-esteem
- Increased problem solving and academic achievement
- Increased comfort with computer technology when computers are used

Successful Cooperative Learning Involves Several Steps

Many teachers fear that cooperative learning is a synonym for controlled chaos. They avoid the strategy because it appears so vague and unstructured. Some of you may have had a bad experience when you tried cooperative learning. I have simplified the steps in the process so you can feel more confident and give it a try.

1. First, decide on a task that can be divided evenly into three or four equal parts. An example would be story editing. The jobs might be Punctuation Editor, Capitalization Editor, Spelling Editor, and Overall Organization Editor. Clearly explain and demonstrate what each job is about.
2. Denote which jobs are which using color-coded posters and tickets. You can change the key for different cooperative learning tasks each time, reusing the posters and tickets (see Figures 27.1 and 27.2).
3. Hand out the tickets to groups of four, and have each student choose a ticket color coded to the job he or she wants. If the students can't decide in three minutes, you will decide.
4. Set a time limit and announce a social skill, such as talking softly, saying please or thank you, sharing materials, calling one another by name, listening, etc.
5. Monitor the groups and check to see that the groups are using the skill.
6. Review with the students how things went, and have them fill out an evaluation of their participation, use of skill, etc. (see Figure 27.3).
7. In middle and high school, experiment with cooperative learning groups even though the class periods may be short. You can set aside time during several sessions and not feel you have to complete the task all in one sitting.

Figure 27.1
Large Color Posters Renamed for Each Task

Key:
Green = Check capitals.
Blue = Check punctuation.
Purple = Check spelling.
Orange = Does it make sense?

Figure 27.2
Color Tickets Coordinated to Tasks

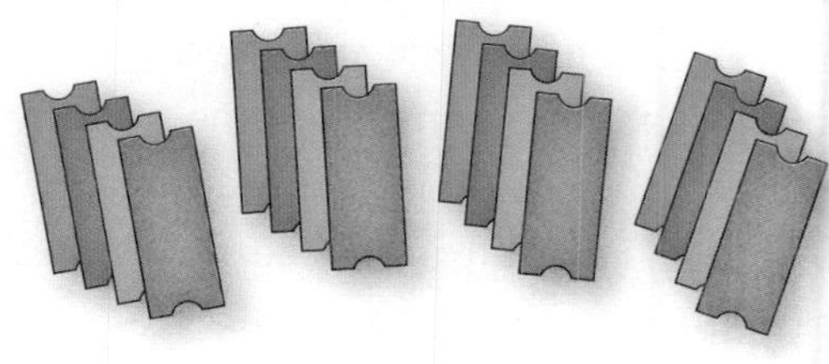

all the other poems in the class briefly.

SUSAN JOHNSON
AP English and Language Arts Teacher
Richwood, West Virginia

(as seen on http://www.LessonPlansPage.com)

TEACHER TALKS . . .

I had a very fractious, difficult class last year because everybody wanted to be the leader and nobody wanted to be a follower. Getting students to do anything together or to cooperate on projects was a nightmare. This year, I have a very compliant group of fifth graders who all want to be followers! They are most content to let me be the leader, and they follow along accordingly. When I had laryngitis a couple of weeks ago, I wrote on the board that I could not speak at all and asked them if they would care to decorate our classroom bulletin board to illustrate our current reading book, My Side of the Mountain*. One hour later, their finished product was absolutely*

(continued on following page)

TEACHER TALKS—*continued*

beautiful to behold, with no help from me other than that I had supplied the paper, scissors, staplers, etc. They worked beautifully together and said please and thank you. Nobody fought, no harsh words were spoken, and the finished product is very creative and well done.

SHANNON VANDERFORD
Fifth-Grade Teacher
West Memphis, Arkansas

(as seen on http://www.LessonPlansPage.com)

AVOID IT!

Avoid the use of generic jobs in your cooperative group planning. Some of the job titles I have heard include Harmonizer, Consultant, Facilitator, and Peacemaker, as well as the more common Materials Distributor, Recorder, and Reporter. The problem with these titles is that they don't pertain to each and every lesson, and that's why cooperative learning frustrates some teachers. Often, the only students who do the actual work are the Recorder and the Reporter. The Materials Distributor is done at the beginning, and the Harmonizer harmonizes without having a real job.

Figure 27.3
Cooperative Learning Feedback/Evaluation

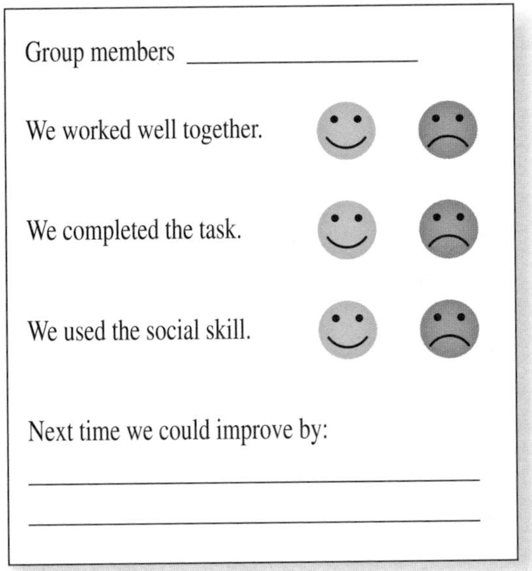

Group members ____________

We worked well together. ☺ ☹

We completed the task. ☺ ☹

We used the social skill. ☺ ☹

Next time we could improve by:

____

____

Reciprocal Teaching

This research-based strategy can be conducted in a cooperative learning group format. Palincsar and Brown (1986) describe reciprocal teaching as an instructional activity that requires a dialogue between teachers and students to facilitate comprehension of text. The dialogue is structured around four jobs, making it conducive to cooperative learning.

There Are Several Jobs in Reciprocal Teaching

Although one student leader can do all four jobs, with input from the group members, the leadership can be distributed equally as follows:

The **Summarizer** summarizes what has been read with the help of the other students or teacher, if need be.

The **Questioner** asks questions to help the group members better understand the passage.

The **Clarifier** clarifies or asks others in the group to better explain what they mean.

The **Predictor** leads the group in a discussion about what may happen next.

APPLY IT!

Think of some activities that you normally use that might lend themselves to a cooperative learning format. Remember that the jobs should be equal. Use a pie chart to create the three, four, or five equal tasks that can be distributed among group members (see Figure 27.4).

Figure 27.4
Pie Charts

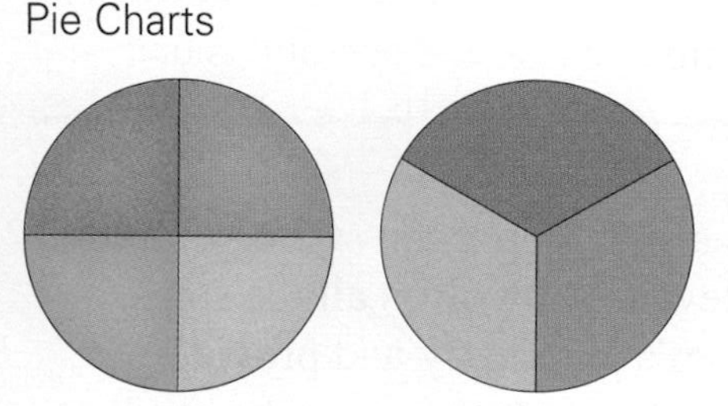

Here Are Suggested Steps for a Reciprocal Teaching Lesson

Reciprocal teaching lends itself to very clearly defined roles and procedures. In fact, it is so structured that you might try this strategy as your initiation into cooperative learning before you try anything more complex.

1. Group students (four per group).
2. Identify students in each group for each of the four roles for the first round.
   Summarizer
   Questioner
   Clarifier
   Predictor
3. Students read ____ paragraphs and use note-taking strategies.
4. The Summarizer draws attention to the key ideas.
5. The Questioner poses questions regarding the selection.
6. The Clarifier addresses puzzling elements and tries to answer the questions that were posed.
7. The Predictor offers guesses about what comes next.
8. Repeat the process for the next ____ paragraphs, switching roles to the right or left.

WATCH IT! video

Reciprocal Teaching

This high school classroom clip explains how reciprocal instruction can be used beyond the reading strategy described in the text described on p. 325. What other sources are there for a reciprocal teaching lesson?

Problem Solving

This is the second research-based strategy that can be conducted in cooperative group format. Other common names you have heard for problem-solving strategies are *inquiry, group investigation,* and what Marzano and colleagues (2004) call *generating and testing hypotheses*.

Inquiry Engages Students in Exploration

Inquiry is the very opposite of listen-and-learn, or pour-and-store, methods of teaching. Rather, it engages students in a process of exploration that requires them to formulate questions and find answers leading to new understanding. The teacher becomes a facilitator instead of the all-knowing guru and is recast as a fellow inquirer or as a mentor or guide.

APPLY IT!

Try out a reciprocal teaching lesson. Use your textbooks as the source of reading material. Model each step along the way before you set the students to the task. Use PowerPoint or the digital projector to demonstrate how to approach the text material. Have your students read along with you. Act out each of the four roles yourself, modeling what kind of statements or questions each group member is likely to say or ask. Check for understanding by having your students work as a whole group to practice each role separately while you give them feedback. Then have them get into their groups, assign a short text passage, set a time limit, and let them go for it. Monitor them and provide corrective feedback if needed. Debrief them and ask for suggestions on how to improve the process. If you need more information, refer to the references at the end of this unit.

This is a very important strategy for all grade levels. It involves all the steps in Bloom's taxonomy and provides opportunities for students to truly act as scientists or social scientists, exploring questions that they formulate and

WATCH IT! video

Motivating through Problem-Based Learning

Students in high school plan a project based at their local airport.

Math Strategies for Problem Solving

Elementary students are encouraged to use problem solving in math to determine average height.

Inquiry Learning

In this video clip, a fourth-grade teacher uses a net-based simulation about endangered tigers along with cooperative learning to engage her students in project-based learning.

Experiential Learning

In this field-based experiential learning activity, middle school students use their senses in a problem-solving strategy exploring plants.

After viewing the video clips, identify the advantages and disadvantages of using a problem- based approach. Would it be difficult for you as a first-year teacher to try problem-based teaching? Why or why not? Design a problem-based lesson plan. What will be your hook?

designing experiments or experiences to validate or negate their initial conceptions or understanding of any given problem.

What Are the Steps in Inquiry?

Although they differ slightly from one another, generally the steps include:

1. A problem or puzzling situation to be solved or resolved
2. Generation of questions or hypotheses
3. An experiment to test hypotheses or study tasks or research to solve a problem
4. Independent and cooperative group research or experimentation
5. An analysis and interpretation of the data
6. A report of the conclusions

UNIT 6

TEACHER TALKS . . .

My fifth-grade students built a model replica of the Wright brothers' 1903 flyer. The model weighed nearly 75 pounds and measured 22 feet by 10 feet. After immersing my students in appropriate literature about the Wright brothers, I was able to introduce the scientific and mathematical components of the project. I instructed my students to use power tools correctly and responsibly and gave them step-by-step instruction about the construction itself. The students decided to paint the airplane red, white, and blue as a tribute to our great nation. My principal, who supported the project from the very beginning, has been my mentor and inspiration for such an undertaking. I proceeded with this project in a manner that would give her and her school recognition for her wonderful leadership and guidance. Any success, in my eyes, was a dedication to her for her generosity. I converted the classroom into a mini

(continued on facing page)

For example, I brought to my methods class a Japanese good luck figure called a *daruma,* as shown in the photo. I asked the students what they thought it was. We listed responses on the board. Then I asked what country or culture might have made it. We listed responses on the board. I asked how we could find out. The students listed several sources of information such as looking at art books and textbooks, asking people, querying members of the anthropology department, and going to the campus museum, among others. I told the students that there was only one object and that I couldn't let it out of my sight. They proposed drawing it, and some photographed it with their digital phones and cameras. We decided that everyone would have the chance before class next time to show their drawings or photos to people they encountered. We organized cooperative groups of four to distribute the four questions that needed to be answered:

Japanese daruma dolls are a sign of good fortune.

1. Is it a special person?
2. When and where was the first one made?
3. What is its purpose?
4. Where are they found in our community?

Excitement was high the next session as we compared answers. Several of the students brought darumas to class, and one student even made one from papier-mâché. Everyone in class had an idea for trying inquiry in his or her field experience, from a gnarled piece of ginger in kindergarten, to a photo of Confucius in sixth grade, to bringing in a dollar bill

AVOID IT!

Avoid being too directive when students are tackling a problem. Part of the strategy involves their ability to work things out for themselves. Intervene when necessary, but challenge them to figure problems out for themselves whenever possible.

Students built a replica of the Wright brothers' airplane.

Teacher Perry Lopez credits his principal as an inspiration.

and exploring the meaning of the symbols on the reverse in a high school government class. We learned this was a strategy that works with all ages.

Summary

The strategies outlined in this chapter are research-based and are generic enough to apply to all grade levels and curriculum areas. Cooperative learning strategies have been shown to be effective with all learners, in particular with English language learners. There are many ways to implement the strategy, but the teacher's careful organization can make the difference between a successful lesson and chaos. The steps for implementing cooperative learning are outlined in this chapter, and another research-based strategy that draws on cooperative learning, reciprocal teaching, is covered as well. Inquiry or project-based learning, another research-based strategy that capitalizes on students' interests, has many different formats and applications. All forms of inquiry learning can engage students in higher-order thinking, research, and the scientific method.

museum and added a puppet show, printing press, family tree, schematics table, raffle table (Wright brothers memorabilia), and an assembly line that re-created a small replica of the flyer. My students became the hosts for other students, district representatives, and parents. My proud students demonstrated that they were able to achieve a high degree of critical thinking.

PERRY LOPEZ
Fifth-Grade Teacher
Bronx, New York

(as seen on http://www.LessonPlansPage.com)

CHAPTER 27

Reflect!

As you read the chapter, you may have found these strategies daunting to implement, especially as a novice teacher. At this point, what do you see as the advantages and disadvantages of both of these strategies? List all your questions and concerns on the chart below. Inquire further into the strategies, using the references at the end of the unit, and ask as many teachers as you can how they implement both cooperative learning and project-based learning.

	Cooperative Learning	Project-Based Learning
Advantages		
Disadvantages		
Questions/concerns		

CHAPTER 28

HOW DO I DIFFERENTIATE INSTRUCTION TO MEET THE NEEDS OF ALL LEARNERS?

> We have become not a melting pot but a beautiful mosaic.
>
> *Jimmy Carter*

Effectiveness Essentials

- You will find that diverse classrooms are the rule rather than the exception.
- Howard Gardner has identified eight facets of intelligence.
- Differentiated learning describes a set of principles that enable you to meet the broad range of readiness, interests, abilities, talents, and skills in your classroom.
- The three components of instruction that can be modified are the content, the process, and the products.
- RTI is a specific approach to differentiated instruction.

STATISTICS

According to a joint report by the National Comprehensive Center for Teacher Quality and Public Agenda (2008), teachers vary in their confidence about teaching a diverse student population:

- 76% of teachers say they learned how to teach diverse students in their coursework.
- 23% say diversity was not covered.
- 39% of teachers say that their diversity training helped a lot.
- 52% say it helped a little.
- 8% say it did not help at all.

Teaching is such a complex profession that I can offer only one assurance in this book—you will have a perfectly successful year if all of your students are cloned from one individual of your choosing. I can make this offer knowing that at some time in the sci-fi future, I may have to pay out, but I feel confident at the moment.

Individual Differences

On that first day of school, the individual differences in your class will jump out at you. Gender and physical differences are only the tip of the iceberg. Beneath the surface are students from different socioeconomic strata; students who come from various family configurations; students with special needs, differing interests, and many abilities; students with different cultural backgrounds, different languages, different learning styles, and different attitudes toward school. This is not a new phenomenon. In one-room schoolhouses of the past, teachers had a similar challenge.

You will find that diverse classrooms are the rule rather than the exception. You can look at this new population

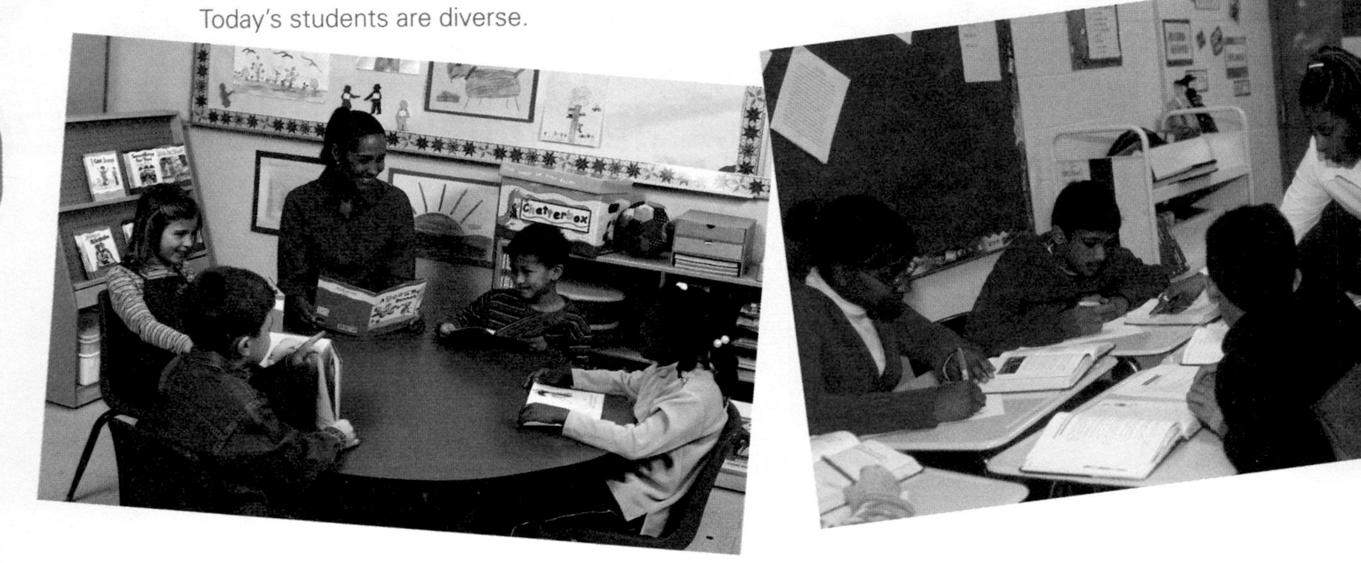

Today's students are diverse.

mythBUSTER

We should always teach to the middle.

In reality, good teachers demonstrate enthusiasm for all students' ability levels. Our passion for our role as teachers is evident and contagious. Students respond to energetic and motivating instructors. While it is easier to prepare lessons for one general group, all students, regardless of ability, deserve high standards and equal representation. In California a teacher must expect the makeup of a class to include RSP (resource) students, English language learners, at-risk students, and nonreaders. Identifying the needs of each individual not only ensures that students receive a quality education but also upholds the integrity of the teacher. We are teachers of all students, not just a select few.

Ingrid Munsterman
Elementary School Principal
Bloomington, California

either as a daunting challenge or as an opportunity to stretch your skills and abilities in new directions while celebrating the multitude of unique individuals relying on you to guide and assess their progress fairly.

The Theory of Multiple Intelligences

One way to understand how your students differ from each other and what each brings to the classroom is through Howard Gardner's theory of multiple intelligences. Gardner's (1993, 2000) work proposes that, instead of a single, fixed intelligence, there are actually eight facets of intelligence. In other words, we are all smart but in different ways. The exciting part of this theory is that teachers can organize learning to take into account the differing intelligences in the classroom.

- **Visual/spatial.** Students with visual/spatial intelligence excel at spatial relationships and learn visually. They enjoy drawing, creating, illustrating, and learning from photographs, videos, and other visual aids.
- **Verbal/linguistic.** Students who have strength in verbal/linguistic intelligence learn best through the language arts: reading, writing, speaking, and listening. These constitute the traditional methods of instruction.
- **Mathematical/logical.** Students who show evidence of mathematical/logical intelligence demonstrate skill with numbers and problem solving. They think abstractly and analytically. They

WATCH IT! video

Incorporating Multiple Intelligences

In this clip of various grade levels, you will see how multiple learning opportunities help teachers reach students with different strengths and learning styles. While teachers do not have to adapt every activity for all of the intelligences, they can offer choices that build on students' styles or stretch them to another style. As you watch the clip, identify the intelligences that you see in the various learning activities.

do well when instruction is logically sequenced.

- **Bodily/kinesthetic.** Students who exhibit bodily/kinesthetic intelligence have good motor skills and are coordinated. They learn best through hands-on activity: games, movement, role play, construction, and manipulation of objects.
- **Musical/rhythmic.** Students who excel in musical/rhythmic intelligence learn through songs, patterns, rhythms, instruments, chants, listening to music, and other forms of musical expression.

WATCH IT! video

Multiple Intelligences

A first-grade teacher demonstrates and discusses how she uses multiple intelligences in a unit on simple machines.

After viewing the video clip, think of an upcoming unit for your grade level or subject matter. Create activities that tap into the multiple intelligences defined here. If you have difficulty, consult some of the works by Howard Gardner listed in the references at the end of this unit. Here are some online multiple intelligences inventories. It would be fun to take them yourself and then administer them to your students. http://www.ldrc.ca/projects/miinventory/mitest.html
http://surfaquarium.com/MI/inventory.htm

- **Intrapersonal.** Students who shine in intrapersonal intelligence are introspective and in touch with their feelings, values, and beliefs. They need time alone to reflect on their learning and how it relates to them.
- **Interpersonal** Students who demonstrate interpersonal intelligence are outgoing, sociable, and people-oriented,

and they learn best by working in groups or interacting with others.

- **Naturalist.** Students whose forte is naturalist intelligence (added in 1996 to the original seven) demonstrate an ability to find patterns in the natural world and the plant and animal life therein. They learn best through classifying and visual discrimination activities, especially when environmental education is involved. Field trips and gardening are two activities they enjoy.

Ideas for Activities

Imagine that your class is studying desert environments. Here are some ideas for activities that would afford opportunities for students to activate the eight intelligences. You can provide your students with a contract that requires them to complete a certain number of activities, each representing a different intelligence to expand their repertoire.

Visual/Spatial

- Paint or draw a desert scene.
- Create a desert collage.
- Watch a video about the desert.
- Construct a desert diorama.

Verbal/Linguistic

- Read a factual book about the desert and write a book report.
- Write a coyote trickster tale after reading some examples.
- Create a desert crossword puzzle using desert vocabulary.
- Write a research report about a desert animal.

Mathematical/Logical

- Design and conduct an experiment to see how much water a small cactus plant needs.
- Classify and categorize the plants found in the desert.
- Locate three deserts on a U.S. map and specify the longitude and latitude of each.
- Make a graph of annual rainfall in three deserts: Gobi, Kalahari, and Sahara.

Bodily/Kinesthetic

- Pantomime desert animals and have the class guess what you are.
- Feel and describe desert plant specimens.
- Fill a bottle with colored sand that you have dyed in desert colors.
- Create a game or sport that can be played in the desert and teach it to the class.

Musical/Rhythmic

- Write a song or jingle about the desert.
- Listen to the theme music from *Lawrence of Arabia*.
- Make a list of sounds you might hear at night in the desert.
- Write a rap about the desert.

Intrapersonal

- Describe how you would feel if you were stranded on a desert island and saw a ship in the distance.

(continues)

Ideas for Activities *(continued)*

- Should the desert tortoise be a protected animal? Why or why not?
- Write a poem about how the desert makes you feel.
- Would you rather live in the desert in a big house or by the sea in a small one?

Interpersonal

- Interview someone who has lived in or visited a desert to get his or her reactions to the experience.
- Debate: The desert tortoise should or should not be protected.
- Write a group report comparing three deserts: Gobi, Sahara, Kalahari.
- In a group, choose a desert and make a desert mural including plants, mammals, insects, birds, and reptiles.

Naturalist

- Make a collection of desert fauna and flora using pictures from the Internet.
- Sort the pictures into categories, as a scientist would do.
- Learn the scientific names of at least 10 desert plants.
- Research Death Valley on the Internet using the National Park Service's website.

DESERT CONTRACT: Name ____________________

Choose three activities

Pantomime a desert animal.	Create a desert diorama.	Write a coyote trickster tale.	Create a desert mural with three others.
Listen to *Lawrence of Arabia* music.	Classify desert plants.	Learn the scientific names of 10 desert plants.	Should the desert tortoise be protected?

Figure 28.1
Sample Contract: Multiple Intelligences

WATCH IT! video

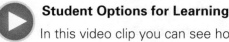

Student Options for Learning

In this video clip you can see how students are given a smorgasbord of options to make learning meaningful. From what you know about multiple intelligence theory, what intelligences do you see represented?

WATCH IT! video

Differentiating Instruction: Giving Students Choices

Choice is integral to the concept of differentiated instruction, especially in terms of how the product will be assessed. Students are given an opportunity to create rubrics. In this clip there are many examples of teachers giving students choices. What are some of them?

APPLY IT!

If you feel very brave, you can design multiple-intelligence–based activity centers and require your students to choose centers, with the directive that they do at least one activity in each center. Make color-coded folders with center names on them, and have students choose a folder and activities that correspond to strengths and/or intelligences that they want to develop. You can name your centers after famous people who exhibit the intelligences:

William Shakespeare Center—Verbal/Linguistic
Albert Einstein Center—Logical/Mathematical
Paul McCartney Center—Musical/Rhythmic
Jacques Cousteau Center—Naturalist
Pablo Picasso Center—Visual/Spatial
Shaun White Center—Kinesthetic
Henry David Thoreau Center—Intrapersonal
Oprah Winfrey Center—Interpersonal

CHAPTER 28

WATCH IT! video

Strategies for Teaching Diverse Learners

A teacher tries to tie instruction to personal experiences of students in order to meet the needs of her diverse learners. After viewing the video clip, what strategies did you see demonstrated? Which strategies would you use to connect learning to your students' experience?

WATCH IT! video

What Is Differentiated Instruction?

This clip is an introduction to differentiated instruction and provides a simple and concise definition. In what other ways do students differ, beyond learning style and expressing themselves?

Differentiated Instruction

Differentiated learning describes a set of principles that enable you to meet the broad range of readiness, interests, abilities, talents, and skills in your classroom. The principles of differentiated instruction as articulated by Tomlinson (2004) provide another perspective on meeting the diverse needs of your students.

Interview With an Expert

Making a Difference

Carol Ann Tomlinson Explains How Differentiated Instruction Works and Why We Need It Now

by Anthony Rebora

Differentiated instruction—the theory that teachers should work to accommodate and build on students' diverse learning needs—is not new. But it's unlikely that anyone has done more to systematize it and explicate its classroom applications than University of Virginia education professor Carol Ann Tomlinson. A former elementary school teacher of 21 years (and Virginia Teacher of the Year in 1974), Carol Ann Tomlinson has written more than 200 articles, chapters, and books, including The Differentiated Classroom: Responding to the Needs of All Learners *and* Fulfilling the Promise of the Differentiated Classroom: Strategies and Tools for Responsive Teaching. *Characterized by a rigorous professionalism and a strong underlying belief in both teachers' and students' potential, her work has given many educators both practical and philosophical frameworks for modifying instruction to meet the individual needs of all students. Anthony Rebora, editorial director of the* Sourcebook, *recently talked to Tomlinson about the theory of differentiated instruction and its use in schools today.*

Differentiated instruction is a term that is interpreted in a lot of different ways. How do you define it, and why is it important for teachers today?

I define it as a teacher really trying to address students' particular readiness needs, their particular interests, and their preferred ways of learning. Of course, these efforts must be rooted in sound classroom practice—it's not just a matter of trying anything. There are key principles of differentiated instruction that we know to be best practices and that support everything we do in the classroom. But at its core, differentiated instruction means addressing ways in which students vary as learners.

The reason I think differentiated instruction is important is that students do vary in so many ways, and our student populations are becoming more academically diverse. They always have been, but they're becoming more so. And the chances are pretty good that this will continue throughout our lifetimes.

As I see it, there are three ways to deal with students' differences. One is to ignore them. We've tried that for years, and we just don't have any evidence that pretending that all kids are alike and teaching them the same things in the same way over the same time period is effective.

The second way is to separate kids out—trying to figure out who's smart and who's not. When we do that, we end up getting the idea that most teachers are supposed to work with "normal" kids, and the kids who are somehow "broken"—if you don't speak English too well, if you have a learning disability, if you're too smart—are put someplace else. But we're finding that this separation process isn't helping in terms of achievement, particularly for the "broken" kids. And there's the problem that the broken kids are often poor and minority, while the kids we see as being in good shape tend to be white and more affluent. So, the division between the haves and the have-nots is being reinforced by schools rather than ameliorated. Finally, sorting kids in this way creates a negative mind-set, to use author Carol Dweck's term. We're basically telling kids from the outset they're too different and that they can't do the work—which is pretty detrimental to their outlook.

So that leaves us with the third, unfortunately less common choice—keeping kids together in the context of high-quality curriculum but attending to their readiness needs, their interests, and their preferred ways of learning. And we have a fairly good body of research to suggest that when you do that the results are pretty impressive. Differentiated instruction assumes a more positive mind-set: Let's assume they can all do good work, and let's attend to the ways that they need us to teach them in order to get there.

(continues)

Interview With an Expert *(continued)*

What are the hallmarks of a well-run differentiated classroom? What are the things you look for when you visit a classroom?

One of the first things I look for are teacher-student connections. Does this seem to be a teacher who is really paying attention to the kids, who's going out of his or her way to study them and understand what makes them tick? To be effective with differentiation, a teacher really needs to talk with the kids, ask them their opinions on things, sit down with them for a minute or two to see how things are going, and listen to them and find out what they are interested in. All that feeds back into instruction. And teacher-student connections not only help teachers plan what to do with kids; they also provide motivation for differentiation: If I can see kids as real individual human beings, I'm going to be much more invested in helping them learn and grow individually.

Another thing I look for is a sense of community in the classroom. Has the teacher pulled this class together as a team? It's helpful to think of a baseball team: Different players play different positions and fill different roles, but they also work together and support each other in working toward a common goal. In the same way, it's really important for kids to come together and understand and appreciate their differences, and to be willing to help one another succeed—as opposed to the cut-throat competition that sometimes goes on in schools.

The third thing I look for is the quality of the curriculum being used. You have to differentiate something. And if what you differentiate is boring enough to choke a horse, you've just got different versions of boredom. If you differentiate something that's murky and not clear regarding why anyone's doing it, then you just generate multiple versions of fog. Or if all you're doing—as unfortunately many teachers feel pressured to do today—is teaching a telephone book of facts in preparation for a test, you're not really providing memorable or useful learning. So teachers who are trying to reach out to kids really need to keep asking themselves about the quality of what they are teaching. This is also a mind-set issue: If I really think all my kids are capable of learning, then I want to give them the most robust materials, not the watered-down stuff.

So what are the key things a teacher needs to think about when developing a differentiated lesson plan?

This gets us further into the core principles of differentiated instruction. One of these is what we call "respectful tasks." This means that everybody's work needs to be equally engaging, equally appealing, and equally important. It's very easy to fall into the pattern of giving some kids no-brainer tasks and giving other kids the teacher's pet tasks. What you really want is every student to be focused on the essential knowledge, understanding, and skill. And for every student to have to think to do his or her work.

Another important principle is that of flexible grouping. This means you don't

UNIT 6

arbitrarily divide students or automatically group them with kids of the same skill level. You need to systematically move kids among similar readiness groups, varied readiness groups, mixed learning-profile groups, interest groups, mixed interest groups, and student-choice groups. In a sense, the teacher is continually auditioning kids in different settings—and the students get to see how they can contribute in a variety of contexts.

Another key to a good differentiated lesson is "teaching up." We do much better if we start with what we consider to be high-end curriculum and expectations—and then differentiate to provide scaffolding, to lift the kids up. The usual tendency is to start with what we perceive to be grade-level material and then dumb it down for some and raise it up for others. But we don't usually raise it up very much from that starting point, and dumbing down just sets lower expectations for some kids.

You alluded to the fact that teachers are under a great deal of pressure to teach mandated standards and to improve standardized test scores. How does differentiated instruction fit into this context?

I think it fits in pretty well actually. As I see it, you've got two choices. One is to say, "Look, all I think I can do is cover this list of skills." But even if that's all you think you can do, it's still better to start where the kid is and help him move from that point instead of trying to skip over gaps.

But what we really know from people who work with good quality curriculum is that the stuff we're being asked to teach kids for the tests is part of a bigger picture of something that helps them make sense of the world. To teach that bigger picture is the second choice. Typically, what we're being asked to teach kids are facts and skills, but you can wrap them in understanding. You give kids a sense of how this makes sense in the world, how it all fits together, how it ties in with their lives, and what they can do with it as people. You don't jettison the facts and skills; you just package them in a way that makes them more interesting to learn, more memorable, more transferable, more useful, and retainable.

No one would ask teachers not to teach what they feel they're responsible for. But you can teach those things in ways that are more meaningful and richer. So what I'm talking about is quality curriculum and my sense of it—and I think this is where most curriculum experts are, too—is that quality curriculum is centered on understandings.

I found it interesting that in The Differentiated Classroom *you say that an effective teacher "must like himself." What do you mean by that?*

When you see purpose in what you do, when you really like what you do, when you get up in the morning ready to make a difference, when you see human beings that are going to be impacted by your work—I think these things enable you to be a fulfilled person. And I think that teachers who really find fulfillment in the classroom feel better about themselves and are more likely to have the courage to reach out to kids and try new things than those who doubt themselves and feel

(continues)

Interview With an Expert *(continued)*

discouraged. And I would guess this is also true of teachers who are more self-efficacious in the first place. You need a certain sense of self-assurance to teach at high levels.

To use differentiated instruction as you discuss it in your books, teachers really have to get to know and understand their students—in terms of their learning styles, interests, strengths, and weaknesses. It seemed to me that this would be very difficult to do if you have five or six classes a day. How do teachers digest all this?

Let me just clarify that I taught for 21 years, so this isn't just something I thought of at a university and never tried in a classroom. I've done it with 150 kids a year. But it is difficult. *Teaching* is difficult. So are many other professions.

But getting to know students in this way isn't really as hard as you think. The key thing is to actively get kids to show you who they are and what their needs are. There are a lot of pretty simple techniques to do this. For example, we have a fairly substantial body of evidence that some of us learn better in creative ways, some in practical ways, and some in analytic ways. To start to gauge where your students fall within this schema, you could create three different journal prompts that all ask the same question—but with one coming at it from an out-of-the-box perspective, one bringing in a life-application aspect, and one in a more methodical or analytic way. Then just ask the kids to respond to the prompt that's best for them personally. More generally, you could give students periodic surveys of the class, asking them what they particularly liked and what they found particularly difficult. It's also good practice for a teacher to keep a kind of journal where they jot down things they learn about kids—about their likes and dislikes, and what they get really excited about—and be able to refer back to it.

Actually, we're hitting on another key principle of differentiation, which is ongoing assessment, meaning that I'm continually checking in on who's where with the knowledge and understanding I'm trying to teach and continuing to track the progress of kids, much the way a hospital would track the blood work or respiration of a patient. There are really a lot of ways to do this, outside of formal quizzes and tests, that aren't tremendously laborious. You start by systematically watching kids, taking good notes, checking work regularly and closely, and asking good questions. It's really as much a predisposition on a teacher's part as anything else.

The growing numbers of English-language learners in schools pose particular challenges for many teachers. In your books, you talk about the ability of differentiated instructors to build "language bridges" to help these students. Can you explain how that's done?

You learn a language through speaking, so making sure these kids participate in discussion groups where they can make a contribution is really very important.

One great way to do this, when possible, is to put a student who is just learning

English in the same group as someone who can serve as a kind of bridge—someone who speaks the same native language but is further along in English. This gives the English-language learner a way to contribute and follow the work.

Another helpful strategy is what we call "front-loading vocabulary." This is when the teacher identifies the half-dozen or so words in a unit that really are central and really give it its meaning. Then you teach this academic vocabulary before the unit begins, so that when the lessons and readings start the kids have something to build on. This is helpful not only with second-language learners but also with students with learning disabilities or below-level vocabulary skills. It helps tremendously with focus and understanding.

A related technique is the use of word walls—which we tend to associate with younger grade-levels but can work well with older students, too. These are simply places on the classroom walls where you list words and definitions and categorize them in word families and in other ways. This gives kids something to refer to and helps them learn words and derivatives. I know a high school teacher in North Carolina who has her students—many of whom are learning English—"adopt" particular words by creating poster-board presentations on them, complete with definitions, pronunciations, and illustrations. Strategies like these really amount to vocabulary-support systems and can help kids create associations and understandings.

Another tried and true technique is to make audio recordings of reading assignments that kids can listen to while they read. Oftentimes, hearing vocabulary in a new language develops more quickly than their reading vocabulary. Graphic organizers can also help English-language learners organize and make sense of ideas in the content.

Teachers often say they don't get enough—or any—training or professional development in differentiated instruction. Why do you think that is?

I think the main reason is that differentiated instruction requires a complex change process for most teachers. It's not something you can show me how to do today and then I can go back and do in my classroom tomorrow. And unfortunately, the professional development models used in most schools aren't conducive to complex, meaningful change or growth. For most schools, a good professional development program is, "Well, shoot, we used two whole staff-development days." But something like differentiated instruction takes a lot more than that. You have to have people in the classrooms with teachers and you have to give teachers opportunities to troubleshoot and work together. And you need a leader who's both approachable and insistent, who commits to the program.

In the book I recently co-authored, called *The Differentiated School*, we actually look at two very different schools—one elementary and one high school—that have moved their entire faculties to differentiated instruction. The one thing that was immediately evident in both schools was that they had

(continues)

Interview With an Expert *(continued)*

leaders who really understood what differentiation meant. And they went about staff development with the understanding that asking teachers to change their practices in this way is a complex thing. Both schools came up with staff-development plans that were sustained and persistent and embedded in the school's culture, with people in charge who never went away. On some level, when you look at those schools, it's almost a no-brainer. Everything they did was entirely sensible—it's just that we almost never do those things systematically and persistently in schools.

Considering the high teacher turnover in many schools and the increasing use of scripted lessons, are you optimistic about the growth of differentiated instruction in schools?

I think I'm sort of a realistic optimistic. I understand how hard change is, and I understand the complexities of schools and school systems. But there's no doubt that our classrooms are becoming more diverse, and that's going to continue. And whether you call it differentiation or something else, we're going to have to reach out to those kids. Educators get this. New ideas in teaching often disappear from the scene fairly quickly because real change is so hard. But I've been working with differentiated instruction for at least 15 years now, and people are sticking with it. It's even starting to take hold, quite effectively, in some good teacher-prep programs, giving young teachers a strong basis for development.

Now, I don't think this is because people just like the way it sounds. I think it's because we all have these kids, in all their wonderful diversity, right there in front of us every morning—and we have to figure how to help them reach their potential. So, I think my optimism comes from what seems to be a sustained interest on the part of educators in reaching out to diverse student populations and a willingness to pursue change even if it doesn't come in a simple formula.

Reprinted with permission from *Teacher Magazine*, September 10, 2008, pp. 26, 28–31.

Focus on the Core Knowledge of Each Subject Area

The core knowledge can be the concepts, skills, and principles that are required of each student, and are also known as the essential standards.

Use Formative Assessment

Teachers need to continuously assess where students are vis-à-vis what they need to learn. The assessment involves not only readiness but also interests and how that student learns best. This is known as formative assessment.

Modify Instructional Components

The three components of instruction that can be modified based on a teacher's ongoing assessment are the content, the process, and the products. You can modify content by choosing the way you input it. You can simplify for those who are not yet ready and enrich the content for those who have

Figure 28.2
Planning Form: Differentiated Instruction

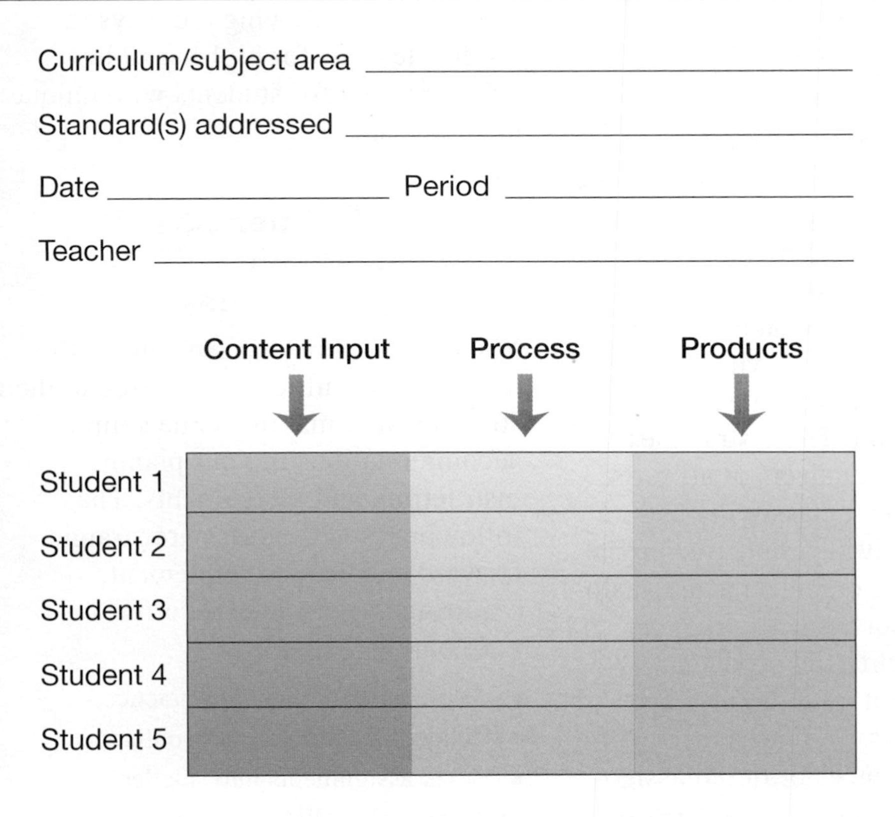
Curriculum/subject area ______

Standard(s) addressed ______

Date ______ Period ______

Teacher ______

	Content Input	Process	Products
Student 1			
Student 2			
Student 3			
Student 4			
Student 5			

TEACHER/PRINCIPAL TALKS FROM A ONE-ROOM SCHOOLHOUSE . . .

As far as the juggling act that is my day in the little schoolhouse—K through 8, 11 students enrolled but no second graders this year—I differentiate instruction all day. I list my students' individual or grade-level assignments for the day on my whiteboard. The students begin working. I walk around and help. At other times, when I do direct teaching, I work with one or two students while all the other students are engaged in their lessons. I use things like books on CD, computer learning time, and assignments that are appropriate and doable to occupy students while I directly teach others. I also have a full-time teacher aide to help out, and she is great! She works mainly with the K–3 grades. She uses the same format I do. At times I do whole-class lessons geared to all levels. Children will often listen to their peers more

(continued on following page)

TEACHER/PRINCIPAL TALKS FROM A ONE-ROOM SCHOOLHOUSE

—continued

attentively than to adults, so I encourage the older students to elaborate on what I am talking about so everyone listens in that way, including the older students. It makes them feel good because they are sharing their knowledge and clarifying what they know, so I build on that or sway the lesson the way I want it to go. I try to let the students talk more than I do, and I find this engages them all. For example, I taught a lesson on writing business letters, and all first through eighth graders wrote a business letter to the president. I talked a bit about friendly letters and then asked, "Why would someone want to write a business letter?" This got the upper graders talking and the younger students listening. Everyone got his or her own letterhead. We used a language arts handbook for the format. All of the students

(continued on facing page)

mastered it. Some ways of varying the input include using:

- Varied level text material
- Supplementary materials
- Varied audiovisuals
- Interest centers
- Varied time allotments
- Technology of all sorts
- Varied instructional strategies
- Cooperative learning
- Varied community resources, such as speakers and field trips

Some of the ways you can modify the process are by helping students make the learning experience relate to their needs and interests and by focusing attention on multiple intelligences.

You can make the material more meaningful (the process) when you include some of the strategies that were covered in this unit. These strategies include graphic organizers of all sorts, group investigation, classifying and sorting, cooperative learning, reciprocal teaching, advance organizers, and analogies and metaphors.

You can modify the product by designing product options for your students based on Gardner's theory of multiple intelligences or tiered assignments. Students can be given a list of options to show their mastery of the content, and you can assess them based on predetermined criteria or rubrics.

Providing for Every Student

You will have students in your class who need extra support in one or more areas. Following are ways to modify lessons for higher and lower achievers and for students with unique challenges.

Teach to the Strengths of Students With Learning Difficulties

You can support your students with learning difficulties by teaching to their strengths and making some simple accommodations in your planning, instruction, and assignments. The following modifications are straightforward and easy to implement, requiring very little extra effort on your part.

- Allow time for plenty of practice.
- Conduct student-teacher conferences.
- Break assignments into smaller, manageable parts.
- Use peer tutors.

- Underline important directions and key words.
- Give shorter assignments, and allow more time for completion.
- Record stories and use other technologies.
- Give immediate feedback and lots of encouragement.
- Use large type on worksheets.
- Keep directions simple, write them out, or give them orally.
- Provide many opportunities for success.
- Provide low-reading-level, high-interest reading material geared to the student's interests.
- Use visuals and manipulative materials when available.
- Use cooperative learning strategies.
- Watch for fatigue and boredom.

Higher-Achieving Students Need Enrichment

It is also probable that you will have students in your class who excel in one or more areas, especially if you subscribe to the theory of multiple intelligences. For these students, more of the same is not acceptable.

- Encourage the reading of library books and perhaps totally individualize the reading and/or math program.
- Encourage individual research, construction, or science projects geared to the student's abilities and interests, for extra credit.
- Provide opportunities to sit in on special unit activities in other classes.
- Introduce new and challenging materials, games, puzzles, and brainteasers.
- Have individual conferences with the student to guide his or her progress.
- Encourage creative responses to stories (e.g., writing to the author, creating a play script from the story, etc.).
- Consider modifying assignments based on multiple intelligences.

Students With Special Physical, Emotional, or Behavioral Needs May Require Individualized Attention

Some students in your class may need differentiated and/or individualized attention because they have special needs related to specific physical, emotional, or behavioral challenges. Individual differences may point to a need for further testing. If you suspect that a student either is gifted or has learning disabilities, notify your principal, who will outline for you the legal requirements for arranging more intensive testing by the school psychologist,

helped me write a letter on the board. The younger students copied the class letter, and the older students added more details to theirs. Then some students went to computers or worked on independent work, and I taught another student her math lesson.

MICHELYN BROWN
Principal and Sole Teacher
Grass Valley, California

TEACHER TALKS . . .

In my third year of teaching general music, I was given a class of children with cerebral palsy to teach. They were all kindergarten age. They were all in wheelchairs, except one. I think there were about six children all together. It was quite a challenge to come up with things they would enjoy and could feel success in accomplishing. One activity we did first thing was to warm up their voices. We would act like we were chewing food and humming at the same time.

(continued on following page)

TEACHER TALKS—*continued*

While they were doing that, they would move their arms up and down to the high and low of their voices. This was something all of them could do, except one . . . Aubrey. Her disability was more severe than the others. She could only make a couple of sounds to denote yes and no. She would sit, and sometimes the teachers who brought the children would make her arms move while we were doing this activity, but sometimes not.

One day, six months into the school year, we started our warm-up as usual, and as I looked around the room, there was Aubrey, on her own, moving her arms up and down with the others. I pointed this out to the teachers, and we were all very excited. That moment had a deep impact on my life as a teacher and a musician. And 19 years later it still inspires me.

DEBORAH LICHFIELD
Middle and High School Music Teacher
St Johns, Arizona

(as seen on http://www.LessonPlansPage.com)

nurse, or special education resource teacher. If you have students in your class with behavioral or physical challenges, you will have a great deal of help from the special education team.

For example, I had a student with a hearing impairment in my methods class, and a student assistant was assigned to sign for him during class. I was very nervous about how I should modify my instruction. I consulted the Office of Students with Disabilities, and staff members offered some simple guidelines such as using the board more, looking at the student when I was talking because he read lips, and writing out all directions for him. That quarter I did some of the best teaching I have ever done! The principles that guided me turned out to benefit all the students. If you are fortunate enough to have students with special needs in your class, seek advice and you will be the better teacher for the experience.

Response to Intervention (RTI)

RTI is a highly specialized outgrowth of differentiated instruction. The method applies instruction with differing intensity, duration, and frequency for different students. According to the National Center for Response to Intervention (2010), RTI "integrates assessment and intervention within a multi-level prevention system to maximize student achievement and to reduce behavior problems. With RTI, schools identify students at risk for poor learning outcomes, monitor student progress, provide evidence-based interventions and adjust the intensity and nature of those interventions depending on a student's responsiveness, and identify students with learning disabilities or other disabilities."

AVOID IT!

Although the number of students in your classroom who fall within the norm may already overwhelm you, direct your attention to those who need your extra effort. Do not hesitate to seek out your resource teacher for suggestions and strategies that can be tailored to the students you have in mind.

In simpler terms, RTI requires that teachers implement research-based instruction, screen all students for academics and behavior, and use researched-based interventions in stages with increasing intensity. According to Howard (2009), the three stages are

1. Whole-class instruction for all students, using flexible grouping and differentiated instruction
2. Small-group instruction for 10 to 15% of the students for 30 minutes per day
3. More individualized instruction for 5 to 10% of the students for 30 minutes per day

During these interventions, which are used in reading and math (and are appropriate for all grade levels, English language learners, and students with special needs), there is continuous data-driven monitoring and assessment of progress.

APPLY IT!

In your district (or potential district), find out how RTI is being implemented. Ask key questions such as these:

1. Is there only one reading (social studies, science, math) book for the grade level?
2. How do teachers differentiate instruction in Stage 1?
3. Who is responsible for working with small groups in Stage 2 and Stage 3: a paraprofessional, a regular teacher, a specialist, or someone else?
4. What are the district's challenges in implementing RTI?
5. What are a teacher's challenges in implementing RTI?
6. If RTI is not being implemented, what are the barriers to implementation?
7. How do the district RTI coordinator or individual teachers monitor progress?
8. How are teachers trained in the RTI model, and what research-based interventions do they use?

Summary

Just as one size does not fit all, one instructional method is not effective for all learners. Differentiated instruction is an approach that suggests adapting instruction to the readiness, skills, abilities, interests, and learning styles of your students. The theory of multiple intelligences posits an

STATISTICS

The Individuals with Disabilities Education Act (IDEA), enacted in 1975, mandates that children and youth ages 3 through 21 with disabilities be given a free and appropriate public school education. According to the U.S. Department of Education's National Center for Educational Statistics (2006),

- 95% of students ages 6 to 21 served under IDEA were enrolled in regular school.
- 3% were served in a separate school for students with disabilities.
- 1% were placed in regular private schools by their parents.
- 0.4% were served in each of the following environments: separate residential facility, home or hospital, or a correctional facility.

TEACHER TALKS . . .

Teaching isn't just about what you teach your students; it's also about what they teach you. When you choose to become a teacher, this brings you into a world of young people who, if you give them a chance, will open up their hearts, share their fears and loves, and make every day special. I have cried with a young woman who had

(continued on following page)

TEACHER TALKS—*continued*

anorexia; visited four kids who were all in mental hospitals at the same time and just wanted a candy bar, a teen magazine, and a hug; witnessed young women with hearing impairments learn to communicate with a grocery store cashier so that eventually they could shop independently; and watched middle school students celebrate "moving on" to high school with the confidence and poise of young men and women. I admit it; I cry every year when I see who they've become. I can't imagine doing anything else with my life.

LAURIE WASSERMAN
Special Needs Teacher
Medford, Massachusetts

(quoted on www.EducationWorld.com)

eight-part conceptual system that gives students choices in how they learn the material, how they express themselves, the products they produce, and the means of assessment that will measure learning. RTI is a very specialized form of differentiated instruction.

Reflect!

What is your primary learning style, and which of the multiple intelligences best describes that style? Which of the multiple intelligences would you choose in order to stretch and extend how you learn? Which of the intelligences are completely opposite to how you learn best? Explain your responses.

UNIT 6

CHAPTER 29

WHAT ARE EFFECTIVE STRATEGIES FOR ENGLISH LANGUAGE LEARNERS?

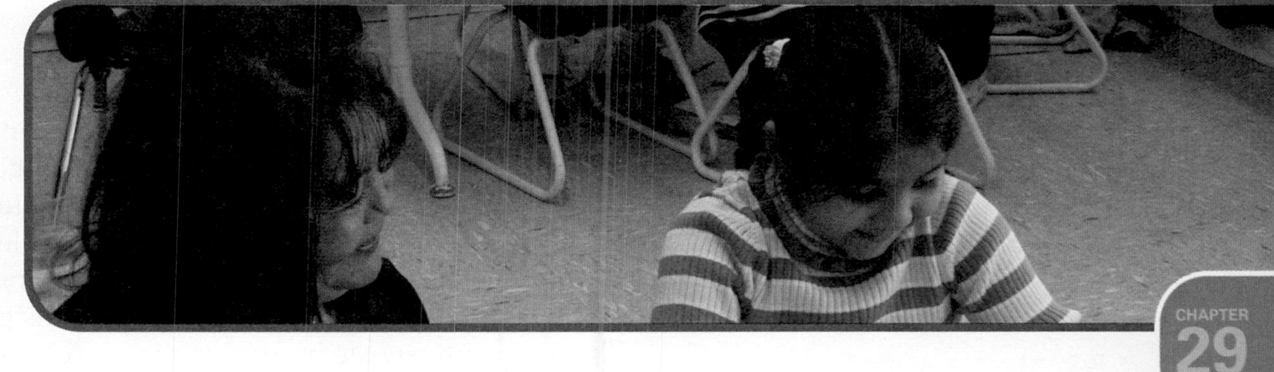

El que sabe dos lenguas, vale por dos.
(He who knows two languages is worth double.)

Spanish maxim

Saber es poder. (Knowledge is power.)

Spanish maxim

Effectiveness Essentials

- Principles of good instruction apply to English language learners.
- Learning about new cultures and new languages is an exciting opportunity for you and your students.
- Culture and language are inextricably linked. Therefore, it is important to help English language learners maintain their own culture and language while learning English and new social norms.
- Multiculturalism should be an integral part of every day in your classroom.
- Sheltered instruction presents grade-level-appropriate content in English using special techniques. SIOP is a research-based approach to sheltered instruction.
- Establish and maintain links with the parents of your English learners.

There is diversity in language and culture at all grade levels.

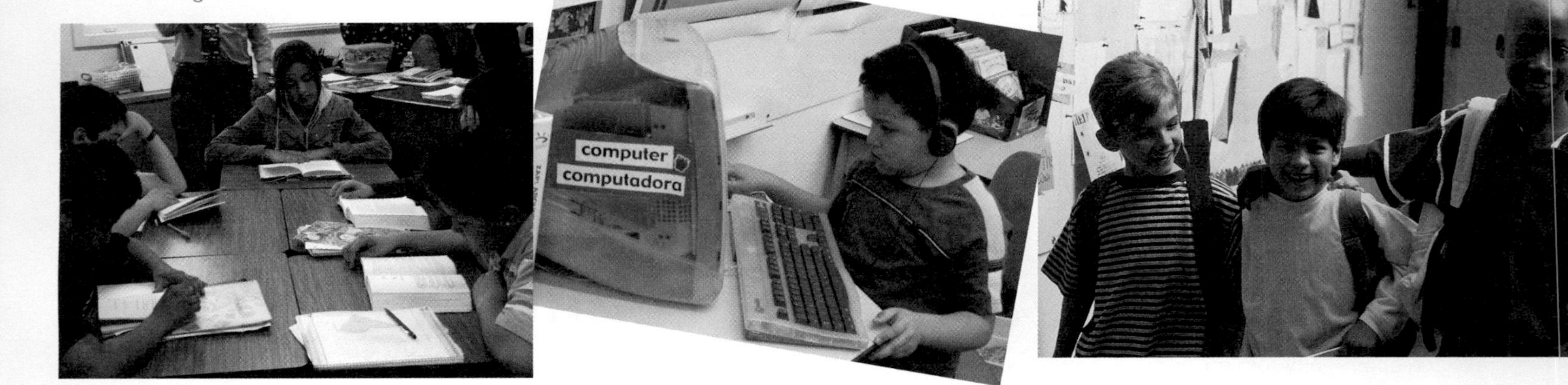

UNIT 6

STATISTICS

The National Clearinghouse on Language Acquisition (Ballantyne, Sanderman, & Levy, 2008) estimates that by 2015 ELL enrollment will reach 10 million and that by 2025 one out of every four students will be an English language learner.

- Today there are more than 5 million ELLs in the United States.
- This number has risen by 57% over the past 10 years.
- Nearly 6 in 10 ELLs qualify for free or reduced-price lunch.
- On tests of reading and mathematics, eighth-grade ELLs' scores are less than half as high as those of English-speaking peers.
- Students from households that speak a language other than English at home lag 20 points behind in high school completion rates.

Increasingly, you will find in your classroom students who are culturally and linguistically diverse. You may be feeling very unprepared as a novice to accommodate them. Given the statistics shown to the left, it is inevitable that you will need to differentiate instruction for the English language learner as well as the other diverse students mentioned in Chapter 28.

Teaching English Language Learners

Principles of good instruction apply to the instruction of English language learners—the task is not as formidable as you may feel it is. Most principles suggest that hands-on, active learning strategies work well with students who are learning English. There are a few accommodations that are specific to this group, however, that will be elucidated in this chapter.

You will be afforded an exciting opportunity to learn about new cultures and even new languages while seeking creative ways to differentiate instruction to meet the needs of your English language learners. Your ELL students will be a valuable resource in helping your entire class improve their English language skills and cross-cultural understanding.

Prepare Yourself

Teachers who have had the experience of learning a foreign language and also have an understanding of students' cultural backgrounds are better equipped to sustain their high academic performance, according to Diaz-Rico and Weed (2010). The implications are clear. If you have had the opportunity to study a foreign language, you will be better prepared to work with your English learners. If you take the time to learn about the cultures represented in your classroom, you will be prepared to teach the students as well.

There are many books, CDs, and kits available to help you learn a different language or improve your ability to converse in the language you studied in high school or college. Take the opportunity to learn some words or phrases. I recently saw a book series that promises that students can learn Spanish, French, Italian, or Chinese in just 10 minutes per day! I currently am improving my college Spanish that way. I challenge you to do the same.

APPLY IT!

Think back to a time when, in terms of language, you were on the outside looking in. It might have been in an immersion middle school language class, on a trip to a foreign country, or in conversation between friends who started speaking a different language and forgot you were there for a few minutes. Write a quick paragraph about how you felt as an outsider.

For me, that moment was a home stay in Japan, where not one of the family members spoke English and I did not speak Japanese. We used dictionaries, pictures, signs, and drawings to communicate. Clearly, I was the student in the household, and I was sensitized to how it might feel to be a student in my class who spoke not a word of English.

Teach Cultural Norms

Culture and language are inextricably linked. It is important to recognize that your students are learning a new culture as well as a new language. The cultural norms of English speakers differ from those in other cultures, and it is important to teach those cultural norms along with the language, as the first Watch It! video clip on the next page explains.

It is also important to help English language learners maintain their own culture and language. This not only

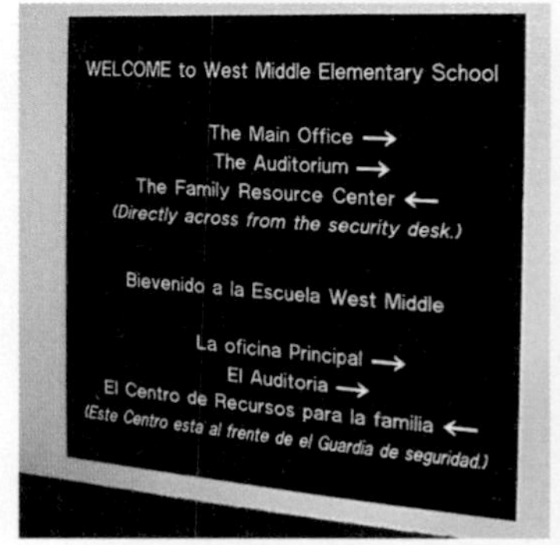

Can you read these?

WATCH IT! video

Teaching Classroom Rules: Everyday Norms of Interaction

When working with English language learners, teachers need to explain the rules of the classroom, demonstrate the way the classroom is organized, and teach and model routines and procedures. English language learners also need to learn about everyday social norms such as eye contact, reading facial expressions, and how far to stand from someone, as well as deeper aspects of culture that may interfere with learning such as the value of time, the concept of beauty, and the roles of family members. This video clip offers some strategies. What strategies will you use to teach the rules of the classroom and common social norms?

WATCH IT! video

Culture Shock

Effects of Culture Shock

In these video clips, the teachers explain that newcomers are scared and overwhelmed by culture shock. How does each teacher make the students feel welcome, safe, secure, and optimistic about their new lives? What else can you do to diminish culture shock in your classroom?

benefits them but also benefits your native English speakers, who can learn new words and customs. Decorate your room with photos, posters, books, and artifacts of the cultures in your classroom. Read-alouds should reflect the diversity of human experience. Crafts, music, foods, and games from all cultures should be highlighted in your curriculum whenever possible.

Learn to Deal With Culture Shock

Newcomers to your class may experience culture shock—that is, feelings of disorientation and frustration that accompany being thrust, often without preparation, into a new country, school, community, and, above all, language. Think about how hard it would be to learn the rules of the road in a new culture without benefit of language to express what you are feeling to your teacher and classmates. Look for

Everyone is welcome here.

feelings and attitudes that signal withdrawal, irritability, confusion, helplessness, etc. Make sure to view the video clips about culture shock and how to facilitate integration. You can acknowledge the feelings yet focus on the positive results of being in a new culture, even if the only aspects of this new culture that the students find positive at first are the different foods and entertainment options. The more sensitively you facilitate the transition and teach the norms and language, the more likely it is that the newcomers will be integrated into the school environment.

Implement Specific ELL Strategies

Most English language learners will be in immersion and sheltered English classes or regular classes. Some English learners may be enrolled in bilingual classes taught by bilingual teachers or in dual language immersion classes, where a percentage of each day is spent learning in both languages and the classes are evenly divided between English learners and native English speakers.

Sheltered English, also referred to as Specially Designed Academic Instruction in English (SDAIE), presents grade-level-appropriate content in English using special techniques. In the immersion and SDAIE programs, the language of instruction is English. The regular teacher, often inexperienced in effective practices for working with English learners, needs support to teach them successfully.

One model of sheltered instruction is the Sheltered Instruction Observation Protocol (SIOP) (Echevarria, Vogt, & Short, 2007). This research-based approach was developed as a way to introduce teachers of English language learners to best practices for concurrently teaching grade-level academic content and delivering explicit instruction in academic language. The model provides an outline for systematic instruction that consists of eight major components: lesson preparation, building background, comprehensible input, strategies, interaction, practice and application, lesson delivery, and review and assessment. Innovative features of the approach include:

- Incorporating a content as well as a language objective in each lesson
- Using supplementary materials to a high degree
- Adapting content to all levels of language proficiency
- Adapting SIOP to all grade levels and curriculum areas
- Connecting lessons to students' experiences and between past and current concepts
- Providing opportunities for student-student interaction such as cooperative learning groups, debates, interviews
- Emphasizing vocabulary throughout the lesson and beyond
- Using many of the hands-on interactive strategies that are outlined in the boxed feature on p. 358

These are just some of the features carefully outlined in the many SIOP books and materials. The components are effective teaching strategies for all students, not just English language learners, and SIOP lesson-planning materials are adaptable to any curriculum area and to students at any grade level or level of English proficiency. Your district may introduce training in the model, and for the individual teacher there are many resources available at the Center for Applied Linguistics website (http://www.cal.org/siop/) and at the SIOP Institute website (www.siopinstitute.net). Also investigate the resources listed at the end of this unit.

Teachers are better prepared to facilitate the language development of second language learners than they realize. According to Johns and Espinoza (1992), teachers often have an intuitive knowledge of the language learning process, which is a good start when combined with a belief that students can learn.

Being able to adapt your instruction is a valuable skill when English language learners are in your classroom. One middle school teacher calls herself the "Overhead Queen." She uses an overhead projector for each paper she gives to her students. They can see exactly what she wants. The visual learners benefit, as do the English learners. She maintains a notebook for each period, organizing the overheads in plastic sleeves and using them from year to year.

Experienced teachers and leaders in the field, such as Peregoy and Boyle (2008), Diaz-Rico and Weed (2010), and Ariza (2010), among others, suggest the tips in the box on the following page to promote English language development in a natural and meaning-centered approach.

Help is available if you are new to these ELL strategies. Confer with teachers and resource personnel at your site or at the district level. Share ideas with teachers who are more experienced than you are. Read factual and fictional accounts about the cultures represented in your classroom. Ask your principal for advice as needed. Avail yourself of the references at the end of this unit.

APPLY IT!

Most of the strategies for English language learners involve excellent teaching practices: hands-on, active learning in a student-centered environment. Think about a lesson you will be teaching at your grade level or in your subject area. How will you differentiate instruction using some of the techniques suggested in the Teaching Classroom Rules: Everyday Norms and Interaction video and in the chapter?

Establish and maintain connections with the parents of your English learners. Check to see if your school district provides informational materials in translation and/or an interpreter during parent conferences. Increasingly, many school districts with diverse populations provide such services. Ask the bilingual coordinator and other bilingual teachers to help you out. Parents often bring a relative or older sibling to translate for them during parent conferences. Use the translation website http://babelfish.yahoo.com for translating simple messages to parents. You can invite parents to share native costumes, foods, music, dance, photos, traditional stories, and family history.

TEACHER TALKS . . .

In Pomona, California, the majority of the third-grade children I taught were ELLs, predominantly Spanish, although I did get to teach two brothers who were from Russia. My favorite moment teaching ever was with one of my ELL students, an eight-year-old Russian boy. There were seven children in his beautiful family, whose life was centered around church, family, and school. Their parents spoke very little English, and I don't speak Russian. One time the kids and parents came to a teacher friend's room, and they all stood around the piano while Dad played and everyone sang Russian songs. When Mark came to my third-grade class, he spoke broken English. He was a bit of a clown and always tried to get people to smile, but he was a hard worker. He moved on and eventually went to middle school. He dropped in on me one March day after Dr. Seuss's birthday. I remember the date because he put my Cat-in-the-Hat hat on his head and thanked

(continued on facing page)

30 Ways to Promote English Language Development

1. Provide direct experiences such as field trips.
2. Include instructional simulations of real-life experiences and role playing.
3. Preview and review material graphically (concept maps, graphic organizers, Venn diagrams).
4. Incorporate substantial oral language opportunities in each lesson.
5. Schedule time for uninterrupted, silent, sustained reading.
6. Encourage the use of student journals and learning logs.
7. Support instruction with technology and audiovisual materials such as DVDs and CDs.
8. Design cooperative learning and collaborative projects.
9. Develop thematic units that integrate curriculum areas.
10. Use maps, graphs, props, concrete materials, visuals, and posters.
11. Dramatize content with gestures and facial expressions.
12. Model clear and understandable written and oral language.
13. Encourage your students to maintain their primary language.
14. Subject your English learners and native English-speaking students to a language unknown to both groups to build empathy.
15. Encourage all students to make personal history and culture books.
16. Recruit native-speaking volunteers or peer mentors.
17. Label objects in the room in all languages represented.
18. Encourage English language learners to keep picture journals.
19. Provide notes (perhaps an outline of the lesson) to students for later review.
20. Allow sufficient time for responses and discussion.
21. Invite your students to share their traditions, stories, and culture with the class.
22. Use research-based active learning strategies described in previous chapters.
23. Use interactive dialogue journals in which students and teachers write to one another in journal format.
24. Encourage choral readings and partner reading.
25. Use reciprocal teaching techniques.
26. Keep routines consistent.
27. Maintain a library of multicultural books.
28. Give clear directions, and review and summarize frequently.
29. Define new words and avoid using idioms and slang.
30. High expectations,
    High expectations,
    High expectations.

CLASSROOM ARTIFACTS

Gaynor Morgan, an 8–12 language arts and EFL teacher in Oostende, Belgium, offers the following lesson designed for English language learners. It can be adapted for English-speaking classes as well.

Title: "The Buzz Poem"
Primary subject and level: language arts, grades 8–12

1. Open a discussion about any topic (five minutes max).
2. Get feedback on feelings (helps with fluency in language).
3. Split class into groups of four or five students.
4. Brainstorm a title and write all suggestions on the board. Agree on a title and the style (rhyming or non-rhyming poem), using the majority choice.
5. Explain that the class will make a joint poem and that with each group each student has two lines to write. The poem can either be split into verses or kept as a continuing poem.
6. Get each student to write two lines of a poem. The group must then decide in which order the lines are going to be—e.g., Johnny's two lines first, then Sarah's two lines, etc. (promotes good teamwork spirit).
7. The group members must then check each other's spelling using dictionaries (good practice for teamwork and precision work).
8. One person in the group will then write out the group's lines on a piece of paper to be handed to the teacher.
9. The teacher, a chosen student, or a chosen person from each group reads out each verse.
10. If facilities allow, photocopy the poem onto a transparency and show the end result on an overhead projector, or photocopy the final poem and give each student a copy of his or her work.

This lesson plan encourages fluency, teamwork, and accuracy but, above all, allows students to show their innermost being without being self-conscious.

(as seen on http://www.LessonPlansPage.com)

me for teaching him to read! If you were to ask me what my most rewarding moment in the classroom was, that would be it.

I use facial expressions and any kind of real examples of what I am explaining. I am not bilingual myself, but I do know a few key terms in Spanish and ASL. I use them to help explain as best as I can. Students and parents seem to like laughing as I butcher the language. This creates a connection between us. It helps me connect with my students when I am interested in their language, and they love to see me mispronounce a word. It lets my students see that I am not afraid to try and make mistakes. They like to teach their teachers things too. If something is just not getting across, I get my other ELL students who understand what I am explaining to try to explain. This makes the student who explains it feel good because he or she is helping, and when students are explaining, they are reinforcing what they have just learned.

MICHELYN BROWN
Currently Principal and Only Teacher
K–8 School
Grass Valley, California

A proud parent shares.

WATCH IT! video

Bringing Students' Culture Into the Classroom

Children's literature is a way of making connections between home and community and the classroom. The diversity of classrooms is reflected in many new books that tell stories of various cultural groups. As you watch this clip, think about some books that you have used that can form the basis of discussion about a culture. How can you gently encourage students who belong to that culture to share whether the book depicts their own experiences accurately?

Creating a Welcoming School Environment for Parents

In this video clip, several approaches to engaging parents of newcomers are articulated. What are some of the ways in which parents are made to feel welcome? Can you add others?

WATCH IT! video

Importance of Valuing Cultures

This video clip points out that teachers should go beyond being *aware* of diversity in the classroom and rather begin to *value* the diverse cultures in terms of what they offer to the classroom community. In what ways is a diverse student population a source of enrichment for the teacher and the other students?

Individuals Within Cultures

In this video clip the teacher cautions that individuals, even within the same culture, are not all the same and that it is important to avoid stereotypical generalizations about the whole group. We can't assume that all members of the culture are the same. We have to look at each student individually and help each reach his or her potential. What cultural stereotypes have you heard? How can you avoid the trap of stereotyping a group by the behavior of a few?

Multicultural Studies

Multiculturalism should be an integral part of every day in your classroom. Multiculturalism should not be an add-on; everyone benefits from learning about other cultures. The importance of valuing the cultures represented in your classroom cannot be overemphasized. You can learn

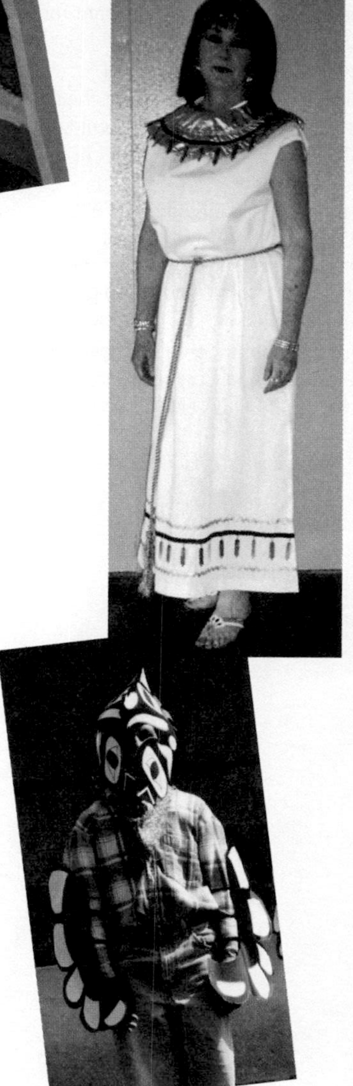

Travel around the world in a day at school.

about your students' traditions, clothing, foods, music, and countries of origin directly from them, and they can learn about yours. Think about how valued a student feels when he or she is asked to share. Consider how enriched everyone in the class will be by the experience.

Where my son teaches—a school designated for global studies—each year, teachers and students create a global fair. Each classroom becomes a different country, and the room is decorated to reflect that place. Activities are set up in each room—crafts, food, art, dance, music, stories, etc. Each student gets a passport at the beginning of the day and travels to four or five countries during the day.

AVOID IT!

Some people speak louder when they meet someone who is learning English. Use the suggestions in this chapter to make your message clearer, not louder. Remember that some English language learners are learning cultural norms as well as a new language. Be sensitive to gestures and body language from them that signal discomfort. Don't expect that they know that in U.S. culture, for example, looking directly at the teacher is a sign of respect. In many cultures, it is just the opposite.

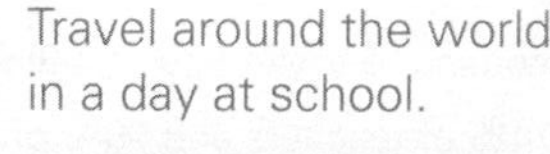

STATISTICS

According to a Met Life (2009) survey,

- 74% of teachers and 79% of principals believe that addressing the needs of ELLs is very important for student achievement.
- 58% of teachers and 61% of principals strongly agree that their schools do a good job of teaching ELLs.
- In schools with at least two thirds of the students identified as ELLs, 75% of teachers and 77% of principals strongly agree that their schools are doing a good job of teaching ELLs.
- Only 25% of students strongly agree that their schools are doing a good job of helping students learn English.

CLASSROOM ARTIFACTS

Fourth-grade teachers Brandi Stephens and Cindy Brewer of Mebane, North Carolina, share the following multicultural lesson plan that illustrates how well-chosen literature can be the hook to teach students about their own cultures. Multiple curriculum standards are incorporated, the lesson is differentiated, and the lesson culminates in a collaborative product.

Title: "What's on Your Quilt?"
Primary subject and level: language arts, grade 3

Essential Questions:

1. What can we learn from studying an author's craft concerning cultures around the world?
2. How can we apply what we learn about Patricia Polacco's works to our own writing styles?
3. How can we apply what we read to our own lives?

Standards and Content Areas:

Language Arts:

Goal 1.04—Increase sight vocabulary, reading vocabulary, and writing vocabulary through wide reading, listening, discussion, book talks, viewing, and studying author's craft.

Goal 2.08—Listen actively by facing the speaker, making eye contact, asking questions to clarify the message, and asking questions to gain additional information and ideas.

Art:

Goal 4.05—Know, discuss, and/or write about how an artist's background and experiences are important in shaping the artist's work.

Math:

Goal 2.02—Identify symmetry and congruence with concrete materials and drawings.

Goal 2.06—Estimate and measure length (inches).

Social Studies:

Goal 2.02—Analyze similarities and differences among communities in different times and in different places.

Description: After reading the story *The Keeping Quilt* by Patricia Polacco, the class will take part in a discussion about the story. For instance, the class will discuss the new words they learned, such as *babushka* (grandmother), and discuss the Russian customs and traditions presented in this book. Next, the class will talk about the significance of the quilt in the story, and the teacher will show the class a quilt that he or she personally designed, while explaining

(continues)

the meaning. This is a great opportunity for the teacher to share his or her background with students. The students will be able to design their own quilts with construction paper. The quilt must represent each individual person, such as where she was born, birth date, hobbies, favorite foods, and so forth. The students will be given squares of construction paper to represent the patches of the quilt that they will glue to the background of the quilt. In addition, students will be encouraged to use markers and crayons to draw and decorate their quilts. The teacher will call attention to the sides of the squares and ask students to measure them in inches. They will notice that each side is the same length (3 inches). Students can share their quilts with the class, and a class quilt can be made by linking them all together and attaching them to a bulletin board to showcase artwork. This is a great activity for encouraging community within the classroom.

Differentiation: Reading the story aloud to the class while showing them pictures from the story will help both auditory and visual learners. Providing an example of the quilt will aid the visual and global learners, while designing the quilts will help kinesthetic learners. Because students produce a visual representation, this project appeals to spatial intelligence. It is good for logical learners because of the math involved. This project is also appropriate for intrapersonal learners because they are creating quilts about themselves.

Assessment: The teacher will assess students through informal observation during class discussions and by viewing the quilts.

Resources:

- *The Keeping Quilt* by Patricia Polacco
- Black or white construction paper for background of quilt
- Multi-colored squares (3-inch sides) for quilt patches
- Glue
- Crayons, markers, or colored pencils

(as seen on http://www.LessonPlansPage.com)

Summary

You will undoubtedly have English language learners in your classroom. This is an exciting opportunity for you and your students to learn about new cultures and to ensure that newcomers feel welcomed and supported because they may be experiencing culture shock as they adapt to a foreign language, a new school, a new community, and a new way of life with its own social norms. While teaching them new skills, remember to celebrate their own culture and help them maintain and share both their own culture and language with their classmates. Sheltered instruction, also referred to as SDAIE, is the most common approach to teaching both English and academic content to newcomers. SIOP is a specially designed and research-based approach to sheltered instruction. Promoting English language development requires that you use a variety of hands-on, well-researched, active-learning strategies. Multiculturalism is not an add-on but an attitude that permeates everything you do in the classroom. Parents of newcomers can be encouraged to participate actively at the school site in a multitude of ways.

Reflect!

Visualize a new student who speaks little English arriving in your classroom midyear. Reflect on the steps you will take to integrate that student into the classroom community, and to orient him or her to the rules, routines, and procedures of the classroom and the norms he or she will need to learn in the greater school community and beyond. How will you ameliorate culture shock and ensure that the newcomer feels welcome, safe, and secure? How will you ensure that the other students are equally welcoming, accepting, and helpful?

UNIT 6 CHECKLIST

Engaging All Learners Checklist	For more information go to:
☐ Am I communicating positive expectations to my students?	Chapter 25
☐ Do I treat all my students equally?	Chapter 25
☐ Am I making an attempt to get to know all my students on a personal level?	Chapter 25
☐ Am I using a variety of research-based strategies, including cooperative learning?	Chapters 26, 27
☐ Do I incorporate multiple intelligences into my lesson plans?	Chapters 22, 28
☐ Have I determined the policies for referring a student with special needs?	Chapter 28
☐ Do I differentiate learning as needed?	Chapter 28
☐ Have I learned strategies to facilitate both language and academic content for the English learners in my classroom?	Chapter 29
☐ Have I prepared materials for parents in their native language or found someone to translate for me?	Chapter 29

Further Reading: Engaging All Learners

Diaz-Rico, L., & Weed, K. (2010). *The cross-cultural language and academic development handbook: A complete K–12 reference guide* (4th ed.). Boston: Allyn & Bacon. This handbook is a key resource for mainstream teachers, K–12, with English language learners in their classroom.

Echevarria, J., Vogt, M., & Short, D. (2008). *Making content comprehensible for English learners: The SIOP model* (3rd ed.). Boston: Allyn & Bacon. This is a valuable resource for teaching ELLs in the regular classroom using the Sheltered Instruction Observation Protocol (SIOP) model. The model is clearly explained, and you can view teaching examples and interviews with the authors and download reproducibles from a CD-ROM that is included. It is appropriate for first-grade through high school teachers.

Friend, M., & Bursuck, W. (2008). *Including students with special needs: A practical guide for classroom teachers* (5th ed.). Boston: Allyn & Bacon. This is a guide to teaching students with special needs in an inclusive setting. It contains many practical suggestions, vignettes, and methods.

Gardner, H. (1993). *Frames of mind: The theory of multiple intelligences* (10th ed.). New York: Basic Books. This book is the original discussion of multiple intelligence theory, the idea that there is there is not one thing called intelligence, but rather several different types of intelligence that accounts for why individuals learn in different ways and demonstrate different skills and talents. The original list of intelligences included seven types: Linguistic, Musical, Logical-Mathematical, Spatial, Bodily-Kinesthetic, and two types of Personal intelligence.

Gardner, H. (2006). *Multiple intelligences: New horizons in theory and practice*. New York: Basic Books. This is an update of the previous book, *Frames of Mind*. In it you will find a description of a ninth intelligence, Existential, defined as reflecting on deep, life questions which Gardner has provisionally added to the eight intelligences he defined in earlier books. (Naturalistic intelligence was added to the original seven in previous works). In this book, Gardner updates his theory's relevance to education and to other arenas in society beyond education.

Haley, M. H. (2010). *Brain-compatible differentiated instruction for English language learners*. Boston: Allyn & Bacon. This book first describes 12 topics that contribute to brain-compatible teaching and learning and differentiating instruction for ELLs.

Herrell, A. L., & Jordon, M. (2008). *50 strategies for teaching English language learners* (3rd ed.). Upper Saddle River, NJ: Pearson Education. This practical book includes 50 strategies teachers of ELLs can use to teach academic content through the language arts. A definition, rationale, and step-by-step procedures accompany each strategy.

Hill, J. D., & Flynn, K. M. (2006). *Classroom instruction that works with English language learners*. Alexandria, VA: ASCD. This text is a thorough resource for helping ELLs at all acquisition levels succeed. The strategies derive from those described in Marzano et al.'s (2004) *Classroom Instruction That Works*.

Marzano, R. J., Norford, J. S., Paynter, D. E., Pickering, D. J., & Gaddy, B. B. (2004). *A handbook for classroom instruction that works.* Upper Saddle River, NJ: Prentice Hall. This is a companion volume to Marzano et al.'s (2004) *Classroom Instruction That Works.* It covers nine different types of research-based instructional strategies. These generic strategies are appropriate for any curriculum area or grade level. The authors provide exercises, brief questionnaires, tips, samples, worksheets, rubrics, and other tools.

Marzano, R., Pickering, D., & Pollack, J. (2004). *Classroom instruction that works: Research-based strategies for increasing student achievement.* Alexandria, VA: Association for Supervision and Curriculum Development. This is a synthesis of what works, and it is easy to read and apply. The most effective teaching strategies are clearly explained in ways that make them applicable in any grade or subject-matter classroom.

Tomlinson, C. (2004). *How to differentiate instruction in mixed-ability classrooms* (2nd ed.). Alexandria, VA: Association for Supervision and Curriculum Development. The second edition provides many field-tested examples of how to differentiate instruction in diverse classrooms by assessing readiness levels, interests, and learning profiles. Many examples of differentiating content, processes, and products of lessons are included.

Informative Websites

One Stop English
http://www.onestopenglish.com/

This website offers lesson plans, free resources, and articles for teachers with English language learners.

The Lesson Plans Page
http://www.LessonPlansPage.com

This website offers ideas and lessons organized by subject and grade level, K–12. If you need an idea, lesson, or complete unit, this is the place to go. You will find educational links, discussion forums, inspirational stories, and much, much more.

Marzano Research Laboratory
http://www.marzanoresearch.com/site/

This is Dr. Marzano's home website. From here you can access classroom tips, new research, products, and books and even get tips from Dr. Marzano emailed to your inbox.

National Association for Bilingual Education
http://www.nabe.org

This professional development and advocacy association for English language learners and families supports and promotes policy, programs, pedagogy, research, and professional development that generate academic success.

Council for Exceptional Children
http://www.cec.sped.org

This official Council for Exceptional Children website provides information on issues, professional development, resources, publications, policy, advocacy, and membership.

Carol Tomlinson, Ed.D.
http://www.caroltomlinson.com

Dr. Tomlinson's website offers books, articles, resources, and more.

UNIT 7

Assessing and Communicating Student Progress

CHAPTER 30

HOW CAN I ASSESS STUDENT PERFORMANCE?

One had to cram all this stuff into one's mind for the examinations, whether one liked it or not. This coercion had such a deterring effect on me that, after I had passed the final examination, I found the consideration of any scientific problems distasteful to me for an entire year.

Albert Einstein

Effectiveness Essentials

- You can design your own easy-to-score diagnostic tests for basic skills and concepts to determine the appropriate starting level for instruction or to assess progress.
- Norm-referenced tests measure student scores in relation to those of other students.
- Authentic assessments focus on the process and continuum of learning, not just on the outcomes.
- Portfolio assessment is an organizational and management system for collecting evidence to monitor student progress.
- Parents and former teachers can provide you with a great deal of information that will be helpful in assessing students' strengths and pinpointing their weaknesses.

Teachers approach student evaluation with trepidation. They often find this particular aspect of teaching difficult because they don't want to hurt students' feelings; they don't feel they know enough about assessment techniques; and they don't know how to factor student effort, as opposed to actual performance, into the grading equation.

Assessment has always been a part of the teaching-learning cycle; therefore, it is a key component of effective practice. Today's standards-based education climate and concomitant high-stakes testing have focused educators' attention on assessment more than ever. Teachers do not teach in a vacuum. At strategic points, they have to determine the effectiveness of their instruction. The feedback teachers receive, based on their assessments, is used to guide further curriculum and instruction decisions. Students also benefit because the assessment data lets them know where they stand in relation to the standards they are expected to reach.

Assessing Your Students

Assessment involves ongoing evaluations of your students' progress on a number of fronts. The process begins with the first day of school. The diagnosis you plan for the beginning of school should be "underwhelming" for you. You will be preoccupied by a multitude of tasks, but diagnosis is very important at the outset and needs your attention. Why? Because you do not want to overestimate or underestimate your students' readiness. You may turn them off if the work is too hard, or you may bore them if they have already mastered the material in another class. You will want to use existing records and some diagnostic measures that are easy to administer and score; short and relevant to your standards-based educational objectives; nonthreatening to the students; and administered in a group rather than individually to save time.

As the year goes on, you can monitor student progress in a number of ways. Assessment generally falls within

WATCH IT! video

Standardized Tests

Gerald Bracey discusses the difference between norm-referenced and criterion-referenced tests. After viewing the clip, define both types of tests, including the strengths and weaknesses of each. What do you think is the best way to effectively measure student progress?

STATISTICS

According to a Met Life (2009) survey, teachers report that academic standards and curricula are stronger than they used to be. However, views on standardized testing are more divergent, with less support among teachers than among principals.

- The number of teachers who rate academic standards in their schools as excellent has doubled from 26% in 1984 to 53% today.
- In 1984, 61% of teachers were in favor of standardized tests to measure student achievement as part of evaluating teacher effectiveness, but today fewer than half (48%) agree that standardized tests are effective in helping them to track student performance.
- In contrast, 79% of today's principals agree that standardized tests help teachers in their schools track student performance.

UNIT 7

TEACHER TALKS . . .

I advise teachers in our district to use an independent reading inventory to assess all new students. Scores for students who were in our district the year before should have been recorded and passed on to the next teacher. Use the IRI to establish a reading and comprehension level for each student. If more information is needed, administer an observation survey. While giving this test, I am able to learn the student's grasp of letter names, sight-word reading vocabulary, written-word knowledge, understanding of hearing and recording sounds during dictation, and understanding of how print works.

I collect writing samples from each student and assess them using a six-trait writing rubric. If I need information on the student's phonics knowledge, I give the 20-word spelling test from Words Their Way *(Bear, Invernizzi, Templeton, & Johnston, 2007).*

JOAN MARIE SMITH
District Curriculum Program Specialist
Colton, California

three general categories or types: norm-referenced, criterion-referenced, and performance-based or authentic. The first two are considered standardized tests because they are administered and scored in a standardized manner. The third type uses rubrics to assess performance, and it is not as easy to control all the variables of administration and scoring. The three types of assessment are all equally important and they all give you essential, albeit different, information.

Norm-Referenced Tests Measure Student Scores in Relation to Those of Other Students

Half of your students will always fall below the 50th percentile by virtue of the bell-shaped curve. Some standardized tests such as the GRE, the SAT, and the Wechsler Intelligence Scale for Children (WISC) are norm-referenced. Many state achievement tests are norm-referenced if they measure students against the group taking the test. The feedback from norm-referenced tests is helpful for comparing classes, schools, and districts in relation to one another. The information you receive as the actual teacher, however, does not tell you precisely where individual students have fallen short or excelled.

Criterion-Referenced Tests Measure Students Against Set Criteria

Like norm-referenced tests, criterion-referenced tests are standardized in that they are administered and scored in a standardized manner. However, instead

mythBUSTER

Standardized tests are the best way to measure progress.

Standardized tests are only *one* way of measuring student progress. It is important to look at the whole child. It is a fact that many children (and adults) do not perform well in testing situations. However, if given the opportunity to demonstrate the same knowledge in an alternative manner, a child may be successful. The true picture of a child's ability contains teacher observations and classroom performance as well as testing achievement.

Joan Prehoda
Principal
Palm Springs, California

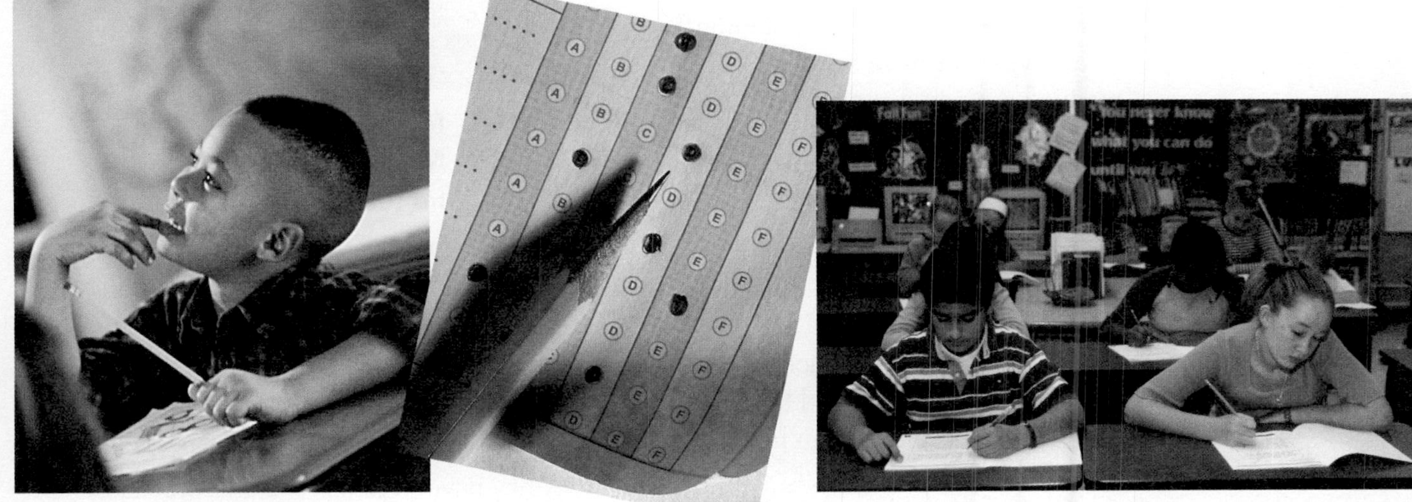

Are your students ready for the test?

of measuring students against one another, criterion-referenced tests measure the students against set criteria. These tests defy the bell curve and assume that every student can achieve a passing score or meet the standard. If this sounds familiar, it is because standards-based tests are a form of criterion-referenced tests. There is a great deal of controversy surrounding high-stakes testing that has been mandated by the No Child Left Behind Act and its reauthorization. If no child is to be left behind, every child should meet the criteria established for passing the standards-based tests. Exit exams are also criterion-referenced tests, with a passing score established that all students are expected to meet or exceed.

Authentic Assessments Focus on the Process of Learning

Authentic assessments, also called performance-based assessments, are not easily standardized and focus on the process and continuum of learning, not just on the outcomes. They take into consideration many more facets or dimensions of a student's progress than do norm-referenced or criterion-referenced standardized tests. Authentic assessments require students to perform real world tasks that show what they have learned vis-à-vis the standards or objectives that have been set. They are evaluated using a rubric with several proficiency levels that are made known to students in advance. All students can succeed at the highest proficiency levels since they know up front what the objective is, what the task is, and how it will be evaluated.

Performance, or authentic, assessment can go a long way toward helping you focus on assessment as an integral part of the teaching-learning cycle. The feedback from authentic assessments will help you determine how much of what you are teaching is getting through to your students. Then you can modify or adapt the instructional process to better meet the needs of your students along the way instead of waiting for a one-time-only standardized test. These assessments can also be fun for your students. For example, students may have to make a model, demonstrate a procedure, or conduct an experiment to show what they have learned. These activities are intrinsically enjoyable in and of themselves.

Five Steps to Authentic Assessment. At first blush you may be a bit intimidated about designing authentic assessments. However, you use authentic assessments all the time—for example, when you observe your students conducting an experiment in a science lab or creating a still-life watercolor based on your

WATCH IT! video

Managing Student Work: Monitoring Progress in Authentic Assessments

In this clip, the teacher gives checklists to the students. Thus, as these fifth graders work on their project, they can assess their own progress at various stages. This kind of formative assessment enables students to check and recheck along the way before they have to turn in the final product. What other kinds of formative assessments are you familiar with (hint: a rough draft is one)?

Forms of Authentic Assessment

In this clip, eighth-grade students work on an invention that will be useful in everyday life. Although a rubric will be used to grade the result, the actual product and its development in stages are part of the authentic assessment process. What products can be assessed with or without a rubric? Is it easier to have the criteria and indicators in place at the outset?

criteria. You observe students' behavior, check on their handwriting, and listen to them read. This is ongoing, and you may not even be aware you are doing it. Authentic assessments could be called "What you have students do every day" assessments. The real challenge is tying the tasks to the standards and scoring the students' work. Here are some steps to help you design an authentic assessment.

1. **Identify what you are assessing.** Look closely at your standards. They will identify *what* students should know or be able to do and at what level. Some specific ideas for assessing the attainment of the standard or objective may jump out at you. For example, if your standard reads, "Students will deepen their understanding of the measurement of solid shapes," you may contemplate a task of actually constructing a pyramid to scale. This becomes your performance objective.
2. **Decide what activity will provide context for assessment.** You may decide that you will indeed have students work in cooperative groups to construct a pyramid, with each member of the group assigned one of three equal tasks that include measuring the pyramid faces and base. Make sure that whatever task you delineate, you have enough materials, supplies, and space. Organize the responsibilities of each task and give very clear directions to avoid confusion.
3. **Define the criteria and let the students in on them.** You can often locate the criteria for attainment of the standard by

WATCH IT! video

Criteria for Evaluating All Grade Levels

In this clip, Dr. James Popham defines rubrics and articulates the steps in creating one. What are those steps? What is the difference between *criteria* and *indicators*?

Part 1: Understanding How to Use a Rubric

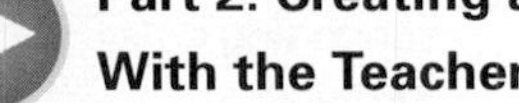

Part 2: Creating a Rubric With the Teacher

Part 3: Referring Back to the Rubric to Stay on Task

In this three-part video clip, second graders are learning the fundamentals of creating and using a rubric. What steps did the teacher take to introduce the rubric to her students? What advantage do you see in having the students participate in creating rubrics?

TEACHER TALKS . . .

We have developed rubrics covering areas from student behavior to academic projects. But before using a rubric at all, I've recommended developing one for something simple and using it as a shared reading and discussion point. After the rubric has been thoroughly worked, then each group writes its own for a group project or group participation. In this way, the students come to own the idea and understanding of a rubric. Anything put into use for greater understanding eliminates the need to go back and reteach. The students have also designed a rubric for family participation at a school family night. The parents really enjoyed it because it gave them a focus for their participation—enabling them to take part in some activities that they might have skipped.

BRENDA DOWNS
Reading Specialist/Literacy Coordinator
Minden, Nevada

looking at the benchmarks that your district has set up. They won't come out of thin air. Focus on the skills and concepts your district or your state has designated as essential. When you are assessing formally, always let the students in on the task and the established criteria and performance levels. The task may be any hands-on activity that you observe or products that the students complete. Let the students tell you what they think a successful project would look like, based on the standard.

4. **Create a rubric.** Your rating system should be based on the criteria you set up along with performance indicators for each of the criteria. You can create your own rubric or use ones designed at your site or district level. I used a free rubric-generating website (www.teachnology.com) to generate Table 30.1. Design fair and simple rubrics since you will be sharing them with your students. Other rubric-generating sites are listed in the references at the end of this unit.

Table 30.1 Rubric for Paragraph Writing

Criteria	4 Points	3 Points	2 Points	1 Point
Topic Sentence	Clear, properly placed, and restated	Either unclear or not placed properly, but restated	Unclear, not properly placed, but restated	Unclear and neither properly placed nor restated
Supporting Details	3 supporting detail sentences	2 supporting detail sentences	1 supporting detail sentence	0 supporting sentences
Mechanics Spelling Punctuation Grammar	No errors	1–2 errors	3–5 errors	6 or more errors
Legibility	Legible in all places	Marginally legible	Illegible in some places	Illegible in all places
Teacher Comments				

5. **Provide feedback.** Translate the results into feedback through anecdotal reports or grades. Decide how the point range on the rubric corresponds to each of the letter grades, or have your rubric's total points add up to a score easily multiplied to give a traditional top score of 100.

You can challenge your students to create rubrics. For example, before sharing the rubric in Table 30.1, I might have shown my students copies of paragraphs I identified as having a wide range of proficiency. I would ask the students to identify the elements of a good paragraph and then ask them (in groups, possibly) to develop four levels of proficiency for each criterion. I would then show them the one I generated by comparison and they could alter theirs if need be. Students can often assess their own work using rubrics.

Creating Rubrics in a Nutshell. Rubrics for common standards are often shared among teachers, so don't reinvent the wheel if you don't have to. Many districts have teams of teachers creating rubrics for the essential standards. Don't be shy! If there are no rubrics for selected standards, either adapt a similar one or create one yourself. Here's how:

1. Share sample assignments with gradations from good to poor with your students.
2. Make a list of criteria for assessing the assignment with the class.
3. Reduce the list of criteria to a manageable few elements.
4. Sketch out approximately four levels of performance for each criterion. These levels can have values attached for easier grading: 3, 2, 1, 0 or 4, 3, 2, 1.
5. Create a draft of the rubric.
6. Apply it to the assignment.
7. Revise and perfect it.

APPLY IT!

Access the website http://www.teachnology.com and create a rubric for one of the performance standards you are required to assess. Then try it out on an assignment in your classroom. If you are already familiar with rubrics and the process for generating them, take this process a step further and involve your students in creating a rubric. Even first graders have created their own writing rubrics!

CLASSROOM ARTIFACTS

A Writing Lesson Plan and Rubric

Title: "Writing Process for Informative Writing"
Creator: Molly Bendorf
Primary subject: language arts
Secondary subjects: science, social studies
Grade level: 3–4
Content area: writing nonfiction research papers
Duration:

- Introduction = 5 minutes
- Activity = 20 minutes
- Closure = 10 minutes

Colorado Standards:

- Reading/writing standard 2: Students write and speak for a variety of purposes and audiences.
- Reading/writing standard 4: Students apply thinking skills to their reading, writing, speaking, listening, and viewing.
- Reading/writing standard 5: Students read to locate, select, and make use of relevant information from a variety of media, reference, and technological sources.
- Reading/writing standard 6: Students read and recognize literature as a record of human experience.

Objectives: At the end of this lesson, students will be able to glean information from text to write an informative paper.

Resources and Materials:

- Nonfiction books, newspapers, magazines, encyclopedias
- Two-column notes sheet for each student
- Index cards for each student
- Numerous informative texts for examples

Differentiation: allow shared writing

Teaching the Lesson:

1. Planning
   - Discuss different ways in which a nonfiction book is written.
     - Share the two-column notes and the index cards to be used in planning.
     - Discuss the planning process.
     - Which plan will be used?
     - How do we plan?
   - Have students help you create a plan. Allow think/pair/share during this time.
   - Have students write their plan based on their topic.
2. Drafting
   - With the whole group write the text from the two-column notes.
   - Show students how to take their information from their plan to create an informative text. Also, make sure students understand the topic sentence and conclusion.
   - Practice writing information in your own words, not just regurgitation from the text.
   - Have students write their draft. If needed for differentiation, work with a group of students and do writing together.
3. Editing
   - Show students how you edit your writing.
   - Have students work in groups to edit each other's writing.

(continues)

4. Publishing
   - After edits are complete, model the publishing technique with students.
   - Allow students to write final copies in ink or on the computer.
   - Have copies of other published works available in the classroom. If none are available, start a collection of published pieces. Students love to see their work.

(as seen on http://www.LessonPlansPage.com)

Research Report Rubric: Science/Social Studies

Category	4 Points	3 Points	2 Points	1 Point
Graphic organizer	Graphic organizer or outline has been completed and shows clear, logical relationships between all topics and subtopics.	Graphic organizer or outline has been completed and shows clear, logical relationships between most topics and subtopics.	Graphic organizer or outline has been started and includes some topics and subtopics.	Graphic organizer or outline has not been attempted.
Notes	Notes are recorded and organized in an extremely neat and orderly fashion.	Notes are recorded legibly and are somewhat organized.	Notes are recorded.	Notes are recorded only with peer/teacher assistance and reminders.
First draft	Detailed draft is neatly presented and includes all required information.	Draft includes all required information and is legible.	Draft includes most required information and is legible.	Draft is missing required information and is difficult to read.
Quality of information	Information clearly relates to the main topic. It includes several supporting details and/or examples.	Information clearly relates to the main topic. It provides 1–2 supporting details and/or examples.	Information clearly relates to the main topic. No details and/or examples are given.	Information has little or nothing to do with the main topic.
Mechanics	No grammatical, spelling, or punctuation errors.	Almost no grammatical, spelling, or punctuation errors.	A few grammatical, spelling, or punctuation errors.	Many grammatical, spelling, or punctuation errors.
Sources	All sources (information and graphics) are accurately documented in the desired format.	All sources (information and graphics) are accurately documented, but a few are not in the desired format.	All sources (information and graphics) are accurately documented, but many are not in the desired format.	Some sources are not accurately documented.
Diagrams and illustrations	Diagrams and illustrations are neat and accurate and add to the reader's understanding of the topic.	Diagrams and illustrations are accurate and add to the reader's understanding of the topic.	Diagrams and illustrations are neat and accurate and sometimes add to the reader's understanding of the topic.	Diagrams and illustrations are not accurate or do not add to the reader's understanding of the topic.
Internet use	Student successfully uses suggested Internet links to find information and navigates within these sites easily without assistance.	Student is usually able to use suggested Internet links to find information and navigates within these sites easily without assistance.	Student is occasionally able to use suggested Internet links to find information and navigates within these sites easily without assistance.	Student needs assistance or supervision to use suggested Internet links and/or to navigate within these sites.

CHAPTER 30

Assessment Using Portfolios

Portfolio assessment is the term that describes an organizational and management system for collecting evidence to monitor student progress. Portfolios include samples selected by the student and teacher as well as reflections about and comments on the work. They may include recordings of students' oral reading at various times during the year, writing samples, homework, tests, artwork, and photos of projects, among other things. Periodically, the students and teacher review portfolio contents and assess progress. This reflective aspect empowers students to make decisions and to evaluate their own progress based on established criteria.

Portfolios are shared with parents at conference time and serve as your data, along with the more objective measures, when you complete report cards. Portfolios can be passed on to the next teacher along with other records or given to the student to take home at the end of the year. It is tangible evidence of how far the student has progressed.

Read all you can about managing portfolios, talk to colleagues, and attend all inservices or seminars on this topic. Some useful resources on authentic assessment are listed at the end of the unit. In these references, you will find very practical advice about portfolio management. Here are a few key timesaving ideas:

1. Take some time each day to examine a few portfolios with the students so the work doesn't get overwhelming. In this way, you can be on a two-week cycle of review.
2. Use sticky notes for comments and add them to the folder, attached to a larger reflection sheet for your expanded commentary.
3. Videotape your class doing oral reports, plays, debates, and other activities. Copies of the tapes can be edited for the students to keep as part of their individual portfolios.
4. Every few weeks, collect recorded reading samples from individual students.
5. Organize writing portfolios on a computer if each student is able to have access. The drafts, edited versions, and final products, along with reviews by peers, the teacher, and even parents, can all be included.

WATCH IT! video

Portfolios and Self-Assessment
A teacher discusses the advantages and management of portfolio assessment in the primary grades.

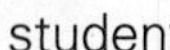

Portfolios
A seventh-grade teacher and a fifth-grade teacher discuss how they assess students using portfolios.

Portfolio Exhibition
A teacher describes a schoolwide exhibition of writing portfolios.

Primary Portfolio
Even younger students can review and report on their work.

High School Writing Folders

High School Portfolios
In these high school examples, students use an organization tool to collect writing samples for review with their teacher.

After viewing the six video clips, discuss the commonalities in approach that you saw. How do the middle school and high school teachers differ in their portfolio management from the primary teacher? What are the advantages of a schoolwide exhibit of the portfolios as opposed to a class exhibit?

APPLY IT!

Gather information about diagnostic testing resources and procedures at your site and district as soon as possible so you don't reinvent the wheel. Teachers' manuals often include relevant diagnostic tests and directions for their administration and interpretation.

Other Diagnostic Tools

Although you may not use all the following data-gathering methods for each student, this list, suggested by experienced teachers, gives you a variety of choices. Completed diagnostic assessments can be added to the student portfolios as well.

TEACHER TALKS . . .

Change your students' view of testing!

This is my first year back in the classroom, after spending 29 years in the medical field. Things have been going really well, except for my students' obvious lack of studying for tests. It was very frustrating for me because my students participate enthusiastically in class, ask plenty of questions, usually complete all their homework assignments correctly, etc. But when test time rolled around, they did not do well. One day I made the comment to them that tests were given not only to test their knowledge of a particular subject but to also test my ability to teach that subject. For some reason, that really got their attention. They began asking questions such as "What's it like to teach?" "How do you know when you are doing a good job?" etc. We had an awesome conversation about teaching, learning, test

(continued on facing page)

Design Your Own Tests

You can design your own easy-to-score diagnostic tests for basic skills and concepts to determine the appropriate starting level for instruction or to assess progress. Speak to other same-subject or same-grade-level teachers. They may have diagnostic and review tests on file that are appropriate for your class as well.

Confer With Other Teachers

To find out more about a student's academic history, seek out a previous year's teacher and present your concerns and questions. You may find that your perceptions are confirmed and the teacher saves you from reinventing the wheel by sharing how he or she was able to reach the student last year. Enlist the help of other resource persons at school: the special education resource teacher, the principal, the school psychologist, or the student study team.

Confer With Parents

Parents can provide you with a great deal of information that will be helpful in assessing a student's strengths and weaknesses. You don't have to wait until formal parent conference times. If you need data that parents can provide, call them and let them know that you need their help in providing the best possible learning situation for their son or daughter. Chapter 34 provides more detail about how you can work with parents to maximize the learning experience for each of your students.

One kindergarten teacher I know interviews each child's parents or guardians during the first few weeks of school, using a nonthreatening set of questions that elicit information about the child's strengths and weaknesses, interests, fears, food preferences, traumas, developmental milestones, health problems, and other concerns. Arrange for an interpreter in these interviews if you need one. These extra efforts result in greater parental cooperation and support and provide a wealth of insightful information not otherwise available.

Check the Cumulative Record

Cumulative records provide continuous and succinct documentation of a student's educational experiences from elementary school through high school. They are used extensively by teachers and other school personnel, since they follow students from grade to grade and provide an easy reference for many aspects of growth and development, academic performance, and behavior in school.

APPLY IT!

Teachers disagree about whether or not to look at cumulative records before they have made their own judgments about a student. What are the pros and cons? What is your position in the debate?

AVOID IT!

Do not make definitive judgments about student achievement just from standardized tests. Gather as much information about a student as you can from all the sources mentioned in this chapter.

Summary

Assessing student achievement is one of the most complex endeavors a teacher, especially a new one, is expected to accomplish. When you multiply this by thirty-plus students, the task seems very difficult. Add to this task your reluctance to pass judgment, limited exposure to assessment courses in teacher prep, and confusion as to how to factor in all the variables and come up with a grade. But this is one area in which a great deal of help is available from your district, your mentors, and your buddy teachers. Testing programs usually have a co-ordinator at the district and school level, and his or her job is to walk you though the various assessments that are required. In your classroom, you can devise your own authentic assessments (and rubrics to grade them) such as projects, performances, experiments, and portfolios. Teachers gather information from various inventories and teacher-made tests as well as from conferences with parents and previous teachers and the cumulative folder.

Reflect!

Obtain the testing schedule from your potential district or school. It will show all the tests you are required to administer. Then ask at least three teachers at your potential grade level or in your subject area what measures they use to assess student achievement. Compare and contrast their answers. Come up with a plan for which types of authentic assessments you will use in addition to the standardized tests that your district requires.

taking, career choices, etc. My students have told me that now they "always think of the teacher being tested" when they are taking tests because of our conversation back in September. I think it helps students to know that testing and feedback are not just part of a process that applies to schoolwork, but they apply throughout life in every profession—and especially in the teaching profession.

SHARON VANDERFORD
Fifth-Grade Teacher
West Memphis, Arkansas

(as seen on http://www.LessonPlansPage.com)

CHAPTER 31

HOW CAN I ASSESS STUDENT INTERESTS AND ATTITUDES?

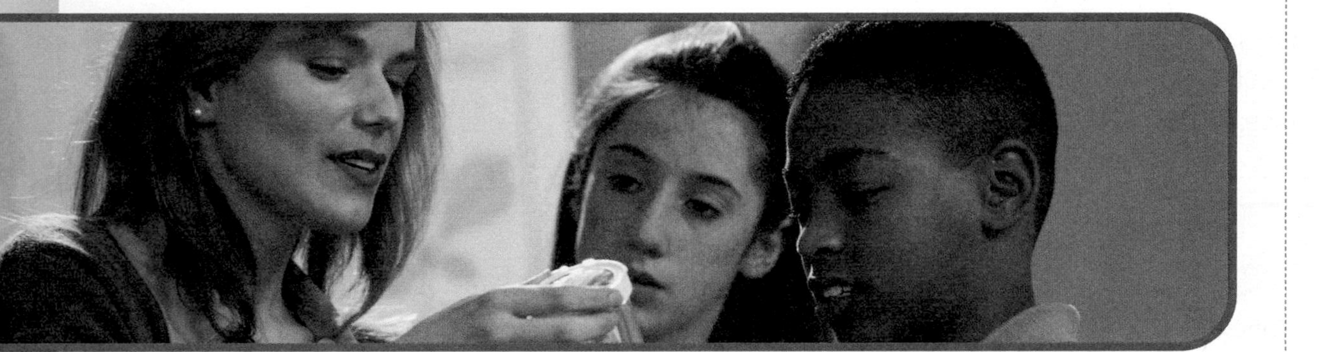

Attitude is a little thing that makes a big difference.

Winston Churchill

Effectiveness Essentials

- Your students can provide you with a wealth of information not obtainable elsewhere and can give you a baseline for building on the diversity in your classroom.
- A number of strategies exist for collecting information about your students that can help you identify their individual needs.

Although much of the focus in education today is on testing and academic progress, your role as assessor doesn't stop there. Gathering feedback from your students and collecting information about them expand your role. Your students are more than numbers or names on a seating chart, and finding out what they are thinking, feeling, and believing is key to your success as a teacher. You are not just teaching in the abstract. You are teaching important content and skills to *students,* and you want to dig deeper to find out who they really are. An inquisitive and sensitive teacher knows that students can provide you with a wealth of information not obtainable elsewhere and can give you a baseline for building on the diversity in your classroom. There are a variety of techniques you can use to collect information about your students' attitudes, especially toward instruction, as well as their interests.

Feedback on Instruction

To improve your instruction, take some time at the end of each class period to gather student feedback. I have found this to be very helpful at all levels of instruction—from elementary to university. Adapt any of these formats or make up your own.

Try a Quick-Write

Have students write a paragraph in response to a probe to evaluate their understanding of a topic. For example, *What was the most important (confusing, troubling, interesting) thing you learned about the Civil War? What was hard to understand?*

Pass the Envelope, Please

Write a question about the lesson on the front of an envelope and pass it around the class. Every student submits a response to the question and places it in the envelope. You can decide whether or not to make this anonymous.

Summarize or Explain

Have students write a paragraph about what they learned during the period. They can be asked to explain the concept in simple terms or to give an example. They can write these paragraphs on index cards or in their notebooks, but you should collect them and read them to see how well they understood the lesson.

Rate the Session

Have the students rate the session in terms of comprehensibility, interest, etc. They can use a scale of 1 to 5 or a yes/no format (see Figures 31.1 and 31.2).

Figure 31.1

Ways to Get Feedback From Middle and High School Students

Tell me what you think:

1. The teacher stated the objective.	Y	N
2. The teacher gave clear directions.	Y	N
3. The lesson was interesting.	Y	N
4. I learned something new.	Y	N
5. The teacher was organized.	Y	N
6. The teacher encouraged us.	Y	N
7. The teacher answered all questions.	Y	N
8. The follow-up assignment was clear.	Y	N

9. What I liked best about the lesson: ____________________.
10. To make the lesson easier to understand, the teacher could have ____________________.

Figure 31.2

Ways to Get Feedback From Elementary Students

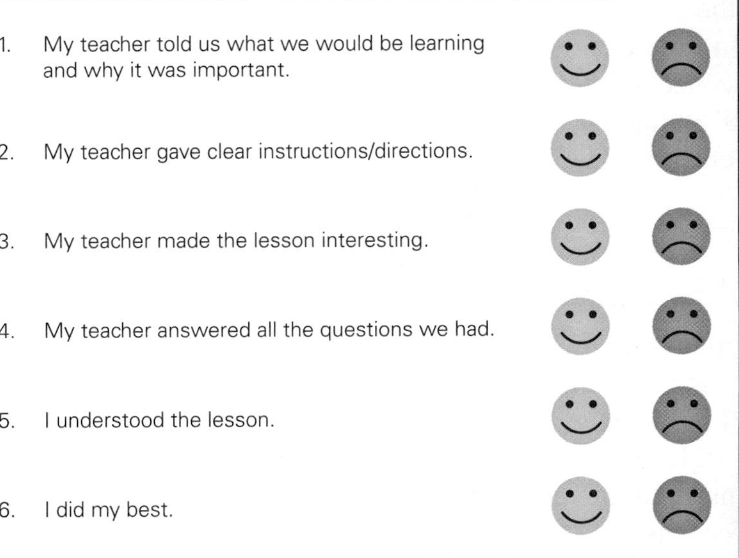

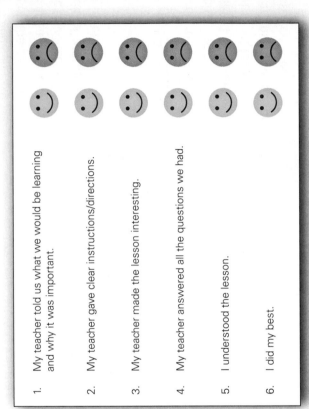

1. My teacher told us what we would be learning and why it was important.
2. My teacher gave clear instructions/directions.
3. My teacher made the lesson interesting.
4. My teacher answered all the questions we had.
5. I understood the lesson.
6. I did my best.

Interviews

Anonymity is the state of not being known, and every student wants literal and figurative recognition. It is understandable when you forget the name or face of a student you had two years ago. It is embarrassing if that student is currently in your class. Some teachers take time during the first weeks to interview each student for a few minutes. Although this is very time-consuming, the face-to-face exchange allows you to ask follow-up questions and individualize the questions to suit each student. Students have a chance to have special time with you, and the interest you show will pay off in instructional matters. You might prepare ahead of time a list of questions from which you draw as appropriate. Make sure that the questions can all be justified as school-related and do not infringe on family privacy. Some sample questions follow:

- What is your favorite family tradition?
- What do you like to do after school?
- What kinds of books do you like to read?
- What would be the best birthday present?
- What are your favorite television programs?
- How much time do you spend watching television each day?
- What are your favorite possessions?
- What subjects do you like best in school?
- What are your least favorite subjects?
- What sports interest you? Do you play on any teams?
- Who is your favorite sports star?
- What faraway place would you like to visit?
- Do you have a pet? Tell me about it.
- What question would you like to ask me about the coming year?
- Describe yourself in three words.
- Tell me one thing you are very good at.
- What new thing would you like to learn to do?
- What do you want to be when you grow up?

Interest Inventories

Students can fill in the inventories themselves or interview a classmate and then fill in the answers. Although this saves a great deal of teacher time, it does not allow the teacher to follow up and give each student individual attention.

Your students' favorite activities can be determined by compiling a long list of choices. Have them use appropriate symbols to mark the ones they are good at and the ones they want to get better at, or the ones they like versus those they don't like at all (see Figures 31.3–31.6).

APPLY IT!

Design an interest inventory, using either interview questions or a self-assessment for the appropriate grade level or subject matter. You can use pictures for younger students.

Figure 31.3
Pictorial Interest Inventory for Young Students

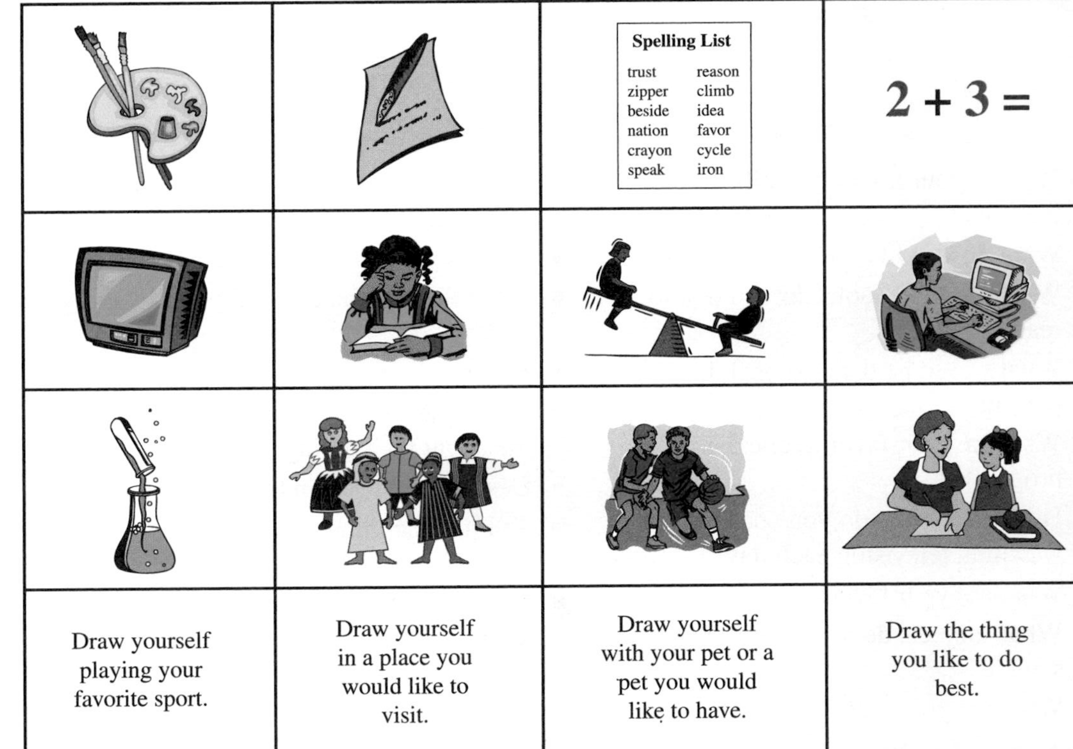

Figure 31.4

Interest Inventory for Middle School Students

Good at ✓	Video games	Skateboarding
Want to get better at ➡	Math	Skiing
Like ♥	Science	Snowboarding
Don't like ✗	Social studies	Basketball
___	Art projects	Baseball
Reading aloud	Science experiments	Swimming
Reading silently	Drawing	Tennis
Singing	Board games	___
Writing stories, poems	Computer work	___
Dancing	Puzzles	___
Speaking in front of the class		*(add your own)*

Figure 31.5

Reading Inventory for Middle or High School Students

1. How many minutes do you spend reading outside of school: each day?______ each week? ______
2. What was the last book you read for pleasure?______
3. Do you have a public library card? How often do you go to the public library?______
4. How many books do you own? Do you have your own bookshelf?______
5. Circle your top choices for genres of books you like to read: historical novels, romance novels, mysteries, science fiction, gothic, sports, textbooks, biographies, other ______.
6. Do you get the newspaper at home? Do you read it? What sections? ______
7. Do you get any magazines at home especially for you? Which ones? ______
8. What do you read online: reviews? news? blogs? Other ______
9. Do you ever download books to read on your computer or other device?______
10. Given your choice, would you rather hold a book in your hand or use a device such as a Kindle or an iPad?______

UNIT 7

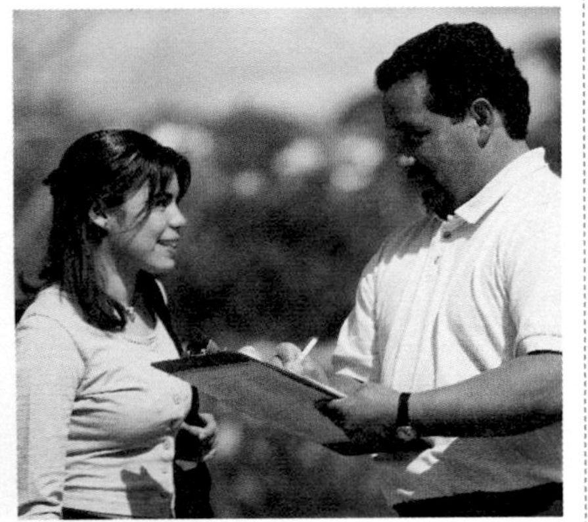

Get to know your students.

Figure 31.6

Reading Inventory for Elementary Students

1. How many minutes do you spend reading or being read to outside of school? Each day?_______ Each week? _______
2. What is your favorite book? ______________________ Why?______________________
3. Do you have a public library card?____________ How often do you go to the public library? ____________
4. How many books do you own? Do you have your own bookshelf?______________________
5. Do you like being read to?______________________
6. What kind of stories do you like to read or havwe read to you? Real or made up? Taking place now or long ago?______________________
7. What topics interest you: sports, real animals, friendship, kids like you, folktales, biographies, fairy tales, information books, mysteries, science fiction, stories from different cultures, history, other?______________________
8. Who is your favorite character from a book?______________________
9. Do you get the newspaper at home? Do you read it? Which sections?______________________
10. Did you ever see a movie based on a book that you read, such as *Charlotte's Web*? Which did you prefer, the book or the movie?______________________

Attitude Inventories

Attitude inventories are self-assessment measures that involve a scaled response from high to low. You might use numbers for your scale or even a progression of faces from happy to sad. Some sample questions follow:

APPLY IT!

Design an attitude inventory appropriate for your grade level or subject area.

- How do you feel about reading in a group?
- How do you feel about coming to school each day?
- How do you feel about math?
- How do you feel about science?
- How do you feel about social studies?
- How do you feel about art?
- How do you feel about listening to music?
- How do you feel about watching television?
- How do you feel about speaking in front of the class?
- How do you feel about being a class monitor or assistant?
- How do you feel about writing assignments?
- How do you feel about working in cooperative groups?
- How do you feel about working on computers?
- How do you feel about taking important tests?
- How do you feel about doing homework?
- How do you feel when you receive your report card?

Autobiographies

Students can write autobiographies as an early assignment. You can structure the task with key questions if students need more direction. These essays will be quite revealing and may answer questions you never even thought to ask.

Sentence Stems

In our local newspaper each week, a teen is highlighted and responds to the following prompts in addition to all the "favorites" such as questions about music, sports teams, junk food, web-sites, etc. You can adapt these ideas to your grade level.

- I go online to . . .
- Few people know that . . .
- One day I will drive . . .
- I will go to college at . . .
- I will work at . . .
- I will live in . . .
- I will vacation in . . .
- I will meet the famous . . .
- With a $____ gift I will buy . . .
- The person who has influenced me most so far is . . .
- My favorite quote is . . .
- I want my classmates to remember me as . . .
- Now I'll describe myself in 20 words or less.

STATISTICS

What American middle and high school students do after school and on weekends (Public Agenda, 2004):

- 66% say they participate in sports activities.
- 62% are in school clubs or extracurricular activities.
- 60% do volunteer work.
- 54% attend religious instruction or a church youth group.
- 52% take lessons in things like music, dance, or art.
- 52% are in an after-school program at school or another locale.
- 37% of high school students have a part-time job.
- 30% get regular tutoring or extra academic or test preparation.
- 19% belong to an organization like the Scouts.

AVOID IT!

Do not ask students questions that would invade their privacy or be embarrassing. Any questions you ask must have the sole intention of providing information to better adapt the curriculum to meet the student's needs. Use your judgment. If you have doubts as to the propriety of a question, seek advice from your principal. Here are some no-nos.

- What does your mom (dad) do for a living?
- Why doesn't your dad live with you?
- Are your parents divorced?
- How many relatives live in your house?

Summary

Gathering feedback from your students regarding your instruction and learning about their interests and attitudes are ways to improve your ability to reach and teach them. You want to dig deeper and find out as much as you can about your students so you can use their interests to motivate them. Knowing their attitudes toward school and your curriculum will enable you to structure your teaching to turn around any negative attitudes and solidify the positive ones. Determine your students' reading interests and attitudes because reading is key to all learning. In this chapter there are many examples of feedback forms and interest and attitude inventories as well as other quick and efficient ways of gathering this information.

Reflect!

Try to answer some of the items on these inventories yourself. It may have been a long time since you were asked these questions. Then you can share your responses with your students, and they will appreciate your willingness to participate along with them.

CHAPTER 32

HOW DO I MANAGE PAPERWORK AND HOMEWORK?

Not everything that counts can be counted,
and not everything that can be counted counts.

Sign hanging in Albert Einstein's office at Princeton University

Effectiveness Essentials

- It's important at the very beginning to establish an efficient system for dealing with paperwork.
- Learn right away what your school district's policies and requirements are for the paperwork that needs to be completed.
- Keep records of all contacts with parents.
- Make accurate and up-to-date entries on student achievement in relation to standards.
- Find creative ways to save time when grading student work.
- Make sure homework is relevant and doable and that it follows the suggested time allocations.

Many teachers report that a major challenge in their school day is dealing with the seemingly endless parade of papers across their desks. The records teachers keep fall into two categories: the official district records and the day-to-day student paperwork, including homework, that needs to be graded so that you can assess student progress. Although some districts use technology for entering grades and generating report cards, some still rely on paper. The more carefully you organize your own assessment and record-keeping procedures at the outset, the less overwhelmed you will be by the additional record keeping dictated by your district.

Official School and District Paperwork

Your school and district requirements for record keeping are demanding yet necessary. The No Child Left Behind Act has mandated very accurate district reporting, and your records of student progress are part of the big picture. There are times when you'll want to hire a part-time secretary when you look at the papers that have covered your desk. School districts generate copious forms. The paperwork goes with the job! You'll learn all about these forms at staff meetings. Some schools provide new teachers with buddies or mentor teachers to help lead you through the maze of forms. Veterans will be happy to explain the forms and offer helpful suggestions.

Set aside a time each day, preferably in the morning before school, to fill in any forms, compose any reports or letters, write your report cards, and do similar chores. Keep a large calendar on which you mark due dates and special events so you can plan ahead and keep on top of any deadlines. The following sections discuss some of the official records you may be asked to keep.

Organize Grade Books and Attendance Books

Many of your records will be kept in a grade book, a marking book, or a

APPLY IT!

Buy a big loose-leaf binder with divider tabs. Begin to collect copies of all the forms you will be required to complete. The tabs will enable you to find what you need at a glance. Some districts even provide new teachers with a guide to the required forms. Keep your binder in a location that is accessible.

computer file. Remember to keep careful attendance records, as these are legal documents. Daily average attendance determines how much money districts receive from the state; and since school attendance is compulsory, your attendance records alert authorities to truancy or more serious problems at home. Each page in a grade book has room for a roster of student names and columns for recording attendance, test grades, and work completed. It's probably best to use a separate page for attendance and for grading each of the major curriculum areas.

You can save yourself some time by simply duplicating class rosters with columns and with the names already typed in. These sheets can be used for innumerable purposes besides grading and attendance, such as checking receipt of field trip permission slips, recording monies collected, and checking off homework. There are many computer grading programs that you can access, but computers crash, so you always want to have a hard copy of all your data.

Keep Accurate Plan Books and Lesson Plans

Practically all schools have a policy regarding the format and length of lesson plans. Some districts require plans to be turned in weekly, some semi-monthly, others not at all. In almost all districts, teachers are required to leave their plan books in school so that substitutes have access to them in case of emergency.

Find out about the policy in your school or district regarding lesson plans and when and if they need to be turned in, if you haven't already done so. This is one of the first questions you should ask as a beginning teacher. Complete your plans in appropriate detail and format and then hand them in on time!

Record Every Parent Conference

It is wise to keep records of all contacts with parents. Keep all correspondence from home, no matter how trivial. If you want to be safe rather than sorry, save copies when you communicate with

APPLY IT!

Buy a card file box and index cards. Use one card for each student to keep records of conferences and telephone calls, or use individual sheets in your loose-leaf notebook. Use index cards of different colors for each class you teach so you can access parent information easily.

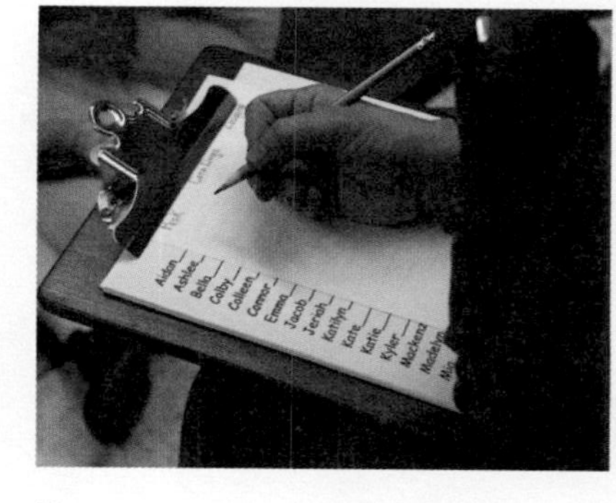

Keep an accurate class roster.

Write down your daily plans.

parents. You can clear up many a misunderstanding if you can produce the evidence by simply opening up your loose-leaf binder or index card file. It is also wise to make a record of all telephone calls to parents, including the date, time, and nature of the call.

Use Standards-Based Records

Teachers stress how important it is to make accurate and up-to-date entries on student achievement in relation to standards. Use district standards-based forms to focus instruction on those concepts and skills required at your grade level. These lists enable you to focus on specific remedial efforts for individuals who have not met the standards. Finally, reporting to parents and enlisting their aid at home becomes easier if you can be quite specific about which standards have been mastered by any particular student and which have not.

Student Paperwork

To be perfectly honest, I love everything about teaching except grading and paperwork. Night after night, we teachers lug home bags full of student papers. The good news is that I became motivated to compile a list of labor-saving suggestions from experienced teachers so I could lighten my load . . . and maybe yours as well. Some are appropriate for all levels, and some are more grade-level-specific. Choosing the type of strategy to deal with the paperwork depends to some degree on the level of thinking the assignment requires. In middle and high school, for example, assignments are geared to the higher levels of Bloom's taxonomy, so the written work is extensive, more complex, and more time-consuming to grade.

Grade on the Spot

As students finish their work, check papers on the spot when it is feasible. Primary youngsters have worksheets that have a reasonable number of items that can be graded right away. Use a "good job" stamp to make the grading fun for elementary students, or apply a sticker to the paper. Secondary grading can be

AVOID IT!

Avoid marking papers with red ink. Because red has been used forever to denote errors, it can immediately make students feel they have failed miserably. You might experiment with different colors, but I prefer using plain pencil.

Figure 32.1
Numerical Grade Book

Number	Name			
1	Cho, Steve			
2	Smith, Jane			
3	Lee, Theresa			
4	Singh, Paul			
5	Stein, Jason			
6	Bloom, Emily			
7	Martinez, Javier			
8	West, Talitha			
9	Lopez, Kathy			

more time-consuming, so use your preparation time or free period to evaluate student work as soon as possible.

Have Students Do the Correcting

Have your students exchange papers or correct their own. One teacher I know assigns students a number in random order that is to be placed on every assignment instead of their name. The students do not know who is who, and the papers can be distributed and then collected in numerical order. If you set up your grade book in numerical instead of alphabetical order, your work is lessened in the marking and the entering-grades phases.

Use Every-Pupil Responses

Use hand signals, choral responses, and individual sets of flashcards to check understanding without having every response written down (see Figures 32.2–32.4). Use thumbs (or pencils) up, thumbs down, thumbs across for agree, disagree, or not sure. Use fingers to denote

Figure 32.2
Thumbs Up and Down

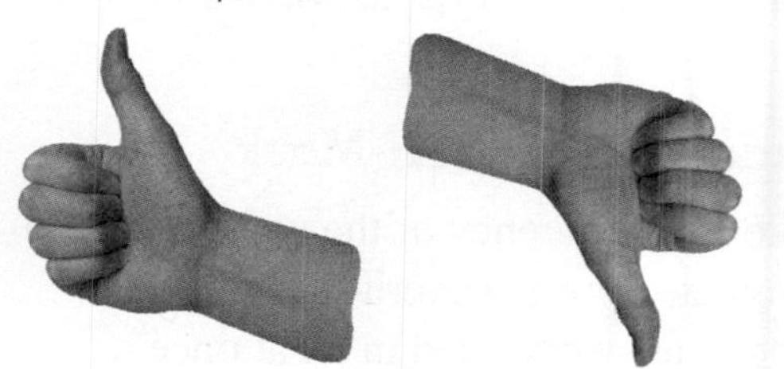

TEACHER TALKS . . .

I'm an English teacher, and I was swamped with papers and in despair. Then I met Dr. Rebecca Daniel of Parkersburg High School in Parkersburg, West Virginia. I adopted her portfolio method. Now, whenever I assign a paper, I add it to a list of writing assignments posted in the room and on my class website. Most of the papers are drafts, but some must be revised and edited until they meet my approval. I have a custom-made rubber date stamp that says, "APPROVED, Mrs. Susan Johnson."

I do not read every paper. There are many ways to validate a student's writing. Some of the papers the students read aloud. Then I make oral comments, and the papers go into the portfolio. Some are peer-edited. Some I skim, make a few comments, and checkmark. A few are stamped. For the stamped essays, the student sits with me, and we go over the essay line by line until it's worthy of my stamp of approval.

(continued on following page)

TEACHER TALKS—*continued*

I have "reading days" when students read their novels, and I bring each person up to my desk one at a time. I also allow them to email me their papers, and I put comments on them using Microsoft Word's comment feature. This is handy because it means that the students and I both have copies of the papers in their various stages of development in our out- and inboxes.

At the end of the grading period, each student turns in his or her entire portfolio with a checklist of all the assignments that I have been generating. This portfolio is half the grade. The other half is made up of quizzes, tests, projects, etc., which add up in the grade book. All I do at this point is flip through and see if all the items are present. If they are, the student gets 100. If he or she is missing an item or two, the grade might be 90 or 80. This check takes me no more than a minute per portfolio.

(continued on facing page)

Figure 32.3
Flashcards

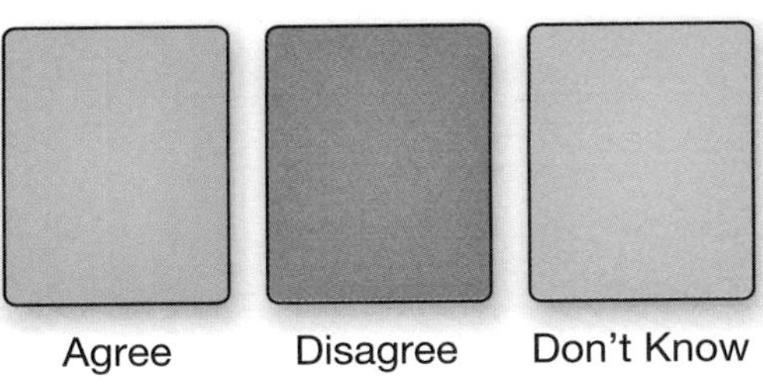

numbers for any mathematical responses. For example, $24 \times 8 =$ ________. Students are asked to hold up the number of fingers representing the number in the ones column, then the tens column and then the hundreds column. You can tell at a glance who needs extra attention.

Try Individual Response Boards

Use individual chalkboards or dry-erase white boards if you have them. Floor tiles with grease pencils work well too. Or laminate response cards made of file folder cardboard and give each student a card, a grease pencil, and a wiper. In each case, the students respond by holding up their plastic cards, tiles, chalkboards, or white boards.

Students Can Self-Mark

Make a transparency of the worksheet and illuminate it on the overhead projector with the answers filled in all at once or one at a time. You will save a great deal of time by following these steps:

1. Make a copy of the worksheet.
2. Fill in answers.
3. Make a transparency.
4. Uncover the correct answers as the students respond.
5. Have them mark their own work or exchange papers with someone.

Figure 32.4
Numerical Response With Fingers

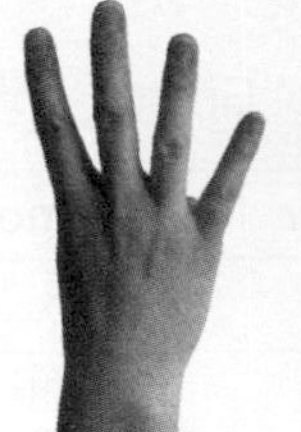

Students respond on individual boards.

Provide Answer Keys

Provide answers on a key or digital projector to all but the last five items. These you check yourself, thus determining if the student has simply filled in the answers or has really mastered the material.

Less Is More

Recognize that you don't have to test each skill or concept with multiple examples when fewer will suffice. If a preprinted worksheet has 25 examples, cut the sheet in half, or tell your students to complete only the odd-numbered ones or the last 10. Or have them do all the examples, but you'll have a fair idea of how they have done if you do only spot checking.

Ask for Parent Volunteers

Engage parent volunteers to help with the marking. This will work only if you have students use numbers instead of names on their papers.

Eyeball Some Assignments

Recognize that not every assignment needs careful attention and, additionally, that not every assignment needs to be returned to your students. You can eyeball the work to check for major error patterns, and honestly tell students that some papers won't be returned but that all are examined.

Review Orally

Review orally as a sponge activity instead of requiring so much written work. This is especially effective at secondary levels when the work is often more conceptual. Tasks such as summarizing the plots of literary selections, reviewing spelling words, defining vocabulary words, and reviewing Constitutional amendments can be accomplished orally.

Review in Eight Boxes

Cochran (1989) suggests that kids make up their own worksheets on papers folded into eighths. In each box, students demonstrate mastery of what they have learned during the day. They can, for example, draw a mammal in box 1, write three nouns in box 2, and solve an addition problem in box 3. In just three spaces you have reviewed three subject areas with a primary class and have very little grading to do at home (see Figure 32.5).

Use Answer Columns

Ask students to use answer columns on their papers to record their final solutions to, for example, math problems.

I like this approach because the students keep up with their papers; I don't. This gives them practice in meeting deadlines and staying organized, and I don't go home anymore loaded down with essays.

I also like it because there are no "A" or "D" papers. Every student works on the stamped essays until they meet with my approval. This is differentiated instruction at its finest. It might take Johnny only one revision to get a stamp, but Janie may require four or five.

Another benefit is that the students have collections of their work in a nicely presented portfolio with my "APPROVED" stamp on it. They are so proud of this—much more than they would be with a handful of papers covered in "Cs" and "Ds." I give them extra credit for turning in the portfolio early, presenting it neatly, and designing a cover sheet.

Finally, I like this system because the student who is failing quizzes and tests can

(continued on following page)

TEACHER TALKS—*continued*

overcome the "F" by working hard on the portfolio. My students with IEPs and those with attendance problems benefit from this system.

SUSAN JOHNSON
High School English Teacher
Richwood, West Virginia.

TEACHER TALKS . . .

Teaching middle school can be a challenge for some and a great pleasure for others. I love it because my students can begin to make their own choices about which way their lives are headed.

I had a student who came into my office last week. She was very concerned about her grade in my class. As an eighth grader preparing for the trials of high school, she knew that she needed to do well. Her grade was slowly slipping below average. This student decided it was time to get to work and find out what she needed to do to pass. So Friday afternoon she came to speak with me.

(continued on facing page)

Figure 32.5
Homework in Eight Boxes

4 + 3 = 2 + 3 = 1 + 3 = 3 + 5 = (Math)	Draw and color 3 yellow balloons and 3 green balloons. How many all together? (Number and color concepts)	Write the letter *Aa* 3 times. (Handwriting)	Color this stop sign. (Social studies safety unit)
Complete this pattern. △●■♥△ _ _ _ _ _ _ _ (Math)	Write your spelling words here. (Spelling)	Draw a picture of the main character in our story. (Reading)	Draw a nest with 4 eggs. (Science—animal homes unit and math)

Instruct them to fold a two-inch-wide column or draw a two-inch-wide line down the right- or lefthand side of their papers to record just their answers. Teachers can quickly scan the answer column for instant feedback, and either grade on the spot or take the papers home to review in their entirety.

Use Rubrics

Use rubrics and have students grade their own work before they turn it into you. The website http://www.teachnology.com can help you generate rubrics. You also can return to Chapter 30 to read more about rubrics (see Figure 30.1).

Try Cooperative Group Grading

Use cooperative groups to peer-edit writing assignments so that you do not have to correct every spelling error, punctuation mark, and capitalization error. In groups of four, assign these tasks: Capitalization Editor, Punctuation Editor, Spelling Editor, and Grammar Editor. There are four papers to edit and each student has a job and a different color pencil for editing. Students pass the paper to the next editor when they have finished their job. Then you are free to focus on the content and organization of the assignments.

Emmer and Evertson (2008) offer some useful suggestions that are applicable to all teachers. They recommend that you become familiar with grading practices in your district, at your school, and in your department and/or team. Most likely, each already has a set of norms. Next, identify how your own ideas about assessment fit in. Consider the percentages that will be awarded for neatness, organization, mechanics, participation, test grades, homework assignments, and other assignments. What will you do about late assignments? Will there be due dates on a master syllabus? Will big projects be broken down into smaller assignments?

Ask yourself the following questions. I do each and every quarter before I type up a final syllabus.

- What are the grading practices in my school?
- What is the weight of each assignment?
- Will I use points, averages, or percentages?
- Are the requirements clear, and are due dates established?
- Will I have a syllabus?
- How will I factor in effort?
- Do I have a grading rubric for each assignment?
- Are the assignments varied so all learners can succeed?
- How will I give feedback to the students, and how soon?
- Will big assignments have incremental deadlines?
- What will I do about late assignments?

Homework Creates More Paperwork

In a perfect world, students sit at a desk every evening in a well-lit, quiet room practicing, reinforcing, and extending the lessons covered during the school day. Their homework is relevant and not busywork, and they focus on the task

I told her that all she needed to do was to complete the assignments that I had given her. I reminded her that at the beginning of the year I had told the class:

"It's your choice! You choose your attitude. You choose how successful you will be in life. It's not teachers, or your parents, or any other adult. We are here to guide you. Ultimately it is your choice!"

The student remembered that advice from the beginning of the year. I reminded her that it was possible to meet her goals. She spoke about how she wanted to make her mother proud. I kindly reminded her that it was her choice to make those who mattered most in her life proud of her.

Now when she walks past me, she reminds me that she is going to raise her grade because it is her choice.

JENNIFER PONSART
Music Director
Davenport, Florida

(as seen on http://www.LessonPlansPage.com)

STATISTICS

According to a Met Life and Harris Interactive (2007) survey,

- 83% of teachers, 81% of parents, and 77% of students indicate that doing homework is important or very important.
- 26% of all students say homework is busywork and unrelated to school work, 30% of secondary students identify homework as busywork, 40% of parents say a great deal of homework is busywork, and 33% of parents say the quality of assigned homework is fair or poor.
- 86% of teachers use homework to help students practice skills or prepare for tests, 80% to develop good work habits, 67% to develop critical thinking skills, and 65% to motivate students to learn.
- Teachers report that they spend an average of 8.5 hours each week doing work related to students' homework. 77% of students, regardless of grade level, spend at least 30 minutes on homework on a typical school day. 45% of students reported spending at least an hour. 77% of students are assigned homework at least three days a week.
- 31% of elementary school students and 11% of secondary school students report that they do nothing else while working on homework. 89% of secondary students are doing other activities while doing homework, including 70% who listen to music and 51% who watch TV.

completely without distractions. Their parents help when needed, and the amount of homework is just right—not too much, not too little.

However, this scenario is far from the truth. As you look at the statistics in the margin on this page, you can see that substantial numbers of students and parents raise concerns about the quality of homework. Too many see it as busywork instead of how teachers see it: as a way to help students practice skills, prepare for tests, and develop good work habits and critical thinking skills.

In too many instances, students have no quiet place to do their homework, often settling for the kitchen table at best or even with no place at all to call a study space. Some will go to the library for want of a homework space, but others will come to class the next day empty-handed. This is especially true for children of poverty, who, aside from having no designated space for homework, have to pitch in with chores such as babysitting or dinner preparation. Some parents are too busy or unfamiliar with the subject matter to help, or too new to English. So instead of meting out a punishment, ask some questions when students come to class without their homework.

Many students who do have a designated homework space are multitasking—that is, listening to music, or watching television or videos, or texting, or talking to friends on the phone. So what can we do? Follow the guidelines of the National Education Association (2002–2010) and assign no more than 10 minutes of homework per grade level. In other words, assign 10 minutes in first grade, 30 minutes in third grade, and so on up to high school, where the average amount of time is 120 minutes, or two hours. It's important to remember that reading should be part of homework at all grade levels. Teachers also need to take into account all of the extracurricular activities kids are engaged in. As part of your interest inventory, ask students to write down for each day of the week the extra activities or responsibilities (work, for example, in high school) they have each day. And at conferences, or as needed, ask the parents about homework routines and whether the work seems doable or is way too heavy a load.

If the statistics are correct, you will bear the brunt of the homework load, spending on average eight and a half hours marking and recording homework. So make sure that the homework is relevant, follows the 10 minutes per grade rule, and is doable.

Interview With an Expert

Homework in the Responsive Classroom: Interview With Cathy Vatterott

by Elizabeth Rich

Cathy Vatterott is an associate professor of education at the University of Missouri—St. Louis. A former middle school teacher and principal, Vatterott learned first-hand about homework struggles as the parent of a child with learning disabilities. Today, her son is a successful college student and she is known as "the homework lady." She earned the title after years of research and writing about homework. She has presented on the topic to over 6,000 educators and parents in the United States, Canada, and Europe.

Her most recent book, Rethinking Homework: Best Practices That Support Diverse Needs *(ASCD, 2009), details a differentiated approach to homework—one that can serve teachers, students, and parents. Vatterott believes that homework needn't stretch into the wee hours of the night, and that teachers shouldn't take a punitive stance against unfinished homework. In fact, Vatterott sees incomplete homework as a crucial window for teachers into the academic and personal needs of students. She also sees an important role for parents in providing feedback to teachers on the struggles of their children to complete homework. We spoke to Vatterott about her homework philosophy and why too much homework can bring about academic failure.*

Are you opposed to homework?

I'm not at all opposed to the idea of homework. I'm opposed to homework that is excessive. I like the 10-minute rule, which is recommended by the Parent Teachers Association and the National Education Association, that kids should have no more than 10 minutes of homework per grade level, per night. In other words, a 1st grader should only have 10 minutes and a 5th grader should have 50 minutes, and so on. To me, that's a good guideline. It's also consistent with the research that shows that for kids who do more than that amount of work, their achievement actually goes down because they get burned out. They get tired. Of course, that doesn't mean that it's going to be the same for every kid. You've got kids that are very focused, who really enjoy doing their homework. They might be able to work longer.

The biggest parent misconception is that a lot of homework is a sign of rigor. A lot of times, parents are like, "If they don't do all of this work, they're not going to get into Harvard." Actually, the research doesn't support that a lot of homework does any good.

In some ways, there are shades of Ruby Payne—whose focus is on poverty's impact in the classroom—in your book. Specifically, you address how some educators attach their own negative, personal attitudes about social class to students who don't complete their homework. How does this play out?

I think when students don't complete their homework, it's easy to blame the student or the parent without really examining what valid reasons there might be for the homework not

(continued on following page)

STUDENT SAYS . . .

For homework tonight I have one page of math and 20 minutes of reading. For math I have to choose which item costs more and then figure out how much more. It will take me about 30 to 40 minutes. My teacher gives me homework so I can learn more, work harder, and think on my own. My mom helps me with my math pages. I usually go up to my room or in another room to read a chapter book. If I don't know what a word is, my mom or dad will help me.

MACKENZIE
Second Grader, Age 8
Aurora, Colorado

STUDENT SAYS . . .

Tonight in math, I have to do problems 3-30 in section 12.1 of my algebra 1 textbook. In history, I have to review the section we have been studying the last weeks for the test that is coming up in a couple of days. Lastly, in English, I have to read a chapter of To Kill a Mockingbird *for our literature circles. I don't have homework in science. It will take me about 45 minutes to an hour to finish.*

My teachers give me homework as sort of study material so that I can be prepared for the upcoming tests. They also give me it to let me try some of the things they were teaching in class on my own.

Homework can be annoying at times, especially if you don't get something, but the feeling after you get it all done almost makes it worth it. You feel like you just got something big out of the way. Every once in a while, I will ask my parents for help if I really don't get something, but it is rare.

ANDREW
Eighth Grader, Age 14
Redlands, California

Interview With an Expert *(continued)*

being completed. Students may not be able to do homework because of home conditions or family responsibilities, not because they are lazy or irresponsible. When teachers fail to understand how poverty or other circumstances can interfere with homework, there can be a tendency to make moral judgments about the student and the parent.

How does poverty interfere with homework?

It's not uncommon that kids who live in poverty don't have a quiet place to work. For instance, where I live, it's not uncommon for there to be a family of five living in a two bedroom apartment. There's no quiet place to work. There is no desk. There are no materials. Like when teachers say, "Oh, go home and cut pictures out of a magazine and then put them together for this." They don't have magazines. That's part of it, but the other part is that children of poverty often have lots of responsibilities at home.

An example that I give is of a teacher who said a 9th grade student told her, "My mom won't let me do homework." And the teacher said, "What do you mean?" And the student responded, "Well, when I get home I have to babysit my brothers and sisters, then I have to cook dinner, and then I have to give them a bath. And then it's time for me to go to bed."

And so when you look at kids in poverty, that's a scenario. When you get to middle school, high school, those kids are making money. They're working to help feed the family. And so they're not doing homework. You also have the population of ELL kids. They get home and their parents don't speak English. There's no help available if they need help. I think those are things that people don't often consider when they look at kids in poverty.

What advice do you have for teachers in these circumstances?

In the book, I have a homework schedule card where the kids write down what they do after school, what they're supposed to do after school, and what responsibilities they have. If the homework is not getting done, investigate why instead of punishing the kids.

You also suggest involving parents in the homework process, including completing questionnaires about how long it takes their children to complete homework assignments. Why is that important?

The parent is the best source of information about what's really going on with homework. Parents can help teachers diagnose whether the work is too hard or too lengthy and can alert teachers to other factors.

What other factors?

In addition to academic issues, the parents also know if it's an organizational issue—for example, if the kid says, "I did it, but I can't find it." Or, if the kid is really frustrated or they've got a lot of other activities going on that are competing with homework. But then there can also be personal things, like does this kid have an anxiety problem? Are there things going on in the family where this kid is depressed?

The parents know if there's this horrible thing going on in the family. Their child's favorite aunt is sick. It's a young kid and their grandmother's in the hospital dying. Stuff like that that teachers don't necessarily know, that parents can communicate back and say, here's what's going on with my kid right now and why they're having trouble focusing. That is helpful to a teacher.

How do you get a parent to comply with a questionnaire, especially when the family could be coping with some of the issues you mention that might be influencing a student's ability to complete work?

You may not be able to get that from the parent. You may have to make a phone call and ask them questions. Yes, sometimes it is hard to get that feedback from the parents. And you may have to just go on the feedback from the kid.

I never understood why we punished kids because their parents didn't sign something. Is that really the kid's fault? Or, is it that the parent just didn't sign it?

You don't believe that homework instills discipline in children; in fact, you stress that homework can negatively affect students' attitudes, their college admissions' test scores, even their admission to college itself. How does this happen?

When students are repeatedly given homework tasks that are too hard for them, frustrations build and students can start to hate learning. When kids are that frustrated, they basically just shut down. We've learned about that from brain research. We've known that frustration shuts down kids' learning. And we know psychologically that's what they do to protect themselves.

You've got kids who were fine in school and all of a sudden they start getting a lot of homework in the 3rd or 4th grade and all of a sudden they're starting to say they hate school and that's a little scary. What if what we're doing here—the overloading of kids or giving kids things they can't do—is causing them to hate school?

No one wants to do something that repeatedly makes them feel stupid. Students may decide it's less painful not to do the homework. When we give students failing grades for not completing homework, it further de-motivates them *and* may make them feel like they are a failure in school. Failing grades in homework often lead to failing course grades which lead to a lower GPA which can make students less competitive for college admissions. Students who give up and stop doing homework may be shortchanging their own development of knowledge and skills, which in turn can cause them to do poorly on college admissions tests.

CHAPTER 32

AVOID IT!

- Avoid arguments about points and criteria by making your grading system clear, fair, and justifiable. I can't emphasize this enough because even very experienced university professors get caught in the grade grievance trap because something wasn't spelled out clearly enough. Students can be great detectives when they set about challenging a grade!
- Avoid holistic grading that you can't justify. Use specific criteria or rubrics instead of saying "I just think you deserved a 'C.'"

Summary

Paperwork is still with us, even as some schools experiment with using technology for grading and reporting tasks. In some districts, grades are being calculated online, and report cards are being generated online as well. But before grades can be calculated, you still have to mark papers manually . . . all those in-class assignments, projects, and homework. Also, you still have official school paperwork to complete. There is no getting around it. Paperwork is part of the job. In this chapter are suggestions for organizing official paperwork and grading more efficiently. The chapter ends with a comprehensive discussion of homework practices.

Reflect!

Which of the grading suggestions in the chapter seem most appropriate for your grade level or subject matter? Ask some colleagues how they save time when they're marking and grading papers. Also ask at least three colleagues what they believe about homework. Then write a short homework policy statement that you can send home to parents. Include information such as

Why you assign homework
The nature of the homework you assign
Approximately how much time homework should take
Due dates (daily or weekly)
How parents can help
How to contact you with questions

UNIT 7

CHAPTER 33

HOW CAN I PREPARE MY STUDENTS FOR TAKING STANDARDIZED TESTS?

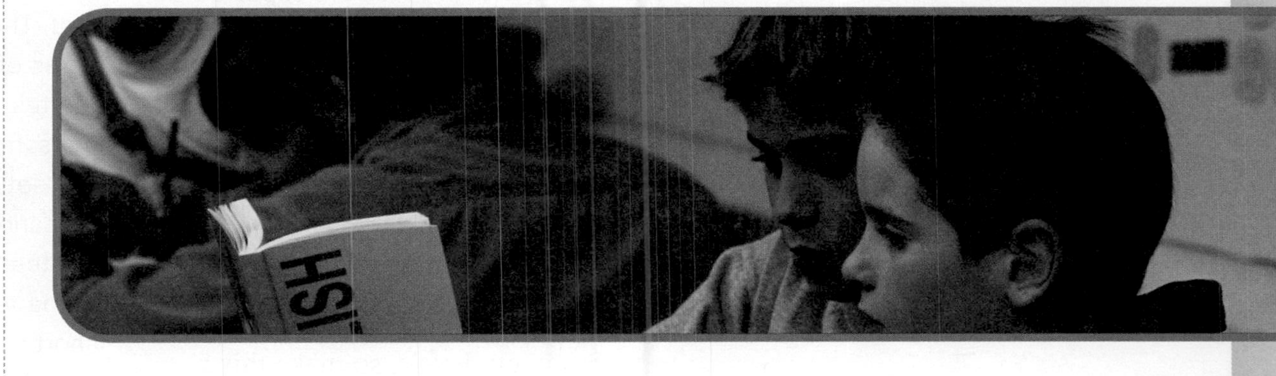

I didn't fail the test, I just found 100 ways to do it wrong.

Benjamin Franklin

But there are advantages to being elected President. The day after I was elected, I had my high school grades classified "Top Secret."

President Ronald Reagan

Effectiveness Essentials

- Prepare your students all year long for high-stakes tests by covering the standards in your instruction.
- Integrate test prep and test-taking skills with your instruction.
- Build up test endurance incrementally by increasing time on task.
- Alert parents and students to the need for students to be well rested and to eat breakfast on test day.

STUDENT SAYS . . .

Teachers would normally give us a packet of old end-of-course questions, and they would tell us what to expect on the test. It's important for the teachers to evaluate what the kids have retained to prepare for the course. Although the tests are basic for that subject, you have to know the subject to be able to progress to the next semester. I feel like these tests are complicated but are rewarding when you pass and move on to the next course.

ADAM
Tenth Grader, Age 15
Lexington, North Carolina

As surely as the daffodils bloom each spring, your school testing coordinator will arrive with packages of standardized tests and test directions. With so much attention on school progress due to NCLB reauthorization, this can be a stressful time for many communities. Schools and districts that do not score well or miss their targets for adequate yearly progress (AYP) on state tests may be sanctioned and lose funding. In extreme cases, principals may be removed. School scores are reported to parents and are published in many newspapers for all to see.

In addition, some districts give other achievement tests such as the Iowa Test of Basic Skills or state achievement tests. Many states also now have high school exit exams, and students who do not pass them may not graduate with a diploma. Students will be attuned to your anxiety levels, so make this a positive and upbeat time, not a nail biter for you or for them! You can help alleviate their anxiety as well as your own by careful attention to standards and sustained test preparation all year long.

You have been preparing your students for these tests all year long by doing your best teaching and adhering to the subject standards. Keep in mind that your students have been engaged in meaningful learning throughout the year and will do their best to make you proud. Excessive worrying won't help.

APPLY IT!

Find out what tests your students will be taking since not all grade levels take every test. Then get a calendar and mark in the dates of the tests in big red letters. Ask the testing coordinator or principal if there are sample tests or materials and teacher booklets that would be useful to you in preparing your students for the format of the test and types of questions asked. Some testing corporations even provide short sample practice tests for students to take. You should inquire sooner rather than later about what test prep materials are available. The more information that your students have about the types of questions and the formats, the less anxious they will feel. Think of this preparation as teaching to the format, not teaching to the test.

Standardized Test Preparation Throughout the Year

Standardized tests, as defined in Chapter 30, are administered and scored in a standardized manner. They can be norm-referenced (comparisons of a student's scores to the group that took the test, resulting in a bell-shaped curve), such as the SAT or ACT, or criterion-referenced (students can all meet the passing scores), such as many state standards-based assessments. For example, in my state, students take the California Standards Test, a criterion-referenced test with five levels of performance for each subject tested: advanced, proficient, basic, below basic, and far below basic. They also take the California Achievement Test, which is a norm-referenced test with scores reported in percentiles for each school and district, and the High School Exit Exam, which is a criterion-referenced test with a set passing score. There are other tests as well for particular subgroups.

Throughout the year, when discussing assignments or administering any kind of test, emphasize that your students need to follow directions closely, budget their time carefully, and check their work

		trustworthiness	fluid
affable	integrity	wily	sticking together
easy flowing			
cunning	cohesive	friendly	

Play word/definition Concentration.

STUDENT SAYS . . .

There are a lot of tests. Most of them are actually pretty easy. Some can be very difficult. Not all of them are important. Some teachers take common assessments as really big tests because they say, "No homework. You have to study. Its worth blah, blah, blah percent of your grade." Some teachers make it a competition between classes for the best grades. It's fun because we like to win.

NIKI
Sixth Grader, Age 12
Redlands, California

TEACHER TALKS . . .

In California, in elementary school, the standardized tests are based on the language arts standards and math standards. I advise teachers to have a thorough knowledge of the standards for their grade level. If the teacher teaches a good curriculum and accounts for the standards being covered, students should have no trouble with standardized tests. It helps to familiarize students with test formatting so that the format does not cause any confusion. Test formatting practice can be done throughout the year or a few weeks before the test.

Besides that, I always emphasize that students should READ, READ, READ, and WRITE, WRITE, WRITE.

JOAN MARIE SMITH
District Curriculum Program Specialist
Colton, California

UNIT 7

Table 33.1 Vocabulary Word Wall

Word	Definition	Synonyms	Antonyms
affable	friendly	genial, pleasant, gracious, amiable	unfriendly, aloof, distant, surly
aggravate	make worse, annoy someone	worsen, inflame	alleviate, soothe, mollify
austere	strict, without decoration	simple, basic, stark	fancy, elaborate, ornate

continually. For vocabulary work, encourage your students to use flashcards and pictographs and to play games such as Jeopardy, Pictionary, and Word-Definition Concentration. Incorporate key skills into your instruction. For example, teach your students to recognize prefixes, suffixes, and root words.

Many teens will be taking the SAT or ACT. The SAT was revised in March 2005 and is 3 hours and 45 minutes long. New to the SAT are a 25-minute essay

APPLY IT!

Build a vocabulary word wall all around the baseboards in your room, encouraging your students to add synonyms, antonyms, and definitions. See Table 33.1.

mythBUSTER

Good teaching can be measured by how well your students do on standardized tests.

I believe good teaching is the ability to provide students with experiences which engage them in the subject matter, help them develop a deep understanding of concepts and processes in the chosen subject, and encourage a love of learning. . . .

The main thing that these sorts of tests show is a student's ability to do well, or poorly, in these sorts of tests!

Shirley Casper
High School Science Teacher
Sydney, Australia

exam and multiple critical reading sections, replacing the older verbal sections. The maximum score is now 2400 instead of 1600. An alternative college entrance exam is the ACT. It assesses high school students' ability to complete college-level work and is composed of multiple-choice tests in English, mathematics, reading, and science, as well as an optional essay test. The writing portion on these exams has caused consternation among students, so you can alleviate anxiety by helping them respond to sample writing prompts. Some students will take review courses and buy numerous review books. You can help all of your students by buying the books yourself and focusing on the format and samples. Even though not all of your students are college-bound, it is important to focus on essential writing skills at all levels.

AVOID IT!

Do not get caught up in the high-stakes testing frenzy. You will be communicating your anxiety to your students. What they need is a cheerleader, a teacher who encourages and builds their confidence—not a worrywart.

Do not assume that students are familiar with the format of standardized tests. Do not assume that students have come to school with a good night's sleep and a full stomach. Make sure you have high-protein stacks available for students prior to the test session.

Ten Suggestions for Standardized Test Preparation

The following 10 suggestions come from experienced teachers and will help you through this stressful time of year. Remember that you have maintained a standards-based focus all year and that your students will rise to the challenge.

1. Do some test preparation each day to avoid the before-test crunch.
2. Integrate test prep with your instruction and make it just another exercise.
3. Teach test-taking skills such as
   - Bubble filling
   - Using scratch paper if allowed
   - Completely erasing any changes in responses
   - Estimating answers in math and checking work
   - Using the process of elimination

STUDENT SAYS . . .

Let's face it: testing's stupid! There, I said it! But really, do we want our kids taking so many tests that they become socially awkward because all they can talk about is the square root of 16? Taking CSTs, SATs, ACTs—you name it! Almost every letter of the alphabet has a test that goes along with it. Taking all those tests will not make our children become geniuses at the age of 12! Sure, we still need to have our children take tests, but not tests that count as 90% of their grade! Testing will probably never change, but when it does, children will be normal again!

JACK
Sixth Grader, Age 12
Redlands, California

- Making reasonable guesses when all else fails
- Webbing an essay response
- Using memory aids such as acronyms
- Reading the questions prior to reading the passage
- Looking for key words in math problems that give clues to the operation
- Using the "does the answer make sense?" test
- Working all the easy ones first
- Pacing
- Reviewing for careless errors

4. Review different types of questions and question formats:
   - Factual
   - Inferential
   - Application
   - Evaluation
   - Opinion
5. Discuss why the right answer is right and how to arrive at the correct response.
6. Discuss why the wrong answers are wrong.
7. Build up test endurance incrementally by increasing time on task.
8. Stress to parents and students the need to be well rested, to eat breakfast, and to wear comfortable clothes on test day.
9. Bring healthy snacks to class on the day of the test.
10. On the day of the test, some teachers give out "magic" cookies, special pencil toppers, or good-luck charms.

APPLY IT!

Ask at least three experienced teachers how they prepare their students to do their best on standardized tests. Create a pre-testing period timeline for implementing these and other suggestions.

Summary

Your students will take a large number of tests all year long, with the most important ones coming in the spring when the entire year's achievement can be assessed, evaluated, and compared to other schools, other districts, and even other states and countries. The test results not only inform instruction but can be used to identify and sanction underperforming schools. Worrying will not help, and you need to prepare your students to do their best throughout the year.

Reflect!

Go to your district's website and search for the required tests, the testing schedule, and any links to practice tests. Then surf the Internet for additional test preparation hints. There are many websites out there that will help you prepare your students for upcoming assessments. Make your own list of test prep ideas that are suitable for your grade level or subject matter and duplicate it for your students to review.

STUDENT SAYS . . .

The biggest, most important standardized test in Massachusetts is the MCAS. Personally I don't like it much. The test is pretty easy for me, but the teachers make us start studying hard for months for it while we might have a much harder class test coming up. So we are wasting time studying for a test that isn't really much different from last year's or even the year before that. I understand that littler kids need to study longer for a test like the MCAS, but not every older kid needs four months to study for these standardized tests.

ERIK
Eighth Grader, Age 13
Brookline, Massachusetts

CHAPTER 34

HOW CAN I ENLIST SUPPORT FROM AND COMMUNICATE WITH PARENTS AND GUARDIANS?

If you want your children to improve, let them overhear the nice things you say about them to others.

Haim Ginott

Effectiveness Essentials

- Your students' parents/guardians play a fundamental role in the educational process.
- Convey in word and deed to parents/guardians that you will treat their child with the same concern and respect as you would your very own.
- A two-way positive communication channel opened early and used regularly throughout the year is the key to success.
- Parent-teacher conferences coincide with report cards, but additional conferences with parents/guardians should be scheduled as needed.

It was my fourth year of teaching and my first year in a university demonstration school. The parents were connected to the university as either students or professors. One non-reader in my sixth-grade class had a father who taught in my doctoral program. "Well, your sixth grader still can't read," I told this parent with trepidation. I was ready to accept all the blame for the previous six years. After all, this father could be my professor next semester! "We don't want to push him; don't worry," said the father. "He'll either learn to read or he won't." The child learned to read and is now a dad with two readers of his own.

Although you may have entered the teaching profession to work with kids, your students' caretakers play a fundamental role in the educational process. It is important to recognize that family configurations are as diverse as the students themselves. Some of your students may have two parents. Some may live with one parent. Some may be raised by a grandparent or other relative. Others may be raised by an unrelated guardian. In all cases, your students' parents or guardians are entrusting their precious offspring to you, and it is the best situation for you and for your students when parents/guardians are on your side, working along with you and not at cross-purposes.

Establishing a Partnership

To engender confidence and gain respect from parents and guardians, convey in word and deed that you will treat their child with the same concern and respect as you would your very own. This attitude will bring out the best that parents/guardians have to give. Engaging their cooperation in the school setting can provide you with a critical mass of support during the rough times and enable you to impart the greatest possible benefit to your students.

Having a majority of the parents/guardians in your corner cheering you on is well worth the time and effort you take in cultivating their support. Parents and guardians, when informed about your goals, program, and procedures, can serve as a valuable backup system. Moreover, they have a right to be informed about a student's progress—both strengths and weaknesses. There are numerous opportunities and processes for encouraging the partnership. Consider the following ways you can strengthen this partnership:

Parent, teacher, and student must work as a team.

TEACHER TALKS . . .

Parents . . . aah . . . parents: perhaps the most crucial yet elusive link to our students' success. Over the years I have found that parents simply want to be listened to and are usually more scared of the teacher than teachers are of them. They are looking toward the teacher for help and expertise. But that's daunting, isn't it? One of the most valuable and educational hours I have ever spent was

(continued on following page)

1. Attend parent organization and parent-teacher organization meetings.
2. Invite parents to volunteer in your classroom.
3. Provide parents with a list of grade-level or subject standards.
4. Accommodate caretakers' work schedules and schedule conferences for siblings on the same day.
5. Read up on cultural norms and learn some welcoming words in languages represented in your class.
6. Encourage parents/guardians to share their life experiences and culture with students in your classroom.
7. Start a lending library of education and parenting books of interest to parents/guardians.
8. Invite parents to shadow their kids during class time and participate in all activities.
9. Send home commendations and awards.
10. Take photos of your students and send copies to parents/guardians.
11. Let parents or guardians know when tests begin, and send home suggestions such as get a good night's rest, eat breakfast, and dress comfortably.
12. Invite parents/guardians to performances, fiestas, debates, award assemblies, etc.

Fostering Communication

Parents/guardians and teachers have a lot to offer and teach one another because they usually share equally the amount of time kids spend awake each day. Parental insight and experience will bring to light additional information that may help you better serve the needs of the student.

A two-way positive communication channel opened early and used regularly throughout the year is the key to success. If the right hand at home knows what the left hand is doing at school and vice versa, how much better both will be at

TEACHER TALKS—*continued*

15 years ago during one of my methods classes, while I was earning my teaching credential. Our class had the opportunity to sit down with a panel of parents and ask them what their expectations were for report cards, homework, parent-teacher conferences, discipline, classroom environment, etc. My advice—do not let these opportunities escape you. Allow your classroom door to be open to parents. Encourage parental involvement. Make those calls home. Write those notes—and not just when Sally has had a bad day, but when she has had a good day. Every time I have had parents in the classroom, they have gained respect and knowledge and have been truly amazed at what we are expected to accomplish each day. They are important allies and need to be aware of the good, the bad, and, yes, even the ugly of daily life in the classroom. Let parents know that they are their child's first and most significant

(continued on facing page)

understanding and doing what is best for the student. Anticipate that every communication with parents, whether oral or written, may need interpretation or translation for those parents whose primary language is not English.

Open Communication Before School Starts

You can start establishing a solid foundation by contacting parents or guardians at the beginning. You don't need to spend a lot of time on these introductory communications, but they will set the right tone when and if you later have to call and deliver unpleasant news.

1. **Phone.** Telephone each parent/guardian during the week preceding the start of the school year. Be brief in making the point—"I care; I want to work with you for your student's sake; let's get together." Few parents/guardians can resist this sincere expression of welcome.

"Just called to say all is well."

2. **Letter.** Type a duplicated letter to each parent/guardian before the school year starts. Make sure to have letters translated into the languages represented in your classroom population and send them appropriately to non-English-speaking parents. Below is an example of such a letter:

Dear Parent or Guardian,

My name is __________ and I will be your son's/ daughter's __________ teacher this year. I'm writing to let you know that I look forward to working with you so that your son/ daughter can develop new talents, skills, and abilities. I really love teaching and will do everything I can to make this year a very successful and happy one.

Our open house is scheduled for the first week in October. If you have any questions or would like to talk with me before then about any of your concerns, please call the school (phone number). I will return your call as soon as possible. I look forward to meeting you in person.

______________________ (name)

______________________ (school)

3. **Interview.** Interview each parent/guardian during the first weeks of

influence and can be their greatest teacher. And remember, when looking and speaking with a student, imagine the parent standing right behind the child.

FRANCESCA DEVEAUX SWEET
First-Grade Teacher
Rialto, California

STATISTICS

According to the U.S. Department of Education's National Center for Educational Statistics (2009),

- 89% of students had parents who reported attending a general school or parent-teacher meeting.
- 78% of students had parents who attended parent-teacher conferences.
- 65% of students had parents who participated in school fundraising.
- 46% of students had parents who volunteered/served on a school committee.
- Parent participation in school-related activities was greater for K–8 students than for 9–12 students.
- Parent participation in school-related activities was higher for students from non-poor families than it was from poor families.
- 95% of K–8 students had their homework checked by an adult.
- 65% of 9–12 students had their homework checked by an adult.

TEACHER TALKS . . .

I establish open communication with parents early in the school year. I ask students to have their parents sign the opening letter I write for students. It's a chatty letter that I love writing each summer in the days before school begins. I always introduce my cats (and describe what they've been doing that summer), and I share my philosophy of education and the English classroom.

At open house, I provide my home email and phone number, and I invite parents to complete a writing assignment: "In 1 million words or less, tell me about your child." I've had hilarious, touching, informative, and crucial information shared.

I also call parents for good reasons—just to tell them their kids did something well, that they have a polite and considerate child, that their kid is improving. . . . Some parents have returned my calls in fear,

(continued on facing page)

school. The interviews will enable you to gather firsthand information about strengths, abilities, health status, developmental milestones, and other factors. Above all, the very act of scheduling the interview conveys that you really care about your students and respect their parents and guardians.

4. **Autobiography.** Encourage parents to sit down with and assist their child in composing the child's autobiography or an autobiographical poem to bring to class on the first day. The format is found in Chapter 7.
5. **Home visits.** Consider making home visits to each of your students. Although this takes a great deal of time, you can gain a lot of information about behavior and home environment. Many parents and guardians will be delighted that you took the time to actually visit their homes.

Communicate on the First Day

Your communication with parents/guardians should probably begin on the very first day if you haven't started sooner. Those who are included from the first day may have fewer questions, comply more readily with requests for assistance, and generally feel better about you and the school.

The content of first-day notes varies according to how much information is provided by the school itself. Your letters can be prepared ahead of time and filed from year to year with only updates added. First-day letters are explained in Chapter 9. Keep your letters, notes, and handbooks short and to the point and avoid using any jargon.

Use Technology to Communicate With Parents

Email is a quick and efficient way of communicating with a parent or many parents at once. You can convey a great deal of information about performances, special events, needed supplies, testing schedule, etc. But beware of sending specific information about academics or behavioral issues using this method. You can't retrieve the email once you push send, and a telephone or direct face-to-face meeting is the best way to convey bad news. You can request email information and provide your own, but respect those parents who don't want to give out their email address. Find a different way to communicate with them and with those parents without any email access.

Your district and school will probably have a website. Websites are very efficient, paperless ways to convey a great deal of information to all concerned parties, including parents. To

WATCH IT! video

Involving Parents

A teacher discusses how she communicates with parents and recruits them for classroom volunteering at parent-teacher meetings and conferences. Her secret is asking them what interests they have so she can match their interests to tasks in the classroom. What are the benefits to kids, the teacher, and the parents? Are there any negatives?

communicate specific information, many teachers set up, with help from the district or school technology resource person, class webpages that are linked from the school website. On your webpage you can list needed supplies, homework assignments, links to subject-matter-related resources, testing dates, special events, open house invitations, parent-conference schedule, and so forth.

Open House Is a Time to Stress Cooperation

Open house may be your first opportunity to meet a majority of the parents and guardians and make a pitch for cooperation. You can increase attendance by having your students write the invitations. Teachers feel it is vital to establish a time during the open house when parents and guardians stop milling and wandering around the room and come together for a brief program. The schedule in a self-contained classroom might look like this:

8:00–8:20 P.M.	Sign the guest book. Walk around the room. Look at texts, materials, and students' portfolios. Play with the computers, etc.
8:20–8:30 P.M.	Program begins.
8:30–8:45 P.M.	Share questions and answers.

When your program begins, you might want to consider covering the following topics and issues:

- Class rules and discipline policies
- Homework policy
- Curriculum overview
- Reporting, grading, conferencing
- Invitation to serve as a room liaison or volunteer
- PowerPoint presentation with student photos
- Students acting out their day

and then cried when I said, "I'm just calling to say how great she is."

CAMILLE NAPIER
Eleventh-Grade English Teacher
Natick, Massachusetts

(quoted on www.EducationWorld.com)

CHAPTER 34

Ten Ideas for a Successful Open House

1. **Refreshments.** Set up a table with some snacks. Food helps create a warm social atmosphere. Note that in some cultures it is traditional to bring food to functions. Some parents and guardians may feel better about attending if they can contribute something, no matter how small. You might extend an invitation, for example, to bring a piece of fruit to cut up and add to a big fruit salad.
2. **Student work.** Have representative samples of each student's work displayed around the room, and have each student's portfolio along with a name card on his or her desk.
3. **Nametags.** Provide nametags for parents and guardians instead of making well-reasoned assumptions about who belongs to whom, which may turn out to be mistaken. Have a space for the names of both caretaker and student.
4. **Schedule.** Write the daily schedule on the board so parents and guardians can actually see what the students do all day or all period long.
5. **Body tracings.** Some teachers have students trace their bodies on butcher paper, color them with tempera paint, cut them out double, stuff and staple them, dress them in clothing brought from home, and prop them up on their chairs.
6. **Sample texts and materials.** Have sample texts and materials out for display. Students enjoy having their parents or guardians look at their books and showing off a special science kit, math lab, computer program, or DVD.

Open house is a great opportunity for communication.

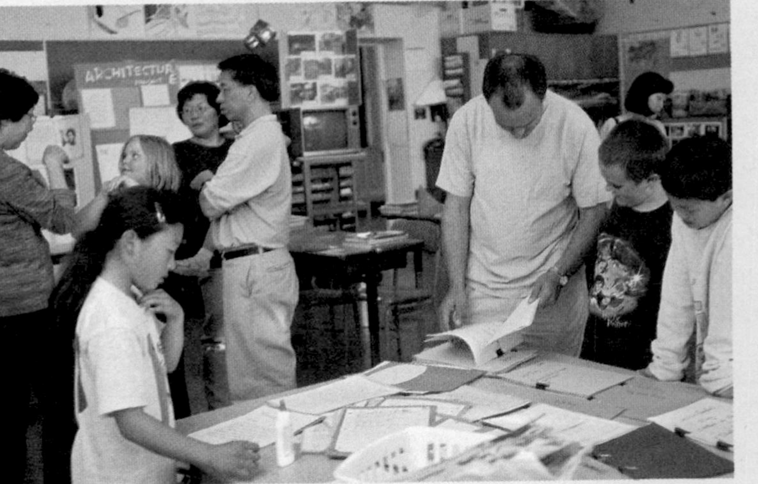

7. **Questions on cards.** At the door, when parents and guardians sign in, provide index cards and encourage them to print their questions on the cards and leave them in a specified box. This will spare parents/guardians the embarrassment of asking what they may consider to be a dumb question. Collect the cards before your program starts, and answer the most frequently asked questions on the spot. Announce your intention to deal with the others in newsletters.
8. **Student guides.** You can make open house into a learning experience for your students when you prepare them as tour guides, pointing out the classroom landmarks and high points. One teacher has a guide of the day, every day, whose responsibility it is to greet and show visitors around the room.
9. **Email and websites.** Promote the use of email and websites to encourage ongoing communication. Let parents and guardians know that if they have and are willing to write their email addresses on the sign-in sheet, you will be able to contact them about general happenings and specific reports on grades, behavior, and other matters. If you have a website, give the address to parents/guardians and ask those with Internet access to communicate with you that way. Otherwise, let them know you will communicate by phone or note.
10. **Handouts.** Provide handouts with all relevant information and in translation if necessary. You can send the information home to parents/guardians who are unable to attend, and those who do attend will be able to have easy reference as needed. Additionally, let them know you will communicate by telephone, notes, and monthly newsletters. Avoid speaking in jargon or acronyms.

In middle school and high school, the parents/guardians generally follow their son or daughter's schedule in an abbreviated way. So if you have a program to present, make it very short because the parents/guardians will need to move on to the next room, which may be far across campus.

Parent/Guardian-Teacher Conferences Should Be Scheduled as Needed

Parent/guardian-teacher conferences coincide with report cards, but additional conferences should be scheduled as needed. The dual goals of such a conference are the exchange

of information about an individual student and the formulation of cooperative strategies to solve any problems. This is a time of high anxiety for both you and the parents or guardians. The parents/guardians are worried about what you have to say, and that's why, no matter what, you should start out on a positive note. You may be worried that you are not qualified to give advice about someone else's child or that parents will attribute any difficulties to your inexperience. You both can relax! This is a partnership in the best interests of the child. On pages 422 and 423 is a checklist to help you have a successful conference.

STATISTICS

According to Herrold and O'Donnell (2008),

- 54% of K–12 students had parents who reported receiving notes or email specifically about their child from the school.
- 91% of students had parents who reported receiving newsletters, memos, or notices addressed to all parents.
- 49% of students reported they had parents who were contacted by telephone.
- 92% of K–12 students had parents who reported receiving information about a student's performance.
- 83% of K–12 students had parents who reported getting information about how to help with homework.
- 75% of K–12 students had parents who reported receiving specific information about class placement.
- 86% of K–12 students had parents who reported receiving information about the parent's expected role at the school.

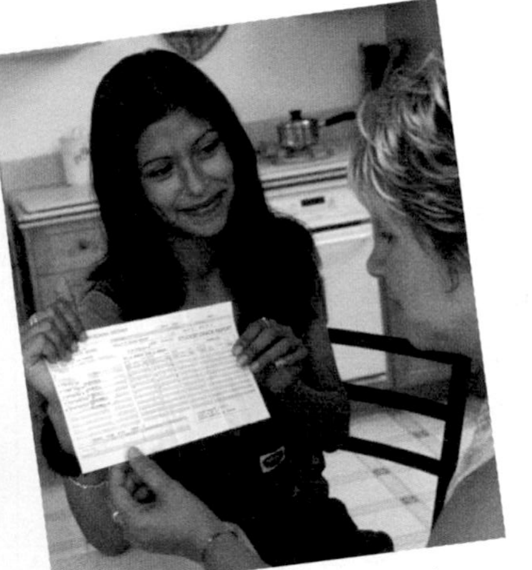

Teachers often share report cards at conferences.

AVOID IT!

Do not be intimidated by parents or guardians. They, like all of us, need to feel significant; and when invited to participate with you as a partner in education, they will jump at the chance. They simply need encouragement to do so. They can participate in big ways, in small ways, in any way at all. They are more intimidated by you than you are frightened of them. Extend a hand to them. It will make a difference to you, to them, and to their kids.

mythBUSTER

Parents and guardians don't want to be involved in school.

Almost all parents want to be involved in their child's education in some way. It just varies how much they would like to participate. I have found that there are three groups of parents or guardians in schools. The first are the "Super Room Parents." These are the parents that want to be in your classroom every day all day if you would let them. Next, you have your "Working Parents." These are the parents that want to be involved but don't know how to do this as a full-time working parent. Lastly, you have the "You-Do-It Parents." These are the parents that are content to let others get involved and want everything to run on automatic.

Super Room Parent. New teachers take advantage of the help. Have a volunteer signup list posted at back-to-school night, and get the helping hands started. Plan for a volunteers meeting soon after to set up a schedule. For new teachers it would be advantageous to have an assistant almost every day. These parents can organize your celebrations, find your donations, and work for you as much as you want (or let them in some cases). On average they are very supportive and work well with small groups, allowing you more time for one on one with your students.

Working Parent. Have a separate signup at back-to-school night entitled "Can Work From Home." You will find that many of your Working Parents love to help this way. At home, they can trace, cut, staple, sort, and do many other tedious things that take time from your day. An easy way to share such tasks is by laminating a large manila envelope and creating a cute and fun cover entitled "Home Helper." In this envelope you can slip in whatever you need done with a quick note giving the parent instructions, and send it home with their child. This makes the parent feel involved and allows you to get more things done.

You-Do-It Parent. It may appear that this set of parents wants nothing to do with your classroom, but once motivated, they can be a great resource. They usually are a big help in donating supplies or money for necessities in your classroom. They like to feel involved without having to do too much hands on. Some parents may need some direct prompting with a phone call rather than just a send-home signup sheet. A highly motivated Super Room Parent can often make the calls to get you the supplies you need.

One final note: All parents and guardians want what is best for their child. As a parent, it can be difficult to have your child away from you for a large part of the day. Having parents involved in the classroom brings peace of mind and fulfillment to the parent, teacher, and student. Create a community where everyone is welcome, and you will find the most successful classroom.

Ivania Martin
Parent and Teacher on Parental Leave
Benicia, California

A parent-teacher conference should start on a positive note.

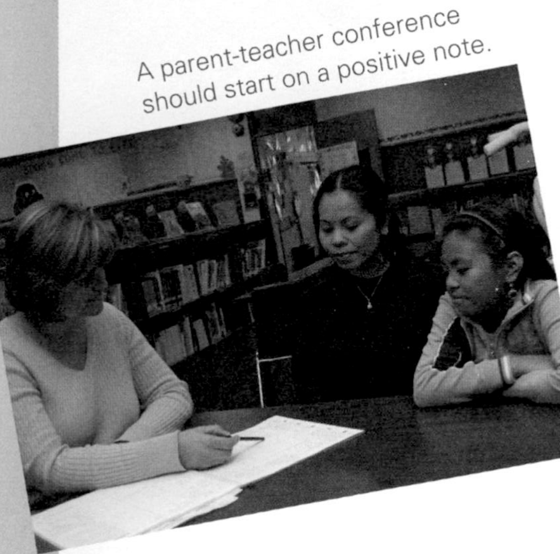

TEACHER TALKS . . .

Each parent comes in not knowing what will be said. All have hope that things are going well. What you have to say should not be the first time you are saying it. In other words, there should be no surprises on conference day. My first question is: "What do you think?" Usually their response is just on target, and it's a great opener to what you have to say.

KRIS UNGERER
Kindergarten Teacher
Riverside, California

A Conference Checklist

Before the Conference

- Confirm the date, time, and place with the parent/guardian.
- Coordinate parent conference schedules with team members in middle school and/or with homeroom/advisory teachers at the high school level and with same-school teachers of multiple siblings.
- Inform parents/guardians ahead of time about the purposes of the conference.
- Have them bring to the conference a list of questions or concerns.
- Arrange for an interpreter if needed.
- Examine the student's portfolio and have your marking book and any anecdotal records accessible.
- Make a list of three or four points to cover, beginning with strengths.
- Think about three adjectives to describe the student.
- Establish a waiting area for early arrivals to maintain confidentiality during the conference in progress.
- Dress professionally in an outfit that will not intimidate.
- Make sure the chairs are adult-sized—even if you have to raid an upper-grade classroom or the teacher's lounge.
- Sit side by side at a table with all of the documentation in front of you.

The Conference Itself

- Start the conference by meeting the parent/guardian at the door.
- Have a space available for coats and umbrellas.
- Be as gracious a host/hostess as you would be in your own home.
- Thank the parent(s)/guardians(s) for coming, and lead them to the conferencing area.
- Start out on a positive note, and find something good to say about the student.
- Begin the six-step process:
  - ☐ Provide data.
  - ☐ Seek information.
  - ☐ Listen actively to parents/guardians.
  - ☐ Synthesize their suggestions with your own.
  - ☐ Devise a plan of action.
  - ☐ Arrange for follow-up.

Teacher Data	Guardian Data
■ Test scores	■ Talents and abilities
■ Academic performance	■ Overall health and concerns
■ Behavior in the classroom	■ Interests, hobbies, sports
■ Social interaction with other students	■ Attitude toward school subject(s)
■ Effort	■ Responsibilities at home
■ Cooperation	■ Homework habits
■ Peer relationships	■ Responses to rules at home

Conference Closure

- Summarize the major points.
- Clarify what action will be taken, if any.
- Set a date for a follow-up note or conference.
- See the parents/guardians to the door.
- Express your sincere thanks for their attendance.
- Make notes about the conference as soon as the parents/guardians leave.
- Take a breather before you start talking to the next set of parents/guardians.
- Send a brief note to each parent/guardian, thanking him or her for attending and listing the major points covered. This can be a fill-in-the-blanks type of note to save time.

Summary

Parents are the first teachers of the students in your class. They will play a key continuing role in their children's education when you form a partnership with them early and often. Recognize the diversity in families, and consider all possible communication avenues such as phone calls, letters, newsletters, interviews, home visits, email, and class websites. Open house and the parent conference are specialized events that enable you to meet and greet parents face to face. These are also times to recruit volunteers.

Reflect!

How will you go about establishing open communication channels with the parents in your class? Which of the suggestions in the chapter seem most appropriate for your grade level and subject matter? Speak to at least three different parents, and ask them what expectations they have for parent-teacher interactions and what kinds of communication, including technology, are most convenient and expedient for receiving news about their child's academic progress and behavior and about classroom events and other information.

TEACHER TALKS . . .

One of the most important secrets to achieving students' success is to get the families involved in the academic process. Parents are important participants who can channel a student's success or failure. To illustrate my point, I would like to share the story of one of my students: After two months of class, she still didn't know any letters or sounds. I tried my best to make her mom understand that it was important for her to get involved in her daughter's education. She listened to me and followed up with my recommendation. After eight months of school, this girl reads at level 14 with great ability to retell stories. To reach high expectations, three components are necessary: student, teacher and family.

MARIA CLEPPE
School Counselor
San Bernardino, California

CHAPTER 34

UNIT 7 CHECKLIST

Assessing and Communicating Progress Checklist	For more information go to:
☐ Have you found out which tests your students will be required to take and when?	Chapters 30, 33
☐ What authentic assessments and diagnostic tools are used at your site?	Chapter 30
☐ Have you checked out what grading practices are the norm at your site?	Chapter 30
☐ Have you gotten a copy of the reporting forms and rubrics?	Chapter 30
☐ Have you made a list of questions for an interest interview or inventory?	Chapter 31
☐ What grading shortcuts seem most feasible to use?	Chapter 32
☐ Have you decided on a pre-testing period timeline for test preparation?	Chapter 33
☐ Are you prepared for parent conferences, or do you need more information?	Chapter 34
☐ Have you familiarized yourself with the cultures represented in your room?	Chapter 34
☐ Have you provided parents with the information they need to help at home?	Chapter 34

Further Reading: Assessing and Communicating Student Progress

Marzano, R. (2006). *Classroom assessment and grading that work*. Alexandria, VA: ASCD. This research-based book offers teachers the tools to design more effective and efficient assessment systems. The book outlines a standards-based, formative evaluation system and answers some of the most pressing questions about assessment and grading.

O'Shea, M., & National Center for Educational Information. (2009). *Pathways to teaching series: Assessment throughout the year*. Boston: Pearson Education. This practical book can help teachers get ready for the assessments they will be required to administer throughout the school year. It includes sensible and realistic information about how to pace the curriculum and prepare for benchmark exams as well as the standards-based cumulative assessments.

Popham, W. J. (2010). *Classroom assessment: What teachers need to know* (6th ed.). Boston: Allyn & Bacon. This text offers a range of assessment techniques that teachers most often use in classrooms. It addresses the mandates of NCLB but focuses as well on alternative assessment tools.

Stiggens, R. J. (2007). *Introduction to student-involved assessment for learning* (5th ed.). Upper Saddle River, NJ: Prentice Hall. This is a comprehensive book about developing assessments that reflect learning. There are clear step-by-step instructions on how to construct all types of classroom assessments and a discussion of what they can and cannot assess.

Vatterott, C. (2009). *Rethinking homework: Best practices that support diverse needs*. Alexandria, VA: ASCD. This book focuses attention on the homework debate and suggests a different approach that ranks quality over quantity, differentiates homework tasks, de-emphasizes grading of homework, and helps students complete homework. Many examples from teachers and schools that implement this approach are included.

Wormeli, R. (2006). *Fair isn't always equal*. Portland, ME: Stenhouse Publications and the National Middle School Association. This book presents a rationale for differentiated assessment and grading and is chock-full of real examples. It answers the fundamental questions about grading and assessment, such as whether to grade homework; how to create test questions; whether to incorporate attendance, effort, and behavior into the grading equation; and so forth.

Assessment Websites

National Education Association

http://www.nea.org/index.html

Find resources about assessment techniques and issues by searching this comprehensive and easy-to-navigate website.

Rubric Generator

http://www.teachnology.com

At this website you can personalize already created rubrics or design your own from scratch.

Pearson Assessment and Information

http://www.pearsonschool.com

This is Pearson Education's website for teaching tools and resources in all curriculum areas, including ESL and ELL, life skills, and assessment.

U.S. Department of Education

http://www.ed.gov/

This website offers information on all aspects of education. Use the search term *assessment* to get the latest updates on the provisions of the reauthorization of the Elementary and Secondary Education Act.

Rubric Generator 2

http://rubistar.4teachers.org/

Users can save and edit rubrics online. Teachers can access the rubrics from home or school or on the road. Registration and use of this tool are free, and all subjects are covered, including art and music.

Education World

http://www.educationworld.com

This is a comprehensive site for teachers and features professional articles on homework, rubrics, assessment, grading, and working with parents. All of the topics covered in this unit as well as other topics covered in this text can be retrieved by way of *Education World's* site and Internet search engine.

CHAPTER 35

WHAT IS REFLECTIVE PRACTICE AND HOW DO I ENGAGE IN IT?

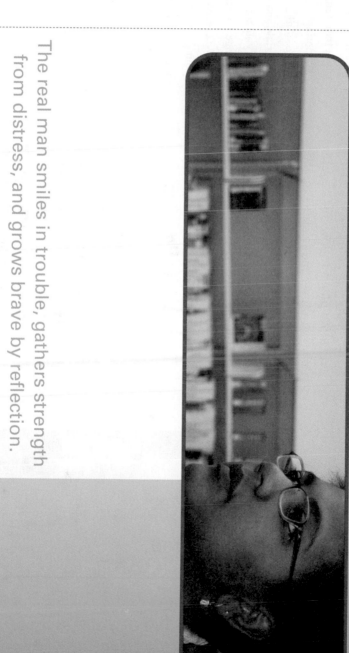

The real man smiles in trouble, gathers strength from distress, and grows brave by reflection.

Thomas Paine

Effectiveness Essentials

- New teachers go through five phases in the induction year.
- The reflective teacher is open to change, takes responsibility for outcomes, and teaches with enthusiasm and openness to diversity.
- There are a number of ways in which a teacher can gain feedback about his or her own teaching that can encourage reflection.

All of the preceding chapters have focused on what you do for your students to make their year rewarding. This unit explores how you can use your insight to make this and future years gratifying for you.

Moir (1990) and colleagues identified five phases in the induction year. You may remember these were described and diagramed in Chapter 3. The *anticipation phase* is characterized by excitement when you land a position. Then comes the *survival phase,* in which you are just happy to keep your head above water. The *disillusionment phase* and the *rejuvenation phase* follow this. A *reflection phase* follows and leads to another *anticipation phase* for the next school year. This chapter spotlights the *reflection phase* and focuses on how you can become a reflective teacher.

Toward Reflective Practice

One of the most important decisions you will make is whether or not you will become a reflective teacher. What is a reflective teacher? Grant and Zeichner (1984) suggest three requisite attitudes for the reflective teacher. They are *open-mindedness,* a willingness to consider and even to admit that you are wrong; *responsibility,* a willingness to look at the consequences of your actions; and *wholeheartedness,* a willingness to accept all students and to practice what you preach.

mythBUSTER

Teachers are born, not made.

New teachers should allow themselves five years. The first year you are totally overwhelmed and a bit confused by all the record keeping, curriculum requirements, and testing schedules and by wondering why you entered the teaching profession! The second year you recognize the materials and manage the schedule. The third year you not only recognize the materials and manage the schedule but are now able to add one or two creative ideas of your own to energize your program. The fourth and fifth years you realize how much fun teaching is and find yourself searching for materials, methods, and opportunities to provide enrichment and enhance the learning experience of your students.

Lynn Sleeth
Former Elementary and Middle School Teacher and Principal
Special Education Teacher
Fontana, California

WATCH IT! video

Succeeding in Your First Year of Teaching

As you watch this clip of a first-year teacher's reflection, take note of the high and low points of her year. If you have completed a first year, what were your high and low points? If you haven't, how does this reflection compare with what you imagine the first year's highlights and challenges might be?

"We have always done it that way" is a saying that is all too common in many fields. You may even hear this at your school site. There is a widely held belief that teachers teach the way that they were taught, and some do so without considering whether those methods were effective. The reflective teacher, on the other hand, discounts the notion that because something has always been done a certain way, it must be good. It may be true that many teaching strategies are as effective today as they were 20 years ago, but the reflective teacher does not take this for granted. Reflective teachers are analytical. They examine what they are doing in light of research and experience, and they seek out feedback in order to grow professionally.

Reflective teachers constantly examine their practice and decide what is best for the current group of students. They can admit they have been mistaken, and they take full responsibility for their decisions. I tell student teachers to realize, "It seemed like the best solution at the time," so they can forgive themselves and learn from their mistakes.

A Five-Point Plan Can Get You Started

As discussed, the reflective teacher is open to change, takes responsibility for

APPLY IT!

Buy a blank journal to write down all your reflections. The first section should be reserved for your teaching credo, no more than 1–2 paragraphs per question. What do you believe makes a good teacher? What do you believe about the way kids learn best? What is your discipline plan? What are your beliefs about parental involvement? From time to time throughout your first year of teaching, look at what you have written and revise it as your belief system grows with your experience. There may be additions, deletions, and revisions. Keep all your versions in your reflection journal.

A TEACHER AND PRINCIPAL TALKS . . .

I applied for National Board status because I felt I had reached a plateau in my delivery of instruction. I knew I could be a better teacher, but I needed the impetus to find out how. Going through the National Board process forced me to take a comprehensive look at my teaching practices and analyze them in detail as they related to national standards and best practices. I truly believe that this year of intense reflection was by far the best professional development I have ever done. That being said, the process is not for everyone. It requires ongoing self-motivation and the ability to recognize one's own strengths and weaknesses. There is no better way to improve one's teaching.

VIRGINIA STRONG NEWLIN
Principal and National Board–Certified Teacher
Rock Hall, Maryland

(quoted on http://www.EducationWorld.com)

CHAPTER 35

STATISTICS

According to the U.S. Department of Education's National Center for Education Statistics (2007–2008),

- Only 2.5% of beginning teachers have earned less than a bachelor's degree.
- Most (77.2%) have earned a bachelor's degree.
- Some (18.2%) have earned a master's degree.
- Very few (2.1%) have earned a degree higher than a master's.

APPLY IT!

In your reflective journal, list at least 10 qualities, skills, or attitudes that make you an effective teacher. Don't be shy! Then write down five areas that you would like to strengthen. Don't be shy here either. What alternatives have you considered? Write these down as well.

outcomes, and teaches with enthusiasm and openness to diversity. Once you decide to be a reflective teacher instead of one who relies on the way things have always been done, how do you take the first steps?

1. Recognize your own implicit theories and beliefs about teaching, learning, and kids. You have gone through your own childhood, schooling, university education, and student teaching. You have read a great deal and heard many diverse theories in classes. Now it's your turn to put it all together.
2. Acknowledge your own strengths and relinquish the notion that you have to excel at everything. Question the way you do things and seek alternatives.
3. Design a five-year plan of goals you would like to achieve, and seek help from all sources (parents, colleagues, local businesses, professional organizations) to reach them.
4. Find ways to love, respect, and treat yourself well. Do not become your own worst naysayer. Teachers are all too quick to dwell on their mistakes and forget all the good. Students have a knack for draining confidence from their teachers. We've all dealt with raised eyebrows, whispers to friends, notes passed, yawns, makeup touch-ups, doodling, bored expressions, wise remarks, clowning around, jokes, etc. You will need to learn to ignore these seemingly hostile manifestations of disinterest. Students may simply be posturing and trying to impress their peers. Do not become discouraged. Seek feedback from the students through a suggestion box in your classroom, and ignore the outward expressions that may not be a reflection on you but rather their need to impress their classmates with their cool world-weariness.
5. Blow your own horn and take every opportunity (conferences, videos,

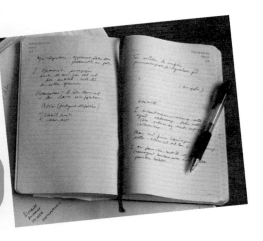

APPLY IT!

Sketch out a tentative five-year plan and keep it in your reflective journal. You can make changes, but keep all the versions.

presentations) to demonstrate your expertise. Viewing your successes through the eyes of the public will help you validate your practice. You will have to acknowledge your own strengths when they are so visible to others. Notify the local media that a special, newsworthy activity is coming up. For example, a third-grade teacher friend of mine also directs the *Nutcracker* ballet each year, and she brought several performers to her school for a special assembly. The local paper carried the story. Make up business cards with your name (see Figure 35.1). Wear a nametag at school. Take and share photos of your classroom activities. Submit a conference proposal.

Engaging in Reflective Practice

Use objective techniques of videotaping or audiotaping lessons to help you reflect on your practice. Also, your students can give you some honest and useful feedback if you ask them. At the end of the school year, one teacher I know has her students write down the three best things about the year, and she rereads them for confidence on the very first day of the following school year. Another has the current class write letters to the next year's class about their experiences. One teacher has her students make report cards for her at the end of the year (see Figure 35.2). The design and categories are of their choosing, and it is a creative way to gather material for reflection.

You may want to design a questionnaire for your students to fill out anonymously at the end of the year. Student responses will provide you with data to ponder before the beginning of the next school year.

Peer coaching or just talking informally with colleagues will help you think about your practice. School-based collaborative teacher reflection should be ongoing, and teachers can become the initiators of their own professional development. When teachers come together with school colleagues to

APPLY IT!

Write a *Dear Me letter* to yourself. Write what you value most about yourself and why you have earned respect from colleagues, family, and friends. Don't be shy. This letter is for your eyes only, and you should keep it in your reflective journal.

Figure 35.1
Teacher Business Card

4th Grade Teacher
Franklin Elementary School
10 School Street
Frankin, NH 00808
ewatson@franklin.edu

Figure 35.2
Report Card for Teacher

Report Card
for
Ms. Davis

Caring	A
Understanding	A
Dedication	A
Fairness	A

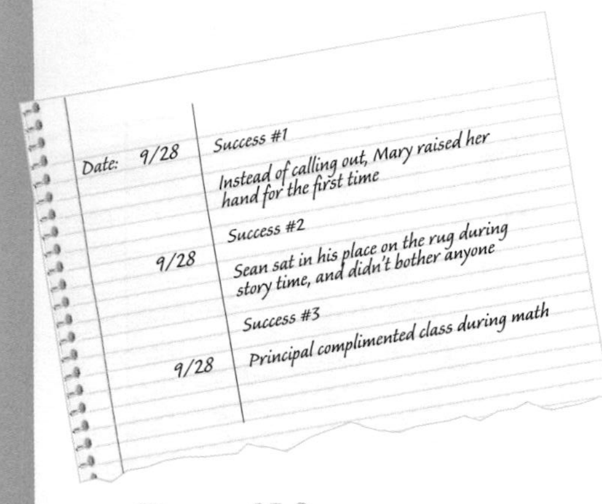

Date: 9/28
Success #1
Instead of calling out, Mary raised her hand for the first time
9/28
Success #2
Sean sat in his place on the rug during story time, and didn't bother anyone
9/28
Success #3
Principal complimented class during math

Figure 35.3
Success-of-the-Day Page From Journal

openly discuss discrepancies between theory and practice and give voice to their opinions, they become intellectually stimulated, less isolated, and more empowered.

Every day jot down your feelings, your successes, your questions, and ruminations about the day in your journal. Keep your reflective journal in your desk drawer, and write down at least three successes every day. When all seems futile, take out your journal and read it from start to finish. That should cheer you up and restore a can-do attitude.

myth**BUSTER**

If I try hard enough, I can reach every student.

I think many teachers enter the classroom thinking that they will be able to rescue all of their students. Then, when they fail, they feel like they aren't good at teaching and might as well quit the profession. Teaching students is not about rescuing them but about giving them the tools to rescue themselves when they need it. It is important that the students know they have choices and that the outcome of their life is based on the choices they make.

Jennifer A. Ponsart
Middle School Music Director
Davenport, Florida

AVOID IT!

Never put yourself down. Even if you have had a very bad day, you need to focus on what went right and how you can ameliorate any problems the next day. There are really no perfect decisions. Recite this to yourself: "It seemed like a good idea at the time." Think back on or rent the movie *Groundhog Day*. Bill Murray was able to relive each day until he got it right. Teachers have this opportunity to start fresh each and every day all year long!

Summary

In your first year there will be ups and downs and in-betweens. Moir (1990) describes the roller-coaster ride of the first year; but in the end, reflective first-year teachers will be looking forward to the next year and will be ready to build on successes and make adjustments where needed. This chapter's five-step reflection plan and ideas for collecting feedback and self-reflection will help you fine-tune your practice.

Reflect!

Start your reflective journal right here by answering these questions. If you are not yet teaching, answer them as if you were.

1. How have I established a caring and positive classroom community?
2. What are some ways I have motivated my students by engaging them in meaningful learning activities?
3. What are some ways I have welcomed and facilitated the language development of English language learners?
4. How have I incorporated students with special needs into the mainstream?
5. How do I encourage parents to form a partnership with me to help their children succeed?
6. What adjustments do I already need to make in my instruction?
7. Make up two more questions and answer them.

CHAPTER 35

CHAPTER 36

HOW DO I ESTABLISH RELATIONSHIPS WITH ADMINISTRATORS AND COLLEAGUES?

Respect your fellow human beings, treat them fairly, disagree with them honestly, enjoy their friendship, explore your thoughts about one another candidly, work together for a common goal and help one another achieve it.

Senator Bill Bradley

Adding "just kidding" doesn't make it okay to insult the Principal.

Bart Simpson

Effectiveness Essentials

- A school is a community within a community.
- Get to know the key personnel at the district office, in the media/technology center, and in the resource center.
- Familiarize yourself with the school norms and operating procedures.
- A successful year depends on an open, honest, and professional relationship with your principal.
- Present yourself as a prepared professional who is positive and enthusiastic about the challenges of the first year.
- Perhaps your greatest allies in your school setting are your colleagues and the school staff.

A school is a community within a community. We all have a primary need to belong and gain acceptance, so you will want to quickly adapt to your adopted community. As the new kid on the block, you will need to orient yourself to the physical environment, get to know the key players, and learn the ropes. You will want to establish productive, positive, and professional relationships with your administrator, colleagues, other staff, and support providers. Good working relationships can make or break the school year.

Getting Oriented

When you arrive at your school, the first thing you need to do is acclimate yourself to the building so you can find your way around. Depending on the size of your school, this could be a daunting task. The second most important thing is to identify the key people in the school. Who will be able to answer questions? Whom do you go to for supplies? Who *really* runs the school?

Find Key Locations

Most schools have campus maps, and you need to ask for one even before school starts. If none is available, take out a piece of paper and start drawing. Annotate it with the following important campus locations:

- Restrooms for your students
- Restrooms for you
- Water fountains
- Teachers' lounge/refrigerator
- Custodians' space
- Cafeteria
- Resource room
- Computer lab
- Gym
- Library
- Nurse's office
- Technology equipment room
- Textbook storage closets
- Assembly room
- Supply room
- School office
- Telephones
- Principal's office
- Counselor's office
- Mailboxes
- Locations of copier, laminator, etc.
- School bus depot
- Your spot for class lineup
- Your spot for emergency lineup
- Place to park your car
- Mass transit stop
- And, of course, your classroom!

TEACHER TALKS . . .

When I started teaching in my high school, it didn't take me long to figure out that the most important people in the school to know were the secretary in the main office and the custodian. They knew all the behind-the-scenes workings of the school, and those are important things to know. It also became very clear which teachers had the most clout, and you didn't want to get on their bad side. But the real power was with the support staff.

MARY K.
High School Teacher, Social Science
Wellman, Iowa

CHAPTER 36

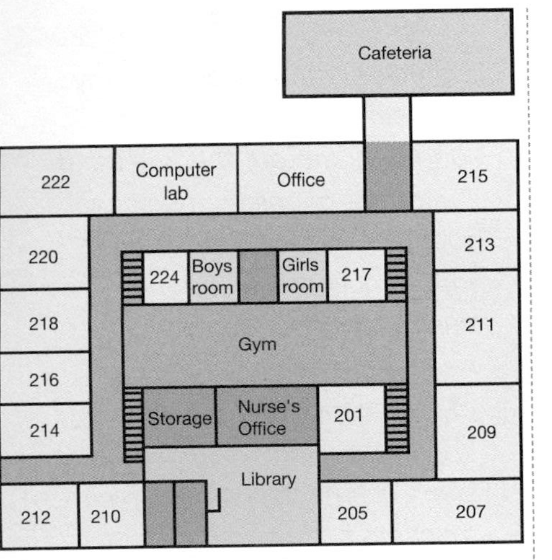

Figure 36.1
Map of a School

The computer lab brings smiles

A teacher's work is never done.

For the first few weeks, you will probably refer to the map fairly often, but in time, it will become less necessary.

Locate Key People

Obtain a staff roster as soon as possible to find out who's who at your site. From time to time, you will be seeking the advice of other professionals and support providers in the school. Knowing them by name will help you develop rapport more easily.

APPLY IT!

Annotate the staff roster as you sit in faculty, team, or department meetings. Not only can you associate names and faces but you can also make a note of any special skills and talents that come to light. For example, who seems to answer every tech question?

Introduce yourself to the key players at school and make notes about the hours and days they are available for consultation and what information they need from you:

- School nurse or health aide
- Community worker
- Special education resource teacher
- Psychologist or counselor
- Bilingual resource teacher
- Reading specialist
- Language and speech specialist
- Library aide
- Technology resource person
- School secretary
- Custodian

Seek out other teachers and take the initiative to introduce yourself. You will need the support they have to offer later, and they will appreciate your support as well.

Get to know the key personnel at the district office, in the technology center, and in the resource center. Don't be shy. You will reap great benefits from just walking in and introducing yourself. Attend school board meetings from time to time, and become familiar with the community leaders and the issues they wrestle with each month.

It won't take long before you identify the movers and shakers at your site. Key players are not always the people with titles. Find out who has influence and who is a leader. Identify those people who seem to make things happen and those whose comments are held in high regard. As with any community, schools have the same political dynamics that play out both in front of and behind the scenes. It may take time to gain an understanding of these dynamics, but this information will prove to be very valuable over time.

Learn Key Procedures

You need to familiarize yourself with the school norms and operating procedures without delay. Some districts provide new teachers with a general policy manual that will answer many of your questions. Questions beget questions, and the answers to these and to all other questions should

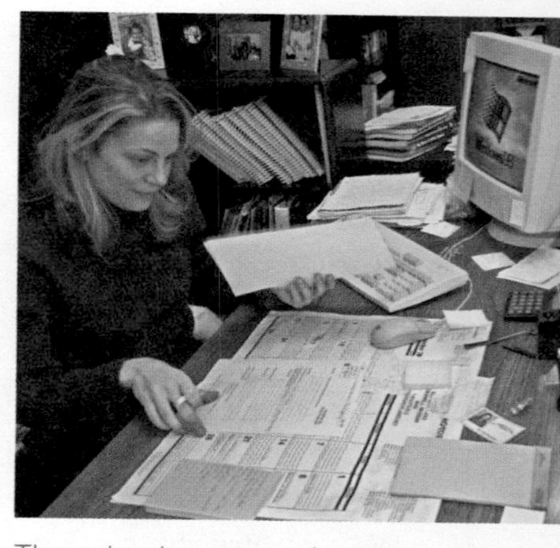

The school secretary is almost always an important resource.

CHAPTER 36

be made a permanent part of your own policy manual. Some of these procedural questions might include the following:

- How do I refer a student for special testing?
- What do I do first if I suspect child abuse?
- How do I get into the school on weekends?
- How does the laminating (copy, die press, bookbinding) machine work?
- How do I sign up to use the multiuse or assembly room?
- How do I order media and technology?
- How many times will the principal visit me, and will I have notice?
- How do I get more desks (books, materials, pencils, etc.)?
- How do I get repairs done in the room?
- What do I do when a student gets sick during class time?

APPLY IT!

Use a loose-leaf notebook and begin to collect all of the policy and procedures documents that cross your desk. Classify them under larger headings and use dividers. Have blank sheets in each section for your own annotations. Prepare a list of questions and get answers to them as soon as possible.

Working With Your Principal and Other Administrators

A successful first year depends on an open, honest, and professional relationship with your principal. You are at least 50% responsible for establishing a productive relationship with your principal and 100% responsible for meeting the expectations that your principal has of you.

PRINCIPAL TALKS . . .

The one quality I try to find is a teacher who will be a kid magnet. Once a student really connects emotionally to the teacher, then the rest will follow! Many things might lead me to believe that the candidate is a kid magnet. Some are based on instinct—a feeling that I get from a young, enthusiastic person who has that "je ne sais quoi," that intangible spark that would attract kids. I also look for people who are involved with kids outside of the school setting, especially music groups, theater, and sports. If I ask the right kinds of questions to let the personality of the candidate emerge, I can usually find this quality if it's there.

Our committee just finished interviewing 26 candidates, and we found three or four with those qualities. All agreed that the candidates have that special something to become superstars—and we will settle for nothing less!

STEVEN PODD
Middle School Principal
St. James, New York

(quoted on www.educationworld.com)

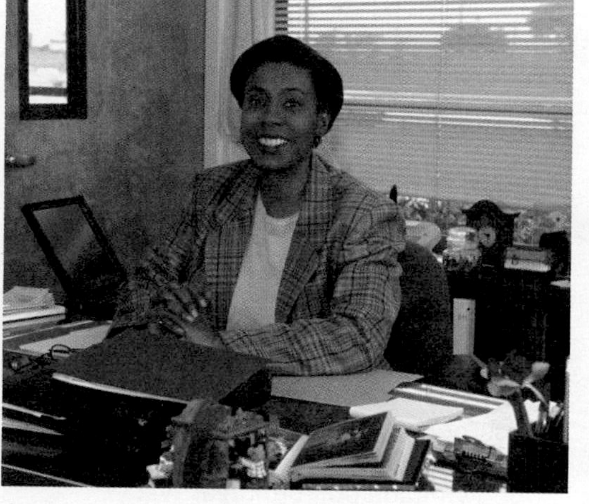
Get to know your principal.

Present yourself as a prepared professional who is positive and enthusiastic about the challenges of the first year. You can demonstrate this overtly through your dress and demeanor. Any first-week difficulties such as overcrowding can be viewed as problems to be solved rather than as tragedies to lament. When requesting changes of any sort, provide an instructional rationale. For example, if you want the unused piano moved into your room, explain that you play piano and use songs to teach concepts.

Working With Other Teachers

Perhaps your greatest allies in your school setting are your colleagues. You may have a formal mentor or you may be assigned buddies, but you definitely will have peers who are ready and willing to help you. They were in your shoes once, and, like most of us, they remember vividly those first years of teaching.

It is important to be friendly to everyone and resist getting pulled into cliques. Try to steer clear of any colleagues you identify as whiners, complainers, or gossips, but remain friendly just the same. There are wonderful opportunities on a staff for collegiality and even deep and lasting friendships.

Contact with your colleagues will help you discover their special talents and skills. Find out who the experts are in various curriculum areas. Who is adept at computer-based instruction?

Work with other teachers.

PRINCIPAL TALKS . . .

- *Surviving your first year is simple if you are not afraid to ask for help. There is no reason to reinvent the wheel. Ask, ask, ask and share, share, share.*
- *To stay organized, you must stay after school and get ready for the next day. This will make your mornings and days run smoother. It will also lower your anxiety because you'll be prepared.*
- *Remember students only have one year to experience this grade with you. Make it the best you can and don't be afraid to ask them how to make it even better. Your students can be one of your best teaching assets.*
- *Don't be a perfectionist when it comes to room environment. Get student work up on the board, and if they are old enough (3rd to 12th grade), let them put it up for you. They will have a sense of ownership.*

(continued on following page)

PRINCIPAL TALKS—*continued*

- *Be firm and fair and always follow through with what you say. You will gain students' respect this way. Remember they don't have to like you, but they should respect you. The easiest way is to show them respect always.*
- *Praise in public and correct in private.*
- *Remember to make time for your home life. Teaching is just a job—not your life. You will be better for the students if you have balance with life and work.*
- *Your principal is your friend! He or she is there to help you succeed. Don't be afraid to ask for help. A reflective first-year teacher is high on a principal's list of desirable traits.*

NINA CONINE
Teacher, K–12 (for 13 years)
Junior High and Middle School Vice Principal (for 2 years)
First-Year Principal
Olivehurst, California

UNIT 8

Ten Ways to Convey a Positive Impression to Your Principal

1. Use great discretion before you send a student to the office for discipline. As a beginning teacher, you want to convey the impression of competence, even though you won't be feeling it all the time.
2. Keep your principal informed at all times so that surprises are kept to a minimum. Discuss problem students with your principal well before the parents storm his or her office. Principals don't like to be left in the dark, and they especially don't want to utter or even think the words, "I don't know anything about this."
3. Share with the principal any letters or communications before you send them home to parents. The principal may notice any policy discrepancies and spare you the embarrassment of having to retract what you have written.
4. Inform your principal about any impending outside activities. Field trips, conferences, inservices, or absences will require that you obtain substitute coverage sooner rather than later.
5. Inform the principal about guest speakers and special presentations. Share with your principal all the wonderful activities you are engaging in with students.
6. Send samples of students' work to the office from time to time. Class newspapers, art projects, stories, and cooked or baked goods will be favorably received.
7. Invite your principal to special events such as plays or debates in your classroom. Your students can design the invitations and escort the principal to a good vantage point upon arrival.
8. Be on time to school and to meetings, and turn in any reports or rosters on or before your deadline. Punctuality rates very high with administrators.
9. Maintain an attractive, orderly, and clean room environment at all times. Your room speaks for your program, especially during a quick walk-through by the principal.
10. Present a positive demeanor. Smiling beats whining and even if you have had a very hard day, remember that, although "this too will pass," an administrator may not forget your downbeat reaction.

AVOID IT!

Don't stay in your room during lunch or recess breaks. It is much more important to socialize and break out of the isolation of the classroom. You need that cup of coffee or glass of juice, not only to refresh yourself but also to feel a sense of belonging with your colleagues.

Do your fair share of committee work, but guard your precious time. Your first year's focus is on your classroom and teaching. Practice tactful ways to decline invitations for extracurricular involvement. Rather than complaining, seek solutions and support from your colleagues.

Who knows every art project ever invented? Who plays guitar and may be willing to swap music for art? Who runs a well-managed classroom? Whom can you go to for science or social studies ideas? You'll discover this information informally. Don't be shy. Ask for help.

The veteran teachers will most likely be delighted if you ask for ideas or help. One or two colleagues may take you under their wing. Swallow your pride and seek them out. This book could not have been written except for the willingness of experienced teachers to share what they have learned either by trial and error or from other teachers.

In middle school, you will probably have an interdisciplinary team to look to for advice. If your school has block scheduling, you will probably be teaming with teachers who are a bit more experienced than you are. In high school, you will probably depend on your department head to guide you through the ins and outs of your first year of teaching. Grade-level colleagues in elementary school will see you through the first year.

Summary

Teachers and school staff are your lifelines during your first years of teaching and beyond. They can teach you not only the stated norms and procedures but also the informal ones as well. Every school has a culture of its own, and you'll want to fit in and learn the ropes as quickly as you can without stepping on toes or making avoidable errors about school customs.

You will probably have an orientation to the school's physical environment, the key people, and the operating routines and procedures. Use your intuition to discern how things actually work and the hidden rules of the school. Find out who is the go-to person who can answer your questions. The school secretary usually is the one who can guide you to the resources you need.

Early on, establish a professional relationship with your principal and show through your professional demeanor, dress, and comments that you are positive, enthusiastic, and ready to meet the challenges of the year ahead.

Reflect!

Think back to a time when you were the newcomer in a context other than a teaching position. Maybe it was a team, a new job, a fraternity or sorority, a charitable organization, a new religious congregation, or a group of fellow tourists. What did you do to become part of the group or the community? What did others do to welcome you? How did you show that you wanted to be included and integrated into the group? What strategies did you use, and in what ways are they applicable to a school setting?

CHAPTER 37

HOW CAN I MANAGE MY TIME AND BALANCE MY LIFE?

Effectiveness Essentials

- Learn to manage your time efficiently both at home and at school.
- A number of planning aids and strategies can help you organize your day.
- Overcome obstacles: perfectionism, procrastination, indecisiveness, and interruptions.
- Stress can derive from the very nature of the teaching profession, the reality of high-stakes testing, and accountability demands.
- There are a number of effective ways to keep stress at bay.

I wasted time, and now doth time waste me.

William Shakespeare

Don't worry about the world ending today.
It's already tomorrow in Australia.

Charles Schulz

YOU'RE INVITED
TO
LYDIA JOHNSON'S
RETIREMENT PARTY!

UNIT 8

In the first few years of teaching, it's not at all unusual to feel sleep-deprived and to wonder how you will juggle every personal and professional demand. Balancing all your responsibilities while establishing yourself in the classroom and your school takes time and can be stressful. But you need to feel assured that eventually, the demands on your time do decrease. In the meantime, there are a number of things you can do to reach a healthy balance.

APPLY IT!

Reflect on why you chose the profession of teaching. Did you want to drive yourself into being a workaholic? Did you want to make sure that each and every lesson is terrific? Write a speech for your future retirement party. What do you want your legacy to be? Only when you decide on a realistic legacy will you be more open to the stress-busting and time-saving suggestions that follow.

Time Management

Time management is a skill you will need to learn. When my student teachers tell me they are burned out, I reply, "How can that be? You haven't even been lit

mythBUSTER

Teaching is a cushy, part-time job.

It is Sunday, my day off, and I just spent three hours doing lesson plans, grading papers, and completing a project for my classroom. I always feel like there is never enough time to do all the things I need to get done as a teacher. I could stay at school for hours after my contract time. But I have learned to manage my time better and to just cut myself off at a certain time each day, whether I am done or not. I say to myself, "Tomorrow is another day!" I always bring home work to grade and lesson plans and projects to complete. There is always something to do that I just can't seem to get done. I put in a lot more time than my contract hours; I think that most teachers do. During time off, I find myself taking extra classes, going to conferences, and constantly thinking about how I can become a better teacher. A teacher's work is never done!

Diane Amendt
Third Grade Teacher
Colton, California

yet!" Beginning teachers often bemoan the lack of time in a day. They spend long hours writing lesson plans, grading papers, and dealing with the day-to-day needs of the job. These tasks can leave you feeling harried as you try to do it all and have it all. Instead, you should take out a crystal ball and look ahead. There will come a time, sooner rather than later, when you are managing your time more efficiently and have more to spend on other aspects of your life.

Manage Your Time at School

It is important to protect teaching and learning time at school. Maximizing teaching and learning time in the classroom will lessen some of the pressure you feel to accomplish your objectives and will ensure that students succeed. The routines suggested in Unit 3 and the additional ones that follow will give you more time on task and fewer repetitions of the new-teacher mantra "I never have time to finish anything."

1. Keep your students on task and away from socializing in order to maximize learning.
2. Sit down and work while your students are working, once they understand the assignment.
3. Routinize your transitions to increase teaching time.
4. Maximize your instructional time by relegating rote practice to homework.
5. Post an agenda on the board and stick to it.
6. Use an alarm clock or a timer to keep yourself focused and away from detours and diversions.

APPLY IT!

The first task you must do when trying to regain some time at school and at home is to honestly record your activities. Choose a typical weekday and in shorthand record what you did in half-hour intervals. Did you chat with a friend on the phone for a half-hour? Did you dawdle over the post-school snack? Did you watch a half-hour *Jeopardy* rerun? Did you pet the cat mindlessly, avoiding the stack of papers on your desk? Could you make more time by adding just one half-hour at the end of the school day for marking papers and tidying your desk? Can you find one half-hour to exercise during your day?

TEACHER TALKS . . .

Mrs. W. was my fifth-grade teacher, and if ever there was a teacher that deserved a gold star, it was she. She did not make me feel defeated. On the contrary, she went out of her way to let me know that I could be whatever I wanted to be. She helped me in so many ways and built my self-concept to the point where I actually did believe that I could do something special. And that is just what I did.

For the past 22 years, I have been a fifth-grade teacher. Because of Mrs. W.'s influence in my life, I am now encouraging students who have had difficulties in their lives to believe that they can overcome and become someone. I have won numerous awards such as Teacher of the Year and have been nominated to Who's Who Among America's Teachers *four times by former students, but I owe it all to one fifth-grade*

(continued on following page)

TEACHER TALKS—*continued*

teacher who believed in me and challenged me to be all that I could be.

CHARLES SKINNER
Science Coach
South Carolina State Department of Education
Cottageville, South Carolina

(as seen on http://www.LessonPlansPage.com)

TEACHER TALKS . . .

An organized teacher means organized and productive students. I was in a classroom and saw this great idea last week. At the front of her room, the teacher has a hanging file system that has seven file folders in it.She can hang the system on a ledge or the overhead cart, and she puts transparencies, examples, and papers she will need for each day of the week in files she has labeled Monday *through* Friday. *In the other two files, she puts extra needed materials. As she writes her lesson plans, she loads each file and puts away the things she has used.*

(continued on facing page)

Teachers are "meeters." Middle school teachers will meet with their teams, and high school teachers may have curriculum or department meetings. Elementary teachers have grade-level meetings. Since you know one another and work so closely together, there is a risk that you will waste time talking about personal issues, complaints, or side issues. Usually meetings have set times dictated by the union and school district, and every minute counts. Try to redirect the conversation diplomatically when it gets off track.

Manage Your Time at Home

Saving time at home is key to your mental and emotional health. At home, try to implement the following 10 steps to conserve time for such important activities as sleeping, exercising, preparing a healthy meal, spending time with your family and friends, or just taking some time for yourself.

1. Commit to balance in your life.
2. Spend fewer hours on computer social networking, YouTube, blogs, and gaming.
3. Prioritize and plan. (Avoid doing extra things like the family reunion or Thanksgiving dinner for 40.)
4. Make to-do lists and use planning aids, especially technology.

5. Overcome obstacles: perfectionism, procrastination, indecisiveness, interruptions.
6. Get rid of clutter and organize your workspace.
7. Socialize with some non-teachers after school hours.
8. Go to sleep and awaken at the same time each and every day.
9. Take up a new hobby like biking, golf, or photography.
10. Travel and share your experiences in the classroom. Keep yourself energized by seeking out new interests.

A cluttered workspace

Make time for your family.

AVOID IT!

Avoid comparing yourself to experienced teachers. Do not overcommit your time to anyone, including friends, family, and community organizations, to name a few groups who would like you to clone yourself so you can give more and more. You have a valid justification for guarding your free time, and you can develop nice ways of extricating yourself from situations that place excessive demands on your time. "I would like to help you out, but during this first year of teaching, I need to focus on my professional responsibilities. Please contact me to serve on that board next year."

Managing Stress

Sometimes the pressure and imbalance of those first years of teaching can be stressful. Stress is like a chameleon, changing its manifestations just as effectively as the lizard changes color. Have you ever felt tired, unable to concentrate, overwhelmed, anxious about going to school, withdrawn, sick to your stomach, unable to sleep, depressed, irritable, insignificant, discouraged? These can all be symptoms of a debilitating state of stress.

Moderate stress is not always bad, but supersized stress or distress serves no purpose. Moderate stress can energize us to get things done. Superstress immobilizes us.

Stress can derive from the very nature of the teaching profession. You may feel discouraged by low pay, high expectations, and the low respect associated with teaching. You can pick up the morning paper most days and read teacher-bashing editorials. Those editorials always get my stress level elevated.

Stress can derive from the reality of high-stakes testing and accountability. Other stress-inducing factors include a sense of isolation, a lack of autonomy,

That way she has everything organized for the next week. This technique helps cut down the stress of teaching because she knows that everything is ready and in a place she can find.

LINDA MEYER
Resource Teacher
San Bernardino, California

TEACHER TALKS . . .

Remember to always expect the unexpected and be ready to respond positively. Keep your cool . . . maybe make it into a teachable moment. I recall teaching first-grade gifted and talented students one morning when a little girl pulled a dead pigeon out of her backpack. She had found it at the bus stop and wanted to help it. So we quickly had an impromptu lesson on birds, their flight mechanisms, their predators, and wildlife in general. Then the students wrote some great stories that went into "Esther's Pigeon Book." Afterward we called the county museum, which agreed

(continued on following page)

TEACHER TALKS—*continued*

to pick up the pigeon to stuff for one of its displays. Meanwhile, the pigeon waited in the nurse's refrigerator.

So what if you learn at the last minute about your class's new computer time, or the five-kid-at-a-time dental checkups, or the canceled library period, or the fundraiser assembly? You have to go with the flow because the students watch your reactions to these changes. It's always good for each one to have an independent folder of math puzzles, writing story starters, or even library books at their tables so that you can all quickly take up the slack. Remember that you can probably fit in that concept you were trying to teach sometime later in the day.

Try to foresee what interruptions might happen during the day, and have a monitor ready to go to the office to pick up or take a note. If he or she is old enough, have a responsible student answer the phone.

(continued on facing page)

Maintaining Perspective

There are a number of ways to maintain a healthy and positive perspective about your professional life and avoid becoming immobilized by stress or negative thinking. Here are some to consider:

1. Set realistic expectations for yourself and your students. Keep careful and up-to-date records, and communicate often with parents and your administrator about your progress with the class as a whole and with individual students.
2. View your students holistically, and recognize that test scores are only one facet of a student's development. Ask yourself, when you are feeling low, "Where was she at the beginning of school? Where is she now?" Justify your program with confidence.
3. Counter any sense of isolation by establishing collegial relationships at school. Make a promise to yourself to socialize during lunch and recess no matter how much work you have. Team with other teachers; plan with other teachers; jog with other teachers. Organize a support group of new teachers that meets once a week during lunch or at someone's house.
4. Students appreciate teachers who have a sense of humor. Use your sense of humor to relieve any tension in your classroom and your own stress level. There are plenty of sources for jokes and humorous stories on the web. Use cartoons or funny photos in your PowerPoint or overhead transparency presentations.
5. Make frequent contact with a mentor or a buddy who has been officially designated, or simply find a friend at school with whom you can talk.
6. Design a learning environment you want to live in for six hours each day. Clean up, organize, and redecorate your room from time to time. Throw things out that are dog-eared or are no longer useful. Play soft music during work time. The room environment is a key factor in how teachers feel about coming to school each day.
7. Devise ways to break the routine for yourself and your students. For example, an elementary teacher might have a backward day when the schedule goes in reverse and so do students' shirts. Other themed days teachers have tried and thoroughly enjoyed include an all-day read-a-thon, crazy-hat day, wearing-slippers day, students-teach-the-class day, bring-your-stuffed-animal-to-school day, and wearing-a-certain-color day.
8. Do some silly things like jumping rope with the kids or playing basketball with them at recess. Bring in a Frisbee and toss it around with them. Take them out for an unexpected walking field trip on the first day of spring. Create new projects like a classroom window garden or a class newspaper. Cook something simple in class.

9. Take a few minutes out of the day for your own relaxation ritual, which may include deep breathing, easy stretching, and muscle-flexing exercises. Or take a few minutes during recess to engage in visual imagery techniques. Regulate your breathing and take a mental trip to a quiet, secluded, peaceful place you have been to or hope to visit. A few minutes in Tahiti or on a hike in the woods during a break will put you in a better frame of mind.
10. Know your limits and be assertively polite about saying no to extracurricular assignments that are not part of your responsibilities.

What is your relaxation ritual?

cascades of paperwork, and a dilapidated physical plant.

Stress can also be caused by poor health choices you make. You know what they are: smoking, drinking, neglecting exercise, and poor eating habits.

Conquer Stress at School

One of the most important things you can do to keep stress at bay is to maintain a positive perspective about your work. When you read negative reports about schools or schooling, you can become stressed out. Do your part to promote respect for teachers. Network with other teachers to brainstorm ways of polishing your profession's image. Parents are your best partners, and they can promote you in the community.

Conquering Stress at Home

You might have to negotiate responsibilities at home to allow yourself more free time. School has a way of consuming teachers, especially new ones, so learn to make yourself top priority. Give yourself time between school and arrival home to unwind, or take a few minutes upon arrival to make the transition. Try to complete most paperwork at school, even if it means staying there to do it. Establish a schedule that gives you some free

If the principal or an administrator walks through, continue teaching with a smile. If it's quiet work time, take a moment to share what you're doing and proudly call her attention to the projects and bulletin board displays.

I hope you're in a school where the intercom is used sparingly. But if not, ask some other teachers to join you in requesting the principal to avoid using it during instruction time.

SHIRLEY CLARK
Retired Third-Grade Teacher
Sun City, California

TEACHER TALKS . . .

My relationship with my peers helps me tremendously with my stress levels. Knowing I have peers who understand the challenges of teaching and keeping a private life really help on days when I feel worn down. I think it is so important to get yourself out of the classroom during lunchtime and spend that time with your peers. Too often, new teachers stay in

(continued on following page)

TEACHER TALKS—*continued*

their classrooms to work and miss opportunities to learn that even veteran teachers struggle to do their best. Also, spending time with veteran peers can help new teachers figure out how to handle themselves with administrators. Listening to how others manage their classrooms and handle difficult or at-risk students is so valuable and needs to be a part of the learning curve. Plus, listening to the anecdotes of others and being able to laugh at situations that only teachers would understand is a stress buster. Teachers are teachers 24/7, so veteran teachers want to help new teachers learn how to survive those first years. This relationship with peers also helps relieve stress at home because spouses who love you want to fix your situation rather than just listen to the griping. Time spent with peers lets you know you are not alone and that everyone has a failed lesson or a student that pushes a teacher's buttons.

MARSHA MOYER
Third-Grade Teacher
San Bernardino, California

nights, even your first year, and use grading shortcuts.

Your personal stress busters are unique to you. They might include attending a sporting event, taking a trip to the day spa, going on a mini-vacation on Saturday, or going out to dinner with a friend. Here are some other low-cost suggestions from teachers to get you started on your own personal rejuvenation plan.

1. Plan a weekend away (or stay home and hibernate).
2. Take up a new hobby.
3. Read a book you "don't have time for."
4. Call a friend and talk out issues that are bothering you.
5. Practice relaxation techniques like meditation or yoga.
6. Spend some time alone.
7. Shop (my personal favorite).
8. Cook a healthy meal and freeze individual portions for lunch.
9. Listen to music or watch a DVD you "don't have time for."
10. Go to the gym, ride a bike, or take a hike.
11. Have your house or apartment cleaned by someone else.
12. Get a babysitter.

Crazy hat, anyone?

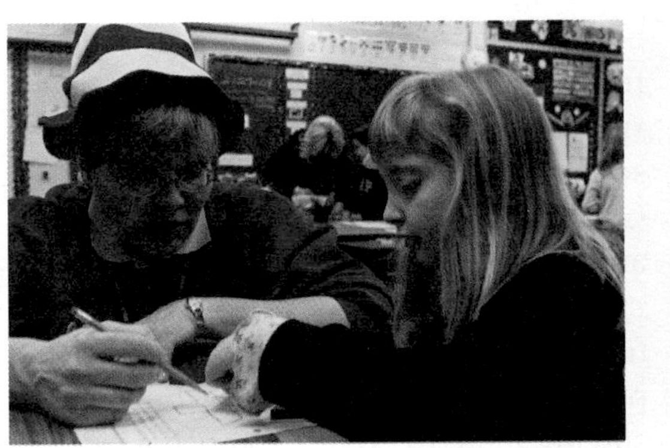

Take time to play with your students.

APPLY IT!

Make a list of at least 10 ways you relax or would like to relax after a day at school. Tape the list on your mirror so you can look at it every day.

AVOID IT!

Do not allow anyone in your life to undermine your career choice. Remember always, whatever the public perception, that you are engaged in significant work that makes a difference in the lives of children and adolescents.

APPLY IT!

Buy a calendar and record all the rejuvenating activities you engage in each month. Make sure that each month your calendar is filled with restorative activities so you can be of sound mind and body for the students in your class. They rely on your well-being more than you know.

Rejuvenation Calendar

Month: ____________

Record All Rejuvenation Activities

Sunday	Monday	Tuesday	Wednesday	Thursday	Friday	Saturday

TEACHER TALKS . . .

Having a sense of humor is important. Don't always take things so seriously. Step back; take a breath. Sometimes I amuse myself with thoughts about a particular situation. At times I can respond to the class with humor. And the support I get from peers is vital to survival. Passing by a colleague in the hall and exchanging certain looks can be a real stress reliever. Who better than a fellow teacher to understand and share your pain?

Also remember to give yourself a break from teaching. Take time for yourself. Do something you like—take a walk, read a book, watch a favorite TV show, etc. All of these can help reduce your stress level. Rome wasn't built in a day, and your classroom won't be either.

JAN CHRISTIAN
First-Grade Teacher
Redlands, California

TEACHER TALKS . . .

New teachers spend every waking moment on school-related tasks: lesson plans, grading, preparing materials for lessons, etc. You need to take one day each weekend for yourself and your family instead of devoting both days to work. On Friday evenings, I enjoy lighting a candle and sipping a glass of sparkling cider as I soak in a bubble bath. Even just 20 minutes for myself makes me feel refreshed and renewed.

BECKY MONROE
Middle School Language Arts Teacher
San Bernardino, California

PRINCIPAL TALKS . . .

I love books of every kind, but my favorite stress reliever is to read a murder mystery. I take time to read every night, even if only for a few minutes. It gets my mind off the hamster wheel of worry for at least a little while and lets me relax enough to fall asleep quickly.

VIRGINIA STRONG NEWLIN
Principal, National Board–Certified Teacher
Rock Hall, Maryland

(quoted on www.EducationWorld.com)

Sundays can be especially stressful if you wait until the last minute to plan for the week. Try to parcel out your planning so you can get it out of the way and have some free, unstructured time to pursue your own interests and hobbies or to catch up on family time or sleep!

Summary

The first year can be challenging as you learn to blend and balance your professional and personal responsibilities in the right proportions. In this chapter there are a number of suggestions for time management to help you set priorities both at home and at school. Stress and burnout are real factors, especially during the first years, when the demands seem unmanageable—that is, before you get a handle on all of your responsibilities. The chapter suggests ways to keep stress at bay.

Reflect!

This chapter describes ways to better manage your time and competing demands and make your life less stressful. Review the suggestions for time and stress management. Which ones appeal to you, and what will you do to implement the suggestions that seem most appropriate for your situation? Outline a plan that makes sense to you.

CHAPTER 38

WHAT PROFESSIONAL OPPORTUNITIES ARE OPEN TO ME?

Effectiveness Essentials

- A profession by its very definition requires continuing education.
- Professional learning communities encourage collaboration to improve student learning.
- Create your own teaching portfolio.
- Get involved with local or regional councils of national professional organizations, and attend conferences.
- Seek out grants that can help you professionally and in the classroom.
- Work with an eye toward applying for National Board certification granted by the National Board for Professional Teaching Standards.

Your work is to discover your work and then with all your heart give yourself to it.

Buddha

TEACHER TALKS . . .

The best teaching ideas are the ones I got from my colleagues. I am always looking for new and innovative teaching strategies, and I continually ask my colleagues for advice or ideas on how to teach a certain topic.

KELLY RUBIO
Fourth-Grade Teacher
Manhattan Beach, California

A profession by its very definition requires continuing education. Even after retirement, you will find yourself keeping up with innovations.

Professional Learning Communities

Professional learning communities or learning teams have come into vogue as a means to improve student learning. As defined by DuFour (2006), "a PLC is composed of collaborative teams whose members work interdependently to achieve common goals linked to the purpose of learning." This definition fits everything from team meetings, to middle or high school department meetings, to school committees, to faculty meetings, or even to school book groups. But DuFour, DuFour, Eaker, and Many (2006) cite certain requirements or "big ideas" that should be core principles of any professional learning community: ensuring that students learn, collaboration for school improvement, and focus on results. In practice, these big ideas translate into a process that requires

1. Collecting data on student learning
2. Identifying strategies to build on strengths and address weaknesses
3. Implementing those strategies and analyzing what works
4. Recycling from step 1 to ensure continuous improvement

Of course, the barriers to effective professional learning teams are time, commitment on the part of teachers and administrators, and a sense of shared responsibility for student learning. But when the goals are limited, focused, and attainable and the evidence of improvement is apparent and concrete, teachers are more likely to continue to participate and persist until larger goals can be identified and reached. The administrators need to make professional learning communities democratic in that everyone is heard, leadership is shared, and consensus is reached.

The specific work of professional learning communities might involve examining the standards and designing lessons or units to meet them effectively, evaluating student work and projects, dealing with classroom management and discipline issues, and so forth. The teams decide what will help them achieve their goals and objectives and may choose to read books and articles, attend inservices, watch webinars, access online workshops, invite district resource persons, and observe one another. The administrators may participate as equals, but their main focus should be coordinating and facilitating the work of the PLCs.

DISTRICT ARTIFACTS

The PLC Journey

We are K–12 instructional coaches in the Professional Development Academy for Hemet Unified School District, and we have been supporting PLCs in our district for the past six years. In the beginning, we were trained at our school sites. The training was optional at the time. Honestly, there was little follow-up, and our teams left the training really not knowing what to do next. The idea of the PLC sounded wonderful, and listening to Becky and Rick DuFour speak and being a part of their training audience was inspiring. But we did not know how or what to do to build a PLC at our own sites.

When we became K–12 instructional coaches, under the leadership of Dr. Martinrex Kedziora, we were more thoroughly trained and supported, and we had extensive opportunities to practice the fine details and functioning operations of what each part of a PLC really is. Once we had a strong understanding of how to create, sustain, and monitor the health of a true PLC, our district made a commitment to a districtwide message of gradually building a PLC. Our plan (and the district's goal), with the facilitation of Dr. Kedziora and Dr. Sally Cawthon, Assistant Superintendent of Student Support Services, was to offer extensive PLC training (10 full days, 5 days per year, over a 2-year period) to each site in the district. Each site selected a PLC team to attend the training. As districtwide coaches, the two of us attended to support the program and engage in the training. At the close of each day, the teams were given tasks to complete for the following training day. The tasks were related and relevant to the journey necessary to developing a healthy PLC team. In addition, each team had a sense of accountability since reporting out and documenting progress was non-negotiable.

Many of the tasks, especially in year 1, focused on building a site's vision and relating all endeavors to student learning and achievement. In the beginning, teams focused on all the reasons that our students were not achieving/learning: poor parent involvement, poor kids, bad tests, English language learning barriers, and so forth. The first step was to support teachers and participants in shifting their perspective of "what we can do, what our students can do, and what we can control." We adhered to the idea that, if we focus on student learning, analyze the student behaviors of learning, and don't engage in "what we can't do," student learning becomes the center of all site and district decision-making processes.

By the end of year 1, teams were interested but not quite ready to conduct on-site focus walks. Teams were analyzing student achievement data from local and site-created

(continues)

STATISTICS

According to a Met Life (2009) survey, almost all teachers participate in some type of collaborative effort with colleagues at their school each week. Teachers average 2.7 hours per week in structured collaboration with other teachers and school leaders. But while elementary and secondary teachers spend almost the same amount of time collaborating with colleagues each week, the type of collaboration differs. Not surprisingly, elementary teachers collaborate with grade-level colleagues, while secondary teachers collaborate with same-subject teachers across grade levels.

Here are some other key findings:

- Two-thirds of teachers (67%) and three-quarters of principals (78%) think that greater collaboration among teachers and school leaders would have a major impact on improving student achievement.
- The most frequent type of collaborative activities are:
  - Teachers meeting in teams to help their students achieve at higher levels
  - School leaders sharing responsibility with teachers to achieve school goals
  - Beginning teachers working with more experienced teachers
- The least frequent type of collaboration is peer observation and feedback. (Only one-third of teachers and principals report that this occurs.)

STATISTICS

Teachers vary in the amount of time spent in structured collaboration per week (Met Life, 2009):

- 24% spend more than 3 hours.
- 17% spend 2 to 3 hours.
- 26% spend 1 to 2 hours.
- 20% spend 31 minutes to 1 hour.
- 12% spend less than 30 minutes.

TEACHER TALKS . . .

PLCs are a powerful way for teachers to collaborate on strategies for meeting the needs of all students. In order for PLCs to truly be effective, teachers must buy in and have the autonomy to make decisions as a team. The administrators must be creative in offering guaranteed and uninterrupted PLC time (usually one full hour per week); and teachers must be willing to step up, set, and maintain meeting norms and agree to leave egos at the door. When done properly, PLCs can be an incredibly empowering format for helping our students learn and achieve.

DAVE EMRICK
Fifth-Grade Teacher
Rialto, California

DISTRICT ARTIFACTS—*continued*

assessments and practicing how to write smart goals. There was an increase in the attention, time, and energy we gave to monitoring student performance. Not all members of each PLC team were on board, but I think at this time the members of each team who were ready to forge forward did, and those who were not were certainly not as vocal about their discontent. Even though the naysayers were not active, engaged members, they supported the team. That is, they were not acting in a manner that would negate or destroy the strength of the team.

Teams who completed year 2 had different levels of health. Some teams completed site-wide focus walks to analyze student performance. Some sites crumbled. Some sites created action plans for the upcoming school year. Each site clearly had different levels of success with the journey, but our district remains committed to the development of the PLC process. I expect there will be additional opportunities for our sites to receive targeted support in the upcoming academic year.

Overall, the biggest challenges of our PLC journey have been the following:

- Time
- Continued enthusiasm after training
- External frustrations sneaking into protected PLC time (layoffs, pink slips, frustration with leadership, confusion, and so forth)
- Personal educational pedagogy (do we really all believe student learning is possible?)

The biggest rewards/benefits have been

- A focus on student learning
- Actually engaging in analyzing student performance based on student work and behaviors
- Increased collaboration (gaining strategies from colleagues to improve professional practice and therefore increasing student achievement)
- Protected time (during trainings) to interact with current research and case studies on the journeys others have taken in their PLC process
- Establishing districtwide common language and discourse conducive to promoting PLCs

Colleen Flavin and Natalie Ruddell
K–12 Instructional Coaches
Hemet United School District
Hemet, California

UNIT 8

Professional Development Opportunities

There are many ways to broaden your knowledge about teaching and learning.

1. Keep reading all you can about teaching and learning, classroom discipline, and management. Some teachers suggest getting subscriptions to magazines that are filled with numerous specific teaching ideas and units. Many can be accessed online as well. At the end of this chapter, you will find a list of periodicals you may want to look for in the resource center or university library and then order for your own professional library.
2. Collaborate with your colleagues and absorb all the information you can. Experienced teachers have made their share of mistakes and can help you avoid some of the common pitfalls. You need only to seek advice and they will be more than happy to share their experiences with you.
3. You may be required by your state credential laws to continue your education right away. Veterans advise that you take the least demanding courses first and none during the first semester of teaching. Your district will likely require you to attend new teacher inservices and meetings that will consume your time during those first few months, in addition to the adjustments you will be going through. You don't want to overcommit yourself.
4. Periodically, take some extended education courses to bone up on some practical aspect of teaching. Take these courses on a need-to-know basis so they are useful to you in your everyday life in the classroom. Consider extension courses with titles such as "100 Ways to Enhance Literature" (or creative writing or science, etc.) or that focus on bulletin boards or using new technologies. Or you might just take a course for fun that has absolutely nothing to do with teaching! "The Care and Feeding of Your Reptile" was one I came across recently.
5. Learn or brush up on second-language skills by studying any of the languages your students speak. Conversation CDs are available in libraries and bookstores, and it would be well worth your effort to speak some simple phrases to your English learners and their parents.
6. Create your own teaching portfolio. You will be able to see your evolution as a professional and have direct evidence, on those bad days, that you really are doing wonderful things. From time to time, you can reflect on your progress,

TEACHER TALKS . . .

PLCs have many benefits:

- *They break down barriers in a safe setting that enables educators to share best practices, analyze student data by subject and/or grade level, and create common assessments—especially formative assessments to help monitor student progress, which can then be discussed, monitored, and adjusted all over again in the PLC.*
- *They allow grade-level teams to work together. That is, they bring together different perspectives on a student's strengths and weaknesses and program strengths and weaknesses and allow for discussion on best practices.*
- *The PLC group can put new practices, schoolwide policies, grade-level policies, or subject-matter changes into place while monitoring and adjusting them.*

(continued on following page)

TEACHER TALKS—*continued*

They also offer challenges:

- *They require team building and trust.*
- *All affected parties must buy in and participate in the early stages.*
- *PLC development and training require budgetary commitment.*
- *All members of a PLC must follow through on planning and implementation.*
- *Participants must schedule regular meetings for data analysis.*

JULIE PRATER
Secondary School Mathematics Coach
Hemet, California

TEACHER TALKS . . .

I have had the opportunity to go through PLC training with two different school sites and found the process to be quite beneficial. The benefits of working in PLCs is that everyone has buy-in. Everyone is part of making decisions that help support student learning. The

(continued on facing page)

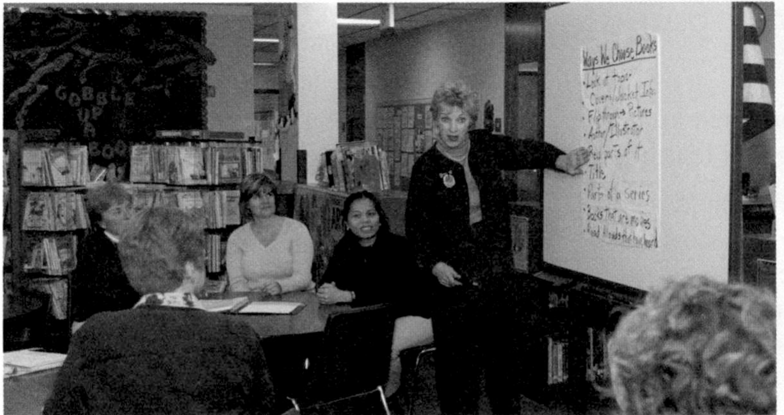

Take advantage of professional development opportunities.

and share your portfolio with colleagues, mentors, administrators, and parents. Include in your portfolio:

- Videos of lessons you have taught
- Samples of pupil products
- Videos of performances
- Photos of special bulletin boards or displays
- Observations and evaluations by your administrator
- Letters from parents
- Notes from your students
- Units you have developed
- Special lesson plans
- Lists of professional books and articles you have read
- Notes and agendas from committee meetings
- Annotated agendas and handouts from conferences and inservices

7. Join local or regional councils of national professional organizations. Read the very informative professional journals they publish. The websites are listed at the end of the chapter. These local councils provide meeting and inservice opportunities.
8. Present at local and national conferences. You can start out by co-presenting with someone who has done this before. Many of the grant and conference presentation opportunities are more available to secondary teachers since there are only a few national organizations solely devoted to elementary concerns. Elementary teachers are usually subsumed within the major subject-area organizations. Choose a curriculum area that you feel is one of your strengths, join the organization that represents that area, and attend meetings.

In time, you can start to submit presentation proposals.

9. Apply for grants of all sorts. Grant monies exist to help you expand your own knowledge and skills as well as to finance projects in your classroom. The challenge is identifying the sources of the grants. Grant forms are pretty simple, and many professional organizations list grant opportunities on their websites. You will also find out about grant opportunities in professional journals. Take advantage of grants to attend seminars and workshops in foreign countries. Combine travel with international conference opportunities. All of my most exciting travel experiences resulted from grants such as Fulbright summer seminars for teachers. Travel grants have taken me to Indonesia, Israel, Vietnam, and Japan.
10. After a few years of teaching, consider applying for National Board certification granted by the National Board for Professional Teaching Standards. National Board certification will give you nationwide access to certification and will carry with it a stipend and, more importantly, a sense of accomplishment. You will need to take certain tests and submit a portfolio, so it's never too early to gather evidence of your accomplishments.
11. Use online resources to participate in webinars, online courses, education blogs, and teacher websites. Read the publications *Education Week* and *Teacher Magazine* online. Use the website *Education World* to research topics of interest to you. Use YouTube to access quality videos on educational topics, and check out archived PowerPoint presentations that have been presented at educational conferences or during webinars. E-learning for professional development has exploded in recent years, and you can download all sorts of great information as needed.
12. Travel when you have vacation time, and use your travels to motivate your students. Recently I have visited the Living Desert Museum in Tucson, Mt. Rushmore in South Dakota, the Custer Battlefield in Montana, the Devil's Tower National Monument in Wyoming, the Lewis and Clark Interpretive Center in Montana, and the Buffalo Bill Historical Center in Wyoming. These travel experiences broaden my own knowledge but also provide an avenue, through photos, artifacts, videos, maps, documents, and interpretive brochures, to engage students. While the content may not link to the standards, there is always some time to introduce students to

TEACHER TALKS . . .

focus of the PLC needs to be on student achievement. Having a process to use data to support student achievement makes it happen. It is important to take time to develop the PLC team: go slow to go fast! The biggest challenge of the PLC is finding time; but once you have everyone on board, teachers are willing to give the time because they see the benefits of working together toward a common goal.

STORME FREEMAN
Beginning Teacher Support and Assessment
Peer Assistance and Review
Hemet, California

TEACHER TALKS . . .

I am a teacher. I have an inner need to make a difference, to matter. My way of making a difference is to strive to inspire people within my circle of influence—primarily my students. I went through the process of becoming a National Board–certified teacher to explore current strategies and best practices available to improve my teaching

(continued on following page)

TEACHER TALKS—*continued*

practice. In this time of our teachers' skills constantly being called into question, I wanted to ensure that I was doing everything I could to prove myself worthy and that I was doing the best for my students and community.

After seven years of teaching I applied to be a candidate. I joined a local support group, collaborated with other teachers and administrators, read everything I could about best practices and strategies, and then began the reflective process. The most rewarding thing about creating a portfolio and taking the National Board test was seeing the growth in student performance from my application of learning. The more I would reflect, plan, and apply what I learned from my students, the more connected they became to the material. The process was a very rewarding professional growth experience. It has long-lasting effects on the teacher experiencing it as well as all those within her circle of influence.

EILEEN MINO
Fifth-Grade Teacher
National Board-Certified Teacher
Colton, California

Eileen Mino asks, "Is National Board certification in your future?"

these exciting places, with the hope that they can be transported out of their familiar environment and learn something new.

Professional Development Resources

Here is a list of professional development resources, including generic teacher websites and magazines; websites and journals for discipline-specific professional organizations; websites for general issues, programs, and technology; and union websites. Many schools subscribe to some of the journals listed and make them available in the library, staff, or resource room. You may find some you want to subscribe to for your own professional library.

Generic Magazines and Websites

Instructor
http://teacher.scholastic.com/products/instructor/

Teaching Pre K–8
http://www.teachingK-8.com

Education World
www.educationworld.com

Middle and High School Teachers' Website
http://712educators.about.com

AVOID IT!

During your first year of teaching, it will be sufficient to limit your professional development options to the essential, required inservices and new-teacher workshops. Ease into the other professional development opportunities, and engage in those activities that will provide practical and sensible solutions to your immediate needs.

Discipline-Specific Professional Organizations and Journals

Social Studies
National Council for the Social Studies
http://www.ncss.org

Social Studies and the Young Learner (elementary)
Middle Level Education (middle school)
Social Education (high school)

Mathematics
National Council of Teachers of Mathematics
http://www.nctm.org

Teaching Children Mathematics (elementary)
Mathematics Teaching in the Middle School (middle school)
Mathematics Teacher (high school)

Science
National Science Teachers Association
http://www.nsta.org

Science and Children (elementary)
Science Scope (middle and junior high)
Science Teacher (secondary)

Reading/Language Arts
National Council of Teachers of English
http://www.ncte.org

Language Arts (elementary)
Voices from the Middle (middle and junior high)
Classroom Notes Plus (secondary)
English Journal (secondary)

International Reading Association
http://www.reading.org

The Reading Teacher
Journal of Adolescent & Adult Literacy

Technology
Computer-Using Educators, Inc.
http://www.cue.org

On Cue

International Society for Technology in Education
http://www.iste.org/

Learning and Leading with Technology

Special Education
Council for Exceptional Children
http://www.cec.sped.org

Exceptional Children
Teaching Exceptional Children

Bilingual Education and English Language Development
National Association for Bilingual Education
http://www.nabe.org

Language Learner

Issues, Practices, and Programs

Association for Supervision and Curriculum Development
http://www.ascd.org

Educational Leadership

National Middle School Association
http://www.nmsa.org

Middle School Journal

TEACHER TALKS . . .

Many new teachers getting ready for their first year have the idea that teaching is going to be easy, but it isn't. The first year is perhaps the hardest year because there are so many things you have to go through such as state certification requirements, administration expectations, not letting your students down, and not giving up after the first day. If you need to, go back to your mentors, college professors, and other experienced teachers to help you through that first year. Observing teaching techniques and going to educator conventions can help you come up with creative ideas for making your classroom an awesome learning experience for your students. It's also important to find an outlet for yourself after school that helps relieve your stress from the day. Remember, every teacher has had his or her first year and made it through, and so will you!

JENNIFER A. PONSART
Middle School Music Director
Davenport, Florida

National Board for Professional Teaching Standards
http://www.nbpts.org

Association for Childhood Education International
http://www.acei.org/jour.htm

Childhood Education

Teacher Organizations/Unions

American Federation of Teachers
http://www.aft.org

American Educator
American Teacher

National Education Association
http://www.NEA.org

NEA Today

Summary

Professionals, by definition, continue their education after initial certification. There are so many ways to broaden your knowledge and skills as a teacher. Participating in a professional learning community (PLC) at school is a powerful way of learning how to best meet the needs of your students. But other continuing educational opportunities abound. You can take courses online or at a local university, participate in webinars, join professional organizations in your specific discipline and read the journals they generate, apply for grants, and travel to broaden your cross-cultural understanding, to name just a few professional opportunities open to you. Create a teaching portfolio and, down the road, apply for National Board certification.

Reflect!

Find out if your local school has ever tried implementing professional learning communities. What were the benefits, and what were the challenges? Would you enthusiastically embrace the idea as a first-year teacher? Which of the other continuing education opportunities would most benefit you as a first-year teacher, and which ones are you likely to pursue?

UNIT 8 CHECKLIST

A Professional Life in Balance Checklist	For more information go to:
☐ Have I decided to become a reflective teacher?	Chapter 35
☐ Will I make a list of my strengths and weaknesses?	Chapter 35
☐ Have I located key places and people at school and in the community?	Chapter 36
☐ Have I begun to establish professional relationships with my principal, the support staff, and my colleagues?	Chapter 36
☐ Have I committed to leading a balanced life?	Chapter 37
☐ Will I accept that I am a work in progress?	Chapter 37
☐ Have I identified my stressors at home and at school?	Chapter 37
☐ Have I explored my state's requirements for continuing professional development?	Chapter 38
☐ Will I create my own teaching portfolio?	Chapter 38

Further Reading: A Professional Life in the Balance

Costantino, P., De Lorenzo, M., & Kobrinski, E. (2008). *Developing a professional teaching portfolio: A guide for success* (3rd ed.). Boston: Allyn & Bacon. This book provides information on how to create and maintain a teaching portfolio, paper or electronic, explaining what should be included, how to reflect on your work, and how to design your portfolio in a creative and engaging manner.

DuFour, R., DuFour, R., Eaker, R., & Many, T. (2006). *Learning by doing: A handbook for professional learning communities at work.* Bloomington, IN: Solution Tree. This handbook presents the rationale for establishing PLCs and defines the steps in establishing a PLC. It includes many handouts and reproducibles.

Losyk, B. (2005). *Get a grip: Overcoming stress and thriving in the workplace.* Hoboken, NJ: Wiley. This book provides tips and strategies for reducing stress through visualization, diet, exercise, etc., to revitalize the mind and body at home or in the workplace.

Morgenstern, J. (2004). *Organizing from the inside out: The foolproof system for organizing your home, your office and your life* (2nd ed.). New York: Holt. This book first discusses the reasons people are disorganized and then goes on to list specific instructions for organizing work and home spaces for maximum efficiency.

Morgenstern, J. (2004). *Time management from the inside out: The foolproof system for taking control of your schedule and your life* (2nd ed.). New York: Holt. In this easy-to-read book, the author discusses the reasons people run out of time and explains how to set realistic goals and use a device called the personal time map to conquer procrastination and lateness.

Singer, J. (Ed.). 2009. *The teacher's ultimate mastery guide: 77 proven prescriptions to build your resilience*. Thousand Oaks, CA: Corwin. This book fosters self-reflection, provides ways to reduce stressors, and includes many practical and entertaining anecdotes.

Professional Development Websites

Professional Development Sourcebook
http://www.edweek.org/tsb/

At this website (run by *Education Week* and *Teacher Magazine*), you can choose a topic and find many possible resources, including free offerings from other websites.

Pearson Professional Development
http://www.pearsonpd.com/webinars/

Pearson lists current webinars and offers an archive of recent webinars on nearly every topic imaginable.

Education World
http://www.educationworld.com/a_curr/index.shtml

Education World lists professional development webinars, courses, and many archived articles.

CHAPTER 39
THE LAST DAYS OF SCHOOL

No more pencils, no more books,
no more teachers' dirty looks.

Nursery Rhyme

There will come a time when you
believe everything is finished.
That will be the beginning.

Louis L'Amour

Effectiveness Essentials

- Maintaining order and interest up until the last day can be challenging.
- Use the time to have some fun with students, but never lose the focus on learning.
- Engage your students' help in reflecting back on the year and assessing what worked and what didn't.

EPILOGUE

TEACHER TALKS . . .

At our school we have what is called an "Exam Jam" (after end-of-grade-tests). We have a theme among our four fourth-grade classes. We rotate the kids throughout the day to different classrooms. For example, we had a fiesta one year—making Mexican-style hats, learning Mexican dances, making fried ice cream, and breaking piñatas.

Teachers can divide up topics, and kids will switch classes. For example, in one class a teacher will do a thematic unit on tornadoes, while another class studies geography. There are so many things that teachers can do to keep students interested, and it's fun for all. I think most everyone is burned out by the end and needs a nice break!

BRANDI STEPHENS
Fourth-Grade Teacher
Mebane, North Carolina

Before closing, I have a few tips for ending the school year. Books such as this one often provide numerous suggestions on how to get through a school year, but they rarely ever talk about how to wind down a school year. In fact, the final days of school are as important as the first days. They are a time for you and your students to reflect on the entire year or semester, and to solidify memories of your time together. It's a time to engage students in projects you didn't have time for all semester or year and to have fun with your class after all the test taking is over. It is time to dismantle your room and to plan for your own free time.

Maintaining Routines and Sustaining Interest

It's really not over until the report cards have been distributed, the tears have been shed, the hugs have been given, and the final goodbyes have been spoken. Your year-end activities will be influenced by the ages of your students, and the way you approach the final day or days will vary accordingly.

Kindergarteners will have no idea that their school year is coming to an end because this is their first year of school. Since very young children don't handle change well and have a great need for structure and security, seasoned kindergarten teachers suggest that you maintain routines, schedule, activities, and the room environment up to the very last day. Your job will be to reassure the little ones and provide a very smooth transition to vacation on that last day. You can read their favorite books; sing their favorite songs; and revisit their favorite field trips, experiences, and memories. Only after they are gone should you dismantle your room. Otherwise, they may be as upset as they were on the first day of school.

On the other hand, your older students will be champing at the bit for vacation to begin. They know what the last day of school means, and they will be counting down the days. Maintaining order and your students' interest can be a serious challenge. However, attendance is mandatory, and you will need to sustain their interest with engaging and motivating activities—for both your sake and theirs.

APPLY IT!

How can you sustain interest in the last days and weeks of school? Brainstorm all the possibilities.

This is the time to introduce some exciting projects since the standardized testing no longer dictates your curriculum. The last days of school may provide opportunities to go beyond the standards and design unique projects that will capture the students' interests and make them anxious to come to school each day.

One teacher, Perry Lopez, creates these projects all year long; but as a novice you probably will feel more comfortable doing large-scale projects such as these at the end of the year, when interest tends to flag. Read the Teacher Talks on this page.

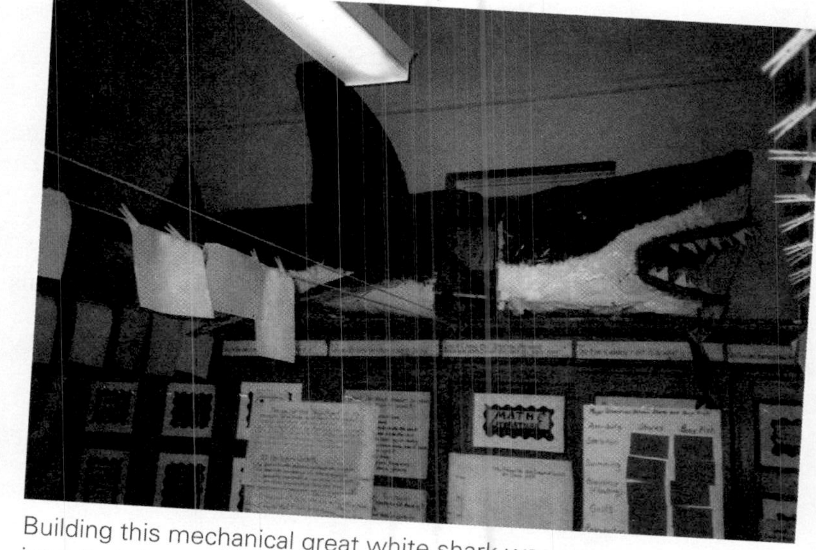
Building this mechanical great white shark was an interdisciplinary project.

Having Fun With Your Students

At the end of the year you can have some guilt-free fun with your students and change both the content and the structure of the day or period. This is the time to try out some different structures, activities, materials, and media. Even though the curriculum has been covered and the standards are all checked off in your planning materials, you still have to make sure that the activities you plan, although fun, are substantive and justifiable to parents and administrators.

One way to ensure that students do not equate fun with goofing off is to assure them that projects are graded up until the very end, when the report cards are distributed and/or sent home. Older students, who are already familiar with your rubrics, can even design their own rubrics to assess the "fun" projects.

Here Are Some Ideas for Elementary School

The list of possible exciting end-of-year ideas is as long as your imagination can make it, but here are some to get you started. Many will relate to the curriculum; others are add-on fun activities that extend the curriculum or create new interests.

TEACHER TALKS . . .

I was able to add an extra curriculum that enhanced my students' higher-thinking skills through interdisciplinary projects within my classroom. Some of our projects included constructing a 23-foot mechanical great white shark, a 17-foot Brooklyn Bridge, a full-scale model of the 1903 Wright Brothers' flyer hanging from the classroom ceiling, and seven 1903 Wright flyer 1/8-scale models.

PERRY LOPEZ
Fifth-Grade Teacher
Bronx, New York

TEACHER TALKS . . .

In my first year of teaching, on the very last day, I was so emotional as I said goodbye to my first graders that I forgot to distribute their report cards. Freud might say I had a hard time letting go. That aside, I had to hand-deliver each and every report card individually that afternoon. That gave me a chance to say goodbye to parents as well.

JASON PAYTAS
First-Grade Teacher
Arcata, California

- Build a diorama reflecting a literature selection.
- Construct story character puppets and re-create stories students enjoyed.
- Study a new topic such as bubbles or anime drawing.
- Take guided walks to collect materials for collages or pressing flowers.
- Design, construct, and fly kites.
- Spend one whole day on each subject.
- Rotate to centers such as crafts, stories, or projects.
- Present unique book talks.
- Participate in scavenger hunts online.
- Create mini skits or plays about subjects students have studied.
- Cook simple recipes or make ice cream.
- Read books about the last days of school, such as
  Last Day Blues (2006) by Julie Danneberg and Judith Dufour Love. Watertown, MA: Charlesbridge.
  The Last Day of School (2006) by Louise Borden and Adam Gustavson. New York: McElderry.

Here Are Some Ideas for Middle and High School

Your older students might enjoy some of the aforementioned activities, but here are some other ideas that might appeal to preteens and teens.

- Compare and contrast the movie version with a book students have read.
- Create mini science, math, or art projects.
- Students use a creative format to review a topic.
- Students "grade" the class—i.e., what did you like most, least about this class?
- Write a letter to next year's students about the class.
- Play games such as basketball against the staff.
- Play year-end *Jeopardy*.
- Become student teachers, and teach the class in pairs or triads based on their interests.
- Develop and implement a community service project.
- Create a commercial, poster, or brochure for the class or course.
- Make a year-end video or PowerPoint with photos of every student.

Reflecting on the Year

The end of school is also a time for creating lasting memories of the year and reflecting back, especially for those students who will be moving on to another school. There are many activities that fall into this category.

- Have the students put together autograph books or anthologies of their writing.
- Create slide shows on PowerPoint with photos and artifacts of the year.
- Have each student create a Power-Point slide of his or her fondest memory.
- Create calendars for next year with photos of main events or activities.
- Have students write autobiographies for a mini yearbook.
- Take a photo of the class or make a collage for everyone to take home.
- Make a book of class records—something unique to each student or awards for each student.

This is also a time for you to reflect back on your year. Look over your class list, and think about your successes and what you might have done differently to better engage each of your students. During your vacation, you can think about what you have learned from the Apply It! activity on the following page.

APPLY IT!

Make a list of at least 10 post-school activities you have planned. They can be simple ones such as "read three mystery books" or as complex as "take a long-awaited trip to a vacation destination."

Dismantling Your Room

To make your life easier next year, use the same care in dismantling your classroom as you did in assembling it. If you do this slowly and enlist the help of your students, the job will be done in a week or less. Remember to wait until school really ends before dismantling the room while your kindergarteners are still there. Carefully pack away your materials, bulletin board items, supplies, etc., in see-through plastic tubs. To be extra meticulous, mark each tub with a list of contents.

Saying Your Goodbyes and Planning Ahead

The last day of school is a celebratory time. You want to celebrate with your students and say your goodbyes to them

EPILOGUE

and to the staff. This might be a time to thank especially helpful staff members with a small token of appreciation or a note. If the staff is having an after school get-together, make sure you attend. Those events bring closure to the year and create a sense of community. Some staffs have one every Friday, but the last one is special. The staff members will probably share their vacation plans, and you should already have some plans, too.

APPLY IT!

Complete these sentence stems, and have each student do the same. Compile them into a list to reflect on during your free time. This feedback will make you a better teacher.

The best three things about this year were . . .
The three projects I liked best were . . .
Five words to describe the students in this class are . . .
This year could have been better if . . .
If I could change the class rules . . .
If I could change the class schedule . . .
We could have used more . . .
We could have used less . . .
The most interesting subjects/ topics were . . .
The most boring subjects/ topics were . . .

STUDENT SAYS . . .

At the end of the year my teacher had Awards Day. This was good because we got to give awards to each other, and it showed how well we did in things through the year.

ERIK
Fourth Grader, Age 9
Brookline, Massachusetts

CHAPTER 40
NOW IT'S TIME TO TEACH!

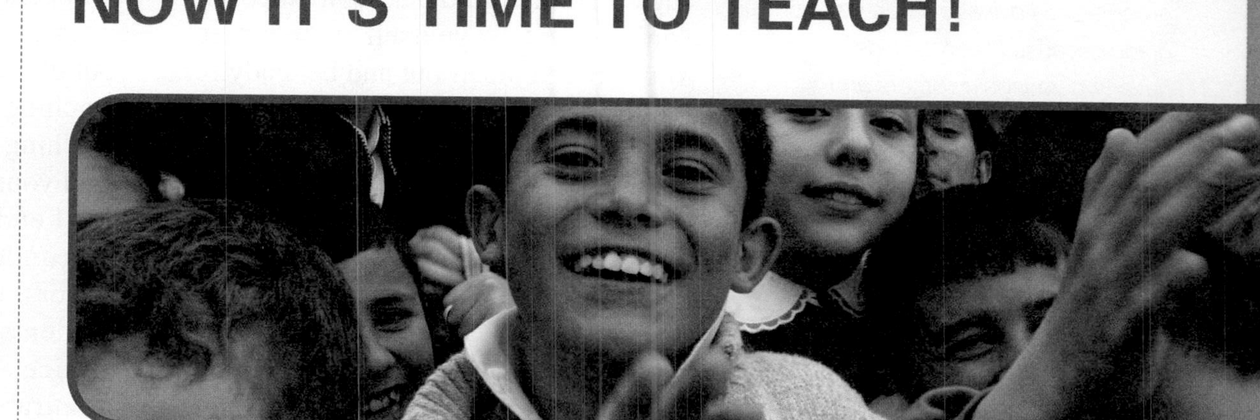

Effectiveness Essentials

- Recognize that there will be good days and bad days and you need to be self-forgiving of mistakes.
- Teaching is a dynamic interaction between you and your students.
- Learn to trust yourself and internalize your own unique teaching style from all the well-intentioned advice you receive.
- Your professional development is a process that can't be short-circuited and will continue as long as you call yourself a teacher.

Anyone who has never made a mistake has never tried anything new.

Albert Einstein

There are no secrets to success. It is a result of preparation, hard work, and learning from failure.

Colin Powell

STUDENT SAYS . . .

I want to be a teacher. It seems like fun and I like to do all of the things teachers do—like teaching, grading, making decorations for the classroom, making charts, and giving stars. I'd like to teach first grade because I like little kids. I have two younger brothers and one younger sister, and I like to play school with them and teach them things I know how to do. My sister Megan thinks I would be a good teacher because she says I'm a great sister, very nice, good with little kids, smart, patient, and treat everyone the same.

My older sister gave me a teacher's kit for Christmas, and I use all of the things in the kit when we play school—an outfit, pointer, letters, numbers, and arithmetic signs. My teacher talks about current events, and I would like to do that with my students. I like talking about real things that are going on in the world, and I would have my students bring in newspaper articles and I'd put them on the bulletin board.

ERIN
Fourth Grader, Age 9
Glenview, Illinois

There will be good days and bad days, so you need to be self-forgiving of mistakes. Don't spend your first week trying to implement every teaching strategy and idea learned in your credential program. Ease up on yourself, and all will fall into place. At all costs, don't overextend yourself at the outset. You'll tire yourself out and be ready for a vacation two weeks into the school year. There are way too many good, qualified teachers in this country who gave up on the profession after only a year because they pushed themselves too hard in the beginning. Be patient! Pace yourself!

This guide will help you take the first tentative steps across the threshold of your teaching career. Your experience will mold and shape you, and you will continue to grow and learn with each successive year.

Teaching is a dynamic interaction between you and your students. The experience will mutually change your lives in both big and small ways. Let your students guide your development as you guide theirs.

You have to trust yourself and internalize your own unique teaching style from all the well-intentioned advice you receive. That said, take the advice contained in this book and in other books as well as the advice offered by colleagues and in courses, and incorporate what works for you.

Your professional development is a process that can't be short-circuited and will continue as long as you call yourself a teacher. Listen, learn, ask questions, but ultimately, during your first year of teaching and beyond, your personal teaching style will emerge and you'll find your own way.

I end with an expression of gratitude to all the teachers, administrators, teacher educators, and students who contributed the practical advice and realistic depiction of this admirable profession. This book could not have been written without your participation. If you would like to be included in the Teacher Talks . . . or Myth Buster! features in the next edition, please contact me at professorellen@roadrunner.com. If your children or students would like to contribute to the Student Says . . . feature, I will send permission slips to them as well.

Now, as my mother used to say when I was starting any new endeavor, "*Put your right foot forward and do it!*"

APPLY IT!

- Review the Effectiveness Essentials that begin each chapter or go back over the entire book. For each chapter, highlight or note those ideas that you will implement. Use your reflection journal to note these ideas, strategies, and activities.
- In your reflective journal, make a list of unanswered questions or concerns and find resources to address them.
- Recite 10 times per day the following wise sayings teachers have suggested:
  - I will be as forgiving of myself as I am of students.
  - I will be realistic and won't dwell on mistakes.
  - This, too, shall pass.
  - Everything is a learning experience.
  - It seemed like the best thing to do at the time.
  - Mistakes are learning opportunities.
  - I'll do my best every day; then I won't worry.

AVOID IT!

The "super-teacher syndrome" is characterized by a debilitating perfectionism. You will make mistakes. We all make mistakes. You can either learn from your mistakes or be paralyzed by them. The quest to be perfect, to be a super-teacher, can be replaced with can-do attitudes.

TEACHER TALKS . . .

I will always remember what one of my professors told me: "You've got to be gentle as a dove yet sly as a fox when dealing with students." He was right! Regardless of what we hope for, our students are thinking up ways to raise our blood pressure. New teachers are a great target because of a lack of experience in the classroom. Whatever age you teach in any subject, stay one step ahead of the kids by thinking like them. I've noticed that they try the same things I did when I was a kid, just with new toys. They always ask me, "How did you know?" I simply reply, "Because once, a long time ago, I tried the exact same things."

JENNIFER A. PONSART
Music Director
Davenport, Florida

Final Teacher Reflections . . .

I have an incurable disease:
I love teaching! I may have contracted it as a preschooler from my parents. I first realized it at age six, when I gathered a group of neighborhood children weekly to teach them. This love has compelled me to see the world with excitement and enthusiasm and develop songs, games, and special ways of inspiring eager minds and challenging others with limited ability or desire. It has connected me to all age levels and a number of cultures and countries. It is unrelenting in its power to increase and harness my imagination. This love grows in intensity as I'm stretched and improved and entreated to move forward. Now that I'm in my eighties, I see no possibility of recovery from or remission of my love of teaching.

BETTY ROSENTRATER
Retired Teacher
Santa Barbara, California

If I had it to do all over again, I'd most definitely still become a teacher. Being a teacher has helped me personally to be more patient, kind, considerate, and understanding. Being a teacher has fostered my ability to learn and grow, to embrace lifelong learning, and to keep current with the many changes taking place in curriculum, education, and technology.

It is important to enter teaching for the right reasons. If you are becoming a teacher to have June, July, and August off, think again. Most summers are filled with courses, inservice training, writing curriculum, and more. If you are becoming a teacher because you love learning and helping others learn, because you want to make a difference in the lives of youth, because you're willing to work hard and against many odds to help students learn, then teaching probably is for you.

ROBIN SMITH
Educational Technology Specialist
Hollidaysburg, Pennsylania

(quoted on
www.EducationWorld.com)

In September 2002, I walked away from a secure, high-paying job in the corporate world to fulfill my lifelong desire to teach. Today I have the job of my dreams, teaching local K–4 students about technology. Although the financial sacrifice (a cut in pay of almost two-thirds) was enormous, I would do it all again in an instant. Why? I am surrounded every day by the two things I love most in the world: children and technology. And extracurricular work outside of school has substantially reduced the financial impact of my career move. I have never been happier.

KEVIN JARRETT
Technology Facilitator, Grades K–4
Northfield, New Jersey

(quoted on
www.EducationWorld.com)

Several years ago, I received a Christa McAuliffe Fellowship, which led me to leave the classroom for a few years to take a position at our state department of educa-tion. Although my experiences there were invaluable because I got to work with teach-ers from all around the state, I missed the classroom. After nearly five years away, I re-turned to teaching fourth grade. I can hon-estly say that the only thing I miss is the longer lunch period. I love being in a school again!

It's true that I don't make a lot of money and the hours are long, but if you like working with children, there is nothing better to do with your life.

KATHLEEN CAVE
Fifth-Grade Teacher
Sparks, Maryland
(quoted on www.EducationWorld.com)

I am a kindergarten teacher who retired and then returned again to teach young children. Someone asked me why I did this. What was it about teaching that captured my heart and drew me back to the classroom? I know what it was. It was the joy. I missed it.

It's the joy that comes as you listen to children sing and then join them as they dance. It's the joy that comes as you hang another drawing on the wall and you see the growth and development you have been waiting to see in this particular child. It's the joy that comes when parents and teachers work together and every single child begins to blossom. It's the joy that comes at the end of the day when you suddenly feel a pull on your hand and one of "yours" comes back to give you that special good-bye hug. It's the joy that comes when these same boys and girls become responsible citizens and treat their classmates with kindness and respect. It's the joy that comes when you know you have done what you were trained to do. You have introduced the children to the joy of learning. You have talked about the joy of a caring heart. You watch as eyes open wide, smiles appear, and confidence grows. They are on their way. Once again, there is joy.

The best joy of all? That's when you put it all together and realize that you do, indeed, make a difference in a child's life. That's what it's all about. That's what teaching means to me.

Remember to look for the joy. It's there. Don't miss it.

ANN KOCHER
Retired Kindergarten Teacher
San Bernardino, California

REFERENCES

Unit 1

Brock, B., & Grady, M. (1996). *Beginning teacher induction programs.* Paper presented at the annual meeting of the National Council of Professors of Educational Administration, Corpus Christi, TX (ERIC Document Reproduction Service No. ED 399361).

Center for Teaching Quality. (2008, November). Teacher working conditions: A review and look to the future. http://www.teachingquality.org/twc. Retrieved July 26, 2010.

Dewey, J. (1933/1993). *How we think: A restatement of the relation of reflective thinking to the educative process.* Boston: Houghton Mifflin.

Futernick, K. (2007). *A possible dream: Retaining California's teachers so all students learn.* Sacramento: California State University.

Hayasaki, E. (2004, August 15). Teachers lose tax breaks for class supplies. *Los Angeles Times,* pp. B1, B9.

Interstate New Teacher Assessment and Support Consortium (INTASC). (2010). Model core teaching standards: A resource for state dialogue. http://www.ccsso.org/intasc. Retrieved July 26, 2010.

Lidstone, M., & Hollingsworth, S. (1992). A longitudinal study of cognitive change in beginning teachers: Two patterns of learning to teach. *Teacher Education Quarterly, 19*(4), 39–57.

Met Life. (2009). 25th annual Met Life teacher survey looks back on more than two decades of education reform. http://www.metlife.org. Retrieved July 26, 2010.

Moir, E. (1990). Phases of first-year teaching. In *California New Teacher Center Newsletter.* http://www.newteachercenter.org/articles.php?p=2. Retrieved September 3, 2010.

National Board for Professional Teaching Standards (NBPTS). (1989). What teachers should know and be able to do: The five core propositions of the National Board for Professional Standards. http://www.nbpts.org/the_standards/the_five_core_propositions. Retrieved July 26, 2010.

National Commission on Teaching and America's Future. (2007). High teacher turnover drains school and district resources. http://nctaf.org/resources/news/press releases/CTT.htm. Retrieved January 20, 2010.

National Comprehensive Center for Teacher Quality and Public Agenda. (2008). Lessons learned: New teachers talk about the jobs, challenges and long-range plans. *Teaching in Changing Times, 3.* http://www.publicagenda.org. Retrieved December 5, 2009.

National Education Association (NEA). (2009). Salary statistics. http://www.nea.org/home/30799.htm. Retrieved July 26, 2010.

U.S. Department of Education. (2002). *No Child Left Behind. A desktop reference.* Washington, DC: Education Publications Center.

U.S. Department of Education, National Center for Education Statistics. (2008). The condition of education, 2008 (NCES 2008-031). http://nces.ed.gov/pubs2008/2008031.pdf. Retrieved July 26, 2010.

U.S. Department of Education. (2009). The American Recovery and Reinvestment Act of 2009: Saving and creating jobs and reforming education. http://www2.ed.gov/policy/gen/leg/recovery/implementation.html. Retrieved August 7, 2010.

U.S. Department of Education. 2010. Race to the Top fund. http://www2.ed.gov/programs/racetothetop/index.html. Retrieved August 7, 2010.

Unit 2

Fisher, A. (1991). *Always wondering: Some favorite poems of Aileen Fisher* (10th ed.). New York: HarperCollins.

Rothstein-Fisch, C., & Trumbull, E. (2008). *Managing diverse classrooms: How to build on students' cultural strengths.* Alexandria VA: ASCD.

Unit 3

Kaiser Family Foundation. (2010). Generation M2. Menlo Park. CA: Author.

Kottler, J. (2003). *Secrets for secondary school teachers: How to succeed in your first year.* Thousand Oaks, CA: Corwin.

Kounin, J. (1977). *Discipline and group management in the classroom.* New York: Krieger.

Public Broadcasting Service (PBS). (2009). Digitally inclined [Survey conducted by Grunwald Associates]. http://www.pbs.org/teachers/_files/pdf/annual-pbs-survey-report.pdf. Retrieved July 27, 2010.

Unit 4

Canter, L., & Canter, M. (2001). *Assertive discipline: Positive behavior management for today's classroom* (3rd ed.). Santa Monica, CA: Canter & Associates.

Dreikurs, R., Grunwald, B., & Pepper, F. (1998). *Maintaining sanity in the classroom* (2nd ed.). Philadelphia: Taylor & Francis.

Glasser, W. (1975). *Schools without failure.* New York: Harper & Row.

Glasser, W. (1998). *Choice theory in the classroom.* New York: HarperCollins.

Jones, F., Jones, P., Jones, J. L., & Jones, F. (2007). *Tools for teaching.* Santa Cruz, CA: Jones & Associates.

Kounin, J. (1977). *Discipline and group management in classrooms.* New York: Holt, Rinehart, & Winston.

Marzano, R., Marzano, J., & Pickering, D. (2003). *Classroom management that works.* Alexandria, VA: ASCD.

Maslow, A. (1987). *Motivation and personality* (3rd ed.). New York: HarperCollins.

National Crime Prevention Council. (2010). Cyberbullying. http://www.ncpc.org/cyberbullying. Retrieved September 5, 2010.

National School Safety Center. (2010). Fact sheet on bullying. http://www.schoolsafety.us/free-resources/bullying-in-schools-fact-sheet-series. Retrieved September 5, 2010.

Nelsen, J. (2000). *Positive discipline in the classroom* (rev. ed.). NewYork: Ballantine.

U.S. Department of Education, Institute of Education Sciences. (2009). Indicators of school crime and safety. http://nces.ed.gov/programs/crimeindicators/crimeindicators2009/key.asp. Retrieved July 27, 2010.

U.S. Department of Education, Office for Civil Rights (2008). Civil rights data collection, 2006. http://ocrdata.ed.gov/ocr2006rv30/xls/2006Projected.html. Retrieved July 27, 2010.

Weinstein, C. S., Tomlinson-Clarke, S., & Curran, M. (2004). Toward a conception of culturally responsive classroom management. *Journal of Teacher Education, 55*(1), 25–38.

Unit 5

Bloom, B., Mesia, B., & Krathwohl, D. (1964). *Taxonomy of educational objectives: The affective domain and the cognitive domain.* New York: McKay.

Biological Sciences Curriculum Study (BSCS). (1997). *Science for life and living* (3rd ed.). Dubuque, IA: Kendall-Hunt.

Charles, C. M., & Senter, G. (2005). *Elementary classroom management* (4th ed.). Boston: Allyn & Bacon.

Davidman, L., & Davidman, P. (2001). *Teaching with a multicultural perspective* (3rd ed.). Boston: Allyn & Bacon.

Free stuff for kids. (2001). Deephaven, MN: Meadowbrook.

Gardner, H. (1993). *Multiple intelligences: The theory in practice.* New York: Basic Books.

Gardner, H. (1999). *Intelligence reframed: Multiple intelligences for the 21st century.* New York: Basic Books.

Hunter, M. (2004). *Mastery teaching: Increasing instructional effectiveness in elementary and secondary schools* (updated by R. Hunter). Thousands Oaks, CA: Corwin.

McNeil, M. (2009, June 10). 46 states commit to common-standards push. *Education Week.* http://www.edweek.org/ew/contributors/michele.mcneil.html. Retrieved July 28, 2010.

U.S. Bureau of Labor. (2010–2011). Occupational outlook. http://www.bls.gov/OCO/. Retrieved July 28, 2010.

U.S. Congress. (2001). No Child Left Behind Act. http://www2.ed.gov/policy/elsec/leg/esea02/index.html. Retrieved July 28, 2010.

U.S. Department of Education. (2009a). Indicators of school reform. http://www2.ed.gov/speeches/2009/06/06222009.html. Retrieved July 28, 2010.

U.S. Department of Education. (2009b). Press release on Race to the Top. http://www2.ed.gov/news/pressreleases/2009/11/11122009.html. Retrieved July 28, 2010.

U.S. Department of Education. (2009c). Secretary Arne Duncan's monthly stakeholder's meeting. http://www.ed.gov/news/speeches/2009/09/0924299.html Retrieved July 28, 2010.

U.S. Department of Education. (2010). Blueprint for reform. http://www2.ed.gov/policy/elsec/leg/blueprint/index.html. Retrieved July 28, 2010.

U.S. House of Representatives. (1994). Goals 2000 Educate America Act. http://www2.ed.gov/legislation/GOALS2000/TheAct/sec102.html. Retrieved July 28, 2010.

Unit 6

Ariza, E. (2009). *Not for ESOL teachers: What every classroom teacher needs to know about the linguistically, culturally, and ethnically diverse student* (2nd ed.). Boston: Allyn & Bacon.

Ausubel, D. (1968). *Educational psychology: A cognitive view.* New York: Holt, Rinehart, & Winston.

Ballantyne, K.G., Sanderman, A.R., & Levy, J. (2008). *Educating English language learners: Building teacher capacity.* Washington, DC: National Clearinghouse for English Language Acquisition.

Cotton, K. (1990). *Expectations and student outcomes: No. 7. School Improvement Research Theory.* Portland, OR: Northwest Regional Laboratory.

Diaz-Rico, L., & Weed, K. Z. (2010). *The cross-cultural language and academic development handbook: A complete K–12 reference guide* (4th ed.). Upper Saddle River, NJ: Prentice Hall.

Echevarria, J., Vogt, M., & Short, D. (2007). *Making content comprehensible for English learners: The SIOP model* (3rd ed.). Boston: Allyn & Bacon.

Gardner, H. (1993). *Frames of mind: The theory of multiple intelligences* (10th ed.). New York: Basic Books.

Gardner, H. (1999). *Intelligence reframed: Multiple intelligences for the 21st century.* New York: Basic Books.

Good, T. L. (1987). Two decades of research on teacher expectations: Findings and future directions. *Journal of Teacher Education, 38,* 32–47.

Howard, M. (2009). *RTI from all sides: What every teacher needs to know.* Portsmouth, NH: Heinemann.

Johns, K., & Espinoza, C. (1992). *Mainstreaming language minority children in reading and writing.* Bloomington, IN: Phi Delta Kappa.

Joyce, B., & Weil, M. (2008). *Models of teaching* (8th ed.). Boston: Allyn & Bacon.

Marzano, R., Pickering, D., & Pollack, J. (2004). *Classroom instruction that works: Research-based strategies for increasing student achievement.* Alexandria, VA: ASCD.

Met Life. (2009). Survey of the American teacher. http://www.metlife.com/about/corporate-profile/citizenship/metlife-foundation/metlife-survey-of-the-american-teacher.html. Retrieved July 28, 2010.

National Center for Response to Intervention. (2010). Essential components of RTI: A closer look at Response to Intervention. http://www.rti4success.org/. Retrieved July 28, 2010.

National Comprehensive Center for Teacher Quality and Public Agenda. (2008). Lessons learned: New teachers talk about the jobs, challenges and long-range plans. Teaching in Changing Times, 3. http://www.publicagenda.org. Retrieved December 5, 2009.

Ogle, D. S. (1986). K-W-L group instructional strategy. In A. S. Palincsar, D. S. Ogle, B. F. Jones, & E. G. Carr (Eds.), *Teaching reading as thinking* (Teleconference Resource Guide, pp. 11–17). Alexandria, VA: ASCD.

Palincsar, A. S., & Brown, A. L. (1986). Interactive teaching to promote independent learning from text. *The Reading Teacher, 39* (8), 771–777.

Peregoy, S., & Boyle, O. (2008). *Reading, writing and learning in ESL: A resource book for K–12 teachers* (5th ed.). Boston: Allyn & Bacon.

Rosenthal, R., & Jacobson, L. (1968/1996). *Pygmalion in the classroom: Teacher expectation and pupils' intellectual development* (rev. ed.). New York: Irvington.

Rowe, M. (1986). Slowing down may be a way of speeding up. *Journal of Teacher Education, 37* (1), 43–50.

Stahl, R. (1990). *Using "think-time" behaviors to promote students' information processing, learning, and on-task participation: An instructional module.* Tempe: Arizona State University.

Tomlinson, C. (2004). *How to differentiate instruction in mixed-ability classrooms* (2nd ed.). Alexandria, VA: ASCD.

U.S. Department of Education, National Center for Education Statistics. (2009). The condition of education, 2009 (NCES 2009-081). http://nces.ed.gov/fastfacts/display.asp?id=16. Retrieved July 28, 2010.

U.S. Department of Education, National Center for Education Statistics. (2010). Percentage of students with disabilities enrolled in regular classrooms. http://nces.ed.gov/fastfacts/display.asp?id=59. Retrieved July 28, 2010.

Unit 7

Bear, D., Invernizzi, M., Templeton, S., & Johnston, F. (2007). *Words their way* (4th ed.). Upper Saddle River, NJ: Prentice Hall.

Cochran, J. (1989). Escape from paperwork. *Instructor, 99* (3), 76–77.

Emmer, E., & Evertson, C. (2008). *Classroom management for middle and high school teachers* (8th ed.). Boston: Allyn & Bacon.

Herrold, K., & O'Donnell, K. (2008). Parent and family involvement in education, 2006–2007 school year. National Household Education Surveys Program of 2007 (NCES 2008-050). Washington, DC: U.S. Department of Education.

Met Life. (2009). Survey of the American teacher. http://www.metlife.com/about/corporate-profile/citizenship/metlife-foundation/metlife-survey-of-the-american-teacher.html. Retrieved July 28, 2010.

Met Life and Harris Interactive. (2007). Survey of the American teacher: The homework experience (ERIC doc. 500012). http://www.eric.ed.gov. Retrieved July 28, 2010.

Public Agenda. (2004). Survey: Sports, arts, clubs, volunteering: Out-of-school activities play crucial, positive role for kids. http://www.publicagenda.org/press_releases/survey-sports-arts-clubs-volunteering-out-school-activities-play-crucial-positive-role-kids. Retrieved July 28, 2010.

U.S. Department of Education, National Center for Educational Statistics. (2009). Contexts of elementary and secondary education: Indicator 30 parent and family involvement in education. http://nces.ed.gov/programs/coe/2009/section4/indicator30.asp. Retrieved July 28, 2010.

U.S. Department of Education. (2010). Blueprint for reform. http://www2.ed.gov/policy/elsec/leg/blueprint/index.html. Retrieved July 28, 2010.

Unit 8

DuFour, R. (2006). *Learning by doing: A handbook for professional learning communities at work.* Bloomington, IN: Solution Tree.

DuFour, R., DuFour, R., Eaker, R. & Many, T. (2006). *Learning by doing: A handbook for professional learning communities at work.* Bloomington, IN: Solution Tree.

Grant, C., & Zeichner, K. (1984). On becoming a reflective teacher. In C. Grant (Ed.), *Preparing for reflective teaching* (pp. 1–8). Boston: Allyn & Bacon.

Met Life. (2009). Survey of the American teacher: Collaborating for student success. http://www.metlife.com/assets/cao/contributions/foundation/american-teacher/MetLife_Teacher_Survey_2009_Part_1.pdf?SCOPE=Metlife. Retrieved July 30, 2010.

Moir, E. (1990). Phases of first-year teaching. In *California New Teacher Center Newsletter.* http://www.newteachercenter.org/articles.php?p=2. Retrieved September 3, 2010.

U.S. Department of Education, National Center for Education Statistics (2007–2008). The beginning teacher longitudinal study. http://nces.ed.gov/surveys/btls/cohort.asp. Retrieved July 30, 2010.

INDEX

A

Acceptance, 160
ACT, 407, 408, 409
Activities
  classification activities, 307, 310, 311
  compliment activity, 111
  discipline clarification activity, 161
  extracurricular activities, 400
  individual differences and, 143
  last days of school activities, 467–468
  meaningful activities, 184–185
  multiple intelligences, 248–249, 335–336, 337
  post-school activities, 469
  self-concept activities, 199
  sponge activities, 185–186, 397
Adaptive technologies, 147
Adequate yearly progress (AYP), 406
Adjectives, students learning each other's names, 76
Administrators, professional dress, 64
Advance organizers, 315–318
Alternative credential programs, 4
Always Wondering (Fisher), 42
American Recovery and Reinvestment Act (2009), 11, 222
American Sign Language (ASL)
  bathroom and water fountain routines, 118, 119
  instructional routines, 130, 131
  nonverbal interventions and, 205, 206
Analogies, 313, 314
Answer columns, 397–398
Application process, for monitors, 137–138
Artifacts on display, classroom climate, 200
ASL. *See* American Sign Language (ASL)
Assessment. *See also* Standardized tests
  attitude inventories, 388–389
  authentic assessment, 370, 371–377
  autobiographies, 389
  criterion-referenced tests, 370–371
  diagnostic assessments, 379–381
  feedback on instruction, 383, 384, 431
  interest inventories, 386, 387, 388, 390, 400
  interviews, 385
  monitoring student progress, 369–370
  norm-referenced tests, 370
  portfolios, 378, 379, 395–398
  standards and, 369
  teacher-made tests, 380
Assigning more work, avoiding, 212
Assumed inadequacy, misbehavior, 172, 175–176
Attendance, record keeping, 392–393
Attention
  group's attention, 187
  misbehavior and, 172–173
Attitude inventories, 388–389
Ausubel, David, 315–316
Authentic assessment
  five steps to, 372–375
  process of learning and, 371–372
  rubrics and, 372, 373
  as type of assessment, 370
  writing lesson plan and rubric, 376–377
Autobiographical bulletin boards, 26, 27, 67
Autobiographies, of students, 389, 416
Autobiography poem, 67, 416

B

Baby picture—guess who?, 100
Back-to-school postcard, 28
Bathroom passes, 117, 118, 119
Bathroom routines, 116–119, 121
Beginning-the-day routines
  ideas for, 112
  predictability in, 110
  rituals of, 110–111
Belonging, sense of, classroom climate, 198
Bilingual coordinators, 357
Bilingual instructional aides, 280–281
Biological Sciences Curriculum Study, 257
Birthday board, 99
Bloom's taxonomy, 244, 245, 306, 326, 394
Bodily/kinesthetic intelligence, 334, 335
Body language
  classroom climate and, 194
  classroom management and, 205–207
Bracey, Gerald, 369
Buddy teacher programs, 14, 21, 22, 392, 439
Bulletin boards
  autobiographical, 26, 27, 67
  baby picture—guess who?, 100
  birthday board, 99
  cohesive classroom community, 140
  current events, 101
  curriculum preview, 42
  designing, 98–99
  ideas for, 99–103
  individual bulletin board spaces, 102
  instructional boards, 100–101
  nonverbal messages of, 97
  purposes of, 99, 100, 103
  reading encouragement, 100
  sharing classrooms, 61
  star(s) of the week, 100
  "Student of the Week," 196, 197
  student self-portraits or silhouettes, 100
  students' photos, 74
  teacher's autobiography, 26, 27, 100
  tooth fairy report, 99–100
Bullying
  cell phones and, 147, 176–177, 180
  classroom policies, 178–179
  cyber bullying, 176–177
Bush, George W., 10, 221
Bystanders, bullying, 177

C

California Achievement Test, 407
California Standards Test, 407
Calling on students, 129, 130, 187
Canter, Lee, 162, 165
Can with name sticks
  for calling on students, 129, 130, 187
  for end-of-the-day compliments, 197
  for monitors, 136
Cell phones
  bullying and, 147, 176–177, 180
  instructional uses of, 148, 153, 158
  parents and, 147, 151, 154
  school policies, 147–148, 151, 157
  texting and, 151, 153, 154
Center for Applied Linguistics, 356
Center for Teaching Quality (CTQ), 19–20
Center rotation chart, 121
Center rotation wheel, 121, 122
Charles, C. M., 283
Charts
  center rotation chart, 121
  circular charts, 314
  comparing and contrasting, 306–307
  computer access charts, 153, 154
  KWL, 239, 301, 302
  pie charts, 325
  pocket chart, 108
  for reward systems, 163, 165, 167
  seating charts, 59, 60, 73, 109, 199, 285
  sequence charts, 314, 315
  "When I Need Help Chart," 127, 128
Choices. *See also* Student decision-making
  classroom climate and, 198–199
  differentiated instruction and, 337
  misbehavior and, 173
Circular charts, 314
Circular configuration, classroom arrangement, 57, 59
Class identity, 139–140
Classification activities, 307, 310, 311
Class job application, 138
Class lists. *See also* Seating charts
  job titles on clothespins for monitors, 137
  record keeping and, 393
Class logo/motto, 39, 139–140
Classmate scavenger hunt, 75
Classroom arrangements. *See also* Bulletin boards
  accessories, 96
  classroom climate and, 198
  classroom management and, 182–183
  decorating the space, 95–103
  dynamic nature of, 94–95
  educational goals and teaching style, 96
  instructional philosophy, 55
  nonverbal messages of, 97–98
  physical space conducive to learning, 93
  private spaces and quiet reading areas, 93–94, 96
  sharing rooms, 61
  student decision-making and, 59–60, 96
  variations of, 55–59
Classroom climate
  classroom meetings, 201–203
  respect and responsibility, 200–201
  teacher expectations and, 302
  thirteen ways to create, 192–200
Classroom management. *See also* Classroom rules; Discipline
  classroom arrangements and, 182–183
  classroom meetings and, 201–203
  cohesive classroom community, 139–140
  culturally responsive, 199–200, 207–208
  effectiveness of, 182
  emotional objectivity and, 189–190
  first day of school, 79
  first year of teaching and, 18
  individual differences and, 183–184
  instruction and, 186–189
  nonverbal interventions, 205–207
  parent/guardian conferences and, 209–210
  planning and, 184–186
  responses to avoid, 210–213
  serious behaviors and, 208–209
  teacher-student relationship and, 182, 192
Classroom meetings
  classroom climate, 201–203
  conflict resolution and, 197–198
  simplified steps for, 202
  substitute teachers and, 288
Classroom rules
  administration of, 83–84
  characteristics of good rules, 81
  cohesive classroom community, 138
  cultural norms and, 82–83
  enforcement, 84
  English language learners, 354
  first day of school, 37, 39, 45, 46, 50
  modeling, 189
  open house and, 417
  parents and, 84–85, 86, 417
  posting of, 82
  serious behaviors distinguished from rule-breaking behavior, 208–209
  seven principles for, 80–85
  student decision-making and, 79, 81, 85
  students with special needs and, 83
Classrooms
  computer-assisted classrooms, 151–154
  "eyes only" tour of, 40
  floor plan for kindergarten classroom, 40
  map of, 41
  movement within, 120–122, 193–194
  sharing, 59, 61
Clustering, classroom arrangement, 56, 57, 60
Cohesive classroom community, routines and schedule, 138–140
Community
  knowledge of, 27–29
  as resource for materials, 273–275
Comparing and contrasting
  classification, 307, 310
  research-based strategies, 306–309
  sorting, 307, 310
Compliments
  classroom climate, 196–197
  compliment activity, 111
Compliment tree, 196
Computer access charts, 153, 154
Computers. *See also* Technology
  access to, 153
  computer-assisted classrooms, 151–154
  curricular and personal objectives supported by, 143, 144
  evaluating software programs, 150
  Internet access in schools, 149
  as learning centers, 152
  rotation schedule for, 153, 154
  student instructional uses of, 145
  ten steps to computer confidence, 149
  as time savers, 143, 144
Computer viruses, 152
Concept maps, 314, 315
Concept webs, 239, 240
Conflict resolution, classroom climate, 197–198
Cooperation
  as low-key intervention, 206
  teacher-parent communication and, 417–419
Cooperative groups
  grading and, 399
  students learning each other's names, 76, 77
Cooperative learning
  classroom arrangement, 56
  classroom climate and, 198
  color-coded posters and tickets, 323
  computers and, 152–153
  feedback/evaluation, 323, 324
  principles of, 321–324
  problem solving and, 326–329
  reciprocal teaching and, 324–325, 326
  steps in, 323
  student achievement and, 301
  teacher expectations and, 301–302
Corporal punishment, 211, 213

Corrective feedback, 298, 299
Criterion-referenced tests, 370–371, 407
Cross-Cultural Consultant, communication norms, 66–67
CTQ (Center for Teaching Quality), 19–20
Cubbies from ice cream vats, 267, 269
Culturally responsive classroom management, 199–200, 207–208
Cultural norms
 classroom rules and, 82–83
 English language learners and, 353–354, 361
 eye contact and, 205, 208
Culture shock, 354–355
Cumulative record, diagnostic assessment, 380, 381
Current events, bulletin boards, 101
Curriculum planning
 changes in, 219
 as continuum, 225–226
 curriculum maps, 229, 230
 familiarity with standards, 224–225
 implementing standards-based curriculum, 227
 long-range planning, 223–230
 managing standards, 226–229
 nested planning, 226
 standards-based planning, 219–223
 unit planning and, 233
Curriculum preview, first day of school, 41–42, 46–47
Cyber bullying, 176–177

D
Dangles, 188
Day planner/calendar, 25–26
Delayed reaction, as low-key intervention, 207
Democratic training
 classroom meetings and, 201–203
 discipline and, 160–161
 modeling respect and, 200–201
Dewey, John, 16
Diagnostic assessments, 379–381
Diaz-Rico, L., 353, 357
Differentiated instruction
 choice and, 337
 classroom arrangement, 56
 classroom management and, 183
 components of instruction, 345–346
 core knowledge and, 344
 defining, 339
 English language learners and, 342–343, 352
 formative assessment and, 344–345
 lesson plans and, 340–341
 modifying for higher and lower achievers, 346–347
 multiple intelligences and, 346, 347
 principles of, 338–344
 Response to Intervention and, 348–349
 standards and, 341
 subject matter/student needs balance, 21
Direct instruction strategies, 315–317
Discipline. *See also* Classroom management; Classroom rules
 behavior modification, 161–165
 bullying, 176–178
 causes of misbehavior, 172–176, 180
 classroom arrangement and, 56
 culture and, 207–208
 first year of teaching and, 18
 instructional aides and, 283
 instructional management and, 186–189
 logical consequences, 161, 165, 167–170
 models of, 160–161
 preventing problems with, 182, 189
 professional dress and, 64
 school norms for, 79–80, 178, 208
 substitute teachers and, 286, 288
 symptoms of other serious behaviors, 178–180
District websites, 28
Diversity. *See also* Individual differences
 cooperative learning and, 322
 differentiated instruction and, 338–348
 multiple intelligences, 246–249, 301, 333–337
 statistics on, 332
 in students, 6, 7, 332
 weekly planning, 245–246
Duncan, Arne, 11, 222, 227

E
Echevarria, J., 356
Educators Progress Service, Inc., 272
Ejection from classroom, 211
Elearning Specialists
 cell phones, 157, 158
 technology use in classrooms, 154–155
Elections, for monitors, 137
Electronic organizers, 25–26
Elementary and Secondary Education Act, 223
Elementary students
 bathroom and water fountain routines, 116, 118
 beginning-the-day routines, 110
 books about school, 43
 bulletin boards, 97, 99, 101
 choosing seats, 59, 60
 classroom arrangement, 57
 classroom rules, 80, 81, 84
 cooperative learning, 322
 curriculum standards for, 226–227
 entering classroom, 108, 109
 feedback from, 384
 generic first-day schedule, 45–46
 last days of school activities, 467–468
 lesson plans, 260
 movement within room, 120
 orientation to school, 40
 portfolios, 379
 positive rewards, 162
 reading inventory for, 388
 student decision-making and, 42
 students learning each other's names, 73–74
 texting and, 151
 unit planning and, 233
 weekly planning and, 243
Emmer, E. T., 399
Emotional objectivity, classroom management, 189–190
Emotions, recognizing possible causes of, 172
Empowerment, conflict resolution, 197–198
Encouragement
 logical consequences and, 161, 165, 167–170
 as low-key intervention, 207
 parent/guardian conferences and, 210
Ending-the-day routines
 closure and, 111–113
 compliment activity, 111
 predictability of, 110
Engagement. *See also* Research-based strategies; Teacher expectations
 classroom management and, 185–186, 187, 188
English language learners
 acknowledgement of students, 44
 audio books for, 148
 bilingual instructional aides, 280–281
 classroom arrangement, 60–61, 97
 cooperative learning and, 321
 cultural norms and, 353–354, 361
 culture shock and, 354–355
 differentiated instruction and, 342–343, 352
 entrance and exit routines, 109
 establishing rapport, 66–67
 gestures, visuals, and peer translators for, 40
 immersion programs, 355, 356
 lesson plans and, 359
 monitorial roles for, 136
 multicultural studies and, 360–363
 promoting English language development, 358
 sheltered English, 239–240, 355–356
 strategies for, 355–359
 unit planning and, 239–240
Entering classroom
 procedure for, 108–109
 routine for, 107–108
Evaluation
 cooperative learning and, 323, 324
 lesson plans, 247
 period evaluation, 112
 of software programs, 150
Evertson, C. M., 399
Every-pupil response techniques, 188, 283, 395–396
Exiting classroom
 lines for, 109
 procedures for, 109–110
Extracurricular activities, 400
Extrinsic motivation, 161, 162
Eyeballing assignments, 397
Eye contact, as nonverbal intervention, 205

F
Federal mandates, 219–220, 224
Feedback
 authentic assessment and, 372, 375
 cooperative learning and, 323, 324
 corrective feedback, 298, 299
 on instruction, 383, 384, 431
 types of, 299
Field trips, 274–275
Figures of speech
 analogies, 313
 metaphors, 312
 research-based strategies, 311–313
 similes, 311, 312
Fire drills, 109
First-aid resource unit, 235–238
First day of school
 acknowledgement of each student, 44
 classroom rules, 37, 39, 45, 46, 50
 community and, 27–29
 curriculum preview, 41–42, 46–47
 easy work for, 44
 gathering resources for, 25–26
 generic elementary first-day schedule, 45–46
 literacy experiences, 42, 43, 44, 53
 motivation of students, 37–38
 nervousness, 36
 orientation to classroom/school, 40–41, 45
 overpreparation, 36–37
 planning classroom arrangement, 29
 preparing for, 25–30
 reaching out to students and parents, 26–27
 routines and schedule, 38–39, 44, 45–47
 setting tone for year, 44–53
 student decision-making and, 42
 teacher expectations and, 46, 79
 teacher-parent communication and, 416
 teachers' editions of textbooks, 30
 teaching supplies, 29–30
 ten basic principles for success, 36–44
First year of teaching
 anticipation phase, 12, 428
 challenges of, 3–4, 7, 16, 17, 18–21
 disillusionment phase, 13, 428
 fear of unknown, 5–6
 instructional needs, 19–20
 practical teaching tasks, 19
 reflection phase, 13, 428–432
 rejuvenation phase, 13, 428
 research versus practical advice, 22–23
 retention of teachers, 10
 subject matter/student needs balance, 21
 survival phase, 12, 428
 teacher preparation and, 2–6
Fisher, Aileen, 42
Flashcards for responses, 396
Flip-flops, 188
Folder storage with cereal boxes, 268, 269
Fragmentation
 instructional management, 187, 188
 unit planning and, 233
Free Stuff for Kids, 272
Free time policy, 130–131

G
Games, for standardized test preparation, 407, 408
Gardner, Howard, 246–249, 301, 333–337, 346, 347
Gender, and bullying, 177, 180
Generating and testing hypotheses, 326
Glasser, William, 22, 162, 176, 201–202
Goals
 educational goals and teaching style, 96
 mistaken goals and misbehavior, 172–176, 180, 208
Goals 2000, 220, 221
Grades and grading
 answer columns, 397–398
 answer keys, 397
 cooperative group grading, 399
 every-pupil responses, 395–396
 eyeballing assignments, 397
 grading on the spot, 394–395
 individual response boards, 396
 oral review, 397
 paperwork, 392–394
 review in eight boxes, 397, 398
 rubrics, 398
 self-marking, 396
 students exchanging papers, 395
Graphic organizers, 146, 307, 313–314, 315
GRE, 370
Group alerting, 126, 188
Group investigation, 326
Group work. *See also* Cooperative learning
 computers and, 152–153
 movement in classroom, 120–122
Grudges, 210

H
Harris Interactive, 400
Help-needed blocks, 127–128
Higher levels of thinking, Bloom's taxonomy, 244, 245
High School Exit Exam, 407
High school students
 bathroom and water fountain routines, 116, 118, 120
 beginning-the-day routines, 110, 111
 books about school, 43
 bulletin boards, 97, 99, 101–102
 choosing seats, 59
 classroom arrangement, 57, 59, 94
 classroom management and, 187
 classroom meetings and, 202
 classroom rules, 79–80, 81, 84–85, 86
 ending-the-period/day routines, 111–112
 entering classroom, 107, 108–109
 exiting classroom, 109
 feedback from, 384
 figures of speech, 312, 313
 generic secondary first-day schedule, 46–47
 labeling papers, 131
 last days of school activities, 468
 materials and equipment, 115, 276
 monitors, 135
 movement within classroom, 120
 orientation to school, 40–41
 penalties and, 164
 portfolios, 379
 positive rewards, 162
 reading inventory for, 387
 reward systems and, 164–165
 serious behaviors and, 208
 serious misbehaviors, 178–180
 standards and, 226, 227
 student decision-making and, 42
 student paperwork and, 394
 students learning each other's names, 75–77
 students needing help, 127
 substitute teachers, 288
 texting and, 151
 weekly planning and, 243
High-stakes testing, 369, 371, 406, 447
Homeroom teachers, 110

Home visits, teacher-parent communication, 416
Horseshoe configuration, classroom arrangement, 57, 59
Humiliation tactics, avoiding, 211–212
Hunter, Madeline, 257

I
Inclusion model, 280
Individual bulletin board spaces, 102
Individual differences. *See also* Diversity
  classroom management and, 183–184
  computers for locating activities supporting, 143
  types of, 332–333
Individuals with Disabilities Education Act (IDEA), 349
Induction programs, 3, 14, 21–22
Inquiry, 326–329
Inspiration (software), 260, 262, 314
Institutional resources, 266
Instructional aides
  appreciation for, 283, 284
  coaching, 283
  orienting, 282–283
  preparing to work with, 281–282
  role of, 280–281, 282, 283
Instructional boards, bulletin boards, 100–101
Instructional management
  in computer-assisted classroom, 151–154
  discipline and, 186–189
  group alerting, 126
  instructional aides, 280–284
  instructional routines and, 125, 126–132
  lesson plans, 247–262
  materials and equipment, 268, 271–277
  overlappingness, 126, 188
  pacing, 126
  planning, 184–186
  principles for, 125–126
  resources and supplies, 264–268
  ripple effect, 125
  satiation, 126
  substitute teachers, 284–288
  transitions, 126, 188–189
  unit planning, 233–241
  weekly planning, 241, 243–247
  withitness, 125
Instructional philosophy, classroom arrangements, 55
Instructional routines
  collection and distribution of papers, 131–132
  controlling noise, 128–129
  effectiveness of, 125
  free time policy, 130–131
  hand raising, 129
  labeling papers, 131
  principles of, 126
  students needing help, 127–128
Interest inventories, 386, 387, 388, 390, 400
Interpersonal intelligence, 334–335, 336
Interstate New Teacher Assessment and Support Consortium (INTASC), 16–17
Interviews
  assessments, 385
  students learning each other's names, 76–77
  teacher-parent communication, 416
Intrapersonal intelligence, 334, 335–336
Intrinsic motivation, 164, 299
Introducers, 67
Introductions
  classroom climate, 195
  teacher-parent communication, 415–416
  teacher-student relationship, 66–67, 69–70, 77
Iowa Test of Basic Skills, 406
iPhone Apps, 151
iPods, for reading, 148

J
Jacobson, Lenore, 295
Jones, F., 22, 162, 205
Jones, F. H., 162, 205, 216
Jones, J. L., 162, 205
Jones, P., 162, 205
Just-in-case kits, 26

K
Kaiser Family Foundation, 142
Kidspiration (software), 262, 314
Kindergarten classroom, floor plan for, 40
Kounin, Jacob, 23, 125, 182, 187, 188
KWL chart, 239, 301, 302

L
Last days of school
  dismantling room, 469
  fun activities for, 467–468
  goodbyes, 470
  maintaining routines, 466–467
  reflecting on year, 496
Legislation, and standards, 220–223
Lesson plans
  differentiated instruction and, 340–341
  district and school expectations, 250, 393
  English language learners, 359
  essential elements of, 247
  5E lesson plan, 257
  generic format for, 250, 256
  lesson plan template, 261
  multicultural lesson plan, 362–363
  organizing, 257, 260, 262
  sample lesson plans, 251–255, 258–259
  seven-step lesson plan, 257
  substitute teachers, 286
  teaching units and, 234
  writing lesson plan and rubric, 376–377
Letter writing, as low-key intervention, 207
Limits, discipline, 160
Lines
  for entering classroom, 107–108
  for exiting classroom, 109
Listening, classroom climate, 194–195
Literacy experiences. *See also* Reading
  first day of school, 42, 43, 44, 53
Logical consequences
  as alternative to punishment, 168–169
  encouragement and, 161, 165, 167–170
  related to offense, 169
  students' success and, 167–168
Lopez, C. L., 148
Lopez, Perry, 467
Lottery, for monitors, 136–137

M
Magazines
  discipline-specific journals, 461–462
  generic, 460
Managers, 67
Marzano, J. S., 182
Marzano, R., 22, 298, 299, 311, 313, 314, 316, 321, 326
Marzano, R. J., 182, 189, 192, 201
Maslow, A., 160
Master schedule, 243–244
Materials and equipment
  book clubs, 272–273
  community as resource for, 273–275
  discount and warehouse mega-stores, 276–277
  freebie guides, 272
  ordering, 268, 271–272
  procedures for distribution and collection, 115–116
  recycled merchandise, 277
  student access to, 115
  teacher and campus stores, 276
Mathematical/logical intelligence, 333–334, 335
Meaningful activities, 184–185
Mentoring programs, 3, 14, 21–22, 244, 392, 439
Metaphors, 312
Met Life, 13, 294–295, 362, 369, 400, 455, 456
Middle school students
  bathroom breaks, 118
  beginning-the-day routines, 110, 111
  books about school, 43
  bulletin boards, 99, 101
  choosing seats, 59
  classroom arrangement, 57, 94
  classroom management and, 187
  classroom meetings and, 202
  classroom rules, 80, 81, 84–85
  cooperative learning, 322
  ending-the-period/day routines, 111–112
  entering classroom, 108–109
  feedback from, 384
  interest inventory for, 387
  labeling papers, 131
  last days of school activities, 468
  literacy experiences, 53
  materials and equipment, 115, 276
  movement within classroom, 120
  orientation to school, 40–41
  penalties and, 164
Middle school students
  positive rewards, 162
  reading inventory for, 387
  serious behaviors and, 208
  standards and, 226, 227
  student paperwork and, 394
  students learning each other's names, 75
  texting and, 151
  weekly planning and, 243
Miller Analogies Test, 313
Mind maps, 316
Misbehavior. *See also* Serious behaviors
  bullying and, 176–178
  causes of, 172–176, 180
  nonverbal interventions, 205–207
  resources in district, 174, 176, 179, 208, 209
  symptoms of other serious behavior, 178–180
Modeling
  classroom climate and, 200–201
  classroom management and, 189, 211
  instructional routines and, 126
  respect, 125, 200–201
Moir, Ellen, 12, 428
Monitors
  assignment of, 136–138, 140
  computers and, 153
  types of, 135–136
Motivation of students
  first day of school and, 37–38
  individual differences and, 184
  misbehavior and, 172–176
  planning meaningful activities and, 184–185
  recognition and, 299
  substitute teachers and, 286
  teacher expectations and, 301
  weekly planning and, 243
Motivation of teachers, 93
Movement within classroom
  classroom climate and, 193–194
  routines for, 120–122
Multicultural studies, 360–363
Multiple intelligences, 246–249, 301, 333–337, 346, 347
Musical rhythmic intelligence, 334, 335

N
Name game, 75
Names
  classroom climate and, 199
  learning students' names, 72–73
  students learning each other's names, 73–77
Nametags/nameplates, 72
National Board for Professional Teaching Standards (NBPTS), 16, 17
National Center for Education Statistics, 12, 304, 349, 415, 430
National Center for Response to Intervention, 348–349
National Clearinghouse on Language Acquisition, 352
National Commission on Teaching and America's Future, 10
National Comprehensive Center for Teacher Quality, 4, 332
National Council for the Social Studies, 224
National Council of Teachers of Mathematics, 224
National Crime Prevention Council, 177
National Education Association, 14, 400, 401
National School Safety Council, 177
Naturalist intelligence, 335, 336
NBPTS (National Board for Professional Teaching Standards), 16, 17
NCLB. *See* No Child Left Behind (NCLB) Act (2001)
Nelsen, Jane, 165, 173, 174, 176, 201–202, 207
New Teacher Project, 4
No Child Left Behind (NCLB) Act (2001)
  curriculum planning and, 220–222
  highly qualified teachers and, 10–11
  high-stakes testing and, 371, 406
  paperwork, 392
  reauthorization of, 223
  research-based strategies, 306
Noise, controlling, 128–129
Noise-level circles, 129
Nonverbal interventions, classroom management, 205–207
Norm-referenced tests, 370, 407
Numerical grade book, 395
Numerical response with fingers, 396

O
Obama, Barack, 11, 221, 222
Objectives
  lesson plans, 247
  teacher expectations and, 298
Ogle, Donna, 239, 301
One-on-one visits, 27
Open body posture, classroom climate, 194
Open house
  ideas for, 418–419
  teacher-parent communication and, 417–419
Openmindedness, 428
Orientation to school and classroom, first day of school, 40–41, 45
Overdwelling, 187–188
Overlappingness, instructional management, 126, 188

P
Pacing, instructional management, 126
Paperwork
  homework and, 399–404
  official school and district paperwork, 392–394
  student paperwork, 394–399
Paraeducators. *See* Instructional aides
Paragraph writing, rubric for, 374
Paraprofessionals. *See* Instructional aides
Parent/guardian conferences, 209–210, 393–394, 400, 419–423
Parents. *See also* Teacher-parent communication
  bathroom routines and, 121
  body language and, 194
  cell phones and, 147, 151, 154
  classroom rules and, 84–85, 86, 417
  diagnostic assessment and, 380
  English language learners, 357
  expectations of, 295
  first day of school and, 26–27
  as guest speakers, 268
  homework and, 400, 402–403
  involvement of, 417, 420–421, 423
  partnership with, 413–414
  portfolios and, 378
  resources from, 266–268, 269, 270
  reward systems and, 164
  student achievement and, 300
  volunteers for marking papers, 397
Parent Teachers Association, 401
Partial outlines, 316, 317, 318
Pass system, for bathroom routines, 117
Pass the envelope, 383
Pavlov, I., 161–162
PBS, 143, 144, 149, 150
PC Viewer, 152
Peer tutoring, 152
Penalties, behavior modification, 161, 164–165
Pencil sharpening, 120
Period evaluation, beginning-the-period/day routines, 112

Personal stories, classroom climate, 195–196
Physical contact, avoiding, 211
Pickering, D., 298
Pickering, D. J., 182
Pictorial Interest Inventory for Young Students, 386
Pie charts, 325
Planning. *See also* Curriculum planning; Lesson plans; Unit planning; Weekly planning
  classroom arrangement, 29
  classroom management and, 184–186
  stress management and, 452
  for success, 25, 184
Playing cards
  for calling on students, 129, 187
  for end-of-the-day compliments, 197
PLCs (professional learning communities), 454–459
Pocket chart, 108
Pollack, J., 298
Popham, James, 373
Portfolios
  assessment and, 378, 379, 395–398
  teaching portfolios, 455, 458
Positive rewards, 162
Power, misbehavior, 172, 173–174, 175
PowerPoints, 146
Praise, encouragement distinguished from, 167, 168, 169
Preferred Activity Time (P.A.T.), 162, 206
President Speaks, Race to the Top, 221
Principals
  discipline norms, 79
  lesson plans, 250
  materials and equipment, 271
  planning oversight and, 244
  professional dress and, 64, 65
  serious behaviors and, 209, 211
  teachers' professional relationship with, 438–439, 440
Prior knowledge, sentence stems, 238, 301
Problem solving
  cooperative learning and, 326–329
  teacher expectations and, 302
Procedures
  for distribution of materials, 115–116
  lesson plans, 247
  planning and, 185
  of schools, 437–438
Professional development opportunities, 455, 456, 458–460, 472
Professional development resources, 460–462
Professional dress
  comfort and, 65
  establishing rapport, 65–66
  first impressions and, 64
  message sent with, 64–65
  playfulness, 65
Professional learning communities (PLCs), 454–459
Professional life
  maintaining perspective, 448–449
  orientation to school, 435–438
  professional development opportunities, 455, 458–460, 472
  professional development resources, 460–462
  professional learning communities, 454–459
  reflective practice, 428–432
  relationship with principal, 438–439, 440
  stress management, 447–452
  time management, 444–446
Professional organizations
  discipline-specific, 461
  standards of, 224, 225
Projection devices, for computers, 152
Projects, classroom arrangement, 56
Proximity, nonverbal interventions, 205–206, 209
Public Agenda, 4, 332, 389
Punishment
  corporal punishment, 211, 213
  logical consequences as alternative to, 168–169
Pygmalion in the Classroom (Rosenthal and Jacobson), 295

Q
Questions, as low-key intervention, 206
Quick-write, 383

R
Race to the Top, 11, 221, 222
Rate the session, 383
Reading. *See also* Literacy experiences
  bulletin boards, 100
  as homework, 400
  iPods for, 148
  reading inventories, 387, 388
  teacher expectations and, 300
Reciprocal teaching, cooperative learning and, 324–325, 326
Recognition reflex, 172
Record keeping
  computers as time savers for, 143
  instructional aides and, 283
  school and district paperwork, 392–394
  serious behaviors and, 209
Reflective practice
  attitudes and, 428–429
  defined, 16
  engaging in, 431–432, 473
  five-point plan for, 429–431
  six-step process for, 17, 18, 23
  standards and, 16–17
  teacher colleagues and, 431–432
Reflective thinking, 16
Report card for teacher, 431
Research-based strategies. *See also* Cooperative learning
  advance organizers, 315–318
  comparing and contrasting, 306–309
  figures of speech, 311–313
  graphic organizers, 313–314, 315, 316
  teacher expectations and, 297–304
Resources and supplies. *See also* Materials and equipment
  district office, 265–266
  locating, 264–268
  school site, 265
Resources specialists, 265, 266, 271
Resource units, 233–234, 238–239
Respect
  classroom climate and, 200–201
  classroom rules and, 50, 80, 81, 83, 85, 86
  discipline and, 39, 161
  logical consequences and, 167, 169
  misbehavior and, 172, 173, 175, 176
  modeling, 125, 200–201
  routines and, 115
  for substitute teachers, 286, 288
Response to Intervention (RTI), 348–349
Responsibility
  classroom climate and, 200–201
  classroom rules and, 80
  discipline and, 39, 160
  logical consequences and, 167
  reflective practice and, 428
  teacher expectations and, 300
Revenge, misbehavior, 172, 174–175
Review in eight boxes, 397, 398
Reward systems
  behavior modification and, 161–165
  charts for, 163, 165, 167
  individual and whole class earnings, 163, 206
  for monitors, 137
Ripple effect, 125
Role playing, as low-key intervention, 207
Rosenthal, Robert, 295
Rothstein-Fisch, C., 82–83
Routines and schedule
  bathroom and fountain, 116–120, 121
  beginning and ending the day, 110–113
  cohesive classroom community, 138–140
  computers and, 153, 154
  entrances and exits, 107–110
  first day of school, 38–39, 44, 45–47
  function of, 106–107
  generic elementary first-day schedule, 45–46
  generic secondary first-day schedule, 46–47
  instructional routines, 125, 126–132
  last days of school, 466–467
  materials and equipment, 115–116
  monitor assignments, 136–138, 140
  monitor types, 135–136
  movement within classroom, 120–122
Rows, classroom arrangement, 56
RTI (Response to Intervention), 348–349
Rubrics
  authentic assessment and, 372, 373
  creating, 374, 375
  grading and, 398
  for paragraph writing, 374

S
Safety, discipline and, 160
SAT, 370, 407, 408–409
Satiation, instructional management, 126
School board meetings, 27
School reform, indicators of, 222
Schools
  bathroom break norms, 117
  books about school, 43
  cell phone policies, 147–148, 151, 157
  discipline norms, 79–80, 178, 208
  district calendar, 243
  instructional aide duties, 281
  key locations, 435–436
  lateness and absence policies, 300
  lesson plan expectations, 250, 393
  map of, 436
  paperwork requirements, 392–394
  planning oversight, 244
  procedures of, 437–438
  staff of, 436–437, 470
  visiting before first day, 27–28
  walking tour for students, 40
  websites of, 28, 416–417
School supply lists, 266–267, 269
SDAIE (Specially Designed Academic Instruction in English), 355–356
Search engines
  instructional uses of, 150
  safety in use of, 146
Seating charts
  classroom arrangement, 59, 60
  classroom climate and, 199
  entering classroom, 109
  learning students' names, 73
  for substitute teachers, 285
"See Me" cards, 207
Self-concept activities, classroom climate, 199
Self-esteem, 160
Self-fulfilling prophecy, 294–295, 296, 297
Self-marking, 396
Sentence stems, 238, 301, 389, 470
Senter, G. W., 283
Sequence charts, 314, 315
Serious behaviors
  discipline and, 178–180
  responses to avoid, 210–213
  rule-breaking behavior distinguished from, 208–209
Sexual harassment, 211
Sheltered English techniques, 239–240, 355–356
Sheltered Instruction Observation Protocol (SIOP), 356
Short, D., 356
Signals, as nonverbal interventions, 206
Silence, controlling noise, 128–129
Silhouettes, 39, 100
Similes, 311, 312
SIOP (Sheltered Instruction Observation Protocol), 356
Smiling, classroom climate, 192–193
Social class issues, classroom management, 207–208
Software programs, evaluation of, 150
Sorting, comparing and contrasting, 307, 310
Specially Designed Academic Instruction in English (SDAIE), 355–356
Spock, Benjamin, 213
Sponge activities, 185–186, 397
Standardized tests
  assessment and, 369, 370, 381
  high-stakes testing, 369, 371, 406
  preparation through year, 407–409
  suggestions for preparation, 409–410
  types of, 406, 407
Standards
  assessment and, 369
  curriculum planning and, 219–223
  differentiated instruction and, 341
  familiarity with, 224–225
  managing standards, 226–229
  overlapping standards in curriculum areas, 228
  reflective practice and, 16–17
  student achievement records, 394
  teacher expectations and, 298
  for teaching profession, 3
  textbooks and, 229
  unit planning and, 233, 234, 240–241
Star(s) of the week, 100
Stress management, 447–452
Student achievement
  cooperative learning and, 301
  differentiated instruction and, 346–347
  parents, 423
  Response to Intervention and, 349
  standards-based records, 394
  teacher expectations and, 294, 295, 297, 300
Student decision-making
  choosing seats, 59–60, 61, 183
  classroom arrangement and, 59–60, 96
  classroom climate and, 198–199
  classroom rules and, 79, 81, 85
  cohesive classroom community, 138–139
  first day of school and, 42
  individual differences and, 183
  monitors, 135–136, 137
  suggestion box, 139
"Student of the Week" bulletin boards, 196, 197
Students. *See also* Elementary students; High school students; Middle school students; Motivation of students; Students with special needs; Teacher-student relationship
  autobiographies of, 389, 416
  calling on, 129, 130, 187
  diversity in, 6, 7, 332
  feedback on instruction, 383, 384, 431
  first day of school and, 26–27, 44
  instructional uses of for computers, 145
  interviews, 385
  keeping up with students' technology use, 146
  learning names, 72–73
  reaction to correction of misbehavior, 172
  saturation point of, 189
  technological devices owned by, 142
Student self-portraits or silhouettes, 100
Student Study Team (SST), 209
Students with special needs
  classroom arrangement, 60–61, 183
  classroom climate and, 197
  classroom rules and, 83
  computers for locating activities for, 143
  differentiated instruction, 348
  free and appropriate public education, 349
  instructional aides and, 280, 281
  monitorial roles for, 136
  substitute teachers and, 286
  technology access of, 147–148
  unit planning and, 240
Student teaching
  supervising teacher and, 4
  unit planning and, 233
Substitute data bank, 286, 287
Substitute teachers
  lesson plans, 286
  preparing for, 284–288

substitute folder, 284–286, 287
supplemental materials for, 286, 288
teaching respect for, 286, 288
Success-of-the-day journal, 25, 26, 432
Suggestion box, 139, 195
Summarization, 383
Super room parents, 421
Suspension, grounds for, 166, 208
Synectics, 311

T

"Take-a-number" method, 127, 128
Talking, controlling noise, 128–129
Tattle Tales box, 195
Teacher attrition, reasons for, 11–12
Teacher business card, 431
Teacher colleagues
curriculum planning and, 229
diagnostic assessment and, 380
locating key people, 436–437
professional development opportunities and, 455, 456
reflective practice and, 431–432
resources and supplies from, 265
working with, 439, 441
Teacher expectations
belief in effort, 299
classroom climate and, 302
connecting learning to personal experience, 301, 302
cooperative learning, 301–302
diverse learning strategies and, 302
effective feedback and, 299
evidence about power of, 295
first day of school, 46, 79
heterogeneous grouping, 301–302
individual differences and, 184
instructional time and, 299–300
interventions, 300–301
outcomes and, 295–297
promoting literacy, 300
providing recognition and, 299
research-based practices for conveying positive expectations, 297–304
self-fulfilling prophecy and, 294–295
specifying objectives, 298
standards and, 298
student achievement and, 294, 295, 297, 300
wait time and, 303
Teacher-made tests, 380
Teacher-only work days, 44–45
Teacher-parent communication
computers used for, 143
first day and, 86, 416
fostering, 414–423
introductions, 415–416
open house and, 417–419
parent/guardian conferences, 209–210, 393–394, 400, 419–423
parent letters, 26–27, 28, 86, 415, 416
technology and, 416–417
Teacher preparation
first year of teaching and, 2–6
recognizing concerns, 13–14
Teacher roles
choice in, 7–8
multiple roles, 6–7
Teacher's autobiography, 26, 27, 100
Teacher-student relationship
classroom management and, 182, 192
establishing rapport, 65–69
introductions, 66–67, 69–70, 77
misbehavior and, 172–176
stability in, 202
students' names and, 72–73
teacher self-disclosure, 68–69
teachers' titles, 67–68
WISHES (welcome, introduction, share hopes, establish standards), 69
Teacher working conditions, 19–20
Teach for America, 4
Teaching profession. *See also* Professional dress; Professional life
diversity in, 6
multiple pathways into, 4
recruiting quality teachers, 10–12
retention of teachers, 10, 11–12
rewards of, 474–475
standards for, 3
Teaching supplies, gathering, 29–30
Teaching units, 233–234, 238–239
Team teaching, 59
Technology
cell phones, 147–148, 151, 153, 154, 157, 158, 176–177
computer-assisted classrooms, 151–154
instructional aides, 281
integrating, 148–150
teacher-parent communication and, 416–417
teaching enhanced with, 142–148
Telephone calls, teacher-parent communication, 415
Textbooks, 229
Texting, 151, 153
Threats, 212–213
Thrusts, 188–189
Time lines, students learning each other's names, 75–76
Time management, 444–446
Time-outs, 211
Token, economies, 162
Tomlinson, Carol Ann, 22, 338–344
Tooth fairy report, 99
Traffic signal, controlling noise, 129
Transitions
group work, 120–122
instructional management, 126, 188–189
structure for, 109
Troops to Teachers, 4
Trumbull, E., 82–83
Truncations, 189

U

Understanding, checking for, 189
Unit planning
adapting unit, 239–240
curriculum integration and, 240–241
designing units, 234, 238–239
resource units, 233–234
teaching units, 233–234
worksheet for, 241, 242
U.S. Bureau of Labor, 283
U.S. Department of Education, 11, 222, 223, 224, 225
U.S. Department of Education, Institute of Educational Sciences, 160, 166, 177
U.S. Department of Education, Office of Civil Rights, 213
U.S. House of Representatives, 221

V

Variety, in instruction, 188, 317
Vatterott, Cathy, 401–403
Venn diagrams, 306, 307
Verbal/linguistic intelligence, 333, 335
Visual/spatial intelligence, 333, 335
Vocabulary word wall, 408
Vogt, M., 356
Volunteers, for monitors, 136

W

Wait time, teacher expectations, 303
Wastebasket access, 120
Water fountain
routines, 116–117, 119–120
Websites
discipline-specific, 461–462
generic, 460
of schools, 28, 416–417
Wechsler Intelligence Scale for Children (WISC), 370
Weed, K., 353, 357
Weekly planning
diversity, 245–246
higher levels of thinking, 244, 245
learning styles, 246–247
master schedule, 243–244
school and district parameters, 241, 243–244
Welcomers, 66
"When I Need Help Chart," 127, 128
Whispering, controlling noise, 128–129
Wholeheartedness, 428
Withitness, 125, 188, 189
Working parents, 421

Y

You-do-it parents, 421

PHOTO CREDITS

iStockphoto.com, pp. 1, 25, 35, 54, 63, 124, 138, 141, 171, 181, 184, 191, 198, 204, 232, 233, 247, 250, 260, 263, 279, 293, 305, 320, 331, 368, 391, 412, 413, 427, 428, 430, 443, 446 (top), 465, 470, 471; Ellen Kronowitz, pp. 2, 11, 66 (right), 74, 82 (middle, right), 96 (left), 98 (both), 102, 114, 137, 139, 163 (all), 186, 196, 226 (both), 243, 361 (all), 460, 467; courtesy of Mark Young, p. 3 (both); Shutterstock, pp. 9, 26 (both), 51, 66 (left), 120, 134, 172 (all), 206 (top left), 410 (bottom), 436 (left); Comstock Royalty Free Division, pp. 15, 20, 49, 59 (top right), 64 (bottom), 187, 192 (top), 194 (left), 202 (left), 264 (left), 296, 352 (right), 371 (left, middle), 382; stock.xchng, pp. 24, 71; Ruddy Gold/Photolibary.com, p. 30; Jupiter Images–FoodPix–Creatas, p. 38; Annie Pickert/Pearson, pp. 41 (top), 99, 101; Fotolia, pp. 41 (bottom), 64 (top), 94 (both), 143 (left), 206 (top right, bottom left), 434, 447, 449; Photodisc/Getty Images, pp. 42, 159, 405; Getty Images, Inc.–Comstock Images RF, p. 52; Scott Cunningham/Merrill, p. 59 (left); Karen Mancinelli/Pearson Learning Photo Studio, p. 59 (bottom); Lori Whitley/Merrill, pp. 70 (left), 100; © Rana Royalty free/Alamy, p. 70 (right); © Blend Images/Alamy, p. 72; Bill Freeman/PhotoEdit Inc., pp. 78, 82 (left); David Mager/Pearson Learning Photo Studio, pp. 96 (middle), 209, 332 (left); EyeWire Collection/Getty Images–Photodisc–Royalty Free, p. 96 (right); Krista Greco/Merrill, pp. 103, 422, 458; Big Box of Art, pp. 105, 218, 453; Michael Newman/PhotoEdit Inc., pp. 107, 355 (right), 388, 436 (right), 439 (bottom); Deborah Schneck, pp. 129, 130, 197, 248; Laura Bolesta/Merrill, p. 136; Valerie Schultz/Merrill, pp. 143 (middle), 280 (left); PunchStock–Royalty Free, p. 143 (right); Getty Images/Digital Vision, pp. 174 (middle), 194 (right); Brand X Pictures/Thinkstock, p. 174 (left); Jupiterimages/Thinkstock, p. 174 (right); Michelle D. Bridwell/PhotoEdit Inc., p. 182 (left); Mary Kate Denny/PhotoEdit Inc., pp. 182 (right), 393 (bottom); courtesy of the Centenary of the Montessori Movement, p. 185 (left); GeoStock/Getty Images, Inc.–Photodisc/Royalty Free, p. 185 (right); Spencer Grant/PhotoEdit Inc., pp. 192 (bottom), 264 (middle); Anthony Magnacca/Merrill, pp. 193, 219 (right), 280 (right), 332 (right), 371 (right), 415, 446 (bottom); David Young-Wolff/PhotoEdit Inc., pp. 200, 210, 277, 355 (left), 420; Patrick Clark/Getty Images, Inc.–Photodisc/Royalty Free, p. 202 (top); © dmac/Alamy, p. 211; Ewing Galloway/Photolibrary.com, p. 219 (left); Joel Rafkin/PhotoEdit Inc., p. 264 (right); provided by Heather Whitley, p. 266; Corbis RF, p. 267 (both); Katelyn Metzger/Merrill, pp. 272, 393 (top); Richard Hutchings/PhotoEdit Inc., p. 276 (left); Mark Richards/PhotoEdit Inc., p. 276 (right); Masterfile Royalty Free Division, p. 281 (left); © Big Cheese Photo LLC/Alamy, p. 281 (right); © Jon Arnold Images/Alamy, p. 328; courtesy of Perry Lopez, p. 329 (both); Hope Madden/Merrill, pp. 351, 352 (left, middle); Amy Etra/PhotoEdit Inc., p. 353 (top); © Larry Downing/ Reuters/Corbis, p. 353 (bottom); © Janine Wiedel Photolibrary/Alamy, p. 360; Brandi Stephens, p. 363; Tony Freeman/PhotoEdit Inc., p. 396; James Shaffer/PhotoEdit Inc., p. 410 (top); Patrick White/Merrill, pp. 410 (middle), 450 (left); Elizabeth Crews/The Images Works, p. 418; Dennis MacDonald/PhotoEdit Inc., p. 437; Bob Daemmrich/ PhotoEdit Inc., p. 439 (top); Cindy Charles/PhotoEdit Inc., p. 450 (right).